The Fascism Reader

The Fascism Reader is a fascinating and wide-ranging introduction to the complex nature, limits, aspects and dynamics of fascism as both ideology and practice. The book draws together classic and recent interpretations to trace the development of the debate on generic fascism.

Exploring fascism in all its diverse manifestations, this book discusses the classic examples of National Socialism in Germany and Fascism in Italy, as well as a series of less familiar movements and regimes, including the Iron Guard in Romania, the British Union of Fascists, Salazar's dictatorship in Portugal and Franco's regime in Spain.

The Fascism Reader explores all the key aspects of fascism including:

*   the essence and limitations of generic fascism
*   the intellectual and ideological dimensions of fascism
*   regimes of fascism as particular models of the exercise of power
*   fascism and society – from anti-Semitism to fascist attitudes to women

This book offers a unique insight into the way in which historiography has approached and interpreted various aspects of fascist experience in interwar Europe.

Aristotle A. Kallis is Lecturer in Modern European History at the University of Bristol. He is the author of *Fascist Ideology: Territory and Expansionism in Italy and Germany, 1992–1945* (Routledge, 2000).

The Fascism Reader

Edited by

Aristotle A. Kallis

Routledge
Taylor & Francis Group

LONDON AND NEW YORK

First published 2003
by Routledge
11 New Fetter Lane, London EC4P 4EE

Simultaneously published in the USA and Canada
by Routledge
29 West 35th Street, New York, NY 10001

Routledge is an imprint of the Taylor & Francis Group

Typeset in Perpetua and Bell Gothic by
Florence Production Ltd, Stoodleigh, Devon
Printed and bound in Great Britain by
TJ International Ltd, Padstow, Cornwall

British Library Cataloguing in Publication Data
A catalogue record for this book is available from the British Library

Library of Congress Cataloging in Publication Data
A catalog record has been requested

ISBN 0–415–24358–0 (hbk)
ISBN 0–415–24359–9 (pbk)

To my parents and my 'extended' family in Greece

Contents

Preface

THE AIM OF THIS READER is to offer insight into the way in which historiography has approached and interpreted various aspects of the fascist experience in interwar Europe. The selection of excerpts featured here represents only a fraction of an extremely wide and constantly expanding body of secondary literature on fascism. The choice of works, however, has resulted from two main considerations: first, to provide a broad coverage of different aspects of the fascist phenomenon, in terms of topics (origins, movements, style of rule, society), methodology (Marxist, liberal, conservative) and countries (Germany, Italy, Spain, Portugal, France, Britain, Austria); and, second, to present different viewpoints vis-à-vis contentious issues or debates that have punctuated the evolution of fascist studies (race, origins of fascism, social attitudes to the fascist regime, membership of the movements, etc.). While some of these debates have concerned the nature of fascism as a *generic* concept, most of the historiography on fascism has focused on its country-specific manifestations, examining their relevance to long-term trends of national past and history.

The selected excerpts include both classic and more recent interpretations in an attempt to trace the development of the bibliography on fascism. The featured material is organised in four parts: the essence and limitations of generic fascism; the intellectual/ideological dimension of fascism; the regime-type of fascism as a particular model of exercise of power; and fascism and society (elites and masses). Part 1 reflects an emphasis on comparative or broad interpretations of fascism, debating the utility and essence of the so-called 'fascist minimum'. Section I [*Fascism – a 'generic' concept?*] comprises a series of generic models of fascism in search for a methodological paradigm, but it also features one of the strongest ever attacks on the concept of generic fascism made by Allardyce. Section II [*What *produces fascism?*] explores the ideological, political and social factors that contributed to the epochal appeal of fascism in interwar Europe. The selected excerpts cover a plethora of aspects – amongst them, the First World War, the crisis of capitalism and of modernity, the disintegration of liberalism, bourgeois aspirations, working class attitudes and generational responses. Parts 2 and 3 offer a combination of singular accounts and comparative approaches, in an attempt to combine breadth of coverage with attention to the particular dynamics of the evolution of autochthonous fascisms. The second part focuses on the ideological-intellectual dimension of fascism and is divided into two sections. Section III [*Fascist ideology – the quest for the 'fascist minimum'*] features a combination of generic accounts of fascist ideology and specific studies of the ideologies of the two 'core' fascist regimes – Fascist Italy and Nazi Germany. Section IV [*Varieties of fascist movements*] deals with a series of case-studies of movements across Europe which did not proceed to the seizure of power but displayed or reproduced traces of fascism's intellectual dimension. The third part refers exclusively to 'fascist' regimes (i.e. political systems which emerged after the consolidation of the power of fascist elements autonomously from other forces). Therefore, the selection reflects an emphasis on Italian Fascism and German Nazism (which are widely seen as the two most developed and radical expressions of the fascist 'new style of politics'). Section V [*Techniques of fascist rule – the exercise of power by the 'regime-model' of fascism*] offers a generic account of totalitarianism and then examines a series of mechanisms which the fascist regimes used in order to consolidate and enhance their power. The selected excerpts cover administration, the role of the party, foreign policy, secret police, corporatism and charismatic leadership. Section VI [*Fascism and anti-Semitism*] concentrates on probably the most controversial feature of racism/anti-Semitism and explores its connection to fascist ideology or national traditions. Finally, the fourth part examines societal attitudes to fascist regimes, both on the elite and the mass level. Section VII [*Society and attitudes to fascism – support, conformity and resistance*] focuses on the attitudes towards the fascist regimes by different sections of the population (social classes, women, youth). The selected excerpts attempt to cover the whole range of attitudes, from enthusiastic support to conformity, apathy and resistance. On the other hand, Section VIII (*Fascism and social elites – complicity and antagonism*) attempts to explore the ambiguous relation between fascist leaderships and traditional elite groups, recording its trajectory from complicity and endorsement of the fascist leaders to disaffection, marginalisation and – in some cases – opposition.

Methodologically, the reader reflects a strong belief in the validity and fecundity of a *comparative* approach to the concept and history of fascism. This statement in itself is far from impervious to criticism. Section A offers some insight into the conflicting views on what fascism is and to what extent comparative analysis can fruitfully be employed to shed light on its nature. There is a further, equally important caveat concerning the rationale behind the way that the term 'fascism' applies to the case-studies featured in this reader. For a start, there is significant and well-documented opposition to generic definitions of 'fascism' (see, for example, Allardyce (**1**), Turner (**45**), Knox (1984: 1–4)). Some may therefore find the extension of the term beyond Fascist Italy problematic and confusing. This is not the place to provide a detailed defence of the methodological premises on which such a generic usage can be predicated – I can only refer to the works of prominent 'genericists', some of whom are featured here (Griffin (**11, 15**), Payne (**5, 16**), Nolte (**12**), Eatwell (**4**), O'Sullivan (**13**), Linz (**3**), etc). The structure of the reader – starting with general questions about the nature of 'fascism' (Sections 1–3) before proceeding to a more in-depth comparison of case-studies in specific fields (Sections 4–8) – aims to offer insight into the different ways that such a comparative approach to fascism can be both justified and criticised, highlighting its strengths, challenges, limitations and possible inadequacies.

However, accepting the validity of comparison is an altogether different story from deciding on a generic definition and choosing appropriate case-studies. *Ideal-types* of fascism can be very different, constantly shifting the dividing line between 'fascism' and 'conventional authoritarianism' or 'para-fascism', and introducing a host of further significant distinctions (for example, Sternhell's differentiation between Nazism and fascism (**14**); Griffin's 'successful' and 'abortive' fascisms; and an often revisited distinction between fascism as ideology and as regime). Ironically, the task of compiling a list of 'core' or undisputed case-studies of fascism has been obfuscated, not facilitated, by the conceptual sophistication of recent generic models. Once again, some may find the inclusion of Salazar's Portugal, Primo de Rivera's or Franco's Spain, Metaxas' Greece and Dolfuss' Austria in a comparative framework for 'fascism' problematic, if not unacceptable. But the 'era of fascism', as Nolte has christened the period between the two world wars, is unique not just because it produced an unprecedented number of radical intellectual currents or movements but also because it established a new 'activist style of politics' (O'Sullivan (**13**)) as an effective alternative to liberalism and an antidote to socialism. The shift from parliamentarism (however flawed) to authoritarian solutions of different varieties – in itself a defining characteristic of the interwar period – became possible through the political interaction between the conservative right and fascism (in the form of either indigenous movements or influence from the already established 'fascist' regimes in Europe). In this sense, there was a significant degree of overlap in the political aspirations of fascists and conservatives (Blinkhorn (**43**)) that often blurred the distinction between them and produced a host of regimes in which the two elements co-existed, on a short- or long-term basis, harmoniously or antagonistically (Kallis 2000). The inclusion of these regimes in this reader does not intend to elide their qualitative differences from the radical, even revolutionary, spirit of fascist ideology or their noticeable lack of fanaticism compared to Nazism or – to some extent – Italian Fascism. But the history of interwar fascism (what Payne calls 'historical fascism' – see Payne 1997) cannot be told without any allusions to the political influence that, first, Mussolini's regime and, later, Nazism or Salazarism exerted on the traditional European right. Understanding many of these regimes' features (corporatism, paramilitary and youth organisations, the cult of the leader, their *palingenetic* discourse (see Griffin (**15**)), etc.) is not possible without the awareness that they were established and continued to operate in a bi-polarised political milieu, in which Italy and Germany gradually came to constitute a dominant pole. This – and not the categorical allusion that they were 'fascist' – is the rationale behind the incorporation of such regimes in this reader.

Comparison, however, does not necessarily presuppose or foreshadow absolute similarity. As Marc Bloch has noted, there are 'similar' phenomena that affect 'different societies' and 'adjacent' societies that experience change in comparable (but not identical) directions (*Mélanges historiques* (Paris, 1963), 1:16–40, quoted in Paxton 1998, n. 22). Thus, when we discuss the historical experience of one country in a particular field, this does not imply that we may assume that all or most 'fascist' regimes followed the same prescription for the same problems or objectives. Section F on race and anti-Semitism highlights this point through a comparison between Germany, Italy and France in their varying degrees of commitment to, and fanatical pursuit of, racial policies. But it is equally important to remember this caveat when dealing with other country-specific excerpts in this reader. Section E offers an overview of some devices used by different regimes to achieve the goal of stable power and social control, by promoting consensus through manipulation and resorting to techniques of institutionalised coercion. In this sense, the function of the Gestapo was unique to Nazi Germany; the Portuguese Estado Novo was a peculiar corporatist experiment underpinned by the country's circumstances and tradition; territorial expansion characterised Hitler's and Mussolini's regimes but is strangely absent from other 'fascist' case-studies; and the 'leader's cult' was choreographed very differently in Germany and Italy (to use the two most emblematic cases). Comparison in this context may help us understand the plurality of techniques employed by different systems to secure power and deal effectively with opposition, but it does not constitute a safe terrain for indiscriminate generalisations about fascism's ideological attributes or its political 'programme' in power.

Equally significant and potentially controversial are the geographical and chronological contours of this reader. This is effectively an anthology of secondary sources on *interwar European* fascism, treating the 1945 watershed as a *terminus ante quem*. The debate about whether fascism is epochal or not and about its European or universal relevance is far from concluded. Some of the extracts make references to the 'survival' of fascism after 1945, its diachronic relevance to crisis-ridden societies and its chances of re-emerging in new forms in the future (**3, 4, 5, 11, 15, 16**); others take up the point made by Nolte (**12**) and emphasise the unique historic qualities of interwar fascism (**6, 9, 10, 29, 43**). This discrepancy is essentially underpinned by the difference between an analysis of fascism as an intellectual current and that of fascism as a result of specific factors present in a peculiar form only in interwar Europe. The former model expands 'fascism' backwards (to the 'proto-fascist' phenomena of the late nineteenth and early twentieth centuries) and forwards (for example, to ultra-nationalist ideologies and movements preaching national rebirth beyond 1945); the latter underlines the uniqueness of these structural factors that produced the 'fascist potential' (Eley (**10**)) in Europe between the two world wars. So we are back to the discussion of what constitutes fascism per se and what the optimal framework for its analysis should be. The debate on fascism, 'neo-fascism' and 'extreme right' (and all these terms have been widely challenged) draws heavily from the conceptual and methodological reservoir of political science and sociology. This is a complication that some disciples of 'traditional history' find unwelcome and anyway peripheral to their emphasis on unravelling fascism's particular record in the 1920s and 1930s. I have not intended this reader to expand its focus beyond 1945, although the inclusion of extracts of an inter-disciplinary nature (**3, 4, 8, 11, 12, 15, 23**) is an oblique statement in favour of what, in my opinion, is a fruitful conjunction of empirical and theoretical analysis for understanding the nature of fascism (Griffin, 'Three Faces of Fascism', *Patterns of Prejudice*, 30 (1996)). Advocates of either 'diachronic' or 'historic' fascism will find relevant material in this reader to test their working hypotheses and challenge those of the other side. Once again, my intention in preparing this work has been to provide stimuli for further scrutiny, not to formulate and promote categorical answers to the problems that make the study of fascism so exciting.

Finally, I should acknowledge that, in the process of selecting the excerpts featured here, I feel that I have perhaps not done justice to many significant genres of historical analysis of fascism, as well as specific works. Obviously there is no such thing as a definitive reader on fascism. Whatever the techniques of choice, however stringent and conceptually sound the criteria for selection and editing, the final content and structure of such a project presuppose a difficult process of inclusion and elimination. Needless to say, the decision to feature forty-eight excerpts from a body of literature comprising thousands of both classic and contemporary works that have stood the test of time and new evidence is difficult and potentially controversial. No two scholars of fascism could conceivably agree on the same short-list of works or the content of the edited texts. But, just like every other similar project, this reader aims to perform a dual task: to introduce students to a selection of key writings on fascism and to provide them with the intellectual stimulus to explore the wider picture of the vast bibliography on its history, country-specific permutations and intellectual qualities. Rather than attempting to be all-inclusive and exhaustive, it concentrates on eight major topics and features lengthier excerpts that reflect a spectrum of different (and often conflicting) historical interpretations. The introductory parts (the longer essay at the beginning and the shorter pieces that precede each section) help to chart the most important historiographical developments, designate issues of controversy, set the extracts in the wider historio-graphical context and point to a host of other significant texts that this reader could not encompass.

Preparing this reader proved to be an exciting but steep learning curve for me. The tasks of locating, choosing, editing, organising and introducing the material, but also the whole process of compiling the final typescript – each had its own specific challenges. The advice and encouragement offered by others at moments of dilemma or crisis provided crucial impetus to this project. I would like to thank Jill Stephenson and Jim Macmillan for all their help, immense support and specific advice on certain aspects of the reader; and Christopher Black for always being willing to provide me with good advice and to share his experience on academic and publishing issues alike. I owe a special thanks to Roger Griffin, who, apart from having been a source of immense academic inspiration for me, has always found time to read typescripts and offer valuable feedback on aspects of my work in general, and of this reader in particular.

The staff at the libraries of the Universities of Edinburgh, Glasgow and Stirling and of the National Library of Scotland have helped me extensively in locating and using the original material. I am particularly indebted to Scott Summers and Nadja Kanellopoulou for being so accommodating to my extensive (and sometimes excessive) requests; and to the staff of the Edinburgh University Computing Services for offering advice on the technical aspects of OCR procedures. Without their help I would probably be still racing against time to complete the typescript.

At Routledge my editor Victoria Peters showed a great deal of understanding and patience in dealing with all my queries and adjustments to the time-scale of the project. Gillian Oliver has managed many aspects of the production process with exemplary flexibility and interest. I am grateful to her and to Helen Brocklehurst for all their advice, information and, above all, encouragement in the painstaking process of dealing with copyrights and permissions. The idea for the project belongs to Heather McCallum, who approached me with the proposal back in the summer of 1999; but I am indebted to the whole History section of Routledge for the way they encouraged my work and ensured that I went through the preparation of this reader as smoothly as possible. A special thanks goes to Ruth Whittington, who saw the book through the final stages of production with huge personal concern, attention to detail, and a skillful combination of subtle pressure and wholehearted encouragement.

During the two years since the inception of the project I spent a significant part of my time at the 204 MGAP unit of the Greek Air Force, as part of my military service. There I had the opportunity to meet a host of people (the overwhelming majority of whom were significantly younger than me) who showed tremendous understanding of my rather unconventional approach to 'military' life. I did not have a proper chance to thank them for their friendship, warmth and patience. Also, the administration of the unit did their best to ensure optimal arrangements, both inside and outside the unit, for my work and research. I consider myself lucky to have spent an otherwise inauspicious part of my life in such an amiable environment. And I am grateful to the Departments of History and Politics of the University of Edinburgh for making my repossession of 'civilian' life so smooth by providing me with the opportunity to resume and, later, expand my teaching activities.

Finally, I am especially indebted to a number of people for whom this book became part of their lives much more than they would desire. Daniel Williams had to endure endless hours of scanning (often round the clock), but he put up with the piercing sound of the electronic equipment with his characteristic good humour and patience. George Pavlakos and Estelle Zinsstag showed a great deal of understanding of my rather anti-social behaviour when I had to devote most of my time to the completion of the project. The same applies to Marc Robertson, who provided me with crucial moral support and practical assistance from the beginning to the final stages of compiling the reader. They were all around when I finished – and I am sure that they felt as relieved and happy as I did!

For any error of fact or judgement in the editorial matter of this reader I *alone* am responsible.

Aristotle A. Kallis
Edinburgh, November 2001

Acknowledgements

The author and publishers would like to thank the following for their permission to reproduce material:

Martin Kitchen, *Fascism*, 1976, Macmillan, reproduced with permission of Palgrave. *Totalitarian and Authoritarian Regimes*, 2nd edition, by J.J. Linz. Copyright © 2000 by Lynne Rienner Publishers. Reprinted with permission of Lynne Rienner Publishers, Inc. R. Eatwell, 'Towards a New Model of Generic Fascism' in *Journal of Theoretical Politics,* 4 (1992), reprinted by permission of Sage Publications Limited. Stanley Payne, 'The Concept of Fascism' in Stein Ugelvik Larsen, Bernt Hagvet and Jan Petter Myklebust (eds.), *Who were the Fascists. Social Roots of European Fascism* (Oslo: Universitetsforlaget, 1980), reprinted with permission of Universitetsforlaget. Robert O. Paxton, 'The Five Stages of Fascism' from *The Journal of Modern History*, 70 (1998), reprinted with permission of the University of Chicago Press and Robert O. Paxton. Palmiro Togliatti, 'On the Question of Fascism', *L'internationale Communiste*, vol. 9 (1928), translated by David Beetham in *Marxists in face of Fascism. Writings by Marxists on Fascism from the Inter-war Period* (Totawa NJ: Barnes & Noble Books, 1984, and Manchester University Press, 1983), reproduced by permission of David Beetham. Charles S. Maier, *Recasting Bougeois Europe: Stabilization in France, Germany and Italy after World War I.* Copyright © 1975 by Princeton University Press. Reprinted by permission of Princeton University Press. Geoff Eley, *From Unification to Nazism: Reinterpreting the German Past,* pp. 254–282, copyright © 1992 by Sage Publications, Inc. Reprinted by permission of Sage Publications, Inc. Ernst Nolte, *Three Faces of Fascism* (Weidenfeld & Nicolson, 1969). Reprinted by permission of the Orion Publishing Group Ltd. Noel O'Sullivan, *Fascism* (JM Dent, 1983) reprinted by permission of the Orion Publishing Group Ltd. Zeev Sternhell, *The Birth of Fascist*

Ideology, copyright © 1991 by Princeton University Press, reprinted by permission of Princeton University Press. Stanley Payne, *A History of Fascism, 1914–1945* (1996, UCL Press and the University of Wisconsin Press), reprinted by permission of Taylor and Francis and the University of Wisconsin Press. Z. Barbu, 'Rumania' in S. Woolf (ed.), *European Fascism* (1968, Weidenfeld & Nicolson), reprinted by permission of Stuart Woolf. Istvan Deak, 'Hungary' in H. Rogger and E. Weber (eds.), *The European Right. A Historical Profile* (1965, University of California Press), reprinted by permission of Istvan Deak. S.M. Ellwood, 'Falange Española, 1933–9' in M. Blinkhorn (ed.), *Spain in Conflict,* copyright © Sage, 1986 reprinted by permission of Sage Publications Ltd. Robert Soucy, *French Fascism: The Second Wave, 1933–39,* © Yale University Press, 1995, reprinted by permission of Yale University Press. Richard Thurlow, *Fascism in Britain* (1986), reprinted by permission of Blackwell Publishing and Richard Thurlow. Reprinted by permission of the publisher from *Totalitarian Dictatorship and Autocracy* by Carl J. Friedrich and Zbigniew K. Brzezinski, pp. 15–26, Cambridge, Mass.: Harvard University Press, copyright © 1956, 1965, by the President and Fellows of Harvard College, copyright © renewed 1984 by Carl Joachim Friedrich. Robert Koehl, 'Feudal Aspects of National Socialism' in *American Political Science Review,* 54 (1960), reprinted by permission of Robert Koehl, Professor of History Emeritus at the University of Wisconsin-Madison. Klaus-Michael Mallmann and Gerhard Paul, 'Omniscient, Omnipotent, Omnipresent? Gestapo, Society and Resistance' in David Crew (ed.), *Nazism and German Society 1933–45* (Routledge, 1994), reproduced by permission of Taylor and Francis and David Crew. Ian Kershaw, *The 'Hitler Myth': Image and Reality in the Third Reich* © Ian Kershaw 1987, reprinted by permission of Oxford University Press. Macgregor Knox, 'Conquest, Domestic and Foreign, in Fascist Italy and Nazi Germany', from *The Journal of Modern History,* 56 (1984), reprinted with permission of the University of Chicago Press. Antonio Costa Pinto, *Salazar's Dictatorship and European Fascism. Problems of Interpretation* (Boulder: Social Science Monographs, 1995), reprinted by permission of Antonio Costa Pinto. Daniel Jonah Goldhagen, *Hitler's Willing Executioners,* copyright © 1996 by Daniel Jonah Goldhagen; Maps copyright © by Mark Stein Studios. Used by permission of Alfred A. Knopf, a division of Random House, Inc., and Little Brown and Company (UK). Michael Burleigh and Wolfgang Wippermann, *The Racial State. Germany 1933–1945* (1991), reprinted by permission of Cambridge University Press. Jonathan Steinberg, *All or Nothing: The Axis and the Holocaust, 1941–43* (1990), reprinted by permission of Taylor and Francis (Routledge) and Jonathan Steinberg, Walter H. Annenberg Professor of Modern European History at the University of Pennsylvania. Mark Neocleous, *Fascism* (1997), reprinted by permission of the Open University Press. R.E. Robertson, 'Race as a Factor in Mussolini's Policy in Africa and Europe', from *Journal of Contemporary History,* 23 (1988), reprinted by permission of Sage Publications Ltd. Susan Zuccotti, *The Holocaust, The French, and the Jews,* copyright © 1993 by Susan Zuccotti. Reprinted by permission of Georges Borchardt, Inc., for the author. B. Wanrooji, 'The Rise and Fall of Italian Fascism as a Generational Revolt', from *Journal of Contemporary History,* 22 (1987), reprinted by permission of Sage Publications Ltd. Tobias Abse, 'Italian workers and

Italian Fascism', from *Fascist Italy and Nazi Germany: Comparisons and Contrasts* edited by R. Bessel (1996), reprinted by permission of Cambridge University Press and Tobias Abse. Detlev J.K. Peukert, *Inside Nazi Germany. Conformity, Opposition and Racism in Everyday Life* (1989), reprinted by permission of Yale University Press and Chrysalis Books. Jill Stephenson, *The Nazi Organization of Women* (Croom Helm, 1981), reprinted by permission of Routledge and Jill Stephenson. Robert O. Paxton, *Vichy France* copyright © 1972 by Robert O. Paxton. Used by permission of Alfred A. Knopf, a division of Random House, Inc. Raymond Carr, *The Spanish Tragedy: The Civil War in Perspective* (Weidenfeld & Nicolson, 1993), reprinted by permission of the Orion Publishing Group and Sir Raymond Carr. Klaus-Jurgen Müller, 'The Structure and Nature of the National Conservative Opposition in Germany up to 1940' in H.W. Koch (ed.), *Aspects of the Third Reich* (Macmillan, 1985) reproduced with permission of Palgrave. Henry A. Turner Jr, 'Big Business and the Rise of Hitler' in *American Historical Review,* LXXV (1969), reprinted by permission of the American Historical Association and Henry A. Turner Jr. Adrian Lyttleton, *The Seizure of Power: Fascism in Italy 1919–1929* (Weidenfeld & Nicolson, 1973), abridged extract reprinted by permission of the Orion Publishing Group. Shlomo Ben-Ami, *Fascism from Above: The Dictatorship of Primo de Rivera in Spain 1923–1930* (1983) © Shlomo Ben-Ami 1983, reprinted by permission of Oxford University Press.

Abbreviations

ACS	Archivo Centrale di Stato
AF	Action Française
BUF	British Union of Fascists
CAUR	Comitato d'Azione per l'Universalità di Roma
CF	Croix de Feu
CGT	Confédération Générale du Travail
CGTU	Confédération Générale du Travail Unitaire
CNT	Confederación Nacional de Trabajo
DBS	*Deutschland-Berichte der Sozialdemokratischen Partei Deutschlands 1934–1940*, 7 vols, Frankfurt-on-Main 1980
DECA	Confederación Española de Derechas Autonomas
EJ	*Encyclopaedia Judaica*
FAI	Federación Anarquiste de Iberia
FET JONS	Falange Española Tradicionalista y de las Juntas de Ofensiva Nacional-Sindicalista
FGC	Fascisti giovanili di combattimento
Gestapo	Geheime Staatspolizei
GIL	Gioventù Italiana del Littorio
GStA	Bayerisches Hauptstaatsarchiv, Abteilung II, Geheimes Staatsarchiv, Munich
GUF	Gioventù universitaria fascista
JAP	Juventud de Acción Popular
JONS	Juntas de Ofensiva Nacional-Sindicalista
JP	Jeunesse Patriot
MSI	Movimento Sociale Italiano

NSDAP	Nationalsozialistische Deutsche Arbeiterpartei
ONB	Opera Nazionale Balilla
OND	Opera Nazionale Dopolavoro
PNF	Partito Nazionale Fascista
PPF	Parti Populaire Français
PSF	Parti Social Français
SF	Solidarité Française
StAM	Staatsarchiv München

Introduction

Fascism in historiography

'Uncomfortable' pasts and controversy in history

WHAT CAME FIRST, history or historiography? Paradoxical though this question might sound, it is one of the most fundamental issues of the philosophy of history. For a long time the positivist historical tradition had appealed to our commonsense perception of time by stating the seemingly obvious: facts come first; their uncovering, narrative and interpretation follow. When E. H. Carr published his celebrated essay *What Is History?* in 1961 (Carr 1987), the idea that the past is conditioned by the present and that facts may tell us different stories about what happened and why it happened, placed the whole debate about history in a new philosophical context which seemed to celebrate diversity of opinion and pluralism over certainty and unwieldy truth. After all, Carr maintained, history thrives on debate, on critical discussion of different views, on controversy and rival conceptions of the past. This view suggested a far more complex relation between the past and history. Rather than simply telling the story of what had happened, historians were also constructing the past through their narratives and diverse interpretations. Controversy was no more an unfortunate side-effect of subjectivity; it was in fact a highly constructive exercise in promoting a deeper and richer understanding of the past.

At the same time, the way we understand history tells us as much about the past itself as about our present. To take one example, *national* history codifies developments of the past in a way that makes sense only from the viewpoint of our current ethnocentricity. The concept of the 'nation' which is prevalent today is therefore projected onto a chaotic past, organising it according to our perceptions and hence constructing a new history along these lines. Inevitably, when social conditions change, when novel ideas are articulated and challenge the old cultural certainties, so our view of the past becomes unsatisfactory, prompting radical reassessments. In this respect, historical interpretation is essentially provisional, a transient statement which by definition cannot claim to represent unassailable 'truth'. Writing history depends on a constant process of re-vision, re-contextualisation, re-construction (Munslow 1997). Thus, new arguments about history always attempt to settle accounts with the past that had been left open by previous historical narratives (Berger, Donovan and Passmore 1999). This is of particular importance when the object of re-examination is what may be called 'an uncomfortable past'. Historic traumas or behaviours which, by present standards, appear unacceptable or misguided (for example, an expansionist war, a painful national defeat, a racist mindset, etc.) often attract the focus of projects aiming to revise conventional knowledge and belief on these subjects. Any 'uncomfortable past' – and especially a recent one – hits raw nerves that reach to the heart of collective memories and identities. On many occasions, dominant historical interpretations of such a past reflect an agonising endeavour to come to terms with the facts themselves, in a way that does not offend the sensibilities of their audience. Of course, as the distance from the events grows, more dispassionate or even radical renditions of the past may find a more accommodating social context in their attempt to rectify, supplement or perhaps challenge historical orthodoxies. But even then, they often prove highly controversial, stirring up acrimonious debates that often transcend academic boundaries and touch upon sensitive political issues (Marwick 1970).

Fascism is an 'uncomfortable past' *par excellence* (Tranfaglia 1996). As an intellectual phenomenon, it appears to have deviated from an ostensible European tradition of humanism, proceeding democratisation and liberal notions of modernity. In the context of national history, it raises awkward questions about continuities with the past, about social attitudes to it and its political legacy for the future. It is not coincidental that views on fascism as a historical 'parenthesis', as intellectually pathological phenomenon alien to both our past and future, had considerable appeal in the immediate postwar period (De Felice 1977: 14–30; Hagtvet and Kühnl 1980: 28; Vincent 1992: 146–8). Fascism was depicted as a distorted, 'bad' form of nationalism, as opposed to a purportedly different, more acceptable official nationalist culture that had predated it (Salvatorelli 1923). It was argued that it had no ideology of its own, depending exclusively on the personal fantasies of its leaders (Rauschning 1939). It was believed that it commanded loyalty only through terror and compulsion, not through any form of social consensus. It was thought that it had no indigenous intellectual roots, having been 'imported' from other countries, and it was allegedly resisted as an alien form of ideology through non-conformity or even organised action. It was conventionally portrayed as counter-revolutionary, anti-modern, socially regressive, intellectually heretical (Horkheimer 1997). In this sense, it was still possible to absolve the past from most of its blame for fascism – and thus liberate the future from the ghost of such an opprobrious historical precedent. It seemed as if fascism could not, and indeed should not, be considered part of the historic continuity of European and individual national histories.

So, when from the early 1960s onwards novel interpretations saw the light of publicity challenging such comfortable orthodoxies in response to new, more stable and open social conditions in many European countries, they sparked off bitter controversies and soon acquired clear political meaning which rendered them even more divisive and explosive. Nothing was left unchallenged – national identity, continuities with the past, the role of social classes and other institutions (state, Church, monarchy), popular memory, the attitude of political and economic elites, long-term foreign policy aspirations. This was the beginning of a painful coming-of-age of post-fascist societies which continues to this day. Of course, many of the arguments that disturbed conventional social views in previous decades have gradually found their way into mainstream historiography – and some of them have acquired the status of the dominant paradigm (Griffin 1998)! The focus of historical revision is constantly shifting, seeking new avenues to challenge our conventional views and propose novel ways of understanding fascism. Available evidence is constantly proliferating and new historical tools or methodologies (for example, oral history, films) offer new viewpoints that enrich and complement the body of existing research into the fascist phenomenon. Yet, even today, more than eight decades since the emergence of the first official Fascist element in Italy, fascism remains a 'conundrum' (Robinson 1981). Its ability to evade unequivocal definitions and interpretations, to arouse strong passions, to sustain older debates and ignite new ones, remains unabated.

Fascism in historiographical perspective

Interwar interpretation (1922–45): Marxist, conservative and liberal early understandings

The urge to explain the rise of fascism and to understand its place in both national and European history is as old as the appearance of fascism itself. Especially after the appointment of the socialist-turned-fascist leader Benito Mussolini as Prime Minister of Italy in October 1922, fascism attracted the attention of various analysts from a broad spectrum of political persuasions, prompting a plethora of Marxist, liberal and conservative interpretations of its causes and prospects for the future. Although it was initially confined to Italy, and arose much earlier than Mussolini himself branded his regime as an 'export' product (1929) (cf. Mussolini 1932), accounts of Italian Fascism – from the right or the left, moderate or radical – did not fail to detect fascism's potential as a pan-European force. In this respect, fascism was examined as an exceptional, violent response to the crisis of interwar liberalism and capitalism, in the extraordinary circumstances of post-First World War insecurity and socialist agitation. Early Marxist accounts generally linked the rise of this novel form of populist dictatorship in Italy to an overall ploy of capitalist forces against the mobilised proletariat. Fascism was perceived as an exceptional type of puppet-regime, prompted by the deep crisis of the world capitalist economy itself and responding to the new international reality created by the 1917 Bolshevik revolution in Russia. The trend towards authoritarianism, Marxist analysts noted, had began in Hungary in 1919, with the violent suppression of the socialist revolutionary efforts of the Bela Kun regime and its replacement by Admiral Horthy's dictatorial system of rule. A similar attempt to crush socialism took place in Germany, when an alliance of liberal, conservative and social democratic elements joined forces against the rule of councils in Bavaria and the Spartacist movement in Germany. In this sense, developments in Italy served as an eloquent confirmation of this trend, as well as a powerful precedent for other countries to follow. Initially, most Marxist commentators exuded a spirit of reassuring optimism about the future – fascism, they argued, was stillborn, an expendable short-term experiment of the elites doomed to collapse through its failure to deliver tangible benefits for its sponsors (De Felice 1970: 36–9; Beetham 1983: 82–7). This, it was expected, would aggravate the crisis of the capitalist system and pave the way for a revolutionary transformation of society along the lines envisaged by Marxist philosophy of history. Of course, such ideas were soon frustrated, first by the resilience of Mussolini's regime in Italy, and second by the subsequent surrender of most European states (not least Germany) to the drive towards dictatorship; a drive which did not strengthen, but in fact gravely undermined, the proletariat's struggle for social change. In the late 1920s the inflexibility and shortcomings of the official Comintern interpretation were becoming obvious even to a number of dissident Marxist analysts. A. Thalheimer based his understanding of fascism on the model of *Bonapartism*, a concept that was derived from Marx's seminal work on the coup d'état of Napoleon III in 1851 France. For Thalheimer, fascism was not an agent of finance capital, but rather the result of a process of neutralisation of social classes which enabled the fascist leadership to build its own independent mass support and centre of power (Beetham 1983: 187–203). In line with Trotsky's analysis of *Bonapartism*, he believed that this process had in fact predated the rise of fascism, going back to Giolittian Italy and the 1930–3 'presidential' cabinets in Germany (Wistrich 1976). But, in general, Marxist interpretations – whether orthodox or dissident – of the interwar period continued to view fascism as a symptom of a much wider problem – capitalism and its ploy to destroy the working class's organisation and fighting power (Beetham 1983). In so doing, they upheld the conventional Comintern argument that fascism should only be targeted within the context of a wider assault on capitalism and of a revolutionary transformation of social structures in accordance with the example set by the Soviet Union (Beetham 1983: 152–3; Degras 1965: 41–3).

This Marxist paradigm was challenged by both liberal and conservative accounts of the interwar period. While Marxist analysts were adamant in castigating fascism as a negative historical experience, the stance of non-Marxist accounts was often ambiguous, if not sometimes sympathetic, especially in the 1920s. This is particularly true of many conservative works which applauded fascism's role as a bulwark to the onslaught of international communism. In the 1920s the Italian regime was praised for restoring order to Italian society and politics, for offering solutions to the country's long-standing economic problems and for reuniting the nation on the basis of an integral nationalism. Fascism seemed to offer the antidote to both the divisive class struggle advocated by Marxism and the fragmentation of society caused by liberal individualism or parliamentary politics (see, for example, Trevelyan 1923; Wells 1933; Ludwig 1982). It was also often regarded as a repudiation of the Enlightenmental tradition of rationality, providing instead a mythic, emotional and therefore more direct form of communication between leadership and the masses. Fascism, it was argued, was a violent response to the decay of European liberalism and its paramount institutions (parliament, political parties, free market, etc.). Some, like O. Spengler (1934), E. Jung (1927), E. Juenger (1922) and F. T. Marinetti (Hamilton 1971: 14, 19–20), saw in it the seeds of cultural and national rebirth after years of terminal stagnation or even disintegration. Its attempt to revive nationalism as the fundamental platform for reorganising social life, its quest for unity, wholeness and discipline, and its resolution (often ruthless) to address chronic domestic problems by providing radical solutions looked promising to the eyes of many conservative interwar analysts (Struve 1973; Sontheimer 1968; Adamson 1993). Although most of them had individual doubts about fascism from the beginning, and later became increasingly disaffected with the fascist movements/regimes, at least initially they provided invaluable support and legitimacy to the fascist experiment.

Ironically, even some prominent liberal commentators displayed a sense of sympathy towards fascism's first steps as a political system. In Italy, the highly respected historian and philosopher B. Croce initially expected Italian Fascism to revive, not destroy, the somewhat stagnant liberal system (Hamilton 1971: 41–4). Another prominent Italian philosopher, G. Gentile, saw in Fascism the remedy for the ethical decay which allegedly befell modern society under liberalism (G. Gentile 1928a and 1928b; E. Gentile 1975: Ch. 6). While, however, Gentile remained loyal to his conversion to Fascism throughout the life span of the Italian Fascist regime (and indeed played a pivotal role in shaping Fascism's political and social ideology), Croce very quickly became disillusioned and followed the path of opposition, like the overwhelming majority of liberal analysts of the interwar period. The liberal critique of fascism differed from its Marxist equivalent in one fundamental aspect: while Marxists perceived fascism as the culmination of a historical process which inculpated both liberalism and social democracy (hence the term 'social-fascists' used by the communists to refer to the social democrats' pro-system attitude), liberals had every reason to defend the liberal system of the past as a positive (if perhaps somewhat flawed) experiment. Marxists did not detect any serious discontinuity in the transition from democracy to fascism; liberals certainly did (Ward 1999: 64–7). Croce was not alone in claiming, both before and after the collapse of the Axis, that fascism had to be examined as a 'parenthesis' in European history. For him it remained a symptom of a serious moral and political malaise which had its roots in the exceptional circumstances of the interwar period (see, for example, Croce 1941).

Transition to post-fascism and the onset of the Cold War

By 1945 the historical fate of fascism had been decided. First, the dismissal of Mussolini by the Fascist Grand Council and King Victor Emmanuel III in July 1943, and then the total defeat of the Nazi armed forces in both east and west epitomised fascism's extinction as a political regime and mainstream ideology. Its two historic figureheads took the secrets of their mortal project to their graves – Hitler committed suicide inside his bunker on 29 April 1945; ironically, just a day earlier, Mussolini was arrested by Italian partisans on his way to Switzerland and executed. The only two surviving interwar dictatorships, Salazar's Portugal and Franco's Spain, hastened to shed symbols and slogans that smacked of fascist persuasion, claiming in their defence that they had remained uncommitted to the Axis project. In a political atmosphere celebrating the painful end of the fascist era and seeking a new political platform for reconstituting post-fascist Europe, there was obviously very little (and marginal) space for nostalgia or rehabilitation. Only a few apologetic accounts of fascism (most of them in Italy, where Fascist sympathisers found refuge in a new political formation, the MSI, the Movimento Sociale Italiano (the Italian Social Movement)) saw the light of publicity and then they remained confined to the fringes of historiography (see, for example, Villari 1959). The post-fascist order was predicated on the paramount moral need to castigate and eradicate fascism. As, however, antagonism between the west and the Soviet Union escalated in the second half of the 1940s, it soon became clear that each side of the victorious wartime coalition understood this need in fundamentally different ways. For the west, post-fascist Europe should be edified on an unequivocal commitment to exactly those values that fascism had defiled – liberalism, democracy, freedom and respect for individual rights. For the Soviet Union, however, transcending fascism entailed a much wider project of radical social transformation. This argument was in line with the interwar Marxist interpretations of fascism as a violent derivative of capitalism's crisis. Accordingly, if fascism had to be eradicated and if society wanted to make sure that it would never resurface in the future, then capitalism itself had to be transgressed, not revamped.

Inevitably, this political-ideological confrontation dominated historiographical production in the two blocs of the Cold War period. Liberal understandings of fascism commanded the majority historiographical and public views in the west; while in the east it was business as usual for Marxist orthodoxies. The restoration of democratic-parliamentary legitimacy to those western countries that had either produced or followed the fascist trend in the 1920s and 1930s dictated the need to exonerate liberalism from any share of responsibility and to reject a reading of national histories in terms of continuity between pre-fascism, fascism and the postwar condition. In this respect, interwar liberal understandings of fascism as a historical 'parenthesis' caused by a general political pathology were instrumental in offering the restored liberal system a new lease of legitimacy. In Germany the rise of Nazism was depicted as a fundamental divergence from the mainstream nationalism of the Bismarckian, Wilhelminian and Weimar regimes, understood better as a side-effect of the economic and political crisis of the interwar period and the bitter feelings caused by the punitive Versailles Treaty. In Italy, the *Resistenza* of 1943–5 provided the historical platform for arguing that Fascism enjoyed no positive support or consensus and could therefore make no claim to represent a continuity of national tradition in modern Italy (Battaglia 1953). In both cases, disproportionate emphasis was placed on the personality of the two fascist leaders and their personal visions and actions, as the key element in explaining away the rise, success and malice of the regimes. This historiographical trend also found strong advocates outside

Germany and Italy, feeding on wartime slogans (for example, Churchill's 'one man alone' rhetoric vis-à-vis the Italian Fascist regime (cf. Macartney 1944)). In France, fascism was widely regarded as a mostly alien import, lacking deep roots in French intellectual traditions and actively resisted by the majority of the population through the networks of resistance in 1940–4 (Aron 1954). At the same time, in those countries where authoritarian but not openly or unequivocally 'fascist' regimes took hold in the interwar period (such as Austria and Greece), attempts were made either to deny the 'fascist' label of these regimes or to compare them favourably to the arguably more extreme German and Italian variants.

In the east, the task of official Marxist historiography was much more straightforward in that respect. The year 1945 signified both the collapse of fascism and the triumph of Marxist teleology, now spreading outside the borders of the Soviet Union to the eastern 'satellite' states. This enormous excision from the previous norm of either authoritarian or liberal system of rule freed national historiography in the east from the task of defending pre-fascist circumstances and choices. In fact, the legitimacy of these newly instituted 'socialist' regimes and of their powerful guarantor (the Soviet Union) rested on exactly this total rejection of the past, this radical new social reality which allegedly redressed not just fascism but also its long-term roots in the capitalist system. While liberal approaches stressed that fascism's main target was the liberal-parliamentary system with its institutions and its modernising drive, Marxist commentators viewed the fascist project as an essentially anti-proletariat exercise, aiming to annihilate the working class's fighting power and organisational strength. Initial Marxist interpretations, in line with liberal equivalents, discerned a blatant, violent anti-modern spirit in fascism; Marxist orthodoxy, however, also dictated a view of fascism as the antithesis of socialism, and hence not just non-revolutionary (Marxists tended to use the word 'revolution' solely in an ethically positive way, involving a categorical improvement in the conditions of the lower social strata) but essentially counter-revolutionary (contrary to the socialist project of the Soviet Union) (Degras 1965: 41–2).

Comparing fascism and Stalinism: the totalitarianist approach

As the ideological conflict between west and east reached new heights in the 1950s, non-Marxist models of interpretation turned to a novel concept of analysis, namely *totalitarianism*. Although the term had first been employed in the context of political science (Arendt 1958; Friedrich and Brzezinski 1956; Schapiro 1972), it soon invaded the historiographical discourse of the west, offering a different viewpoint on the analysis of interwar fascism. Totalitarianism related to the exercise of power and therefore to regimes and not to fascism as either intellectual entity or social movement. It focused on a checklist of certain features (leadership, terror, propaganda, all-embracing party, etc. – see 23) and thus invited immediate comparisons between Nazism, Italian Fascism and the Stalinist regime in the Soviet Union (Hagtvet and Kühnl 1980). Although D. Germino attempted to introduce the totalitarian approach to the study of Italian Fascism, claiming that the regime's 'totalitarian' project depended on the all-embracing character of the Fascist party (Germino 1959), most commentators suggested a much closer affinity between Nazism and Stalinism, with the Italian case regarded as a peripheral and not fully developed form of totalitarianism (Friedrich and Brzezinski 1956: 100f.).

The significant impact of this approach, especially in the USA, owes a lot to the international political setting of the era. It provided a conceptually sophisticated way not just to explain fascism in a wholly negative light (as the mood of the postwar era dictated) but also to link it with the Soviet system of rule and thus discredit the socialist project as well. Perhaps its political agenda was a little bit too transparent at times to win converts from the less partisan quarters of historians and political scientists; perhaps its emphasis lay more on explaining the Soviet system of rule in comparative terms and less on a coherent model for the interpretation of fascism itself. The claim that the Stalinist and Nazi systems were '*basically* alike' (Friedrich and Brzezinski (23)) was cautious enough not to exaggerate the similarities and not to discount the fundamental differences (of ideology, outlook and political objectives) between the two systems; but the emphasis on the actual mechanisms and devices of the 'totalitarian dictatorship' (a truly novel political system according to the disciples of this approach, linked to the effects of modernity on twentieth-century society, such as technology and mass mobilisation) misconstrued the importance of ideology in providing fundamentally different motivations and stimulating diverse expectations in each of the 'totalitarian' systems. This said, however, the totalitarian approach exerted significant influence, if not so much as an overall theory for understanding fascism, at least on the conceptualisation of the fascist experience *as regime*. Historiography turned its attention to whether actually the fascist systems of rule aspired to be, and indeed whether they succeeded in becoming, totalitarian in their policies and grip upon their indigenous societies. It also offered invaluable insight into the structures and functioning of the fascist system of rule, thus introducing a distinction between fascism as intellectual movement and fascism as political regime.

The challenge to orthodoxy: Fritz Fischer, A. J. P. Taylor and the issue of continuity in national history

Yet, as was mentioned earlier, societal change is unkind to old certainties. The start of the 1960s found most European societies on the much more reassuring territory of political stabilisation and economic boom. As the actual historical distance from 1945 grew, so the psychological grip of the fascist experience upon collective conscience became looser and less suffocating. The 1960s proved to be a decade of intense questioning and bold rethinking in both west and east (short-lived though it turned out to be there, as the events of 1968 in Czechoslovakia left little hope for potential imitators). The moral need to censure fascism as an unequivocally pernicious phenomenon and to present it (as liberal historiography had endeavoured to do) as a parenthesis in national and European history gave way to more dispassionate readings of the events, greatly assisted by the increasing availability of documentary evidence. This new trend redrew the map of the historiography on fascism, and through it the view of the past itself. In 1961 the German historian Fritz Fischer published an exhaustive account of Germany's path to the First World War (Fischer 1967). In it he presented his main thesis that the world power aspirations of the Bismarckian and Wilhelminian elite sectors of German society created a political milieu which endorsed aggressive policy-making and indeed war. This assumption was real political dynamite for a number of different reasons. First, it attacked the conventional historiographical view that the First World War had been the result of misconceptions and miscalculations by all major European powers, which led to an uncontrollable 'sliding' into the war in August 1914. By attributing a large share of responsibility to Germany, Fischer demolished the basis for all subsequent German attempts to castigate the view put forward by the Versailles Treaty that Germany alone bore the responsibility for the First World War (Fischer 1975). Second, by examining the Bismarckian and the Wilhelminian Reichs in terms of continuity, Fischer did not shy away from shifting part of the blame to the structures and aspirations upon which the modern German state had been constituted by Bismarck. Third, he provided a methodological alternative to the conventional diplomatic account of the events that led to war in 1914 from the viewpoint of internal politics, paying particular attention to domestic pressures which rendered war an increasingly more appealing course of action (Fischer 1974 and 1975). But the real *tour de force* in Fischer's account lay in the wider implications of his continuity thesis. Indirectly in the beginning but more openly in his subsequent works (Fischer 1986), he suggested that these world power aspirations and domestic structures survived into the interwar period, thus linking 1914 to 1939. For the dominant German historiography of that period, so intent upon presenting Nazism as a parenthesis in national history and salvaging at least the Bismarckian Reich from any major share of responsibility for the events of the first half of the twentieth century, Fischer's arguments amounted to real heresy – and indeed were received as such by an outraged majority inside the German historical profession (Koch 1972).

Again in 1961 came the second blow – A. J. P. Taylor published a deliberately provocative account of the origins of the Second World War in which he twisted the continuity thesis in an altogether different direction (Taylor 1961). In his customary sardonic style, Taylor presented Hitler as a conventional nationalist German politician, not as an exceptional figure of unique qualities and aspirations. For him, the war of 1939 was an undesirable development, caused by diplomatic 'miscalculations' by the Great Powers; but Nazi Germany's initial aspirations did not differ from those of Bismarckian or Wilhelminian nationalism. Continuity also reigned supreme in Taylor's interpretation, but it was a continuity of banality, writ large by external circumstances and human errors. Again, such an analysis flew in the face of most of the certainties of postwar western historiography on fascism – the uniqueness of Hitler's distorted worldview, his alleged sole responsibility in forcing a general war upon Europe, his departure from traditional German notions of nationalism, expansion and prestige, even his desire to go to war against Poland. While Fischer disturbed a powerful *domestic* consensus about how the 'uncomfortable past' of Nazism should be viewed (Ritter 1969–73), Taylor appeared blasphemous in the face of the very certitudes of postwar understandings of Nazism, Hitler and the course of German history. The portrayal of Hitler as a mainstream German nationalist, not dissimilar to his predecessors of the Bismarckian and Wilhelminian Reich (or even the politicians of the Weimar Republic!), struck at the heart of the prevalent view that the answers to the lethal savagery of Nazism lay exclusively in Hitler's personality, his psychopathology and distorted personal view of history (Martel 1999).

Both these debates (continuity and role of the leader) found perceptive (but not always willing) listeners in countries outside Germany. Painful questions about national history and long-term domestic trends have been raised ever since throughout Europe, albeit not to the extent that they were in Germany after Fischer. But historiography in the 1960s broadened its horizons in other ways too. Interest in the general features of fascism as both ideology and political regime produced a number of publications which examined the fascist experience in different countries. New, innovative interpretations of the intellectual derivation and nature of fascism suggested for the first time that fascism did possess some sort of ideology, which was rooted in a dissident current of late-nineteenth-century European thought but became particularly relevant and radical in the exceptional circumstances of the interwar crisis (Mosse 1966; Hamilton 1971). At the same time, sociological research opened up a new avenue of interpretation, arguing that fascism could perhaps form an alternative path to the modernisation of those societies which did not follow the 'orthodox' liberal path to modernity (Lipset 1965; Moore 1966, 1978). A sense of deviation from historical norm was particularly strong with regard to Germany, with its belated unification, rapid industrialisation, survival of atavistic political structures and weak middle-class development. This view of German historical development as peculiar gave rise to the discussion of an alleged German 'special path' (*Sonderweg*). A host of authors, both inside (Dahrendorf 1967; Wehler 1975) and outside (Mosse 1966; Stern 1961) Germany, focused on different aspects of the country's alleged 'backwardness' – political institutions, social structures, culture.

To some extent these issues were imported into Italy, with which Germany shared late state-formation and uneven socio-economic development. But, in general, the breadth and depth of historical revision in Germany did not find serious disciples in other European countries burdened with a form of 'fascist' past. Even in Italy, the only serious discussion of the issue of continuity came from Marxist historiography, not from the liberal majority view, which continued to defend the positive character of the country's development from the *Risorgimento* until 1922. It was Marxist historians, such as G. Procacci (1965), who identified the 1914–15 period as the real fracture in modern Italian history, establishing the foundations of an 'exceptional' kind of regime, authoritarian and unaccountable to democratic institutions, thus presaging the capitulation of the Italian middle class to the allure of Fascism – an interpretation still in line with the official Comintern analysis of fascism as a tool of capitalism with the complicity of the middle strata (see above). Strikingly, no such debate gained much currency in Austria, despite its particular susceptibility to different forms of 'fascist' phenomena in the interwar period (of which Austrian National Socialism was but the most extreme manifestation) (Merkl

1980; Schum 1980). While the establishment of communism in eastern European countries, such as Romania and Hungary, released the official (Marxist) historiography from the intricate task of defending a long-term national past, western states such as Germany, Italy and Austria had to live with it, no matter how difficult it was to explain the rise of fascism within this context. Therefore, insinuations about fascism's relevance to long-term national history touched raw nerves, subverting the efforts to reconstruct a positive sense of postwar national identity. And if Germany, in the end, appeared significantly more responsive to such painful revisions of the conventional view of the past, it was primarily because the collapse of Nazism in 1945 was widely experienced as a historical fracture – prompting a new beginning for the postwar Federal Republic. A discredited past disparaged the notion of a national identity drawing legitimacy from it (Fulbrook 1999a and 1999b; Iggers 1991). In its place, postwar Germany attempted to erect an essentially a-historical *ersatz*: a form of 'constitutional nationalism', based upon the fundamental departure from anti-liberalism and authoritarianism that the new constitution (Basic Law) represented. And even if Fischer's provocative assumptions galvanised opposition from those who feared the total discrediting of Germany's post-unification identity, this proved a short-lived backlash in a society much more amenable to a dispassionate reinterpretation of its past. Italy, by contrast, succeeded in rescuing a sense of national identity through the collapse of Mussolini's regime in 1943, the switch of allegiance from Axis to the Allied bloc and (perhaps even more importantly) the emergence of a powerful resistance movement in the 1940s (*Resistenza*). In a similar way, the view of Austria as an essentially invaded and occupied country by its powerful Nazi neighbour appeared a much stronger historical motive than, say, the enthusiastic crowds which lined the streets in March 1938 to greet Hitler and the parading German armed forces. Upon such arguments and memories both Italy and Austria could rescue a form of national feeling based on the past in the postwar era in a way that Germany could not (and, in fact, was not allowed to).

Perhaps this difference goes a long way towards explaining why it was once again Germany where one of the most persisting postwar taboo issues about fascism was brought under scrutiny. In 1967 R. Dahrendorf declared that the extent of social change under Nazi rule amounted to no less than a revolution (Dahrendorf 1967). A year earlier, this same notion had been put forward in superlative terms by another scholar, the American D. Schoenbaum, in a book-length publication which readily associated Hitler with the idea of a 'social revolution' even in its title (Schoenbaum 1966). Such a view was obviously anathema to Marxist historiography, which continued to view the very term 'revolution' in ethical terms, involving a positive change which, by implication, was only meaningful in a socialist context and with the active participation of the proletariat (as allegedly was the case in 1917 Russia). But it was also a particularly dubious claim to make in the context of the postwar liberal moral inclination to depict fascism as a wholly malignant phenomenon. Even if the use of the term 'revolution' was less ideology laden in liberal than in Marxist historiography, it still conjured up images of a more positive social reality than the post-fascist world was willing to discuss or admit. Until the 1960s, fascism was largely depicted, in west and east alike, as a reactionary force (Griffin 1998: 1–16).

Some western commentators would perhaps go as far as admitting that, through (but not because of) fascism, some European societies underwent a deep social transformation after 1945. But this was regarded as more of a secondary effect, caused by the destructive experience of fascism, than a primary result of fascist intentions (cf. Rauschning 1940). In this sense, the articulation of the notion that fascism had effected a 'revolutionary' programme of social change was a breakthrough in the evolution of fascist studies, introducing an interesting (if not always fruitful) debate about fascism's 'revolutionary', 'reactionary' or 'counter-revolutionary' nature (Mommsen 1979; Weber 1979).

The shift to national history: new foci, new methodologies, new challenges

The 1970s witnessed a historiographical disaffection with all-embracing accounts of fascism as a generic concept, a sense of distrust towards grand theories, and a shift of attention to more in-depth and long-term interpretations of fascism in its various national contexts. In this renewed emphasis on country-specific accounts, the impressive increase in the available primary evidence (as a result of both releasing previously classified documents and exploiting new archives and research tools) produced a series of landmark works which took stock of significant debates on the previous decades and offered new directions in the study of indigenous fascism. Unsurprisingly, it was once again Nazi Germany and Fascist Italy that attracted the bulk of historiographical energies, even if in most cases the underlying theme of analysis was each regime's specificity and uniqueness. The proliferation of accounts of single regimes or movements of the interwar period produced a highly complex landscape, in which the overriding focus on difference seemed to doubt the futility of comparison and synthesis. What was common methodological practice in the past, namely accepting the validity of fascism as a generic phenomenon and focusing on similarities across its various case-studies, now became a liability. First, disproportionate emphasis on Germany and Italy had produced theories of fascism which were derived from either of these two regimes and thus were inappropriate for dealing convincingly with regional variations or even with fundamental differences between Nazism and Italian Fascism themselves. Second, the generic models of fascism that came to attention in the 1960s rested on rather basic generalisations about the nature of fascism, lacking in theoretical elaboration and failing to impart a coherent set of overall definitions and criteria for comparison (Griffin 1998: 12–13). In fact, some of their main assumptions proved inaccurate. The idea that fascism was a heavily middle-class phenomenon, the image of monolithic structure and organisational rigidity of the regimes, the allegedly omnipotent role of the leaders, came increasingly under attack in the 1970s as new, more layered evidence came to the fore. What remained as the common denominator of such a disparate group of movements and regimes was now regarded as too general and abstract to possess any real heuristic value.

In historiographical terms, the 1970s produced a mixed image of innovation, reassessment and retrenchment, in a milieu already highly susceptible to generating controversies. An increasing number of historians abandoned the traditional model of political–diplomatic analysis and shifted their methodological emphasis to social structures and attitudes within the societies that nurtured fascist phenomena in the interwar period. New areas of investigation – such as patterns of decision-making (Mommsen 1966 and 1977), social and economic policy (Milward 1979; Mason 1975 and 1993b), the role of different social groups (classes, women, youth), and local studies – offered alternative fruitful ways of approaching fascism 'from below' in a way that took account of the traditional Marxist emphasis on socio-economic factors without the customary ideological stiffness of official communist historiography in the east. In Germany, a number of historians (Broszat 1981; Schieder and Dipper 1976; Mommsen 1977) used the 'structuralist' model of analysis to challenge the persistent conventional assumptions about Hitler's role in the Nazi system and about the alleged ideological coherence of Nazi policies, as well as about the overall functioning of the regime (see, for example, Hildebrand 1973 and 1979; Jäckel 1972). The result, predictably, was controversy and a somewhat artificial polarisation of historiographical opinion (Kershaw 1995: Ch. 6). A group of prominent historians, including K. D. Bracher (1976), K. Hildebrand (1976) and A. Hillgruber (1973), reacted strongly to what they perceived as an undue dismissal of the achievements of conventional historiography. Social history, it was argued, was not appropriate for the analysis of a phenomenon (fascism) so dependent on the visions of its leaders and on such an extraordinary commitment to a sense of ideological purpose. The subsequent entrenchment of views behind clearly recognisable labels (*structuralism* for the former; *intentionalism* for the latter) did not leave enough room for individual nuances. M. Broszat, for example, did not altogether dismiss the intellectual validity of Hitler's ideas about *Lebensraum*, although he understood its function in the Nazi discourse as an 'ideological metaphor', powerful enough to convey a vague but emotive meaning to a German society conditioned to succumb to its symbolic signification (Broszat 1970 and 1981). At the same time, T. Mason, despite his extensive work on social issues and focus on structural determinants of Nazi policy-making, conceded a high degree of ideological intention to Hitler and advocated the 'primacy of politics' over economics in the Nazi system (Mason 1968). But such subtleties were brushed aside in the face of the deepening fracture between intentionalists and structuralists in Germany – a fracture that has remained beneath historiographical debates until the present day. The discussion about the influence of ideology upon action and policy-making appeared equally relevant to the case of Italian Fascism. While postwar historiography had generally underlined the crucial role of Mussolini in defining the regime's physiognomy and political agenda (Bosworth 1998: Ch. 3), many commentators had also depicted the Duce as an unscrupulous opportunist, a master of propaganda and political deceit. It was G. Salvemini who had provided the first systematic interpretations of the regime along these lines in the 1930s and 1940s (Salvemini 1952 and 1953). Taylor made rudimentary comments about Fascist Italy's lack of clear programmatic substance (Taylor 1961). But the most vehement rebuff of Mussolinian intentionalism came from D. Mack Smith, who in a series of works on interwar Italy consistently reduced the Duce to what could be described as a political clown, devoid of any ideological priorities or political seriousness (Mack Smith 1969 and 1981). Inside Italy, a variant on the intentionalist-structuralist debate started unfolding in the 1970s – in fact, more and more historians there started detecting a sense of general 'programme' in Mussolini's domestic and foreign policy which challenged the conventional approach of Mussolini as an opportunist (for example, Alatri 1963; Rumi 1974); but the dismissive view of Salvemini and Mack Smith also continued to be highly influential. There was simply not enough passion in this debate, at least compared to the acrimonious controversies it generated in Germany. The general impression was that the Fascist regime in Italy, whether ideologically motivated or not, lacked the sense of determinism and missionary zeal that permeated its Nazi equivalent. Given that the prevalent historiographical mood of the 1970s showed growing disaffection with general theories about fascism and focused on the singularity of fascist experience in different countries, such a conclusion seemed to fit the bill perfectly.

In the same period, France experienced a somewhat painful detachment from its Gaullist myths and the particular sort of history associated with them. The powerful nationalist imagery of Resistance, with General de Gaulle as its uncompromising leader, had produced a version of the past in which the Vichy regime appeared as the culmination of French decline, before liberation ushered in a period of renewal (de Gaulle 1954–9). This was a comforting reworking of national history, largely absolving the Fourth (1944–58) and Fifth (since 1958) Republics from the pressing burden of historic accountability for Vichy and collaboration. The 'so-called' Vichy state, as Gaullist historiography used to refer to it, implied the existence of a parenthesis in recent French history for which the French nation should not assume any moral responsibility (Aron 1954). There was also a feeling of pride in that France had defended its democratic institutions successfully in the 1920s and 1930s against the onslaught of fascism. Fascism, Rémond maintained in 1952, had no intellectual roots in France and constituted a forced import which never carried much conviction with the French population (Rémond 1982). At the same time, the classic accounts of Vichy France appeared more concerned with the way Vichy allegedly shielded France from the most lethal excesses of Nazi policy and continued to view the issue of collaboration as relevant only to a small minority of the French population and its leaders. Even Pétain, Aron argued, should be seen in a somewhat favourable light, because his regime sustained those conditions which would enable France to make a decisive, positive step to liberation in 1944 (Aron 1954). This view of the past, however, came under increasing attack in the 1970s, when the psychological grip of de Gaulle's legacy began to slacken. This was reflected in a number of publications both on interwar French 'fascist' movements and on the Vichy regime which appeared more willing to discuss the relevance of France's 'uncomfortable' interwar past (collaboration, anti-Semitism, native 'fascist' groups) to the overall intellectual and political development of the nation (Frey 1999). It was R. Paxton's ground-breaking work on the Vichy regime, published in 1972, which provided the first systematic and authoritative attack on the Gaullist myth of the French as a nation of resisters (Paxton 1972 – see **41**). This process of reassessment would become more extensive, fruitful and – inevitably – controversial in the

1980s, but the roots of dissent from the conventional Gaullist narratives may be easily located in the post-1968 period, which witnessed the first cracks in the previously unassailable political legacy of de Gaulle himself.

The debate on the specificity of Italian Fascism: A. J. Gregor and Renzo De Felice

Although the shift to country-specific accounts of fascism set the historiographical tone throughout the 1970s, certain constants about the nature of fascism as a generic concept had largely survived the revisionist assaults of the previous decades. If, for example, fascism had ceased to be perceived as a purely anti-revolutionary and anti-modern form of socio-political experience, it was nevertheless still regarded as a genus of the right-wing political culture (Griffin 1998: 9–12). The publication of a volume on the European right by H. Rogger and E. Weber suggested a high degree of continuity between the late-nineteenth- and early-twentieth-century radical right, on the one hand, and the various fascist or quasi-fascist phenomena of the interwar period (Rogger and Weber 1965). It was E. Nolte who insinuated a more complex intellectual relation between fascism and the conventional left–right fracture, describing it as essentially anti-socialist but also ideologically cognate to Marxism (Nolte 1965 – see **12**). E. Weber examined fascism in a generic framework and came to the conclusion that it could be best understood as an activist phenomenon, a doctrine produced through action based on a constant fusing of right- and left-wing themes (Weber 1964). But in 1979 A. J. Gregor published a highly controversial account of Italian Fascism as a form of mass-mobilising 'developmental dictatorship', more suited to Italy's twisted path to modernity than the conventional western model of liberal democracy (Gregor 1979a). Obviously, Gregor's argument had absorbed the revisionist view of fascism as a modernising political force, a view that had been first articulated in his previous works (see, for example, Gregor 1974b). Yet, his own interpretation was extraordinary in a host of different ways. It acknowledged fascism's intellectual debts to socialist thought and questioned its conventional identification with the right. Then, on the basis of this argument, he made an emphatic distinction between Nazism and Italian Fascism, the latter being discussed in a much more positive light than the former. Above all, however, Gregor provided perhaps the most emphatic endorsement of intentionalism in the Italian context by maintaining that Fascism possessed a highly coherent, autonomous and cogent ideological profile. For him, Mussolini was an influential political thinker who came up with a remarkably original and eclectic system of ideas from both the left and the right. In fact, Gregor viewed the Fascist leader as a dissident Marxist, increasingly disaffected with the socialist party line and attracted to the dynamics of the idea of nation, but also loyal to the fundamental socialist themes of revolutionary change and mass mobilisation. He based his assertion on extensive research on the intellectual development of the Duce, with a particular emphasis on his transformation from the maximalist socialist of 1912 to the Fascist leader of 1919–22 (Gregor 1979b). It was exactly at this point that Gregor's interpretation diverged from the norm. While the bulk of liberal historiography on Italian Fascism suggested that Mussolini had broken with socialism, if not in 1914–15 (during the *intervento* campaign) then definitely by the end of the First World War (Vivarelli 1967), he portrayed Mussolini's intellectual development in terms of essential continuity and consistency, marrying his belief in fundamental socialist principles with a strong rejection of materialism and a growing fascination with radical nationalism.

Perhaps Gregor overstated both his arguments – Mussolini's intellectual consistency and Fascism's ideological coherence – and this might explain why he remained almost a lone voice in the historiography on fascism, without succeeding in exercising significant influence on subsequent interpretations (Bosworth 1998: 79–80). His work, however, was emblematic of a much wider tendency, especially inside Italy, to re-examine Fascism in more positive terms and in antithesis to Nazism. In this context, the 1970s witnessed a broad conservative retrenchment vis-à-vis Italy's 'uncomfortable' Fascist past. In 1975 R. De Felice (author of a massive biography of Mussolini whose publication commenced in 1965 and went on for almost thirty years and seven volumes until his death in 1997 – see De Felice 1965–97) saw the text of his interview with M. Ledeen published in a short volume with the title *Interview on Fascism* (De Felice 1975). In it he excelled in making a host of extraordinary and highly controversial revisionist claims, which have been hotly debated to this day. As De Felice was also impressively prolific as an author, the articulation and restatement of his portentous views in numerous subsequent publications continued to amaze and stir controversy throughout the 1980s and 1990s (see below). For a start, De Felice deplored the legacy of the *Resistenza* for the postwar Italian Republic, condemning its disproportionate emotive imagery as a serious distortion of national history and as the cause of the Republic's subsequent ills. He also bemoaned what he perceived as the violent termination of Italy's identification with a positive sense of nationalism as a result of Fascism's systematic discrediting in postwar historiography. For De Felice, post-Fascist Italy was in desperate need of an alternative model to the 'anti-Fascist' myth of the *Resistenza* – a sort of 'anti-"anti-Fascist"' orthodoxy which would revise the conventional liberal and Marxist accounts of Mussolini's Italy as a reactionary, destructive and overall negative stage of the country's recent history (De Felice 1979). In line with Gregor's controversial analysis, he detected a positive modernising legacy in Fascism, mainly originating from its early days as a radical movement which, in sharp contrast to Nazism, was forward-looking and essentially revolutionary. This revolutionary-modernising angle, he argued, was of course mitigated when Fascism evolved as a regime and system of rule, but was reinvented during the last two years of Mussolini's life, in the so-called Republic of Salò (De Felice 1975 and 1977). While the majority of historiographical accounts viewed the history of this puppet state in strongly negative terms (as a protectorate of Germany, highly anti-Semitic and solely depending on the use of terror over the population – see Mayda 1978), De Felice expressed a certain sympathy with what he understood to be Mussolini's last effort to go back to the origins of Fascism and extenuate a part of it in the eyes of subsequent Italian generations.

All this already amounted to a revision of the ideological fabric of postwar historiography on Italian Fascism so gigantic and groundbreaking that it could not go unnoticed. But De Felice had no intention of stopping here. Mainly through the numerous pages of his volumes on Mussolini's biography but also in other peripheral publications, he continued his relentless attack on the 'anti-Fascist' version of Italian history. His inherent anti-socialism (fuelled by the polarised political climate of the 1970s and 1980s in Italy) induced him to see Fascism's struggle for order and security through the destruction of socialist fighting power in 1919–25 as an essentially positive development (De Felice 1966 and 1968). He also argued that the Fascist regime enjoyed a considerable degree of social support ('consensus') throughout its life span, culminating in 1936 in the aftermath of the occupation of Adis Abeba and the declaration of the Italian empire (*Impero*). Even the Republic of Salò, he argued, commanded the loyalty of a sector of the population – an argument which was designed to strike at the heart of the Resistance myth and its assertion that it constituted a popular, trans-class uprising against Fascism and Mussolini personally. But De Felice also deplored the absence of a true national consciousness in the Italian bourgeoisie, that sense of duty to the *patria* which had been so conspicuous in Germany but dissolved in Italy during the years of the war. In this respect, he perceived his task of revising the conventional view of Fascism as a contribution to something he (and a growing number of historians from the 1970s onwards) believed to be the optimal course for the future – the re-establishment of a sense of national unity and identification with the national past that sharply diverged from the 'divisive' and embellished legacy of the *Resistenza*.

De Felice, like Hildebrand and Bracher in Germany, advocated with characteristic passion the need to return to a history from above, dismissing the methodological fecundity of social history. His work was the apotheosis of neo-positivism, an unconditional commitment to accumulating new archival sources, quoting extensively from documents and speeches, writing a history of what actually happened through evidence. He was often accused (not unfairly) of a headstrong over-reliance on the sources, taking words at face value without either paying sufficient attention to the context in which they had been enunciated, or interpreting them in a critical way (see, for example, Tranfaglia 1995). His revisions galvanised both liberal and Marxist historiography, generating new debates in the somewhat barren (at least by comparison to Germany) historiographical landscape on Italian Fascism. But, unlike what happened in Germany in the 1980s (see below), conservative reappraisals in Italy proved significantly more influential and plausible, outlasting many of their most vehement critics of the 1970s. Until his death De Felice continued to support his revisionist model with a host of new personal publications and a powerful academic network of loyal disciples, both inside Italy's historical establishment and internationally. And, in the end, whatever arguments on Italian Fascism have seen the light of day since the 1970s, they were largely compelled to take a clear (critical or sympathetic) stance vis-à-vis his version of history and his methodological fixations.

New Marxist approaches: Stamokap historians

In defiance of the general trend towards country-specific accounts of fascism, Marxist approaches struggled to uphold the idea that fascism should be examined in generic terms. The fundamental premise that fascism should be treated as a wider problem of capitalist crisis and transformation remained largely unassailable, even in the most sophisticated Marxist accounts of the 1970s. But an increasing body of Marxist historiography, especially in the west but to some extent also in the east, absorbed the new empirical evidence and responded to the calls for revision, or at least elaboration, of the orthodox line of interpretation. Even the powerful *Stamokap* (a bizarre acronym derived from *Staatsmonopolistische Kapitalismus,* state-monopoly capitalism) historical guild of East Germany acknowledged the need for a more nuanced restatement of its thesis (Beetham 1983; Iggers 1991; Dorpalen 1985). Ever since the late 1960s Eichholtz and Czichon had detected significant divisions within finance capital in Nazi Germany, thus rendering previous generalisations about an allegedly unified bloc of big business untenable (Eichholtz 1971; Czichon 1972; Eichholtz and Gossweiler 1980). At around the same time, the view from Hungary (arguably the least 'orthodox' country of the communist bloc in eastern Europe) appeared to have taken stock of historiographical developments outside the socialist world – one of the most resilient constants of the Marxist model of fascism, its predominantly middle-class character, became the subject of scrutiny and revision. Of course, it would be ideologically inconsistent with the overall Marxist theory of history to endorse the arguments put forward by western historians about fascism's trans-class character (which implied that it succeeded in making inroads into the proletariat too!). But the idea that fascism was 'autonomous' from any particular social class, that it developed its political profile in relative autonomy (and often divergence) from middle-class aspirations, invaded the Marxist discourse on fascism (Vajda 1976). Understandably, the margins for revision were significantly larger in the western world, where Marxist commentators felt less bound by any sort of ideological duty to dogmatic continuity. It was, therefore, in France that the sociologist N. Poulantzas (1974) produced a highly sophisticated interpretation of generic fascism which eloquently recorded the changes that had taken place in the Marxist camp. Poulantzas elaborated the idea of fascism's 'relative autonomy' from any particular social class by defining it as an 'exceptional' form of capitalist-imperialist regime in a situation of deep crisis. He shed light on the way that a certain elite of the fascist party (and not the party as a whole) had infiltrated and corroded the state, thus generating a new system of rule, fairly autonomous from either initial fascist aspirations or the interests of any individual social group. Through this process of gradual change, Poulantzas argued, fascism ensured a certain degree (and impression) of continuity with the liberal past which guaranteed its internal stability and offset the danger of its immediate collapse (Caplan 1977).

The idea of continuity between fascism and a flawed version of liberalism like the one experienced by most European countries in the first decades of the twentieth century had a mixed fate in various national historiographies. While, as we saw, it became a common theme in Germany, it still appeared far from universally accepted in France and, especially, Italy. In this respect, the gap between Marxist and liberal interpretations was still obvious and unbridgeable. In Italy, the work of the celebrated leader of the Communist Party A. Gramsci (who had spent many years in prison during Fascist rule, only to be released shortly before his death in 1937) continued to exert an influence of almost mythical proportions over the historiography of the left (Gramsci 1971). His interpretation of Fascism as the result of a long-term pathology in the course of Italian history prompted him to focus on the legacy of the *Risorgimento*. In contrast to most liberal historians, who viewed (and in fact continue to do so) the Italian unification as a positive historical development, Gramsci attacked it as a *rivoluzione mancata* (missed revolution), burdening modern Italy with a flawed social and political legacy for the future (Clark 1977). The debate on the nature of the *Risorgimento*, although not directly relevant to the analysis of Fascism, did implicate the interwar period in a wider discussion about continuities in modern Italian history (Riall 1994: 63–75). While liberal historians, like R. Vivarelli and S. Romeo, continued to advance interpretations which handled Fascism in parenthetical terms and cherished the liberal tradition of the modern Italian state (Vivarelli 1981; Romeo 1963 and 1978), left-wing historiography insinuated that the deeper reasons behind the capitulation of the Italian state to Fascism in 1922–5 lay in the long-term shortcomings of Liberal Italy, stretching back to the time of national unification. It was Trotsky, after all, writing in the 1930s, who had detected the origins of a Bonapartist type of regime in the Giolittian (ostensibly liberal) period (Hayes 1992). While, however, Italian liberals were extremely defensive about the legacy of the *Risorgimento*, the merits of Liberal Italy and the moral validity of the country's participation in the First World War, non-Marxist historians elsewhere appeared more willing to perceive continuities between liberalism and Fascism. When, for example, R. J. B. Bosworth suggested that Italy's decision to enter the war in 1915 was motivated by a not-all-that-dissimilar notion of nationalism to the one underpinning the Fascist expansionist pursuits in the 1930s, his views were summarily brushed aside by the majority of Italian liberal historians (Bosworth 1979 and 1983). The attempt to introduce categories of analysis that were first rehearsed in Germany (for example, Fischer's idea of long-term continuity) stumbled upon a sense of pride in Italy's 'liberal' past, in the legacies of Cavour, Mazzini and Garibaldi; by contrast, modern Germany's foundation myth was Chancellor Bismarck, a man of strong Prussian authoritarian tendencies with no liberal credentials. The analogy, it was implied, was erroneous – Fascism was different from Nazism, in the same way that the overall course of modern Italian history shared very little with that of modern Germany (cf. Chabod 1963b).

Attempts at synthesis: the comparative study of fascism in the 1970s and its critics

So, with all these country-specific accounts and the inclination to focus on differences rather than fundamental similarities between 'fascist' interwar movements and regimes, where did the 1970s leave the concept of *generic* fascism? If fascism as a

historical phenomenon had enjoyed wide publicity in the 1960s, with both new interpretations and viewpoints suggesting a more complex picture of its nature and
relevance than the one initially suggested, the 1970s ended on a sombre note. In an
article published in 1979 G. Allardyce denounced the term 'fascism' as a generic
concept, arguing that its use and abuse by postwar historiography had deprived it of
any heuristic value. Nazism, in his view, possessed unique characteristics and
dynamics that set it clearly apart from any other extreme phenomenon of the
interwar period (Allardyce 1979). In fact, he was not the first to evince this argument – ever since the end of the war the Nazi regime had attracted special attention
for the unprecedented scale and ferocity of its use of terror (epitomised in the policies of the 'Final Solution'). Taylor's suggestion that Italian Fascism was a 'fraud'
by comparison (Taylor 1961), albeit exaggerated, reflected the mood of a wide
section of historiography which tended to view Fascism as less serious and extreme
than Nazism. But Allardyce did not simply reiterate this thesis; he also struck at the
heart of the belief that 'fascism' was an appropriate term for a series of interwar
radical regimes in Europe. This was essentially the methodological assumption
behind the all-embracing anthologies of 'fascist' phenomena which were published
throughout the 1960s (Woolf 1968; Weber 1964; Carsten 1967); and Allardyce
summarily dismissed it as both unhelpful and misleading.

These were indeed inauspicious years for historical generalisations and comparative methodologies. P. M. Hayes and A. Cassels attempted to sustain the debate on
generic fascism (Hayes 1973; Cassels 1975), suggesting a distinction between
Nordic and southern variants of fascism – the former influenced by Nazism and the
latter emulating Italian Fascism. But, overall, it seemed that Allardyce's scathing
attack on the generic model of analysis in 1979 summed up accurately the prevalent mood of scepticism that marked the 1970s. However, in the second half of the
decade, the time was ripe for a major reassessment of the course of historiography
on fascism. The proliferation and elaboration of interpretations was so impressive
that the need for some sort of digest, summarising past developments and making
new paths for future analysis, became evident. In 1976 W. Laqueur published a
volume that brought together two different types of contributions: first, country-
specific essays that outlined the major historiographical developments in the
study of indigenous fascism (including, for the first time, references to populist
regimes of South America – Hennessy 1979); and second, general expositions of
various aspects of generic fascism. Two of these expositions, Z. Sternhell's piece
on fascist ideology (1979) and J. J. Linz's essay on the nature of fascism (1979)
provided new stimulating ways of rehabilitating the concept of generic fascism. On
the one hand, Sternhell discussed a model of fascist ideology which was largely
derived from Fascist Italy and (in line with Gregor's interpretation) paid particular
attention to its mixed intellectual origins (located both in radical nationalist and in
dissident socialist bodies of thought), thus rejecting the conventional identification
of fascism with the right. But Sternhell also echoed the tendency of the 1970s to
treat Nazism as a genus of its own, distinct from any generic model of fascism
(Sternhell 1979: 328). In this sense, Nazi Germany was regarded as unsuitable for
educing general conclusions about the nature of fascism as a whole. Linz, on the

other hand, saw Italy as the intellectual cradle of fascism but was less willing to limit the application of his model by excluding Nazi Germany. His interpretation owed a lot to his sociological background — fascism, he argued, was a 'late-comer' in the already overcrowded spectrum of political ideologies, struggling to occupy an autonomous space and define its ideological character independently. This, for him, explained why fascism was essentially a negative phenomenon, an assortment of oppositions (to socialism, liberalism, democracy, etc.) which alone gave it a partic- ular meaning of its own (Linz 1979: 29–39). Linz also linked fascism's wide appeal to its very distinct 'style' of political conduct and eclectic ideology, which together proved very successful in mobilising a broad section of the population regardless of class, age group or previous political affiliation (cf. 3).

Did all this amount to some form of exoneration of generic fascism, after the barren years of the 1970s, despite Allardyce's gloomy story? Hindsight, based on developments in the subsequent two decades, provides an affirmative answer. The year 1979 saw another ground-breaking publication, this time from G. L. Mosse and again in the form of a collection of essays on country-specific aspects of fascism. In his introduction to the volume, Mosse provided a masterly analysis of fascist ideology and political practice in generic terms. A disciple of the history of ideas himself and author of works on the intellectual origins of Nazism, he adopted the view that fascism was derived from a unique blend of radical right-wing and socialist themes, a 'scavenger' determined to provide a new synthesis that was capable of transcending both liberalism and Marxism in pursuit of a 'third way' (Mosse 1979). Like Linz, Mosse saw no reason to exclude Nazism from his definition and coverage of his volume, but discussed it critically in comparison not just to Italy, but also to the experience of fascism in Austria, France and Scandinavia. A year later, S. Payne (a scholar with particular research interests in Francoist Spain (Payne 1961, 1980b and 1986)) supplied a book-length reinstatement of generic fascism, based on a highly sophisticated model of fascist ideology (Payne 1980a: 6ff. – cf. 5). This model, as Payne admitted, was a sort of 'ideal type' which applied to varying degrees to different case-studies. But he saw country-specific individual variations as a challenge and incentive for further elaboration, not as precluding comparative analysis. His model of fascist ideology was tripartite (negations, ideology, style), absorbing views that had been articulated before him (Linz's and Mosse's influence here is evident).

Therefore, the start of the 1980s reflected an impressive pluralism of approaches to fascism, a deep epistemological division amongst historians of the period as to what constituted fascism, and a wider deliberation on the most constructive way forwards. The country-specific model of analysis continued to appear unassailable, but the dismissal of the generic nature of 'fascism' had not gone unchallenged by a minority of commentators. At the same time, the rehabilitation of fascism's generic dimension continued to be fraught with competing suggestions as to which regimes or movements were 'fascist' and which should be excluded from the general defini- tion. The conventional view of Nazism and Italian Fascism as the two most prominent case-studies of fascism was questionable for some (Sternhell 1979; Allardyce 1979; De Felice 1977), upheld by others (Payne 1980a; Linz 1979 and

1980; Mosse 1979), and regarded as too restrictive by a third group (the discussion of other regimes/movements in Laqueur's reader suggested an extension of the sample outside Europe and in the post-1945 period). Opponents of the generic approach underlined this puzzling diversity of definitions and foci in arguing that such a model was methodologically flawed and essentially unhelpful. There were still, however, glimpses of hope for the genericists. The year 1980 saw the publication of one of the most sophisticated, comprehensive and constructive collections of essays on fascism (Larsen, Hagtvet and Myklebust 1980). In almost 800 pages of dense, lucid analysis, the volume brought together some of the most elaborate interpretations of fascism, which remain impressively relevant even today. Following Laqueur's structure, the volume featured essays on both the generic dimension of fascism and on national case-studies from interwar Europe. Unlike its precursor, however, it was less concerned with summing up bibliographical developments or with extending the focus of analysis beyond Europe; instead, it provided mainly novel interpretations of various aspects of the fascist experience, with an exhaustive coverage of European fascisms, from Germany and Italy to Spain and Portugal, and from Belgium to the Nordic countries. Of particular importance for the reinstatement of generic fascism was R. Kühnl's discussion of the various theories of fascism and J. J. Linz's more elaborate exposition of his 'later-comer' thesis, four years after its first airing in Laqueur's reader (Linz 1980). An extraordinary feature of this new collective volume was its even-handed treatment of both the most prominent 'fascist' case-studies (Italy, Germany) and the more marginal peripheral phenomena (for example, the Arrow Cross of Hungary, the Iron Guard of Romania, the Rexists of Belgium, the People's Patriotic Movement of Finland, etc.). In so doing, the volume shed light on the plurality of fascist-like movements in the countries of interwar Europe, their individual differences and their often hostile relations – even within the same country. Instead of taking their 'fascist' character for granted (as many of the collective works of the 1960s used to do), the contributions discussed the relations of these movements/regimes with conservative, Catholic, traditional authoritarian and radical leftist ideological strands. Thus, a far more complex picture emerged, in which fascism was compared (but not identified) with more conventional forms of dictatorship or populist right-wing phenomena that emerged in the interwar period.

France and the fading of the Gaullist legacy: the 'Sternhell controversy'

And then all went quiet on the 'generic' front. For a decade or so the search for more elaborate explanatory models of generic fascism entered (with only a few, isolated exceptions (O'Sullivan 1983; Wippermann 1983)) a historiographical twilight zone, leaving the plateau empty for even more country-specific approaches, more narrow foci and more controversies about fascism's relation to national past. This trend produced mixed results – sometimes invigorating a healthy reassessment of conventional myths about a country's 'uncomfortable past' but often generating a historiographical parochialism, an idolatry of national uniqueness and – occasionally

– apologetic views about national past. France, where historiographical orthodoxies had more or less withstood the first wave of revision in the 1970s, experienced a psychological chasm with its Gaullist past. The proliferation of studies on interwar French 'fascist' movements and parties (Croix de Feu, Faisceau, Doriot's PPI etc.) unmasked their much higher degree of ideological affinity to fascist ideas (Sternhell 1980). The traditional view of fascism as alien to France's intellectual traditions gave way to an acknowledgement that, as Z. Sternhell put it, the country was perhaps the best place for the incubation of fascism (Sternhell 1980: 479–89; cf. Sternhell 1986). Emphasis was placed on dissident radical ideological strands of the Third Republic as precursors of a particular French variant of fascist thought – amongst many, Sorel's national syndicalism, irrationalism and glorification of violence as revolutionary technique; Boulangism's fusion of nationalism with socialist rhetoric in opposition to the Republic; the Action Française's radical nationalism and anti-liberalism (a movement that had attracted the attention of Nolte in the 1960s (Nolte 1965: 29–141)); and G. Le Bon's ideas on charismatic leadership. Fascism was, therefore, not an import of external ideas but a culmination of certain native radical trends of the late nineteenth century which withstood obscurity, influenced other countries (for example, Italy) and re-emerged with a vengeance in the 1920s under-pinning the various French 'fascist' phenomena of the interwar period. The classic accounts of the 1950s and 1960s, largely inspired by the Gaullist myth of over-whelming opposition to German occupation and very limited complicity by a small minority of 'traitors', subsided in favour of a more dispassionate and potentially upsetting picture of a higher degree of collaboration and less resistance. R. Paxton's and M. R. Marrus' detailed works on the Vichy regime exposed the willingness with which the administration of southern France succumbed to Nazi anti-Semitic obses-sions and actively assisted the systematic persecution of the Jewish population of France (Marrus and Paxton 1981). G. Bertram built upon S. Hoffmann's distinc-tion between 'active collaboration' with the Nazis and 'informal' forms of casual collaborationism with the authorities, thus offering a significantly more layered picture of the variety of attitudes towards the moral dilemma between resistance and complicity (Bertram 1980; S. Hoffmann 1974). This was also the essence of the approach of J. F. Sweets, who focused more heavily on the notion of resistance but once again came upon the same distinction between organised/active and unoffi-cial/casual opposition to the Vichy regime (Sweets 1986). Thus, the study of the Vichy period became the stepping stone for revisiting two different sensitive issues – first, the intellectual roots of native anti-Semitism in France, portraying the excesses of the 1940s as the culmination of pre-existing trends, evident in the polit-ical discourse of the Third Republic (for example, the Dreyfus affair of 1893–8); and second, the broad spectrum of popular dispositions towards the 'collabora-tion–resistance' dilemma which could not be unravelled by the somewhat simplistic Gaullist 'either–or' scheme (Frey 1999: 205–16).

There were still, however, powerful clusters of Gaullist myths which continued to hold the official state discourse of the French Republic hostage. It was the first socialist president of the Fifth Republic, F. Mitterrand, who refused to accept the anniversary of the round-up of the Jewish population of Paris in 1944 as an official day of remembrance for the French nation, with the justification that the Republic could not bear the responsibility for crimes committed under the allegedly alien Vichy 'non-state'. Mitterrand, himself burdened with his alleged personal 'uncomfortable past' dating back to his links with the Vichy administration, appeared unwilling to push forward a final settling of accounts with this chapter of French history, seeking instead a form of obliteration and excision of these years from the nation's collective memory (Frey 1999; Conan and Rousso 1994). Such a resistance to attempts to 'historicise' the Vichy regime originated from a view of this period as an exceptional phase in modern French history, in which conventional ideas of patriotism and devotion to the nation had been suspended or distorted in the face of extraordinary circumstances that had forced a – much larger than previously believed – part of the French population to adopt a moral stance irreconcilable with the prevailing attitudes of the postwar French Republics.

It was, therefore, not surprising that the publication of Z. Sternhell's groundbreaking account of French interwar fascism in 1983 aroused such bitter controversy, culminating in a series of court charges for defamation against the historian. Sternhell argued that interwar France was saturated with ideological trends and political formations that could certainly be described as 'fascist'. He also linked the vulnerability of French intellectual and political life to fascist ideas as highly responsible for the collapse of French resistance against the advance of the Nazi forces in 1940 and for the country's smooth administrative adaptation to the occupation. His interpretation unleashed the 'Vichy ghost' – as the painful reassessment of this period was commonly referred to in the 1980s – suggesting a far higher degree of ideological continuity between the Third Republic and the administration of the two French areas in the early 1940s. But controversy did not stop there. Sternhell's carefully chosen title for his book, *Neither Right nor Left*, suggested a summary rejection of the conventional view of fascism as predominantly a genus of extreme right-wing ideology (Griffin 1998: 9–10; Eatwell 1995: Ch. 1). This theme, that fascism can be best understood as a revision of Marxism, he elaborated in a number of subsequent publications. He rejected Marxism's traditional dependence on materialism and the concept of class in favour of a radical form of nationalism and a mythical, irrational style of political mobilisation (Sternhell 1987 and 1994). For Sternhell, fascism should be seen as a revolutionary force, ideologically coherent and eclectic, seeking an alternative route to social transformation beyond orthodox Marxism, liberalism, conservatism or social democracy.

Apart from its sensitive political repercussions, the so-called 'Sternhell controversy' stimulated a wider historiographical debate amongst historians of fascism. Some, like A. Costa Pinto (1986) and R. Wohl (1991), remained largely unimpressed by the facility with which Sternhell branded a host of disparate interwar French movements and parties as 'fascist', in spite of their significant individual differences and their often sceptical attitude towards Nazi Germany and, to an extent, Fascist Italy. Although in a subsequent publication Sternhell provided his own definition of fascism along the lines presented in his *Neither Right nor Left* (Sternhell 1987), his critics reproached him for his unsubstantiated claims and his rather tenuous use of the term 'fascism'. Others, like R. Soucy (1986 and 1995), attacked his unconventional interpretation of 'fascism' as a revision of Marxism in a radical (and revolutionary) nationalist direction as ignoring fascism's actual political agenda once in power. They reminded their readers that the first taste of most fascist regimes was to destroy the organisational structures of the socialist left and to co-operate with certain sectors of the ruling elites in defence of – and not in fundamental opposition to – the existing social order. It was perhaps more accurate, Wohl stated, to say that fascism was *both* left and right in doing justice to its intellectual eclecticism (Wohl 1991), but in its government practice it remained a predominantly anti-socialist and anti-liberal force, more intent on destroying the labour movement and on offsetting the danger of a socialist revolution than on systematically pursuing a far-reaching vision of revolutionary transformation of its own.

De Felice and anti-'anti-Fascism'

With so much revision let loose and so extensive a questioning of national past, a further group of scholars of French history reacted to what they perceived as a wholesale discrediting of any positive form of identification with the nation. Echoing similar concerns to De Felice's passionate pleas for reinventing a positive sense of national identity through history (see above and below), J. Nora lamented the erosion of belief in the French nation as a constructive force behind recent national history (Nora 1984–92). Rather than discussing the essence of recent revisions of the postwar Gaullist view of the past, Nora seemed to reject its alleged excesses and its negative consequences for national unity (Jackson 1999: 243–4). With the De Felicean machinery of academic production in full motion in the 1980s (the fifth volume, covering the 1936–40 period, was published in 1981 (De Felice 1981), followed by other books on Mussolini, writings on the Resistance and a major revision of his 1961 publication on the Italian Jews (De Felice 1988)), a similar debate continued to unfold in Italy throughout the 1980s before reaching its peak in the 1990s. What De Felice and his disciples had set out to achieve was a rewriting of the history of Fascism starting from the premise that 8 September 1943 (the day Italy switched her allegiances from the Axis to the anti-fascist alliance) and the subsequent years of the *Resistenza* amounted to a 'national catastrophe' which seriously undermined the development of a postwar healthy identification with national history (Bosworth 1998: 200–2). The world had to wait until 1990 and 1997 (the years when the last two volumes of Mussolini's biography for the 1940–5 period were published) to find out De Felice's detailed view of events (De Felice 1990 and 1997), but his 'anti-"anti-Fascist"' project continued to evolve throughout the 1980s and to command the loyalties of a growing number of Italian historians. In 1980 R. Quartararo published an impressively detailed account of Fascist foreign policy in the 1930s in which she attributed Mussolini's eventual shift to the Axis and belligerence to the misguided British foreign policy of complacency and marginalisation of Italy as a potential ally (Quartararo 1980). Echoing De Felice's main argument about Mussolini's 'realism' (Knox 1995) and lack of clear commitment to the Axis until the very end, Quartararo portrayed a Duce desperately clinging to the possibility of some form of understanding with the west before turning as a last resort to Germany and war. Whilst A. Del Boca fought a solitary historiographical war to expose the excesses of Italy's colonial policies in the 1930s (extermination of the Sanussis in Libya, use of poison gas in Ethiopia) (Del Boca 1969 and 1976; cf. Rochat 1973), De Felice reiterated his view that the Ethiopian campaign was Mussolini's 'masterpiece' (De Felice 1974: 758ff.). His contribution to the treatment of the Jews under Italian Fascism underlined the idea that Italy – in contrast to Germany – was significantly more humane towards minorities, both inside Italy and in the occupied areas (De Felice 1988).

At a time when international historiography seemed so intent upon advancing the view that Nazi racial policies were unique and unprecedented in both brutality and extent, De Felice's picture of the Italian nation as a 'gentle people' seemed a fairly plausible inference based on comparison. That it was exploited, however, in order to advance De Felice's obsession with a more sympathetic view of the Fascist past (and his previous themes about Fascism's 'modernising' tendencies and Mussolini's 'revolutionary' intentions bear witness to this) was an altogether different matter. His assault on the moral validity and historical legitimacy of the 'anti-Fascist orthodoxy' of postwar Italy did have a positive effect, generating a fresh look at the events of the 1940–5 period and introducing the view of the *Resistenza* as a far-from-universal struggle of the Italian nation against the last vestiges of Fascism (Levy 1999; Tranfaglia 1996; Zapponi 1994). Reactions from the 'anti-Fascist' camp did come to the fore, questioning De Felice's relativisation of the moral choices with which the Italians were confronted in 1943–5. G. Quazza and N. Tranfaglia attacked his ideological motives and his literal reading of only those sources that endorsed his argument (implying that he had also discounted 'anti-Fascist' sources in his accounts) (Quazza 1976; Tranfaglia 1984). For them, the Resistance remained a morally valid choice against the evils that Fascism had inflicted upon society for two decades, vindicated by the postwar commitment to democratic institutions and respect for individual rights. Yet, in the much more polarised political climate of postwar Italy (accommodating both a strong Communist Party and a direct rebranding of the Fascist legacy, namely the MSI (Chiarini 1991)), De Felice's revisionist views found significantly more auspicious circumstances for commanding broader loyalties than, say, in France or Germany.

Sonderweg and Historikerstreit in Germany: Nazism, national identity and the Holocaust

Parochialism was not the exclusive unfortunate preserve of Italian historiography. After two decades of unparalleled (in both breadth and depth of coverage) constructive revisionism, Germany experienced a similar form of historiographical introversion in the 1980s. Of course, many of the new ideas that had been articulated during previous years had found their way into mainstream historiography, enriching its methodological apparatus and broadening the horizons of research. The intentionalist–structuralist debate (see above) continued to be a defining issue of interpretation, but there was evidence that the need for synthesis between the two methodologies and outlooks was accepted by a growing number of historians (Kershaw 1995; Mason 1981). Another important debate on the nature of Nazism (and, by implication, of fascism in general), that concerning *modernity*, displayed a similar pattern of convergence and synthesis. In 1984 J. Herf attempted to bridge the gap between those detecting a modernising outlook in Nazism and those rejecting it on the basis of the regime's appalling political objectives (Herf 1984). Herf put forward the term 'reactionary modernism', stating that the Nazi system endorsed modernity as a means (for example, technology) to a horrifying anti-modern end. At the same time, the idea of a German *Sonderweg*, rooted in the allegedly unconventional evolution of the Bismarckian and Wilhelminian Reichs, was waning (Steinmetz 1999). In the early 1980s D. Blackbourn and G. Eley published a volume on the alleged peculiarities of German history, in which the various contributions argued convincingly that the differences between Germany and Britain had been exaggerated (Blackbourn and Eley 1984). They suggested that, although the Kaiserreich possessed unique qualities, it was an essentially bourgeois phenomenon. It was also shown that many of the more eccentric phenomena of pre-Nazi German history (eugenics, imperialism, etc.) had parallels in the western world (see Blackbourn 1991). Similar criticisms against the alleged overstatement of Germany's historical 'peculiarities' were put forward by another collection of essays, this time by Blackbourn and R. J. Evans, which was published at around the same time (Blackbourn and Evans 1991). The idea of overall continuity between Wilhelminian and Nazi Germany – which had stirred so much controversy in the 1960s – was now the majority historiographical view. The real issue, as Eley put it, was the mechanisms through which certain ideological trends survived and became radicalised in interwar Germany while others (democracy, liberalism, political rationality, social democracy) proved stillborn and were eventually rejected (Eley 1983).

However, the line between constructive reassessment of an 'uncomfortable past' and distorting relativisation is often too easy to transcend. This was a lesson which historians on Italian Fascism had already learnt through De Felice's revisionist manoeuvres (Tranfaglia 1996: 65–96), and now it was Germany's turn to experience a moral mystification about its own past. When in 1986 E. Nolte published an article in one of Germany's most respected conservative broadsheets, he chose a rather eloquent title – 'The Past that will not Pass Away' (Nolte in Knowlton and Cates 1993: 18–23). What he was essentially alluding to was the need to redimension Germany's collective sense of guilt for the Nazi period. Like De Felice and his school, Nolte believed that the distance from the events of the interwar period should stimulate more dispassionate interpretations which could challenge the 'myths' (Nolte himself had used the term in another publication of similar content in 1985 (Nolte 1985)) of the postwar majority view. In principle, his plea seemed to suggest the opposite of De Felice's prescription – instead of focusing solely on national history, Nolte advocated the judiciousness of an unbiased analysis of the Nazi past within the wider framework of the crisis of European society in the interwar period. But, like De Felice, he subscribed to the fundamental belief that the lack of a national historical consciousness in postwar Germany lay at the heart of its allegedly uncertain identity and direction (Fulbrook 1999a). In other words, Nolte attempted to advance a theoretically fruitful end (reassessment of Germany's past in a less morally laden way) in a rather questionable and distorting way (by relativising the excesses of the Nazi regime). His main argument (elaborated in a book-length publication which appeared in 1986–7) focused on what he described as a pan-European 'civil war' between Bolshevism and the forces of fascism (Nolte 1987). This momentous conflict, for him, was not simply about ideologies or politics; it was also a clash of cultural models, of forms of civilisation. Bolshevism and Nazism represented the two extreme poles of this 'civil war', and their antipodean nature preordained their final, lethal confrontation. It is exactly at this point that his revisionist ploy backfired in the most spectacular way. He chose to focus on the origins of the Nazi genocidal programme against the Jews, by far the most emotive, hotly debated and unequivocal aspect of unprecedented Nazi brutality. Whilst denying neither its extent nor its shocking cruelty, he essentially advocated that it was a sort of pre-emptive irrational reaction to the spectre of 'Asiatic' barbarism (Nolte in Knowlton and Cates 1993; Nolte 1985: 36). Why 'Asiatic'? Here Nolte constructed his interpretation on the basis of two separate arguments. First, the 1915 Turkish genocide of the Armenians had been widely reported in Germany as an 'Asiatic' form of barbarism – and he assumed (with little corroborating evidence) that Hitler and his entourage shared this view. Second, the Bolsheviks had allegedly displayed similar 'Asiatic' traits – they had resorted to a widespread type of 'class annihilation' against their ideological enemies and had also purportedly used similar techniques against the German prisoners of war during the German–Russian conflict. In this sense, the Nazi extermination programme was reactive – a spasmodic response to the ghost of 'Asiatic' barbarity, targeting the Jews, who, in Hitler's distorted worldview, were the main force behind the Bolshevik system in the Soviet Union. Thus, for Nolte, the singularity of the 'Final Solution' had been blown out of any proportion; it was unique in means (the gas chambers) but not in conception, since the Bolsheviks had previously attempted an allegedly comparable annihilation scheme against 'class' enemies and threatened to repeat it against the defeated Germany.

Nolte's ideological edifice was not an isolated incident. Since the early 1980s the debate about the renationalisation of German historical consciousness had made significant inroads into both the historical profession of the Federal Republic and – to some extent – the official government discourse (Fulbrook 1999b; Friedländer 1987a and 1987b; Kershaw 1995: Chs 8, 9). Yet, the public dissemination of his revisionist theses from the pages of a widely read newspaper was indeed sensational, signifying an attempt to take the debate out of its academic confines and render it more accessible to the wider public. A similar logic underpinned the equally public (from the pages of another broadsheet, *Die Welt*) denunciation of this sort of revisionism by the distinguished liberal philosopher J. Habermas a few weeks later (Habermas in Knowlton and Cates 1993). Habermas dismissed the essence of Nolte's scheme, arguing that this type of renationalisation of German historical consciousness was essentially apologetic, resulting in an inadmissible relativisation of Nazi crimes. But, above all, Habermas censured what he believed was a concerted ploy of conservative historians of the new right to articulate a new, distorted view of the Nazi past. Evidence of this, he argued, could be found in the recent works of another two prominent historians of the Third Reich, A. Hillgruber and M. Stürmer. In 1986 Hillgruber (who in the 1970s had played an active role in questioning the method-ological validity of social history in defence of the more conventional interpretation of Nazism 'from above' – see above) had published a long essay focusing on the conduct of the retreating *Wehrmacht* troops on the eastern front (Hillgruber 1986). There he had some extraordinary things to say about the motives behind the terror unleashed by the defeated Nazi forces. In his view, the behaviour of the German armed forces could not be understood on its own terms. Rather, it was the result of a peculiar combination of separate factors. On the one hand, Hillgruber conceded, the bulk of the Nazi troops in the east resorted to 'unimaginable crimes' in the concentration camps. On the other hand, however, he also detected a desperate attempt to defend the 'centuries-old German settlement area' of East Prussia against the then impending danger of irreversible loss. This, in his view, was meant to consti-tute a well-intentioned contribution to safeguarding the future of the German nation and of the country's 'great-power' status against the onslaught of Bolshevism. In this sense, he concluded, 1945 should not be explained solely in terms of 'liberation' (Hillgruber in Knowlton and Cates 1993: 155–61). Hillgruber also had something to say on another two fundamental historiographical issues. First, as a renowned intentionalist, he was conditioned to place primary emphasis for the regime's decisions on Hitler's personal worldview. This proved exceptionally useful in his revisionist schemes vis-à-vis the origins of the 'Final Solution'. For now Hillgruber could attribute the ideological zeal behind the widespread extermination programme against the Jewish populations in the east to Hitler's own racial fixations and not to a general acceptance of his genocidal ideas by the German civilian population or soldiers. In fact, his analysis evinced sympathy with the unfortunate position of the German troops in the east and attempted to explain the brutality of the *Wehrmacht* as the secondary consequence of the imperative need to concentrate on the task of serving what then seemed to be the 'national interest', i.e. the war effort against the Red Army and the advance of Bolshevism (Hillgruber in Knowlton and Cates 1993: 155–61). Second, Hillgruber revisited the debate about the historic singularity of the Holocaust. Like Nolte, he did not dispute the horrifying dimensions of the geno-cidal programme, but rather chose to question its uniqueness. He reminded his readers that the record of appalling mass crimes committed by the Stalinist regime (both before the war and during the Red Army advance in eastern Europe in 1944–5) was well documented. Therefore, he concluded, historians had two choices: either 'judge more leniently the methods that the Stalinist regime employed for the purpose of defence against the German attack' or 'judge (these) crimes of the same "quality" that the National Socialist leadership committed in the course of its war of annihi-lation' (Hillgruber in Knowlton and Cates 1993: 159ff.). Inevitably, he believed that the latter choice would result in the repudiation of the claim that the Nazi 'Final Solution' was indeed unique.

Habermas' third target, M. Stürmer, had not been directly involved in what the philosopher had called 'apologetic tendencies'. His plea for a redefinition of German national identity by a sort of 'higher meaning', only to be found in a healthy patriotism and pride in the nation, was in fact closer to the Gaullist model of patriotic nationalism than to Nolte's relativising acrobatics (Stürmer 1983). But Stürmer was a fervent opponent of the view that modern German history should be understood in terms of continuity between the unification and Hitler (Stürmer 1990). He also believed that a 'land without history' like Germany was destined to seek artificial meaning for manufactured 'myths' – and the myth of anti-fascism, he claimed, had distorted the past by bestowing undue praise on the communists for allegedly 'liberating' Germany in 1945 (Stürmer in Knowlton and Cates 1993). For Stürmer, the sort of 'constitutional nationalism' that Habermas had suggested as the only acceptable form of national consciousness for Germany was an essential but not sufficient condition for providing the Germans with a solid identity. In this sense, the 'search for a lost past . . . is morally legitimate and politically necessary' (Stürmer in Knowlton and Cates 1993: 196–7). This was the sort of renationalisation of German historical consciousness that Habermas and other left-liberal historians of the Federal Republic (H.-U. Wehler, J. Kocka and H. Mommsen in Knowlton and Cates 1993; Bartov 1987: 336ff.; Bartov 1996) were not prepared to accept without a fight.

This acrimonious exchange, known as the *Historikerstreit* (literally, the historians' quarrel) lingered on until 1987 and stimulated a series of publications which continued well into the 1990s. Its intellectual fecundity has been widely questioned (Evans 1989: 25–46, 86–7; Kershaw 1995: Ch. 9; Fulbrook 1999b) – its legacy for German historiography on Nazism even more so. Perhaps Habermas gave too much prominence to a set of views that otherwise would have been destined to remain on the fringes of historiographical debates in Germany; perhaps he even read too much intrigue into three relatively autonomous publications. After all, revisionism (in the sense of revisiting conventional 'truths' about the past) did not deserve the bad name it acquired in the Federal Republic as a result of the *Historikerstreit*. The acerbity of the debate resulted in a partisan division of the German historical profession and in a call to take sides – Kocka, Mommsen, Jäckel, Winkler, Broszat versus Nolte, Hillgruber, Fest, Stürmer, Hildebrand, Weißmann. But the crux of the debate, however distorted by polemics and personal antipathies, remained crucially relevant – and not just for Germany: how to deal constructively with an 'uncomfortable' national past without forgetting, denying or embellishing it (Berger 1999). As the discussions about 'renationalising' historical consciousness in many European countries in the 1980s showed, there was simply no straightforward way to attain such a goal.

With the exception of Germany, Italy and France, most European countries with some form of 'fascist' past did not share such historiographical anxieties, thus largely avoiding acrimonious controversies regarding the interpretation of their native phenomena (see, for example, Payne 1986; Griffin 1998: 1–16). There were few exceptions to this norm – few but significant. In 1971 P. F. Sugar published a collection of essays on 'minor' fascist variants in the 'successor' states of central and southern Europe, in which he introduced the term 'native fascism'. In it a series of essays on lesser-known and often neglected movements, from Poland to Yugoslavia, examined the causes of their emergence and success/failure, thus making a significant contribution to the comparative analysis of fascism. The implication of using the term 'fascism' in this context was equally significant. For Sugar appeared to suggest that the prevailing obsession with Italy and Germany and the restrictive use of the term 'fascism' by the bulk of historiography had obscured the influence that Nazism and Italian Fascism had exerted on the political discourse of many other European countries, and the way that this influence had been adapted to the specific 'native' conditions of each of them (Sugar 1971). The message from Sugar's volume was not that the reviewed movements/regimes were identical to the 'classic' fascist case-studies, but that the emergence of such native phenomena in eastern and southern Europe during the interwar period owed a lot to the adaptation of the fascist experience to the particular conditions, problems and expectations of these countries.

S. Ben-Ami's work on Primo de Rivera's dictatorship in Spain (first published in 1983) was another sophisticated example of how a work on a 'minor' regime can also be employed in order to make a contribution to the wider discussion on the nature of interwar fascism (see **47**). This was the culmination of Ben-Ami's research on 1920s Spanish history since the late 1970s (see, for example, Ben-Ami 1979). For him Primo's dictatorship was not a conventional relapse from a flawed democratic system to military dictatorship of the sort that Spain had repeatedly experienced in the nineteenth and twentieth centuries. Instead, *primoderiverismo* became a precedent for the authoritarian right in both Spain and other countries experiencing belatedly the painful transition to modernity. Primo's *pronunziamento* and the regime instituted by him (1923–9) possessed a series of features that distinguished it from the more conventional military dictatorships of the past: for example, the existence of a proto-fascist movement (Union Patriotica) which Primo himself founded in 1924 on the basis of a corporatist philosophy – a movement seen by many as a precursor of the Falange Española of the 1930s; and the 'false (populist) mobilization of the masses' under Primo, which Ben-Ami considered a crucial aspect of fascism. In this respect, Ben-Ami concluded, *primoderiverismo* did constitute a proto-fascist phenomenon, a 'transitional' regime that paved the way to the right's experiments with populist (mobilisational) variants of dictatorship in the 1930s – not just in Spain but also in other European countries which were comparable in socio-economic terms (for example, Yugoslavia, Romania and Greece).

These exceptions notwithstanding, in a period when interest in grand theories of fascism remained a marginal concern of historiography and country-specific accounts constituted the unassailable norm of historical analysis, there was no real impetus for discussing the similarities and differences of peripheral interwar regimes or movements with reference to any overall fascist model. In most cases, the analysis of indigenous cases of radical nationalist ideology or authoritarian rule was primarily concerned with discussing their relevance to long-term national trends and far less with their relevance to 'core' fascist phenomena as experienced in Italy or Germany (Payne 1986: 163–6). The 1980s confirmed a schism in the historiography of the interwar period: while historians in countries with an 'uncomfortable past' seemed preoccupied with the historicisation of native phenomena in the context of long-term national history (the development of an indigenous right, the strength of elites, the 'singularity' of their country's path to modernity, the issue of national identity), commentators studying fascism from an external perspective appeared more willing to take up comparative analysis and discuss individual phenomena with regard to a general 'fascist' theory, regardless of whether they upheld or rejected such a theory (Griffin 1998: 14–16). These issues, and the way they were accommodated in the historiographical discourse of European countries (Austria, Spain, Portugal, Britain), will be reviewed in Section III. Here it suffices to note that the impressive growth of historiographical interest in interwar movements and regimes in the 1980s seemed to contribute to the conspicuous disintegration of the concept of generic fascism. Whether out of conviction or lack of interest, 'fascism' was overshadowed by a notion that each interwar case-study was singular, more relevant to the course of national history than to any Europe-wide trend or influence.

The revival of generic fascism in the 1990s

Such was the extent of this decline that in 1991 T. Mason – himself a disciple of the country-specific model and author of seminal works on Nazism's and Italian Fascism's social history – produced a brief essay with the title 'Whatever Happened to Fascism?', which was subsequently reprinted in a volume discussing new trends in the analysis of National Socialism (Mason 1993b). Although he had remained generally cautious about the fruitfulness of general theories of fascism in the 1970s and 1980s, Mason evinced a sense of alarm and mystification with the direction of recent historiographical debates and, most importantly, with the essence of the *Historikerstreit* in Germany. He dismissed Nolte's attempt to focus his analysis on the 'genocidal' aspect of National Socialism and thus relate Germany to Stalinist Russia and even to Pol Pot's Cambodia (Kocka in Knowlton and Cates 1993: 85–92). He reiterated his belief that fascism remained an essentially interwar phenomenon (a view which, paradoxically, had been systematically put forward by Nolte in the 1960s!) and that comparative analysis was desperately needed in order to understand the forces behind the Europe-wide capitulation to anti-liberalism and authoritarian rule in the 1920s and 1930s. Mason concluded his essay with a passionate appeal for an end to introversion and historiographical parochialism by stating that events such as Cambodia's 'class' genocide or Turkey's persecution of the Armenians were 'extraneous to any serious discussion of Nazism; Mussolini's Italy is not' (Mason 1993b: 260).

Once again, it was historians with no direct involvement in the country-specific debates on the 1980s who endorsed Mason's concerns and opted for comparative, generic analysis. In 1990 M. Blinkhorn published a collection on the relations between 'fascists' and 'conservatives' in interwar Europe (Blinkhorn 1990). This was an important contribution to the revival of interest in generic fascism, since it brought together up-to-date contributions on the various manifestations of 'fascism' in a host of European countries, ranging from Italy and Germany to Austria, Portugal and Greece. The conceptual framework of the volume was highly sophisticated, avoiding the superficial generalisations of the comparative accounts of the 1960s and paying sufficient attention to the complex relation between fascism and conservative right. Three years later, R. Griffin produced a fascinating taxonomy of generic fascism as both an ideological phenomenon and a system of rule (Griffin 1993a and 1993b – cf. 11). His interpretation rested upon the premise that fascism was a form of mass-mobilising 'palingenetic ultra-nationalism', intent upon carving a 'third way' between liberalism and socialism. Another prominent disciple of generic fascism in the 1990s was R. Eatwell, who shared Griffin's notion of 'third way' but focused more heavily on the extreme, aggressive 'holistic-nationalist' aspect of fascist ideology (Eatwell 1992, 1993, 1996a and 1996b – cf. 4). Both agreed, however, on the need to view fascism as a true revolutionary phenomenon and a coherent system of ideas and values, which should not be confined to one historical period or place (i.e. interwar Europe) and whose relevance to contemporary political discourses of the extreme right had to be carefully accounted for. Then, in 1997 S. Payne published the most comprehensive commentary so far of the various interwar 'fascist' regimes in Europe (Payne 1997). Apart from the exhaustive, even-handed treatment of the diverse manifestations of fascism, from the core fascist case-studies (Italy and Germany) to peripheral regimes and radical movements that never came to power, Payne's most recent work has built upon the merits of his 1980 sophisticated definition of fascism (see above) in order to produce what he called a new 'retrodictive theory of fascism' (Payne 1997: 487–95). In this explanatory model Payne identified a series of factors that contributed to fascism's appeal in the 1920s and 1930s, distinguishing between economic, political, economic, social and international parameters. He chose to focus his analysis on the 1919–45 period, acknowledging that most of these factors, which had been so instrumental in fascism's success in the interwar period, were thwarted after 1945; but he suggested that, ideologically and intellectually, fascism survived the collapse of its reference regimes in Italy and Germany before reinventing itself in the postwar political discourse.

Recently, Griffin described the convergence of views between himself, Eatwell and Payne as a trend amounting to a sort of 'new consensus' (Griffin 1998: 14–16, 50–5). In spite of these authors' individual differences in focus, conclusions and wording, they seem to share a determination to take fascist ideology seriously, to provide highly elaborate generic models of interpretation and, above all, to salvage the debate on generic fascism after almost two decades of dilapidation. At the same time, a growing interest in comparative analysis of Fascist Italy and Nazi Germany produced a substantial body of publications. R. Bessel's edited volume brought together prominent historians of the two regimes in an attempt to detect significant similarities and analyse constructively their individual differences (Bessel 1996). A. De Grand published a concise account of what he called the 'fascist style' of politics, again discussing the two core fascist case-studies in comparative terms (De Grand 1995). R. Paxton introduced a typology of fascism based on the notion of evolution and consolidation, from a dissident intellectual trend to movement to party and, finally, to regime with the Nazi and Italian Fascist cases as the most developed forms of fascism (Paxton 1998). M. Knox combined his interest in long-term features of Italian and German societies with a fresh focus on the two regimes' expansionist policies in the 1930s and early 1940s (Knox 1984, 1996 and 2000 – see **29**). Interestingly, the conventional totalitarian approach – which had experienced a kind of revival in the 1980s, especially in Germany and Italy – came under closer scrutiny in a volume edited by I. Kershaw and M. Lewin on Nazism and Stalinism (Kershaw and Lewin 1997). The comparative framework of this publication revealed some interesting similarities but also substantial divergences in both the ideas and the practice of the two regimes. Indirectly, this conclusion seemed to strengthen the view that fascism (and Stalinism for that matter) was much more than totalitarianism had suggested in the past, that it deserved an autonomous place in the history of modern political ideologies. It now seemed that understanding fascism had a lot less to do with the study of the Soviet Union than with the comparative analysis of the various interwar dictatorships and radical movements in Europe – and, in this context, the comparison between the two reference regimes of Fascist Italy and Nazi Germany appeared the most appropriate, if not obvious, method.

Perhaps Griffin's optimism about the 'new consensus' was somewhat premature. National debates about the soundness or not of a wide renationalisation of historical consciousness continued in the 1990s with the same acerbity and artificial polarisation. Introversion – so conspicuous in the historiographical production of those countries still at odds with their own 'uncomfortable past' – remained too powerful to succumb to the less politically exciting task of trans-national comparisons. This, as we saw earlier, was essentially left to those historians with an external viewpoint and a far smaller vested interest in serving the needs of purely national history – Griffin himself acknowledged that the 'loosely instituted school' of the 'new consensus' depended on the works of predominantly Anglo-Saxon historians, with Z. Sternhell being the odd one out, because of his long residence in France (Griffin 1998: 15–16). Again, there were few notable exceptions. A. Costa Pinto's monograph on Salazar's regime in Portugal, first published in the early 1990s (Costa Pinto 1995 – see **30**) provided a fascinating example of how the recent elaboration of the theories of fascism could be applied to the study of a regime that was not a straightforward case of 'fascism' – and vice versa. Costa Pinto did not attempt to equate *salazarismo* (which he analysed as a form of para-fascist dictatorship 'from above' and 'without party') with Nazism or Italian Fascism. But he devoted the first part of his book to discussing how historiographical developments in the field of generic fascism could be fruitfully employed in the study of interwar Portuguese history. Whilst primarily concerned with Salazar and his regime, Costa Pinto's publication also made a significant contribution to the understanding of para-fascism itself – namely to the investigation of a host of regimes in interwar Europe that remained entrenched in the political and social tradition of conventional authoritarianism but emulated 'fascist' themes and adopted the new style of politics pioneered by Mussolini in the 1920s and developed by Hitler in the 1930s. But, overall, a great number of historians of the period continued to be enthralled by the intricate (and politically sensitive) questions of national identity and native fascism's relevance to national past.

The quest for a 'positive' historical national identity in Italy and France

In Italy, the historiographical foci in the 1990s were not significantly different from those of the previous decade – anti-Fascism, the myth of the *Resistenza* and, unavoidably, De Felice himself (Zapponi 1994; Painter 1990). It has been argued that what Nolte's revisionist scheme failed to do in Germany, De Felice and his school achieved in Italy – to endow their revisionism with the aura of a majority view. The cataclysmic events in eastern Europe bolstered De Felice's instinctive anti-communism and conferred upon his 'anti-"anti-Fascism"' an even more militant, uncompromising tone. The collapse of the Italian First Republic amidst a pandemonium of corruption allegations against the *partitocrazia* (literally, partyocracy, the rule of the parties) nurtured his distaste for the political and moral fabric of the postwar Italian state. In 1990 he published the sixth volume of Mussolini's biography, covering the 1940–3 period, and embarked on compiling his much-anticipated seventh volume on the Republic of Salò and the Resistance (De Felice 1990). The following year, on the twentieth anniversary of his original interview with M. Ledeen, he gave a second one, dominated by a strong defence of his positivist methodology (exhaustive dependence on, and quoting of, the sources), warning against the alleged dangers of subjective interpretation (De Felice 1995). In this interview, he also offered some insight into the content of his then forthcoming (and anxiously anticipated) last volume of Mussolini's biography. His death in May 1996 appeared to condemn his massive biographical project – a work born out of real conviction, as N. Zapponi noted (Zapponi 1994: 560–1) – to the status of a monumental *non-finito*. But De Felice had left behind loyal and highly adept disciples, who collected and edited his manuscripts in a seventh volume which appeared a year later. Through the pages of this posthumous publication De Felice provided an account of the last years of Mussolini's life (until 1944) that exceeded even the expectations of his adherents. He once again referred to the 'fateful 45 days' between the dismissal of Mussolini and the signing of the Italian armistice on 8 September 1943 as a 'national catastrophe' (De Felice 1997: 72ff.). For De Felice, the period of the *Resistenza* can be described in terms of a 'civil war', and a class one for that matter, not dissimilar to the ideological conflicts that afflicted many Balkan states after their liberation from the Axis forces. His analysis focuses on the factional character of the fighting (communists versus Fascists), which allegedly left the majority of the Italian population unimpressed, apathetic and eventually hostile to both groups (De Felice 1997: 87f.). The ensuing 'civil war', he argued, was an essentially partisan conflict between the supporters of the Salò Republic and the communists, leaving the majority of the Italian population not just apathetic but confused and dismayed. Here, De Felice's analysis evinced a sense of moral ambiguity: he rejected outright the 'anti-Fascist' depiction of the *Resistenza* as a struggle of good against evil, opting instead for an interpretation that spoke of the two offspring of the same pathology of Italian society. Inevitably, he viewed the end-result, the victory of the Resistance and the total discrediting of Mussolini, as the triumph of a one-dimensional view of the country's past, politically flawed and morally incapable of uniting the Italian nation in the postwar era. With these caveats, De Felice returned to his favourite subject of historical consciousness. He launched a scathing attack on the post-1945 *partitocrazia* as the result of the partisan 'civil war' that Resistance was in his view and once again urged historians to seek a new form of legitimacy for the Italian state in its national tradition. He was convinced that the 'Stalinist communists of Togliatti' who hijacked the Resistance movement could not claim that they represented a truly national 'anti-Fascist' cause, bound as they were to the *Diktats* of their Soviet allies (De Felice 1997: 253). The result, as he put it, was the total depletion of national consciousness during 1943–5, the capitulation to the whims of a divisive partisan culture and the artificial suppression of any form of usable national past by the postwar First Republic (De Felice 1997: 169; De Felice 1990: 828).

De Felice was not alone in noting that the collapse of the postwar political system in the early 1990s cried out for Italian identity to be freed from the 'myths' of the Resistance in favour of a positive renationalisation. In fact, it was E. Galli della Loggia who became the torchbearer of this revisionism in the 1990s. In 1996 he published a book-length analysis of the transition from Fascism to the First Republic with the eloquent title *The Death of the Patria* (Galli della Loggia 1996). Echoing De Felice's scathing aphorisms about the *Resistenza* and the 'fateful 45 days' of 1943, Galli della Loggia argued that the death of the Italian 'nation-state' was the artificial and calamitous result of the period of the Resistance, whose partisan character and domination of the postwar debate on Fascism had rendered any form of constructive identification with national history practically unusable. He deplored the discrediting and demise of old traditional symbols of the post-unification Italian nation-state: the monarchical tradition, the military, the legacy of the *Risorgimento* itself. It is not surprising that Galli della Loggia followed the *Historikerstreit* debate in Germany and indeed supervised the Italian translation of Hillgruber's controversial study of the retreating *Wehrmacht* soldiers on the eastern front (see above). Like De Felice, he believed that the moral choices during that period were not as straightforward or clear-cut as postwar 'anti-fascism' had portrayed them. His revisionism was aimed at the one-sided attribution of the roles of saviours, victims and villains in a postwar historiography which had, in his view, only too hastily and obstinately set upon demolishing any positive identification with the nation-state (Galli della Loggia 1996; Levy 1999: 266–8).

Not that such views went unchallenged. E. Gentile did support De Felice's view that the Fascist regime commanded the loyalties of a significant part of the Italian population through the 'totalitarian' aspirations of the Fascist Party (PNF) (E. Gentile 1986 and 1997); but, although he too talked of the 'decline of the national state', he attributed this effect to the attempt of the Fascist regime to monopolise the Italian nationalist traditions (E. Gentile 1994 and 1995). Thus, the discrediting of the Fascist 'totalitarian state' brought about the automatic demise of the Italian 'nation-state' per se. At the same time, the belligerent tone of De Felice's 'anti-"anti-Fascism"' galvanised more layered interpretations from the 'anti-Fascist' camp in the 1990s. C. Pavone's seminal work on the *Resistenza*, a combination of oral history and political analysis, did concede that the Resistance amounted to a 'civil war' but argued that the cause of the 'anti-Fascist' struggle was a worthy one (Pavone 1991). G. E. Rusconi saw the rise of the Northern League as a direct threat to the unity of the Italian state and defended the legacy of the Resistance as the ethical and historic glue that could counter present-day separatism (Rusconi 1993). M. Viroli detected in the *Resistenza* the rise of a feeling of patriotism (as opposed to nationalism) which had bestowed upon the Italians a sense of positive civic identity as an antidote to the discrediting of identification with national history (Viroli 1995). This new 'anti-Fascist' trend in historiography did not deny the exaggeration of the 'myth' of the Resistance itself after the war; but it defended the moral validity of the 'anti-Fascist' choice and perceived the disintegration of national historical consciousness as successfully replaced by new forms of identification with Republican, civic and European loyalties (Levy 1999: 268–9).

In France, the 'past that does not pass away', as E. Conan called the Vichy regime (Conan and Rousso 1994), continued to dominate the historiographical debates on France's relation to its own 'fascist' past. Numerous new studies on the nature of the Vichy regime ('fascist' or not?) and, especially, its anti-Semitic record, continued to be published, stimulating a debate that, albeit less concerned with the need to renationalise historical consciousness than in Italy or Germany, remained heated throughout the 1990s (Jackson 1999). The Gaullist view of a healthy identification with national history did command the loyalties of a certain sector of French historians, who reacted to what they saw as an 'exaggerated' focus on French anti-Semitism. This, they believed, projected a negative view of national history which endangered national unity. But such calls were too far from representing the majority view. The most conventional reaction to the 'Vichy syndrome' pertained to its perhaps overzealous effort to exorcise the moral stigma of anti-Semitism by placing disproportionate emphasis on the so-called 'Jewish' perspective at the expense of other, equally indefensible, aspects of Vichy violation of human rights. While an increasing number of works paid tribute to the victims of the regime's anti-Semitism (see for example, R. Paxton's 1997 work on the Jews of Marseilles, or R. H. Weisberg's 1996 analysis of the legal sophistication of exclusionary Jewish laws under Vichy rule), the focus shifted to new complex issues, such as the idea of solidarity between the French population and the Jews (Hallie 1979) and the debate as to who really was a 'collaborator'. The previously rather simplistic dichotomy between the 'resisters' (majority) and 'collaborators' (minority) was revisited, allowing for arguments that spoke of a largely apathetic group in the French population which could not be accommodated in the conventional 'either–or' model. P. Burrin's masterly account of occupied France detected a highly intricate web of far more nuanced French attitudes to the 1940 defeat, attitudes that did not allude to clear moral choices between collaboration or resistance (Burrin 1993). Inevitably, however, the issue of collaboration and anti-Semitism became intertwined, causing confusion as to whether an active anti-Semite of the Vichy period was indeed automatically culpable of complicity with the fascists. Those who reacted to the alleged hijacking of the analysis of Vichy by anti-Semitism were eager to point out that the equation of anti-Semites and collaborators was misleading – just as in Italy not all 'anti-Fascists' were democrats, in France not all anti-Semites were 'collaborators'. Such distinctions were initially intended to highlight what many historians regarded as the secondary importance of anti-Semitism for the whole 'resistance–collaboration' debate about the Vichy regime. Yet, this proved to be a far more controversial basis for rewriting the history of this period, raising awkward questions about what constituted a real 'patriot' in the interwar years, how much anti-Semitism was an active choice of the Vichy (French) officials and population or a simple case of passive complicity with a Nazi-instigated policy, and whether a usable French identity can be constructed on such a divisive, guilt-ridden view of national past, where the history of sub-groups (in this case, the Jews or, today, the immigrants) allegedly erodes the continuity of collective overall identity (Jackson 1999: 239–40). Here, the general question of renationalising historical conscious-ness is articulated in a more cautious way compared to its rather flagrant assertion in Italy and Germany – but it is still projected as a powerful alternative to the frag-mentation of *national* historical identity and the allegedly disproportionate emphasis on the so-called 'Judaeo-centric' perspective on fascism. The belated recognition of the 'Vélodrome d'Hiver' arrest of more than 12,000 Jews in 1942 as a day of national commemoration by President Jacques Chirac in 1995 was intended to rectify the previously ambiguous attitude of the French Fifth Republic towards Vichy and its anti-Semitic record. As E. Conan and H. Rousso noted, it was ironic that a Gaullist president contributed to the demolition of the Gaullist postwar myth of the Vichy 'non-state' through a symbolic gesture that his socialist predecessor, François Mitterrand, had refused to concede on the basis of an essentially Gaullist view of France's past (Conan and Rousso 1994). The result was predictable – while the majority of the French population saw this recognition as an opportunity to reflect on the country's anti-Semitic past, the disciples of renationalising French contem-porary historical identity commented unfavourably on the benefits of such a divisive and disconcerting perspective on what they believed to be only a part of France's national past.

   This debate remains an extremely sensitive one, requiring historians to perform very refined narrative manoeuvres on a highly slippery terrain. There is indeed a fine line between an overall constructive redimensioning of the importance of anti-Semitism for the general interpretation of fascism, on the one hand, and overtly apologetic accounts, aiming to relativise the significance or extent of the event itself (the extermination of the European Jewish populations), on the other. It is true that so-called 'Holocaust revisionism' (denying that there was a 'systematic' Nazi plan for the annihilation of the Jews, that the gas chambers ever existed and that the quoted figures of 6–11 million victims are accurate) has been constructed on the argument that this 'Judaeo-centric' account of the events, supported by a powerful 'industry of sorrow', has allegedly produced an extremely biased and distorting view of the past, full of exaggerations and substantial inaccuracies (Eatwell 1995). Although such views remain confined to the very fringes of the historiography of fascism, they do cast a shadow on every call to redefine the relation between fascism and anti-Semitism. It is also true that emphasis on the racial-genocidal features of Nazi policy (especially after 1940) have provided the necessary methodological ammunition to those who have attempted to relativise the brutality of other 'fascist' regimes (for example, Galli della Loggia and De Felice in Italy, who argued that

Italian Fascism could not be compared to Nazism in that respect; and the more careful works of Steinberg (1990) and Goglia (1988)) and thus attack any notion of generic definition of fascism on these grounds. The classic study of Nazi racial utopia by W. Wippermann and M. Burleigh reached a similar conclusion about the validity of comparing Nazism to other interwar 'fascist' regimes simply because virulent, eliminationist anti-Semitism was so central to the Nazi worldview (Burleigh and Wippermann 1991). Therefore, when prominent 'genericists' such as Griffin and Payne attempted to argue that anti-Semitism, albeit so fundamental for the understanding of the Nazi variant, should not be regarded as a prerequisite for a general theory of fascism (Griffin 1993b: 48; cf. Neocleous 1997, Ch. 2), they seemed to stumble upon a widespread – historiographical and popular – association between fascism and anti-Semitic ideology. The crux of the genericists' arguments points to anti-Jewish sentiment being prevalent in the nationalist traditions of most European countries long before fascism appeared on the political scene in the interwar period. In fact, as A. Lyttelton (a prominent Italianist and author of a classic account of the Fascist take-over of power) has rightly pointed out, the odd one out in this respect was not Germany but Italy – a country with a strikingly limited anti-Semitic feeling in sharp contrast to most other European states of the interwar period (Lyttelton 1996: 12–13). Those who oppose a radical distinction between Nazi Germany and other interwar 'fascist' dictatorships or movements on the basis of anti-Semitism have indicated that this element was part of a wider long-term nationalist tradition which fascism inherited and radicalised, but definitely did not invent (Neocleous 1997: Ch. 2). Therefore, distinctions made exclusively on that basis appear somewhat oblivious of native fascism's relation to national past and obscure a host of conspicuous similarities between interwar 'fascist' phenomena in many other fields.

Holocaust again: the 'Goldhagen controversy' in Germany

With this debate in full swing in the 1990s it is hardly surprising that the major controversy of the decade originated from the publication of a book on the Nazi 'Final Solution'. In the mid-1990s D. Goldhagen published a massive study of the ideological motivations and political execution of the Nazi genocidal programme against the European Jewry. The title he chose for his account – *Hitler's Willing Executioners* – reflected in itself the controversial, highly provocative nature of his argument (Goldhagen 1996 – 31). For Goldhagen, the 'Final Solution' was the end-result of a particular *German* ideological-cultural tradition which had been bent on the idea of Jewish annihilation long before Hitler assumed power and sought his own racial utopia. He therefore shifted the focus of interpretation from the debate on fascism's general ideological traits to Germany's specific development in the nineteenth and twentieth centuries – a development which, in his view, rendered a genocidal form of anti-Semitism more acceptable to extremely wide sections of the German population (Goldhagen 1996). Hitler's 'willing executioners', he argued, were not just the conventional race-maniacs of the SS, the Nazi Party or the traditional anti-Semitic right; in fact, as Goldhagen boldly asserted, the majority of the

German population were culturally conditioned to accept and justify the goal of anni-
hilating the Jews without Nazi instigation or indoctrination. In this respect, he
concluded, Germany presented a unique model of malicious anti-Semitism, capable
of envisaging genocide as a radical but reasonable solution to what was widely
perceived as a 'problem' by conventional wisdom. This model set Germany apart
from other European states and transformed Nazi genocidal anti-Semitism into a
problem of the country's long-term cultural deviation from the European norm.

It is not difficult to see why Goldhagen's interpretation provoked so much controversy, both inside Germany and internationally. This was, in many ways, the last
major debate of the twentieth century on fascism, albeit originating from a book
that focused more heavily on German history rather than on fascism itself. In
Germany the book was mainly criticised for lack of analytical sophistication.
Through the pages of the broadsheet *Die Zeit* (a newspaper that, as we saw, had
published numerous contributions on the *Historikerstreit* in the 1980s) Germany's
most prominent historians commented on Goldhagen's radical reinterpretation of the
Holocaust (*Die Zeit*, 1.1996). In a country so intent upon paying a sort of continuing moral debt to the millions of Jewish victims of its Nazi past and afflicted by
the kind of revisionism that the *Historikerstreit* had (unsuccessfully but blatantly)
articulated, this book received extremely cautious verdicts – emphasising the factual
soundness of Goldhagen's analysis but castigating its rather simplistic link between
clichéd anti-Semitic views (undoubtedly prevalent amongst the German population
at that time) and active, zealous genocidal action (Wehler 1997; Berger 1999).
Outside Germany, the debate on *Hitler's Willing Executioners*, albeit concerned with
the issues of continuity in German history and the country's cultural *Sonderweg*
in the issue of anti-Semitism, extended to the overall relevance of Goldhagen's arguments to the wider discussion of the nature of fascism, in country-specific or generic
terms. It is true that his concern to expose the peculiarities of the *German* path to
genocide was used by many historians, particularly in Italy, to uphold the distinction between an allegedly 'evil' Nazism and a more benign native version of fascism.
In such a framework, this was a particularly welcome interpretation that could be
advantageous in fostering a sense of positive identification with national history in
a way that, after Goldhagen's book, was no longer available in Germany (cf. De
Felice 1990: 470ff.). Yet, beyond the myopic motives of such an ambivalent quest,
Hitler's Willing Executioners seemed to suggest that the differing attitude of the
various interwar 'fascist' regimes to anti-Semitism can be best understood in the
context of long-term national history. Fascism as such reflected, rather than devised,
native nationalist trends and shaped its special, country-specific profile according to
them. In acknowledging this, the field was at last free for a more constructive discussion of the significant similarities between the various interwar 'fascist' phenomena
in so many other areas, such as charismatic leadership, nationalist fervour, activism,
irrationalism and anti-liberalism.

Moreover, the Goldhagen controversy had quite a significant impact on the
internal historiographical debate in Germany and, in particular, on the fate of the
sort of revisionism that Nolte introduced in the 1980s and the likes of R. Zittelmann
and K. Weißmann sustained in the 1990s (see, for example, Zittelmann 1995;

Weißmann 1993 and 1995). The massive commercial success of the translated edition of Goldhagen's book in the reunified Federal Republic appears to have demolished the intellectual and moral validity of the project to 'normalise' the perception of Nazism and thus promote the 'renationalisation' of historical consciousness in Germany (Berger 1999: 258–61). New trends in this direction, like the argument that the launching of 'Operation Barbarossa' against the Soviet Union in June 1941 was a sort of pre-emptive war against an enemy state preparing to unleash total war against the Third Reich and Europe as a whole, seem to have lost the game of emotional manipulation (Wippermann 1997: 59–79). Of course, certain sectors of the German right have not laid down their intellectual weapons. The exhibition on the brutality of the *Wehrmacht* in the Second World War attracted both immense public interest and vehement criticisms for its alleged unfair depiction of the German troops as 'criminals'. Here, echoes of the kind of emotional sympathy that Hillgruber had evinced in his work on the retreating *Wehrmacht* troops on the eastern front (see above) still appeared capable of galvanising strong emotional support for a renationalised historical consciousness. On the whole, however, the debate on Goldhagen's flawed model for interpreting the Holocaust released a wave of positive energy in the direction of transcending the 'uncomfortable' national past and cherishing the emancipation of a post-national democratic, tolerant culture in the postwar Federal Republic.

PART ONE

Generic fascism

The search for definitions and explanations

SECTION I

■ Fascism – a 'generic' concept?

IN THE EIGHT DECADES since its first appearance in Italy the concept of 'fascism' has been done, undone and redone numerous times. From the first official Comintern understandings of it in the early 1920s as a counter-revolutionary tool of monopoly capitalism to the liberal ideas of a historic 'aberration' and to the most recent, conceptually sophisticated attempts to define it in its own terms, research on fascism has found it easier to discuss fascism's various permutations than to define the term itself. Since the 1970s there have been numerous attempts to codify the plurality of interpretations of what fascism really was, to distil the expanding bibliography on the subject and produce clear taxonomical categories (Kühnl 1980; De Felice 1977; Vincent 1992); but the quest for a fascist 'paradigm', that is, a generally accepted definition of fascism, has remained elusive. The initial basic split between Marxist, liberal and conservative explications has been further compounded by a host of subsequent different methodological models and conceptual discrepancies, which – ironically – intended to solve the riddle of defining 'fascism' but effectively obfuscated the debate about its character.

Disagreement has focused on a plethora of key questions. Was fascism an ideology or a system of rule? Was it a phenomenon of the interwar period or a system of thought that survived the collapse of Nazism and Italian Fascism? Was it European or did it affect other parts of the world too (for example, Latin America)? Was it revolutionary in its goals or reactionary, regressive or even counter-revolutionary? Or, even more fundamentally, does the term 'fascism' hold any analytical value for describing the experience of so many (and different) countries? This last question was raised in the 1970s, after the dramatic postwar growth of interest in the study of fascism had produced a litany of conflicting definitions without any hint of generating consensus on the horizon. It was Gilbert Allardyce (1) who vented his frustration with the absence of clear methodological standards in employing the term 'fascism' by the bulk of historiography. His unequivocal rejection of the validity of the term marked the nadir of the debate on the nature of fascism. For it cast a shadow not simply on the bewildering variety of available interpretations but – more alarmingly – on the relevance and desirability of a debate conducted on such a flawed conceptual basis. In other words, Allardyce suggested that the lack of a precise, intelligible subject matter had rendered all the subsequent questions and controversies about the nature, goals and extent of fascism essentially immaterial. More recently, Macgregor Knox (1984 and 2000) did not shy away from describing the scene of fascist studies as a 'deserted battlefield littered with the burnt-out, rusting hulks of failed theories'. Such a disparaging statement was accompanied by a reaffirmation of the value of comparative research, especially with regard to Fascist Italy and Nazi Germany. A closer scrutiny of Knox's thesis shows how his scepticism towards the concept of fascism diverges from the objections raised by Allardyce in 1979. For Knox simply rejects the value of the quest for an all-embracing definition of 'fascism' but accepts that some case-studies (for example, the two major interwar dictatorships in Italy and Germany) can be fruitfully analysed in comparative terms. A similar conceptual postulate underpins the volume edited by Richard Bessel (1996), whose endorsement of comparative analysis did not presuppose – or indeed seek to elaborate – a generic definition of 'fascism' extricated from the experience of Fascist Italy and Nazi Germany. In this sense, Knox's criticism of 'generic fascism' reflects a different approach to the study of 'fascist' movements and regimes – one which understands the rise of Fascism and Nazism as the end-result of a particular historic path that the two countries had followed after their (late) national unifications.

Against such a formidable challenge the defence of 'fascism' was conducted on various levels, albeit without the congruity necessary to dispel the doubts about the substance of the debate. The most fundamental problem was deciding to what extent fascism was a *generic* phenomenon, requiring comparative analysis of its various permutations within a single conceptual framework, or was the product of disparate *indigenous* conditions and historical trends. Ernst Nolte (see **12**) had pioneered the case for a generic approach to fascism as ideology in the 1960s, combining Nazism, Italian Fascism and the Action Française in his comparative analysis of fascism. For Nolte, 'fascism' was an intelligible and useful label, befitting the experience of various European countries in the interwar period. He also suggested that fascism was an 'epochal' phenomenon, confined to the period between the two world wars and unsuitable as a general (diachronic) category. For Marxist historiography, on the other hand, fascism's generic dimension was related to the capitalist system that produced it in the first place; in this sense, as Martin Kitchen (**2**) has argued, fascism is inherent in the postwar system and its violent reappearance (in mutated form) cannot be ruled out. In the 1980s and 1990s the renewed interest in the study of fascism produced a series of new accounts and definitions that shed further light on fascism's generic nature, producing what Griffin (1998) called 'new consensus' in the fray of fascist studies. The pioneering work of Juan J. Linz and Zeev Sternhell in the 1970s and 1980s paved the way for the elaboration of the generic analysis of fascism. In the last decade, Roger Griffin, Roger Eatwell and Stanley Payne displayed a firm commitment to the understanding of fascism as a coherent ideological system with its own revolutionary agenda in search of a 'third way' beyond the established universal creeds of liberalism and socialism. For the representatives of the 'new consensus', fascism constitutes a system of specific values, whose origins lay in dissident intellectual trends of the nineteenth and early twentieth centuries and whose political relevance extends to our days, albeit in a different form from that of the interwar period. Individual differences, of course, persist: Linz (3) stressed the 'anti' character of fascism – its emphatic negation of main tenets of the established ideologies of the nineteenth century – in an attempt to define itself more clearly in the already overcrowded spectrum of political thought; Eatwell (4; also 1996b) defined fascism in terms of a 'holistic' nationalism in search of a revolutionary 'third way' beyond the conventional categories of left and right; Payne (5) analysed fascism as a unique example of a revolutionary mass movement, with its negations, specific goals and distinctive style. The essence, however, of the 'new consensus' approach lies in its unequivocal endorsement of the generic nature of 'fascism' and in its analysis on its own individual terms, as an autonomous system of values which was coherent enough to be treated like any other established '-ism'.

In a landscape of constant diversification and controversy, it would have been unrealistic to expect that the 'new consensus' would succeed in producing an uncontested fascist paradigm. Dissenting voices have continued to question the soundness of any form of generic approach to the study of fascism. In a recent article Robert O. Paxton (6) has underlined the importance of understanding fascism not simply in ideological terms, but also in its transformation from ideology to movement, party and finally regime. Such a dynamic definition still falls within the wider category of a generic interpretation; but it departs from the insistence of the 'new consensus' that fascism remains an essentially *ideological* phenomenon and that its interwar characteristics should be analysed as epochal features of an intellectual movement that should not be confined to them. Other commentators have attacked the generic interpretation on the basis that it has failed to account for the significant ideological variations of the different fascist phenomena in the 1920s and 1930s. Focusing on difference rather than on similarity has been a facile task – the two reference fascist phenomena of the interwar period in Germany and Italy diverged on significant issues, such as their attitude to modernity, their use of systematic violence and extermination policies, the extent of their grip over their respective societies, the personality and background of their leaders, and the cultural models of their societies. The issue here is whether the core of generic 'fascist' values can sufficiently accommodate such country-specific disparities or are eclipsed and invalidated by them. The 'new consensus' has attempted to square this methodological circle by devising an 'ideological minimum', namely a specifically 'fascist' kernel of ideas and values that underpinned the various national permutations of fascism but were interpreted and formulated differently in each case. Its critics, however, remain largely unimpressed.

Chapter 1

Gilbert Allardyce

GENERIC FASCISM: AN 'ILLUSION'?

■ from **WHAT FASCISM IS NOT: THOUGHTS ON THE DEFLATION OF A CONCEPT**, *American Historical Review*, 84 (1979), pp. 367–8, 370, 378–9, 381–2, 184–5, 187–8

In 1979 Gilbert Allardyce launched a vehement assault on the use of the term 'fascism' by postwar historiography. Using categorical statements ('fascism is not a generic concept', 'fascism is not an ideology', 'universal fascism is an illusion'), he called for the concept of 'fascism' to be 'de-modeled, de-ideologized, de-mystified, and . . . de-escalated', in an attempt to salvage some (albeit very limited) heuristic value in it. Allardyce reserves strong words for those urging an understanding of fascism in intellectual terms, but also for the 'anti-fascists' of the time who employed the term in purely ideological-political terms without any attention to historical accuracy. Interestingly, Allardyce endorses Nolte's thesis (**12**) that 'fascism' should be confined to the interwar period – but once again as a lesser evil, allowing us some control over the use of the term.

'**P**ERHAPS THE WORD FASCISM should be banned, at least temporarily, from our political vocabulary,' S. J. Woolf wrote in 1968.[1] Historians who have confronted the problem of defining this mulish concept may sympathize with this modest proposal. Unfortunately, the word 'fascism' is here to stay; only its meaning seems to have been banned. Nevertheless, the German philosopher-historian Ernst Nolte is probably correct in stressing that historians do not have the responsibility to invent new terms simply because the existing ones seem inadequate. But they do have the responsibility to confess how truly inadequate the term fascism has become: put simply, we have agreed to use the word without agreeing on how to define it. This article is concerned with the reasons for this unfortunate state of affairs.

Although some scholars attempted from the start to restrict the use of the term fascism to Mussolini's movement in Italy, most have joined in a process of proliferation that began as early as the 1920s. After Mussolini's success, observers thought they recognized men and organizations of the same type arising in other nations. From this beginning emerged a popular image of fascism as an international movement, a phenomenon that found purest expression in Italy and Germany, but also appeared in a wide number of other countries. When stripped of national trappings, it is commonly believed, all of these movements had a common characteristic that was the essence of fascism itself. Although that essence is difficult to define, the prevailing hope is that continuing research will eventually reveal the nature of fascism more clearly. Thus, while the thing itself continues to elude us, the name goes on as before.

Edward R. Tannenbaum has observed that the study of fascism appears to instill in scholars a particular compulsion for reductive logic, a tendency to relate the phenomenon to a single and central significance.[2] They usually 'reduce' it, however, to a significance that is very large indeed. From the beginning writers seem to have felt compelled to deepen fascism's importance, to 'see through' its ideas and rationalizations, and to explain it in terms beyond the fascists themselves. The movement appeared simply too aberrant, too demagogic, too empty of ideas and honest motives to be taken at face value: fascism had to be 'deciphered.' Ernst Nolte has noted that, when Mussolini deserted socialism to support Italian intervention in the First World War, his old Marxist comrades immediately asked a question that was elaborated thereafter into the socialist conception of fascism: 'Who is paying?'[3] Thus was created, virtually by reflex, the first interpretation of fascism. Others followed, but most continued in the same way to conceive of fascism as an agent of someone or something and invariably portrayed it in literature written between the world wars as a force in itself brutal, opportunistic, and unintelligent, but momentous in what it revealed of the society that gave it birth. In large part, contemporary historians have continued this process of intellectual inflation. Whether they envision fascism as the tool of class interests or the expression of more impersonal forces – the revolt of the masses, the moral crisis of civilization, totalitarianism, or the modernization process – they generally understand it in terms of something more fundamental and important to history. Rarely, on the other hand, is it understood in terms of what the 'fascists' themselves declared it to be. Communist ideas are interpreted seriously, complains one political scientist; fascist ideas are merely 'interpreted.'[4]

This elevation of fascism as a historical concept places considerable strain on the rules of evidence. The burdens of research necessarily restrict the number of personalities and organizations that historians of fascism can investigate with sufficient competence and depth, and thus the effort to develop general theories inevitably carries them beyond the limits of specific knowledge. Unfortunately, the diversity of these personalities and organizations is such that general theories formed from the study of certain samples are often contradicted by the study of others. The more we know in detail, the less we know in general. Few historians, however, have lost confidence that further research will unearth the 'missing link' that unites the different individuals and parties in a generic fascism. Somewhat like the search for the black cat in a dark room, this search presumes that there is something to be found in the dark void. In this sense the notion of generic fascism exists in faith and is pursued by reason. In a way, the problem is reminiscent of the philosopher's world of universal forms and real objects. If so, few concepts are more in need of Ockham's razor than fascism. Only individual things are real; everything abstracted from them, whether concepts or universals, exists solely in the mind. There is no such *thing* as fascism. There are only the men and movements that we call by that name. [. . .]

First of all, fascism is not a generic concept. The word *fascismo* has no meaning beyond Italy. Yet it was applied from the beginning to movements that arose in other nations, movements whose fate it was to be interpreted in terms of Mussolini's organization. Such parties presumably corresponded to foreign 'models,' first the Blackshirts, and later the Nazis. 'They claim that we are fascists, but they know that this is a lie,' protested Jacques Doriot, the leader of the *Parti populaire français*, in 1937. 'We do not think that the regime of Hitler or Mussolini can be fitted to our country.'[5] Such men, however, could no more get rid of the word in their time than historians can be rid of it today. Even those outside Germany and Italy who adopted the term for their own political purposes came to recognize the curse of its association with things foreign. Oswald Mosley, leader of the British Union of Fascists, contended that his own movement was a form of English patriotism that became so confused in the public mind with alien powers that it was denounced as unpatriotic. Students of politics, of course, must always distinguish between movements already in control of the state and those still competing for power. Few were more aware of the difference than the so-called fascists themselves. Mosley complained in later life that, whenever some success appeared possible in the 1930s, his organization received a 'knock-down blow' from the actions of Hitler and Mussolini themselves, blustering into some new European crisis for purely national interests and spreading alarm and opposition in England.[6] 'Patriotic traitors' like Mosley and Doriot were alternately inspired and anguished by the two dictators, imitating them at one minute and denying their influence at the next. On the one hand, they drew support from the secret subsidies of Rome and Berlin; on the other, they suffered the hatred of a public enraged by Italian and German aggression. In this sense, international relations between such leaders were always 'brutal friendships'.

That the slogan, 'nationalists of the world unite,' involves a logical impossibility is a common observation. In the 1930s, however, ideological battles had a logic of their own. Between 1933 and 1936, when Rome and Berlin competed for influence over organizations in other countries and when Mussolini stood guard at the Brenner Pass to prevent Nazi expansion into Austria, the popular image of fascism remained largely bipolar. Fascists were either Blackshirts or Nazis: they looked for inspiration either to Rome or to Berlin. With the Axis alliance, however, rivalries became blurred; and, during the ideological crusade that began with the Spanish Civil War, antifascists everywhere created a fascist model of their own – an international fascism of jackboots, barbed wire, and corpses: irrational, anti-Semitic, totalitarian, and genocidal. Fascists were fascists, and Mussolini and Hitler were their prophets. [. . .]

Secondly, fascism is not an ideology. To contemporary observers, 'fascist' ideas appeared somehow incommensurate with the spirit and spontaneity of fascist action. So suddenly had fascism broken upon Europe, so extraordinary was its appearance, and so shocking its deeds that scholars at first resisted the conclusion that its essence could be contained in a system of ideas. One could demonstrate, for instance, that virtually every 'fascist' idea dated back at least to the nineteenth century or, in some cases, to the origins of political thought itself. Fascism, seemingly, must derive from more explosive material. A force so cataclysmic and unforeseen could only have been generated from the catastrophes of our own century: the First World War, Bolshevism, and the Great Depression.

More recently, however, this 'big bang' theory of fascism has given way to the arguments of a number of intellectual historians that the real substance of fascism was to be found in its intellectual content. Some in particular have claimed to discover the origins of fascist thought in the intellectual revolt against liberalism and Marxism between 1870 and 1914, when a collection of European thinkers, obsessed by a fear of mass democracy and moral decadence, developed a philosophy of will, emotion, soil, and blood. Fascism, in this way, acquired a history, a connection with what are sometimes described as 'prefascist' ideas and thinkers existing before the movement itself. These historians attempt not only to identify a body of ideas, an 'ideology' of fascism conceived as more or less analogous to the conventional ideologies of liberalism or socialism, but also to comprehend its psychological pull, to 'understand' fascism by means of an intuitive grasp upon the consciousness of its adherents. They seek to understand fascism by understanding its appeal. In extending its intellectual origins into the nineteenth century, they seek the reasons why men came to the movement itself in the twentieth century. George Mosse, for instance, admitted that the mental shock of the First World War was necessary to provide the popular base of fascism but insisted nevertheless that the thought of the nineteenth century conditioned this response in the European mind.[7]

The 'big bang,' it seems, was ignited by a long fuse. Most scholarly efforts to trace the ideas involved have been exercises in good old intellectual history. In raw form, the method proceeds as follows: first the researcher isolates an idea in the thought of a reputed fascist ideologue; next he finds an earlier thinker who appears to have originated, possessed, or transmitted the idea; and, by connecting one with the other, he assigns to the earlier thinker a place in the philosophical tradition leading to fascism. This 'precursor' is then often dubbed a 'prefascist' or 'protofascist.' Edward R. Tannenbaum recently presented a terse critique of such procedures: 'The observation that two successive things are similar does not prove that the later one has a direct connection with the earlier one. To assert such a connection without empirical proof is a logical fallacy: *post hoc, ergo propter hoc*. And to use the similarities as evidence is to argue in a circle.'[8] [. . .]

In the beginning, Mussolini reportedly considered fascism to be strictly 'our thing,' a product unique to Italian genius and temperament, and clearly marked 'not for export.' Little definition, therefore, was required – nor were all fascists sure there was one. 'I am fully aware,' admitted one of the Duce's ideologues in 1925, 'that the value of Fascism as an intellectual movement baffles the minds of many of its followers and supporters and is denied outright by its enemies.'[9] In his informative study, *Universal Fascism*, Michael Ledeen noted that, since the doctrine was so vaguely defined, Blackshirt lieutenants were confused about how to distinguish between heresy and conformity in Italian thinking. With the rise of Hitler, however, came a 'profound change.' Rome was confronted with a foreign 'fascism' that was, at the same time, an ideological rival in the struggle for influence over fledgling movements emerging in other countries. At stake, Mussolini was told by his propagandists, was his place in history as the creator of fascism. The challenge he faced was the problem of fascism itself, the problem of giving transcendent meaning to an

Italian expression, of finding an international definition for a phenomenon previously defined in national terms. In addition, there was the problem of defining it against Nazism, a force reviled at Rome as pagan, anti-Semitic, and alien to the fascism originated by Italians. 'Fascist after fascist,' according to Ledeen, 'wrote of the folly of racist doctrine, stressed the humanistic and religious components of Italian fascism, and attacked Hitler.'[10] In his famous encyclopedia article in 1932 and through his representatives two years later at the international fascist congress at Montreux in Switzerland, the Duce attempted to define 'universal fascism,' to pre-empt the role of its prophet, and to establish Italy as its spiritual – and financial – source. But this effort to bring meaning and order to fascism was no more successful than the others.

The Montreux Congress, called to establish the principles of fascist unity, divided instead on the Jewish question. Before departing, the delegates managed to agree on common articles of faith in the monolithic state, economic corporatism, something called the 'national revolution,' and, above all else, the proposition that each nation must solve its problems in its own way. This creed was so general, concluded Ledeen, that most elements of the extreme Right in Europe could have agreed to it as well, including traditional corporatist groups within the Catholic Church. Disappointed, the Italians thereafter let this first project for universal fascism lie dormant. In 1936, however, diplomatic events brought Hitler and Mussolini into a marriage of convenience that soon generated the need for a matching ideology. The Axis alliance, historians now recognize, was based on a personal relationship between two very different men, companions without communication, each needing the cooperation of the other and each resigned as a result to tolerating the inflexible opinions that divided them.[11] The dictators were more interested in minimizing their ideological differences than in debating them. More important were things that could bring them together, ideas and enemies that would give 'fascist' meaning to a politicomilitary association between two grasping partners. Here Nazism, obsessed from the beginning with Germanic notions of a world-historic mission, offered more possibilities than the opportunistic creed of the Blackshirts. Thus, Mussolini incorporated into a revised version of universal fascism racial politics and the 'crusade against Bolshevism,' issues previously of little importance at Rome.[12] To this, the antifascists of Europe added dimensions of their own, and the revised version became the standard version, the popular conception of the ideology of fascism. 'During the thirties . . . ,' recalled Stephen Spender, 'Fascism meant dictatorship, censorship, the persecution of the Jews, the destruction of intellectual freedom. To be anti-Fascist was to be on the side of humanity. Conversely, to be Fascist meant to be against it.'[13] [. . .]

As with most things in the study of fascism, the German and Italian movements have supplied the main evidence for interpretations of fascist ideas. Unfortunately, we will be no more successful in comprehending other groups in terms of these two ideological forms than we have been in the past when attempting to comprehend them in terms of one form. It is probably true that every proclaimed fascist organization drew inspiration from both the German and Italian parties and some imitation was therefore inevitable, but most such organizations had the ambition to create their own national versions of the same thing, movements expressing the uniqueness of their own national character and traditions. When Mussolini invited the leader of the *Falange Española*, José Antonio Primo de Rivera, to attend the international fascist congress at Montreux in 1934, he flatly refused. The Falange was not fascist, he protested, it was Spanish.[14]

The time has come for historians to admit what Mussolini himself was forced to recognize: universal fascism is an illusion. Whether in one form or another, fascism was not an ideology in the style of the great nineteenth-century ideologies, that is, a thought system that provided a theoretical outlook upon experience. Some observers have remarked that this very absence of ideology was what doomed fascism to virtual extinction after 1945. It had nothing for men to carry forward, no key to knowledge, no view of history, no ideal for the future. Nor was it connected to anything permanent in society. It represented the outlook of neither a social class, an economic interest, nor a social organization.[15] The movements we call fascist were not historical accidents. They were conceived and nurtured in the womb of society. Yet, when they appeared, they were also a kind of 'happening,' a collection of forces in motion, at once spontaneous and imitative, committed and unprincipled, extroverted and self-absorbed. I remarked earlier that there is no such thing as fascism per se; there are only the men and organizations that carry that name. When they were defeated, or when their moment was over, fascism passed into history with them. [. . .]

'Fascism offers an ideal meeting ground for historians, political scientists, sociologists and economists,' S. J. Woolf suggested in 1967. 'It enables them to refine the precision of their methodological tools and test the validity of their hypotheses.'[16] In reality, however, social scientists go away from most conferences on the subject more confused than when they arrived. Stanley G. Payne has concisely described the reason: 'The term fascism can be applied to the entire broad genus only at the cost of depriving it of any specific content.' In this connection, I can summarize somewhat ungrammatically the conclusions to the present article: the concept of fascism should be de-modeled, de-ideologized, de-mystified, and, above all, de-escalated. It will not be the first time that an 'ism' has been discovered to embrace things unique and too diverse to be defined in terms of general categories or specific ideas. 'We came to believe that this word "romanticism" was only a word,' wrote the French poet Alfred de Musset in 1836. 'We found it to be beautiful, and it seemed unfortunate that it meant nothing.' Yet the word romanticism has been retained to refer to a movement of men and ideas in a particular historical epoch. They are men and ideas that we have been conditioned, perhaps without sufficient reason, to associate together but that most of us acknowledge are recognizably distinct; and they will probably always elude collective definition. The word fascism deserves a similar fate.

Because fascism is 'dead,' seemingly swallowed up and consumed by the Second World War, Ernst Nolte has reasoned that we can set limits to its history and designate the period 1919–45 as the 'era of fascism.' The memory of the Final Solution will, most likely, always keep fascism immediate and alive for scholars of the human sciences, and no doubt resistance will continue against permitting the record of its deeds to become 'only history.' There is, nevertheless, something to recommend the idea of confining the term fascism within the time limits that Nolte defined. Full of emotion and empty of real meaning, the word fascism is one of the most abused and abusive in our political vocabulary. Unlike the word romanticism it is not found to be beautiful. But it is similar in that it means virtually nothing. Yet the term fascism is probably with us for good. The object, therefore, is to limit the damage.

Placing it within historical boundaries at least provides a measure of control, restricting the proliferation of the word in all directions, past and present, and preventing it from distorting political rhetoric in our own time. Fascism must become a foreign word again, untranslatable outside of a limited period in history.

I have argued here that fascism must become recognized as merely a word within this limited period as well, undefinable beyond the individuals and organizations that it is used to identify. No doubt those who believe that further research will ultimately provide a universal definition of fascism are likely to interpret this article as a counsel of despair. Where they are concerned, it is meant to be a counsel of despair. The search for the meaning of fascism has yielded few convincing results to those social scientists concerned with forming general theories on human experience. For historians, the best advice is not to despair over the present direction of research but to follow it. Research is leading toward the disintegration of what remains of 'uni-fascism' as a generic or ideological concept and the replacement of it with a fascism at once more simple and more difficult: more simple in that the term is becoming disentangled from universal abstractions, more difficult in that it covers a bewildering variety of political expressions. The task, therefore, is to study these political expressions just as they are, while recognizing that the name given them is less intelligible than we would like it to be. Anyway, there is no perfect history any more than there is a real fascism.

Notes

1   Woolf, Introduction to S. J. Woolf, ed., *European Fascism* (New York, 1969), 1.
2   Tannenbaum, *The Fascist Experience: Italian Society and Culture, 1922–1945* (New York, 1972), 3.
3   Nolte, *Three Faces of Fascism*, trans. Leila Vennewitz (New York, 1966), 16.
4   A. James Gregor, *The Ideology of Fascism* (New York, 1969), 14.
5   *La Liberté* (PPF newspaper), June 25, 1937.
6   Mosley, *My Life* (London, 1968), 292.
7   Mosse, 'Fascism and the Intellectuals,' in Woolf, *The Nature of Fascism*, 246.
8   See Tannenbaum's joint review of Zeev Sternhell, *Maurice Barrès et le nationalisme français* (1972) and of Robert Soucy, *Fascism in France: The Case of Maurice Barrès* (1972), in *American Historical Review*, 78 (1973): 1478–80.
9   Alfredo Rocco, 'The Political Doctrine of Fascism,' in Carnegie Endowment for International Peace, *International Conciliation*, no. 223 (1926): 408.
10   Ledeen, *Universal Fascism* (New York, 1972), 101.
11   F. W. Deakin, *The Brutal Friendship: Mussolini, Hitler, and the Fall of Italian Fascism* (New York, 1962); and Mack Smith, *Mussolini's Roman Empire* (New York, 1976), 53–54, 129–30, 142–43.
12   Informative here is the neglected article of Phillip Cannistraro and Edward Wynot; see their 'On the Dynamics of Anticommunism as a Function of Fascist Foreign Policy,' *Politico: Revista de Scienze Politiche*, 38 (1973): 645–81.
13   See Spender's foreword to Alastair Hamilton, *The Appeal of Fascism* (New York, 1971), x.
14   For his press release, see Charles F. Delzell, ed., *Mediterranean Fascism 1919–1945* (New York, 1970), 278.

15   Eugen Weber, 'France,' in Hans Rogger and Eugen Weber, eds., *The European Right* (Berkeley and Los Angeles, 1965), 125.
16   Woolf, Introduction to his *The Nature of Fascism*, 4–5.

Chapter 2

Martin Kitchen

FASCISM AND THE CAPITALIST SYSTEM: A MARXIST VIEW

■ from *FASCISM*, London and Basingstoke, 1976, pp. 83–91

Martin Kitchen's concept of generic fascism shows how an essentially Marxist methodology may be usefully employed in the fray of fascist studies. Although the author departs from the orthodox Comintern notion of fascism as simply a tool of monopoly capitalism, he sees fascism as a product of capitalism (though not 'an inevitable stage' of its development). He also emphasises the prevalence of the anti-socialist/labour/proletariat orientation of fascism, as well as its close alliance with the traditional industrial, political and military elites. Kitchen also provides a tax-onomy of interwar dictatorships, in which he shows considerable scepticism about the extension of the term 'fascism' beyond Germany and Italy. Given his identification of fascism with capitalism, the author believes that the survival of the capitalist system after 1945 does not rule out the re-emergence of fascism in the event of a 'crisis', though with a fundamentally different form, programme and style of politics.

T HE TIME HAS COME TO SALVAGE something from the wreckage and to list certain criteria which will enable us to determine whether or not a regime or a political movement can be called fascist.

Firstly, fascism is a phenomenon of developed industrial states. If capitalism has not reached a certain level of development the particular relationships between classes which are characteristic of fascist movements are not possible. Only in advanced capitalism can there be a powerful capitalist class, a large and organised working class with a potentially revolutionary ideology which calls for a radical restructuring of society, and a large petite bourgeoisie which is caught in the con-tradictions between capital and labour and is unable to find any way out of its social, economic and political dilemmas. Fascism is the product of capitalist society, and for all its anti-capitalist rhetoric, particularly in its early stages, it is unwilling and unable to surpass that society. Fascism is not identical with capitalism, as it is held to be in certain extreme theories of fascism, but there exists between capitalism and fascism a non-identical identity. Fascism is potential within late capitalism, but for that potentiality to become manifest a particular set of historical and social circumstances, which are detailed below, are necessary. Fascism is thus not an inevitable stage through which capitalism is bound to pass.

Secondly, fascist movements are triggered off by a severe socio-economic crisis which threatens a considerable section of society with loss of status and even economic ruin, and which plunges society into a widespread feeling of uncertainty and fear. Confidence in the existing political system and its representatives is shattered and bourgeois-democratic forms no longer seem adequate to master a crisis which appears to threaten the entire structure of society. In every case there is a direct correlation between economic crisis and the rise of fascism, but once again it must be emphasised that fascism is not response by a capitalist society to an acute crisis. All capitalist-countries produced fascist movements after the crash in 1929 but in most of these countries they were movements of the lunatic fringe, and parliamentary regimes, usually of the moderate right, were able to contain and control the crisis without any major quantitative or qualitative changes. It is in countries where the social and political balance is extremely unsteady as a result of specific historical and economic circumstances that a socio-economic crisis of this magnitude can lead to the establishment of a fascist regime.

Thirdly, fascism is a response to a large and organised working class which, through its political parties, whether communist or social democratic, have made significant demands on industry and on the bourgeoisie. Fear of the demands of the working class is a major factor in the mass support for fascist movements and their financing by the capitalist elite. Many felt that it was better to be black (or brown) than red, and the elite was determined to destroy the organisations of the working class. However, fascism is only possible when the socialist working class has suffered severe defeats, such as those in Italy in 1920 and in Germany between 1918 and 1923, and when the socialist parties are so badly divided between themselves as was the case with the communists and the social democrats. Although most fascists saw themselves as defending society against this threat from the left, in fact fascism was, strictly speaking, an offensive against the working class. Fascism attacked a working class that had already been defeated and demoralised. Thus, although a large, organised and menacing working class is a necessary precondition of fascism, it must have spent its forces before fascism can succeed. A united and determined working class is the major safeguard against fascism.

Fourthly, fascism recruits its mass following from a politicised, threatened, and frightened petite bourgeoisie. Artisans, small independent businessmen and farmers who are threatened by monopolisation and severely hurt by the economic crisis flock to the fascists, attracted by their political rhetoric, in the hope of finding economic and social salvation, where they join forces with white-collar workers and lower civil servants who are determined to ward off the immanent threat of being cast down into the ranks of the proletariat. In some instances they are joined by members of the 'aristocracy of labour' who no longer identify with the working class and see in fascism a means of enhancing their social status.

Fifthly, fascist regimes are characterised by an alliance between the fascist party leadership and the traditional elites of industry, banking, the bureaucracy and the military [Note: see the excerpts in Section VIII]. We have seen that this relationship is a two-way affair. The fascist parties were not simply manipulated by the capitalist elite, and the fascist leadership did not establish the undiluted primacy of politics which reduced the old elites to the level of being the mindless executive organs of political extremists. The community of interests between the functional elite and the fascist leadership resulted in a significant change in the relationship between the leadership and the party. Party members who stressed the social revolutionary aspects of fascism, and who represented the political aspirations of the radical petite bourgeoisie in their demand for a 'second revolution', were purged, and the fascist party stripped of its influence and reduced to the role of social integrator. However, the very existence of a mass party was a powerful weapon which could be used by the leadership, if necessary, to threaten and cajole the old elites when differences over means led to conflict at the top. Attempts by [Heinrich] Brüning and [Franz von] Papen to establish authoritarian regimes which had no mass base had failed, so that the fascist solution seemed to be the only viable alternative. The fascist executive enjoyed a certain degree of independence, and often acted in ways that were inimical to sections of industry. The alliance between these two centres of power was thus always close, but it was by no means always harmonious.

Sixthly, the social function of fascism was to stabilise, strengthen and, to a certain degree, transform capitalist property relationships and to ensure the social and economic domination of the capitalist class, which felt threatened, which was divided among itself as to the best means of overcoming the crisis and which was prepared to relinquish some of its political power in order to maintain its privileged position. It can be argued that in this respect fascism is little different from conservatism, which also aims to strengthen and perpetuate the social status quo. The social basis of the support for conservative and extreme right-wing parties is similar. Both factions of the political right subscribe to a vague anti-modernist ideology and a pronounced anti-socialism. Neither show any genuine concern for the fate of their petit bourgeois followers. The significant difference between the two is that conservative regimes, however far to the right they may be, operate within the bounds of legality and of established political practice. Fascist regimes, on the other hand, employ the utmost terror against their opponents in order to achieve their social, political and economic goals. This terror is particularly directed against the organisations of the labour movement. In this limited sense Dimitroff's definition of fascism as open terror by the most reactionary sectors of capitalist society is perfectly correct.

Seventhly, therefore, fascism is a terror regime which dispenses with all the trappings of parliamentary democracy. No opposition whatsoever is allowed, either within or without the fascist movement. The presence of opposition forces, however ineffectual and powerless they may be, is incommensurate with fascism and is evidence of an authoritarian regime which may, nevertheless, contain strong fascist elements. It is, however, inadmissible to take this terror regime as the sole most significant aspect of fascism, as does the theory of totalitarianism. The function and the social basis of this terror distinguish fascism sharply from other forms of terror regime, such as the Soviet Union in the Stalin era.

Eighthly, fascist movements use ideology deliberately to manipulate and divert the frustrations and anxieties of the mass following away from their objective source. Fascist ideology is characterised by an emphasis on essentially irrational concepts such as authority, obedience, honour, duty, the fatherland or race. Fascists proclaim the existence of a true community, based on blind obedience and the leadership principle. The main thrust of this ideology is against socialism. It claims to stand for those with property, however small and insignificant that property might be, against those who threaten to take that property away from them. Such a form of anti-socialism amounts to an attack on the very concept of an emancipatory society. The masses are further controlled by the emphasis on the hidden enemies who have sinister designs on society and who threaten the longed-for sense of community. Almost any group, or collection of groups, will fulfil this function, be they Jews or blacks, intellectuals or Jehovah's Witnesses, Gypsies or foreigners. Such groups are relatively weak and unable to defend themselves, and provide excellent scapegoats for the ills and failures of society. Fascists are also able to justify their own short-comings and failures, and the hardships which they impose on the masses, by conjuring up the vision of a host of enemies at home and abroad who are determined to crush the regime. Thus further sacrifices and efforts can be demanded so that the fascist 'new order' can be finally established.

Ninthly, fascist regimes pursue aggressive and expansionist foreign political aims. This imperialism is justified in terms of military necessity — so that the state may be secure against the menace of its envious neighbours and be prepared for the 'battle of the world-views'. It is also justified in terms of economic necessity — so that economic autarchy can be achieved and the problems of capitalist reproduction overcome. There is also a strong social imperialist moment. The conquest of new land diverts the tensions and frustrations of society away from their objective source, it provides a national purpose and goal, and it can be used to compensate the masses for the privations and the sufferings of the past.

Tenthly, the degree of intensity of any of these above points is determined by the level of capitalist development and the resulting problems which the fascist regime is called upon to overcome. Thus German fascism was far more brutal, aggressive and totalitarian than Italian fascism, because Germany was both a more developed and a more antagonistic society. The crisis of 1933 was thus more acute than the crisis of 1922, and the German fascist regime had at its disposal more sophis-ticated techniques for mass control, terror and expansion.

If we accept these ten distinguishing marks of fascism how can they be applied to categorise fascistic regimes? If fascism is a phenomenon of highly developed indus-trial states, then clearly the military dictatorships of South America and of the under-developed countries of Africa and Asia cannot be termed 'fascist'. Such regimes lack the mass support which characterises fascist movements, even though they are often adept at mobilising the masses. To a considerable extent they uphold a feudal rather than a capitalist mode of production. They do not have the pro-nounced imperialist ambitions of fascist states, for they are often themselves in a state of imperialist dependency. They frequently lack the instruments of sustained terror and control, and tend rather to indulge in outbursts of uncontrolled brutality and violence. Even the Argentina of Perón, which is frequently described as fascist, was supported by a fundamentally different class alignment and had a quite different function from a fascist regime. Similarly the bestial counter-revolutionary regime in Chile, although showing striking similarities with fascism in a number of aspects, is quite distinct from the fascist model.

The regimes of Spain and Salazar's Portugal and the 'clerical fascism' of Austria before the *Anschluss* are even closer to the fascist model. But even here there are significant differences. In Spain the fascist party, the Falange, never attained the size nor enjoyed the independence of the fascist mass parties in Italy and Germany, and was always controlled and manipulated by a military clique. Franco's regime initially rested on the support of the army, the police and the bureaucracy, rather than on the party. Ideology was the province of the church rather than the Falange. The socially dominant class was the semi-feudal landowning aristocracy. The level of capitalist development was modest. In Portugal these restorative and conservative tendencies in the dictatorship were even more pronounced. The *'Heimwehr* fascism' of Austria, which has yet to be given a detailed scientific analysis, was also something of a hybrid between fascism and ultra-conservatism. Not until 1938 and the *Anschluss* did Austrian fascism approach the true fascist model, but that was not the result of the inner dynamics of Austrian society, but rather the military, political and economic dominance of Nazi Germany.

Similarly the right-wing dictatorships of inter-war Europe lacked many of the essential ingredients of fascist regimes. Poland, Romania, Greece and Yugoslavia were ruled by varying forms of military dictatorship of a conservative type which, although they suppressed the left, never went as far as the totalitarian dictatorships of the fascist type. All of these countries had fascist movements, but they remained on the fringe of the radical right until, in some cases such as Hungary, Croatia and Slovakia, they gained power thanks to German armies of occupation. They were thus imported regimes which did not reflect the social structure and political dynamics of the countries which they dominated.

Although the regimes of Nazi Germany and fascist Italy provide the best examples of fascism in action it would be a serious mistake to limit a definition of fascism to these two forms, or even to the period between the two World Wars. Such a definition would make it impossible to analyse fascist dangers in the present day. The fact that changing circumstances are liable to produce differences in fascist movements, at least at the phenomenological level, has led many writers to talk of 'neo-fascism'.

It can be argued that the changed circumstances of the capitalist world since 1945 are such that talk of the end of the epoch of fascism may seem a trifle premature. The capitalist world had been reduced and weakened. The vast increase in the power and influence of the Soviet Union and its dependent states, of China and the whole socialist world which now comprises one third of the world's population has greatly reduced the relative strength of the capitalist world. This tendency is further intensified by the fact that the vast majority of the former colonies have found relative independence. An intolerable strain is placed on the advanced industrial states by the determination of some countries producing essential commodities such as petroleum to command the maximum possible price. In such changing circumstances the classical bourgeois liberal state has undergone some significant changes, and has been obliged to adapt itself to new contingencies. The problem therefore is whether the ruling elites in the advanced capitalist countries have the situation so well in hand

and have developed new techniques of government which will make a fascist regime unnecessary, even in situations of grave crisis, or whether an exceptional regime will be established, the techniques of 'crisis management' having failed.

Modern capitalist states are indeed far better equipped than ever before to deal with economic and social crises. The state is prepared to intervene in the workings of the economy to a degree which would have been inconceivable in the inter-war years. The techniques employed to control the effects of economic problems, although in many ways deficient, have greatly improved, and governments are now more ready to use them. The techniques of mass communication have made even more startling advances, enabling a higher degree of control so that an ideological consensus is more easily achieved. Advertising is only one of the more obvious ways in which the individual is manipulated, rendered uncritical and made to absorb a view of the world which serves to maintain and strengthen the status quo.

The similarity between these techniques and those of fascist regimes has led certain ultra-left writers to argue that contemporary capitalist practice is a sinister and concealed form of fascism. Fascism is then seen as that form of domination which maintains the capitalist mode of production in an advanced capitalist society which is threatened by a crisis which challenges and brings into question the principles on which that society is based. In contemporary capitalism, according to this version, opposition groups are fully integrated into the system, the working class is so totally absorbed with economistic concerns that it no longer has any fundamental political demands to make and has completely lost its revolutionary *élan*; parliamentary democracy, freedom of speech and the diverse offerings of the media merely complete the process of control and manipulation. If such an analysis were true then it is of little interest whether contemporary capitalism is labelled 'fascist' or whether one asserts that fascism is an antiquated and outmoded form of control that is no longer necessary. The political consequences that can be drawn from such an analysis are either total resignation as a pseudo-political stance, Eastern mysticism or the rigmarole of the drug culture providing a suitable ideological cover, or irrational outbursts of anarchic putschism. The inevitable failure of either tactic is then used as further evidence of the sinister repressive quality of society, and thus reaffirms the original ideological stance.

Such a reading of the contemporary scene, which commanded a considerable following in the 1960s, has since been proved empirically false. Economic crises, runaway inflation, mass unemployment, racial tensions, the growth of political radicalism and unsuccessful foreign adventures have placed a tremendous strain on many countries. A tendency to strengthen executive power is most noticeable in the Gaullist constitution and in the American presidency, particularly as it was under Nixon. Neither regime could be considered fascist, although they were often accused of it, and their fascistoid tendencies were controlled and contained in large part by the existence of strong pockets of democratic tradition of both a liberal and a socialist nature, which put up a determined resistance to any further encroachments on those liberties and freedoms without which no anti-fascist struggle is possible.

A new fascism is bound to adapt itself to a new situation. This is already apparent in the fascistic movements such as the N.P.D. in Germany, the M.S.I. in Italy or the National Front in Britain. Their style is not as rowdy and violent as that of their predecessors. They are more concerned to appear respectable. Anti-semitism, although often present, is less pronounced. Immigrant workers are frequently blamed for economic problems such as unemployment. Anti-communism takes the place of anti-capitalism [*Note: the text was written in the 1970s, long before the collapse of the communist bloc in eastern Europe*]. Fascist mass-movements, if they reappear, will probably be more restrained and civilised, but they will be no less menacing. When the manipulation of mass opinion is no longer sufficient to maintain the consensus then the state repression of the opposition groups may well be deemed necessary. Again this need not imply the physical brutality of previous fascist regimes, but may well be of a more subtle and insidious nature. For all the talk of 'structurally immanent state fascism' a mass party, a charismatic leader and a distinct ideology will still be necessary. The nature of all three components is likely to be quite distinct from their historical forms. Such differences combined with a changed economic, political, social and psychological situation may, perhaps, make it more meaningful to speak of 'neo-fascism'. A theory of neo-fascism would take the essential features of the fascism of the past, examine how these factors are likely to have changed, and see under what socio-economic crisis situations in contemporary advanced capitalism such drastic measures are likely to be employed. But [. . .] the danger of fascism is still with us [. . .] [because] the socio-economic system which produced fascism to overcome its difficulties still exists, the problems which it faces still remain acute.

Editor's note

The cabinets of the period 1930–3 (before the appointment of Hitler) were:

Bruning	24 March 1930	–	30 May 1932
Papen	31 May 1932	–	14 November 1932
Schleicher	2 December 1932	–	28 January 1933

Chapter 3

Juan J. Linz

FASCISM AS 'LATECOMER': AN IDEAL TYPE WITH NEGATIONS

■ from *TOTALITARIAN AND AUTHORITARIAN REGIMES*, Boulder and London, 2000, pp. 220–7

Juan J. Linz sees fascism as a 'latecomer' on the scene of political ideologies – and hence better defined by its opposition to the established ideologies. However, he also emphasises fascism's 'future-oriented' character as opposed to a conventional, back-ward-looking 'reactionary' understanding. Linz's 'ideal type' of fascism makes a distinction between negative ('anti-') goals, positive (only in contrast to the 'anti-positions') objectives and elements of a 'new style of politics'. He also underlines the significance of mobilisational techniques employed by fascism – an element that distinguishes it from other authoritarian systems (even in those cases, such as the Iberian peninsula and the Balkans, where this mobilisation remained limited compared to Nazi Germany).

THE NATURE AND DEFINITION OF FASCISM itself is a subject of lively debate (Lipset, 1960; Nolte, 1968a; Linz, 1976). We would characterize fascism as an ideology and movement defined by what it rejects, by its exacerbated nationalism, by the discovery of new forms of political action and a new style. The anti-positions of fascism are essential to its understanding and its appeal, but they alone do not account for its success. Fascism is antiliberal, antiparliamentarian, anti-Marxist, and particularly anticommunist, anti- or at least aclerical, and in a certain sense antibourgeois and anticapitalist; while linking with the real or imagined historical national tradition, it is not committed to a conservative continuity with the recent past or a purely reactionary return to it but is future-oriented. Those negative stances are a logical outcome of its being a latecomer on the political scene, trying to displace liberal, Marxist, socialist, and clerical parties and win over their supporters. They are also the fruit of the exacerbated nationalism that rejects the appeal to class solidarity across national boundaries and puts in its place the solidarity of all those involved in production in a nation against other nations, seizing on the notion of the proletarian nation: the poor countries against the wealthy plutocracies, which happened to be at that time also powerful democracies. Communist internationalism is defined in this context as the enemy. The latent hostility to a church that transcends the national boundaries and whose divisive effect on the national community with the struggle between clerical and secularizers interferes with the goal of national greatness, hostility that becomes bitter hatred in cases like Nazism, is another logical consequence that differentiates the fascist from other conservative antidemocratic parties. To the extent that modern capitalism is, particularly in its financial institutions, part of an international system, fascists tend to idealize preindustrial strata like the independent peasant, the artisan, and the entrepreneur, particularly the founder directing his own firm (Mosse, 1964; Winkler, 1972). Masonry, as an organization emphasizing links across nations and closely identified with the liberal bourgeois, secularized strata that created the democratic liberal regimes, is another obvious enemy. Anti-Semitism in the Europe of the turn of the century, particularly Eastern Europe (Pulzer, 1964; Massing, 1949), had a long tradition, and wherever there were Jews fascism seized on those tendencies, stressing the anational, cosmopolitan character of the Jews and particularly of Zionism.

Those negative appeals, however, had a kind of distorted positive counterpart. The anti-Marxism is compensated by an exultation of work, of the producers of *Faust* and *Stirn*, 'hand and brain,' in that way appealing to the growing white-collar middle class, which rejected Marxist demands that it should identify with the proletariat (Kele, 1972). The populism of fascism leads it to support welfare-state policies and to engage in loose talk of national socialism, socialization of the banks, etc., which justifies in fascist authoritarian regimes economic interventionism and the development of an important public sector in the economy. The anticapitalism that appeals to precapitalist and petit bourgeois strata is redefined as hostility to international financial stock exchange and Jewish capitalism and as exultation of the national entrepreneurial bourgeoisie. The emphasis on a national common good, which rejects the assumptions of individualism, is easily combined with hostility to the free play of interests of economic liberalism and finds expression in protectionist and autarchic economic policies that appeal to industrialists threatened by international competition. The hostility of a secularized intelligentsia of exacerbated nationalists to clerical politics and their competition with Christian democratic parties for a similar social basis account for the anticlericalism that gets combined with an affirmation of the religious tradition as part of the national, cultural, historical tradition. Already the Action Française in secularist France had taken this path, appealing to the Catholics who rejected the secularizing, liberal democratic state. The Iron Guard, the only successful fascist movement in a Greek Orthodox country, confronted with the denationalized, secularized bourgeoisie and an influential Jewish community, was the fascism that most directly linked with religious symbolism. In the case of Germany the confused programmatic statements about positive Christianity and the identification of many Protestants with a conservative state religion were used by the Nazis, but ultimately the racist ideology became incompatible with any commitment to Christianity (Lewy, 1965; Buchheim, 1953). The anti-religious stands of Marxism and particularly communism in the Soviet Union allowed the fascists to capitalize on the ambivalent identification with the religious heritage. The anticlericalism facilitated the appeal to secularized middle classes unwilling to support the clerical and Christian democratic middle-class parties, while their antiliberalism, anti-Masonic, and even anti-Semitic stands, combined with their anticommunism, facilitated the collaboration with the churches when they came to power. The antibourgeois affect, the romanticization of the peasant, the artisan, the soldier, contrasted with the impersonal capitalism and selfish bourgeois rentiers, appealed to the emotional discontent of the sons of the bourgeoisie, the cultural critics of modern industrial and urban society. The rejection of the proletarian self-righteousness and the bourgeois egoism and the affirmation of the common national interests above and beyond class cleavages exploited the desire for interclass solidarity developed among veterans of the war (Linz, 1976; Merkl, 1975) and the guilt feeling of the bourgeoisie, and served well the interests of the business community in destroying a labor movement that threatened its privileges and status. The populist appeal to community against the pragmatism of society, *Gemeinschaft* versus *Gesellschaft,* had considerable appeal in democratic societies divided by class conflict and mobilized by modern mass parties.

The deliberately ambiguous and largely contradictory appeals we have just described would have been, and were, unsuccessful in those societies in which war and defeat had not created a serious national crisis. In the defeated nations or in those which, like Italy, although victors, felt unjustly deprived of the fruits of their victory, an upsurge of nationalism was channeled by the new parties. The efforts to establish an international political order through the League of Nations under the leadership and to the benefit of the Western, capitalistic, plutocratic democracies became another issue in the armory of the fascists. The lack of coincidence between the national-cultural boundaries and those of the states, the irredenta on the borders, and the existence of nationalities that had not become nation-states, combined with the pan-nationalist movements, were another source of strength for fascism, particularly in the case of Nazis.

Fascist ideology had to reject totally the assumptions of liberal democratic politics based on pluralist participation, the free expression of interests, and compromise among them rather than the assertion of the collective interests above individuals and classes, cultural and religious communities. The obvious distortion of the idea of democracy in the reality of the early twentieth century and the incapacity of the democratic leadership to institutionalize mechanisms for conflict resolution provided the ground for the appeal of fascism. On a less lofty level, all the interests threatened by a powerful labor movement with revolutionary rhetoric, particularly after some of its revolutionary attempts had been defeated, could support the fascist squads as a defense of the social order. In societies that had reached the level of political, economic, and social development of Western Europe, that defense could not be left to the old institutions – the monarchy, the army, the bureaucracy, and the oligarchical political elites. In that context the fascist ideology offered a new alternative, which promised the integration of the working class into the national community and the assertion of its interests against other nations, if necessary through military preparedness and even aggression (Neumann, 1963). This position would appeal to veterans not reintegrated into civil society and army officers and would neutralize the armed forces in the course of the struggle for power.

Neither the ideological appeals nor the interests served by or expected to be served by fascism are sufficient to account for its rapid success. Fascism developed new forms of political organization, different from both the committee electoral-type of parties and the mass-membership, trade-union-based socialist parties, as well as the clerically led religious parties. It was the type of organization that, like the communist counterpart, offered an opportunity for action, involvement, participation, breaking with the monotony of everyday life. For a generation that had lived heroic, adventurous actions of war and even more for the one that had lived that experience vicariously, due to its youth, the *squadrismo* and the storm troopers offered welcome relief. Many of those who found their normal careers and education disrupted by the war and economic crisis, and probably some of the unemployed, provided the party with many of its activists, whose propaganda and direct action in support of specific grievances – of farmers to be evicted, peasants onto whom the labor unions were imposing the employment of labor, industrialists threatened by strikers – gained them support that no electoral propaganda could have achieved. This new style of politics satisfied certain psychological and emotional needs like no other party could except some forms of cultural protest and to some extent the communists.

Finally, fascism is characterized by a distinctive style reflected in the uniforms – the shirts – which symbolized the break with bourgeois convention, the individualism of bourgeois dress; and the mass demonstrations and ceremonies, which allowed individuals to submerge in the collective and escape the privatization of modern society. The songs, the greetings, the marches, all gave expression to the new myth, the hopes, and illusions of part of that generation.

This ideal-typical description of fascism as a political movement ignores national variants in ideology, appeal, social basis, and alignments on the political scene. We cannot go into the complex question of whether National Socialism, with its extreme racism, its biologic conception of man, fits into the broader category of fascism (Nolte, 1963; Mosse, 1964, 1966), particularly since many fascists felt quite critical of Nazism and many Nazis felt ambivalent toward Mussolini and his movement (Hoepke, 1968). Our view is that National Socialism, particularly the northern left wing of the movement, rather than 'Hitlerism,' fits into the more general category (Kühnl, 1966). Nazism did not reject the identification as fascism, but it also acquired unique characteristics making it a quite different branch of the common tree into which German ideological traditions (Mosse, 1964; Sontheimer, 1968; Lukácz, 1955) had been grafted and one that had its own distinct fruits. The strength of that branch growing with the resources of German society made it an appealing competitor of the first fascist state.

The ambiguities and contradictions of the fascist Utopia, combined with the inevitable pragmatic compromises with many of the forces it initially criticized, account for the failure of the model, except in Italy (to a certain point) and in Germany. To have been successful the initial nucleus would have had to gain support in all strata of the society and particularly among the working class in addition to the peasantry. However, the organizational penetration, except perhaps in Hungary, Rumania, and (if we consider Perónism as a deviant of fascism) in Argentina, of the socialist, communist, and anarcho-syndicalist (in Spain) labor movements was such that such hopes were condemned to failure. In some countries the Catholic peasantry, middle classes, and even many workers had identified with clerical and/or Christian democratic parties in the defense of religion and found in the social doctrine of the Church an answer to many of the problems to which fascism presumed to be a response. Unless deeply scared by unsuccessful revolutionary attempts, disorganized by continuous economic crises – inflation, depression, unemployment, and bankruptcies – or uprooted by war, the middle and upper-middle classes remained loyal to old parties (including, before the March on Rome, most of the Italian south) in countries like France, Belgium, the Netherlands, Scandinavia, and the UK (Linz, 1976; Kaltefleiter, 1968; Lepsius, 1968). Fascism's success in these countries was a minority, largely generational phenomenon, strengthened in nationalist border areas and gaining broader support in crisis periods. The heterogeneous basis and the failure to gain strata to which its appeal was directed, ultimately explainable by its latecomer role on the political scene, led the leaders to an unremitting struggle to gain power and to a policy of opportunistic alliances with a variety of established groups and a- or anti-democratic conservative forces, which in turn hoped to manipulate its popular appeal and youthful activist following for their own purposes. In societies that had experienced a serious crisis but no political, social, and economic breakdown comparable to czarist Russia, this meant that the way of power was open only in coalition with other forces, particularly the conservative authoritarian parties like the Partito Nazionalista in Italy and the DNVP in Germany, the powerful antilabor interest groups, and the army, and by neutralizing the churches. Such groups well entrenched in the establishment and the state could provide men more capable of governing than were the activists of the first hour. The result was the establishment of authoritarian regimes – with a seriously limited and muted pluralism – with a single party whose rule ranged from fairly dominant and active, approaching in some moments the totalitarian model, to regimes in which it was only a minor partner in the coalition of forces, or absorbed like in Portugal, or suppressed, like in Rumania. Only in Germany would the party and its many – and competing – organizations become dominant. In all of them fascism introduced a mobilizational, populist component, a channel for some degree and some types of voluntary political participation, a source of ideological discontent with the status quo and justification for social change, which differentiates authoritarian mobilizational regimes from other types. Even where that mobilization was ultimately deliberately demobilized, like in Spain (Linz, 1970), the half organic-statist, half bureaucratic-expert-military authoritarian regime emerging after the 1940s would never be the same as for example the regime of Salazar, where fascism as we have characterized it never had taken root.

The struggle against a powerful, particularly a social democratic, labor movement and the effort to undermine the authority of a democratic state exacerbated the romantic love for violence into an end in itself and generally, consciously or unconsciously, transformed the movement into an instrument of vested interests (often verbally and even sincerely denounced), transforming the 'national integrative revolution' into hateful counterrevolution. The Marxist interpretation (Abendroth, 1969; Mansilla, 1971; *International Journal of Politics*, 1973; Galkin, 1970; Lopukhov, 1965), while inadequate to explain the emergence of the ideology, its complex appeal, and its success in capturing the imagination of many youthful ideologists and misunderstanding the motivation of the founders and many leaders, is largely right in the analysis of the 'objective' historical role played by fascism (Neumann, 1963). This obviously does not mean to accept the thesis that the fascists were the hirelings of capitalism based on subsidies that started coming only when the party had gathered strength and in proportion to its success relative to other anti-Marxist parties, or that fascism was the last possible defense of capitalism, or that in power it only and always served its interests. Even less does it absolve the Marxist movement of having undertaken and failed in revolutionary attempts to gain power in relatively democratic societies or of holding onto a maximalist revolutionary rhetoric that mobilizes its enemies and prevents the democratic governments from functioning effectively – a policy that prevents the government from imposing the order desired by those supporting it, while not making a serious effort to impose (at least in part) the policies favored by those movements by participating actively in democratic policymaking by either supporting or even entering government. Fascism, among other things, is a response to the ambivalence of the Marxist ideological heritage toward the importance of political institutions, toward 'formal' liberal democracy, toward reform rather than revolution. Mussolini reflected this dialectical relationship when he said that if the red menace had not been there it would have had to be invented. The anti- or at least a-democratic behavior of the left made possible the more effective one of the right, even when in turn the manipulative attitude of the liberals toward democratic institutions explains the reaction of the left.

Fascist-mobilizational authoritarian regimes are less pluralistic, more ideological, and more participatory than bureaucratic-military or organic-statist regimes with a weak single party. They are further from 'liberalism' and closer to 'democracy,' further from individual freedom from political constraint but closer to offering citizens a chance to participate, less conservative, and more change oriented. Probably the greater ideological legitimacy and the greater mobilization of support made them less vulnerable to internal opposition and overthrow than other types of authoritarian rule, and in fact only external defeat destroyed them.

References

Abendroth W (1969) *Faschismus und Kapitalismus: Theorien über die soziale Ursprunge und die Funktion des Faschismus* (Frankfurt am Main)

Buchheim H (1953) *Glaubenskrise im Dritten Reich: Drei Kapitel Nationalsozialistischer Religionspolitik* (Stuttgart)

Galkin A (1970) 'Capitalist society and fascism', *Social Sciences*, 1: 128–38

Hoepke K-P (1968) *Die deutsche Rechte und der italienische Faschismus* (Düsseldorf)

Kaltefleiter W (1968) *Wirtschaft und Politik in Deutschland: Konjuktur als Bestimmungsfaktor des Parteiensystems* (Cologne)

Kele M H (1972) *Nazis and Workers: National Socialist Appeals to German Labor, 1919–1933* (Chapel Hill, NC)

Kühnl R (1966) *Die nationalsozialistische Linke 1925–1930* (Meisenheim am Glan)

Lepsius R (1968) 'The collapse of an intermediary power structure: Germany 1933–1934', *International Journal of Comparative Sociology*, 9: 289–301

Lewy G (1965) *The Catholic Church and Nazi Germany* (New York)

Linz J J (1970) 'From Falange to Movimento-Organización: the Spanish single party and the Franco regime 1936–1968', in Huntington S and Moore C (eds) *Authoritarian*

Politics in Modern Societies: The Dynamics of Established One Party Systems (New York)

Linz J J (1976) 'Somes notes towards a comparative study of fascism in socio-historical perspective', in Laqueur W (ed.) *Fascism: A Reader's Guide* (Harmondsworth)

Lipset S M (1960) 'Fascism – left, right and centre', in Lipset, *Political Man: The Social Bases of Politics* (Garden City, NY)

Lopukhov B R (1965) 'Il problema del fascismo italiano negli scritti di autori sovietici', *Studi Storici*, 6: 239–57

Lukácz G (1955) *Die Zerstörung der Vernunft* (Berlin)

Mansilla H C F (1971) *Faschismus und eindimensionale Gesellschaft* (Neuwied)

Massing P W (1949) *Rehearsal for Destruction: A Study of Political Anti-Semitism in Imperial Germany* (New York)

Merkl P H (1975) *Political Violence under the Swastika. 581 Early Nazis* (Princeton NJ)

Mosse G L (1964) *The Crisis of German Ideology. Intellectual Origins of the Third Reich* (New York)

Mosse G L (1966) *Nazi Culture. Intellectual, Cultural and Social Life in the Third Reich* (New York)

Neumann F (1963) *Behemoth: The Structure and Practice of National Socialism, 1933–1944* (New York)

Nolte E (1963) *Der Nationalsozialismus* (Munich)

Nolte E (1968a) *Die Krise des liberals Systems und die faschistischen Bewegungen* (Munich)

Pulzer P G J (1964) *The Rise of Political Anti-Semitism in Germany and Austria* (New York)

Sontheimer K (1968) *Antidemokratisches Denken in der Weimarer Republik* (Munich)

Winkler A (1972) *Mittelstand, Demokratie und Nationalsozialismus. Die Politische Entwicklung von Handwerk und Kleinhandel in der Weimarer Republik* (Cologne)

Chapter 4

Roger Eatwell

A 'SPECTRAL-SYNCRETIC' APPROACH
TO FASCISM

■ from **TOWARDS A NEW MODEL OF GENERIC FASCISM**,
Journal of Theoretical Politics, 2 (1992), pp. 172–7, 178–80, 182–4, 185–6,
187, 189

Like Griffin, Roger Eatwell underlines the importance of studying fascism as an intellectual phenomenon and not simply as the sum of its interwar practical
manifestations and 'style'. The novelty of the following excerpt lies in its assertion
that fascism should be studied not in the conventional 'left–right' model, but with
what Eatwell calls a 'spectral-syncretic' approach. A further important aspect of
Eatwell's methodology is the distinction between core elements of fascism (such as
nationalism and corporatism) and other features (charismatic leadership, single
party) which characterised the 'classic fascist model' of the interwar perior but
should not be regarded as prerequisites of fascism in diachronical terms.

T HE FIRST [CONSIDERATION in order to conceptualise fascism
precisely] is the need to distinguish between *ideology and propaganda*. The definitions of these terms are highly contested, but here they are treated as
unproblematical. An ideology is a set of basic ideas and policies about the organization of society. Propaganda refers more to ways of gaining support for a movement/
regime based on such ideas, though not always by revealing their true nature. An
example helps illustrate the importance of this distinction. A recent original attempt
to define fascism has seen it as a form of 'palingenetic ultra-nationalism' (Griffin,
1991). This approach manages to incorporate into a basic definition two appeals that
had both ideological and propagandistic aspects. Nationalism was crucial to fascism,
but it was seen in significantly different ways by fascists (see below). The rebirth,
Phoenix, image too was important because it could be interpreted in at least two
ways. It could symbolize the rebirth of something which had already existed; in other
words it had a conservative or reactionary dimension. On the other hand, it could

be a radical-revolutionary symbol of the need to create something new out of the ashes of the old.

In order to help solve the problem of distinguishing between ideology and propaganda, it is important to add four further analytical devices about the form of fascist ideology. First, is the difference within a self-styled 'revolutionary' ideology between its *critique* of existing society/and vision of its *Utopia*, and its view of the *transition* to the new system. As the argument develops, it will be seen that a significant flaw in previous analyses of fascism has been a failure to perceive that even classic fascism, let alone European neo-fascism, encompassed different views on the nature of the transition. Yet a narrow view of the transition has been encompassed into generic definitions of fascism.

This can be seen even more clearly by considering a second device to illustrate the difference between ideology and propaganda. This is the importance of distinguishing between *intellectual* and *activist* fascism. The former category does not imply any necessary academic imprimatur. The point is more that some fascists sought to create and offer a serious level of debate about both current and more metapolitical issues. Others, especially the leaders, sought more either to influence, or themselves were, street-fighters, activists. It is symptomatic of academic attitudes to fascism that the main focus has been on the latter. (Would those seeking to refine the concept of conservatism pay great attention to the *ideas* of Reagan or Thatcher, or the views, psychological dispositions, yet alone 'style' of their party activists?)

Third, there is the difference between fundamental *principles* and the specific *context*. As already noted, fascism was a latecomer to the political system, and had problems defining ideological 'space'. This meant that fascism was both an ideology undergoing rapid mutations and a movement/regime that was always likely to make tactical compromises (the same point could be elucidated by making another distinction: between a more fundamental ideology and more pragmatic programme). Individuals could also join fascist movements, especially those in power, without being committed to key fascist principles. For example, Carl Schmitt, the 'Crown Jurist' of the early Third Reich, was in many ways a Catholic conservative, moved by opportunism (Bendersky, 1983). National contexts are also important, as even within inter-war Europe there were significant socio-economic differences within countries. Indeed, there is a danger in all generic models of separating ideas from specific historical context, and thus producing a false picture.

It might be added that since 1945 some of the more intellectual European neo-fascists have sought to develop doctrine in important ways. Their activities also illustrate the way that fascism at times has felt it best to hide its fundamental principles. This points to a final analytical device: the distinction between its *esoteric* and *exoteric* appeal. The former refers to the ideological nature of discussion among converts, or in closed circles. The latter refers more to what it is considered wise to say in public. Thus contemporary European neo-fascist groups with aspirations to electoral success try to hide from the wider public the potentially damaging fact that some leaders are Hitler-worshippers (Billig, 1978). There is also an external dimension. Both Franco and Perón in the immediate post-1945 years found it expedient to play down the more fascist side of their regimes in order to court international, especially American, opinion.

The spectral-syncretic model

The problem of producing a model of generic fascism can best be understood by considering it within the context of four themes: (a) 'natural history'; (b) geo-politics; (c) political economy; and (d) leadership, activism, party and propaganda. The problems of list-approaches have already been considered, and the above four themes are not proposed as a new form of list. Rather they are issues through which it is possible to see both the central syntheses of fascism and the spectrum of positions which could derive from this. Hence, it is called the 'spectral-syncretic' model.

It is based on a study of primarily European fascism, both as a movement and as a regime. It is particularly important not to ignore the former. Whilst it is vital never to lose sight of what fascist regimes actually did, policy should not necessarily be seen as providing the true key to fascist ideology. The two classic regimes were relatively short lived and, like communism in the Soviet Union, they found it necessary at times to accommodate both internal and external forces. Thus post-1945 intellectual fascists have sometimes claimed that inter-war fascism exhibited 'immaturity and incoherent ideology' (*Rising*, No. 4, 1983, 5). Moreover, fascism in Italy during its closing stages sought a return to the early movement's radicalism, and some of the more thoughtful European neo-fascists have held that both the Hitler and Mussolini regimes betrayed, or deformed fascism by accommodating more conservative groups. Some attention is thus also paid to European neo-fascist views, especially as they highlight the possibility of a fascist ideology which is dialectical, which reacts to a changed world. Indeed, far too much discussion of fascist ideology sees it as locked in a narrow time-periodization. (Must the conservative heirs of Burke be judged solely within the intellectual and social context of Britain at the turn of the 19th century?!) The model itself is thus a spectral-syncretic distillation of different phases of fascism. As such it tries to limit the problem which afflicts some ideological models, namely a tendency to focus exclusively on the more interesting fascist intellectuals, like Drieu La Rochelle, who, according to one leading critic, had minimal influence over actual fascist leaders and parties (Allardyce, 1979: 378).

Natural history

There is something dangerous about talking of 'in the beginning' when discussing fascist ideology. Those present at the creation of the first 20th-century fascist movements were political activists, individuals who were mainly lightweight theoretical magpies, borrowing from diverse sources, and developing ideas to accommodate both contextual and principled changes. Moreover, in view of the violence and atrocities which characterized fascism from the outset, it is important to underline that many of its activists need understanding in terms of psychopathology rather than political theory. Nevertheless, a relatively constant set of ideas and debates can be discerned among early fascists – from which most other positions subsequently tended to derive. Arguably the most central of these in early 20th-century Europe were views on what could be termed 'Natural History', which were linked to the idea of the creation of a 'new man'.

The idea of nature as a model of human existence exercised a profound attraction on Nietzsche, whose thought influenced many fascists (though it was corrupted in the process). The word 'nature' occurs throughout Hitler's *Mein Kampf*, but he was only picking up a theme to be found earlier within Italian Fascism, and intellectuals linked in some way to Fascism. The Mussolini-Gentile entry in the 1932 *Enciclopedia Italiana* begins by arguing that 'In order to know men it is necessary to know man; and in order to know man it is necessary to know reality and laws' (Mussolini, 1936: 68). These laws were partly derived from views about human nature, and a tendency to use biological explanations can be found in many fascist writers. These views derived mainly from the late 19th-century attack on positivism, and more specifically from Social Darwinism.

Fascism was influenced by Social Darwinism in at least two senses. The first was the emphasis on a hierarchical, evolutionary chain. Man was not born equal, nor was he essentially rational. He was easily swayed, and tended to be lazy, to lack goals, to be decadent. As Valois's thought shows, fascism in a sense reversed Rousseau. In nature man was an ignoble savage until civilized by strong leaders. Fascism held that man needed to be welded into a new community, with a less materialist set of goals. At the core of this community would be the traditional, male-dominated family, but in terms of wider values there would be dramatic changes. Indeed, even the emphasis on family was countered by youth organizations, which in some ways threatened the autonomy of the family. The new community fascism sought would end the alienation and decadence which came from the individualistic, mercenary and inherently divisive liberal democratic-capitalist form of society. Fascism thus sought to remake man, not least in a more martial form. For the second aspect of Social Darwinism which was picked up by fascism was more the emphasis on survival of the fittest, the need to maintain a society based on the willingness to wage war, or at least healthy enough to avoid falling into the false cosiness of individualistic-materialistic domesticity. [. . .]

Fascism's more general philosophy of history can be glimpsed through the views of Rocco, an Italian Fascist professor of law. He held a typical cyclical vision. This was no liberal or Marxist linear view of history as the story of progress. Rather, it was a tale of the unending struggle of state authority against centrifugal forces of disintegration. Italian Fascism's interest in Ancient Rome was not simply a question of using its glories for propaganda purposes. The fall of Rome was important as a source of historical lessons. Rome fell because of decadence and a lack of discipline (see, in particular, Evola's works on the decline of 'Traditional' society). It was defeated by less sophisticated, but more virile primitive peoples who had not experienced the debilitating effects of domesticity.

Yet this was no fatalist cyclical philosophy. In the Classical world decadence was regarded almost as a law of nature. Civilizations rose and fell with recurring regularity. Fascism synthesized natural and historical arguments by adapting vitalist and activist ideas. The human will was capable of freeing man, and shaping destiny and history. Or more exactly, the will of a small number of those born to rule could bring about such changes. Following Machiavelli and Pareto, these natural rulers were not necessarily equated with the existing ruling elite. Indeed, a central aspect of the fascist critique was the belief that existing elites had failed in important ways. History thus reinforced the biological views: it taught a whole series of lessons about what man was like, and how societies developed. For example, it confirmed the importance of property: did not each regiment at Verdun fight to defend its own 'patch'! (Valois, 1921: 265 ff.). For Gentile, history showed how the rise of secularism and individualism had destroyed faith and heroism. He saw fascism as the continuation of the struggle between the idealist spirit of Mazzini and the materialist scepticism of Giolitti, the two souls of Italy (Gentile, 1961: 15–50). More generally, history was seen to show the need for elites. Bourgeois conceptions of history were wrong: it was great men, exercising power and vision who produced significant changes. History was sometimes even taken to show that a particular nation had a unique destiny (Poliakov, 1974). [. . .]

Geopolitics

Papini argued that development to higher forms requires some sacrifice of the mass, of little man (Lyttelton, 1973: 24). Ideas such as duty and sacrifice were central to fascism, but the point being highlighted here is that fascism was not the pure celebration of the people to be found in more populist thought. This was not simply a question of the inherent inequalities in people. There was at times even a kind of contempt for the masses.

This raises the vital problem of how the basic unit of the people, the community, was perceived. The standard answer is that the nation, or race was this unit. Indeed, fascism is universally portrayed as the very epitome of hyper- or ultra-nationalism. However, whilst this is a vital perspective, there is a misleading aspect to the focus on nationalism [and racism, especially as such views were pervasive in European culture (Mosse, 1978)]. If nationalism is conceived in ethnocentric rather than polycentric terms, how is it possible to explain the thousands who volunteered from many countries to fight with the Nazis against Bolshevism? (Degrelle, 1969).

The Mussolini-Gentile entry in the 1932 *Enciclopedia Italiana* noted that the nation is '[n]ot a race, nor a geographically determined region' (Mussolini, 1936: 72). This was accompanied by the view that the nation does not constitute the state so much as the state makes the nation. The boundaries of the nation were thus fluid, and a form of Fascist Internationalism appears at least as early as 1930. Later, the Salò Republic's constitution encompassed a form of Europeanism. However, this internationalism did not encompass a view of equal-community with, say, black Africans. Indeed, parts of Africa were seen as ripe for colonization. On the other hand, Italian Fascism had no indigenous theory of racial superiority (the tall, blond, Aryan male eulogized in Nazi propaganda was hardly designed to appeal in southern Mediterranean cultures, though it might be added that Nazi leaders hardly corresponded to this ideal either). Moreover, central to the Italian colonial idea was a quest for land to provide work and opportunities. The theme of colonies as something to be exploited was a minor one (De Felice, 1976: 65–7).

National Socialism placed much greater emphasis on biology and race, though some Nazis did not hold deep-rooted anti-semitic views. Hitler held that 'The Jewish doctrine of Marxism rejects the aristocratic principle of Nature' (1969: 60), whilst simultaneously arguing that Jewish materialism lay behind capitalism. To explain this paradox, Hitler held that there was a Jewish conspiracy to destroy Western civilization. In the words of the propaganda film, *The Eternal Jew* (1940), 'This is no religion . . . this is a conspiracy against all non-Jews, of a cunning, unhealthy, contaminated race' who believed that they were the 'Chosen People'. This view owed much to Rosenberg's anti-semitism, which was more cultural, holding that Jews were a distinct race, from which dangerous cultural characteristics could be deduced (Rosenberg, 1982). On the other hand, Eckhart saw Jewishness as something spiritual, a materialistic bent which exists in everyone. Thus, whereas the former views were inherently genocidal, Eckhart's interpretation pointed more to the need for Germany to retain a sense of 'Jewishness'. In terms of actual policy, Jews were allowed to leave Germany as late as 1940 (though having suffered terrible persecution), and Nazi policy until the start of the war seems to have been to make Europe as a whole 'Jew Free' through forced emigration (Marrus, 1989).

Although Nazi racism was based mainly on biology, it was not uniquely nationalist. Biological argument was in some ways a geopolitical defence of all Aryan peoples, and involved an embryonic Europeanism (Herzstein, 1982). In the short run, there was the threat from Bolshevism, not just at home, but in terms of Bolshevik hordes from the East. Bolshevism's ideological commitment to class politics, ultimate equality, internationalism and other principles was anathema to most fascists.

Nevertheless, it is important not to lose sight of the nationalist theme. Nationalism, like racism, also had a mythical dimension (much less true of Europeanism, which appealed more to the 'intellectuals'). Thus, following Sorel, the crucial point was not the prior truth or logic of an argument, but its ability to motivate and thus take on an objective force. As a radical ideology, a central question for classic fascism was how to rouse the masses from their slumbers. Here again the influence of natural and historical arguments combined. From natural arguments fascists derived a belief that people wished to combine in like groups, that they were only fulfilled in such groups. History taught that one of the great mobilizers of the people was racism or nationalism. Thus Hitler in *Mein Kampf* clearly stresses the role of anti-semitism in attracting working-class support in turn-of-the-century Vienna (1969: 51, 90 ff.). The impact of the First World War, when left-wing dreams of proletarian unity shattered in the face of mass jingoism, offered a far more important pointer.

Before the Second World War, these factors led many in Germany and Italy to the idea of the need for a new empire, or *Lebensraum* (the idea of 'Eurafrica' lingered on after 1945). Marxist critics have often seen such policies as a reflection of the influence of business on fascism, in particular the quest for new markets and sources of cheap labour at a time of declining profits. However, studies of Nazi policy in particular have shown that its East European vision was largely developed before significant business donations were made to the party. More important were the desires both to counteract Bolshevism and to provide a basis for the economic health of the state. For most fascists, this was not a step on the path to world domination, though Nazi imperialism had rather confused motives (Smith, 1986). Hence both Germany and Italy could sign a pact with Japan, which did not threaten their interests, but which shared a common fear of the Soviet Union. Some were also interested in pacts with Arab countries, though here motives encompassed anti-semitism and economic interests too. British and French fascists similarly tended to have no concept of world domination, more a sense of 'natural' spheres of interest. Among the smaller European countries a few fascists dreamed of new, or restored empires, but most were realistic of their state's potential. Their fascism tended, therefore, not to be expansionary (with the exception of the specific 'rectification' of boundaries, somewhat capriciously drawn by the post-1918 peace treaties). [. . .]

A common belief among fascists was that capitalism produced not just alienation, but was enslaving. Mosley saw capitalism as unfreedom, holding that the beginning of liberty is the end of economic chaos. Thus economic revival, not possible under free market capitalism, was essential to increase positive freedom. José Antonio's key speech on 29 October 1933 argued in a similar vein:

> the liberal state came to offer us economic slavery, saying to the workers, with tragic sarcasm: 'You are free to work as you wish. . . . Since we are rich, we offer you the conditions that please us; as free citizens, you are not obliged to accept them . . . ; but as poor citizens you will die of hunger.'
>
> (Payne, 1962: 38)

The liberal state included parliamentary institutions as well as capitalism. Such 'democratic' forms were universally despised by fascists, though they could use them where it suited their purposes. Parliamentary politics were seen as leading to weakness and lack of authority. The multi-party systems which characterized much of Europe were seen as part of this cancer, especially as they helped create false social divisions.

So what did fascism propose to replace this despised capitalist-liberal-democratic system? The answer, according to previous commentators, is the strong state. Certainly Mussolini and Mosley wrote extensively about the state, though there were a few fascists, like Brasillach, who seemed suspicious of permanent central authority (Tucker, 1975). Exactly what was meant by this strong state, however, was not always clear. It has been claimed that 'Never did . . . any major Nazi writer before 1933, prophesy a dictatorship' (Lane and Rupp, 1978: xii). In *Mein Kampf* Hitler wrote that '[t]he state is a means to an end' (1969: 357), adding little about what a Nazi state would be like. In terms of state theory it is interesting to consider the Action Française, given the usual high level of its theorizing. Many commentators have not seen this group as fascist, mainly on account of its lack of mass-mobilizing policies. However, in 1923 Maurras called Italian Fascism close cousins even twin sisters to his group; if he later stressed differences with fascism this stemmed mainly from a need to fend off other French nationalist groups by avoiding any tainting with foreign doctrine, and later by his anti-Germanism. Interestingly, Maurras called for a decentralization of government and less Jacobin etatisme, though this was to be under elite control.

Italian fascists often talked of creating a totalitarian state in a positive sense, meaning in particular the achievement of social unity. However, it is particularly important when discussing political and economic forms to be wary of separating propaganda from ideology for two main reasons. First, like Marxism, fascism was more a critique- and transition-based ideology than a utopian one. It was notably vague about basic economic and political institutions. Indeed, it has been claimed that 'When the Nazis took office, they had no coherent economic programme'

(Noakes and Pridham 1974: 375). Second, there was a philosophical explanation for this as well as the obvious historical point that the classic fascist movements went relatively quickly from small opposition groups to running the government. This was the Bergsonian idea, common among some fascists, that all is flux, that ultimate reality is a continuous, unpredictable process of creation which could not be grasped by the intellect but only intuited, lived. This was hardly a philosophy suited to the practicalities of government, and policy-oriented fascist thinkers developed more concrete ideas. [. . .]

The most consistently advocated socio-economic institution by fascists in Europe was corporatism. Indeed, one leading authority on France has argued that 'Every French fascist movement in the interwar period posited corporatism as the answer to Marxism' (Soucy, 1986: 160–1). Corporatism was meant to institutionalize social unity by linking workers, management and the state. Italy created the facade of such a system, as did Franco's Spain and Salazar's Portugal. Hitler wrote in *Mein Kampf* of a 'future economic parliament or chambers of estates' (1969: 546), but the Nazis never created an elaborate facade of corporatism. Rather, as in Italy, corporatist rhetoric was used to hide the brutal suppression of free trade unions by the state. This points to dangers in seeing corporatism as a key defining aspect of fascism, especially as the term is open to significantly different interpretations. For example, was the system essentially authoritarian-statist, or more syndicalist. Moreover, some European neo-fascists have been highly critical of corporatism, arguing that it managed to combine the worst aspects of capitalism and socialism/communism: namely continuing division between workers and employers on the one hand, and increasing state bureaucracy on the other (*Vanguard*, No. 18, 1988: 14–15). [. . .]

Leadership, activism, party and propaganda

[. . .] The idea of a strong leader seems implied by fascism's theoretical views on hierarchy. More concretely, d'Annunzio and the short-lived example of his Fiume Republic acted as an important mediator between Nietzsche and early Italian Fascism. D'Annunzio's eulogies to superman and his vitalist ideas that life has its highest expression in the active, decisive leader, clearly influenced Mussolini. Rocco, an important figure in the creation of the Italian corporate state, believed that the great heroes were conqueror-legislators like Napoleon and Mussolini: men who won not just historic battles, but who created new principles under which to live (Lyttelton, 1973: 32).

Nevertheless, it is important to question whether fascism necessarily involves a single, strong leader. The hierarchical view is perfectly consistent with an emphasis on collective leadership. Thus the *Faisceau* was governed by a committee and developed no *Führerprinzip*. Indeed, the Strassers thought that the leadership principle was a foreign import rather than a central idea, and the Hitler-cult was limited during the first years of the NSDAP, as was Caesarism in early fascism. Bardeche (1961) even wrote that Mussolini had died from Caesarism. A non-ideological perspective is also necessary in considering leadership. The Hitler-cult was used both for propagandistic purposes and to help strengthen the leader's position vis-à-vis rivals. [. . .]

A key argument in rejecting some regimes as fascist has been their lack of a single, organizationally important, political party. For example, the Salazar regime lacked such a party until 1930, and it subsequently played no major role. Thus one major commentator has argued that the claim that Salazar's *Estado Novo* was fascism without the party is 'something of a non-sequitur' (Payne, 1986: 172). This is also a common reason for rejecting Latin American regimes such as Perón's as fascist. Another feature common to these examples is the transition to power. Unlike Italy and especially Germany, where fascist parties gained notable election successes before coming to power, these regimes tended to be based on some form of military coup.

However, the emphasis which is normally accorded to the role of party and the means of coming to power must be considered carefully. Nothing in fascist ideology necessarily committed it to coming to power through a mass movement; indeed, a case could be made for the opposite. Fascist ideology implied the need for some form of authoritarianism and control after coming to power, but this did not necessarily have to be based on a party. It is highly debatable how significant the Italian Fascist Party was, especially after 1928. Indeed, the 1932 *Enciclopedia Italiana* claimed that 'Outside the State there can be neither individuals nor groups (political parties . . .)' (Mussolini, 1936: 71).

The classic fascist model, therefore, needs understanding within a specific European context. The Italian Fascist and Nazi parties emerged at a particular stage in the development of political activity. This was a new age of mass meetings, of a mass electorate. Gone were the party politics of elite factions and limited franchise. But the age had not yet dawned of postmodernist privatization, of political consultants advising on the 'cool' medium of television, rather than the 'hot' medium of the great rally. [. . .]

Conclusion

Most attempts to produce a generic definition of fascist ideology have been linked to a particular conception of where fascism stands on the left-right spectrum. It is normally seen as 'extreme right', though right-wing terminology is often used erratically, and fascism is sometimes also conceived as 'radical right', 'far right' and 'ultra right'. Moreover, left-right terminology fails to bring out that ideologies are better seen as multidimensional, and that at some levels there can be significant overlaps between ideologies (Eatwell, 1989).

One recent definition from a major commentator holds that: 'fascism was primarily a new variety of authoritarian conservatism and right-wing nationalism which sought to defeat the Marxist threat and the political liberalism which allowed it to exist in the first place' (Soucy, 1991: 163). Such a definition completely fails to see fascism's radical side. In an attempt to solve this problem, others have seen fascism as 'neither left nor right', as a doctrine of the 'revolutionary centre' (notably Sternhell's major works, 1978, 1983). The problem here is the opposite one; such approaches fail to see fascism's right-wing aspect.

The approach delineated above tries to resolve this problem by seeing fascism as a spectral-syncretic ideology. In other words, there was a series of core themes in European fascist ideology, notably synthesis, but these did not produce a unique set of conclusions. Some commentators, notably Sternhell, have already stressed Valois's formulation of: nationalism + socialism = fascism. However, there are misleading aspects to this formula. Moreover, fascism sought a much broader set of syntheses. Among the most important were: between a conservative view of man constrained by nature and the more left-wing view of the possibilities of creating a 'new man'; between a commitment to science, especially in terms of understanding human nature and a more anti-rationalist, vitalist interest in the possibilities of the will (one of the factors which attracted the philosopher Heidegger to Nazism was his belief that the fall into an inauthentic mode of existence in modern society was reversible); between the faith and service of Christianity and the heroism of Classical thought; between private property relations more typical of the right and a form of welfarism more typical of the left. The Mussolini-Gentile entry in the 1932 *Enciclopedia Italiana* underlines this point when it notes that fascism was '[a]nti-positivistic, but positive', that the fascist state was 'the synthesis and unity of all values' (Mussolini, 1936: 69, 71).

References

Allardyce, G. (1979) 'What Fascism Is Not: Thoughts on the Deflation of a Concept', *American Historical Review* 84: 367–98.

Bardeche, Maurice (1961) *Qu'est que le fascisme?* Paris: Les Sept Couleurs.

Bendersky, Joseph W. (1983) *Carl Schmitt: Theorist for the Reich*. Princeton, NJ: Princeton University Press.

Billig, M. (1978) *Fascists*. London: Harcourt.

De Felice, R. (1976) *Fascism*. New Brunswick, NJ: Transaction Books.

De Felice, Renzo (1977) *Interpretations of Fascism*. Cambridge, MA: Harvard University Press.

Degrelle, Leon (1969) *Hitler pour 1000 ans*. Paris: La Table Ronde.

Eatwell, R. (1989) 'Part One: Approaching the Right' in R. Eatwell and N. O'Sullivan (eds) *The Nature of the Right*. London: Pinter.

Gentile, G. (1961) *Il fascismo: antologia di scritti critici*. Bologna, Il Mulino.

Griffin, Roger (1991) *The Nature of Fascism*. London: Pinter.

Herzstein, R. (1982) *When Nazi Dreams Come True*. London: Abacus.

Hitler, Adolf (1969) *Mein Kampf*. London: Hutchinson.

Lane, B. M. and L. J. Rupp, (eds) (1978) *Nazi Ideology before 1933*. Manchester: Manchester University Press.

Lyttelton, Adrian (1973) *Italian Fascisms: From Pareto to Gentile*. London: Jonathan Cape.

Marrus, Robert (1989) *The Holocaust in History*. London: Penguin.

Mosse, George L. (1978) *Toward the Final Solution*. New York: Howard Fertig.

Mussolini, B. (1936) *Scritti e discorsi di Benito Mussolini: (1932–33)*. Milan: Ulneo Hoepli.

Noakes, Jeremy and Pridham, Geoffrey (eds) (1974) *Documents on Nazism, 1919–1945*. London: Jonathan Cape.

Payne, Stanley G. (1962) *Falange. A History of Spanish Fascism*. London: Croom Helm.

Payne, Stanley G. (1986) 'Fascism in the Iberian World', *Journal of Contemporary History* 21: 63–77.

Poliakov, L. (1974) *The Aryan Myth*. London: Chatto and Windus.

Rosenberg, Alfred (1982) *The Myth of the Twentieth Century*. Torrance: Noontide Press.

Soucy, Robert (1986) *French Fascism: The First Wave, 1924–1933*. New Haven, CT: Yale University Press.

Soucy, Robert (1991) 'French Fascism and the Croix de Feu: A Dissenting Interpretation', *Journal of Contemporary History* 26: 159–88.

Sternhell, Zeev (1978) *La droite révolutionnaire, 1881–1914. Les origines françaises du fascisme*. Paris: Seuil.

Sternhell, Zeev (1979) 'Fascist Ideology', in W. Laqueur (ed.), *Fascism: A Reader's Guide*. Harmondsworth: Penguin, 325–406.

Sternhell, Z. (1983) *Ni droite, ni gauche*. Paris: Editions du Seuil.

Tucker, W. R. (1975) *The Fascist Ego: A Political Biography of Robert Brasillach*. Berkeley: University of California Press.

Valois, G. (1906) *L'homme qui vient*. Paris: Nouvelle Librairie Nationale.

Valois, G. (1921) *D'un siècle à l'autre*. Paris: Nouvelle Librairie Nationale.

Chapter 5

Stanley G. Payne

FASCISM AS A 'GENERIC' CONCEPT

■ from **THE CONCEPT OF FASCISM**, in Stein Ugelvik Larsen, Bernt
Hagtvet and Jan Petter Myklebust (eds), *Who Were the Fascists? Social Roots
of European Fascism*, Bergen, 1980, pp. 14, 19–24

Stanley Payne's analysis of 'generic fascism' appeared in 1980 and constitutes one
of the earliest attempts to define a working 'fascist minimum' whilst acknowledging
potential difficulties in devising an all-embracing model of analysis (cf. Allardyce
(1)). His tripartite typology borrows heavily from J. J. Linz's earlier work (cf. 3). On
the basis of this typology (which Payne regards as non-exhaustive but producing a
new synthesis that distinguished fascism from right-wing authoritarianism) he identifies six main 'varieties of fascism' (a debt to Eugen Weber's 1964 work with the
same title). He also introduces a clear distinction between fascist movement and
regime, adding that the limited experience of the latter does not provide us with an
all-round idea about the essence of fascism (in contrast to R. O. Paxton's excerpt (6)).

EVER SINCE THE MARCH ON ROME, political analysts and historians
have tried to formulate an interpretation capable of explaining the phenomenon
of European fascism. As the only genuinely novel or original form of radicalism
emerging from World War I and one that seemed to involve multiple ambiguities
if not outright contradictions, fascism did not readily lend itself to monocausal explanation or a simple unified theory. For more than half a century the debate has gone
on, and there is still no general consensus regarding an explanatory concept.[1]

The principal theoretical concepts of fascism have been directed primarily either
toward a definition of the underlying nature of this species of politics, its overall
significance, or more commonly, the principal sources or causes that gave it life. For
convenience's sake, they may be summarized in nine categories:

1   A violent, dictatorial agent of bourgeois capitalism.
2   The product of a cultural or moral breakdown.

3   The result of neurotic or pathological psychosocial impulses.
4   The product of the rise of amorphous masses.
5   The consequence of a certain stage of economic growth, or historical sequence of national development.
6   A typical manifestation of twentieth-century totalitarianism.
7   A struggle against 'modernization'.
8   The expression of a unique radicalism of the middle classes.
9   The denial that such a thing as 'generic fascism' ever existed due to the extreme differences between putatively fascist movements, and hence denial of the possibility of a general concept of 'fascism'. [. . .]

The need for a criterial definition of generic fascism

The only attempt at a comprehensive description of the full range of European fascist movements remains Ernst Nolte's *Die Krise des liberalen Systems und die faschistischen Bewegungen* (Munich, 1968). In it Nolte recognized the need for some sort of 'fascist minimum' – a set of criteria that could set standards according to which a given political movement might be objectively recognized and defined as fascist, or not. He suggested six points or criteria:

*   Anti-Communism
*   Anti-Liberalism
*   Anti-Conservatism
*   Leadership Principle
*   Party-Army
*   Aim of Totalitarianism

This criterial description represented a significant advance in clarity over preceding informal and off-hand suggestions that other writers made merely in passing. Nonetheless, it seems to me inadequate in the following respects; a) While it recognizes the distinctive fascist negations, it fails to deal fully with characteristic goals and program (if indeed such existed) or to define what at the time seemed most striking about fascists – their particular style and choreography; b) The reference to fascist anti-conservatism, while essentially correct, tends to blur the fact that fascists always had to rely at least momentarily on rightist allies to come to power; c) Though all fascistic parties tended toward strong personal leadership, it may be misleading to impute to them the predominantly German character of the *Führerprinzip*; d) Most fascist parties sought, but never achieved, a genuine 'party-army'; e) The goal of totalitarianism is an ambiguous formulation, difficult to define or apply; f) The distinctively fascist form of nationalism and political radicalism cannot be understood without reference to the ultimate goal of some form of imperialism or at least a drastic realignment of the nation's status and power relations in the world.

Given the difficulty in arriving at a common definition of the putatively fascist movements, it is always possible that the extreme nominalists and skeptics could be right, and that a true 'fascist minimum' did not exist. Against such skepticism, we have the relative agreement of the majority of contemporary observers in the 1930s that a new form and style of politics had emerged in the radical new nationalist movements of Europe customarily called fascist, a position generally adopted by the majority of scholars and analysts since. But what were the basic common qualities generally referred to by this label? We are still left with the problem of an adequate description.

A possible typological description of generic fascism

It seems possible, at least hypothetically, to achieve this goal through a typological description of the principal features held in common by the movements we refer to as fascist – thus establishing justification for our use of the generic concept – while at the same time taking into account valid arguments by critics of the generic concept through recognition that such a common description does not by any means exhaust the inventory of major characteristics or goals of individual movements. It would only define the minimal characteristics that they had in common as distinct from other types though specific fascist groups sometimes had other beliefs, characteristics and goals of major importance to them that did not contradict the common features of generic fascism but were simply added to them or went beyond them.

If an analogy were made for morphological purposes, fascism would then be understood to constitute a certain political species, one of about half a dozen that compose the broader genus of modern revolutionary mass movements. In order to arrive at a criterial definition applicable to the species, it then seems appropriate to follow a suggestion made by Juan J. Linz and identify a) the fascist negations, b) common points of ideology and goals, and c) special common features of style and organization.

A The fascist negations

* Anti-liberalism
* Anti-communism
* Anti-conservatism, but of a more qualified nature, with a degree of willingness to compromise at least temporarily, with rightist groups and principles.

B Ideology and goals

* Creation of a new nationalist authoritarian state not merely based on traditional principles or models.
* Organization of some new kind of regulated, multi-class integrated national economic structure capable to some extent of transforming social relations, whether called national syndicalist, national socialist or national corporatist.
* The goal of empire or a revolution in the nation's relationship with other powers.
* Specific espousal of an idealist, voluntarist creed, normally involving the attempt to realize a new form of modern, self-determined secular culture.

C Style and organization

- Emphasis on esthetic structure of meetings, symbols and political choreography, stressing romantic and/or mystical aspects.
- Attempted mass mobilization with militarization of political relationships and style, and with the goal of a mass party militia.
- Positive evaluation of – not merely willingness to use – violence.
- Extreme stress on the masculine principle and male dominance, while espousing an organic view of society.
- Exaltation of youth above all other phases of life, emphasizing the conflict of generations, though within a framework of national unity.
- Specific tendency toward an authoritarian, charismatic, personal leadership style of command, whether or not to some degree elective.

Space precludes full discussion of the components of this inventory, but it can perhaps serve as a guideline to explain in most cases what serious scholars refer to as fascist movements, while recognizing that it can be used as an analytical tool only as a relatively integrated whole. There is no implication that every single characteristic in the inventory was unique to fascist movements, for most individual facets might be discovered to have existed individually or partially within a number of other radical groups. The uniqueness of fascism as a political species was rather that only fascist-type movements shared each of these characteristics (if in varying degrees) jointly and simultaneously: the suggested typology will be of use in identifying a specific movement as fascist only if the group in question exhibits not merely most but all or almost all of the qualities described.

The varieties of fascism

As explained, identification of a typology is not intended to imply that within the species of fascism all groups were fundamentally about the same and did not differ greatly among themselves with regard to further national characteristics, beliefs, values and goals above and beyond those minimal features which they all held in common. Much confusion has resulted from the assumption that if fascism is to be identifiable as a generic phenomenon it must somehow be regarded as a uniform type bearing essentially homogeneous traits, whereas in fact it was a broad species that included widely varying subtypes or subspecies.

Among the subspecies or 'varieties of fascism', in Eugen Weber's telling phrase, a minimum of six may be identified:

1   Paradigmatic Italian fascism, pluralistic, diverse and not easily definable in simple terms. Forms to some extent derivative appeared in France, England, Belgium, Hungary, Austria, Romania and possibly even Brazil.
2   German National Socialism, a distinct and remarkably fanatical movement, and the only one of the entire species to achieve a total dictatorship and so to begin to develop its own system. Somewhat parallel or derivative movements emerged in Scandinavia, the Low Countries, the Baltic states and Hungary, and more superficially in several satellite states during the war.

3   Spanish Falangism. Though to some extent derivative from the Italian form, it became a kind of Catholic and culturally more traditionalist type that was more marginal to the species.
4   The Romanian Legionary or Iron Guard movement, a mystical, kenotic form of semi-religious fascism that represented the only notable movement of this kind in an Orthodox country and was also marginal to the species.
5   Szalasi's 'Hungarist' or Arrow Cross movement, somewhat distinct from either the Hungarian national socialists or Hungarian proponents of a more moderate and pragmatic Italian-style movement, momentarily perhaps the second most popular fascist movement in Europe.
6   Abortive undeveloped fascisms attempted through bureaucratic means by right-wing authoritarian regimes, mainly in Eastern Europe during the 1930s. None of these efforts, however, produced fully formed and complete fascist organizations.

The need to distinguish between fascist movements and fascist regimes

Much of the confusion about defining a typology of fascism has stemmed from the failure to distinguish between fascist movements and regimes. Nearly all fascist parties failed to develop beyond the movement stage, and even in Italy the fascist party never assumed full power over the government and all the institutions of the country. Hence in the case even of Mussolini one cannot speak of a total party regime system as in Nazi Germany or Communist Russia.

In the absence of examples other than Nazi Germany of situations in which fascist-type parties came to full power or totally dominated regimes, it must be recognized that we are speaking of certain generic tendencies in the form of movements, but not of systems. This also says much about the limitations of the appeal and strength of fascism, even in the supposed 'fascist era' and underlines the fact that the historic significance of the whole phenomenon was primarily bound up with Hitlerism and not with generic fascism.

The distinction between fascism and right authoritarianism

Much of the confusion surrounding the identification and definition of generic fascism has lain in the failure to distinguish clearly between fascist movements and the nonfascist (or sometimes protofascist) authoritarian right. During the period of World War I and after there emerged a new cluster of conservative authoritarian forces in European politics that rejected moderate nineteenth century conservatism and simple old-fashioned traditional reaction in favor of a more modern, technically proficient kind of new authoritarian system that spurned both leftist revolution and fascist radicalism. The new right authoritarian groups have often been confused with fascists because both were authoritarian and nationalist and up to a point were opposed to many of the same things (leftists and liberals). Moreover, circumstantial alliances were made between fascists and new rightists in a number of countries, especially in Germany, Italy and Spain, but also elsewhere. Nonetheless, the fact that communists and liberals are both opposed to fascism and rightism and have sometimes formed circumstantial alliances in a number of countries since 1935 has not generally led most analysts to the false conclusion that communism and liberalism are the same thing.

Similarly, the distinction between fascism and right authoritarianism should be clearly understood for purposes of analysis, taxonomy and conceptualization. The basic differences might be synthesized as follows:

(a)   The new authoritarian right was anticonservative only in the very limited sense of a qualified opposition to the more moderate parliamentary forms of conservatism.

(b)   The new right advocated authoritarian government, but hesitated to embrace radical and novel forms of dictatorship and normally relied either on monarchism or Catholic neocorporatism, or some combination thereof.

(c)   In philosophy and ideology, the right was grounded on a combination of rationalism and also religion, and normally rejected the secularist irrationalism, vitalism and neoidealism of the fascists.

(d)   The new right was based on traditional elites rather than new formations of déclassé radicals, and aimed their tactics more at manipulation of the existing system than toward political conquest from the streets.

(e)   The new right never projected the same goals of mass political mobilization.

(f)   Whereas the fascists aimed at changes in social status and relations, the new right explicitly intended to maintain and affirm the existing social hierarchy, if anything increasing the degree of dominance of established groups.

(g)   The new right tried to rely a great deal on the army and was willing to accept praetorian rule, rejecting the fascist principle of militia and mass party militarization. [. . .]

Some ingredients of a more empirical and comprehensive concept of fascism

It has been said that the chief weakness of the classic interpretations of fascism has been their tendency toward a kind of theoretical monocausality and reductionism. A more adequate concept of the phenomenon must be able to take into account a wide variety of factors, and interpret the problem in terms of its particular historical setting or environment. 'Finance capital' can never explain fascism, since the overwhelming majority of the political expressions of finance capital from the nineteenth century to the present have had nothing to do with generic fascism. That a 'cultural crisis' existed in Europe during the early twentieth century is beyond dispute, but the formulators of the 'cultural crisis' theory have neither given us an accurate definition of the fascist culture produced in this atmosphere nor a fully viable explanation of why such a cultural ambience should necessarily result in significant fascist movements in some countries but not in others.

After the works by Gregor,[2] Jaeckel[3] and Hildebrand[4] the oft-repeated assumption that fascist movements lacked recognizable ideologies or a kind of cultural

Weltanschauung of their own seems increasingly doubtful. A more empirically valid concept of fascism in the future must thus take into account the background and development of the new ideas of fascist culture and ideology in the period 1910–40 with the same rigor and precision being demonstrated in the study of social mobilization and class support.

Clearer analysis is required of the political, social, economic, and national/historical variables involved in those countries where the fascists achieved significant mobilization (e.g., 15 per cent or more of the vote), compared with similar factors in other European countries where this support did not exist. A more exact definition of the unique structural and cultural problems of South and Central European countries in the 1920s and 30s and their relationship to fascist strength (or its absence), may serve to elucidate to what extent fascism was merely a conjunctural historical phenomenon or whether it is likely to be paralleled or approximated by new forces in the future, whether in Western countries or the new polities of the Third World.

Notes

1   There are two useful anthologies that have collected statements of some of the leading interpretations: Ernst Nolte, ed., *Theorien über den Faschismus* (Cologne, 1967), and Renzo de Felice, ed., *Il fascismo: Le interpretazioni dei contemporanei e degli storici* (Bari, 1970). The latter is more thorough and complete, and contains more extensive analysis. The most incisive critique of the standard interpretations is A. James Gregor, *Interpretations of Fascism* (Morristown, N.J., 1974). Gilbert Allardyce, *The Place of Fascism in European History* (Englewood Cliffs, N.J., 1972), presents a briefer anthology. See also H. A. Turner, Jr., *Reappraisals of Fascism* (New York, 1975).

2   A. James Gregor, *Interpretations of Fascism* (Morristown, N.J., 1974).

3   Eberhard Jaeckel, *Hitler's Weltanschauung* (Middletown, Conn., 1972).

4   Klaus Hildebrand, *The Foreign Policy of the Third Reich* (Berkeley–Los Angeles, 1974), and also Norman Rich, *Hitler's War Aims* (New York, 1974), 2 vols.

Chapter 6

Robert O. Paxton

FASCISM AND ITS EVOLUTION 'IN TIME': FIVE STAGES

■ from **THE FIVE STAGES OF FASCISM**, *Journal of Modern History*, 70 (1998), pp. 2–7, 8–11, 12–13, 16, 17–22

Robert Paxton's recent article is significant both as a useful review of the major debates on the nature of generic fascism (first part of the excerpt) and as a novel framework for studying fascism's various permutations in interwar Europe (second part). For him fascism as ideology or movement is fundamentally different from fascism as regime. He therefore proposes a five-stage analysis of fascism: formation of movement, creation of party, seizure of power, exercise of power, radicalisation/entropy. Unlike the 'fascist [ideological] minimum' of Griffin, Payne and Eatwell, Paxton's model of interpretation is dynamic and concerned with fascism's evolution 'in time'. The featured excerpt also provides brief critiques of the 'middle-class' thesis (cf. Lipset (8)) and of the 'totalitarian' approach (cf. Brzezinski (23); Linz (3)).

FIVE MAJOR DIFFICULTIES stand in the way of any effort to define fascism. First, a problem of timing. The fascist phenomenon was poorly understood at the beginning in part because it was unexpected. Until the end of the nineteenth century, most political thinkers believed that widening the vote would inevitably benefit democracy and socialism. Friedrich Engels, noting the rapid rise of the socialist vote in Germany and France, was sure that time and numbers were on his side. Writing the preface for a new edition in 1895 of Karl Marx's *Class Struggles in France*, he declared that 'if it continues in this fashion, we will conquer the major part of the middle classes and the peasantry and will become the decisive power.'[1] It took two generations before the Left understood that fascism is, after all, an authentic mass popular enthusiasm and not merely a clever manipulation of populist emotions by the reactionary Right or by capitalism in crisis.[2]

A second difficulty in defining fascism is created by mimicry. In fascism's heyday, in the 1930s, many regimes that were not functionally fascist borrowed elements of fascist decor in order to lend themselves an aura of force, vitality, and mass mobilization. They were influenced by the 'magnetic field' of fascism, to employ Philippe Burrin's useful phrase.[3] But one can not identify a fascist regime by its plumage. George Orwell understood at once that fascism is not defined by its clothing. If, some day, an authentic fascism were to succeed in England, Orwell wrote as early as 1936, it would be more soberly clad than in Germany.[4] The exotic black shirts of Sir Oswald Mosley are one explanation for the failure of the principal fascist movement in England, the British Union of Fascists. What if they had worn bowler hats and carried well-furled umbrellas? The adolescent skinheads who flaunt the swastika today in parts of Europe seem so alien and marginal that they consti-tute a law-and-order problem (serious though that may be) rather than a recurrence of authentic mass-based fascism, astutely decked out in the patriotic emblems of their own countries. Focusing on external symbols, which are subject to superficial imita-tion, adds to confusion about what may legitimately be considered fascist.

This leads to the third problem with defining fascism, posed by the dauntingly wide disparity among individual cases in space and in time. They differ in space because each national variant of fascism draws its legitimacy, as we shall see, not from some universal scripture but from what it considers the most authentic ele-ments of its own community identity. Religion, for example, would certainly play a much greater role in an authentic fascism in the United States than in the first European fascisms, which were pagan for contingent historical reasons.[5] They differ in time because of the transformations and accommodations demanded of those movements that seek power. A little circle of dissident nationalist syndicalists, such as those whom Zeev Sternhell studies, functions differently from a party in search of alliances and of complicities within the country's elites. Disparate in their symbols, decor, and even in their political tactics, fascist movements resemble each other mainly in their functions (a point to which we shall return).

A fourth and even more redoutable difficulty stems from the ambiguous rela-tionship between doctrine and action in fascism. We shall have to spend much more time with this problem than with the others. As intellectuals, almost instinctively, we classify all the great political movements – all the 'isms' – by doctrine. It is a time-honored convention to take for granted that fascism is an 'ism' like the others and so treat it as essentially a body of thought.[6] By an analogy that has gone largely unexamined, much existing scholarship treats fascism as if it were of the same nature as the great political doctrines of the long nineteenth century, like conservatism, liberalism, and socialism. This article undertakes to challenge that convention and its accompanying implicit analogy.

The great 'isms' of nineteenth-century Europe – conservativism, liberalism, socialism – were associated with notable rule, characterized by deference to educated leaders, learned debates, and (even in some forms of socialism) limited popular authority. Fascism is a political practice appropriate to the mass politics of the twen-tieth century. Moreover, it bears a different relationship to thought than do the nine-teenth-century 'isms'. Unlike them, fascism does not rest on formal philosophical positions with claims to universal validity. There was no 'Fascist Manifesto,' no founding fascist thinker. Although one can deduce from fascist language implicit

Social Darwinist assumptions about human nature, the need for community and authority in human society, and the destiny of nations in history, fascism does not base its claims to validity on their truth.[7] Fascists despise thought and reason, abandon intellectual positions casually, and cast aside many intellectual fellow-travelers. They subordinate thought and reason not to faith, as did the traditional Right, but to the promptings of the blood and the historic destiny of the group. Their only moral yardstick is the prowess of the race, of the nation, of the community. They claim legitimacy by no universal standard except a Darwinian triumph of the strongest community.

Fascists deny any legitimacy to universal principles to such a point that they even neglect proselytism. Authentic fascism is not for export.[8] Particular national variants of fascism differ far more profoundly one from another in themes and symbols than do the national variants of the true 'isms.' The most conspicuous of these variations, one that leads some to deny the validity of the very concept of generic fascism, concerns the nature of the indispensable enemy within Mediterranean fascisms, socialists and colonized peoples are more salient enemies than is the Jewry.[9] Drawing their slogans and their symbols from the patriotic repertory of one particular community, fascisms are radically unique in their speech and insignia. They fit badly into any system of universal intellectual principles. It is in their functions that they resemble each other.

Further, the words of fascist intellectuals – even if we accept for the moment that they constitute fundamental philosophical texts – correspond only distantly with what fascist movements do after they have power. Early fascist programs are poor guides to later fascist policy. The sweeping social changes proposed by Mussolini's first Fascist program of April 1919 (including the vote for women, the eight-hour day, heavy taxation of war profits, confiscation of church lands, and workers' participation in industrial management) stand in flagrant conflict with the macho persona of the later *Duce* and his deals with conservatives. Similarly, the hostility of the Nazi Twenty-Five Points of 1920 toward all capitalism except that of artisan producers bears little relation to the sometimes strained though powerfully effective collaboration for rearmament between German business and the Nazi regime.[10]

Sternhell responds to this line of argument by asserting that every political movement deforms its ideology under the constraints of exercising power.[11] Fascism, however (unlike Stalinism), never produces a casuistic literature devoted to demonstrating how the leader's actions correspond in some profound way to the basic scriptures. Being in accord with basic scriptures simply does not seem to matter to fascist leaders, who claim to incarnate the national destiny in their physical persons.

Feelings propel fascism more than thought does. We might call them mobilizing passions, since they function in fascist movements to recruit followers and in fascist regimes to 'weld' the fascist 'tribe' to its leader.[12] The following mobilizing passions are present in fascisms, though they may sometimes be articulated only implicitly

1   The primacy of the group, toward which one has duties superior to every right, whether universal or individual
2   The belief that one's group is a victim, a sentiment which justifies any action against the group's enemies, internal as well as external

3   Dread of the group's decadence under the corrosive effect of individualistic and cosmopolitan liberalism
4   Closer integration of the community within a brotherhood (*fascio*) whose unity and purity are forged by common conviction, if possible, or by exclusionary violence if necessary
5   An enhanced sense of identity and belonging, in which the grandeur of the group reinforces individual self-esteem
6   Authority of natural leaders (always male) throughout society, culminating in a national chieftain who alone is capable of incarnating the group's destiny
7   The beauty of violence and of will, when they are devoted to the group's success in a Darwinian struggle

Programs are so easily sacrificed to expediency in fascist practice that, at one point, I was tempted to reduce the role of ideology in fascism to a simple functionalism. Fascists propose anything that serves to attract a crowd, solidify a mass following, or reassure their elite accomplices. That would be a gross oversimplification. Ideas count in fascism, but we must be precise about exactly when and how they count. They count more at some stages than at others. At the beginning, their promise of radical spiritual-cultural renewal and restored national community helps fascists recruit a broad and varied public, including some respectable intellectuals.[13] Early fascist ideas helped amplify the disrepute of the liberal values to which the broad middle classes had largely adhered before World War I. But it is only by distancing themselves from those elements of the early radical programs that were threatening to conservatives that certain fascist movements have been able to gain and exercise power. [. . .]

The fifth and final difficulty with defining fascism is caused by overuse: the word 'fascist' has become the most banal of epithets. Everyone is someone's fascist. Consider Rush Limbaugh's 'feminazis.' A couple of summers ago, I heard a young German call Western-sponsored birth control programs in the Third World 'fascist,' forgetting that the Nazis and the Italian Fascists were, for once, agreed in encouraging large families – except, of course, among those considered either eugenically or racially inferior. Those people were condemned to sterilization, if not worse.[14] The term 'fascist' has been so loosely used that some have proposed giving it up altogether in scholarly research.[15]

Nevertheless, we cannot give up in the face of these difficulties. A real phenomenon exists. Indeed, fascism is the most original political novelty of the twentieth century, no less. It successfully gathered, against all expectations, in certain modern nations that had seemed firmly planted on a path to gradually expanding democracy, a popular following around hard, violent, antiliberal and antisocialist nationalist dictatorships. Then it spread its 'politics in a new key' through much of Europe, assembling all nationalists who hated the Left and found the Right inadequate.[16] We must be able to examine this phenomenon as a system. It is not enough to treat each national case individually, as if each one constitutes a category in itself. If we cannot examine fascism synthetically, we risk being unable to understand this century, or the next. We must have a word, and for lack of a better one, we must employ the word that Mussolini borrowed from the vocabulary of the Italian Left in 1919, before his movement had assumed its mature form.[17] Obliged to use the word fascism, we ought to use it well.

Unfortunately much scholarly work on fascism complicates things still further by two very widespread errors of approach. First, most authorities treat generic fascism in a static manner. With several remarkable exceptions – I think particularly of Pierre Milza and Philippe Burrin – they look for a fixed essence: the famous 'fascist minimum.'[18] Second, most works consider fascisms in too isolated a manner, without sufficient sustained reference to the political, social, and cultural spaces in which they navigate. Together, these two common errors of approach produce what we might call 'bestiaries' of fascism. Like medieval naturalists, they present a catalog of portraits of one beast after another, each one portrayed against a bit of background scenery and identified by its external signs.[19]

We can get beyond the 'bestiary' approach by adopting three quite simple historical strategies. One is to study fascism in motion, paying more attention to processes than to essences. Another is to study it contextually, spending at least as much time on the surrounding society and on fascism's allies and accomplices as on the fascist movements themselves.[20] The more actively a fascist movement participates in the political life of its country, the less one can understand it in isolation. It is ensnared in a web of reciprocal influences with allies or rivals in its country's civil society. Finally, we can put the disconcerting malleability of fascisms in time and in space to good use. That malleability is not necessarily an obstacle to understanding. It may even make understanding easier, by making comparison possible. Comparison is 'a way of thinking more than a method,' and it works better when we try to account for differences than when we try to amass vague resemblances.[21] Comparison works revealingly with fascisms, since every Western society has contained at least some marginal example. Their different fates across time and space in neighboring settings should help us to identify the principal factors in the varying success of specific cases, and even to isolate the constants.[22]

But one must compare what is comparable. A regime where fascism exercises power is hardly comparable to a sect of dissident intellectuals. We must distinguish the different stages of fascism in time. It has long been standard to point to the difference between movements and regimes. I believe we can usefully distinguish more stages than that, if we look clearly at the very different sociopolitical processes involved in each stage. I propose to isolate five of them:[23] (1) the initial creation of fascist movements; (2) their rooting as parties in a political system; (3) the acquisition of power; (4) the exercise of power; and, finally, in the longer term, (5) radicalization or entropy. Since different kinds of historical process are involved in each stage, moreover, we must deploy different scholarly strategies in the analysis of each. Consider the first stage. First-stage fascism is the domain of the intellectual historian, for the process to be studied here is the emergence of new ways of looking at the world and diagnosing its ills. In the late nineteenth and early twentieth centuries, thinkers and publicists discredited reigning liberal and democratic values, not in the name of either existing alternative – conservative or socialist – but in the name of something new that promised to transcend and join them: a novel mixture of nationalism and syndicalism that had found little available space in a nineteenth-century political landscape compartmented into Left and Right (though retrospect may reveal a few maverick precedents). This first stage is the part of the fascist elephant that scholars have found most congenial as a subject; examining one limb, of course, may mislead us about the whole beast. [. . .]

The second stage – rooting, in which a fascist movement becomes a party capable of acting decisively on the political scene – happens relatively rarely. At this stage, comparison becomes rewarding: one can contrast successes with failures. Success depends on certain relatively precise conditions: the weakness of a liberal state, whose inadequacies seems to condemn the nation to disorder, decline, or humiliation; and political deadlock because the Right, the heir to power but unable to continue to wield it alone, refuses to accept a growing Left as a legitimate governing partner. Some fascist leaders, in their turn, are willing to reposition their movements in alliances with these frightened conservatives, a step that pays handsomely in political power, at the cost of disaffection among some of the early antibourgeois militants.

[. . .]

At the third stage, the arrival in power, comparison acquires greater bite. What characteristics distinguished Germany and Italy, where fascism took power, from countries such as France and Britain, where fascist movements were highly visible but remained marginal? We need to recall that fascism has never so far taken power by a coup d'etat, deploying the weight of its militants in the street. Fascist power by coup is hardly conceivable in a modern state. Fascism cannot appeal to the street without risking a confrontation with future allies – the army and the police – without whom it will not be able to pursue its expansionist goals. Indeed, fascist coup attempts have commonly led to military dictatorship rather than to fascist power (as in Romania in December 1941).[24] Resorting to direct mass action also risks conceding advantages to fascism's principal enemy, the Left, which was still powerful in the street and workplace in interwar Europe.[25] The only route to power available to fascists passes through cooperation with conservative elites. The most important variables, therefore, are the conservative elites' willingness to work with the fascists (along with a reciprocal flexibility on the part of the fascist leaders) and the depth of the crisis that induces them to cooperate.

[. . .]

The fourth stage – the exercise of power – is conditioned by the manner in which fascism arrives in power. The fascist leaders who have reached power, historically, have been condemned to govern in association with the conservative elites who had opened the gates to them. This sets up a four-way struggle for dominance among the leader, his party (whose militants clamor for jobs, perquisites, expansionist adventures, and the fulfillment of elements of the early radical program), the regular state functionaries such as police commanders and magistrates, and the traditional elites – churches, the army, the professions, and business leaders.[26] This four-way tension is what gives fascist rule its characteristic blend of febrile activism and shapelessness.[27]

The tensions within fascist rule also help us clarify the frontiers between authentic fascism and other forms of dictatorial rule. Fascist rule is unlike the exercise of power in either authoritarianism (which lacks a single party, or gives it little power) or Stalinism (which lacked traditional elites).[28] Authoritarians would prefer to leave the population demoralized, while fascists promise to win the working class back for the nation by their superior techniques of manufacturing enthusiasm.[29] Although authoritarian regimes may trample due process and individual liberties, they accept ill-defined, though real, limits to state power in favor of some private space for individuals and 'organic' intermediary bodies such as local notables, economic cartels, families, and churches. Fascism claims to reduce the private sphere to nothing, though that is propaganda (which has been quite successful, moreover, even with scholars).[30] Stalin's Communist Party governed a civil society radically simplified by the Bolshevik Resolution; under Hitler in contrast the party, the bureaucracy, and the traditional elites jostled for power. Even if Stalin's techniques of rule often resembled those of fascism, he did not have to concern himself with concentrations of inherited autonomous social and economic power.

[. . .]

In the long run (the fifth stage), fascist 'dual power' can evolve in either of two directions: radicalization or entropy. Mussolini's regime subsided toward routine authoritarianism after the establishment of the dictatorship in 1925–26, except during colonial campaigns. The Ethiopian War (1935–36) set off a 'rivoluzione culturale' and 'svolta totalitaria' in which the Fascist regime tried to shape the fascist 'new man' by instituting 'fascist customs,' 'fascist language,' and racial legislation.[31] Within the sphere of colonialist action, first in Libya and then in Ethiopia, the party's arbitrary rule and policies of racial discrimination were free to set the tone.[32] The radicalism of Italian Fascism's early days reappeared at the end of the war in the phantom Republic of Salò that governed the north of Italy under German tutelage after September 1943. Nazi Germany alone experienced full radicalization. A victorious war of extermination in the East offered almost limitless freedom of action to the 'prerogative state' and its 'parallel institutions,' released from the remaining constraints of the 'normative state,' such as they were. In the 'no-man's-land' of what had been Poland and the western parts of the Soviet Union they put into application their ultimate fantasies of racial cleansing.[33] Extreme radicalization remains latent in all fascisms, but the circumstances of war, and particularly of victorious wars of conquest, give it the fullest means of expression.[34]

Focus on processes and discrimination among stages – this article's principal methodological proposals – casts a clarifying light on many specialized themes in the study of fascism. Social composition, for example, evolves with successive stages. Any study that proposes a single, fixed social composition inherent in fascism is flawed.[35] It also becomes doubtful that we can identify a single unchanging fascist aesthetic that would apply to all the national cases.[36] The macho restoration of a threatened patriarchy comes close to being a universal fascist value, but Mussolini advocated female suffrage in his first program, and Hitler did not mention gender issues in his Twenty-Five Points.[37]

Having picked fascism apart, have we escaped from the nominalism of the bestiary only to fall into another nominalism of processes and stages? Where is the 'fascism minimum' in all this? Has generic fascism evaporated in this analysis? It is by a functional definition of fascism that we can escape from these quandaries. Fascism is a system of political authority and social order intended to reinforce the unity, energy, and purity of communities in which liberal democracy stands accused of producing division and decline. Its complex tensions (political revolution versus social restoration, order versus aggressive expansionism, mass enthusiasm versus civic submission) are hard to understand solely by reading its propaganda. One must observe it in daily operation, using all the social sciences and not only intellectual-cultural history, and, since it is not static, one must understand it in motion, through its cycle of potential (though not inevitable) stages. [. . .]

Notes

1   Friedrich Engels, 1895 preface to Karl Marx, *Class Struggles in France (1848–50)*, in *The Marx–Engels Reader*, ed. Robert C. Tucker, 2nd ed. (New York, 1978), 571.

2   In the 1970s, Western Marxists criticized Stalin's interpretation of fascism and found an alternate tradition in August Thalheimer, the Austro-Marxists, and Antonio Gramsci. See, e.g., Nicos Poulantzas, *Fascism and Dictatorship* (London, 1974); and Anson Rabinbach, 'Toward a Marxist Theory of Fascism and National Socialism,' *New German Critique*, no. 3 (Fall 1974): 127–53. Wolfgang Wippermann surveys the German case in 'The Postwar German Left and Fascism,' *Journal of Contemporary History* 11 (October 1976): 185–219, and in *Fascismustheorien zum Stand der Gegenwartigen Diskussion*, 5th ed. (Darmstadt, 1989).

3   Philippe Burrin, 'La France dans le champ magnétique des fascismes,' *Le Débat* 32 (November 1984): 52–72.

4   George Orwell, *The Road to Wigan Pier* (New York, 1961), 176. See also 'The Lion and the Unicorn' (1941), quoted in *The Collected Essays, Journalism, and Letters of George Orwell*, ed. Sonia Orwell and Ian Angus (New York, 1968), 3:93.

5   S. G. Payne, *A History of Fascism, 1914–45* (London, 1997), 490, 518, considers fascism inherently anticlerical; religious fundamentalisms, he asserts, are more likely today to produce authoritarianism than neofascism. In practice, however, fascisms can be close to churches identified with the national cause, as in Croatia, as Payne himself shows. W. Laqueur, *Fascism: Past, Present, Future* (New York, 1996), 95, 148–51, posits a closer link between religious fundamentalism and neofascism.

6   Roger Griffin (*Nature of Fascism*, London, 1993) and Roger Eatwell (*Fascism: A History*, London, 1996) assert vigorously that fascism is to be understood as a doctrine. The most ambitious effort is Griffin's, he overcomes the problems of variation and contradiction by paring the fascist minimum down to national regeneration. Even Payne's more narrative *History* says 'reading fascist programs' is his methodological starting point (pp. 11, 472).

7   A recent brief review of these assumptions within Nazism, with an extensive bibliography, is found in Michael Burleigh and Wolfgang Wippermann, *The Racial State: Germany 1933–1945* (Cambridge, 1991), chap. 2.

8   Michael A. Ledeen, *Universal Fascism: The Theory and Practice of the Fascist International, 1928–1936* (New York, 1972), explores Mussolini's short-lived

attempt to gather the other fascist movements around himself in an international organization. Hitler manifested little interest in his foreign disciples, showing notable reluctance to entrust the governance of conquered territories to Quislings like the original in Norway (out of power until 1942), Mussert in Holland, and Degrelle in Belgium. A recent study is Martin Conway, *Collaboration in Belgium: Léon Degrelle and the Rexist Movement* (New Haven, Conn., 1993).

9   Emilio Gentile, *The Sacralization of Politics in Fascist Italy*, trans Keith Botsford (Cambridge, Mass., 1996), 24–25, examines the ritual purificatory burning of captured socialist materials by the *squadristi*.

10   Current authors still sometimes claim that the Nazis violated the aspirations of big business. See, for example, Payne, *History*, 190. In fact, most business leaders, whose negative memories of Weimar and the Depression were still fresh, swallowed their reluctance about Nazi autarky and thrived handsomely on rearmament. Peter Hayes, *Industry and Ideology: IG Farben in the Nazi Era* (Cambridge, 1987), finds an 'intersection, not an identity, of interests' (p. 120). Daimler-Benz enjoyed particular favor with the regime. See Bernard P. Bellon, *Mercedes in Peace and War* (New York, 1990). The most important common interest, of course, was the emasculation of the labor movement. These issues are magisterially treated by Charles Maier, 'The Economics of Fascism and Nazism,' in his *In Search of Stability. Explorations in Historical Political Economy* (Cambridge, 1987), pp. 70–120.

11   Zeev Sternhell, *The Birth of Fascist Ideology: From Cultural Rebellion to Political Revolution* (Princeton, N.J., 1994), 231, argues that actions conflict with programs no more extensively with fascism than with other political currents.

12   I draw these terms from Marc Bloch's description in summer 1943 of the two political systems then engaged in a life-and-death struggle: 'the tribe that a collective passion welds to its leader is here – that is, in a republic – replaced by a community governed by laws.' Marc Bloch, 'Pourquoi je suis républicain,' *Les Cahiers politiques*, Organe du Comité général d'études de la Résistance, no. 2 (July 1943), one of the 'écrits clandestins' published in *L'Etrange défaite* (Pans, 1993), 215. He evoked the same distinction in *L'Etrange défaite,* 176. Hitlerism 'remplace la persuasion par la suggestion emotive.'

13   Walter L. Adamson, 'Modernism and Fascism: The Politics of Culture in Italy, 1903–1922,' *American Historical Review* 95 (April 1990): 359–90, holds that the principal effect of Mussolini's association with modernist intellectuals was the legitimation this lent early Fascism (p. 361). 'The important issue is not the content of fascist ideology but the cultural sources of fascist rhetoric and of the secular-religious aura it sought to project' (p. 363).

14   Gisela Bock, *Zwangssterilisation im Nationalsozialismus: Studien zur Rassenpolitik und Frauenpolitik* (Opladen, 1986) (. . .), Atina Grossmann, 'Feminist Debates about Women and National Socialism,' *Gender and History*, 3 (Autumn 1991): 350–58.

15   Henry A. Turner, Jr., doubted that generic fascism is a valid or useful concept in 'Fascism and Modernization,' in *Reappraisals of Fascism*, ed. Henry A. Turner, Jr. (New York, 1975), 132–33. Gilbert Allardyce pushed skepticism furthest in 'What Fascism Is Not: Thoughts on the Deflation of a Concept,' *American Historical Review* 84 (April 1979): 367–88.

16   The term is from Carl Schorske, *Fin-de-siècle Vienna* (New York, 1980), chap. 3.

17   The term *fascia* was used by syndicalists in the 1890s, as in the *fasci siciliani*; it emphasizes the solidarity of brothers in action. Pro-intervention syndicalists

brought the word into the nationalist lexicon during World War I, as in the *Fasci de Difesa Nazionale* in Ferrara, to whose journal, *Il Fascia*, Mussolini contributed in 1917. The form *fascismo* seems to be Mussolini's own invention in 1919.

18   Pierre Milza, *Fascisme français: passé et présent* (Paris, 1987), presents a four-stage model of fascism; Philippe Burrin, *La Dérive fasciste* (Paris, 1986), elegantly traces the itineraries by which Jacques Doriot, Marcel Déat, and Gaston Bergery, steering between blockages and opportunities, shifted from the Left to fascism. Most recent authors seek some 'fascist essence.' Payne, *History*, 487–95, while rejecting any monocausal or reductionist theory, presents 'elements of a retro-dictive theory of fascism' that apply to movements as well as to regimes; Laqueur, *Fascism*, finds fascism like pornography, in that 'it is difficult – perhaps impossible – to define in an operational, legally valid way,' but nevertheless presents 'the essence of fascism' (pp. 6, 13–21); in *The Nature of Fascism*, Griffin proposes a 'new ideal type' of fascism defined as 'a genus of political ideology whose mythic core in its various permutations is a palingenetic form of populist ultranationalism' (p. 26); for Eatwell, fascism is a 'coherent body of thought' (p. xvii) whose 'essence' is a 'form of thought that preaches the need for social rebirth in order to forge a holistic-national radical Third Way' (p. 14).

19   An extreme case of this genre, Anthony Joes, *Fascism in the Contemporary World: Ideology, Evolution, Resurgence* (Boulder, Colo., 1978), includes practically every mass-based dictatorship in the developing world.

20   A superior example is Adrian Lyttelton, *The Seizure of Power: Fascism in Italy, 1919–1929*, 2nd ed. (Princeton, N.J., 1987).

21   Raymond Grew, 'On the Current State of Comparative Studies,' in *Marc Bloch Aujourd'hui: Histoire comparée et sciences sociales*, ed. Hartmut Atsma and André Burguière (Paris, 1990), 331.

22   Marc Bloch, a great exponent of comparison in history, distinguished two kinds: the juxtaposition of similar phenomena in different cultures, such as feudalism in the West and in Japan; and the parallel study of 'neighboring and adjacent soci-eties' having known 'change in the same direction.' Marc Bloch, 'Pour une histoire comparée des sociétés européennes,' *Revue de Synthèse* 46 (1928): 15–50, reprinted in Marc Bloch, *Mélanges historiques*, 2 vols. (Paris, 1963), 1:16–40. This second type of historical comparison, confronting different outcomes for the same process in two neighboring regions, is the sharper tool. One thinks of the two halves of the *département* of the Sarthe, one republican and the other counter-revolutionary, compared so fruitfully by Paul Bois, *Paysans de l'ouest* (Paris, 1971); and of Maurice Agulhon's comparison of the different reception of republicanism in the early nineteenth century in two regions of the Var, one of them 'virtually immobile' and the other 'touched by the fever of industrial development': *La République au village* (Paris, 1979), 32.

23   Milza proposes four stages: a first fascism, that of marginal movements of intel-lectuals from both Right and Left; a second fascism, that of militant activists on the road to power; a third fascism, exercising power; and a fourth, under the pres-sures of war.

24   Payne, among others, considers authoritarian military dictatorships the most effec-tive barrier, historically, against fascist acquisitions of power. See Payne, *History*, 250, 252, 312, 321, 326, 395, 492.

25   Interwar fascists could remember how a general strike had frustrated the Kapp Putsch in Germany in 1920.

26   Racial hygiene has recently proven a fruitful subject because it links Nazi practice to professional interests. See Michael H. Kater, *Doctors under Hitler* (Chapel Hill, N.C., 1989); Robert Jay Lifton, *The Nazi Doctors: Medical Killing and the Psychology of Genocide* (New York, 1986). Burleigh and Wippermann, 353, n. 1, advocate, convincingly, a more anthropologically informed study of how fascist regimes interacted with specific social groups.

27   Perspicacious contemporaries saw this compound quality of fascist rule as a 'dual state,' in which the 'normative state' jostled for power with a 'prerogative state' formed by the party's parallel organizations. See Ernst Fraenkel, *The Dual State* (New York, 1941); and Franz Neumann, *Behemoth* (New York, 1942). The compound nature of fascist rule has been conceptually refined since the 1970s by the 'polyocratic' interpretation. See Martin Broszat, *Hitler's State* (London, 1981); Hans Mommsen, in many works, including *From Weimar to Auschwitz*, trans. Philip O'Connor (Cambridge, 1991); and *Der Führerstaat: Mythos und Realität*, ed. Gerhard Hirschfeld and Lothar Kettenacker (Stuttgart, 1981). For an analagous reading of Fascist Italy, see Emilio Gentile, 'Le rôle du parti dans le laboratoire totalitaire italien,' *Annales: Economies, sociétés, civilisations* 43 (May–June 1988): 567–91; and Philippe Burrin, 'Politique et société: Les structures du pouvoir dans l'Italie fasciste et l'Allemagne nazie,' *Annales: Economies, sociétés, civilisations* 43 (May–June 1988): 615–37. For 'shapelessness,' see Hannah Arendt, *The Origins of Totalitarianism*, 2nd ed. (New York, 1958), 389–390, 395, 398, 402. She credits the term to Neumann, *Behemoth*.

28   Juan J. Linz has made the classic analysis of authoritarianism as a distinct form of rule: 'An Authoritarian Regime: Spain,' in *Mass Politics: Studies in Political Sociology*, ed. Erik Allard and Stein Rokkan (New York, 1970), 251–83, 'From Falange to Movimiento-Organización: The Spanish Single Party and the Franco Regime, 1936–1968,' in *Authoritarian Politics in Modern Societies: The Dynamics of Established One-Party Systems*, ed. Samuel P. Huntington and Clement Moore (New York, 1970), 'Totalitarian and Authoritarian Regimes,' in *Handbook of Political Science*, ed. Fred I. Greenstein and Nelson W. Polsby (Reading, Mass., 1975), vol. 3, esp. pp. 264–350. As for totalitarianism, Arendt included Stalin and excluded Mussolini, as did Carl Friedrich and Zbigniew Brzezinski, *Totalitarian Dictatorship and Autocracy* (Cambridge, Mass., 1956). By the late 1960s, the totalitarianism concept had come to seem a Cold War artifact and remains in use today mainly in popular language. See Benjamin R. Barber, 'The Conceptual Foundations of Totalitarianism,' in Carl J. Friedrich, Michael Curtis, and Benjamin R. Barber, *Totalitarianism in Perspective: Three Views* (London, 1969). See now Ian Kershaw and Moshe Lewin, eds., *Stalinism and Nazism: Dictatorships in Comparison* (Cambridge, 1997).

29   The borders between the two kinds of regime are blurred here, for, in practice, neither gets its wish. Faced with aroused publics, authoritarians as well as fascists may attempt to create a Durkheimian 'mechanical solidarity.' Paul Brooker, *The Faces of Fraternalism: Nazi Germany, Fascist Italy, and Imperial Japan* (Oxford, 1991). Fascists may achieve no more than a 'superficial' and 'fragile' consent. Victoria De Grazia, *The Culture of Consent: Mass Organization of Leisure in Fascist Italy* (Cambridge, 1981), 20 and chap. 8, 'The Limits of Consent.' The most meticulous study of German public opinion under Nazism, Martin Broszat's 'Bavaria program,' concluded that it was atomized and passive. See Ian Kershaw, *Popular Opinion and Dissent in the Third Reich: Bavaria, 1933–1945* (Oxford, 1983).

30   Robert Ley, head of the Nazi Labor Service, said that the only private individual in the Nazi state is a person asleep. Arendt believed him. See *Origins*, 339.

31   The terms are Renzo De Felice's in *Mussolini: Il Duce: La stato totalitario, 1936–1940* (Turin, 1981), 100; for this and other controversial judgments by Mussolini's principal biographer, see Borden W. Painter, 'Renzo De Felice and the Historiography of Italian Fascism,' *American Historical Review* 95 (April 1990): 391–405.

32   Claudio Segrè, *The Fourth Shore: The Italian Colonization of Libya* (Chicago, 1974); Denis Mack Smith, *Mussolini's Roman Empire* (New York, 1976); Luigi Preti, 'Fascist Imperialism and Racism,' in *The Ax Within*, ed. Roland Sarti (New York, 1974), 187–207.

33   In the debate about what drove radicalization, the artificial distinction between 'intentionalists' and 'functionalists' has been resolved, most effectively by Christopher Browning, in favor of an interaction between the leader's intentions and competitive harshness among subordinates who count on his approval. Browning's most recent analysis is *The Path to Genocide: Essays on Launching the Final Solution* (Cambridge, 1992).

34   Omer Bartov makes a somewhat different point about how the special conditions of the Russian campaign inured the Army as well as the SS to brutality. See *The Eastern Front, 1941–1945: German Troops and the Barbarization of Warfare* (New York, 1986), *Hitler's Army: Soldiers, Nazis, and War in the Third Reich* (New York, 1991).

35   Stein U. Larsen, Bernt Hagtvet, and Jan Petter Myklebust, eds., *Who Were the Fascists? Social Roots of European Fascism* (Oslo, 1980), surmounts this problem better than most. Current work shies away both from class and from Hannah Arendt's classless mass, preferring to explore links with more particularly defined groups: professions, clubs, fraternities, and other 'intermediary bodies.' See Rudy Koshar, 'From *Stammtisch* to Party: Nazi Joiners and the Contradictions of Grass Roots Fascism in Weimar Germany,' *Journal of Modern History* 59 (March 1987): 1–24; and, more generally, Rudy Koshar, *Social Life, Local Politics, and Nazism: Marburg, 1880–1935* (Chapel Hill, N.C., 1986).

36   Susan Sontag made an interesting effort to extract the elements of a fascist aesthetic from the work of Leni Riefenstahl: 'Fascinating Fascism,' in Susan Sontag, *Under the Sign of Saturn* (New York, 1980), but it may apply mainly to German culture.

37   Still basic in English is Jill Stephenson, *Women in Nazi Society* (New York, 1975); Burleigh and Wippermann have an up-to-date chapter on women in Nazi Germany and, more innovatively, one on men. George Mosse, *The Image of Man: The Creation of Modern Masculinity* (New York, 1996), culminates with Nazi Germany. Essential for Italy is Victoria De Grazia, *How Fascism Ruled Women: Italy, 1922–1945* (Berkeley and Los Angeles, 1992).

SECTION II

■ What produces fascism?

T HE QUESTION 'WHAT PRODUCES FASCISM?' is closely linked to the discussion of the contingent factors that prompted the formulation of its doctrine and allowed its ideological and political representatives to exercise wide influence and enjoy high levels of political appeal in interwar Europe. The validity of studying fascism as an intellectual phenomenon (in the fashion of the 'new consensus') has proved extremely functional in understanding fascism's ideological debts to, and derivation from, pre-existing strands of dissident radical nationalist thought, stretching back to the second half of the nineteenth century (see, for example, Sternhell (**14**)). This said, exclusive reliance on the ideological production of fascism might produce misleading impressions about the importance of actions and events in shaping its character. To mention but the most conspicuous examples, the Florentine avant-garde revolt, the *völkisch* nationalist discourse in Wilhelminian Germany, the radical ideas of the *Action Française* and a host of dissident intellectuals like Sorel and Le Bon in France and of Lueger and Vogelsang in Austria all pointed to a novel, utopian and mythical form of nationalism that rejected the rational 'normality' of mainstream (that is, liberal and conservative) discourses and was obsessed with a more holistic approach to the social and political life of the nation. However, to interpret affinity and a certain degree of intellectual continuity as direct causality is misleading (cf. Allardyce (**1**)). Fascism was indeed a sort of culmination of this ideological trend, but not its pre-determined end-result or its automatic derivation. Until the outbreak of the First World War, it remained an essentially marginal phenomenon, confined mainly to intellectual circles and considered as largely irrelevant to the pivotal social and political reality of the time. Without the dramatic consequences of the First World War and the seismic events of 1917 in Russia this intellectual current of nationalism might as well have remained a footnote in the history of European ideas.

Such exceptional factors and developments, heavily influencing the general socio-economic and political milieu of interwar Europe, provide invaluable insight into the forces that transformed the two decades between the two world wars into what may be termed a 'fascist epoch' (Nolte (12)). However, they rest on historical generalisations which do not account for another fundamental question – why fascism appeared only in certain countries and why it achieved differing degrees of appeal or political success across Europe. There are obvious distinctions that have to be made between Italy and Germany (where fascism was catapulted to power), Britain and France (where fascist ideology proved an insufficiently powerful vehicle to mobilise the population or attract the support of the elites), and a large group of other countries (where fascism did achieve some success but failed to occupy an autonomously dominant position in the national political discourse). A number of interpretations have stressed the varying degree of impact that certain general developments had on specific societies: for example, the economic crisis after the war or the Depression from 1929 onwards; the feeling of 'national humiliation' that afflicted those countries that came out of the Great War with the label 'defeated'; the flaws in the operation of political liberalism and the degree of commitment to its values by the population and the elites alike; the level of socialist mobilisation and of the perceived 'threat' of a communist revolution; and finally, the degree of 'modernisation' (and its subsequent side-effects on society) within a certain socio-political system.

Inevitably, different models of interpretation have diverged in the significance that they place upon each of these (and other) factors. Overall, Marxist accounts tend to emphasise the crisis of the world capitalist system (and the violent responses it generated from the elite groups in defence of their dominant status in society) as the key to understanding the capitulation of many European countries to the allure of fascism (3, 7). They stress the vulnerability of the lower strata of the middle class (what has been generically called the *petty bourgeoisie*) to the promise of order, stability and elimination of working-class agitation – a promise particularly seductive to a group that had been 'sandwiched' between the traditional elites and the growing proletariat in danger of losing its identity and status in a society experiencing the effects of economic crisis and fluidity. Most early interwar Marxist interpretations (the official Third International position on fascism, but also the early writings of Antonio Gramsci, Palmiro Togliatti, Mátyás Rákosi and others) exuded a premature arrogance towards the chances of the long-term viability of Italian Fascism, based on the view that fascism had essentially failed to deliver tangible benefits to its elite sponsors. As Rákosi wrote in 1925, 'the worst period is over', believing strongly in the capacity of the Communist Party in Italy to regroup and crush the Fascist dictatorship, which was allegedly devoid of any popular base. Such optimism, however, evaporated in the second half of the 1920s, under the weight of the evidence that Fascism as regime possessed both the organisational apparatus and a sort of popular base to ensure its survival. The admission that Fascism was indeed a popular movement contradicted early Marxist interpretations of the Fascist regime as the exclusive product of elite aspirations and support. Gramsci and Togliatti acknowledged the existence of a genuine popular base in Fascism, although (like most Marxist commentators) they identified it with the petty bourgeoisie. To take August Thalheimer as an example, he criticised the initial orthodox Third International position of 'fascism as the dictatorship of capital' by pointing out that the most advanced capitalist states in Europe did not develop a form comparable to Italian Fascism. In this sense, Thalheimer argued, stages of economic development were not indicators of the vulnerability of a society to fascism (cf. Kitchen (2)).

The idea that fascism was essentially a 'middle-class' phenomenon proved one of the most persisting orthodoxies in the postwar era for Marxist and liberal interpretations alike (though for very different reasons). For the former, the predominance of 'class' as a device for historical analysis hindered an understanding of fascism's capacity to appeal to different social groups, including, to an extent, the urban and rural working classes. Palmiro Togliatti (7) affirmed the significance of the middle-class popular base of fascism, underlining how it strengthened its political power and transformed it into an indispensable tool of elite counter-revolution against the proletariat. For the latter (liberal), especially in the first two decades after the war, the key factor was a sort of moral decay, disintegration of the cultural and social matrix of European civilisation (see, for example, Croce 1946; Meinecke 1950). Even the subsequent sociological interpretations of fascism in the 1960s displayed a methodological veneration for class-based discourse in analysing the origins and nature of fascism. Seymour Martin Lipset (8) analysed it as the product of the 'extremism of the middle classes', a movement of the social *déclassés*, which developed either in a right-wing (the more conservative regimes in Portugal, Hungary, Austria), a left-wing (Perónism in Argentina) or a combined direction (Nazism, Italian Fascism, etc.).

While Lipset (and other sociologists, such as Organski (1965) and Barrington Moore (1966, 1978)), approached fascism as a phenomenon linked to general conditions of social development and 'modernisation' (cf. **39, 47**), arguing that as such it is not a strictly defined historical category of the interwar period, historical interpretations emphasised the *specific* conditions that explain the rise of fascism in the two decades between the two world wars. Charles Maier (9) focused on the 1920s and attempted to link the rise of fascism in certain countries to particular conditions of crisis in bourgeois society and culture. Geoff Eley (10) located the roots of fascism in the crisis of the world capitalist system of the 1920s and 1930s, coupled with the disintegration of the liberal political order and the threat of socialism. For him, fascism developed in 'dynamically capitalist societies' where the existing political system proved incapable of managing the crisis and providing much-needed social cohesion in the uncertainty that followed the First World War and the crisis of confidence in liberalism. Finally, Griffin's piece (11) draws attention to a set of historical and social preconditions that – together – explain why fascism succeeded in acquiring mass support and even political power in some countries but failed in others (such as Britain and France).

Chapter 7

Palmiro Togliatti

AN INTERWAR MARXIST ANALYSIS OF FASCISM: TOGLIATTI AND ITALIAN COMMUNISM

■ from **ON THE QUESTION OF FASCISM**, *L'Internationale Communiste*, 9 (1928), 324–36, translated in David Beetham (ed.) *Marxists in Face of Fascism: Writings by Marxists on Fascism from the Inter-war Period*, Totowa, NJ, 1984, pp. 136–48

Alongside Antonio Gramsci, Palmiro Togliatti was the patriarch of Italian communism and of the PCI (Partito Communista Italiano). He produced several analyses of Fascism in Italy throughout the 1920s and 1930s which showed an increasing tendency to take Mussolini and his movement/regime more seriously than the initial Comintern understandings suggested. In the following extract from an article published in 1928 Togliatti acknowledges that Fascism indeed had a significant social base (mainly rural and urban bourgeoisie); however, it gradually lost the initiative to the more reactionary 'big bourgeoisie and landowners', thus becoming the political pivot of the dominant classes within Italy. Note how sceptical Togliatti is about generalising the experience of Italy into a theory of generic fascism, applicable to other countries.

[. . .]

BUT FASCISM WAS NOT SIMPLY capitalist reaction. It embraced many other elements at the same time. It comprised a movement of the rural petty-bourgeois masses; it was also a political struggle waged by certain representatives of the small and middle bourgeoisie against a section of the traditional ruling classes; it was an attempt to create a comprehensive organisation, covering the whole country, to regroup a fraction of the urban petty bourgeoisie under the direction of *déclassé* elements (ex-officers, unemployed professionals); finally it was a military organisation which claimed the ability to take on the regular armed forces of the state with some probability of success. Embracing all these elements, besides capitalist reaction, fascism's development was bound to be complex. It was absolutely naive to believe that capitalism would have used this movement as a tool intended to break the strength of the proletariat, except with the intention of subsequently casting it aside so that it could continue in power itself, reverting to its customary procedures and employing the same institutions, the same politicians, the same methods as before. Yet the complexity of the fascist phenomenon ensured that the evolution of the movement was not determined exclusively by the aims of the bourgeoisie and the landowners, but was also influenced by other motives of a quite different character, and by other impulses which arose from the very heart of the movement and which at certain moments even attempted to control it.

The over-simplification displayed by our Party [*the PCI*] had two consequences which did us great harm. First of all, we did not realise that it would have been possible to prevent fascism conquering certain elements of the petty bourgeoisie; more precisely, we could have helped accentuate the contradictions in this movement at the heart of the petty bourgeois masses. Besides, we had not taken account of the fact that the conquest of power by the fascists could not take place without a fairly violent struggle between them and a section of the old ruling classes. Right up until the eve of the event, and while it was actually taking place, we denied the possibility of a fascist *coup d'état*. As can be seen, these were consequences of considerable political importance.

Let us take another example. In 1924 people started to become clearly aware that the developments that had occurred in the economic structure of French capitalism demanded political changes in a reactionary direction. The political positions of the big industrial and financial bourgeoisie had to be strengthened, in order to assure them an undisputed hegemony. It was then that certain apparent militants of the French Communist Party launched the pronouncement: 'Fascism is here, fascism has arrived'. In fact the arrival of fascism has till now been delayed, and it only appears in France in a very weakened form. All the same the reaction is self-evident. In the course of this period a real political transformation had undoubtedly taken place, though not by a direct mobilisation of petty-bourgeois strata assembled around the more reactionary groups of the bourgeoisie. Nor has it even manifested itself in a struggle against the traditional ruling groups of the centre and right, or against parliament; nor has it taken the form of illegal violence directed against the workers' organisations, nor of a conquest of power by recourse to illegal extra-parliamentary methods that are characteristic of fascism. The reaction has been carried out quite differently, by means of an absorption of the left petty-bourgeois groups into a reactionary political bloc, led by members from the traditional ruling classes. This has led to the necessity of complicated manoeuvres, resulting in parliamentary compromises which include even the Socialists. Besides, the repression of the workers was arranged by the normal agencies of the bourgeois 'democratic' state. It is possible, and could even be considered certain, that the final outcome will be the same; but the methods employed, and the course of development are profoundly different. Now, it is impossible to carry out any serious policy, or even any 'policy' at all, by considering only the final outcome, and taking no account of the course of events and the different stages traversed. In the case that we have just examined, certain political errors committed by the PCF in the course of the past few years (among others its failure to recognise in time the development of a clear split between the vanguard of the working class and the political formations of the petty bourgeoisie) may well have been caused by a mistaken assessment of the course which French political life had taken in its development towards reaction.

Let us turn, then, to a critical examination of certain characteristic features of Italian fascism, the 'typical' fascism; we shall then see how far it is possible to generalise, and what conclusions can be drawn, from the Italian experience. In the first place we can say that fascism is the most thoroughgoing and systematic form of reaction that has so far emerged in the countries where capitalism has reached a certain level of development. This assertion is not based on the terrorist atrocities, nor on the large number of workers and peasants assassinated, nor on the cruelty of the methods of torture applied on a vast scale, nor on the severity of the sentences handed out. It is based on the systematic and total suppression of all forms of autonomous organisation on the part of the masses. It may be that other countries, especially those where reaction was installed after the checking of a revolutionary struggle at the point of insurrection, have witnessed a larger number of victims and a harsher terror. But no other country has seen such a radical suppression of any possibility for the masses of creating their own autonomous organisations, under whatever form, as has Italy. In no country has the struggle for the destruction of formal democratic liberties been waged in such a consistent manner, and with such effectiveness.

How are we to explain this side of Italian fascism that is so characteristic? It would be absurdly mistaken to look for the causes in the exceptional savagery of fascism's purposes and those of its most obvious militants, or to discover there that species of collective sickness which the feeble ideologists of pure democracy and idiotic pacifism have been pleased to designate by the term 'militaristic psychosis' and 'disease of violence', etc. The total suppression of democratic liberties, such as the freedom of assembly, of expression, of association, the right to strike, direct universal suffrage, etc., alongside the prohibition against setting up autonomous mass organisations, corresponds to a specific necessity of Italian capitalism and its stabilisation.

Italy is a very poor country. Capitalism there, although it has reached a considerable level of development, has been undermined by the contradictions inherent in imperialism, and has a wretchedly weak structure. During the whole period of the development of the bourgeois state prior to the world war, the ruling classes had been compelled to take account of the growing pressure exerted by the abundant working population of the towns (proletarians and artisans) and the countryside (agricultural labourers, poor and middle peasantry), a population that was continually on the increase. Only in the years immediately preceding the war was it possible for the bourgeoisie, thanks to a favourable economic situation, to corrupt a small fraction of the proletariat, which could consider itself privileged in comparison with the great mass of workers and above all the poor peasants, who were the most heavily oppressed and exploited. The crisis after the war drove the internal contradictions of Italian capitalism even deeper, and these found expression in violent conflicts. From that moment the conditions which had allowed the existence of a labour aristocracy ceased to hold. The profit margin reserved for the benefit of the capitalists was squeezed. The pressure of the masses on the apparatus of bourgeois power and of capitalist production broadened and intensified. The process of capitalist stabilisation was bound thereafter to lead rapidly to desperate economic and political pressures (more rapidly than in other European countries where the bourgeoisie, being richer and stronger, could afford the luxury of a greater room for manoeuvre). In the economic field, the stabilisation could take no other form than the one it took after the advent of fascism to power: penetration of finance capital into the whole economic life of the country, in an attempt to reduce the internal contradictions that obstructed a rapid stabilisation – a savage reduction of wages; hateful exploitation of consumers; unprecedented taxation of petty-bourgeois producers. This economic programme could not have been realised if the working population, and especially the proletariat, had not already been deprived of every possibility of collective action; this is the reason why fascism's victory was rapidly followed by a fundamentally reactionary transformation in the whole political life of the country.

The reactionary character of fascism in respect of its consequences is thus first of all the expression of an economic necessity and of a process whose causes must be traced in the sphere of the relations of production. The tendency of Italian capitalism not only to become reactionary (a tendency present in all countries in the imperialist epoch), but to make use of fascism from the outset, and subsequently to identify with it, derives directly from its distinctive structure and from the special features of the crisis which it underwent. It is impossible to predict if fascism, in the form it has taken in Italy, can become established in another country, unless one first takes the trouble to analyse carefully its capitalist system, and likewise its relations of production and those of its dominant classes.

[. . .]

To sum up on this first point, I think it is possible to reach the following conclusions: on one side, one of the essential characteristics of fascism is that it is a reactionary regime driven to its logical extremes; on the other side, we must not forget that this characteristic derives from the special economic and class relations that exist in Italy. It is this particular situation that has determined the direction in which Italian fascism has developed. So if we wish to be prudent and anticipate the methods, the limits and the types of reactionary transformation that modern capitalist society can undergo, we should above all not lose sight of the economic situation.

The second important characteristic of fascism, besides its reactionary nature, is that it is closely bound up in its origins and evolution with a certain configuration of class relations; in saying this I am thinking not only of the major antagonistic classes of modern society, bourgeoisie and proletariat, but also of the relations that these two principal classes maintain with the intermediate classes which move about between the two. On this point, however, it would be particularly mistaken to be satisfied with general formulae. It is necessary to examine the class relations with great care, taking account of their development.

At the outset the social basis of fascism lay in certain strata of the rural and urban petty bourgeoisie. In more precise terms, its basis in the countryside was made up mainly from the middling peasants, farm managers and share-croppers, who were exasperated by the absurd policy of the Socialist organisations. The Socialists proclaimed the Maximalist programme in the countryside, including the socialisation of the land. In their practical activity they took no account of the existence or the interests of the intermediate strata of the rural petty bourgeoisie; they made no attempt to construct a political alliance between the proletariat and these strata; they did not even try to neutralise them. In the towns, as well, fascism rested at first on the petty bourgeoisie; these were partly artisans, skilled workers and shop-keepers, partly also elements displaced because of the war (ex-officers, the disabled, commandos, volunteers). If one considers on which side the aspirations of these social circles were directed, one can see that the interests of some drew them towards the anti-proletarian struggle, whereas the objective situation of others and even their rudimentary inclinations were anti-capitalist. It has already been shown elsewhere that historically the intermediate social groups can sometimes ally them-selves with the bourgeoisie, and sometimes, depending on the precise circumstances, with the proletariat. It is true that among the strata which formed the basis of fascism at the outset there existed an anti-proletarian tendency; on the other hand they had no intention of fighting to establish the dictatorship of large industrial and financial capital. Which then was the element that prevailed, and decided the general orientation and development of the movement? As is well known, it was the anti-proletarian tendency that clearly had the upper hand. The big bourgeoisie and landowners succeeded in drawing fascism to their side for the attainment of a deci-sively reactionary objective. This did not happen, however, without opposition, hesitations and compromises. Only after passing through a whole series of stages were the big bourgeoisie and the landowners able to influence the movement in a decisive manner. And even when they succeeded in attaining their ends, they could not prevent fascism from developing and maintaining the character of a politically autonomous movement, and it was in this capacity that it set out on the conquest of power, dispossessing a section of the old ruling class.

On the basis of the whole period preceding the advent of fascism to power and, in general, of the whole history of its evolution, one can say that 'the factor that consistently determined the direction of fascism's development, and that ended with the major say in its administration was clearly the big bourgeoisie; while on the other hand the forms of its evolution were determined – apart from the particular histor-ical context – by the petty-bourgeois social composition of the fascist movement'.

Such a conclusion should provoke us to considerable caution in generalising from the Italian experience, above all when it comes to extending the political implica-tions that can be drawn from it. There is little likelihood of seeing a movement analogous to Italian fascism arising in a historical and social context that is quite different, especially in a country where capitalism is very strong. Certain aspects of the Italian phenomenon may reappear, and the general reactionary direction of the political transformation in bourgeois society may remain, but it will be difficult to find again the essential features characteristic of fascism. Above all it will be difficult to find again a situation like that in Italy, where we saw reaction take the form of a mass movement, thanks to a sudden and complete change in the attitude of the middle classes. A movement of the 'fascist' type, like the one in Italy, would have the greatest difficulty in conquering power elsewhere. Before announcing that a country is becoming fascist, therefore, it is always necessary to see if the situa-tion of the country concerned allows for the repetition of the two fundamental factors that have been expounded above. Profound researches are hardly necessary to prove that in general these conditions only pertain in states with a weak economic structure, lacking political equilibrium, in which there is an abundance of middle- and petty-bourgeois strata. It is in fact countries of this type that, in the course of the last few years, have experienced developments of a truly fascist kind, or very similar to fascism (the Balkans, Lithuania, Poland).

If we now examine the period following the conquest of power, we see that the contradiction mentioned, between the social basis of fascism and its political results, does not disappear, but on the contrary becomes accentuated. The inescapable consequences of capitalist stabilisation impose themselves. Fascism finds itself obliged to carry out in brutal fashion, and without reservation, the policy of finance capital, of large industry and the banks, to the detriment of the majority of the working population. This creates a permanently unsettled state in the social base of fascism itself, and hence in turn the necessity of a reactionary pressure that operates with increasing intensity in certain directions. Some political elements could profit from an abandonment of fascism by discontented groups among the petty bourgeoisie. These groups mostly derive from the productive petty bourgeoisie (artisans, peasant farmers, share-croppers, farm managers, small traders), who resent in their distinctive way the consequences of the dictatorship of finance capital. Hence these political elements become the direct enemies of fascism, since they threaten to strike right at its foundations; and thus at certain moments the reaction becomes particularly infuriated against them. Thus fascism 'legally' dissolved the freemasons, for example, and the reformists in the same way, before it dissolved the Communist Party. This does not mean that the anti-fascist bourgeoisie and petty bourgeoisie have been persecuted more harshly than the revolutionary workers. Exactly the opposite has happened. But it shows that fascism needs to develop special measures against these organisations of the petty bourgeoisie, so as to impress them and prevent them from striking at its vulnerable point.

One of the most interesting facts to note, furthermore, is that fascism was obliged to become reactionary in its own internal organisation after the conquest of power; it was compelled to effect a quite rapid and far-reaching transformation in its structure and social composition. The principal forms of this process that we have been able to identify so far are the following:

1   The supporters among the petty-bourgeois producers abandon fascism little by little. Henceforward the membership of the Party is predominantly composed of the non-producing petty and middle bourgeoisie (state functionaries, professional fascists, etc.). This fact is particularly important as it heralds a change in the balance of forces in the countryside.

2   The fascist cadres are almost completely changed. In place of the former blackshirts, the 'fascists of the first hour', are the direct representatives of the big bourgeoisie (industrialists, bankers, landowners, and their agents), who occupy the leading posts in the Party.

3   The Fascist Party gradually absorbs a part of the general staff of all the old parties of the bourgeoisie and petty bourgeoisie.

4   At the same time democracy is completely eliminated at the centre of the Fascist Party, and replaced by a system of government from above.

In consequence of this process, fascism proves itself conclusively to be not only an instrument of reaction and repression, but also a centre of political unity for all the dominant classes: finance capital, large industry, the landowners. It identifies itself with Italian capitalism in the present period of its evolution. The Fascist Party thus tends to lose the character of an autonomous movement of certain intermediate social strata that it had to begin with, and becomes, along with its organisation, intimately fused with the economic and political system of the dominant classes.

Chapter 8

Seymour Martin Lipset

FASCISM AS 'EXTREMISM OF THE MIDDLE CLASS'

■ from *POLITICAL MAN: THE SOCIAL BASES OF POLITICS*
London, Melbourne, Toronto, 1959, pp. 132–5, 136–40, 174–6

Seymour Martin Lipset's analysis of the social bases of fascism is regarded as the most emblematic statement of the traditional view of fascism as a 'middle-class' phenomenon. Although such a view has been widely challenged ever since (see, for example, Eley (10); Paxton (6)), Lipset's argument nevertheless contains an interesting analysis of fascism as an 'extremist' protest movement of the middle strata in large-scale capitalist countries with a strong labour movement (cf. Kitchen (3)). The featured excerpt underscores the need to understand the concept of extremism not simply in terms of the 'left–right' divide, but across the ideological spectrum (including the centre, where fascism is situated, according to Lipset, because of its opposition both to big business and to socialism). Note, however, his branding of 'para-fascist' cases (Austria, Franco's Spain) as non-revolutionary and therefore constituting an 'extremism of the right'.

T HE POLITICAL AND SOCIOLOGICAL analysis of modern society in terms of left, center, and right goes back to the days of the first French Republic when the delegates were seated, according to their political coloration, in a continuous semicircle from the most radical and egalitarian on the left to the most moderate and aristocratic on the right. The identification of the left with advocacy of social reform and egalitarianism; the right, with aristocracy and conservatism, deepened as politics became defined as the clash between classes. Nineteenth-century conservatives and Marxists alike joined in the assumption that the socio-economic cleavage is the most basic in modern society. Since democracy has become institutionalized and the conservatives' fears that universal suffrage would mean the end of private property have declined, many people have begun to argue that the analysis of politics in terms of left and right and class conflict oversimplifies and distorts reality. However, the tradition of political discourse, as well as political reality, has forced most scholars to retain these basic concepts, although other dimensions, like religious differences or regional conflicts, account for political behavior which does not follow class lines.[1]

Before 1917 extremist political movements were usually thought of as a rightist phenomenon. Those who would eliminate democracy generally sought to restore monarchy or the rule of the aristocrats. After 1917 politicians and scholars alike began to refer to both left and right extremism, i.e., Communism and fascism. In this view, extremists at either end of the political continuum develop into advocates of dictatorship, while the moderates of the center remain the defenders of democracy. This chapter will attempt to show that this is an error – that extremist ideologies and groups can be classified and analyzed in the same terms as democratic groups, i.e., right, left, and *center*. The three positions resemble their democratic parallels in both the compositions of their social bases and the contents of their appeals. While comparisons of all three positions on the democratic and extremist continuum are of intrinsic interest, this chapter concentrates on the politics of the center, the most neglected type of political extremism, and that form of 'left' extremism sometimes called 'fascism' – Perónism – as manifested in Argentina and Brazil.

The center position among the democratic tendencies is usually called liberalism. In Europe where it is represented by various parties like the French Radicals, the Dutch and Belgian Liberals, and others, the liberal position means: in economics – a commitment to *laissez-faire* ideology, a belief in the vitality of small business, and opposition to strong trade-unions; in politics – a demand for minimal government intervention and regulation; in social ideology – support of equal opportunity for achievement, opposition to aristocracy, and opposition to enforced equality of income; in culture – anticlericalism and antitraditionalism.

If we look at the supporters of the three major positions in most democratic countries, we find a fairly logical relationship between ideology and social base. The Socialist left derives its strength from manual workers and the poorer rural strata; the conservative right is backed by the rather well-to-do elements – owners of large industry and farms, the managerial and free professional strata – and those segments of the less privileged groups who have remained involved in traditionalist institutions, particularly the Church. The democratic center is backed by the middle classes, especially small businessmen, white-collar workers, and the anti-clerical sections of the professional classes.

The different extremist groups have ideologies which correspond to those of their democratic counterparts. The classic fascist movements have represented the extremism of the center. Fascist ideology, though anti-liberal in its glorification of the state, has been similar to liberalism in its opposition to big business, trade-unions, and the socialist state. It has also resembled liberalism in its distaste for religion and other forms of traditionalism. And, as we shall see later, the social characteristics of Nazi voters in pre-Hitler Germany and Austria resembled those of the liberals much more than they did those of the conservatives. [. . .]

'Fascism' and the middle class

The thesis that fascism is basically a middle-class movement representing a protest against both capitalism *and* socialism, big business *and* big unions, is far from original. Many analysts have suggested it ever since fascism and Nazism first appeared on the scene. Nearly twenty-five years ago, the economist David Saposs stated it well:

> Fascism . . . [is] the extreme expression of middle-classism or populism. . . . The basic ideology of the middle class is populism. . . . Their ideal was an independent small property-owning class consisting of merchants, mechanics, and farmers. This element . . . now designated as middle class, sponsored a system of private property, profit, and competition on an entirely different basis from that conceived by capitalism. . . .
>
> From its very inception it opposed 'big business' or what has now become known as capitalism. Since the war the death knell of liberalism and individualism has been vociferously, albeit justly sounded. But since liberalism and individualism are of middle-class origin, it has been taken for granted that this class has also been eliminated as an effective social force. As a matter of fact, populism is now as formidable a force as it has ever been. And the middle class is more vigorously assertive than ever. . . .[2] [. . .]

As the relative position of the middle class declined and its resentments against on-going social and economic trends continued, its 'liberal' ideology – the support of individual rights against large-scale power – changed from that of a revolutionary class to that of a reactionary class. Once liberal doctrines had supported the *bourgeoisie* in their fight against the remnants of the feudal and monarchical order, and against the limitations demanded by mercantilist rulers and the Church. A liberal ideology opposed to Throne and Altar and favoring a limited state emerged. This ideology was not only revolutionary in political terms; it fulfilled some of the functional requirements for efficient industrialization. As Max Weber pointed out, the development of the capitalist system (which in his analysis coincides with industrialization) necessitated the abolition of artificial internal boundaries, the creation of an open international market, the establishment of law and order, and relative international peace.[3]

But the aspirations and ideology which underlay eighteenth- and nineteenth-century liberalism and populism have a different meaning and serve a different function in the advanced industrial societies of the twentieth century. Resisting large-scale organizations and the growth of state authority challenges some of the fundamental characteristics of our present society, since large industry and a strong and legitimate labor movement are necessary for a stable, modernized social structure, and government regulation and heavy taxes seem an inevitable concomitant. To be against business bureaucracies, trade-unions, and state regulation is both unrealistic and to some degree irrational. As Talcott Parsons has put it, the 'new negative orientation to certain primary aspects of the maturing modern social order has above all centered in the symbol of "capitalism". . . . The reaction against the "ideology" of the rationalization of society is the principal aspect at least of the ideology of fascism.'[4]

While continuing conflict between management and labor is an integral part of large-scale industrialism, the small businessman's desire to retain an important place for himself and his social values is 'reactionary' – not in the Marxist sense of slowing down the wheels of revolution, but from the perspective of the inherent trends of a modern industrial society. Sometimes the efforts of the small business stratum to resist or reverse the process take the form of democratic liberal movements, like the British Liberal party, the French Radicals, or the American Taft Republicans. Such movements have failed to stop the trends which their adherents oppose, and as another sociologist, Martin Trow, recently noted: 'The tendencies which small businessmen fear – of concentration and centralization – proceed without interruption in depression, war and prosperity, and irrespective of what party is in power; thus they are *always* disaffected. . . .'[5] It is not surprising, therefore, that under certain conditions small businessmen turn to extremist political movements, either fascism or antiparliamentary populism, which in one way or another express contempt for parliamentary democracy. These movements answer some of the same needs as the more conventional liberal parties; they are an outlet for the stratification strains of the middle class in a mature industrial order. But while liberalism attempts to cope with the problems by legitimate social changes and 'reforms' ('reforms' which would, to be sure, reverse the modernization process), fascism and populism propose to solve the problems by taking over the state and running it in a way which will restore the old middle classes' economic security and high standing in society, and at the same time reduce the power and status of big capital and big labor.

The appeal of extremist movements may also be a response by different strata of the population to the social effects of industrialization at different stages of its development. These variations are set in sharp relief by a comparison of the organized threats to the democratic process in societies at various stages of industrialization. As I have already shown, working-class extremism, whether Communist, anarchist, revolutionary socialist, or Perónist, is most commonly found in societies undergoing rapid industrialization, or in those where the process of industrialization did not result in a predominantly industrial society, like the Latin countries of southern Europe. Middle-class extremism occurs in countries characterized by both large-scale capitalism and a powerful labor movement. Right-wing extremism is most common in less developed economies, in which the traditional conservative forces linked to Throne and Altar remain strong. Since some countries, like France, Italy, or Weimar Germany, have possessed strata in all three sets of circumstances, all three types of extremist politics sometimes exist in the same country. Only the well-to-do, highly industrialized and urbanized nations seem immune to the virus, but even in the United States and Canada there is evidence that the self-employed are somewhat disaffected.

The different political reactions of similar strata at different points in the industrialization process are clearly delineated by a comparison of the politics of certain Latin-American countries with those of Western Europe. The more well-to-do Latin-American countries today resemble Europe in the nineteenth century; they are experiencing industrial growth while their working classes are still relatively unorganized into trade-unions and political parties, and reservoirs of traditional conservatism still exist in their rural populations. The growing middle class in these countries, like its nineteenth-century European counterpart, supports a democratic society by attempting to reduce the influence of the anticapitalist traditionalists and the arbitrary power of the military.[6] To the extent that there is a social base at this stage of economic development for extremist politics, it lies not in the middle classes but in the growing, still unorganized working classes who are suffering from the tensions inherent in rapid industrialization. These workers have provided the primary base of support for the only large-scale 'fascist' movements in Latin America – those of Perón in the Argentine and Vargas in Brazil. These movements, like the Communist ones with which they have sometimes been allied, appeal to the 'displaced masses' of newly industrializing countries.

The real question to answer is: which strata are most 'displaced' in each country? In some, it is the new working class, or the working class which was never integrated in the total society, economically or politically; in others, it is the small businessmen and other relatively independent entrepreneurs (small farm owners, provincial lawyers) who feel oppressed by the growing power and status of unionized workers and by large-scale corporative and governmental bureaucracies; in still others, it is the conservative and traditionalist elements who seek to preserve the old society from the values of socialism and liberalism. Fascist ideology in Italy, for example, arose out of an opportunistic movement which sought at various times to appeal to all three groups, and remained sufficiently amorphous to permit appeals to widely different strata, depending on national variations as to who were most 'displaced.'[7] Since fascist politicians have been extremely opportunistic in their efforts to secure support, such movements have often encompassed groups with conflicting interests and values, even when they primarily expressed the needs of one stratum. Hitler, a centrist extremist, won backing from conservatives who hoped to use the Nazis against the Marxist left. And conservative extremists like Franco have often been able to retain centrists among their followers without giving them control of the movement.

In the previous chapter on working-class authoritarianism I tried to specify some of the other conditions which dispose different groups and individuals to accept more readily an extremist and demonological view of the world. The thesis presented there suggested that a low level of sophistication and a high degree of insecurity predispose an individual toward an extremist view of politics. Lack of sophistication is largely a product of little education and isolation from varied experiences. On these grounds, the most authoritarian segments of the middle strata should be found among the small entrepreneurs who live in small communities or on farms. These people receive relatively little formal education as compared with those in other middle-class positions; and living in rural areas or small towns usually means isolation from heterogeneous values and groups. By the same token, one would expect more middle-class extremism among the self-employed, whether rural or urban, than among white-collar workers, executives, and professionals.

[. . .]

The social bases of fascism

[. . .] While all the varieties of antidemocratic mass movements are of equal interest, I have tried here to establish the usefulness of the tripartite distinction by examining the social bases of different political movements. Data from a number of countries demonstrate that classic fascism is a movement of the propertied middle classes, who for the most part normally support liberalism, and that it is opposed by the conservative strata, who have, however, at different times backed conservative antiparliamentary regimes. The conservative regimes are, in contrast to centrist ones, nonrevolutionary and nontotalitarian. In a conservative dictatorship, one is not expected to give total loyalty to the regime, to join a party or other institutions, but simply to keep out of politics. Though the dictatorship of the Austrian clerical conservatives has been described as fascist, the differences between it and its Nazi successor are abundantly clear. Similarly, although Franco is backed by the Spanish fascists – the Falange – his regime has been dominated by conservative authoritarians. The party has never been allowed to dominate the society; most institutions remain independent of the state and the party, and the opposition is not asked to conform or join, only to abstain from organized opposition.

Although a distinction may be made among these movements analytically, in any given country there is considerable overlap, as in the case of the Spanish Nationalists. Basically revolutionary movements like Nazism did secure some support from conservatives who agreed with its nationalistic and anti-Marxist aspects. Italian Fascism represented a coalition of both centrist and conservative extremism led by a pure opportunist. It would be a mistake, however, to conclude from the absence of movements which are purely one or the other variety that the analytic distinction is of merely speculative interest. Recent political movements – Poujadism, McCarthyism, Gaullism – all exhibit particular characteristics associated with the nature of their social base. If we want to preserve and extend parliamentary democracy, we must understand the source of threats to it, and threats from conservatives are as different from those originating in the middle-class center as these are from Communism.

Extremist movements have much in common. They appeal to the disgruntled and the psychologically homeless, to the personal failures, the socially isolated, the economically insecure, the uneducated, unsophisticated, and authoritarian persons at every level of the society. As Heberle puts it, such movements are supported by 'those who for some reason or other had failed to make a success in their business or occupation, and those who had lost their social status or were in danger of losing it. . . . The masses of the organized (Nazi) party members consisted therefore before 1933 largely of people who were outsiders in their own class, black sheep in their family, thwarted in their ambitions. . . .'[8] As far back as the 1890s, Engels described those who 'throng to the working-class parties in all countries' as 'those who have nothing to look forward to from the official world or have come to the end of their tether with it – opponents of inoculation, supporters of abstemiousness, vegetarians, antivivisectionists, nature-healers, free-community preachers whose communities have fallen to pieces, authors of new theories on the origin of the universe, unsuccessful or unfortunate inventors, victims of real or imaginary injustice . . . honest fools and dishonest swindlers.'[9] It is often men from precisely such origins who give the fanatical and extremist character to these movements and form the core of believers.[10] But the various extremist movements, like their democratic alternatives, wax or wane depending on whether they can win and retain the support of the strata whom they are trying to represent and lead. It is impossible to understand the role and varying success of extremist movements unless we distinguish them and identify their distinctive social bases and ideologies much as we do democratic parties and movements.[11]

Notes

1   In spite of the complexities of French politics, the foremost students of elections in that country find that they must classify parties and alternatives along the left–right dimension. See F. Coguel, *Géographie des élections françaises de 1870 à 1951*, *Cahiers de la fondation rationale des sciences politiques*, No. 27 (Paris: Librairie Armand Colin, 1951).

2   David J. Saposs, 'The Role of the Middle Class in Social Development: Fascism, Populism, Communism, Socialism,' in *Economic Essays in Honor of Wesley Clair Mitchell* (New York: Columbia University Press, 1935), 395, 397, 400. An even earlier analysis by André Siegfried, based on a detailed ecological study of voting patterns in part of France from 1871 to 1912, suggested that the petty bourgeoisie who had been considered the classic source of French democratic ideology were becoming the principal recruiting grounds for extremist movements. Siegfried pointed out that though they are 'by nature egalitarian, democratic, and envious . . . they are fearful above all of new economic conditions which threatened to eliminate them, crushed between the aggressive capitalism of the great companies and the increasing rise of the working people. They place great hopes in the Republic, and they do not cease being republican or egalitarian. But they are in that state of discontent, from which the Boulangisms marshal their forces, in which reactionary demagogues see the best ground in which to agitate, and in which is born passionate resistance to certain democratic reforms.' André Siegfried, *Tableau politique de la France de l'ouest sous la troisième république* (Paris: Librairie Armand Colin, 1913), 413.

3   See also Karl Polanyi, *The Great Transformation* (New York: Farrar and Rinehart, 1944).

4   Talcott Parsons, 'Some Sociological Aspects of the Fascist Movement,' in his *Essays In Sociological Theory* (Glencoe: The Free Press, 1954), 133–34. Marx himself pointed out that 'the small manufacturer, the small merchant, the artisan, the peasant, all fight against the (big) bourgeois, in order to protect their position as a middle class from being destroyed. They are, however, not revolutionary, but conservative. Even more, they are reactionary, they look for a way to reverse the path of history,' quoted in S. S. Nibon, 'Wahlsoziologische Probleme des Nationalsozialismus,' *Zeitschrift für die Gesamte Staatswissenschaft*, no. 1 (1954), 295.

5   Martin A. Trow, 'Small Businessmen, Political Tolerance, and Support for McCarthy,' *American Journal of Sociology*, 64 (1958), 279–80.

6   For an analysis of the political role of the rapidly growing Latin-American middle classes see John J. Johnson, *Political Change in Latin America – the Emergence of the Middle Sectors* (Stanford: Stanford University Press, 1958). The different political propensities of a social group at successive stages of industrialization are indicated by James Bryce's comment in 1912 that 'the absence of that class of small landowners which is the soundest and most stable element in the United States and in Switzerland and is equally stable, if less politically trained, in France and parts of Germany, is a grave misfortune for South and Central America.' This may

have been true in an early period, before the impact of large-scale organization of the farms meant economic competition for small farmers and added them to the rank of the potential supporters of fascism, as the data on Germany and other countries discussed here show. See James Bryce, *South America: Observations and Impressions* (New York: Macmillan, 1912), 533.

7   A comparison of the European middle class and the Argentine working class, which argues that each is most 'displaced' in its respective environment, is contained in Gino Germani, *Integration política de las masas y la totalitarismo* (Buenos Aires: Colegio Libre de Estudios Superiores, 1956). See also his *Estructura social de la Argentina* (Buenos Aires: Raigal, 1955).

8   R. Heberle, *From Democracy to Nazism* (Baton Rouge: Louisiana State University Press), 10.

9   Friedrich Engels, 'On the History of Early Christianity,' in K. Marx and F. Engels, *On Religion* (Moscow: Foreign Languages Publishing House, 1957), 319.

10 See G. Almond, *The Appeals of Communism* (Princeton: Princeton University Press, 1954), Chaps. 9 and 10, esp. pp. 258–61.

11 In emphasizing the consistencies in the type of extremist politics associated with various social groupings, I do not mean to assert that such findings permit a high order of political prediction. As Reinhard Bendix has pointed out: 'The point is not that certain types of farmers in relatively industrialized countries are poten-tial fascists *or* communists, but that they have a certain propensity to radicalization under conditions of acute distress. When such radicalization will eventuate and which way it will turn, the analyst of social stratification is not in a position to predict. His knowledge does enable him to estimate the relative chances for such a development, but only in the sense that certain types of farmers are more likely to be affected than others. Obviously, local conditions, historical antecedents, the acuteness of the crisis, and the intensity of the organizational drive on the part of a totalitarian movement will play a role and can be judged only in specific cases.' R. Bendix, 'Social Stratification and Political Power,' in R. Bendix and S. M. Lipset, eds., *Class, Status and Power* (Glencoe: The Free Press, 1956), 602.

Chapter 9

Charles S. Maier

THE COLLAPSE OF THE 'BOURGEOIS EQUILIBRIUM' OF THE 1920s AND THE RISE OF FASCISM

■ from *RECASTING BOURGEOIS EUROPE: STABILIZATION IN FRANCE, GERMANY AND ITALY AFTER WORLD WAR I*, Princeton, NJ, 1975, pp. 579–84, 586, 591–3

Charles Maier's account of bourgeois society in interwar Germany, Italy and France offers an interesting perspective on the forces that underpinned the relative stability of the 1920s and its collapse in the 1930s. He analyses the way that a conservative 'bourgeois equilibrium' was reconstructed after the First World War through corporatist practices that aimed to minimise the fighting power of the socialist left by establishing ways of collaboration between industry and labour. This equilibrium, Maier contends, was undermined by the uncertainty of the middle classes (the main losers of the two inflationary crises of 1914–24 and 1929 onwards) and their search for defence. There was, however, a crucial difference between Italy and Germany: while in the former, pre-industrial elites turned to fascism as a substitute for a flawed liberalism and backward economy, in the latter, Nazism arose out of animosity to the corporatist structures of the advanced-capitalist Weimar Republic.

The structure and limits of stability

STABILITY IS A RELATIVE TERM. Even the briefest glance at politics, labor relations, and the international economy reveals that no bright sunlit years separated Dawes plan from Depression. How can one write of meaningful stabilization, some might object, in view of the Nazi takeover and the violence and war that lay ahead? I would disagree. A discernible equilibrium among economic interests, classes, and nations finally emerged after many false starts. A combination of coercion, payoffs, and exhaustion produced a broad political settlement. The equilibrium was certainly hostage to continuing American prosperity and the control of German national resentments. But the collapse of the structure does not mean that we must abandon study of the plans and foundation. They could serve for less rickety edifices.

It would also be foolish to deny the conservative political achievement of the late 1920s. After mid-decade – with the return of Poincaré, the election of President Hindenburg, Britain's return to gold and easy weathering of the General Strike, the silence of suppression in Italy – the passions of domestic conflict abated. Conferences between nations began to yield agreements and not merely endless wrangling. Locarno, Geneva, and The Hague produced only transient results, yet the public read in them a spirit different from the constant disputes before 1924. Statesmen now argued over incremental issues of more or less: would occupied German territory be evacuated sooner or later? How quickly would reparations be scaled down? How much of Europe's debt would Washington write off? Exhaustion and frustration attended such bargaining, but cataclysm was not invoked. A Western economy linchpinned upon American participation was functioning again. Savings were reconstituted, even though the great squandering of 1914–1918 cost at least a decade of development. For those who wrote or performed, a new republic of letters seemed at hand. Harry Kessler chatted at cafes about Proust and Valéry, flitting among the celebrities of a culture that embraced Berlin and Paris. When in October 1929 he noted the death of Stresemann, he also recalled that Diaghilev and Hofmannsthal had been taken in that same year: 1929 . . . '*wahrhaftig eine année terrible.*'[1]

Throughout this book our task has been to understand how the reconstruction of a conservative, 'bourgeois' equilibrium was achieved across the unparalleled violence, costs, and passions occasioned by World War I. This has sometimes meant departing from the events that were most conspicuous to stress conflicts that were more prosaic but often more decisive. Elections, for instance, usually made less difference than contemporaries, or historians, thought they did; the Ruhr invasion may have changed little that would not have otherwise occurred; such brief explosions as the Kapp Putsch or the Occupation of the Factories altered even less. It would be grossly inaccurate to say that these events signified nothing, for they signified a great deal in the sense of making manifest underlying tension and conflict. But they altered little, demolished few arrangements that were not already undermined. Their institutional legacy was slight.

This is not to claim that nothing had changed or that life in the late 1920s recreated *la belle époque*. In fact, just restoring the facade of stability required significant institutional changes. It is worth mustering them in summary review.

1   Whether under liberal or authoritarian auspices, group conflict was being resolved by what – with some reluctance – we have termed corporatist approaches. In other words, social priorities were increasingly decided not by traditional elites nor by the aggregation of voters' preferences. Elections resolved less than the day-to-day bargaining between industry and labor or among different business, agricultural, and party interests. If these groups failed to negotiate coherently or did not set clear priorities – the French situation in the mid-1920s – policy was becalmed in a Sargasso of ineffective parliamentarism.

The key to consensus or mere civic peace was either forcible suppression or constant brokerage. Any major organized interest could disrupt a modern economy or imperil social order, hence had to be silenced by duress or granted a minimum of demands. The need for brokerage switched the fulcrum of decision making from the legislature as such to ministries or new bureaucracies. During the war, ministries of munitions had developed into economic planning agencies. Under men of ambition and energy such as Rathenau, Loucheur, and Lloyd George, they extensively regulated the labor market and the allocation of scarce raw materials. They co-opted private business in this task, sharing public powers to increase the scope of regulation.[2] Although war-time controls were not retained, the 1920s did not simply revert to the degree of market freedom prevailing before 1914. The Weimar Inter-party Committee and Ministry of Labor, the Fascist Grand Council and Ministry of Corporations, in a lesser way the French Coal Agency and Ministry of Commerce (and if Herbert Hoover had had his way, the U.S. Department of Commerce) took on new political tasks. Parliamentary decision making never recovered fully from the eclipse into which it had fallen during the war. By 1925 governments collected and spent perhaps 20 to 25 percent of national income, in contrast to about half that share before the war. Parliaments did not work well in deciding how to levy this new burden. They worked even less well in trying to adjust the internal burdens of currency depreciation and revaluation. Traditional parties had taken form around earlier issues, and they proved too divided internally for this invidious allocation.

2   From 1918 until about 1924 the chief *political* objective for most bourgeois forces, parties or interest groups, amounted to exclusion of the socialists from any decisive influence on the state. Bourgeois resistance outran opposition to specific social democratic programs, which were generally moderate and reformist. Rather, the working-class parties represented a threat to what was seen as good order just by their new prominence and potential power. Later in the 1920s coalitions with social democrats did become acceptable, but only when social democracy acquiesced in the economic conceptions of its bourgeois partners. If the socialist left seriously presented its own economic objectives on the national level, alarmed conservatives fought back. They resorted either to decentralized but simultaneous boycotts of government bonds and money (as in France), or to concerted political opposition to taxation within the terms of coalition politics (as in Germany), or to extralegal coercion (as in Italy). In the face of such opposition, social democratic forces could not maintain positions of leadership or even parity at the national level. As Engels had foreseen shortly before his death in the 1890s, the socialists had wagered on legality while their opponents were prepared to indulge in violence. Turati recalled the prediction when his party majority foreswore reformism.[3] What more touching tribute to the nineteenth-century liberal belief in the *Rectsstaat* than that European social democrats should have been its most tenacious defenders!

3   A defining characteristic of the corporatist system that we have sought to analyze was the blurring of the distinction between political and economic power. Clout in the marketplace – especially the potential to paralyze an industrial economy – made for political influence. Consequently, economic bargaining became too crucial to be left to the private market, and state agencies stepped in as active mediators. Not surprisingly, labor questions became some of the most crucial tests of political stability. The economic issues were grave in their own right, but they also represented political disputes. The trade-union movements, more precisely the non-

Catholic federations, represented the arm of social democracy in the marketplace and were combated as such. If the union federations contributed to the political influence of social democracy, however, they also increased its liabilities during a period of economic recession and unemployment. Working-class forces that were defeated in the marketplace were usually administered blows in the political arena as well.

(a)   The first major setback after the war was the limitation of factory representation, such as was embodied in works councils. The council movement had promised a restructuring of capitalism from the work-place outward. Even after its messianic transformation failed to materialize in 1918–1919, factory representation still beckoned the working class. Factory representation was elective; it was responsive to immediate grievances; it offered a foothold on issues of management. But the 1920s brought one defeat after another for plant representation. In France the movement hardly got started; in Germany the councils were legally restricted in scope; in Italy they were conceded by Giolitti as a diversionary measure and were eliminated by Fascist union leaders – who could not capture their majorities – in concert with industrialists. Fascist union leaders in Italy and later in Germany did not abandon the idea of entrenching their own agents in the factory. But Mussolini (and later Hitler) had no more reason to sanction powerful plant delegates than had earlier leaders.

The last major phase of the Italian controversy developed during the spring of 1929 as Fascist union leaders, who had been set back by the 'unblocking' of their confederation the previous fall, initiated a new campaign to install factory trustees. Only the trustees, claimed the labor leaders, could prevent industrial managers from abusing the legislation that protected workers. Their campaign culminated in a syndicalist congress at Milan's Lyric Theatre at the end of June and early July, after which Mussolini intervened to restore discipline. In a series of extensive 'Intersyndical' conferences from July 6 to 12, the union leaders accused the industrialists of hostility to fascism and evading collective contracts. Mussolini recognized the validity of the charges, but refused to install the factory trustees. Instead he talked about the need for rationalization and technical improvements. Over a summer of debate the union leaders were forced to retreat, abandoning the claims to plant representation and becoming more receptive to schemes for rationalization that they had earlier characterized as exploitative. By its September meeting the Intersyndical Committee unanimously rejected the principle of factory delegates.[4]

(b)   The upshot was characteristic of the capitalist economies in general and not just the fascist system. If the 1920s began with the left pressing for democratization of the factory, it ended with the right calling for rationalization, Americanism, Fordism, the Bedeaux plan, or equivalent nostrums. All these systems claimed that labor could be utilized as another form of capital, subject to efficient analysis and organization. The trade conditions of the late 1920s, which impelled export competitions and cost cutting, made these schemes attractive. But the right also seized upon scientific management as a political weapon. Invocations of 'the organization of labor' really became appeals to factory autocracy in the name of industrial efficiency. Europeans of the left and right gave excess credit to scientific management as the motor of American prosperity and social harmony, because it fitted their respective ideological premises. The left decried a more subtle means of exploitation; businessmen on the right celebrated its efficiency. European industrialists in particular sought a system of labor control that did not entail just an outdated reassertion of factory paternalism. They could not resurrect the *Herr im Hause*, but the impartial engineer and technician of management could provide the same authority.[5]

(c)   While the right defeated worker delegation in the factory, it had to accept certain transformations as irreversible. Entrepreneurs in fascist Italy and Weimar Germany had to come to terms with some continuing trade-union organization and accept collective bargaining. No matter how hollow the forms of labor representation might become under fascism, businessmen could not simply eliminate them entirely. Of the three countries considered here, France alone lagged in the obligation to recognize collective bargaining, as did the United States outside Europe. Both nations, though, would enforce union contracts by the mid-1930s. The Matignon agreements and the Wagner Act imposed requirements on French and American entrepreneurs similar to those of the Stinnes-Legien and Palazzo Vidoni agreements. The reader will rightly object that only the external forms were alike, but that the thrust of democratic and fascist regulation was antithetical. Still, the form was important, for it signified that fascist as well as democratic regimes had to negotiate collective settlements and group bargains. Fascist labor delegates might be spurious representatives for Turin's metalworkers or the *braccianti* of Emilia, but they still retained some influence as a bureaucratic interest group in a political system that claimed to subsume and resolve all social conflict.

Nonfascist societies had to purchase the cooperation of the working class as well as compel it. The left won peripheral rewards in the re-arrangement of power in the 1920s. Social democrats retained important political control at the municipal and state level. They won important extensions of social insurance from conservative governments in Britain, France, and Germany. These countries also accepted foreign policies aimed at softening the outcome of 1918: a goal that the left had sought since the Armistice. The achievement was largely symbolic – the spirit of Geneva – but important nonetheless.

4   In the long run the major possibility for social consensus derived from a slow transformation of the principles of class division. Class consciousness was undergoing a double evolution. In the world of work, identification as proletarian or bourgeois was becoming less compelling than interest-group affiliation, less a principle of common action in the economic arena. Yet the world of production was only one reference point for social stratification and political loyalties, and one of diminishing importance throughout the twentieth century. While European socialism appealed to man as worker from its origins, the European Right sought to make social roles outside the sphere of production the major determinants of political allegiance. Insofar as party competition followed divisions in industry and commerce, the right

could not outbid the traditional left. On the other hand, the right could appeal to man insofar as he was concerned as consumer or as saver about the value of money, as a newspaper reader about the prestige of his nation-state, or even as a commuter about his rights to uninterrupted tram service. Work experiences did not become more unified; a few still commanded, many still followed orders. But mass transit, the cinema, radio, vacations, less formal dress made workplace identity less encompassing and facilitated new collective consciousness.

It was ironic that fascism should encourage this development. For fascism boasted that it had superseded the empty liberal abstractions of citizenship to regroup men as producers. Syndicalism and corporatism supposedly followed from the priority of *homo faber*. In fact, fascism and the right in general increasingly appealed to men outside the workplace. Fascist culture, political rallies, collective gymnastics, and Blackshirts were calculated to build a new unity. Whereas the left celebrated man's liberation and rationality in the world of work, the right appealed to audience-man. As the concept of the 'proletariat' had once replaced 'mob' or 'rabble,' so now, for social theorists, 'masses' replaced proletariat. By the latter 1920s, former socialists who had become discouraged at the attrition of their support discovered the same appeal to 'instinctual' rather than rational loyalties in a neosocialism that verged towards fascism.[6]

In retrospect, the left's stress on plant representation and work councils can be interpreted as a last effort to reinstall a producer's consciousness among the old working class. It was rebuffed, and the centrality of work experience as a political rallying point failed with it. It was fitting that observers pointed to Mussolini's *dopolavoro* and Hitler's *Kraft durch Freude* as characteristic contributions of fascist labour policy. Both were regimentations of leisure. Bureaucratically, the *dopolavoro* served as one more organization to pit against the fascist labour unions. But it also amounted to a major attempt to alter class perceptions and experiences.

[. . .] Two major sorts of tension arose to imperil and then undermine the equilibrium of the 1920s. The very corporatism that facilitated political stability simultaneously imposed fundamental dilemmas. One was the difficulty of reconciling the conflicting priorities of the international economy and domestic needs. The other involved the fate of those who were battered by the very corporate restructuring around them.

1   While the issues of inflation and revaluation encouraged corporatist organization, they also imposed limits to the degree of stability that might ultimately be achieved. Equilibrium remained hostage to the discrepancy between the demands of an international economy and the pressures for compromise between groups at home. [. . .]

2   The inflationary decade from 1914 to 1924 had brought together strong unions and big business in a price-wage spiral at the expense of the middle strata of society. Unfortunately, the deflationary *Konjunktur* thereafter did not reassure the middle strata. Income streams might be reconstituted, but the 80 percent write-off in currency values on the Continent was confirmed and not recovered. The movement toward the concentration of enterprises and the growth of large firms also struck at

middle-class independence. The number of independent proprietors declined. Even if income for these beleaguered middle-class groups remained steady, their sense of independence and patrimony must have been eroded.

Ultimately, the unorganized losers — whether old middle-class artisans, shop-keepers, small producers, marginal farmers burdened with debts, or the new middle class of clerical workers and office employees — felt the need for defense. Losers both in inflation and revaluation, their reaction was to attack the corporatist collaboration of labor and industry. Unable to organize in a cohesive economic phalanx, for they faced diverse markets, they could still organize politically. The results would combine hostility to liberalism and organized labor with a vague rhetorical anti-capitalism. Weimar Germany could not survive this new strain; France could — among other reasons, because the less developed corporatist organization of her society evoked a less intense right-radical response. The Radical Socialist constituency avoided fascism in the 1930s for the same reason that it had endured economic confusion in the 1920s: the continuing viability of economically archaic modes of livelihood. French democracy was to remain buffered by the society's proverbial reluctance to organize.[7]

If National Socialism is viewed in the perspective of Weimar's corporatism, it becomes evident how different it remained from Italian fascism. The difference takes us to the heart of the developments underway in the 1920s. At the beginning of the decade Italian fascism emerged as a new, coercive way of reestablishing a scaffolding for elites once the old one had corroded with mass suffrage and the war. It involved a coalition between traditional leadership groups and new middle-class allies as well as a young, urban bourgeois cadre mobilized since Intervention. Nazism grouped some of the same elements, but the mix was different, as were the reasons for its success. Before the seizure of power the role of traditional elites may well have been smaller in Nazism, the middle-class objectives more predominant. In the absence of more than a few local studies, estimates of social composition must remain risky. But statements about function are possible. In Italy fascism remedied a defective organization of middle-class and elite elements. If Italy had earlier developed a liberal corporatism to replace her antique parliamentary and party structure, fascism might well have appeared unnecessary for bourgeois defense. On the other hand, if Germany had not passed through the crucible of capitalist corporatism, Nazism might have seemed unnecessary for middle-class viability. Italian fascism substituted for prior organization in the political arena or marketplace; German Nazism arose in resentment against the organization that seemed to dominate.[8]

Nazism thus testified to the success of restoration in the 1920s. The elites of industry and land succeeded too well in the Weimar Republic: by engineering their restoration within a corporatist framework, they provoked a grass-roots rebellion against the capitalist marketplace — against all its liberal rules of the game as well as its economic outcomes. While Italian fascism testified to the preindustrial formation of the Italian elite, Nazism reflected what was simultaneously most retrograde and most modern: retrograde, because in Germany the guild usages of the pre-Napoleonic era — the stress on municipal independence, estatist divisions, elaborate self-enclosed associations — were carried forward to clutter up the twentieth-century sociopolitical landscape; modern, because corporate capitalism and corporatist pluralism have increasingly prevailed as forms of social organization since the 1920s in all Western societies. Nazism tried to build off pre-industrial corporatism and annul the more recent. It ended by destroying the first and leaving the second largely unscathed. [. . .]

Notes

1   Harry Graf Kessler, *Aus den Tagebüchern 1918–1937* (Munich, 1965), 288.

2   See Paul A. C. Koistinen, 'The "Industrial-Military" Complex in Historical Perspective: World War I,' *Business History*, 41 (1967), 378–403; E. M. H. Lloyd, *Experiments in State Control at the War Office and the Ministry of Food* (London, 1924), 18–26, 259 ff.; W. Oualid and Charles Picquenard, *Salaires et tarifes, conventions collectives et grèves: La politique du Ministère de l'Armament et du Ministère du travail* (Paris, 1928); Gerd Hardach, 'Französische Rüstungspolitik 1914–1918,' in Heinrich August Winkler, ed., *Organisierter Kapitalismus. Voraussetzungen und Anfänge* (Göttingen, 1974), 101–116; Alberto Caracciolo, 'La crescita e la trasformazione della grande industria durante la prima guerra mondiale,' in Giorgio Fuà, ed., *Lo sviluppo economico in Italia* (Milan, 1969), 197–212; Luigi Einaudi, *La condotta economica e gli effetti sociali della guerra italiana* (Bari, 1933), 99–178.

3   Friedrich Engels, 'Introduction' [1895], to Karl Marx, *The Class Struggles in France, 1846 to 1850*, Karl Marx and Friedrich Engels, *Selected Works*, 2 vols.

4   Sessions of the Comitato Centrale Intersindacale in ACS, Rome: Carte Cianetti, B. 4; controversy followed in Piero Melograni, *Gli industriali e Mussolini. Rapporti tra Confindustria e fascismo dal 1919 al 1929* (Milan, 1972), 276–311.

5   For the European industrialists' exploitation of scientific management, see Charles Maier, 'Between Taylorism and Technocracy: European Ideologies and the Vision of Industrial Productivity in the 1920s,' *Journal of Contemporary History*, v. 2 (1970), 54–59, including further citations; also André Philip, *Le problème ouvrier aux états unis* (Paris, 1927), 39–87, for a social democratic evaluation; cf. Dzherman M. Gvishiani, *Organization and Management: A Sociological Analysis of Western Theories* (Moscow, 1972), 174 ff., for the latest specimen of a Russian interest beginning with Lenin. On the roots of Nazi labor policy in Weimar's entrepreneurial attitudes, see T. W. Mason, 'Zur Entstehung des Gesetzes zur Ordnung der nationalen Arbeit, vom 20. Januar 1934,' Bochum Symposium paper, June 1973.

6   Hendrik De Man, *Zur Psychologie des Sozialismus* (Jena, 1926), 137–57. Cf. Robert Michels, 'Der Aufstieg des Faschismus in Italien,' *Archiv für Sozialwissenschaft und Sozialpolitik*, 52 1 (1924), 71. [. . .] Recent approaches to the problem in: E. R. Tannenbaum, *The Fascist Experience: Italian Society and Culture* (New York, 1972); Gino Germani, 'Fascism and Class,' in S. J. Woolf, ed., *The Nature of Fascism* (New York 1969), 65–96; Renzo De Felice, *Le interpretazioni del fascismo* (Bari, 1972), 113–144.

7   Heinrich August Winkler, *Mittelstand, Demokratie und Nationalsozialismus* (Cologne, 1972), and Winkler, 'Extremismus der Mitte? Sozialgeschichtliche Aspekte der nazionalsozialistischen Machtergreifung,' *Vierteljahreshefte für Zeitgeschichte*, xx, 2 (1972), 175–191, for the best recent syntheses of the huge literature on Nazism and middle-class resentment. For a prediction that the French middle classes in the 1930s must provide a reservoir for fascism, see Leon Trotsky's *Whither France?* [1936] (New York, 1968), 12–24.

8   Cf. De Felice, *Le interpretazioni del fascismo*, 256–266, for an emphasis on German-Italian parallels in mobilizing the resentments of the *ceti medi*. For a resume of what studies exist on social composition of the Italian Fascist Party (which became more 'respectable' and upper-echelon between 1925 and 1928), see Renzo De Felice, *Mussolini il fascista*, vol. II, *L'organizzazione dello stato fascista, 1925–1929* (Turin, 1968), 188–192; and Adrian Lyttelton, *The Seizure of Power: Fascism in Italy 1919–1929* (London, 1973), 54–71, 303–305; the most recent study on Germany is Jeremy Noakes, *The Nazi Party in Lower Saxony 1921–1933* (London, 1971). Cf. William S. Allen, *The Nazi Seizure of Power: The Experience of a Small German Town* (Chicago, 1965) and the review of earlier literature in Seymour Martin Lipset, *Political Man* (New York, 1963), 127–151. Cf. Charles S. Maier, 'Strukturen kapitalistischer Stabilität in den zwanziger Jahren: Emmgenschaften und Defekte,' in Winkler, ed., *Organisierter Kapitalismus*, 206–208.

Chapter 10

Geoff Eley

FASCISM AS THE PRODUCT
OF 'CRISIS'

■ from **WHAT PRODUCES FASCISM: PRE-INDUSTRIAL
TRADITIONS OR A CRISIS OF THE CAPITALIST STATE?**, in his
From Unification to Nazism: Reinterpreting the German Past, London and New
York, 1992, pp. 256–8, 268–9, 271–4, 275–6

Geoff Eley has written extensively on the development of the German right since
unification (1871) and, more particularly, the transition from the authoritarian
structures of the Wilhelminian period to Nazism. He has also dealt with the continuities between the Wilhelminian radical nationalist organisations and the NSDAP.
In this excerpt Eley criticises the notion of a German special historical path
(*Sonderweg* – see Introduction). For him the emergence of Nazism was not simply
the result of the survival of pre-industrial social structures in Germany, but rather
the product of a twin crisis – of elite representation and of popular loyalty to the
state. Note Eley's critique of the 'middle-class' thesis; and his belief that fascism
cannot be properly understood in purely intellectual-ideological terms.

O NE OF THE COMMONEST EMPHASES in the literature is a kind of
deep historical perspective, which proceeds from the idea of German, and to
a lesser extent Italian, peculiarity when compared with the West. In this case the
possibility of fascism is linked to specific structures of political backwardness. These
are themselves identified with a distinctive version of the developmental process,
and are thought to be powerful impediments against a society's ultimate 'modernization'. This 'backwardness syndrome' is defined within a global conceptual
framework of the most general societal comparison. It stresses 'lateness' of industrialization and national unification and their complex interaction, predisposing
towards both a particular kind of economic structure and a far more interventionist
state. The divergence from 'Western' political development is usually expressed in
terms of the absence of a successful 'bourgeois revolution' on the assumed Anglo-
French model, an absence which facilitates the dominance after national unification
of an agrarian-industrial political bloc with strong authoritarian and anti-democratic

traditions. The failure to uproot such 'pre-industrial traditions' is thought to have obstructed the formation of a liberal-democratic polity, and in general this is taken to explain the frailty of the national liberal traditions, and their inability to withstand the strains of a serious crisis. In recent social science this perspective stems from (amongst others) Barrington Moore, Alexander Gerschenkron and the discussions sponsored by the SSRC Committee on Comparative Politics. In contemporary Marxism it has drawn new impetus from discussion of the ideas of Antonio Gramsci. But in both cases the analysis may be traced back to the end of the last century.[1] It exercises a profound influence on how most historians tend to see the problem of fascism, though frequently at a distance, structuring the argument's underlying assumptions rather than being itself an object of discussion.

The argument was put in an extreme, discursive form by Ralf Dahrendorf in *Society and Democracy in Germany* (Garden City, NY, 1967; originally published in Germany, Munich 1965), which deeply influenced a generation of English-speaking students of German history. It has also functioned strategically in a large body of work dealing with the imperial period of German history (1871–1918), whose authors write very much with 1933 in mind. One of the latter, Jürgen Kocka, has recently reaffirmed Dahrendorf's argument in a particularly explicit way, which highlights the specific backwardness of German political culture.[2] Thus in Kocka's view 'German society was never truly a bourgeois society', because the 'bourgeois virtues' like individual responsibility, risk-taking, the rational settlement of differences, tolerance, and the pursuit of individual and collective freedoms were much 'less developed than in Western Europe and the USA'. Indeed, the chances of 'a liberal-democratic constitutional development' were blocked by a series of authoritarian obstacles. Kocka lists the great power of the Junkers in industrial Germany and the feudalizing tendencies in the big bourgeoisie; the extraordinary power of the bureaucracy and the army in a state that had never experienced a successful bourgeois revolution and which was unified from above; the social and political alliance of the rising bourgeoisie and the ever-resilient agrarian nobility against the sharply demarcated proletariat; the closely related anti-parliamentarian, anti-democratic, and anti-liberal alignment of large parts of the German ruling strata. In fact, the 'powerful persistence of pre-industrial, pre-capitalist traditions' pre-empted the legitimacy of the Weimar Republic and favoured the rise of right-wing extremism.

These arguments, which are conveniently summarized in Kocka's essay, are representative for the generation of German historians who entered intellectual maturity during the 1960s, in a fertile and (for the time) liberating intellectual encounter with the liberal social and political science then in its North American heyday. This is particularly true of those historians who have explicitly addressed the question of Nazism's longer-term origins, for whom figures like Karl Dietrich Bracher, Wolfgang Sauer, Ernst Fraenkel, Martin Broszat, M. Rainer Lepsius and Dahrendorf provided early intellectual examples.[3] Here, for instance, is Hans-Jürgen Puhle summarizing the argument in terms which correspond precisely to the ones used by Kocka. Fascism is to be explained by the specific characteristics of a society 'in which the consequences of delayed state-formation and delayed industrialization combined closely together with the effects of the absence of bourgeois revolution and the absence of parliamentarization to form the decisive brakes on political democratization and social emancipation'.[4]

It should be noted that this approach to the analysis of fascism is advanced as an explicit alternative to Marxist approaches, which for this purpose are reduced by these authors polemically and rather simplistically to a set of orthodox variations on themes bequeathed by the Comintern, in a way which ignores the contributions of (amongst others) Poulantzas, the Gramsci reception and Tim Mason.[5] Thus in a laboured polemic against the German new left Heinrich August Winkler gives primary place in his own explanation of Nazism to pre-industrial survivals, which in other (healthier) societies had been swept away. This was the factor which explained 'why certain capitalist societies became fascist and others not'.[6] Or, as Kocka puts it, adapting Max Horkheimer's famous saying: 'Whoever does not want to talk about pre-industrial, pre-capitalist and pre-bourgeois traditions should keep quiet about fascism'.[7]

[. . .]

[D]espite the over-representation of the petty bourgeoisie, fascist parties were always more eclectic in their social recruitment than much of the literature might lead us to suppose. Two observations in particular might be made. On the one hand, peasants proved especially important to a fascist party's ultimate prospects, because the transition from ideological sect to mass movement was achieved as much in the countryside as the towns. This was true of both Italy (1920–1) and Germany (1928–32). Conversely, some of the smaller fascist movements owed their weakness to the country population's relative immunity to their appeals. This applied both to Norway and Sweden, where farmers kept to the established framework of agrarian-labour co-operation, and to Finland, where neither the Lapua movement (1929–32) nor its successor the IKL (Isänmaallinen Kansanliike – Patriotic National Movement) (1932–44) could break the hold of the Agrarian Union and Coalition Party on the smaller farmers.[8] But, on the other hand, it is also clear that many fascist panics acquired significant working-class support. The best example is the Nazi Party itself, with its 26.3 per cent workers in 1930 and 32.5 per cent in 1933. But though higher than the working-class membership of the Italian Fascist Party (15.4 per cent in 1921), this was by no means exceptional. Both Miklós Lackó and György Ránki show that the Hungarian Arrow Cross won much support from workers, in both the more proletarian districts of Budapest and the industrial areas of Nógrád, Veszprém and Komárom-Esztergom.[9]

There is a tendency in the literature to play down the importance of this working-class support in the interests of the 'petty-bourgeois thesis', especially in the German case, where the research is extensive. Certainly, we can admit that the Nazis made most progress amongst specific types of workers. Tim Mason lists 'the volatile youthful proletariat' in the big cities, who went straight from school to the dole, who lacked the socializing education of a trade union membership, and who provided many of the SA's rank-and-file support; the 'uniformed working class' in public employment, especially in the railways, post office and city services; and those in the small-business sector of provincial Germany, 'where the working-class movement had not been able to establish a stable and continuing presence'.[10] It seems clear that the Nazis failed to breach the historic strongholds of the labour movement – the urban industrial settings that contained the 8 million or so wage-earners who voted habitually for the SPD and KPD – and had to be content with those categories of workers the left had failed (or neglected) to organize.

Yet this was surely significant enough. Though not a sufficient basis for contesting the left's core support, it deprived the latter of a necessary larger constituency. As Mason points out, between 1928 and July 1932 the combined popular vote of the SPD and KPD fell from 40.4 per cent to 35.9 per cent, and it was progressively unclear how they were to break through the 'sociological, ideological, religious and, not least, sex barriers' that defined the 'historic' working class in Germany. Mason suggests, in fact, that under the conditions of economic crisis after 1929 these barriers were virtually impassable. By eliminating the chances for either reformist legislation or effective trade union economism, the depression 'robbed the working-class movement of its anticipatory, future-directed role for the working class in general', and 'to the degree that industry and trade shrank, the potential constituency of the workers' parties stagnated'. The effect, Mason concludes, was a disastrous 'narrowing of the political arena of the working class movement'.[11]

[. . .]

It is time to draw some of these threads together. My comments have clearly been concerned mainly with the strong German and Italian cases, with occasional reference to fascist movements elsewhere. I have also [. . .] confined myself to a particular aspect of the overall problem, namely the 'coming to power' of indigenously generated fascist movements, rather than the less compelling examples of the smaller imitative or client movements, or the dynamics of established fascist regimes. In so doing I suggested that the specificity of the fascist movements resided in a particular capacity for broadly based popular mobilization – a distinctive ideology or style of politics, as the preceding paragraph puts it. Fascism is more extreme in every way. It registered a qualitative departure from previous conservative practice, substituting corporatist notions of social place for older hierarchical ones, and ideas of race community for those of clerical, aristocratic and bureaucratic authority. These and other aspects of fascist ideology are intimately linked to its broadly based popular appeal. Fascism is an aggressively plebeian movement, espousing a crude and violent egalitarianism. Above all, fascism stands for activism and popular mobilization, embracing everything from para-military display, street-fighting and straightforward terror, to more conventional forms of political activity, new propagandist forms and a general invasion of the cultural sphere. It is negatively defined against liberalism, social democracy and communism, or any creed which seems to elevate difference, division and conflict over the essential unity of the race-people as the organizing principle of political life.

At the same time, fascism was not a universal phenomenon, and appeared in strength only in a specific range of societies. In explaining this variation there are two main emphases. One is the deep historical perspective discussed in relation to Jürgen Kocka. At some level of explanation the structural factors stressed by the latter are clearly important and might be summarized as follows: accelerated capitalist transformation, in a dual context of simultaneous national state formation and heightened competition in the imperialist world economy; the coexistence in a highly advanced capitalist economy of large 'traditional' sectors, including a small-holding peasantry and an industrial-trading petty bourgeoisie, 'deeply marked by the contradictions of capitalist development';[12] and, finally the emergence of a precocious socialist movement publicly committed to a revolutionary programme. This complex over-determination (the 'contemporaneity of the uncontemporary', or 'uneven and combined development') characterized both German and Italian history before the First World War, articulated through the interpenetration of national and social problems. Most of the primary analytical traditions share some version of this framework (for example, the political science literature on state formation and the related theories of developmental crises, the particular works of Gershenkron and Barrington Moore, and most of the analogous literature within Marxism).

However, German historians have given this structural argument an additional formulation, which is far more problematic. Evaluating German development (or 'misdevelopment', as they call it) by an external and linear model of 'modernization', which postulates an ultimate complementarity between economic growth and political democratization (which in Germany, for peculiar reasons, was obstructed), such historians stress the dominance in German public life of 'pre-industrial' ideological traditions. The absence of a liberal political culture is thought to have permitted the survival of traditional authoritarian mentalities which enjoyed strong institutional power bases, and which could then be radicalized under the future circumstances of an economic or political crisis. Thus a 'reactionary protest potential' is created.[13] Fascism draws its support either directly from 'traditional social strata', or from newer strata (like white-collar employees) supposedly beholden to 'traditional' ideas. This essentially is Jürgen Kocka's argument.

Though not incompatible with a modified version of the above, the second approach stresses the immediate circumstances under which the fascists came to power. Here we need to mention the impact of the First World War, the nature of the postwar crisis in the European revolutionary conjuncture of 1917–23, the unprecedented gains of the left (both reformist and revolutionary), and the collapse of parliamentary institutions. Together these brought a fundamental crisis in the unity and popular credibility of the dominant classes, which opened the space for radical speculations. Here again, although one was the major defeated party and the other a nominal victor in the First World War, the German and Italian experiences were remarkably similar in these respects. In both cases the radical right defined itself against the double experience of thwarted imperialist ambitions and domestic political retreat, each feeding the other. In both cases the postwar situation was dominated by the public accommodation of labour, whose political and trade union aspirations appeared to be in the ascendant: trade unions acquired a new corporative legitimacy; socialists attained a commanding presence in large areas of local government; the national leaderships of the SPD and PSI occupied the centre of the political stage; and substantial movements to their left (first syndicalist and then communist) added an element of popular insurgency. In both cases, too, liberal or parliamentary methods of political containment were shown to have exhausted their potential, guaranteeing neither the political representation of the dominant classes, nor the mobilization of popular consent. In such circumstances fascism successfully presented itself as a radical populist solution.

In other words, fascism prospered under conditions of general political crisis, in societies which were already dynamically capitalist (or at least, which possessed a dynamic capitalist sector), but where the state proved incapable of dispatching its organizing functions for the maintenance of social cohesion. The political unity of the dominant classes and their major economic fractions could no longer be organized successfully within the existing forms of parliamentary representation and party government. Simultaneously the popular legitimacy of the same institutional framework also went into crisis. This way of formulating the problem – as the intersection of twin crises, a crisis of representation and a crisis of hegemony or popular consent – derives from the work of Nicos Poulantzas and its subsequent reworking through the extensive and continuing reception of Antonio Gramsci's ideas into the English language.

[. . .]

The problem of defining fascism is therefore not exhausted by describing its ideology, even in the expanded sense of the latter intimated above. Fascism was not just a particular style of politics, it was also inscribed in a specific combination of political conditions (themselves the structured, mediate effect of complex socioeconomic determinations), namely the kind of dual crisis of the state just referred to. Now, that kind of crisis is normally associated with the Great Depression after 1929, but the postwar crisis of political order between 1917 and 1923 was equally important. The global ideological context of the Bolshevik Revolution and its international political legacy gave enormous impetus to the radicalization of the right, and the more vigorous fascist movements generally arose in societies which experienced serious left-wing insurgencies after 1917–18.

[. . .]

Fascism may be best understood, therefore, as primarily a counter-revolutionary ideological project, constituting a new kind of popular coalition, in the specific circumstances of an interwar crisis. As such it provided the motivational impetus for specific categories of radicalized political actors in the immediate aftermath of the First World War, embittered by national humiliation, enraged by the advance of the left. As working-class insurgency defined the capacities of the existing liberal politics to achieve the necessary stabilization, this radical-nationalist cadre became an important pole of attraction for larger circles of the dominant classes and others who felt threatened by the reigning social turbulence. In Italy, where the socialist movement was generally further to the left than in Germany, and where no equivalent of the SPD functioned as a vital factor of order, this process of right-wing concentration around the redemptive potential of a radical-nationalist anti-socialist terror was far more advanced. But later, in the renewed but differently structured crisis of 1929–34, a recognizable pattern recurred. Elsewhere a similar scenario was scripted, but indifferently played out. Spain and possibly Austria were the closest examples of a similarly enacted fascist solution. Other countries certainly generated their own fascist cadres – in some cases very large (say, France, Finland, Hungary, Romania), in some quite small (say, Britain, Scandinavia). But the severity of the political crisis, and the resilience of established political forms, determined the broader attractions of the fascist ideology.

Notes

1   For discussions of these analytical traditions, see: D. Blackbourn and G. Eley, *Mythen deutscher Geschichtsschreibung*, and J. A. Davis (ed.), *Gramsci and Italy's Passive Revolution* (London, 1979). For valuable examples see: A. Gerschenkron, *Economic Backwardness in Historical Perspective* (Cambridge, 1962); B. Moore, *Social Origins of Dictatorship and Democracy* (Boston, Mass., 1966); C. Tilly (ed.), *The Formation of National States in Western Europe* (Princeton, NJ, 1975); R. Grew (ed.), *Crises of Political Development in Europe and the United States* (Princeton, NJ, 1978); and B. Hagtvet and S. Rokkan, 'The conditions of fascist victory', in S. U. Larsen, B. Hagtvet and J. P. Myklebust (eds), *Who Were the Fascists? Social Roots of European Fascism* (Bergen, 1980), 131–52, which links the 'violent breakdown of competitive mass polities' to a complex 'geoeconomic-geopolitical model', in which a country's early 'geopolitical position', its 'semi-peripheralization' in the world economy, and its manner of unification supply the vital preconditions for the emergence of fascism.

2   J. Kocka, 'Ursachen des Nationalsozialismus', *Am Politik und Zeitgeschichte*, 21 June 1980, 9–13.

3   K. D. Bracher, *The German Dictatorship: Origins, Structure and Consequences of National Socialism* (Harmondsworth, Middx, 1973; original German edition 1969); W. Sauer, 'National Socialism: totalitarianism or fascism?', *American Historical Review*, vol. 73 (1967), 404–24, and 'Das Problem des deutschen Nationalstaats', in H.-U. Wehler (ed.), *Moderne deutsche Sozialgeschichte* (Cologne, 1966), 407–36; E. Fraenkel, *The Dual State* (New York, 1941); M. Broszat, *Der Nationalsozialismus: Weltanschauung, Programm und Wirklichkeit* (Stuttgart, 1960); M. R. Lepsius, 'Parteiensystem und Sozialstruktur: Zum Problem der Demokratisierung der deutschen Gesellschaft', in G. A. Ritter (ed.), *Deutsche Parteien vor 1918* (Cologne, 1973), 56–80; R. Dahrendorf, *Society and Democracy in Germany* (London, 1967). By 'German historians' in this context I mean historians in West Germany. It is hard to say exactly how broad this generational experience was, partly because the ideological fronts have changed again since the early 1970s, leaving the most self-conscious exponents of avowedly 'social-scientific' history (e.g. as represented in the controlling group of the journal *Geschichte und Gesellschaft*) feeling relatively isolated within the West German historical profession as a whole. But for a fairly representative example of literature and authors at the height of the earlier liberalizing trend (several of the contributors have since moved quite markedly to the right), see M. Stürmer (ed.), *Das kaiserliche Deutschland. Politik und Gesellschaft 1870–1918* (Düsseldorf, 1970).

4   H.-J. Puhle, *Von der Agrarkrise zum Präfaschismus* (Wiesbaden, 1972), 53. The constipated nature of this sentence is an accurate (even benevolent) reflection of the original German.

5   The literature on Gramsci is now enormous. Among the most useful discussions of what he had to say about fascism in particular are the following: A. Davidson, *Antonio Gramsci: Towards an Intellectual Biography* (London, 1977), 185–201; W. L. Adamson, *Hegemony and Revolution. Antonio Gramsci's Political and Cultural Theory* (Berkeley, Calif., 1980), 71–101; C. Buci-Glucksmann, *Gramsci and the State* (London, 1980), 295–324; P. Spriano, *Antonio Gramsci and the Party: The Prison Years* (London, 1979); Davis (ed.), *Gramsci and Italy's Passive Revolution*. For the work of Tim Mason the following are most important: 'The primacy of politics –

politics and economics in National Socialist Germany', in S. J. Woolf (ed.), *European Fascism* and *The Nature of Fascism* (London, 1968), 165–95; *Sozialpolitik im Dritten Reich* (Cologne, 1977); 'Zur Entstehung des Gesetzes zur Ordnung der nationalen Arbeit vom 20. Januar 1934: Ein Versuch über das Verhältnis "archaischer" und "moderner" Momente in der neuesten deutschen Geschichte', in H. Mommsen, D. Petzina and B. Weisbrod (eds), *Industrielles System und politische Entwicklung in der Weimarer Republik* (Düsseldorf, 1974), 322–51; 'Intention and explanation: a current controversy about the interpretation of National Socialism', in G. Hirschfeld and L. Kettenacker (eds), *Der 'Führerstaat': Mythos und Realität* (Stuttgart, 1981), 21–42; 'Open questions on Nazism', in R. Samuel (ed.), *People's History and Socialist Theory* (London, 1981), 205–10.

6   H. A. Winkler, 'Die "neue Linke" und der Faschismus: Zur Kritik neomarxistischer Theorien über den Nationalsozialismus', in H. A. Winkler, *Revolution, Staat, Faschismus. Zur Revision des Historischen Materialismus* (Göttingen, 1978), p. 116, and esp. pp. 74–83. Winkler's essay 'German society, Hitler and the illusion of restoration, 1930–33', in Mosse (ed.), *International Fascism,* 143–60, puts a similar point of view.

7   Kocka, 'Ursachen des Nationalsozialismus', 11. For exactly similar arguments, see Puhle, *Von der Agrarkrise,* 53, and H.-U. Wehler, *Das deutsche Kaiserreich 1871–1918* (Göttingen, 1973), 238 ff., 226.

8   For discussions of agrarian fascism in Italy and Germany, see J. Baglieri, 'Italian Fascism and the crisis of liberal hegemony, 1901–1922', and N. Passchier, 'The electoral geography of the Nazi landslide', in Larsen, Hagtvet and Myklebust (eds), *Who Were the Fascists?,* 327 ff., 283 ff. The Scandinavian essays in the same volume are especially useful and show how illuminating the comparison with smaller and more marginal fascisms can be. For Norway: J. P. Myklebust and B. Hagtvet, 'Regional contrasts in the membership base of the *Nasjonal Samling*'; H. Hendriksen, 'Agrarian fascism in eastern and western Norway: a comparison'; S. S. Nilson, 'Who voted for Quisling?' For Sweden: B. Hagtvet, 'On the fringe: Swedish fascism 1920–45'. For Finland: R. Alapuro, 'Mass support for fascism in Finland'; R. E. Heinonen, 'From people's movement to minor party: the People's Patriotic Movement (IKL) in Finland 1932–1944'. See Larsen, Hagtvet and Myklebust (eds), *Who Were the Fascists?,* 621–50, 651–6, 657–66, 735–8, 678–84, 689 ff.

9   Figures for Germany and Italy are taken from S. Payne, *Fascism. Comparison and Definition* (Madison, Wis., 1980), 60 f. An additional 23.4 per cent could be considered in the Italian case, accounting for agricultural labourers. For Hungary, see M. Lackó, 'The social roots of Hungarian fascism: the Arrow Cross', and G. Ránki, 'The Fascist vote in Budapest in 1939', in Larsen, Hagtvet and Myklebust (eds), *Who Were the Fascists?,* 395–400, 401–16.

10   T. Mason, 'National Socialism and the working class, 1925–May 1933', *New German Critique,* no. 11 (Spring 1977), 60–9.

11   ibid., 59, 65.

12   R. Fraser, 'The Spanish Civil War', in Samuel (ed.), *People's History and Socialist Theory,* 197.

13   J. Kocka, *White Collar Workers in America 1890–1940. A Social-Political History in International Perspective* (London, 1980), 252.

Chapter 11

Roger Griffin

PRE-CONDITIONS FOR FASCISM'S SUCCESS

■ from *THE NATURE OF FASCISM*, London and New York, 1993b, pp. 208–12

In this first excerpt from *The Nature of Fascism* Griffin discusses the necessary preconditions for fascism's socio-political success. The existence of a native tradition of ultra-nationalism and/or foreign models for imitation, of a relatively developed but structurally weak liberal political culture, of a limited consensus to democracy and liberalism, of adequate 'political space' for a novel radical phenomenon such as fascism, and finally of pure luck – all are considered as crucial in creating a favourable conjuncture for fascism's victory. These conditions, Griffin argues, help us understand why fascism succeeded in Italy and Germany but not in 'stable pluralistic societies' such as Britain and France.

Socio-political determinants of fascism's success

(a) The presence either of native currents of ultra-nationalism, or of fascist 'role models' to build on

FASCIST POLITICAL MYTH is unable to become a nucleus of extra-systemic political energies in a particular country unless the forces of secularism and pluralism have already taken root there, and given rise to either (i) currents of non-fascist ultra-nationalism which palingenetic mythopoeia can turn into components of a revolutionary ideology, or (ii) indigenous or foreign examples of fascism to draw on.

Negative corroboration of this principle is provided by interwar Japan. Here secularization had been inadequate to allow a *radically* palingenetic myth to emerge, with the result that the powerful currents of ultra-right myth which surfaced as a result of the nation's profound structural crisis generally flowed in neo-conservative channels. Further negative corroboration is implied in twentieth-century Latin America, demonstrating how rare it is for populist right-wing energies, even when abundant, to take an outright fascist form, unless elaborate schemes of decadence and rebirth have become as well established as an integral part of the cultural and intellectual tradition as they were in *fin-de-siècle* Europe. For example, in Paraguay, which lacked a proto-fascist sub-culture, such energies found an outlet in the political Catholicism of the *Febreristas* rather than in fascism proper, while the Peruvian *Apristas* never aspired consistently to become the kernel of a 'new order'. Brazil, however, had seemingly been through enough of its own 'revolt against positivism' to lay the socio-cultural foundations necessary for Salgado's Integralism to take off.*

Positive confirmation of this pattern can be seen in the fact that all the most significant examples of original fascist movements which we have encountered (for example in Italy, Germany, Romania, Finland, Brazil, South Africa) emerged when genuinely palingenetic political aspirations were able to legitimate themselves by invoking components of indigenous populist ultra-nationalism, so that with hindsight the latter can be seen to have prepared the ground for the fascist formulations.

An important basis on which some interwar fascists could build was the presence of a native tradition of pre-1914 proto-fascism, for example national syndicalism in Italy, currents of *völkisch* thought in Germany, the revolutionary syndicalist wing of the *Action Française* in France, Afrikaner nationalism in South Africa. In the same way, post-war fascists were able to draw on any national variants of fascism which flourished before 1945 ('nostalgic fascism'). Another important potential source of fascist mythopoeia has been the existence of 'ready-made' foreign examples on which to model the ideological programme, organization, style and tactics of a local variant. In the interwar period up to 1933 these were predominantly Fascism (for example in Britain, Brazil) and thereafter Nazism (for example in South Africa, Norway).

Since 1945, while such interwar movements as the Iron Guard, *Rex* and the Falange have sometimes been lionized in fascist publicism, it is Nazism which has proved to be the most important source of mimetic fascism. [. . .] [W]hat results in such cases can vary considerably from slavish imitation to creative adaptation. The post-war period has also demonstrated that ideologues are far from being trapped in the past and have been able to create new variants of palingenetic ultra-nationalism. At the same time it has underlined the fact that the mere existence of a nucleus of fervent fascist ideologues and activists is far from sufficient to create a revolutionary movement of any significance.

(b) Adequate political space in a 'modern' society undergoing a structural crisis

Because fascism is literally unthinkable where what (from a Euro-centric point of view) are seen as 'modern' forces of populist politics and nationalism are weak, it cannot emerge wherever 'pre-modern' political systems are largely intact (for example traditional or absolutist societies unaffected by liberalization). Even in societies where secularization and democratization have had an impact, and pockets of fascist myth have formed, they can only become the nuclei of significant political forces when the myth can evoke a credible and desirable alternative order to sectors of the general public at large. A precondition for this is a major structural dysfunction at the heart of the existing system, whether owing to the complex strains of 'modernization' (as in interwar Brazil), or to the acute socio-economic and political tensions arising from war (as in Europe after 1918), or economic collapse (for example in Europe after 1929). A negative corroboration of this is the numerical insignificance and marginal impact of those theorists and activists who make up fascism's natural constituency in stable pluralistic (or 'Westernized') societies.

However, even such a conjuncture of factors will not be enough to generate a powerful fascist *movement* if it is precluded adequate space by other political forces. This is illustrated by the case of interwar Bulgaria, which in the early 1920s hosted a mass agrarian movement under Stamboliisky and a potent military and monarchical ultra-right, while IMRO (Internal Macedonian Revolutionary Organization), the Macedonian separatist movement, developed a powerful Bulgarian irredentist faction. Hence, although the country was undergoing a severe structural crisis and had a vigorous *völkisch* subculture (two vital preconditions for the emergence of a native fascism) potential recruits for fascism either as a populist or a cadre force tended to be already 'catered for', and such a force was in any case denied room in which to thrive. As a result native fascist movements, such as the mimetic Nazi group led by Tzankov, got nowhere, especially after Boris III tightened his grip on power in the early 1930s by installing an authoritarian (and superficially fascistized) regime from above (see Fischer-Galati, 1980; Groueff, 1987). The imposition of state communism in 1944 completed the picture: fascism had been systematically denied political *Lebensraum*. Authoritarian regimes based on military, monarchical, personal or presidential dictatorship have all proved equally lethal to fascism's micro-climate (as would be one based on religious fundamentalism).

On the other hand, there were a number of structurally weak liberal democracies in the interwar period (for example in Spain, Romania, Brazil, Hungary, Latvia, Estonia) where a contest for hegemony took place between the palingenetic and non-palingenetic ultra-right. In these cases fascism had the space to develop a substantial following, but lost out to anti-fascist authoritarianism, even if the fundamental antagonism between them was camouflaged to the untrained eye because the regimes which eventually took over adopted fascist trappings (thereby becoming what we have called 'para-fascist'), and in the case of Spain and, temporarily, in Romania, cynically co-opted the most powerful fascist movement into the state apparatus. There is no precedent for fascism prevailing over non-fascist authoritarian forces, a pattern confirmed by the fate of Japan's own prolific ultra-right under Imperial government.

In principle, then, fascism's *only* chance to take off without being crushed is in a relatively advanced liberal democracy undergoing a structural crisis without a strong non-fascist ultra-right poised to take over. Not only does the pluralism of such a society guarantee considerable political space in which competing ideological movements can develop, but liberalism's commitment to such values as materialism, internationalism, party politics and racial tolerance means that it can more easily be equated by ultra-nationalists with a corrupt, decadent system needing to be destroyed and replaced. However, even when a liberal democracy of this sort is riven by major structural tensions (as was generally the case in interwar Europe), this will only become a nomic crisis on a scale necessary for fascism to mount a serious assault on state power if another condition is fulfilled.

(c) An inadequate consensus on liberal values

So far we have argued that Fascism can only break out of its marginalised position as part of the 'lunatic' right if it operates in a secularizing and pluralist society struck by crisis. It will only stand a chance of carrying out a successful revolution in a liberal democracy caught in a particularly delicate stage of its evolution: mature enough institutionally to preclude the threat of a direct military or monarchical coup, yet too immature to be able to rely on a substantial consensus in the general population that liberal political procedures and the values which underpin them are the sole valid basis for a healthy society.

Latin America, Africa and the Far East provide abundant examples of fragile democracies being snuffed out by military dictatorships incapable of pursuing anything as sophisticated as a new order, and this pattern obtained in the interwar period in the Iberian peninsula and much of Eastern Europe. By contrast those European countries in the interwar period in which civic and political culture had over time become extensively humanized and liberalized (for example Britain, France, Sweden) were not seriously challenged by fascism because parliamentary government remained generally, though of course not universally, assumed to be the only legitimate force which could take the action necessary to deal with structural crises, no matter how severe.

Arguably there have only been four countries where fascism briefly grew into a significant opposition movement within a liberal democracy in this vulnerable transitional state: Italy (1918–22), Germany (1918–23, 1929–33), Finland (1929–33), and South Africa (1939–43). The examples of Finland and South Africa underline the fact that, to make matters worse for those who hanker after neat 'nomothetic' generalizations to apply to fascism, a conjuncture of the three preconditions which we have identified as necessary for it to become a credible revolutionary force is by no means 'sufficient' to ensure that it finally seizes power. It is here that a final factor comes into play.

(d) Favourable contingency

Clearly chance or (from the fascist point of view) 'destiny' plays a crucial role in enabling fascism to 'take off' in the first place and develop momentum as a revolutionary movement thereafter. A number of contingent factors relating to the internal dynamics of the fascist movement itself condition how credibly it is able to present itself as an alternative to the prevailing 'system' to potential followers such as the personal qualities of its leadership (especially the 'charismatic' appeal of any undisputed leader who emerges), the energy which it invests in attracting a popular following and its flair for propaganda and self-advertisement. Underlying all these factors, of course, is the most contingent factor of all: human psychology. The 'elective affinity' with fascism experienced by every individual involved in it, from the leader to the most lukewarm fellow traveller, is the product of unique psychological predispositions which are reducible to tendencies, patterns and types only at a high level of generality and tentativeness.

As for the external forces acting on fascist movements, the fate of the handful which have been strong enough to mount a direct challenge to state power ultimately depended on the way the state reacted to the threat it posed. As we have stressed, authoritarian regimes were ideally placed to crush or absorb the challenge. In the case of the four liberal democracies which we have identified as the most vulnerable to the fascist revolution, the outcome was decided by a host of chance factors, ranging from crucial decisions taken by key individuals to the vagaries of the electoral system. In the event both internal and external contingent factors conspired to close the door on fascism in Finland and South Africa, while in Italy and Germany they worked in conjunction with the other three preconditions which I have identified to allow it into the citadel of power. Though scores of other fascist movements have arisen where the first precondition was fulfilled, none of them have got as far because the others were not.

References

Fischer-Galati, S., 1980. Introduction to Part 4, in Larsen, S. U., Hagtvet, B., Myklebust, J. P. (eds), 1980. *Who Were the Fascists? Social Roots of European Fascism,* Universitetsforlaget, Bergen.

Groueff, S., 1987. *The Crown of Thorns. The Reign of King Boris III of Bulgaria 1918–43,* Madison, New York.

Editor's note

*   Integralism was started by Plinio Salgado and Gustavo Barroso and became a significant political force in Brazil in the 1930s. In 1937 the Estado Novo (New State) was created with a strong corporatist and anti-liberal physiognomy. The Integralist movement was suppressed the following year.

PART TWO

Fascist movements

Ideology and variations

■ Fascist ideology – the quest for the 'fascist minimum'

FOR MANY RESEARCHERS, talking of 'fascist ideology' amounts to a monumental contradiction in terms. Since the 1920s the official Comintern interpretation of Italian Fascism, and the outpouring of subsequent orthodox Marxist critiques of generic fascism, converged on a summary dismissal of fascism's autonomous ideological character and substance. In line with the early understandings of Mussolini's and Hitler's regimes as artificial façades concealing the unabashed victory of monopoly capitalism, postwar orthodox Marxist interpretations generally showed very little inclination to acknowledge any ideological originality in fascism – and even less interest in studying it as an intellectual category. In the immediate postwar period the revelation of the extent of the unprecedented brutality and atrocity inflicted upon Europe by the Nazi genocidal factory induced a mood of demonisation, of approaching the fascist experience as an exceptional case of human pathology that could only be understood on its own terms and in direct reference to the invidious personal obsessions of the fascist leaders. Hermann Rauschning's (1939, 1940) analysis of Nazism as a 'revolution of nihilism' divulged the sense of acute uneasiness which postwar historians experienced in their efforts to conceptualise the horrifying record of fascist aggression and war. But it also reflected a belief that fascism did not possess an ideology in the conventional sense of the word – what took place under fascist rule resulted from a terminal breakdown of even the most fundamental values of human life and dignity in a paranoid quest for a self-destructive chimera. Such a reading received further intellectual ammunition from the contributions of psycho-analytical studies of fascism, ranging from Wilhelm Reich's (1946) complex analysis of the links between sexual repression and mass mentality to a host of publications attempting to decipher Hitler's monomaniac fixations on the basis of his psychological development and personal experiences.

In this sense, the efforts of a – small – number of liberal western historians in the 1960s to engage with the question of fascism's ideological essence was both ground-breaking and daring. Eugen Weber (1964) and Ernst Nolte (1965) endeavoured to extricate fascism from the status of an exceptional historic phenomenon and incorporate it into the analysis of the radical intellectual traditions of Europe in the nineteenth and twentieth centuries. Nolte (12) examined fascism as a phenomenon specific to the interwar period, closely related to the experience of the First World War and the Bolshevik revolution of 1917 in Russia. This was, however, just the beginning. In the following three decades a growing number of commentators demonstrated a determination to take fascism's ideological substance more seriously, to analyse it comparatively and produce increasingly elaborate (if far from convergent) models for an understanding of fascism as an autonomous ideological phenomenon. In 1983 N. O'Sullivan (13) identified 'core' elements in generic fascism which he collated in a typology of fascist ideology. In the 1990s Roger Griffin used the term 'new consensus' to highlight the relative convergence of the works of highly distinguished historians of fascism – like Zeev Sternhell, Juan Linz, A. James Gregor, Stanley Payne, Roger Eatwell and himself – on a mould of interpreting fascism as a unique ideological articulation of radical revolutionary nationalism, 'third way' politics and holistic social organisation. This body of interpretations seemed to accept that fascism did possess a coherent ideological core, and one that linked it to pre-existing dissident radical intellectual traditions in Europe, thus departing from the earlier understandings of the fascist experience as an aberration of European historical development in a value-free, nihilistic and essentially reactionary direction. Methodologically, the disciples of the 'new consensus' referred to a fascist 'ideological minimum' – a list of features that distinguish fascism as an intellectual phenomenon from other kindred ideological strands. Z. Sternhell (14) linked fascism's intellectual origins to a revision of Marxism that started in France in the late nineteenth century and was first completed in Italy towards the end of the First World War. R. Griffin (15) identified the ideological nucleus of fascism in a unique synthesis of ultra-nationalism, populism and the myth of rebirth (*palingenesis*). S. Payne (16) constructed a list of fascism's core ideological and stylistic/ organisational features, stressing that fascism's specificity lies in their unique combination, not in their individual originality. Therefore, the over-representation of this model of analysis in this section originates from two dissimilar considerations: first, that the interpretations produced by the 'new consensus' constitute the most sophisticated defence of the existence of a congruous 'fascist ideology' and possess invaluable heuristic value; second, that they differ in their individual prescriptions as to how we should understand the gist of this 'fascist ideology'.

'New consensus', however, does not signify overall consensus. The elaboration of an ideal-type of generic fascist ideology by the disciples of the 'new consensus' has not – as yet – resulted in a palpable general reorientation of fascist studies towards an assessment of the generic ideological aspects of interwar fascism. Opposition to the study of fascism as a meaningful ideological category has remained largely unaffected by the efforts of historians since the 1960s to salvage fascism from the disrepute of constituting action without vision and substance. Two main frames of analysis have questioned the validity of the approach that the 'new consensus' has attempted to systematise. The first reverts to the initial postwar rebuff of fascism's alleged ideological foundations. The calls of Roberto Vivarelli (1991) that fascism should be studied only through its actions suggests that any effort to identify some sort of ideological vision and then employ it as a matrix for interpreting fascism's evolution and policy-making is methodologically sterile and flawed. The second frame of analysis does not necessarily reject the existence of some ideological substance in fascism, in Germany, Italy or elsewhere. The objection in this case refers to the *connection between ideas and action*, that is, ideology and policy. In the Introduction (pp. 12–14) I briefly reviewed the 'intentionalist–stucturalist' controversy, which has dominated historiography on Nazism since the 1960s but has also made some modest inroads into the literature on Italian Fascism. While the intentionalists insist that awareness of the ideological visions and programmes of the fascist leaderships is an invaluable tool for understanding the unfolding of fascist actions and the reasons behind key choices of the leaderships, structuralists (or functionalists) perceive these actions as contingent on a series of exogenous factors which nullify the influence of ideological motives and intentions on decision-making (see, for example, Mommsen 1997). In other words, structuralists claim that the ideology–action problem in fascism is far more complicated than the intentionalist linear interpretation of how vision underpinned decisions. With all these caveats, the debate about the role of fascist ideology in the process of unravelling the fascist 'conundrum' is more relevant and contentious than ever.

Chapter 12

Ernst Nolte

THE 'ERA OF FASCISM' AND THE UNIQUENESS OF FASCIST IDEOLOGY

■   from *THREE FACES OF FASCISM*, New York and Toronto, 1969, pp. 18–19, 20–2, 40, 537, 539–40, 548–9

Albeit published in the 1960s, Ernst Nolte's *Three Faces of Fascism* remains one of the most accomplished studies of the ideological character and political history of fascism in interwar Europe. The following excerpt discusses three of Nolte's most significant theses in his understanding of fascism. The first pertains to the 'epocality' of fascism – the idea that the period between the two world wars may be legitimately called the 'era of fascism' in recognition of the novelty of this political phenomenon. The second concept refers to the importance of the 1917 Bolshevik revolution in understanding the rise of fascism in Europe – hence his dictum that 'without Marxism there is no fascism'. Finally, the last part of the excerpt discusses Nolte's view of fascism as a 'metapolitical phenomenon', an event whose understanding obligates a new framework of thought that departs from the conventional categories for analysing European history.

T O   I N Q U I R E   I N T O   T H E   N A T U R E   of the 'era of fascism,' then, means to add the specific problem of a still much-disputed term – the scholarly discussion of which has barely begun – to the overall difficulty which every periodization entails. On the other hand, it is obvious that the question of fascism cannot be separated from the question of its era, since no universally acknowledged and meaningful concept of the era between 1919 and 1945 exists. Even if the term 'fascism' is taken strictly as a name, that is, to describe an isolated phenomenon, the question remains of the extent to which events in Italy were *not* – in spite of their incalculable worldwide effect – epochal. Whichever way we look at it, the common nature of the inquiry into fascism and the era is inescapable, and it is our task to define the concepts and review the facts.

However, the order in which the thematic material is placed is governed by one helpful limitation. Even though fascism existed after 1945 and has continued to exist since that time, and even though it is still capable of arousing bitter conflicts, it cannot be said to have real significance as far as the image of the era is concerned unless the term be stripped almost entirely of its traditional connotation. Thus the very subject of this study precludes any reference to events of the present day.

Hand in hand with this limitation goes a very tangible advantage; for contemporary history, in so many respects at a disadvantage when compared with its older sisters, has at its disposal a virtually ready-made division of eras, enabling us to trace the course of fascism deductively.

To use the term 'era of the world wars'[1] and imply the period from 1914 to 1945 would certainly not be valid for all time; but seen from the present day, the dates of August 1, 1914, and May 8, 1945, represent such profound cleavages in history that their epoch-making character has never been denied. What is disputed (aside from how to divide the subsections) is the context into which the epoch is to be placed and the point in time at which the cataclysmic caesura represented by the outbreak of war caused the new constellations to mature and acquire their first self-awareness. The most important of these concepts imply an answer to the question, whether the chronological and formal criterion might not be augmented by a more meaningful one. It should be enough to enumerate three of the best-known of these concepts:

1   The era of the world wars forms part of an age of revolutions and profound social changes, an age of which the most visible starting point was the French revolution.[2]

2   The immediate roots of this era are to be found in the period of imperialism. It was during this time that all the conflicts developed which merely achieved their climax with the outbreak of war.[3]

3   It was not until 1917 that World War I ceased to be simply a conflict of national states. With the entry of the United States into the war and the Bolshevik revolution, the constellation became a universal one: a general state of civil war and the future splitting of the world into two are already discernible in outline.[4] [. . .]

There is no doubt that the year 1917 represented a cleavage which cut deep into its own time and far into the future. But it is equally certain that the two great powers whose emergence was marked by this cleavage soon withdrew to their own native ground. When the American people opted against Wilson in 1920 it chose two decades of a new isolationism; the skepticism Lenin felt toward the 'workers' aristocracy' of the West was soon confirmed. It turned out that the victory of bolshevism in Russia did not prevent its defeat on all the social battlefields of Europe, if it did not in fact actually cause it. Starting not later than 1923, the year of the failure of the last revolts in Germany, the Communist parties were operating everywhere more to the advantage of their enemies' cause than to their own. The Soviet Union became once more an unknown country on the periphery of the world, and Europe was once more the arena of world events. But was it likely that after that fearful interlude the participants should remain quite the same?

The war, the revolution, imperialism, the emergence of the Soviet Union and the United States, were not locally confined phenomena. Neither could a movement which came into being as an outcome of the war, a movement which fought revolution with revolutionary methods, which radicalized imperialism, and which saw in the Soviet Union (and in 'Americanism' too, although with less emphasis) the greatest of all threats, be called a locally confined phenomenon, no matter how many differences might be attributable to it due to local conditions. This movement would have found its place in the Europe of the postwar period even if Mussolini and Hitler had never lived. No term other than 'fascism' has ever been seriously proposed for it. This word has the drawback of being simultaneously name and concept; it has the advantage of being without concrete content and of not, like German National Socialism, implying an unjustifiable claim. It is not the business of scholarly investigation to invent a new term just because the one commonly used cannot satisfy all requirements.

If, then, fascism can be defined as a new reality which did not exist before World War I, or only in rudimentary form, the obvious next step is to declare it to be the characteristic political trend of an era in which, owing to the withdrawal of the two recently emerged 'flanking powers,' Europe can be regarded once more as the focal point of the world. Out of four principal powers in this Europe two, as we know, became fascist within ten years, and after ten more years a continent which had become almost totally fascist (or so, at least, it seemed) had torn the two 'flanking powers' from their isolation and challenged them to battle.

When a historian speaks of the 'era of the Counter Reformation' he does not imply that the Counter Reformation was the dominant force in all areas of the then known world and that it met with no resistance, nor is he obliged to believe that it contained the seeds of the future. He does not even have to regard it as 'necessary.' In order to describe a period marked by powerful religious elements he simply uses the religious phenomenon which, being central to this trend, represented its most novel and thus most typical manifestation. In the same way, if we are to name an era marked by political conflicts after the most novel phenomenon in the center of events, we cannot do otherwise than call the era of the world wars an era of fascism.

This definition of the era is not new, and so should not be surprising. At various times it has been used (explicitly or implicitly) by leading representatives of the most disparate parties.

At the peak of his reputation and independence during the years 1930 to 1935, Mussolini often said that fascist ideas were the ideas of the age and that within a few years the whole of Europe would be fascist. On all sides he descried, it seemed to him, 'fascist ferments of the political and spiritual renewal of the world';[5] he defined fascism as 'organized, concentrated, authoritarian democracy on a national basis,'[6] and did not hesitate to claim for it anything in the world that demanded a strengthening of state power and intervention in the economy.

[. . .]

Neither antiparliamentarianism nor anti-Semitism is a suitable criterion for the concept of fascism. It would be equally imprecise to define fascism as anti-communism, but it would be obviously misleading to use a definition which did not adequately stress, or even entirely omitted, this basic criterion. Nevertheless, the identifying conception must also be taken into account. Hence the following suggests itself:

FASCISM IS ANTI-MARXISM WHICH SEEKS TO DESTROY THE ENEMY BY THE EVOLVEMENT OF A RADICALLY OPPOSED AND YET RELATED IDEOLOGY AND BY THE USE OF ALMOST IDENTICAL AND YET TYPICALLY MODIFIED METHODS, ALWAYS, HOWEVER, WITHIN THE UNYIELDING FRAMEWORK OF NATIONAL SELF-ASSERTION AND AUTONOMY.[7]

This definition implies that without Marxism there is no fascism, that fascism is at the same time closer to and further from communism than is liberal anti-communism, that it necessarily shows at least an inclination toward a radical ideology, that fascism should never be said to exist in the absence of at least the rudiments of an organization and propaganda comparable to those of Marxism. It enables us to understand the extent to which there can be states of fascism: according to the evolution of the ideology and the predominance of one of its two chief components, the pseudosocialist or the elite – that is, race – element; according to the degree of determination in, and the more or less universal nature of, the will to destruction; and according to the energy of execution. The decisive factors, however, are starting point and direction, for this concept is a 'teleological' one, and even the most marked differentiation of stages does not do away with the unity of its essential nature.

Finally, this definition enables us to make concrete distinctions and identifications: neither the Pan-Germans nor Stoecker's Christian Socialists come under it; on the other hand, there is no reason to maintain that every opponent of Hitler in his party or in the other groups of the extreme Right was a non-Fascist.

[. . .]

Fascism has been defined on three levels. On the first level it was examined as an internal political phenomenon and described as 'anti-Marxism' seeking to destroy the enemy by the development of a radically opposed yet related ideology and the application of nearly identical, although typically transformed methods; always, however, within the unyielding framework of national self-assertion and autonomy. This definition is valid for all forms of fascism.[8]

The second definition, which describes fascism as the 'life-and-death struggle of the sovereign, martial, inwardly antagonistic group,' no longer looks at it as a manifestation within politics, but sees in it the natural foundation of politics itself brought to light and to self-consciousness. This definition could only be unequivocally demonstrated by the radical-fascist form and could be adequately illustrated within the context of this derivation.

On the third level – the least accessible and the most fundamental – fascism was termed 'resistance to transcendence.' This definition could be derived from fascism's oldest as well as its most recent forms: it describes fascism as a metapolitical phenomenon. It can be neither illustrated by historical details nor demonstrated by simple considerations. It requires a new departure in thought if it is not to remain a mere suggestion in the semiobscurity of approximate insight.

[. . .]

The term 'transcendence' has been chosen here to demonstrate the scientific intention behind the relating of philosophical and historical thematic material. Moreover, it seems more appropriate than any other to denote that uniform and yet intrinsically differing fundamental process of which such terms as 'faith' or 'emancipation' merely reveal certain aspects.

It is true, of course, that no philosophical agreement exists as to the interpretation of this term. 'Transcendence' is sometimes used to denote 'God' or 'ultimate reality,' and is thus placed in opposition to man even when it embraces him along with everything else and is to that extent not merely an object; the opposite of this transcendence is immanence, the sphere of the within-worldly and the nondivine – a sphere to which man is in thrall as long as he is unable to raise himself to transcendence by thought, prayer, or faith.

But it is from this theological interpretation of transcendence that we can derive that neutral structural concept which is to be the foundation of what follows. For if in the welter of questions and answers a common element exists on which all thinkers from Parmenides to Hegel agree, it is the distinction between those things which are partial and dependent on time and place and the 'One' ('existence,' 'nature,' 'God'), which contains none of the negative characteristics of finite being and which therefore alone completely fulfills the absolute meaning of existence: in other words, the distinction between a *finite* and an *eternal* existence. It is on this distinction that the whole emphasis rests. But there is an analogous distinction in man who with his highest capacity – that of thought – can reach out to eternal existence, although as a being among beings he is shackled to his finite environment. For thought alone can form the concept of the whole as distinct from all that exists and all that is individual.[9]

[. . .]

In summing up the following definitions may be given:

Theoretical transcendence may be taken to mean the reaching out of the mind beyond what exists and what can exist toward an absolute whole; in a broader sense this may be applied to all that goes beyond, that releases man from the confines of the everyday world and which, as an 'awareness of the horizon,' makes it possible for him to experience the world as a whole.

Practical transcendence can be taken to mean the social process, even its early stages, which continually widens human relationships, thereby rendering them in general more subtle and more abstract – the process which disengages the individual from traditional ties and increases the power of the group until it finally assails even the primordial forces of nature and history. However, since it is only possible to experience it as transcendence when it reaches its universal stage, the concept is usually limited to this stage. As a synonym the term 'abstraction of life' can be used, as against 'abstraction of thought' for theoretical transcendence.

A phenomenon will be called transcendental in which transcendence achieves dominant form, or which adopts a specific relationship to it. But (with an ambivalence already present in Kant) a method of observation will also be called transcendental when it seeks to uncover the transcendental nature of an object which in the case of a political phenomenon may be called 'metapolitical.' [. . .]

It has now become evident what fascism actually is. It is not that resistance to practical transcendence which is more or less common to all conservative movements. It was only when theoretical transcendence, from which that resistance originally emanated, was likewise denied that fascism made its appearance. Thus fascism is at the same time resistance to practical transcendence and struggle against theoretical transcendence. But this struggle must needs be concealed, since the original motivations can never be entirely dispensed with. And insofar as practical transcendence from its most superficial aspect is nothing but the possibility of concentration of power, fascism pursues its resistance to transcendence from within that transcendence and at times in the clear consciousness of a struggle for world hegemony. That is the transcendental expression of the sociological fact that fascism has at its command forces which are born of the emancipation process and then turn against their own origin. If it may be called the despair of the feudal section of bourgeois society for its traditions, and the bourgeois element's betrayal of its revolution, now it is clear what this tradition and this revolution actually are. Fascism represents the second and gravest crisis of liberal society, since it achieves power on its own soil, and in its radical form is the most complete and effective denial of that society.

It is precisely in this broadest of all perspectives that the observer cannot withhold from fascism that 'sympathy' of which we have spoken. This sympathy is directed not toward persons or deeds, but toward the perplexity underlying the colossal attempt to overcome that perplexity, which is the most universal characteristic of an era whose end cannot be foreseen. For transcendence, when properly understood, is infinitely remote from the harmlessness of safe 'cultural progress'; it is not the couch of the finite human being, but in some mysterious unity his throne and his cross.

Nevertheless, fascism as a metapolitical phenomenon still serves as a means of understanding the world today: only when liberal society, after steadfast and serious reflection, accepts practical transcendence as its own although no longer exclusive product; when theoretical transcendence escapes from its ancient political entanglements into genuine freedom; when Communist society looks at itself and its past with realistic but not cynical eyes and ceases to evade either one; when the love of individuality and barriers no longer assumes political form, and thought has become a friend of man – only then can man be said to have finally crossed the border into a postfascist era.

Notes

1   E.g., Ludwig Dehio, 'Deutschland und die Epoche der Weltkriege,' in *Deutschland und die Weltpolitik im 20. Jahrhundert* (Munich, 1955).
2   E.g., Waldemar Besson, 'Periodisierung, Zeitgeschichte,' in Fischer-Lexikon, Vol. XXIV, *Geschichte* (Frankfurt a.M., 1961).
3   E.g., Bans Herzfeld, *Die moderne Welt*, Vol. II (Braunschweig, 1960).
4   Hans Rothfels, 'Sinn und Aufgabe der Zeitgeschichte,' in *Zeitgeschichtliche Betrachtungen* (Göttingen, 1959).

5   *Opera Omnia di Benito Mussolini* (Florence, 1951), XXVI, 45.

6   *Ibid.*, XXIX, 2.

7   In its isolated form the definition lays no claim to originality. The basic paradox is already contained in the term 'conservative revolution.' Gustav Adolf Rein, in *Bonapartismus und Faschismus* (Göttingen, 1960), describes fascism as counter-revolution on the soil of revolution. The definition comes to life only within the framework of the study as a whole.

8   For the Action Française, however, only inasmuch as, in opposing the republic, it was combating the socialist revolution which allegedly was bound to arise out of the democratic soil.

9   The earliest classical example of this train of thought is Parmenides' poem with its basic idea of: 'For it is [truly only] the [nothingness] being' 'For the same [of identical limitless nature] is thought and being.' Closely linked with this is the definition of sensuality as 'unseeing eye' and 'tempestuous hearing,' as well as of ordinary men as 'twin heads' and 'undiscriminating rabble.' Parmenides completely ignores any possible connection between truth and opinion, thought and sensuality, and thus also history.

Chapter 13

Noel O'Sullivan

FIVE MAIN TENETS OF FASCIST IDEOLOGY

■ *FASCISM*, London, 1983, pp. 131–3, 134–6, 138–9, 149–50, 161–2, 167–71

Although Noel O'Sullivan's earlier work on fascism predates many major works on fascist ideology that appeared in the 1980s and 1990s, it does share with them an interpretation of fascism as a revolutionary 'third-way' discourse between (or beyond) capitalism and socialism. O'Sullivan rejects the notion that fascist ideology was a 'monstrous deviation' from the west's intellectual tradition; but he also identifies five major themes that he perceives as 'distinctly fascist' (corporatism, revolution, the leader principle, messianic faith, autarky). These themes underpinned, in his view, the specific fascist 'activist style of politics' – a novel style of social mobilisation and political behaviour that distinguished the fascist experience from the traditional western state.

IT HAS BEEN ARGUED THAT, far from being a monstrous deviation from the western political tradition, the fascist *Weltanschauung* stands in a direct line of continuity with it. To stress this continuity would be misleading, however, if it meant minimizing the importance of ideas which may properly be regarded as distinctively fascist, in the sense that they figure more prominently within the fascist *Weltanschauung* than in any other form of activist ideology. It is for this reason that five ideas in particular must now be given more detailed consideration than they have so far received, even though they are not peculiar to fascist ideology but are part and parcel of the activist style of politics at large.

The first idea, which remains controversial down to the present day, is the fascist concept of the corporate state as a 'third way' between capitalism and socialism. The second is the fascist rejection of reason and stability in favour of a stress upon myth and dynamism which culminates in the ideal of permanent revolution. The third is the so-called leader principle. Although this principle is now a familiar ingredient in activist movements throughout the world, it was fascism which originally proclaimed it to be the key to the organizational structure of the movement regime with which the activist style of politics seeks to supersede the traditional western state ideal. The fourth idea is the messianic concept of a redemptive mission. The fifth, and last, idea is that of creating an autarkic (i.e. self-sufficient) state through a programme of world conquest. Blended into one great intellectual mish-mash, these five ideas provide the structure of the fascist *Weltanschauung*.

1 Corporatism

The most important claim made by fascism was that it alone could offer the creative prospect of a 'third way' between capitalism and socialism. Hitler, in *Mein Kampf*, spoke enthusiastically about the 'National Socialist corporative idea' as one which would eventually 'take the place of ruinous class warfare';[1] whilst Mussolini, in typically extravagant fashion, declared that 'the Corporative System is destined to become the civilization of the twentieth century'.[2] [. . .]

Corporatism in the fascist sense, by contrast, is a concept which is ultimately intelligible only within the all-embracing vision of an organic, spiritually unified and morally regenerated society. Within this context corporatism refers, more especially, to the various economic policies and institutions by which the union of employers and workers is to be brought about. What mainly characterizes these policies and institutions is an attempt to unite both groups by means which will imbue them with a desire for mutual self-sacrifice in the national interest. Fascists claim, more generally, that only the organic society created by these measures would offer true freedom, by which they mean a release from the petty, egoistic concerns of everyday life and an opportunity for total devotion to the nation and its leader.

This, at least, is true of Italian Fascism; the Nazi corporatist ideal was different, mainly because Nazi doctrine required that economic considerations should be completely subordinate to racial ones. As Werner Sombart made clear in his book *German Socialism* (1934), the ultimate aim was 'a total ordering of the German Volk', which must 'above all be uniform, born from a single spirit and extended from a single central point systematically over the entire social life'. In other words, the Nazi aim was to submerge all groups – peasants, workers and employers alike – in one racially pure organic society (*Volksgemeinschaft*). It was corporatism in this romantic, *völkisch* sense, rather than corporatism in the more economically rational sense in which Italian thinkers tend to present it, which accounts (for example) for such measures as the abolition of independent trade unions and their replacement by the Labour Front in the Law for the Organization of National Labour of 20 January 1934. The primary function of this reform, as of all other Nazi economic reforms, was the purely ideological one of fabricating a sense of emotional participation in the mythical Nazi racial community. Those who persisted in emphasizing the economic aspects of corporatism were either repudiated by the regime or – as in Gregor Strasser's case – murdered.

[. . .]

Italian corporatism, by contrast with the Nazi version, was generally confined to the economic sphere. For that reason, it has often been regarded as an altogether more constructive attempt to create a 'third way' between capitalism and socialism. Its *non-völkisch* emphasis on economic re-construction and state planning meant, in particular, that Italian propaganda could present Fascist corporatism as a universally applicable solution to the socio-economic cleavages inherent in all modern mass-industrial societies. On closer inspection, however, even Italian theorizing about corporatism completely fails to bear out any of the ambitious claims which Fascists were fond of making for it. Mussolini's own speeches and writings, for instance, are a complete muddle, containing at least three different and incompatible interpretations of the idea.

According to one of his interpretations, corporatism was intended to offer an entirely new conception of the function of the state. On this view, not only the traditional cleavage between state and individual but also the more modern division of industrial society into contending classes, were to be overcome by reconciling both within the framework of the corporation. The corporation, as Mussolini explained to the Senate on 14 November 1933, was to act as a cramp (*un vincolo*) that bound all members of society together in a single common faith. According to Fascist cant, the new corporate basis of social and political life would facilitate creative individual self-expression, on the one hand, whilst also facilitating the elimination of the wasteful laissez-faire system by a new, more positive ideal of state intervention directed towards securing communal goals, on the other. In practice, of course, the Fascist vision of a corporatist society based upon the self-regulation of producers under the aegis of the state was merely a veil for despotism. Mussolini himself acknowledged this when he explained that corporatism in this sense was only relevant to a totalitarian state like the Italian one, since the reforms it would require were so all-pervasive that the corporatist system could not possibly work within the context of limited politics.[3]

According to a second interpretation, however, the corporatist system was not tied to one particular political system but could be exported to any industrialized country in which individuals and groups wished to use the state as a non-coercive device for maintaining voluntary self-discipline (*autodisciplina*). This view, which was originally put before the Senate in a speech on 13 January 1934,[4] was subsequently embroidered by Mussolini in a way which identified corporatism with domestic socialism, on the one hand, and with a militant programme of national expansion, on the other.[5] Corporatism in this sense was obviously just a formula for warmongering, and Fascist 'socialism' was merely another name for the collectivism required by a war economy.

Finally, Mussolini made a third claim, according to which corporatism meant not so much a new function for the state, or a new kind of social order, as an entirely new conception of the form and structure of the state. Corporatism, according to this view, was the only form of democracy appropriate to the twentieth century. The corporatist system alone, it was held, would make the state structure truly representative by ending a fundamentally divisive parliamentary system based upon geographical particularism and upon divisive political parties. In place of this unsatisfactory system there would be an organic one, in which a corporatist parliament represented 'natural' (i.e. economic) social groups instead of abstract geographical and political ones.[6] In line with this manner of thinking, the remnants of the Italian Parliament were abolished in 1938 and replaced by a corporatist parliament. The result of this supposedly new 'organic' conception of the state, as might be expected, was merely a further enhancement of Mussolini's dictatorship, rather than the creation of an alternative to parliamentary democracy. The kind of politics which characterized the new organic state (or, as it was sometimes called, 'functional democracy'), may be gleaned from the Proceedings of the Chamber of Fasces and Corporations, 27 April 1940. From these we learn that, 'The Chamber and public galleries broke out with an enthusiastic ovation. The cry of *"Duce", "Duce"* resounded through the hall again and again. The Duce responded with the Roman salute. The assembly then sang *"Giovinezza"*. The President ordered that the Duce should be saluted, and the Chamber answered with a powerful *"A Noi"*. When the Duce left his seat, the National Councillors crowded around him with enthusiastic and continual acclamations.' [. . .]

2 Permanent revolution

Whilst corporatism lent a veneer of respectability to the Italian regime, the most remarkable feature of the fascist *Weltanschauung* is to be found elsewhere. It consists in the essentially fluid and dynamic conception of life and the world which fascism sought to oppose to both liberal and socialist political theory, as well as to the traditional forms of conservative ideology.

A dramatic illustration of the initial incomprehension encountered by the new view of life even amongst fascists themselves may be found in a conversation which took place between Hitler and Herman Rauschning in 1934. The core of National Socialism, Hitler explained to Rauschning, 'is a revolutionary creative will that needs no ideological crutches'. This, he added, is what primarily distinguishes the Nazi revolutionary ideal from the Marxist one. Rauschning, however, was not at all clear about what the Nazi 'revolutionary creative will' actually was, and he was therefore compelled to ask Hitler to explain. Hitler tersely observed that, 'It has no fixed aim.' To Rauschning, whose views were of a traditional conservative kind, this aimless dynamism was so novel that Hitler was obliged to elaborate a bit further upon the nature of the Nazi revolution. 'We are a movement,' he informed Rauschning, adding that, 'Nothing could express our nature better. [Unlike the Marxists] we know that there is never a final stage, there is no permanency, only eternal change . . . the future is an inexhaustible fount of possibilities of further development.'[7] [. . .]

3 The leader principle

The leader principle is now a familiar part of all contemporary activist regimes. Fascism, however, is the only modern ideology to place the explicit cult of a leader at the very centre of its teaching. The central significance of the principle in the fascist *Weltanschauung* can best be brought out by considering the three different functions which it performs.

For fascism, the first and most crucial of the leader's functions is to serve as a symbolic embodiment of the myth which shapes the historical destiny of his people. A single example will illustrate how radically this conception of leadership differs from that to be found within other modern ideologies. The example in question relates to the significance of a political speech. In liberal and socialist ideology, the purpose of a speech is primarily the rational one of instructing the listeners. Within fascist ideology, by contrast, the purpose of a speech (as Hitler himself put it) was to open the gates to the heart of the *Volk*, as with the blows from a hammer.[8] For fascism, in other words, the leader's task is no longer to instruct his listeners but to arouse their emotions, in a way which encourages them to 'live out' the fascist myth, rather than to examine it critically.[9]

In order to perform this first function the fascist leader must ensure that his movement is free from the disputes over the relationship between theory and practice which bedevil other ideologies. To achieve this internal harmony he must claim to be infallible in all matters of fascist faith, morality and politics. Consider, for example, the blunt terms in which Hitler felt obliged to spell out the doctrine of infallibility to Otto Strasser, in the course of a head-on clash over the scope of the leader principle which occurred in 1930. According to Strasser, the leader was ultimately subordinate to the Party, which was the true organ of Nazi infallibility. 'The Idea (i.e. the ideology)', Strasser asserted, 'is divine in origin, whilst men are only its vehicles, the body in which the Word is made flesh. The Leader is made to serve the Idea, and it is to the Idea alone that we owe absolute allegiance.' By contrast with the Idea, he maintained, 'The leader is human, and it is human to err.' Hitler's reply to this impertinent critique of his personal infallibility was brief and unequivocal. 'You are talking monumental idiocy,' he snarled. 'You wish to give Party members the right to decide whether or not the Führer has remained faithful to the so-called Idea. It's the lowest kind of democracy, and we want nothing to do with it! For us the Idea is the Führer, and each Party member has only to obey the Führer.'[10] In Italian Fascism, the same point was asserted still more directly; in the words of the Fascist Decalogue, 'Mussolini is always right.' [. . .]

4 The messianic mission

[. . .] Messianic fanaticism, it will immediately be objected, is not peculiar to the modern world, let alone to fascism; on the contrary, it will be said, it may be traced back to antiquity. Thus the Jews regarded their God, Jehovah, not merely as the God of Israel, but as the God of all nations and all history. What distinguishes messianic fanaticism of this kind from the fascist type, however, is the fact that the Jews never claimed that their messianic status derived from any intrinsic excellence or merit on their part; they claimed only that God, by a free act of grace, had chosen Israel for his people, regardless of any peculiar merit of their own. Until the advent of modern nationalist doctrine, all messianic movements conformed to this pattern; they derived their mission, that is, from a source outside the chosen people rather than from a claim to intrinsic superiority over other peoples. Since it was the claim to intrinsic superiority which was to be exploited by fascism, it is necessary to consider how this idea entered the western political tradition.

The idea that one people might be intrinsically superior to another is in fact a relatively recent one, which appeared in Europe only towards the end of the eighteenth century. Until that time, the primary conception of order was of an international civilization to which all particular states and individuals were subject. In practice, this civilization was identified with the supra-national order of 'Christendom', whose cosmopolitan status was embodied in theories of natural law which can be traced back as far as classical antiquity. At the end of the eighteenth century, however, there appeared a new conception of international order which revealed an increasingly marked tendency to reject the ideal of an overriding, universal order of civilization in favour of a stress upon the intrinsic value of particular national cultures. From that time down to the present day, the western world has been confronted by two potentially incompatible conceptions of order, one of which is universal, whilst the other is more or less nationalistic.

[. . .]

Long before the appearance of Mussolini and Hitler, in short, the European world had become familiar with extravagant claims to a messianic mission advanced by activist politicians within every European nationalist movement. To this tradition of messianic nationalism, fascist ideology added no new intellectual ingredient. Even Nazi racialism involved no novel departure from the tradition, since claims to racial superiority had frequently jostled alongside the more usual nineteenth-century nationalist claims to cultural superiority. Whilst fascism added nothing of substance to the earlier messianic tradition, however, it nevertheless modified that tradition in one vital respect: it destroyed the complacent assumption that nationalism was a basically progressive doctrine which was inseparably connected with the twin ideals of individual liberty and international harmony.

5 Autarky

The belief that a world composed of democratic, self-determining nation-states would inevitably be a peaceful and harmonious one derived a considerable part of its intellectual appeal from an important but dubious assumption about the likely impact of modern economic development upon the international order. It is this assumption that must now be briefly considered.

The assumption, whose implausibility was not exposed until the advent of fascism, was that the world-wide growth of industry and commerce would gradually soften national rivalries and in that way intensify the overall trend towards world peace. It was this delusion which inspired, for example, the influential nineteenth-century Saint-Simonian school, whose doctrine provides a good illustration of the aspect of modern progressive orthodoxy in question. According to Saint-Simonian doctrine, once the industrialization process is properly organized it will necessarily create 'a state in which the different nations scattered over the face of the earth appear only as parts of a vast workshop, labouring under a common impulse to achieve a common goal'.[11] Unfortunately, what progressive sentiment of this kind failed to appreciate was that the concept of national self-determination was susceptible to two conflicting interpretations, which carried with them entirely different practical implications for economic policy.

On the one hand, self-determination might be taken to imply peaceful economic policies which aimed at preventing excessive dependence upon foreign countries for crucial raw materials. This, for example, was how the American statesman, Alexander Hamilton, interpreted the principle of national self-determination in 1791, when he submitted a report to the House of Representatives in which he urged the American government to adopt a policy of economic autarky. 'Not only the wealth, but the independence and security of a country', Hamilton stated, 'appear to be materially connected with the prosperity of manufactures.' Therefore, he concluded, 'Every nation, with a view to these great objects, ought to endeavour to possess within itself all the essentials of natural supply.' From this it followed, he observed, that the policy of the American Government should be the promotion of such manufactures 'as will tend to render the United States independent of foreign nations for military and other essential supplies'.[12]

On the other hand, this moderate and flexible approach might be rejected in favour of an entirely opposite interpretation of the economic implications of national self-determination. Instead of being confined to securing peacefully what Hamilton called 'the essentials of natural supply', self-determination might instead be interpreted to mean the achievement of total economic self-sufficiency. A state which adopted the latter interpretation would then have to choose between two different ways of implementing it. One way was by minimizing its needs, in order to permit it to withdraw from the international order; the other was by a programme of world domination aimed at securing complete control over all the resources of the earth. It was this latter interpretation of the principle of national self-determination to which fascist ideology was openly committed, as both Hitler and Mussolini made clear.

In a conversation with Otto Strasser on 22 May 1930, Hitler vehemently rejected Strasser's demand for the creation of economic autarky by policies which would insulate Germany from the rest of the world. Replying to Strasser, Hitler insisted that Germany must acknowledge its dependence upon the world economic order, since, 'We are bound to import all important raw materials, and we are not less bound to export the goods manufactured by us . . . we cannot stop this nor do we wish to.' The proper task of the Nazi party, he continued, is therefore 'to organize on a large scale the whole world so that each country produces what it can best produce while the white race, the Nordic race, undertakes the organization of this gigantic plan. Believe me, National Socialism as a whole would be worth nothing if it were restricted merely to Germany and did not seek the supremacy of the superior race over the entire world for at least a thousand to two thousand years.' This then was what the Nazi programme of economic autarky implied. In Hitler's eyes, of course, it did not amount to a programme of domination or exploitation, since 'the lower race is destined for tasks different from those of the higher race'. The lower race would accordingly be grateful, if it were sufficiently intelligent, for the rational reorganization of the world which Hitler proposed to bring about.[13]

Like Hitler, Mussolini also adopted the militant, expansionist version of the autarkic ideal. In the course of outlining his policy and ideas for the future in 1936, for example, Mussolini explained that, 'Italy can and must attain the maximum of economic independence for peace and war. The whole of the Italian economic system must be directed towards this supreme necessity, on which depends the future of the Italian people . . . This plan is determined by one single consideration: that our nation will be called to war.'[14] Mussolini's demand that Italy should be given a 'place in the sun' through the creation of a new Roman Empire, however, was at once more vague and less brutal than Hitler's expansionist programme. The Italian regime, indeed, was notable for the sheer ineptitude of its efforts to convert the Fascist economy into a self-sufficient military unit. In practice, what happened was that a regime which had always depended more upon ideological propaganda than upon deeds finally fell foul of its own mythology. This propaganda, whose purpose had been to vaunt Italy's superiority over other nations, succeeded in the end only in convincing Mussolini himself that victory would be almost effortless. Accordingly, he made no order for general mobilization, and even left Italian munitions production in a half-hearted condition, in order that the factories should be ready for the production of civilian goods which would be necessary to compete with Germany in the post-war economic boom which he expected to follow upon victory. To treat all this (in S. J. Woolf's phrase) as no more than 'cheerful pragmatism'[15] or, worse still, as a positive contribution to the 'modernization' of Italy, is wide of the mark. The fact is that Mussolini's autarkic policies kept the overall rate of Italian economic growth at almost the same level for two decades, and made sense only as a device for maintaining the economy and the masses in the barrack-room state of unity which Hitler, in a more successful way, imposed upon Germany.

The fascist policy of economic autarky is nevertheless instructive. Throughout the nineteenth century, as was just observed, the principle of national self-determination had generally been regarded as a natural extension of the democratic ideal of popular sovereignty, and hence as an important stage in the creation of a world without war. In 1919, the principle had been made the foundation of the peace settlement and the basis of the new democratic world order which it was intended to bring into existence. What fascism revealed was that the principle of national self-determination could never provide the foundation for a stable world order. Far from being a pacific principle, national self-determination might well be used to justify messianic claims to cultural superiority, on the one hand, and unlimited claims to world domination in the interest of achieving economic autarky, on the other. Once again, however, the sole novelty of fascist ideology in this respect lies in the fact that the fascists alone openly professed militant policies which other activists – most notably communist regimes – pursue without explicitly acknowledging it.

Notes

1   Hitler, *Mein Kampf* (New York: Hutchinson Publications, 1969).
2   In Denis Mack Smith, *Italy: A Modern History* (Ann Arbor, Michigan, 1969), 395.
3   See E. Barker, *Reflections on Government* (London, 1967), 348–9.
4   ibid., 349.
5   ibid., 350.
6   ibid., 354–5.
7   H. Rauschning, *Hitler Speaks* (London, 1939), 175–6.

8   G. L. Mosse, *The Nationalization of the Masses* (N.Y., 1975), 201.

9   ibid.

10   J. Noakes and G. Pridham, eds., *Documents on Nazism 1919–1945* (London, 1974), 98.

11   Quoted by E. Halévy in *The Era of Tyrannies* (N.Y., 1965), 60.

12   In J. Braunthal, *Need Germany Survive?* (London, 1943), 36.

13   Norman H. Baynes, *The Speeches of Adolf Hitler* (Oxford, 1942), vol. 1, 774–5.

14   Quoted in A. William Salomone, *Italy, From the Risorgimento to Fascism: An Inquiry into the Origins of the Totalitarian State* (Newton Abbot, 1970), 296–7.

15   Eugen Weber, *Varieties of Fascism: Doctrines of Revolution in the Twentieth Century* (Princeton, 1964), 142.

Chapter 14

Zeev Sternhell

FASCIST IDEOLOGY: A DISSIDENT REVISION OF MARXISM?

■ from *THE BIRTH OF FASCIST IDEOLOGY: FROM CULTURAL REBELLION TO POLITICAL REVOLUTION*, Princeton, NJ, 1994, pp. 5–6, 8, 9–11, 12, 23–4, 27–8, 31, 32, 33–4

Zeev Sternhell is a most unusual disciple of the notion of generic fascism. Although his *Birth of Fascist Ideology* aims to identify the ideological core of fascism as a 'general European phenomenon', he makes clear that his understanding of fascism does not include Nazism. The reason for this emphatic distinction becomes clear in the following excerpt. For Sternhell believes that fascist ideology rests on a synthesis between organic nationalism and a 'revision' of Marxism in an anti-material, non-internationalist direction. This synthesis was first accomplished in Italy and France, where nationalism was combined with the traditions of revolutionary syndicalism to produce the first articulation of a genuine 'national socialism'. Sternhell notes, however, that the crisis-ridden Italian society of the early twentieth century provided a more suitable milieu for the osmosis of these radical ideas that was complete (as Fascism) by 1918.

FASCISM CAN IN NO WAY BE IDENTIFIED with Nazism. Undoubtedly the two ideologies, the two movements, and the two regimes had common characteristics. They often ran parallel to one another or overlapped, but they differed on one fundamental point: the criterion of German national socialism was biological determinism. The basis of Nazism was racism in its most extreme sense, and the fight against the Jews, against 'inferior' races, played a more preponderant role in it than the struggle against communism. Marxists could be converted to national socialism, as indeed quite a number of them were; similarly, national socialism could sign treaties with Communists, exchange ambassadors, and coexist with them, if only temporarily. Nothing like this, however, applied to the Jews. Where they were concerned, the only possible 'arrangement' with them was their destruction.

Certainly, racism was not limited to Germany. At the end of the nineteenth century, biological determinism developed in a country like France too; but if it was a factor in the development of the revolutionary Right, racism in its French variant never became the whole purpose of an ideology, a movement, and a regime.

In fact, racial determinism was not present in all the varieties of fascism. If Robert Brasillach professed an anti-Semitism very close to that of Nazism, George Valois's 'Faisceau' had none at all; and if some Italian Fascists were violently anti-Semitic, in Italy there were innumerable Fascist Jews. Their percentage in the movement was much higher than in the population as a whole. As we know, racial laws were promulgated in Italy only in 1938, and during the Second World War the Jews felt much less in danger in Nice or Haute-Savoie, areas under Italian occupation, than in Marseilles, which was under the control of the Vichy government.

Racism was thus not a necessary condition for the existence of fascism; on the contrary, it was a factor in Fascist eclecticism. For this reason, a general theory that seeks to combine fascism and Nazism will always come up against this essential aspect of the problem. In fact, such a theory is not possible. Undoubtedly there are similarities, particularly with regard to the 'totalitarian' character of the two regimes, but their differences are no less significant. Karl Bracher perceived the singular importance of these differences, which Ernst Nolte (this was his chief weakness) completely ignored.[1]

Having clarified this question, let us now return to our definition of fascism. If the Fascist ideology cannot be described as a simple response to Marxism, its origins, on the other hand, were the direct result of a very specific revision of Marxism. It was a *revision* of Marxism and not a *variety* of Marxism or a *consequence* of Marxism. One of the aims of this book is to study this antimaterialistic and antirationalistic revision of Marxism. It is absolutely necessary to insist on this essential aspect of the definition of fascism, for one can scarcely understand the emergence of the fundamental concepts of fascism and of the Fascist philosophy and mythology if one does not recognize, at the same time, that it arose from an originally Marxist revolt against materialism. It was the French and Italian Sorelians, the theoreticians of revolutionary syndicalism, who made this new and original revision of Marxism, and precisely this was their contribution to the birth of the Fascist ideology.

In this respect, the rise of fascism was one of the aspects of the intellectual, scientific, and technological revolution that overtook the European continent at the turn of the twentieth century. This revolution changed the prevailing way of life to a degree hitherto unknown, transforming the intellectual climate as well as social realities. All of a sudden, one saw the inadequacy of the social and economic laws Marx propounded. Confronted with problems that the previous generation had not even envisaged, the new generation proposed totally unexpected solutions.

Consequently, anyone who regards fascism as no more than a byproduct of the First World War, a mere bourgeois defensive reaction to the postwar crisis, is unable to understand this major phenomenon of our century. A phenomenon of civilization, fascism represents a rejection of the political culture prevailing at the beginning of the century. In the fascism of the interwar period, in Mussolini's regime as in all other western European Fascist movements, there was not a single major idea that had not gradually come to fruition in the quarter of a century preceding August 1914.

Although an ideal prototype of a disruptive ideology, fascism cannot be defined only in negative terms. Undoubtedly, fascism rejected the prevailing systems: liberalism and Marxism, positivism and democracy. This is always the case; a new ideology and an emerging political movement begin by opposing the systems of thought and political forces already in place. Before offering its own vision of the world, Marxism began by opposing liberalism, which a century earlier had risen up against absolutism. The same was true of fascism, which conflicted with liberalism and Marxism before it was able to provide all the elements of an alternate political, moral, and intellectual system.

In the form that it emerged at the turn of the century and developed in the 1920s and 1930s, the Fascist ideology represented a synthesis of organic nationalism with the antimaterialist revision of Marxism. It expressed a revolutionary aspiration based on a rejection of individualism, whether liberal or Marxist, and it created the elements of a new and original political culture.

[. . .]

Thus, antimaterialism, a direct assault on liberalism and Marxism, at the beginning of this century represented a third revolutionary option between the two great systems that dominated the political life of the period and that, over and above all their differences, nevertheless remained the heirs of the eighteenth century. Fascism was antimaterialism in its clearest form. But if it was opposed to liberalism and Marxism, it took from liberalism a respect for the power and vitality of the mechanisms of the market economy, and from Marxism a conviction that violence was the motive force of history, which was governed solely by the laws of war.

[. . .]

These were the two great supporting pillars of the Fascist edifice, which, taken as a whole, represented a coherent, logical, and well-structured totality. [. . .] The first of the two essential components of fascism to appear on the political scene of the end of the nineteenth century was tribal nationalism, based on a social Darwinism and, often, a biological determinism. In France, this type of nationalism was found in its clearest form in the work of Maurice Barrès, Edouard Drumont, Charles Maurras, and the representatives of Action française.[2] In Italy, Enrico Corradini demonstrated, in a truly fascinating manner, the evolution of Italian nationalism from the time, still close, of the struggle for independence. From the end of the nineteenth century, the new nationalism truly expressed the revolt against the spirit of the French Revolution. The gulf that divided Corradini from Mazzini, or Barrès, Drumont, and Maurras from Michelet, reveals the distance between Jacobin nationalism and that of *la Terre et les Morts*, the Land and the Dead. This formula of Barrès was in fact only the French counterpart of the German formula *Blut und Boden* (Blood and Soil), and it showed that the old theory, consecrated by the French Revolution, that society was made up of a collection of individuals, had been replaced by the theory of the organic unity of the nation. In this respect, the system of thought developed in France by the generation of the 1890s was scarcely different from the one that grew up in the same period on the other side of the Rhine. The nationalist fervor of the French writers of the time was in no way inferior to that of their contemporary Heinrich von Treitschke, the celebrated theoretician of German nationalism at the end of the nineteenth century. Drumont and Wilhelm Marr, Jules Guérin, the marquis de Morès, Adolf Stöcker and the Austrian Georg von Schonerer, Georges Vacher de Lapouge and Otto Ammon, Paul Déroulède and Ernst Hasse, the head of the Pan-German League, were as alike as peas in a pod.

We are here in the presence of a general European phenomenon. For this new nationalism – which was situated at the opposite pole from the one that, from the French Revolution to the Commune of Paris, had attempted a synthesis of the 'religion of the fatherland' with the religion of humanity – the nation was an organism comparable to a sentient being. This 'total' nationalism claimed to be a system of ethics, with criteria of behavior dictated by the entire national body, independently of the will of the individual. By definition, this new nationalism denied the validity of any absolute and universal moral norms: truth, justice, and law existed only in order to serve the needs of the collectivity. The idea of society as something isolated and shut in, a violent antirationalism, and a belief in the supremacy of the subconscious over the forces of reason amounted to a truly tribal concept of the nation.

[. . .]

This cult of deep and mysterious forces that are the fabric of human existence entailed as a necessary and natural consequence the appearance of a virulent anti-intellectualism. For this school of thought, the fight against intellectuals and against the rationalism from which they drew their nourishment was a measure of public safety. There were a great many nationalists at the turn of the century who, like those of the interwar generation, constantly attacked the critical spirit and its products, opposing them to instinct, intuitive and irrational sentiment, emotion and enthusiasm – those deep impulses which determine human behavior and which constitute the reality and truth of things as well as their beauty. Rationalism, they claimed, belongs to the 'deracinated'; it blunts sensitivity, it deadens instinct and can only destroy the motive forces of national activity. Barrès believed that only the emotional content of a situation had any real value; for him, the process of what is known as thought took place on the level of the unconscious. He concluded from this that to attack the unconscious was to divest the national organism of its substance. Consequently, in order to ensure the welfare of the nation, one had to turn to the people and exalt the primitive force, vigor, and vitality that emanated from the people, uncontaminated by the rationalist and individualist virus. For the revolutionary Right of 1890 as for that of 1930, the incomparable merit of popular opinion was its unreflecting spontaneity, springing from the depths of the unconscious. At the turn of the century as on the eve of the Second World War, these were the new criteria of political behavior.

Since the masses were truly the nation, and since the primary aim of politics was to ensure the nation's integrity and power, nationalism could not accept that the social question should remain unsolved. Barrès, the major theoretician of this 'Latin nationalism,' which was even more genuine than 'Latin Marxism,' was one of the first people to understand that a 'national' movement can exist only if it ensures the integration of the most disadvantaged strata of society. At the same time, he understood that a 'national' movement cannot be Marxist, liberal, proletarian, or bourgeois. Marxism and liberalism, he claimed, could never be anything other than movements of a civil war; a class war and a war of all against all in an individualistic society were merely two aspects of the same evil. As a result of this way of thinking at the end of the nineteenth century there appeared in France a new synthesis, the first form of fascism. Barrès was one of the first thinkers in Europe to employ the term 'national socialism.'[3]

[. . .]

The second main component of fascism, which, together with antiliberal and antibourgeois nationalism, made up the Fascist ideology, was the antimaterialist revision of Marxism. This revolt, which involved both the non-conformist extreme Left and the nationalist Right, allowed the association of a new kind of socialism with radical nationalism.

[. . .]

Since the Marxist prophecies showed no sign of coming to pass in the foreseeable future, and since the capitalist economy, on the contrary, was in excellent shape, it was difficult to conclude, like Kautsky, that socialism was an economic necessity. Capitalism, in short, did not seem to carry in itself the seeds of its own destruction. It followed in the dissident's view, that in order to destroy bourgeois society one first had to develop the factors favorable to class struggle; and then, still more important, one had to introduce to Marxism new elements that would *artificially* produce the effect of division, of permanent violence, of insidious warfare not produced by capitalism – a capitalism that was far more dynamic and efficacious than Marx had thought or than most of his disciples had wanted to believe, a capitalism that had shown itself capable of adapting to all conditions of production. Moreover, even when a conflict did arise, the bourgeoisie and the socialist parties that spoke in the name of the proletariat, because they operated in a liberal democratic regime and could function only according to the logic of the system, hastened to reach a compromise that would satisfy the immediate needs of the proletariat. In this way, any combativeness that existed in the working masses was neutralized. According to the Sorelians, this produced a fundamental incompatibility between socialism and democracy which necessitated the immediate destruction of the existing system.

In this situation, the dissidents came to the conclusion that the revolution could take place only if three conditions were met simultaneously. These three elements, or rather, these three series of elements, taken together and as a single whole, constituted revolutionary syndicalism. It was the totality that counted, and this totality finally developed into national syndicalism and then into fascism. As we said at the beginning of the introduction, this evolution, which took place during the first twenty years of this century, forms the subject of this book.

The first of the three elements that ensured the development of Fascist thought was the idea that the revolutionary dynamic was dependent on the market economy, which was regarded as representing the universal laws of economic activity.

The second element was the introduction of new and very special types of cata-lysts into Marxism. [. . .] Marxism was a system of ideas still deeply rooted in the philosophy of the eighteenth century. Sorelian revisionism replaced the rationalist, Hegelian foundations of Marxism with Le Bon's new vision of human nature, with the anti-Cartesianism of Bergson, with the Nietzschean cult of revolt, and with Pareto's most recent discoveries in political sociology. The Sorelian, voluntarist, vitalist, and antimaterialist form of socialism used Bergsonism as an instrument against scientism and did not hesitate to attack reason. It was a philosophy of action based on intuition, the cult of energy and *élan vital*.

This was the very original solution Sorel proposed for overcoming and super-seding the crisis of Marxism. Since the free play of economic forces was unable to start up the revolutionary process, psychology had to compensate for the deficiency of economics. One had to summon the deep forces of the unconscious and of intu-ition and to mobilize these sources of energy that formed the greatness of ancient Greece, of early Christianity, and of the armies of Napoleon. One needed myths – myths being 'systems of images' that can neither be split up into their component parts nor refuted. Proletarian violence was a myth that aimed to produce a contin-uous state of tension leading to breakdown and catastrophe, an insidious state of war, and a daily moral struggle against the established order. In this way, Sorel sought to rectify Marx by introducing irrational elements into Marxism. Myths and violence were key elements in Sorel. They were not expedients but permanent values, as well as being means of mass mobilization suited to the needs of modern politics. There was thus a progressive shift in the main emphasis of Marxist doctrine: psychology replaced economics as the motive force of revolutionary activity.

The third principle of revolutionary revisionism was the destruction of the liberal democratic regime and its intellectual norms and moral values. Since recent history had shown that democracy was simply a swamp in which socialism had become bogged down, the labor movement had to be freed from the dominance of the socialist parties, and all connection between the workers' syndicates and socialist political institutions had to be severed. In short, one had to destroy the democratic system as a whole.

[. . .]

Thus, it was quite natural that a synthesis would arise between this new socialism, which discovered the nation as a revolutionary agent, and the nationalist movement, which also rebelled against the old world of conservatives, against the aristocrats and the bourgeois, and against social injustices and which believed that the nation would never be complete until it had integrated the proletariat. A socialism for the whole collectivity and a nationalism that, severed from conservatism, proclaimed itself as being by definition the messenger of unity and unanimity thus came together to form an unprecedented weapon of war against the bourgeois order and liberal democracy.

That was the nature of the synthesis that produced fascism. The Sorelians contributed the idea of a revolution that must eradicate the liberal democratic regime and its moral and intellectual norms without destroying all the structures of the capi-talist economy. To the world of traders and hair splitters they opposed another, all heroism and virility, where pessimism and puritanism were made into a virtue — a world in which the sense of duty and sacrifice was glorified. The new society would be dominated by a powerful avant-garde made up of an aristocracy of producers joined to a youth avid for action. Here we come upon the great discovery Sorel made: the masses need myths in order to go forward. It is sentiments, images, and symbols that hurl individuals into action, not reasonings. It was likewise from Sorel in particular and the Sorelians in general that fascism borrowed something else: the idea that violence gave rise to the sublime. Fitted out in this way revolutionary action could now overcome all the resistances of the material world.

[. . .]

With regard to political theory, the fascist synthesis was already clearly expressed around 1910–1912 in publications like *La lupa* in Italy and the *Cahiers du Cercle Proudhon* in France. After the first manifestations of the Fascist synthesis in France, the war was needed in order that a situation should exist in Italy that would enable this movement of ideas to be transformed into a political force.

Indeed, for reasons related to a semipermanent crisis that prevailed in Italian society at the beginning of the century, this synthesis flourished in Italy and became a political force. Sorel was regarded as a patriarch, an authority, and a continual inspiration. It was the pure Sorelians, the proponents of an ethical, vitalist, and voluntarist revisionism, the advocates of creative and moral violence, who formed the real ideological core of fascism and provided it with its initial conceptual framework. The first biography of Sorel, by Agostino Lanzillo, appeared in Italy in 1910. It was again among the youth in the Italian universities that his theories, mingled with scientific data, took root.

[. . .]

In Italy the synthesis of nationalism with revolutionary syndicalism was based on the same principles as in France: on one hand, a rejection of democracy, Marxism, liberalism, the so-called bourgeois values, the eighteenth-century heritage, internationalism, and pacifism; on the other hand a cult of heroism, vitalism, and violence. Robert Michels, one of the outstanding figures of revolutionary syndicalism, an Italianized German and one of the foremost theoreticians of fascism until his death in 1936, said that in order to shatter the conservatism of the masses, a vitalist and voluntarist ethic was needed, and an elite able to lead the masses into combat. Michels is known not only for his contribution to Fascist ideology, but also for his pioneering work *Political Parties*, which even today is a classic of political science. Together with Pareto and Mosca, he brought to fascism the support of the new social sciences.

[. . .]

Not all Italian revolutionary syndicalists became Fascists, but most syndicalist leaders were among the founders of the Fascist movement. Many even held key posts in the regime founded by the most famous fellow traveler of revolutionary syndicalism, Benito Mussolini. In 1909 Mussolini declared that he had become a syndicalist during the general strike of 1904, but in fact, at the time of his exile in Switzerland between 1902 and 1904, his connections with the revolutionary syndicalists were well established. Before 1905, he collaborated in the *Avanguardia socialista*, read Sorel and Pareto, and was decisively influenced by theoreticians and leaders of revolutionary syndicalism such as Olivetti, Panunzio, Alceste de Ambris, and Filippo Corridoni. Mussolini soon became one of the best-known leaders of Italian socialism. A charismatic personality, at once an intellectual and an outstanding leader, he quickly rose in importance. From being a provincial socialist leader, he became the head of the revolutionary Left of the Socialist party and the editor of *Avanti!* At that period, in the European socialist parties, the task of editor was reserved for a dominant personality, for one of the leading figures, if not for the head of the party himself. Jaures, Blum, Vanderwelde, Bernstein, Kautsky, Plekhanov, and Lenin were all editors. During this period, Mussolini often crossed swords with heretics who preferred to leave the party or who were dismissed, especially in connection with the political decisions of the organization. A chapter of this work is devoted to Mussolini, his political activities, and his ideas. It is nevertheless necessary to point out at this stage that his opposition to the revolutionary syndicalists concerned only political tactics, not major ideological options. From the beginning of his association, Mussolini in effect subscribed to the fundamental principles of revolutionary syndicalism.

In 1913 the socialist leader rejoined the people who had shaped his thinking. When he seemed to have reached the peak of his ascension within the party, Mussolini did something unexpected: he began to publish a journal with the symbolic name Utopia, opening its pages to the dissidents that the party had excluded from its ranks a few years earlier. This was a quite calculated step that reflected the deep intellectual crisis through which the socialist leader was passing at that time. At the end of his soul-searching and under the pressure of the dramatic events of the summer of 1914, Mussolini put an end to the ambiguity that for two years had characterized his relationship with the leadership of the party he was supposed to guide at the time of the European war. The leader of the socialist Left quit the party and joined the revolutionary syndicalists, who were already organized in aggressive and vociferous pressure groups and demanded Italy's participation in the Anglo-French alliance. The ideological crisis Mussolini passed through had begun long before the war and had no connection with it, but the war brought it to a head. Like all European socialists, Mussolini had to cease wavering. A heroic socialism extolling vitalistic values had always captured the heart of this young man who had fought democratic socialism from his first day of political activity. Twelve years after he had started in the wake of Arturo Labriola, Mussolini found practically all the revolutionary syndicalists in the interventionist movement. But the war also added something else: the mobilizing power of nationalism. When the armistice arrived, Mussolinian fascism was almost complete. In any case, he had already incorporated the ideas of revolutionary syndicalism.

Notes

1   See K. D. Bracher, 'The Role of Hitler: Perspectives of Interpretation,' in W. Laqueur, ed., *Fascism: A Reader's Guide. Analyses, Interpretations, Bibliography* (Berkeley and Los Angeles: University of California Press, 1976), 217ff.

2   On the Action française, see V. Nguen's remarkable *Aux Origines de l'Action française. Intelligence et politique à l'aube du XXe siècle* (Paris: Fayard, 1991); C. Capitan Peter, *Charles Maurras et l'idéologie d'Action française* (Paris: Ed. du Seuil, 1972), and E. Weber, *Action française* (Stanford, Calif.: Stanford University Press, 1962). See also Z. Sternhell, *Maurice Barrès et le nationalisme français* (Paris: A. Colin, 1972; new paperback edition: Brussels: Ed. Complexe, 1985), and *La Droite révolutionnaire. Les Origines françaises du fascisme* (Paris: Ed. du Seuil, 1978) (new paperback edition: Points-Histoire, 1985).

3   M. Barrès, 'Que faut-il faire?' *Le Courrier de l'Est*, 12 May 1898.

Chapter 15

Roger Griffin

FASCISM: 'REBIRTH' AND 'ULTRA-NATIONALISM'

■ from *THE NATURE OF FASCISM*, London and New York, 1993b, pp. 32–9

Roger Griffin's work on generic fascism is the most conceptually sophisticated and methodologically consistent attempt to devise a model for accommodating generic fascism. This is why his work is represented by two excerpts in this reader. In the following extract from his authoritative *Nature of Fascism* he defines the 'fascist minimum' (the nucleus that all fascist case-studies had in common in distinction to other nationalist or rightist currents) as 'palingenetic populist ultra-nationalism'. Griffin acknowledges that each component of this definition is not specific to fascism – instead, fascism's uniqueness lies in the combination of these elements in a new synthesis. Note that, unlike Nolte, Griffin extends the chronological and geographical scope of the term 'fascism' to the post-1945 period and to other continents besides Europe.

'Palingenetic myth' and 'populist ultra-nationalism'

(a) Palingenetic myth

THE FIRST OF THESE COMPONENTS is perhaps one of the most common ingredients of human experience, despite the highly uncommon, not to say obscure, name we have given it here, namely the myth of renewal, of rebirth. Etymologically, the term 'palingenesis', deriving from *palin* (again, anew) and *genesis* (creation, birth), refers to the sense of a new start or of regeneration after a phase of crisis or decline which can be associated just as much with mystical (for example the Second Coming) as secular realities (for example the New Germany). Even in the spheres of theology and biology the term is unusual, not to say obsolete in modern English (see the *Oxford English Dictionary*), though it would be a mark of the heuristic value of this book to fascist studies if it eventually underwent its own palingenesis as a term of current social scientific usage. It was used extensively in this way by the French theorist Ballanche (1833) in his *Palingénésie sociale* and is occasionally applied by Italian academics in the context of fascism just as I propose to do here (for example Gentile, 1975, 5; Lazzari, 1984, 55). I intend to employ it as a generic term for the vision of a radically new beginning which follows a period of destruction or perceived dissolution.

The most obvious well-head of palingenetic myth in the wider sense is religion. The resurrection of Jesus Christ places one such myth at the very centre of a whole faith (a point I make with due deference to readers for whom this is a 'lived' reality: like ideology, myth is identifiable as such only by someone who is cognitively and spiritually 'outside' it). Notions of metaphorical (to believers, metaphysical) death and rebirth pervade the symbolism of baptism, communion, and Easter celebrations, while generations of Christian mystics have elaborated intricate verbal, pictorial and ritual mythologies to invoke the reality of spiritual rebirth on a higher plane of being after dying to the world of the flesh. Palingenetic myth is also central to the 'political religions' which Christianity has inspired in the past, notably the millenarianism exhaustively studied by Cohn (1970) and in which Sorel saw a major example of myth's power to act as an agent of historical change.

Again we must stress that an important premise to the way generic fascism is being approached in this book is that secular palingenetic myth is not derived from religious myth but is simply the expression of an archetype of the human mythopoeic faculty in secular form. In any case it is absurd to assume that the symbolism of death and renewal is peculiar to Christianity or even the 'West'. It is a central motif of religious, mythical and magical thought encountered literally the world over. Different aspects of its prevalence in cosmological thinking, mystical imagery and ritualistic practice have been extensively documented by Eliade (for example 1964, 1971), Jung (for example 1958), Frazer (1957), Schnapper (1965) and Campbell (1968, 1990). It became a well established topos in secularizing societies as well, especially from the mid-nineteenth century onwards, once renegades from the official Western cult of progress became convinced that the decadence gripping society was not inexorable but could be reversed (see Swart, 1964; Fromm, 1963, ch. 6; E. Weber, 1982). One example is Dostoevsky's vision of Russia becoming a Third Rome (see Voegelin, 1952, 113), a notion also explored with quite different connotations by Mazzini.

The theme of regeneration can set the tone for economic projects (for example the 'New Deal'), or architectural schemes (for example the megalomaniac architectural projects of Ceausescu, or the high-rise solutions to slum housing favoured by the town-planners of the sixties). In modern art, too, the myth of rebirth is a familiar theme. It surfaces, for example, in D. H. Lawrence's obsession with regeneration (which led to his adoption of the phoenix as a personal symbol) and in the preoccupation of many modern writers with achieving a new sense of (non-linear) time (for example Kermode, 1967). It need hardly be added that palingenetic myth was central to the Renaissance vision of the West's cultural history, as the term itself testifies. The longing for regeneration can also express itself in quests for the transformation of consciousness, whether of the sort aspired to by the Flower Power generation (for example Reich, 1971), or in modern psycho-therapy (for example in Jungian, EST or rebirthing therapy). It may express itself in something as commonplace as the urge to 'turn over a new leaf' or the sense of magic personal regeneration which accompanies falling in love after a period in an emotional wilderness.

However, it is the power which palingenetic myth can display in the arena of political ideology which concerns us in the present context. Significantly one of the most universal and multivalent symbols of palingenesis, the phoenix, was frequently used in medieval, and even in classical times, to refer to entire eras of secular history when a period of decay had burgeoned into one of 'dynastic, social and political' renewal (Reinitzer, 1981, 82). In modern society, too, moments in history when an old order seems doomed to total annihilation still create the ideal climate for palingenetic myth (even if it is not specifically expressed through the imagery of the phoenix) to be projected on to the contemporary situation and crystallize the hopes that a 'new era' is dawning. Thus it was that members of the French National Assembly felt that their 'liberal' revolution represented the 'regeneration of the world' (see Skocpol, 1985, 88), and that liberal intellectuals nurtured visions of a new world order in the darkest days of the Second World War (for example Buchman, 1941; Wells, 1942; Dawson, 1943; Croce, 1944). The EEC was born partly out of highly pragmatic geopolitical considerations, but also from utopian dreams of a regenerated Europe united by common economic and social goals (for example Schuman, 1963), while *perestroika* owed much of its initial success at home and favourable reception abroad to the way it conjured up mythic visions of Russia's metamorphosis into a liberal and capitalist democracy. (The Russian Revolution itself had originally been a profound palingenetic event – see Stites, 1992.)

'Dark' green politics, too, are a rich source of palingenetic myth, scenarios countered with rhapsodic evocations of a new global order if structural changes are introduced in time (see Capra, 1982).

Obviously the most spectacular manifestations of palingenetic politics in recent history were provided during the autumn of 1989, when state communist regimes in several East-bloc countries were dramatically overthrown. Within the space of a year, history had generated yet another shape of George Bush's dream of a 'New World Order' (which strikes an ominous note into those who see it as *pax Americana*). Ironically, this heady vision, which outstrips in scope even that of another American president, Woodrow Wilson, at the end of the Great War, grew out of the (First-)world crisis brought about when Saddam Hussein lived out territorial ambitions reinforced by a political ideology saturated with palingenetic myth. [. . .] Incidentally, none of these examples have anything to do with political religions, even if late in the day Hussein started cynically blending elements of (Islamic) 'religious' politics into his self-legitimation. Against this background, the expression 'palingenetic myth' comes to denote the vision of a revolutionary new order which supplies the affective power of an ideology, even if, as in the case of liberalism and communism, its ultimate goal is a society which is dynamic but neither violent nor war-like. When this is a political ideology it will centre on a new society inaugurated through human agency and not a millenarian vision of a new world in a metaphysical and supra-historical sense. At the heart of palingenetic political myth lies the belief that contemporaries are living through or about to live through a 'sea-change', a 'water-shed' or 'turning-point' in the historical process. The perceived corruption, anarchy, oppressiveness, iniquities or decadence of the present, rather than being seen as immutable and thus to be endured indefinitely with stoic courage or bleak pessimism, are perceived as having reached their peak and interpreted as the sure sign that one era is nearing its end and a new order is about to emerge.

A characteristic sub-myth of such hopes of transformation is the idea that a 'new man' is destined to appear, a politicized version of the archetypal 'hero myth'. For example, the 'new communist man' was a well-known figure in the Marxist-Leninist evocation of the new era (and was satirized in Wajda's *Man of Steel*) and is still encountered in recent works informed by socialist hopes of renewal (for example Rossi-Landi, 1990, 89; Attwood, 1990). Here again it is possible to find strictly religious analogies, as in the cosmological speculations of medieval Christian poets about the New Man (for example Silvestris, 1978; Alan of Lille, 1973) or *homines noves* (see Voegelin, 1952, 112), cultural parallels (cf. the late 1980s magazine cult of the 'new man'), as well as 'purely' aesthetic equivalents, as in the longing for the 'New Man' in German Expressionism (see Riedel, 1970; Gordon, 1987). Voegelin is thus misleading when he insists on seeing the frequency of the concept in modern ideologies as a symptom of 'eschatological extravaganza' (Sandoz, 1981, 242).

Though etymologically 'palingenetic political myth' could be taken to refer to a 'backward-looking' nostalgia for a restoration of the past (that is rebirth of the *same*), its value as a term in the analysis of ideologies would be diminished if it were to be extended to ultra-conservative or reactionary movements which involved no sense of revolutionary progress or 'new birth'. It is well known that a similar ambiguity is inherent in the word 'revolution', which within a cyclic scheme of history meant returning to an idealized vision of an earlier stage of society. But in an era dominated by linear conceptions of time and progress, 'revolution' now generally denotes the emergence of a substantially new order of society, no matter how much it is inspired by historical precedents or the myth of a past golden age. In palingenetic political myth (which is secular in orientation even when 'religious politics' are involved) the new order will be created within a secular and linear historical time. The arrow of time thus points not backwards but forwards, even when the archer looks over his shoulder for Guidance on where to aim. It is with the particular connotations of political myth and this radically non-restorationist sense of a *'new birth' occurring after a period of perceived decadence* that I propose to use the term 'palingenetic' in this study. Even with these qualifications, however, we are clearly dealing with a phenomenon which in medical terms might be termed 'non-specific' in that it can be a symptom of all but the most nostalgic ideologies in their utopian, revolutionary phase. It is only in combination with the next political term that it serves to designate something peculiar to fascism.

(b) Populist ultranationalism

One of the pervasive ideological forces in the shaping of modern history is nationalism, and if anything its virulence shows every sign of increasing rather than diminishing. It may well be that the history of the next few decades will be substantially shaped by the conflicts between centrifugal liberal nationalisms with a pacifistic and universalistic orientation on the one hand and centripetal illiberal nationalisms of a violent and separatist impetus on the other. The prospects of achieving any substantive 'green revolution' in time to save the ecosystem clearly depends partly on the triumph, or at least predominance, of the former.

However, as a taxonomic term in the social sciences 'nationalism' is, like 'ideology', a victim of its own success. It has been identified as an ingredient in a wide range of conflicting political systems and ideologies and has generated a plethora of sub-categories, such as 'tribal', 'pan-ethnic', 'dynastic', 'religious', 'liberal', 'communist', 'Third World', 'imperialist', 'Enlightenment', 'Romantic', 'integral' nationalisms (see Minogue, 1967; Smith, 1979; Alter, 1989). This rampant 'diversification' stems from the fact that the root concept 'nation' admits a wide range of definitions according to whether the criteria invoked are religious, geographical, historical, constitutional, cultural, linguistic, ethnic or genetic. Moreover, even when the same criteria are used, the connotations of the term necessarily vary according to the particular historical and political conditions which relate to the grouping in question. For example the core entity undergoes significant semantic shifts as we consider in turn 'British', 'Welsh', 'Arabic', 'African', 'Islamic', 'Aboriginal' nationalisms.

To refine the term so that it becomes useful for the investigation of fascism I propose to use the more specialized sub-category 'populist ultra-nationalism'. I follow Eley (1980, 281) in using 'populist' not to refer to a specific historical experience (for example late nineteenth-century American or Russian Populism) but as a generic term for political forces which, even if led by small elite cadres or self-appointed 'vanguards', in practice or in principle (and not merely for show) depend on 'people power' as the basis of their legitimacy. I am using 'ultranationalism', which already has some currency in the political sciences, to refer to forms of nationalism which 'go beyond', and hence reject, anything compatible with liberal institutions or with the tradition of Enlightenment humanism which underpins them. It approximates to what has also been referred to as 'integral' (Alter, 1989) or 'radical' (Eley, 1980) nationalism.

Combined into a single expression, 'populist ultra-nationalism' precludes the nationalism of dynastic rulers and imperial powers before the rise of mass politics and democratic forces (for example that of the Habsburgs or the Pharaohs), as well as the populist (liberal) nationalism which overthrows a colonial power to institute representative democracy (for example that of Mazzini in the Italian *risorgimento* and of many Czechoslovakians in late 1989). In other words, populist ultra-nationalism rejects the principles both of absolutism and of pluralist representative government. In Weberian terms (see M. Weber, 1948) it thus repudiates both 'traditional' and 'legal/rational' forms of politics in favour of prevalently 'charismatic' ones in which the cohesion and dynamics of movements depends almost exclusively on the capacity of their leaders to inspire loyalty and action (see Roth, 1963, for the notion that populist revolutionary movements in which myth in the Sorelian sense plays a central role are essentially charismatic). It tends to be associated with a concept of the nation as a 'higher' racial, historical, spiritual or organic reality which embraces all the members of the ethical community who belong to it. Such a community is regarded by its protagonists as a natural order which can be contaminated by miscegenation and immigration, by the anarchic, unpatriotic mentality encouraged by liberal individualism, internationalist socialism, and by any number of 'alien' forces allegedly unleashed by 'modern' society, for example the rise of the 'Masses', the decay of moral values, the 'levelling' of society, cosmopolitanism, feminism, and consumerism. For the sake of succinctness 'ultra-nationalism' will henceforth be used exclusively with the qualifying connotations of 'populist' outlined here.

Defined in these terms, numerous forms of ultra-nationalism can be seen to have emerged since the breakdown of absolutist *ancien régimes* and 'the rise of the masses': in the many movements of racism and xenophobia which operate within liberal democracies while completely rejecting the pluralism and universal human rights on which these are based (for example the Ku Klux Klan, anti-immigration leagues in several EC countries); in those separatist nationalisms which eschew the liberal goal of instituting substantive democratic institutions after secession (for example those which have arisen in Azerbaijan now that the bonds holding together the Soviet Union are weakening); in the many nationalistic authoritarian regimes which have attempted to maximize genuine popular consensus rather than reign simply through manipulation and terror (for example the regimes of Vargas, Perón, Schuschnigg, Qadhafi) – which are to be distinguished from the pseudo-populism of many other modern dictatorships which cultivate the illusion of popular consensus as the justification for their despotism (for example Marcos, Pinochet, Pol Pot, Ceausescu, Saddam Hussein). Genuinely populist ultra-nationalism plays a determining role, too, in generic fascism.

The 'fascist minimum': palingenetic ultra-nationalism

When the terms palingenetic ultra-nationalism are combined they delimit each other in such a way that, like 'nation-state', or 'social democracy', they become a relatively precise political concept. Just as the combination of two lenses in a telescope can bring a distinct object suddenly into focus, the binomial expression which they create defines a genus of political energy far more circumscribed than the vast areas of phenomena embraced by them separately, namely one whose mobilizing vision is that of *the national community rising phoenix-like after a period of encroaching decadence which all but destroyed it.*

To treat a mythic core based on this vision as the 'fascist minimum' is an example of what Max Weber called 'idealizing abstraction' at work. For both components have been identified independently in previous scholarship without being consciously combined within a synthetic ideal type. Nationalism (by which scholars clearly mean a profoundly illiberal form which corresponds to what we have called ultra-nationalism) is practically the only common denominator of all previous accounts of fascism's definitional characteristics, whether proposed by Marxists (for example Frolov, 1985, 194) or non-Marxists (for example E. Weber, 1964, 17–25; Hayes, 1973, 51–62; Linz, 1979, 28–9; Mosse, 1980, 189; O'Sullivan, 1983, 161–7; Sternhell, 1986, 148; Payne, 1980, 7).

Independent corroboration for the centrality of its 'palingenetic' component is inevitably far more patchy, but Payne alludes to it when under the heading 'ideology and goals' he includes the creation of a 'new nationalist authoritarian state', a 'new . . . integrated economic structure', a '*new* form of modern, self-determined, secular culture' (Payne, 1980, 17 (**5**); my emphasis). Implicit recognition of it can likewise be detected when Smith (1979, 54) acknowledges that fascism offered 'a new solution to the old nationalist problems of the decay and decline of community' and associates this with the theme of the 'new fascist man'. In similar vein Mosse's 'general theory of fascism' (1979, ch. 1) states that the 'new fascist man provided the stereotype for all fascist movements' (ibid., 26), and a number of other scholars see the concept of the new man as a central fascist myth (for example, ibid., 82, 128, 265–7; Cannistraro, 1972, 130; De Felice, 1982, 214). Mosse also takes seriously fascist claims to represent a revolutionary 'Third Force' in European history in which 'utopianism and traditionalism' merged (op. cit., 8). Sternhell goes even further. He sees as the central thrust of fascist ideology the awakening of 'a desire for reaction and regeneration that were simultaneously spiritual and physical, moral, social and political' in an all-embracing 'revolt against decadence' (Sternhell, 1979, 356–7). In fact the whole thrust of the major essay on fascist ideology in which he makes the observation is the recognition of the centrality of what we have called 'palingenetic myth' to the ethos of fascism (ibid., 325–406).

References

Alan of Lille. 1973. *Anticlaudius* (trans. James Sheridan), Universal, Toronto.

Alter, P., 1989. *Nationalism*, Edward Arnold, London.

Attwood, L., 1990. *The New Soviet Man and Woman. Sex-role Socialization in the USSR*, Macmillan, London.

Ballanche, P. S., 1833. *Palingénésie sociale: prolégomènes*, Vol. 4 of *Oeuvres complètes*, Bureau de l'encyclopédie des connaissances utiles, Paris.

Buchman, F., 1941. *Remaking the World*, William Heinemann, London.

Campbell, J., 1968. *The Hero with a Thousand Faces*, Princeton University Press, Princeton.

Campbell, J., 1990. *The Hero's Journey*, Harper, New York.

Cannistraro, P. V., 1972. Mussolini's cultural revolution: fascist or nationalist?, *Journal of Contemporary History*, Vol. 7, Nos. 3–4.

Capra, F., 1982. *The Turning Point*, Wildwood House, London.

Cohn, N., 1970. *The Pursuit of the Millennium*, Palladin, London.

Croce, B., 1944. *Per la nuova vita dell'Italia. Scritti e discorsi 1943–44*, Ricciardi, Naples.

Dawson, C., 1943. *The Renewal of Civilization,* National Peace Council, London.

De Felice, R., 1982. Fascism, in P. V. Cannistraro (ed.), *A Historical Dictionary of Italian Fascism*, Greenwood Press, Westport, Connecticut, London.

Eley, G., 1980. *Reshaping the German Right. Radical Nationalism and Political Change after Bismarck*, Yale University Press, New Haven.

Eliade, M., 1964. *Shamanism: Archaic Techniques of Ecstasy*, Routledge & Kegan Paul, London.

Eliade, M., 1971. *La Nostalgie des Origines*. Méthodologie et Histoire des Religions, Gallimard, Paris.

Frazer, J. G., 1957. *The Golden Bough*, Macmillan, London.

Frolov, I., 1985. *Dictionnaire Philosophique*, Editions du Progrès, Moscow.

Fromm, E., 1963. *The Sane Society*, Routledge & Kegan Paul, London.

Gentile, E., 1975. *Le Origini dell'ideologia Fascista*, Laterza, Bari.

Gordon, D. E., 1987. *Expressionism: Art and Idea*, Yale University Press, New Haven.

Hayes, P. M., 1973. *Fascism*, George Allen & Unwin, London.

Jung, C. G., 1958. *The Undiscovered Self,* Routledge & Kegan Paul, London.

Kermode, J. F., 1967. The modern apocalypse, in *The Sense of an Ending*, Oxford University Press, Oxford.

Lazzari, G., 1984. Linguaggio, ideologia, politica culturale del fascismo, *Movimento Operaio e Socialista*, Vol. 7, No. 1.

Linz, J. J., 1979. Some notes towards the comparative study of fascism, in W. Laqueur (ed.), *Fascism: A Reader's Guide*, Penguin Books, Harmondsworth.

Minogue, K. R., 1967. *Nationalism*, B.T. Batsford, London.

Mosse, G. L., 1980. *Masses and Man*, Howard Fertig, New York.

O'Sullivan, N. K., 1983. *Fascism*, J. M. Dent & Sons, London.

Payne, S. G., 1980. The concept of fascism, in S. U. Larsen, B. Hagtvet, J. P. Myklebust, 1980. *Who Were the Fascists?*, Universitetsforlaget, Bergen and Oslo.

Reich, C., 1971. *The Greening of America*, The Penguin Press, Harmondsworth.

Reinitzer, H., 1981. Vom Vogel Phönix, in W. Harms and H. Reinitzer (eds), *Natura loquax*, Peter D. Lang, Frankfurt-on-Main.

Riedel, W., 1970. *Der neue Mensch*, Bouvier und Co. Verlag, Bonn.

Rossi-Landi, F., 1990. *Ideology,* Oxford University Press, Oxford.

Roth, J., 1963. Revolution and morale in modern French thought: Sorel, and the Sorelians, *French Historical Studies*, Vol. 3, No. 2.

Sandoz, E., 1981. *The Voegelinian Revolution*, Louisiana State University Press, Baton Rouge, London.

Schnapper, E. B., 1965. *The Inward Odyssey,* George Allen & Unwin, London.

Schuman, R., 1963. *Pour l'Europe*, Nagel, Paris.

Silvestris, B., 1978. *Cosmographia*, ed. P. Dronke, Brill, Leiden.

Skocpol, T., 1985. Cultural idioms and political ideologies in the revolutionary restructuring of state power: a rejoinder to Sewell, *Journal of Modern History*, Vol. 57, No. 1.

Smith, A., 1979. *Nationalism in the Twentieth Century*, Martin Robertson, Oxford.

Sternhell, Z., 1979. Fascist ideology, in W. Laqueur (ed.), *Fascism: A Reader's Guide*, Penguin Books, Harmondsworth.

Sternhell, Z., 1987. Fascism, in David Miller (ed.), *The Blackwell Encyclopedia of Political Thought*, Basil Blackwell, Oxford.

Stites, R., 1992. *Revolutionary Dreams. Utopian Dreams and Experimental Life in the Russian Revolution*, Oxford University Press, Oxford.

Swart, K. W., 1964. *The Sense of Decadence in Nineteenth-century France*, International Archives of the History of Ideas, The Hague.

Voegelin, E., 1952. *The New Science of Politics*, University of Chicago Press, Chicago and London.

Weber, E., 1982. Decadence on a private income, *Journal of Contemporary History*, Vol. 17, No. 1.

Weber, E., 1964. *Varieties of History*, D. Van Nostrand, New York.

Weber, M., 1948. *From Max Weber* (ed. and trans. by H. H. Gerth and C. Wright Mills), Routledge & Kegan Paul, London.

Wells, H. G., 1942. *Phoenix. A Summary of the Inescapable Condition of the World Reorganization*, Secker & Warburg, London.

Chapter 16

Stanley Payne

THE IDEAL TYPE OF FASCISM: A 'RETRODICTIVE THEORY'

■ from *A HISTORY OF FASCISM, 1914–1945*, London, 1997, pp. 487–95

Stanley Payne's 'retrodictive' theory of fascism constitutes an ideal type. He warns the reader that 'not all of these factors existed in every (fascist) case', but most of the factors he lists did characterise the host of fascist groups in interwar Europe. His subsequent analysis of his theory discovers discrepancies (for example, Romania developed a strong fascist movement although it had come out of the First World War as one of the biggest victors in territorial terms) and discusses them critically. Interestingly, Payne also links the absence of some of these factors in specific movements to their eventual failure either to attract mass following or to acquire power. A reference to the 'era of fascism' towards the end of the excerpt alludes (critically) to Ernst Nolte's view of fascism as an 'epochal' phenomenon (see **12**).

Elements of a retrodictive theory of fascism

T HE SEARCH FOR AN ADEQUATE theory or interpretation of fascism has generally ended in failure, so that over the years the residue left by such discussions has come to resemble, in MacGregor Knox's phrase, the remains of a desert battlefield littered with abandoned or burned-out wrecks. Most theories of fascism can be easily shown to lack general or even specific validity. They mostly tend toward the monocausal or reductionist and can either be disproved or shown to be inadequate with greater or lesser ease. Moreover, most of those who deal with fascism are not primarily concerned with a common or comparative category of diverse movements and/or regimes but refer exclusively or primarily to German National Socialism, which reduces the scope and application of such arguments.

It is doubtful that there is any unique hidden meaning in, cryptic explanation of, or special 'key' to fascism. It was an epochal European revolutionary movement of the early twentieth century of great complexity, fomented by the new ideas and values of the cultural crisis of the fin de siècle and the ideology of hypernationalism. Fascism possessed distinctive political and social doctrines, as well as economic approaches, but these did not stem from any one source and did not constitute an absolutely discrete new economic doctrine. Fascist movements differed more widely among themselves than was the case with various national movements among other political genera. Fascism was not the agent of any other force, class, or interest or the mere reflection of any social class, but was produced by a complex of historical, political, national, and cultural conditions, which can be elucidated and to some extent defined. Above all, fascism was the most revolutionary form of nationalism in Europe to that point in history, and it was characterized by its culture of philosophical idealism, willpower, vitalism, and mysticism and its moralistic concept of therapeutic violence, strongly identified with military values, outward aggressiveness, and empire.

On the basis of broad inductive study of the principal fascist movements, it should be possible to arrive at the constituents of a kind of retrodictive theory of fascism – that is, an elucidation of the particular circumstances that would have to have existed in an early twentieth-century European country in order for a significant fascist movement to have developed. Such movements – gaining the support of as much as about 20 percent or more of the electorate – emerged in only five countries: Italy, Germany, Austria, Hungary, and Romania. The only other two lands where significant fascist movements developed were Spain and Croatia, but the growth of Spanish fascism developed only after incipient civic breakdown and then civil war – circumstances of such crisis as to cloud the issue there – whereas in Croatia the Ustashi had remained a comparatively small movement before Hitler overran Yugoslavia and awarded power to Pavelic as a second choice.

The elements of such a retrodictive theory would include many factors, including the cultural, political, social, economic, and international. Obviously not all these factors existed in every case where a significant fascist movement developed, but the great majority of them did, and the absence of certain factors may explain the ultimate failure of one or two of the stronger movements.

The cultural roots of fascism lay in certain ideas of the late nineteenth century and in the cultural crisis of the fin de siècle. The chief doctrines involved were intense nationalism, militarism, and international Social Darwinism in the forms that became widespread among the World War I generation in greater central Europe, coupled with the contemporary philosophical and cultural currents of neoidealism, vitalism, and activism, as well as the cult of the hero. Fascism developed especially in the central European areas of Germany, Italy, and the successor states of Austria-Hungary most affected by these cultural trends. It was also to be found in varying degrees outside greater central Europe, but elsewhere fascism was more effectively counterbalanced by opposing cultural influences. The impact in France may have been nearly as great as in central Europe, since some of these concepts originated there. Yet the overall effect in France was less, because the ideas were counterbalanced by other elements and because the overall sense of crisis was less acute. Moreover, most of the other variables were scarcely present in France. The case of

Romania is somewhat peculiar, for the fin de siècle crisis seems initially to have been less intense there. Among the smaller Romanian intelligentsia, nonetheless, the general sense of crisis grew after World War I. A Marxist response was ineffective for domestic political and for geopolitical reasons, while more moderate nationalist populism proved ineffective. Spain was another peripheral country in which the effect of the fin de siècle crisis was weaker, and in fact fascism had little presence there before the final breakdown of 1936.

Cultural factors

1   Comparatively strong influence of the cultural crisis of the fin de siècle
2   Preexisting comparatively strong currents of nationalism
3   Perceived crisis in cultural values
4   Strong influence (or challenge) of secularization

Political factors

1   A comparatively new state, not more than three generations old
2   A political system that temporarily approximates liberal democracy but has existed for no more than a single generation
3   A fragmented or seriously polarized party system
4   A significant prior political expression of nationalism
5   An apparent danger, either internally or externally, from the left
6   Effective leadership
7   Significant allies
8   In order to triumph, a government that is at least semidemocratic at the time of direct transition to power

Social factors

1   A situation of pronounced social tension or conflict
2   A large sector of workers and/or peasants-farmers that are either unrepresented, underrepresented, or outside the main party system
3   Major middle-class discontent with the existing party system because of either underrepresentation or major party/electoral shifts
4   Existence of a Jewish minority

Economic factors

1   Economic crisis either of dislocation or of underdevelopment, caused by or nominally imputable to war, defeat, or 'foreign' domination
2   A sufficient level of development in politics and economics to have neutralized the military

International factors

1   A serious problem of status humiliation, major status striving, and/or under-development
2   Existence of a fascist role model

Fascism could not become a major force in countries where a reasonably signifi-cant nationalist ideology or movement had not preceded it, at least by half a generation if not more. So radical and intense a doctrine could gain momentum only as the second stage in ongoing nationalist agitation and mobilization. This was the case in each example of a vigorous fascist movement, while the virtual absence of any previously mobilized nationalism in Spain was a major handicap for the Falange that could not be overcome under seminormal political conditions.

Fascism seems also to have required the kind of cultural space opened by a process of secularization or, in one or two cases, the challenge of a kind of secular-ization not otherwise being met. In most of the more heavily secularized countries, conversely, fascism was not a challenge either because the secularization process had been effectively completed or because most of the other preconditions did not exist. In a number of central European countries, fascism was able to take advan-tage of the space left by secularization, and it was less successful in nonsecularized areas. In Spain, political Catholicism sought to meet the challenge of leftist secular-ization directly, and under seminormal political conditions it had no need of fascism. In Romania, however, fascism itself provided perhaps the main political challenge to secularization, creating a hybrid religious fascism, though necessarily of a semi-heretical character. The core fascist movements were anticlerical and fundamentally even antireligious, but this was not so much the case in the geographically and developmentally more peripheral areas. As the main example of a nominally reli-gious or Christian fascism, the Legion of the Archangel Michael was the most anomalous of fascist movements, for the somewhat heretical or potentially schis-matic character of its mysticism nonetheless did not obviate its peculiar religiosity.

In every case, the significant fascist movements emerged in comparatively new states, none more than three generations old. In general, fascism was a phenomenon of the new countries of the 1860s and 1870s – Italy, Germany, Austria, Hungary, and Romania – their unsatisfied status strivings, defeats, or frustrations, and late-developing political systems. Fascism has sometimes been called the product of a decaying liberal democracy, but that notion can be misleading. In no case where a liberal democratic system had been established either before World War I or had existed for a full generation did the country succumb to fascism. This, rather, was a significant phenomenon only in certain relatively new countries during the period in which they were just making, or had very recently made, the initial tran-sition to a liberal democracy that was as yet unconsolidated. Simultaneously, and again seemingly paradoxically, conditions approximating liberal democracy were in fact necessary for fascist movements to develop and flourish. They did not function as Communist-style insurrections but as broad European nationalist movements which required the liberty to mobilize mass support – liberty offered only by condi-tions equivalent to, or closely approaching, liberal democracy.

Another, and fairly obvious, requirement was fragmentation, division, or sharp polarization within the political system. Countries with stable party systems, such as Britain, France, and the Low Countries, were largely immune to fascism. The larger fascist parties required not merely some preparation of the soil by a pre-existing movement of intense nationalism but also significant fragmentation or cleavage among the other forces. A partial exception to this stipulation might appear to be the rise of the Arrow Cross in Hungary during the late 1930s, in a situation in which Horthy's government party still enjoyed a nominal majority. In this case, however, the system was one of only semiliberal democracy at best. The elitist ruling party was increasingly unpopular and maintained its status to that point only by sharp electoral restrictions, accompanied by some corruption. Fascism (or more precisely the multiple national socialisms, in the Hungarian nomenclature) thus became the main vehicle for a deeply felt popular protest that had few other means of expression. The structure of the Hungarian electoral system stood apart from that of most other European parliamentary regimes.

The existence of a menace from the left – either real or perceived – has often been held necessary for the rise of fascist movements, and this is generally correct. Italian Fascism could probably never have triumphed without the specter, and the reality, of revolutionary social maximalism. Germany was the home of the strongest Communist party in Europe outside the Soviet Union, always perceived as a serious threat by many. In the minds of others, the broad base of support enjoyed by German Social Democrats only added to the problem. The even greater strength of socialism in Austria was at first a basic catalytic factor there, while the Spanish Civil War represented the ultimate in left–right polarization.

Conversely, the left would not seem at first glance to have played an equivalent role in Hungary and Romania, but certain other features of politics in these countries must also be kept in mind. At the beginning of the interwar period, Hungary was briefly the only country outside the Soviet Union ruled by a revolutionary Communist regime. This colored Hungarian politics for the next generation, exacerbating anticommunism and antileftism in general and also helping to create the conditions in which only a radical nonleftist movement such as Hungarian national socialism would have both the freedom and the appeal to mobilize broadly social discontent. In Romania, the Communist Party was effectively suppressed and the Socialists weak, but Romania now shared a new border with the Soviet Union, which never in principle recognized the Romanian occupation of Bessarabia. Anticommunism thus remained a significant factor in Romanian affairs, and Soviet seizure of Bessarabia and Bukovina in 1940 (together with Hitler's award of much of Transylvania to Hungary) created the condition of extreme trauma in which Antonescu and then the Legion could come to power.

Fascist movements were no different from other political groups in needing effective leadership. In fact, because of their authoritarian principles they required a strong leader – with at least some degree of ability – more than did more liberal forces. Not all the leaders of the larger fascist movements were charismatic or efficient organizers, Szalasi being perhaps the best negative example. But in many cases leadership was a factor in helping to determine the relative success of the movement, even though other conditions were more determinative. The difference between the relative success of a Mosley and a Szalasi did not lie in their respective talent and ability but in the totally distinct conditions of their two countries.

Leadership was more important the higher any particular fascist movement rose. It became vital for any serious attempt to take power, except in the cases where Hitler simply awarded authority to puppets of limited ability such as Pavelic and Szalasi. When Horia Sima, a relatively incompetent leader, was awarded a share of power in Romania, he was unable either to consolidate or to expand it. Given the inability of fascist parties to employ insurrectionary tactics because of the institutionalized character of European polities, allies were in every case essential for taking power. No fascist leader ever seized power exclusively on his own, as leader of a fascist movement and no more. Since semilegal tactics were required, and even the most popular fascist movement never gained an absolute majority, allies — who almost always came from the authoritarian right — were indispensable in bringing a fascist leader to power and even to some extent in helping to expand that power.

Though fascism battened on the weakening of democracy and consensus, it was important for such movements that relative pluralism and some degree of a representative process be preserved up to the time of initially taking power. Without conditions of at least relative freedom — even if not the purest constitutional democracy — a fascist leader could not expect to be able to take power (again, with the standard exception of Hitler's puppets). Authoritarian government closed the door to fascism in Austria and Portugal, in Vichy France, and in a number of eastern European countries. Authoritarian government also controlled and limited the participation of fascists in power in Romania and Spain, subordinating them in the latter and eventually eliminating them altogether in the former.

As far as international circumstances are concerned, significant fascist movements took root in countries suffering from severe national frustration and/or ambition, or in some cases a combination of both. The classic examples of fascist movements battening on a national sense of status deprivation and defeat were the national socialisms, German and Hungarian. To a lesser degree, the whole complex arising from the sense of a *vittoria mutilata* (mutilated victory) in Italy stimulated the growth of Mussolini's movement, though it was not necessarily the prime cause thereof. In Spain, the Falange finally benefited not merely from the challenge of the revolutionary left in 1936 but also from the strong, if paranoid, perceptions of the roles of foreign ideologies and powers therein. Once more the Romanian case seems anomalous, for, despite an ignominious military effort, Romania was one of the biggest winners in World War I, doubling in size and being awarded more territory than it could digest. The deprivation perceived by Romanians did not stem from military defeat or loss of territory (as in Germany and Hungary) but from the failure to achieve dignity, development, and national unity or integration, from the perception of a breakdown in culture and institutions as much as in politics.

Another international factor of importance was the existence abroad of a fascist role model, at least in the case of nearly all the movements except for those in Germany and Italy. To prosper, any fascist movement had to develop autochthonous roots, but foreign examples were factors in encouraging the majority of them, for only in Italy and Germany did they develop absolutely on their own. Conversely, it was of course also true that a fascist movement primarily (rather than only secondarily) dependent on foreign example, ideology, inspiration, or funding was not likely to develop much strength of its own, and thus all the purely mimetic movements — with the exception of Austrian Nazism and perhaps the partial exception of Spanish Falangism — failed.

No aspect of the analysis of fascist movements has generated more controversy than the issue of social bases and origins. It is true that fascism had little opportunity in stable societies not undergoing severe internal tensions. A significant degree of internal stress or social conflict was a sine qua non, but that is about as far as agreement has gone. There is relative consensus that the lower middle class was the most decisive social stratum for fascism, but even this has been somewhat exaggerated. Italian Fascism, for example, had approximately as much support from workers, farmers, and farm laborers during its rise as it did from the lower middle class, the mesocratic stratum coming to dominate membership only after formation of the dictatorship. The decisiveness of different social classes varied from case to case and country to country. The lower middle class was ultimately the most important social sector for the movements in Germany, Austria, Italy, and probably Spain. In these cases, the failure to represent or incorporate the lower middle sectors adequately in the liberal system was important, together with the fragmenting of middle-class parties in Germany and Spain.

In Hungary and Romania, the role of the middle and upper classes was significant primarily for the leadership. The ordinary members were more likely to be peasants and workers. In these countries, it was the failure to incorporate or represent the lower classes that provided available space for mass social recruitment.

In the majority of cases, the existence of a Jewish minority was important for the development of the movement as well. In Italy, on the other hand, this proved to be irrelevant, the Fascist Party itself being disproportionately Jewish. In Poland and Lithuania, conversely, the presence of Jewish minorities as large or even larger than those in Hungary and Romania did not 'elicit' significant fascist movements, though a great deal of less lethal anti-Semitism existed. Once again, no single factor is of crucial importance by itself, but only insofar as it converged, or was unable to converge, with other influences.

In economic structure, influence, or development, no single key common to all significant fascist movements can be found. Such a movement was powerful in one of the best educated and most advanced of European countries, and also in one of the most backward and illiterate. Those seeking to explain the social and economic basis of Hitlerism have often referred to the very high German unemployment statistics of 1930–33, but equally high unemployment existed in various other countries that did not develop significant fascist movements, and the percentage of unemployed was almost as high in the democratic America of Hoover and Roosevelt.

The only economic common denominator was that in every country in which a strong fascist movement was found, there existed a broad perception that the present economic crisis stemmed not merely from normal internal sources but also from military defeat and/or foreign exploitation. The further down the development ladder, the greater the economic hatred of the 'capitalist plutocracies.'

One factor concerning the level of development that was more clear-cut was the need for the country to have achieved a plateau in economic and political development in which the military was no longer a prime factor in political decisions. Otherwise the Mussolini and Hitler governments would probably have been vetoed as both irrelevant and even as harmful by a politically dominant military. Such military powers largely throttled fascism in eastern Europe.

Not one of the factors providing elements for a retrodictive theory was of any great significance by itself, or even in combination with one or two others. Only if the majority of them converged in a given country between the wars was it possible for a truly fascistogenic situation to develop.

To recast the retrodictive design in simpler and shorter terms, then, we can say that the necessary conditions for the growth of a significant fascist movement involved strong influence from the cultural crisis of the fin de siècle in a situation of perceived mounting cultural disorientation; the background of some form of organized nationalism before World War I; an international situation of perceived defeat, status humiliation, or lack of dignity; a state system comparatively new that was entering or had just entered a framework of liberal democracy; a situation of increasing political fragmentation; large sectors of workers, farmers, or petit bourgeois that were either not represented or had lost confidence in the existing parties; and an economic crisis perceived to stem in large measure from foreign defeat or exploitation.

Fascism was, as Nolte, Mosse, Weber, and Griffin have explained, a revolutionary new epochal phenomenon with an ideology and a distinctive set of ambitions in its own right. It was also the product of distinctive national histories, being primarily confined to the new nations of the 1860s – new state systems that had failed to achieve empire and status, and in some cases even reasonable economic development. Sufficient conditions existed for strong fascisms in those countries alone, the only exception being the sudden rise of fascism in Spain amid the unique civil war crisis of 1936 – itself sufficient explanation of this apparent anomaly in the Europe of the 1930s.

Conversely, sufficient conditions for the growth of fascist movements have ceased to exist since 1945, even though the number of neofascist or putatively neofascist movements during the past half century has been possibly even greater than the number of genuine fascist movements during the quarter century 1920–45. [. . .]

To call the entire period 1919–45 an era of fascism may be true in the sense that fascism was the most original and vigorous new type of radical movement in those years, and also in the sense that Germany for a time became the dominant state in Europe. The phrase is inaccurate, however, if it is taken to imply that fascism became the dominant political force of the period, for there were always more antifascists than fascists. Antifascism preceded fascism in many European countries, and among Italian Socialists – in their opposition to Mussolini's early 'social chauvinism' – it almost preceded the original Fascism itself. Down to 1939, antifascists, both voters and activists, always outnumbered fascists in Europe as a whole.

Crises and semirevolutionary situations do not long persist, and fascist movements lacked any clear-cut social class or interest basis to sustain them. Their emphasis on a militarized style of politics, together with their need for allies, however temporary the association, greatly restricted their opportunities as well as their working time, requiring them to win power in less than a generation and in some cases within only a few years. The drive of a fascist movement toward power threatened the host polity with a slate of political war (though normally not insurrectionary civil war) quite different from normal parliamentary politics. No system can long withstand a state of latent war, even if a direct insurrection is not launched. It either succumbs or overcomes the challenge. In the great majority of cases the fascist challenge was repelled, though sometimes at the cost of establishing a more moderate authoritarian system. At any rate, the 0.7 percent of the popular vote won by the Spanish Falange in the 1936 elections was much nearer the norm than the 38 percent won by the Nazis in 1932.

SECTION IV

■ Varieties of fascist movements

THE TEMPTATION TO DEDUCE THEORIES and models of generic fascism from the experience of Fascist Italy and/or Nazi Germany is often irresistible, perhaps even methodologically justifiable. After all, there are many compelling reasons to treat the movements and systems of rule that emerged in these two countries as the arch-priests of the new 'conquering creed' of the twentieth century, as Mussolini described fascism (Mussolini 1932, in Oakeshott 1949: 178ff.). First of all, the very term 'fascism' is indisputably the intellectual property of the *Duce*, his own patented contrivance which he subsequently branded as an 'export product', suitable for the regeneration of other countries too. Then, the consolidation of the NSDAP after 1928 and the establishment of the Nazi system after the *Machtergreifung* (seizure of power, January 1933) created an increasingly powerful source of inspiration for kindred movements and aspirations across Europe. If fascism remained essentially a peculiarly Italian experiment in the 1920s, stimulating mixed responses from outside commentators – ranging from outright admiration and imitation to scepticism or even flat rejection – the advent of Nazism in Germany transformed the novel phenomenon of revolutionary, organic 'palingenetic' (Griffin 1993b) nationalism to the status of a major alternative to liberalism and socialism. The attraction in the 1930s was obvious, in the sense that fascism had become not just internationalised but also the defining characteristic of the political operation of two Great Powers. This provided fascism with powerful publicity, the aura of resilience and the status of dominant worldview – a perfect recipe for attracting further attention and inspiriting new disciples throughout Europe.

Thus, the methodological dilemma that underpins any analysis of interwar fascism relates to the way a workable definition of 'fascism' can be fashioned. The task of identifying appropriate case-studies of fascism has always generated bitter controversies without producing an unequivocal set of criteria for distinguishing fascism from more conventional forms of authoritarianism and conservatism. In a continent with so many varied traditions and historical trajectories it is impossible to accommodate the emergence of fascism as the result of a single set of circumstances. Fascism was corporatist in western and central Europe (especially in countries with strong traditions of social Catholicism), but not necessarily in the east. It was essentially secular in Italy and Germany but not in Romania, Austria or Portugal. It was racist in the Nordic countries but far less so in the south. It was anti-Semitic in Germany, Romania, France and Britain but not actively so in Hungary or Greece – even less so in Italy. Fascism, essentially a *national* prescription for domestic problems, reverberated the different histories of the various corners of the European continent; and, unlike in the case of the Socialist International, these differences proved an overwhelming obstacle to efforts to create a common 'fascist' Directory under the aegis of Mussolini's Italy at Montreux in 1934 (see 1).

Identifying the most appropriate 'fascist' cases depends on the definition of fascism each commentator chooses to apply to the vast pool of comparable radical interwar movements. A 'purist' definition of fascism is more likely to produce a very short list; a more flexible approach, on the other hand, will result in a far longer catalogue, encompassing variants which could frustrate any effort to construct an all-embracing definition of fascism. The choice of excerpts in this section is underpinned by a distinction between *endogenous*, authentic national variants of fascism and mimetic movements. The second category encompasses phenomena which were directly inspired by the German and/or Italian paradigms and sought to emulate their features in a strict, uncritical way as part of a wider pan-European crusade spearheaded by the two reference fascist regimes (and the Axis after 1936). This category (with offspring in almost every country, especially in the 1930s, albeit usually with limited membership and political influence – see Merkl 1980) is excluded in favour of the endogenous movements, which display a variety of ideological and political peculiarities, heavily influenced by their respective indigenous traditions.

Three excerpts discuss the emergence of what may be termed 'central/eastern European' fascism (or, to use a term introduced by P. F. Sugar, 'fascism in the successor states' of the dissolved Habsburg empire). Although by no means the only 'fascist' entities in their respective countries (smaller groups, most of them openly mimetic, also operated with limited influence and support), the Iron Guard in Romania and the Arrow Cross in Hungary have attracted the attention of research on comparative fascism, because of their ideological specificity and their popular appeal. The former was characterised by a spirit of Orthodox mysticism and self-sacrifice, a virulent anti-Semitism and a powerful discourse of spiritual regeneration (Barbu (17)). The latter developed its own version of the fascist worldview (Ferenc Szalasi's ideology of *Hungarism*) with strong missionary elements, expansionist ambitions and an elitist attitude which derived its legitimacy from the alleged historic 'greatness' of the Hungarian nation in the past (Deák (18)). Austria (Lewis (19)), on the other hand, offers an interesting comparison between nativist strands of fascism (the Heimwehr and the subsequent Christian Social corporatist state with its one-party structure) and a radical mimetic National Socialist movement (the

Austrian NSDAP). Three further excerpts feature varieties of 'western' European fascism. The first deals with the Spanish Falange (Ellwood (**20**)), a movement that exemplifies a palingenetic discourse impregnated with strong Catholic values and a radical militaristic spirit, committed to an all-out struggle against socialism and corrupt liberalism in search of a 'third-way' political solution to Spain's political deadlock in the 1930s. Interestingly, the Falange constitutes an example of a fascist movement that succeeded in participating in power structures (through its co-operation with Franco's Nationalist forces and its establishment as the only party of the Francoist regime). By contrast, the two last pieces discuss the emergence and failure of fascism in two mature liberal democracies of western Europe. In France fascism expanded over two decades, from the early 1920s to the late 1930s, before finding a political outlet in the form of the Vichy regime in 1940. As R. Soucy points out (**21**), it was saturated with a radical notion of integral nationalism and the quest for social rebirth. For Soucy, France, far from being a barren intellectual territory for 'imported' fascist ideas, experienced two main 'waves' of native fascism but succeeded in upholding the liberal-democratic system until German occupation in 1940. Britain, on the other hand, experienced the formation of a movement (Oswald Mosely's BUF) which combined an openly mimetic stylistic outlook (especially after Mosley's trip to Italy in the early 1930s) with a decidedly autochthonous ideological discourse and political orientation (Thurlow (**22**)). Both excerpts address the complex question of why these indigenous and highly elaborate varieties of fascism failed to exert lasting political influence on their national system and failed (in both electoral and political terms) to challenge effectively the dominant position of the mainstream right in the 1920s and 1930s (cf. (**11**)).

Chapter 17

Z. Barbu

ROMANIA: THE 'IRON GUARD'

■ from **RUMANIA**, in S. Woolf (ed.) *European Fascism*, London, 1968, pp. 50–3, 55–6, 60–4

As Z. Barbu stresses, the Romanian fascist variant – Corneliu Codreanu's Iron Guard – was one of the few 'wholly fascist' movements to exercise power without outside intervention and help. It was also one of the most successful fascist parties in electoral terms. In the following excerpt Barbu analyses the rather unconventional social composition and ideological outlook of the so-called Legionaries in their political trajectory from a small dissident radical group to a big party, its short-lived collaboration with General Antonescu's regime (1940) and its eventual violent suppression by the latter (1941). The author also discusses the paradox of Romanian fascism – that it arose in a country that came out of the First World War with the undisputed label of 'victor' (i.e. with unprecedented territorial gains at the expense of both Russia and Austro-Hungary).

THE ORIGINS OF RUMANIAN FASCISM can be traced back to 1919, and generally speaking to the period of social turmoil following the first world war. The first thing to be mentioned, however, is that Rumania was not a defeated country. Nor was she disappointed and frustrated as was Italy. On the contrary, by a stroke of luck, Rumania came out of the war somehow dizzy with her success: as the result of the peace treaty of Versailles all the provinces in which the Rumanians constituted a majority – Transylvania, Bucovina and Bessarabia – were united in a new Rumanian national state with a population of over seventeen millions. Thus, Rumanian fascism was not the outcome of national defeat. This does not mean, however, that Rumanian fascism was in no way the child of collective confusion and anxiety. As recent studies of mental disorders and of suicide in particular have shown, sudden riches and sudden poverty produce similar results. If the analogy can be stretched so far, Rumania found herself in the position of the *nouveau riche*, with a territory five times bigger than that of the Old Kingdom, and with a population not only considerably larger, but also highly heterogeneous in traditions and ways of life. The problem therefore, was one of organization and unity. What were the unifying factors, and what was the basis for consensus and solidarity in the new community? Questions such as these aroused considerable anxiety. This was reflected in the political situation of the country which was marked by vague democratic populist ideologies and even vaguer democratic reforms – with one exception, the extension of electoral rights to all males over the age of 21. The spectrum of political parties was rich, colourful and highly changeable. One structural feature, however, seemed to be constant: an almost empty 'centre', with the large traditional political parties to the Right, and a very small Social Democratic and even smaller Communist Party to the Left. Electorally, there was no sign of political radicalization.

That the birthplace of the Iron Guard was Moldavia has its own significance. Ever since the creation of the first independent Rumanian state (1859) with its capital in Bucharest, the Moldavians have given signs of wounded pride. One way in which they showed this was by a retreat into provincialism and by slightly demonstrative nationalism. Even more significant is the fact that, at this period, Moldavia had a relatively large Jewish population, larger than that of any other Rumanian province. And last but not least was its geographical position adjoining Bessarabia, recently incorporated in the Rumanian state, and thus highly aware of, and sensitive to the threat of communism. As will be seen later, communism as an idea and a threat from outside played a considerable part in the rise and development of Rumanian fascism, despite the fact that – unlike Germany or Italy – she never had a strong marxist party. Historical circumstances apart, the Iron Guard owed its existence to one man who had been its indisputable leader for almost twenty years. This was Corneliu Zelia Codreanu.

[. . .]

In 1919, Codreanu started his student life in Jassy, the capital of Moldavia. From the start his cultural and political development was deeply influenced by Professor A. I. Cuza, a sort of Rumanian Julius Streicher, obsessed by the Jewish threat to the purity of Christian girls. Cuza was also a skilled demagogue and the inspirer and leader of a small political organization which consisted at the time mainly of students. The programme of the organization was nationalistic-racist and was centred around three main points: (1) The unity of all Rumanians in an ethnic national state from which foreigners were to be eliminated or where they would be deprived of positions of social and political responsibility; (2) the emancipation of the peasants, not so much through economic reforms, badly needed at the time, as through political education; (3) by far the best known point of the programme: the solution of the 'Jewish Problem'. In this context Cuza advocated the complete segregation of the Jews and antisemitic violence as a means to this end.

Cuza was Codreanu's mentor of the Right, but nothing that Codreanu learned from him was strikingly new. Cuza served mainly as a catalyst for his nationalism and antisemitism. There was, however, in Jassy at that time, another political mentor, a much more interesting figure towards whom Codreanu throughout his life conserved a warm feeling of respect and admiration. This was a certain Constantin Pancu, a manual worker with intellectual and political aspirations, who managed to organize around himself a small group consisting of one lawyer, one priest, one student and about thirty skilled manual workers. To the extent that Pancu's group possessed any political programme, it can be described as a vague version of national socialism, with a strong emphasis on the first term. At any rate, what held the group together was an obsession, a sort of action-anxiety – the defeat and final destruction of the communist organizations which were apparently gaining ground in many local industrial enterprises. 'Apparently' is a key word here for, according to some views, communism – or rather the threat of communism – did not play any considerable part in the rise of Rumanian fascism. This may be so, but it is worth recording that Codreanu speaks about thousand-strong communist crowds demonstrating on the streets of Jassy. Though of short duration, Codreanu's membership of Pancu's group provided him with an excellent opportunity to learn and rehearse a role for which he soon became famous. It gave him his first opportunity to organize people and lead them into action, which in this case consisted of street demonstrations and fights. But above all he learned one thing which became a basic tactical principle of the Iron Guard, namely, that violence, organized and sustained violence, pays rich political dividends. Pancu's group specialized in strike-breaking activities and Codreanu excelled in this.

[. . .]

During a short term of imprisonment, in 1923, he had his first vision: the Archangel Michael came to him and urged him to dedicate his life to God as revealed by the Rumanian Christian tradition.[1] A few years later (1927) he founded the 'Brotherhood of the Cross', an elitist body, which he placed at the centre of his party. To indicate the nature of this organization it is necessary to mention that, apart from the Archangel's revelation, Codreanu was inspired by an old Rumanian tradition. Such forms of privileged and mystic associations, or rather communions, between two or more people existed and maybe still exist among Rumanian peasants. The association is highly ritualized and often those entering upon it have to taste each other's blood in order to become brothers, 'unto life and death'. The Brotherhood of the Cross conformed in many ways to this pattern of human relations in which the primary ties of blood are symbolically resurrected. The Brotherhood of the Cross was the mystic body of the Iron Guard, open only to the few and the elect. Those worthy of membership had to undergo a primitive ceremony, a *rite de passage*. They were summoned to a secret place, and after an incantational ritual which took place at a late hour of the night they made a formal vow pledging their life to the cause and the 'Captain'.

In 1926, as a result of a quarrel between Codreanu and Cuza, the League of National Christian Defence was dissolved, and in 1927 there came into being the first independent political organization of Codreanu's movement, the Legion of the Archangel Michael. This was a prototype of fascist organization. To start with, it had no political programme. 'The country is dying for lack of men and not for lack of programmes' were the words used by Codreanu at the foundation meeting of the Legion. If I may advance an idea, the *legionari* constituted a psychological rather than a political group: the basic trait of their organization was a state of mind. The main points in their programme were, 'Faith in God', 'Faith in the Mission' and 'Love for each other'. All these were 'cultist' in character, and required specific tests and trials and particularly specific states of mind. This is even more clearly revealed by the fourth point in their programme; 'Love of songs'. [. . .] [M]usic, vocal music above all, was a basic element of the *legionaris'* way of life. All their meetings started and ended in incantational rituals of song and often dance.

[. . .]

It is now time to return to the political activities and success of the Iron Guard. [. . .] [T]he League of National Christian Defence won six parliamentary seats in the election of 1926. This represented 120,000 votes. In 1931, the Legion of the Archangel Michael won less than two per cent of the electorate and according to the Rumanian constitution this meant no representation in parliament. One year later, however, it won five seats. This was the first serious warning of its political potential and the government reacted swiftly by dissolving the Legion as a political party. This allowed the legionaries to pose once more as victims. The proof is that, in 1937, when they were recognized again as a political party under the name 'All for the Fatherland' they gained sixty seats, representing more than sixteen per cent of the electorate. This placed the Iron Guard in the second place – after the National Peasant Party – among the political parties of the country. In 1938, the organization was dissolved once more and its leadership decimated by the dicta-torial regime of King Carol. Between April and December 1939, more than 1200 legionaries, including Codreanu, were arrested and lost their lives in circumstances which have remained to a great extent obscure. The official version was that they were shot while trying to escape. Although it never recovered from this blow, the Iron Guard appeared once more in the political arena. This was in 1940–1 when Rumania had for the first time a *legionari* government. It was in fact a coalition government of the military group of General Antonescu and the surviving elements of the Iron Guard under the leadership of Horia Sima. The coalition did not work, and after an abortive *putsch* and revolution, in early 1941, the legionaries were eliminated from the government and their leadership was again decimated.

The political career of the Iron Guard can be summed up in two points. First, between 1931 and 1940 it increasingly became one of the most important political forces in Rumania. Second, with the exception of Italian fascism and German Nazism, it was one of the few wholly fascist movements to come to power and form a government. How can one explain this success?

In answering such a question, it is useful to recall one of the best known inter-pretative models of sociological studies of fascism. According to this model, fascism is a middle-class phenomenon expressing the interests of either the upper middle class, i.e. their expansionist-imperialistic aspirations as well as their apprehensions about the economic implications of liberal democracy, or the specific interests of the lower middle classes in their struggle against 'big capital'. Sometimes these two hypotheses are combined, and the interpretative model is amplified with other variables, such as the level of industrialization of the community as a whole, and the degree of politicization of the masses and of the working classes in particular.

The difficulty about applying such interpretative models to Rumania of the inter-war period is that the middle classes were numerically small, as well as ideologically, politically and socio-culturally ill-defined. Something like eighty per cent of the population were peasants while the industrial workers constituted a tiny and poorly organized minority. The difficulty is increased when one takes into account the ideology of the Iron Guard with its systematic attack on urban bourgeois values and ways of life.

All this makes it necessary to abandon for Rumania, at least for the moment, the theoretical hypothesis regarding the middle-class character of fascism and to look more closely at the social composition of the Iron Guard at the levels of leadership, party membership and electoral support. Naturally it must be borne in mind that one is dealing here with an authoritarian organization; hence the level which counts most is that of leadership.

From the very beginning, the leadership was dominated by two categories of people, intellectuals and youth. For lack of more adequate documentation, the best one can do to illustrate this point is to refer to the data offered by Weber from the analysis of two groups in terms of their occupation and age. The first consists of 251 legionaries interned in Buchenwald between 1942 and 1944, the second of 32 legionaries executed at Vaslui in September 1939. Though for obvious reasons these cannot be considered as representative samples, the following figures seem to be indicative of both the composition of the leadership and the membership of the organization as a whole. Taking the two groups together, intellectuals repre-sented between forty and fifty per cent, including students who alone represented almost thirty per cent, professions and public servants. The average age in the first group was 27.4. Particularly young was the top leadership. For instance, in 1931 Codreanu was thirty-two, Motsa twenty-nine, Marin twenty-seven and Stelescu twenty-four. The question of the social origins of the Legion's leadership and its membership in general presents considerable difficulties. As Weber rightly points out, the middle-class element (state employees, professionals, and even tradesmen and shopkeepers) seems at first sight to dominate. But one particularly relevant point needs to be noted: their connection with the traditional rural population and way of life is direct, almost uninterrupted. Codreanu was the son of a schoolteacher and the grandson of a peasant, Motsa the son of a priest and grandson of a peasant. This applies to the leadership at all levels and on the whole to the so-called middle-class element of the Legion.

All this throws considerable doubt on the class membership, let alone on the class identity of the legionaries. It is very likely that we are dealing here with a psychological rather than a social group. Most of its members were climbing up the ladder of social hierarchy in the direction of the middle class. But the point is that they had not yet arrived, they had not yet broken away from their rural traditional background. On the whole they were a marginal group and it was their condition of marginality rather than their class interests and consciousness which determined their political behaviour. What follows is an attempt to demonstrate this point.

The prominent part played by the intelligentsia in the history of the Legion can in itself be taken as a symptom of marginality, of classlessness, as Mannheim would put it. To this general condition can be added a series of more specific ones. First of all, the kind of intelligentsia we are dealing with belonged to an emerging, newly born society without a clear sense of solidarity and identity, and certainly without a stable system of stratification. Furthermore, they belonged to a society in which the upper as well as the urban strata were traditionally associated if not identified with outsiders, Turks, Hungarians, Germans, Greeks and Jews. This says a great deal about the social position, objective or subjective, of Rumanian intelligentsia and of legionary intelligentsia in particular. In reality they could not and did not belong anywhere, and escaped reality by inventing their society and reference group. For example, Codreanu identified himself with the 'people', an idealized community which he never defined except in vague and abstract terms such as 'unity', 'purity', 'Christianity'. It was an unhistorical entity including all Rumanians who had existed in the past and would exist in the future. Even more characteristically, Motsa, after rejecting the corrupt social reality of his time, identified himself with the 'old world', the legendary past of his nation. This is an important point which should occupy a central place in any detailed study of Rumanian fascism. The most one can do here is to point out that the reference group of the legionaries, of the intellectuals in particular, was an imaginary one. It was an ideal society in which the legend of an old traditional Rumanian community loomed large. The predominant utopistic element in this image of society was of a moral religious character, with brotherly unity and love as the basis of communal life.

The only element which linked this image of society to reality was the rural community of the Rumanian village. As has often been said, the legionaries were 'idealists' in that they 'struggled to maintain and indeed to introduce into Rumanian society of the interwar period the morality and social solidarity of a traditional community and primary group. They were the arch-enemies of secularization, urbanization and industrialization. Moreover, they tried to maintain – in an idealized form, of course – the elements of a pre-market and pre-individualized society. Nobody who lived in Rumania during this period can forget the eerie and anachronistic character of a legionary demonstration. It was something between a political protest, religious procession and a historical *cortege*. The middle and indeed the core of the demonstration consisted of a well-organized body of young people in uniform – the 'green shirts'. It was normally headed by a group of priests carrying icons and religious flags. Finally, all this was followed and surrounded by men and women in national traditional dress. It is significant that the Captain normally appeared in traditional Moldavian dress, though the green shirt was the official uniform of the Legion.

Note

1   In 1926 Codreanu murdered the prefect of Galatsi, Manciu.

Chapter 18

Istvan Deák

HUNGARY: HORTHY, GÖMBÖS AND THE 'ARROW CROSS'

■ from **HUNGARY**, in H. Rogger and E. Weber (eds) *The European Right: A Historical Profile*, London, 1965, pp. 364–5, 377–81, 383–6, 388–92, 394–5, 399–401

Istvan Deák's essay on Hungary appeared in a collection entitled *The European Right*. It is, therefore, particularly interested in the ideological and political connections between the traditional right (what Deák calls the 'Horthy Right') and the indigenous fascist formations (Böszörmény's National Socialists and Szálasi's Arrow Cross). The extract chronicles the experiments of the conservative-authoritarian right with formations of the Hungarian radical nationalist right, their uneasy cohabitation and the eventual collapse of the Horthy regime in the 1940s, which heralded the short-lived rule of the Arrow Cross under the tutelage of Nazi Germany. Note that the Arrow Cross received more than a third of the national vote in the 1938 elections, making it the second most successful fascist party in interwar Europe in electoral terms.

BETWEEN 1919 AND 1944 there were two Rights in Hungary. One may be called the Horthy Right, and the other, the Right of the National Socialist movement. While the Horthy Right tolerated the existence of a multiparty parliament, suffered and occasionally fostered a Social Democratic party and socialist trade unions, and, though anti-Semitic, almost succeeded in saving the lives of the country's considerable Jewish population, it was the aim of the National Socialist Right to destroy all of this.

Nothing shows better the dominance of the Right in Hungarian politics than the fact that Admiral Horthy's regime was never even remotely threatened by a popular movement of the Left. On the contrary, in the decisive years 1938–1944 the few leftist parties proved to be Horthy's loyal supporters against Germany and the National Socialists. Even the underground Communist movement in the 1940s saw its only chance of success in temporary cooperation with the Horthy government.

It is no less indicative that most of the accumulated social discontent – and there was infinite reason for complaint – was expressed not so much through the leftist movements as through the regime's radical rightist opposition.

The opposition between the Horthy Right and the National Socialists was something of a class struggle. The final victory of the National Socialists in October, 1944, also meant the beginning of a still unfinished social revolution.

The stability of the Horthy regime (it was overthrown in October 1944, not so much by the Hungarian Nazis as by German troops) was owing to the skill of the Hungarian police, of course, but also to the genuine loyalty of large segments of society and to the rather hopeless imbecility of the Radical Right, especially its leader, Ferenc Szálasi. But, perhaps even more, the Horthy regime owed its stability to the fanatical patriotism that characterized most Hungarians, rich and poor, Christian and Jew alike. Indeed, no greater accusation could be raised against a person in Hungary than that he was 'un-Hungarian,' a term that implied cowardice, treason, cunning, and lack of chivalry; in short, it implied Swabian (German), Czech, or Romanian, but not Hungarian, behavior. Judged by these standards, Hungary's Radical Right often came dangerously close to being un-Hungarian, and ultimately deprived itself of an overwhelming popularity.

[. . .]

Reinforced by foreign capital, Hungary became relatively prosperous [in the 1920s]. This happy age, however, ended as it did everywhere with the great depression. Then, under the impact of declining industrial production, the collapse of wheat prices, the growing despair of the land-owning class, and the unemployed young intelligentsia, the Bethlen system collapsed.[1] After an unsuccessful experiment with another conservative politician, the Regent, in September, 1932, appointed General Gyula Gömbös as prime minister. This marked the return to power of the counter-revolution's radical wing.

Gyula Gömbös of Jákfa was considerably younger than Bethlen (thirty-three at the time of the counterrevolution), and, unlike him, without any political experience in 1919. Nor was he an aristocrat, but the son of well-to-do Swabian peasants, who simply usurped a title of nobility. He had been a captain on the General Staff of the Austro-Hungarian army, from which he emerged a fierce Hungarian chauvinist. During the counterrevolution Gömbös had been one of Horthy's loyal supporters and the spokesman of the younger officers. Unlike Bethlen, he hated the Habsburgs and, in 1921, had organized the armed defense against troops loyal to King Charles. Later, resigning his army commission, he entered politics, first in the Party of Unity then at the head of the small Party of Racial Defense, dedicated to anti-Semitism. (One of the members of this party was Endre Bajcsy-Zsilinszky, who, in the 1940s, became the head of the anti-German resistance movement and was executed by the Hungarian Nazis.)

In 1928, having acquired sufficient nuisance value, Gömbös was taken back into the Government Party and, a year later, became Minister of Defense. He celebrated this appointment by promoting himself from captain to lieutenant-general. Vain and aggressive, Gömbös was not without a certain charm and talent; he was also hopelessly sentimental. Discovering the glories of Italian fascism, he groomed himself for the position of dictator – under the regent, of course – and imitated the *duce* in his outward appearance. As a dictator, he was confident he would rid Hungary of the Jews and Freemasons; he would spread happiness by providing the workers with jobs and the peasants with land.

Gömbös's appointment by the regent was owing to the pressure of a large group of younger counterrevolutionaries and some businessmen who had been extremely dissatisfied with Bethlen's fulfillment of the peace treaty with the Allies, his 'philo-Semitism,' and with the whole parliamentary system. Gathered in scores of secret and semisecret patriotic associations (as far as any secret could be kept in Hungary, where journalists had keen ears and where everyone was privy to everyone else's moves), these people cultivated the spirit of 'national revival.' The patriotic organi-zations, such as the Awakening Hungarians or the more mysterious EKSZ (Etelköz Association), were generally constructed along a supposedly ancestral tribal pattern. New members took fearful oaths of unconditional obedience to their 'chief-tains,' and swore to die rather than to divulge the associations' secrets or to abandon the pursuit of a 'great, Christian and racially pure Hungary.' Actually, as the pogroms ended in 1920, these groups became mere political clubs, with member-ship advisable for all who aspired to a civil service career. On the fringes of these associations officiated the Turanians, priests of a new Hungarian mystical creed; they worshipped, with various degrees of conviction, a certain Hadür, or War Lord, supposed god of the ancient Hungarians. For good measure, this brotherhood of the Turanians (that is, of the Turkish and Ural-Altaic 'races') attempted to prove that such ancient peoples as the Persians, Hittites, Egyptians, and particularly the Sumerians, were the Magyars' direct ancestors, and that Jesus himself must have been Turanian. From this deep fount of wisdom, many a Hungarian National Socialist was later to drink.

Although usually harmless, some of these patriots, Gömbös included, flirted with the idea of a coup d'etat whenever they saw the 'ideas of Szeged,' that is, of the counterrevolution, downtrodden by Bethlen and his Jewish-liberal-aristocrat cohorts. In 1923, for instance, some of Gömbös's friends, if not Gömbös himself, negotiated with Hitler for *putsches* to be carried out simultaneously in Bavaria, Hungary, and perhaps in Russia as well. The execution of the plan was thwarted by the police, who from the outset had been privy to it. In the words of police presi-dent Hetényi, his intervention became necessary only after 'the gentlemen had ignored repeated warnings to stop this nonsense.' The conspirators received light sentences of honorary confinement and were immediately released; Gömbös was not even indicted. This official leniency was in line with the government's habitual policy toward 'patriotic' offenders, especially if they happened to be gentlemen. Only later, when lower-class National Socialists were engaged in subversive action, were harsher measures applied against the radical Right.

Once in power, Gömbös proved surprisingly weak. He was undoubtedly restrained by the now thoroughly conservative regent, by all the forces of the old, by Hungary's economic and military weakness, but his own weakness must have been no less a factor. In any event, he did not abolish parliament, did not set himself up as a dictator, and toward the Jews he 'extended his friendly hand.' The proudly announced ninety-five-point program of his government was even made available in an English version (*The National Programme of the Hungarian Government* [Budapest:

1932]). It reads like a curious litany of promises and their simultaneous denials. It envisaged, for example, a 'reform of the electoral law on the basis of the secret ballot,' but with the proviso 'that at the same time the great national ideals of the Hungarian people must be safeguarded'; and it promised freedom of the press 'as long as the press faithfully serves the interests of the nation.'

The four years of the Gömbös government (1932–1936) brought no major reforms. What they did bring was a change in political atmosphere. The aristocratic restraint of Bethlen gave way to the demagogy of Gömbös. In his first address as prime minister he said: 'I stand here before you as your Leader. I might lead you on a new path, but do not fool yourselves by expecting miracles. Our path will be a steep, rocky, thorny one, but I feel, I know, that it will lead us to the goal. Hungarians! My brothers! Ignite the candle of trust at the life-fire of my soul that burns for you, my nation! Spread this illumination!'

Under Gömbös the state became more authoritarian. A form of press censorship was introduced; heavily subsidized newspapers were created to present the government's point of view; a system of informants was built up; the secrecy of mail was violated. There was also a changing of the guard in the civil service and the army, especially in the General Staff, with a great number of 'Gömbös boys,' partly of Swabian origin, taking over the key posts. This process was speeded up after May, 1935, when Gömbös was in a position to 'make' the elections and thus bring into parliament a strong contingent of his own followers. In foreign policy, Gömbös took a fatal step by committing the country to a German-Italian orientation. In his enthusiasm, he saw Central Europe divided among Germany, Italy, and Hungary, and pressed Hungary's friendship upon the two great powers.

Gömbös died in 1936, but the dangers of this step to the Right were clearly recognized by the saner segment of Hungarian society. Slowly and hesitantly, the conservative wing of the Government Party established a working agreement with the Left-opposition. Though never publicly acknowledged, a new front came into being, of the Bethlen wing of the Government party, the Christian party (with royalist tendencies), the resurrected Smallholders' party, the Social Democrats, and various liberal, democratic elements. A strange conglomerate indeed, but a durable one. It lasted as long as the Regency. These aristocrats, nationalists [. . .] Jewish financiers, democratic intellectuals, politically educated peasants, and representatives of the organized workers, included the country's most reactionary as well as its most enlightened and progressive groups. They were united by fear of German expansion, and of domestic dictatorship. In the puzzling Hungarian pronaos, from then on determined by the country's relationship with Germany, this front definitely constituted the Left. Against them were lined up the rightist elements in the Government Party, the National Socialists, many civil servants, the unemployed and unemployable young 'diploma holders,' almost the entire officer corps, a great part of the petite bourgeoisie, and many of the workers and agricultural laborers. And while this 'Left' talked of domestic peace, order, and historical values, the Right argued social reform, an end to feudalism and capitalism, and the necessity of a close alliance with a triumphant Germany.

[. . .]

The Gömbös conspiracy of 1923 was by no means the only extreme rightist undertaking of the Bethlen period. It has been mentioned here only because it was characteristic of the 'gentleman era' of the radical Right, with its secret, conspiratorial activities and its lack of popular appeal – for the *putschist* of the 1920s was just as reluctant to appeal to the masses and thus stir up dangerous waters as was Bethlen himself. The first popular agitator, Zoltán Böszörmény, emerged during the great depression. His political party, although awkward and helpless, was also National Socialism's most original, most characteristically Hungarian version.

Böszörmény, born in 1893, was the son of a bankrupt landowner. His youth was a succession of odd jobs that turned him, successively, into an apprentice, a messenger, a worker, and a porter. In 1919 he joined the counterrevolution; later he dabbled in journalism and managed to enter the University of Budapest, where he was elected leader of the patriotic student fraternities. Böszörmény was also a poet, and to peddle his patriotic verses he employed a couple of agents who later became his party's organizers.

In 1931, if his confessions are to be believed, Böszörmény visited Germany, where he met Hitler and was instantly converted by him. On his return, he published a manifesto and announced the birth of the Hungarian National Socialist Workers' party, the first of a great many undertakings bearing the same or similar names. As his party's emblem, Böszörmény chose the crossed scythes. He never doubted his destiny. In 1932, he wrote:

> Even among the giants of intellect I am a giant, a great Hungarian poet with a prophetic mission. . . . My heart shudders at the cry of pain of Hungarian mothers. . . . I have listened to the call of the sweetest mother of all, Mother Hungary, and – answering it – I started off on the road, abandoning all worldly goods and happiness. . . . I knew well that my fight, begun without arms, would be ruthless: a fight to the teeth-gnawing bitter end.

To this, he later added: 'This is the fullness of time, and the lonely poet, the Man, who always stood alone, departs to oppose the destructive forces of Money. . . . One Man against the whole world.'

For the time being, the 'tribune,' who – in his own words – was ready 'to caress but also to have hundreds of thousands executed without batting an eyelash,' became the favorite target of the Budapest satirical newspapers. Yet, among the peasants of Eastern Hungary, his message spread fast.

[. . .]

In Gömbös' Hungary, the Scythe Cross did not have a chance. By the end of 1932, Böszörmény boasted of twenty thousand party members and, supported by some boisterous storm troopers, he made several attempts to run as candidate at parliamentary by-elections, but the customary vigilance of the local authorities prevented him from collecting the necessary number of 'recommendations' for candidacy. Only once did he manage to stand for election and then he won only a few hundred votes. The party's weekly was occasionally suppressed and the Leader himself condemned to short prison terms which, however, he never served.

Böszörmény's ideology is not easy to define. He was against Jews, Bolsheviks, and liberals, and for his own dictatorship, land reform, and 'justice for the poor.' In the 'Ten Commandments of the Storm Troopers,' published in 1935, he exhorted his followers to violence, in language enriched by Hitlerite slogans and magic Turanian terms. He described his comrades as 'Gardeners of the Hungarian race, fateful Death Reapers of the Jewish swine and their hirelings . . . opponents of all Habsburg aspirations,' but history records no serious evidence of Scythe Cross violence, and its one attempt to act failed miserably.

A regular peasant rebellion was planned for 1, May 1936, when three million peasants were to march on 'sinful' Budapest and raze it to the ground. In one peasant town of the great Hungarian plains a few thousand peasants actually met on the appointed day, but they were easily dispersed by the ubiquitous gendarmes. Several trials ensued. Böszörmény and his principal codefendants were given relatively light sentences, varying from a few months to two and a half years in prison; none of them was placed in custody, and Böszörmény was allowed to escape to Germany in the spring of 1938. He was the first of many Hungarian National Socialists to seek asylum from the Horthy authorities in Hitler's Germany.

The mass trial of the Scythe Cross rank and file presented a disheartening spectacle. Altogether 700 peasants were arrested, and 113 of them judged at a single trial. All declared themselves ready to die for the 'Idea,' but were unable to provide the judge with further elucidation. 'Out of a hundred defendants,' wrote Kovács, '98 owned neither house nor land. . . . They wore torn trousers, miserable short overcoats or old sheepskin vests; none of them wore a shirt.' The judge permitted most of the defendants to return to their poverty.

By the time Böszörmény's movement was suppressed, he was no longer in the forefront. National Socialism had shifted to the cities, especially to Budapest, where socially acceptable leaders turned it into a more consequential political force.

[. . .]

In Hungary's troubled history, perhaps no politician was subjected to such extremes of abuse and of idolatry as Ferenc Szálasi. In C. A. Macartney's *History of Hungary*, 1525–1945, the author describes Szálasi as one of the strangest and most interesting characters of contemporary Hungarian history. While his many enemies spared no invective in denouncing him, Macartney writes that he inspired a personal devotion among his followers 'such as no other Hungarian of his age could equal, and after his death they carried on the cult of him, passing his words from hand to hand, speaking of him as early Christians spoke of the Messiah.'

[. . .]

Although this is too tolerant a judgment, it is certain that Szálasi was no hireling of Hitler. In his childish conceit, he considered Hungary Germany's equal partner in a new Europe. He was convinced that the Hungarians, 'this little people,' could reorganize Europe if only they would follow him. 'I have been selected by a higher

Divine authority to redeem the Magyar people – he who does not understand me or loses confidence – let him go! At most I shall remain alone, but even alone I shall create the Hungarist State with the help of the secret force that is within me.' Szálasi coined the word 'Hungarist' (*Hungarista*) to designate his principles and program. It indicated that his National Socialism was different from that of the Germans. It also made Szálasi's movement invincible for, while his Arrow Cross party could be and often was suppressed, the 'Hungarist Movement' would continue to live in the hearts of his followers.

It must come as no surprise that this superpatriot was also of foreign descent. Szálasi's father was of Armenian, and his mother of mixed Slovak-Magyar, stock. His father was an NCO in the Austro-Hungarian army. Like so many other sons of noncommissioned officers, Szálasi chose an officer's career. He served on the front during the late years of World War I; in postwar Hungary he was permitted to enter the General Staff College from which he graduated with highest honors. It was in the General Staff College, where such activity was encouraged, that Szálasi began to write on political and economic subjects. But he was already a major on the General Staff when, in 1933, he published, without permission of his superiors, his 'Plan for the Construction of the Hungarian State.' As the plan seemed to do injustice to Magyar aspirations, he was severely reprimanded for insubordination. He then addressed a memorandum to Prime Minister Gömbös, criticizing the government's policy. This angered Gömbös, who had no use for officers – besides himself – in politics. Apparently, the Prime Minister nevertheless attempted to win Szálasi over, offering him a mandate in the coming elections, but Szálasi put forward impossible conditions. In March, 1935, he resigned his army commission and founded his first political movement, the Party of National Will. He was then thirty-eight years of age. He stood twice for election, but was handsomely defeated. He then decided (1936) never again to run as a candidate.

On April 16, 1937, he was for the first time arrested and the party headquarters, comprising two rooms, were sealed. The police found a total of 420 *pengös* ($84) in the party treasury. The court sentenced him to three months in honorable confinement for anti-Semitic agitation, but he was never called to serve the sentence, although it did bring his name before the public. The nebulous statements on social reform he made at the trial won him many sympathizers. Soon after that he visited Germany, which caused the Budapest liberal press to credit him with Germany's favor. Membership in his party, renamed the Arrow Cross Party-Hungarist Movement, grew rapidly to twenty thousand by the summer of 1937. In October of the same year, he effected a merger of most National Socialist parties in an impressive demonstration held in Budapest. The merger lasted only a few weeks, but no one now doubted Szálasi's political importance. Yet his sudden popularity was hard to explain. He was neither a good speaker, nor a good organizer; but his sincerity and undoubted honesty kindled admiration, perhaps because such qualities were rare in contemporary Hungarian politics. He was fond of visiting, à la Hitler, in every corner of the country, where he amazed and charmed his followers by remembering their names. His popularity among women was one of his great assets. More important were his connections in the officer corps. Indeed, the younger officers who formed the bulk of the General Staff were impatient for political and social reform, which, they felt, was mandatory in view of the coming war. They besieged the regent with warnings against the leftist and Jewish agitation, and insisted that he implement a 'new, determined, uncompromisingly Christian, national and popular policy.' This meant in essence that the regent should curtail parliament and impose further restrictions on socialists and Jews. The officers negotiated with Szálasi and counted on him, but most of them were still reluctant to entrust him with political power.

The regent himself was aware of Szálasi's activity and, although he consistently refused to give an audience to his factious officer, he allowed the chief of his military cabinet to seek out Szálasi and inquire into his intentions. Szálasi made his views clear: the regent should 'take charge of the country,' that is, he should stage a *putsch* with the help of the army, and nominate Szálasi prime minister. But the regent refused to listen.

The year 1938 promised to be stormy. Rumors of a coming rightist coup were circulating and were played up enormously by a near-hysterical liberal press; the Arrow Cross flooded the streets of Budapest with leaflets, announcing Szálasi's impending triumph. The regent himself was booed by students and officers at a gala performance in the Budapest Opera. At parliamentary by-elections, some of Szálasi's younger lieutenants ran successfully against the candidates of the Government Party and half a dozen Smallholder deputies left their party to join the National Socialist movement. In addition, the Arrow Cross now seemed to have almost unlimited funds. Through some Hungarian agents and through the German minority in Hungary, German money flowed into the coffers of the radical Right. Some influential Budapest newspapers changed hands and endorsed a National Socialist program. Szálasi knew nothing of these transactions, but then he was above such petty considerations.

Finally, the regent took matters in hand. In May, 1938, he dismissed the hesitant Darányi, Gömbös' immediate successor, and appointed Béla Imrédy prime minister. Imrédy was a financial expert and had the reputation of being a liberal and an Anglophile. He subsequently disappointed the regent because of his violent anti-Semitism and his aspirations to dictatorship, but for the Arrow Cross his appointment was a great blow. Imrédy, like Gömbös, had no use for other leaders and least of all for the unruly Arrow Cross. A week after his appointment he forbade all employees of the state to be members of political parties; as there were very few civil servants with leftist sympathies, this was designed as a measure against the Right.

Next, Szálasi was arrested. This time the government meant business; he was indicted for subversive activity, and sentenced to three years' hard labor. On August 27, 1938, he was taken to Szeged prison from where he was not to emerge for over two years. From then on, until the German occupation in March, 1944, the Arrow Cross was subjected to almost continual harassment. Its newspapers were suspended, its meetings forbidden, some of its leaders imprisoned, hundreds put in internment camps, there to outnumber by far the Communist prisoners. The German press reacted with violence to such persecution and hailed Szálasi as a martyr. At home, the Arrow Cross went into the new elections with his name on its banner. The parliamentary elections of May, 1939 (the first since 1935), were held with secret balloting in accordance with a law adopted a year earlier. The National Socialists scored a great success. Out of 259 seats the Government Party won a comfortable 183, but the National Socialists increased the number of their mandates to

49 (Szálasi's Arrow Cross alone received 31 mandates). The Social Democrats and the Smallholders were defeated. They won 5 and 14 seats respectively. Worse still, the majority of the Government Party had clearly rightist sympathies.

The popular vote was even more favorable to the Arrow Cross: out of a total of approximately 2,000,000 votes, they scored 750,000. In Budapest the National Socialists obtained 72,385 votes, as opposed to 95,468 for the Government Party and 34,500 for the Socialists. 'Red' Csepel, Budapest's most industrialized suburb, elected two National Socialist deputies.

In the new parliament the Arrow Cross deputies became the government's first true opposition. They remained, of course, completely impotent but they posed as the people's champions; between 1939 and 1944 their parliamentary speeches repeatedly harped on the plight of Hungary's poor. The extreme Right spoke with fire and conviction. No longer did it have to parrot the Horthy Right's slogans; it had its own ideology, formulated by Ferenc Szálasi.

[. . .]

Szálasi was a devout Catholic; his vaguely Turanian Christ was the King of all Hungarians. The Hungarist state was to be based on a 'Christian moral order' where atheism and nondenominationalism would not be tolerated. On the other hand, Church and state would be separated, and education taken out of the hands of the religious orders. A 'political Church' had no place in the 'Hungarist order.' His religious orthodoxy was not necessarily shared by his followers. The party intellectual, Dr. Pal Vágo, for instance, was violently anticlerical; he accused the Church of propagating a Jewish version of Christianity. Dr. Vágo considered himself an expert in biblical studies and was able to prove that Christ was a Scythian (and thus a Turanian), and so were all the early Christians.

In Szálasi's opinion women and children were two of the 'seven pillars of the nation.' The concept of illegitimate birth was to be abolished, and divorces restricted to cases of 'national interest.' Church weddings were to constitute the only legal act of marriage, civil marriages were to be forbidden. Women were to remain at the hearth. 'The basis of Hungarism is the family . . . the head of the family is its warrior, the mother its soul, the child its weapon, and the youth its symbol.' As for the Jews, alien to Hungarians in both spirit and physique, they were to find themselves a new home. Szálasi insisted he was no anti-Semite, but an 'a-Semite,' a fact that did not prevent him from publicly referring to the Jews as a pestilence, and believing in the existence of an anti-Christian Jewish world conspiracy as formulated in the 'Protocols of the Elders of Zion.'

[. . .]

The release of Szálasi from prison in September, 1940, did not mean the beginning of a triumphant rise to power. On the contrary, his party's strength appeared to have passed its zenith. Factional struggle became more violent and several of Szálasi's lieutenants deserted him, charging him with insanity or embezzlement of party funds. Furthermore, the government was more firmly in the saddle than ever. The territorial gains made between 1938 and 1941, and Hungary's involvement in the war, commanded national unity and order; this the government was resolved to enforce.

[. . .]

In May, 1944, Szálasi had had his much-sought-for audience with the regent, but there had been no agreement between them (regarding Szálasi's demands for power-sharing). Upon the appointment of Lakatos, the Arrow Cross had finally decided on action. Abandoning his previous loyalty to the regent, Szálasi began negotiations with the Germans, offering his services and warning them of Horthy's surrender plans. Veesenmayer, the German plenipotentiary, who had a very low opinion of Szálasi, was slow to come around to the Arrow Cross point of view; but even he gave in when the SS Command in Hungary decided that Szálasi alone, of all Hungarians, remained a true friend of Germany. Clearly, the surrender of the Hungarian troops, now fully involved in operations against the Russians, would have caused the collapse of German defenses. Szálasi was therefore groomed for a take-over, and preparations were made for the day when Horthy would announce his surrender. This came when Horthy, following an agreement concluded in Moscow, made the armistice public in a radio address on October 15.

Perhaps no political turnabout was more poorly prepared. There were no troops in Budapest to defend the regent; the Hungarian generals were taken by surprise; the socialist workers and the resistance movement had not been given the promised arms. The armistice was literally the undertaking of Horthy and his immediate family with the help of a few trusted officers and a few conservative politicians. (The latter, like Bethlen, emerged from their hiding places for that occasion.) The exclusiveness of Horthy's undertaking was motivated not only by a very justified fear of betrayal, but by the clique character of the whole Horthy system. The true Left, particularly the Social Democrats, had always been regarded as instruments, never as serious partners. On the decisive day, Horthy remained isolated. The great majority of the officers disobeyed Horthy's orders; commanders loyal to the regent were arrested. The Germans acted rapidly: the radio station and the royal palace were seized by a few tanks; Horthy was placed in custody and forced to withdraw his orders. German arms were distributed to the Arrow Cross and, before the people of Budapest could recover from their surprise, the formation of an Arrow Cross government under Szálasi was announced. In his first order of the day, Szálasi exhorted the nation to a final effort against the Russian invaders.

Szálasi's reign was a sad epilogue to a tragic story. Insisting on legal sanctification of his coup, and using his enforced appointment by the regent, Szálasi had himself accepted as prime minister by a rump parliament, and, subsequently, proclaimed himself National Leader. On November 3 he took a solemn oath to the Holy Crown in the Royal Palace.

Note

1   Count István Bethlen became prime minister of Horthy's authoritarian aristocratic regime in 1921 and remained in office until 1931. The Prime Ministers under the Horthy regime in Hungary were:

1921–1931	István Bethlen
1931–1932	Mihaly Karolyi
1933–1936	Gyula Gömbös
1936–1938	Kalman Daranyi
1938–1939	Béla Imrédy
1939–1941	Count Pal Teleki

Chapter 19

Jill Lewis

AUSTRIA: 'HEIMWEHR', 'NSDAP' AND THE 'CHRISTIAN SOCIAL' STATE

■ from **CONSERVATIVES AND FASCISTS IN AUSTRIA, 1918–34**, in M. Blinkhorn (ed.) *Fascists and Conservatives*, London, 1990, pp. 98, 99–105, 106–7, 108, 110–11, 114

Jill Lewis' essay examines the relations (ideological and political) between the Christian Social Party of Dolfuss and Schuschnigg, on the one hand, and fascism. Conventional approaches to the Austrian Ständestaat have tended to underline its Catholic, anti-Nazi/fascist character. Lewis, however, challenges this notion, arguing that the character of the Christian Social regime can be accurately described as a distinct brand of indigenous fascism – 'Austrofascism'. The excerpt concludes that the destruction of parliamentary democracy in interwar Austria was the main weapon against socialism, and not a defensive move against the rise of the Austrian Nazis.

T HE AUSTRIAN FIRST REPUBLIC was founded in 1918 following the collapse of the Habsburg Empire and was officially destroyed by the German invasion in 1938. The term 'First Republic', however, actually encompasses three political phases: the democratic republic (1918–33), the dictatorship (1933–4) and the 'Austrofascist' *Ständestaat* (1934–8).[1] Throughout most of this twenty-year period the national government was dominated by the Christian Social Party. The purpose of this chapter is to examine the relationship between that party and the growth of fascism in Austria. It will be argued that the Christian Social leadership swung towards fascism in the late 1920s as a result of domestic political and economic problems, developing in the process a form of 'Austrofascism' that was distinct from both German and Italian fascisms. Essential to this argument is the debate within Austria on the still politically contentious term 'Austrofascism'. [. . .]

Although Austria ceased to be a parliamentary democracy in March 1933, its democratic constitution was not officially overturned until May 1934. It was then replaced by a corporate constitution designed to create a 'Social, Christian, German state, Austria, founded upon estates under strong authoritarian leadership': the

Ständestaat Parliament was replaced by six councils: those of state, culture, the economy and the provinces, plus a federal diet and assembly. The first four possessed only advisory powers, while the membership of five out of the six was nominated by either the Chancellor's office or the president. The exception was the federal diet, whose members were chosen by the provincial governors and financial officers, the mayor of Vienna and, in the absence of a Viennese financial officer, a person 'well informed about the city's finances'. The apparent independence of this body was illusory, for the governors were appointed by the Chancellor and the financial officers by the governors.[2] All council members had to be 'loyal citizens' as proved by their membership of the Fatherland Front. The Front, therefore, controlled political participation. It also represented the mass element in Austrofascism, mediating in labour disputes and organizing demonstrations of loyalty. By 1936 its membership was 2 million, in part because it was impossible to obtain a job or unemployment benefit without quoting a Fatherland Front number.[3]

[. . .]

The nature and origins of the *Ständestaat* are controversial issues in Austrian historiography, despite – or perhaps because of – the fact that until recently academic research into the entire period has been badly neglected. The very term '*Ständestaat*' is contentious for, although it was the official title of the Austrian state between 1934 and 1938, it invokes an image of a pre-industrial society or, more concretely, a society unfettered by modern class divisions, while also emphasizing its Catholic roots. This image, which the state itself sought to foster, still pervades much of the writing on the period, especially that which rejects the whole notion of Austrofascism. For instance, while the corporate nature of the 1934 constitution may be indisputable, many historians draw an emphatic distinction between the 'Catholic' corporatism of Austria and the 'fascist' corporatism of Mussolini's Italy or Hitler's Germany. The Austrian constitution was influenced, they argue, by the 1931 papal encyclical *Quadragesimo Anno*, and was adopted not as a move towards fascism but as a defence against it.[4] The Austrian government resorted to dictatorship in 1933 as an act of national self-protection at a time of crisis. Parliament had become unworkable and Hitler's assumption of power in Germany and National Socialist regional electoral victories at home in 1932 both indicated a growing domestic threat. Had the democratic constitution remained, new national elections would have been called and these, it was feared, would have swept the Nazis to power.[5] Austrian corporatism was therefore inherently anti-Nazi and, by extension, anti-fascist. The outward expression of fascism, the destruction of Parliament, the political opposition and the unions, and the establishment of the Fatherland Front, reflected instead a traditional conservative dictatorship which adopted the trappings of fascism for pragmatic reasons – in order to appease both the Italian fascists and the Heimwehr, on whom the government relied for support. But the structural base and dynamism of 'true' fascism were missing.

This view, and the entire approach on which it is based, have been challenged by Klaus-Jörg Siegfried. Their proponents, he alleges, have concentrated excessively upon external (i.e. German and Italian) forces promoting Austrian fascism, and insufficiently upon internal economic factors.[6] He argues that the economic instability of the 1920s, the inflation of 1922–3, the stabilization crisis, shortage of capital, and the weakness and eventual collapse of the banking system forced Austrian industry, and hence the government, to increase their reliance on Anglo-French capital. This necessitated accepting the investing states' condition of renouncing all possibility of a customs union with Germany. The resultant split of 1932 in the ruling alliance between the Christian Social and Pan-German parties jeopardized bourgeois control of Parliament.[7] The *Ständestaat*, therefore, arose from a crisis of capitalism, with the function of maintaining bourgeois power while destroying the Socialist labour movement and so reducing the social costs of labour. The 'clerical dictatorship' was thus a form of fascism.

Siegfried differs from most historians in adopting a functional rather than a descriptive concept of fascism itself. Questioning the use of typological definitions or models, he points out that, in the Austrian context, these concentrate on *German* characteristics of fascism and the National Socialist system imposed after 1938. From this starting-point it is simple to isolate those aspects of the *Ständestaat* which differed from National Socialism and then conclude that the earlier system was not fascist.

This has been common practice in the study of Austrofascism. For example, the *Ständestaat* was authoritarian but never fully totalitarian, allowing the Catholic Church internal autonomy.[8] Anti-clericalism was completely absent. The mass movement, the Fatherland Front, was not a source of the dictatorship but was created only after it had been declared.[9] There was no attempt to restructure the economy because, although a corporate system existed on paper, it was never fully implemented.[10] Nor was there any policy of autarky or militaristic imperialism, both of which characterized the domestic and foreign policies of Nazi Germany and Fascist Italy.[11] More doubtful is the assertion that the *Ständestaat* was not supported by industry and finance but rested upon the Church and army.[12] Clearly the *Ständestaat* did not conform to the models of fascism which are frequently used as definitions: according to such criteria it was at most an alliance between the fascist principles of the Heimwehr and the clerical conservatism of the Christian Social Party, designed to preserve 'the social and religious traditions of Austria' against the 'revolution of nihilism' from both left and right and to 'restore Austria's traditional social structure':[13] conservatism cloaked in fascist attire.

Yet, as Siegfried has pointed out, the very use of such rigid, descriptive definitions is problematical, since they depend so heavily upon the specific circumstances in which German National Socialism in particular developed that they effectively preclude comparative analysis. This is uniquely true in the case of Austria, where similar cultural characteristics and a shared language tend to mask basic differences between the two countries, such as those involving the political roles during the nineteenth century of religion and nationalism. In any case, some of the criteria used to dismiss 'Austrofascism' are of dubious validity even when applied to the two 'true' fascisms of Italy and Germany. Examples of this are the insistence on a functioning corporate economy, full totalitarianism and anti-clericalism, all of which would be difficult to establish in the Italian case.[14] Even where the models do reflect 'true' fascism, they ignore political, cultural and economic differences which might give rise to *varieties* of fascism. For instance, the Austrian economy was small, structurally weak, relied heavily on foreign capital and trade, and lacked the diversity which would have allowed a policy of economic autarky. Rather than ruling out the possibility of fascism, this simply suggests that an Austrian fascist regime would adopt other economic policies in an attempt to promote domestic capital.[15] The final criticism of the typological approach is that although its users are scrupulous in attempting to define 'fascism', the term which is frequently adopted in its place, namely 'conservatism', has received far less analytical attention and frequently lacks any definitional rigour whatsoever.

This last point is amply illustrated by the case of the Christian Social Party which, with its Catholicism, influential monarchist wing and strong rural support, is commonly held to have represented the 'conservative' as distinct from the 'nationalist' or 'socialist' camps in Austrian politics.[16] Yet the party had other characteristics which undermine the appropriateness of the 'conservative' label, especially when this is used to distinguish it from the 'fascism' of the Heimwehr. These include a radical populist tradition and a corporatist ideological strand which became increasingly influential in the 1920s as the economy floundered and class tensions increased, and had much in common with the Heimwehr. It was this which led to the Austrofascism of the *Ständestaat*. In terms of the narrow descriptive definitions of fascism, Christian Socialism remained essentially conservative with fascist overtones. As we have seen, however, narrow definitions cannot accommodate the idea of different forms of fascism and have become academically sterile. A wider approach is needed.

[. . .]

The remainder of this chapter will seek to demonstrate this by establishing (1) that Christian Social populist traditions fostered a distinct form of fascist thought which contributed to the creation of the *Ständestaat*, (2) that the Heimwehr's role was as support for the Christian Social leadership and not as a competitive or dominant force; and (3) that the object of the *Ständestaat* was to undermine the strength of the working class. Austrian fascism was doubtless less radical and less successful than its German counterpart, but fascism it nevertheless remained.[17]

Central to this argument is the political role of religion within the Christian Social Party. Although in the Republic the links between the party and the Church establishment were unusually strong, this had not always been so. The original Christian Social movement had been distinctly anti-establishment, stemming from the revolt of the Viennese petty bourgeoisie after the 1873 stock market crash and depression. This had presented a former Liberal politician, Karl Lueger, with the opportunity to galvanize the newly enfranchised 'five gulden' men into a movement able to challenge and eventually defeat the Liberal Party in Vienna's council elections.[18] Lueger's own charisma was one reason for his success, but another was the platform on which he built his campaign: a bombastic religious anti-Semitism with which he won the support of anti-Liberal, anti-capitalist elements within the petty bourgeoisie, as well as the lower clergy.[19]

Linked to Lueger's movement was the Catholic neo-romantic corporatism of Karl Vogelsang. Both Lueger and Vogelsang based their politics on hostility towards anti-Catholicism, modern capitalism and – most important for Lueger – the Liberal Party which was associated with both.[20] There were also sharp differences between them, especially regarding religion. Vogelsang developed a highly Utopian, backward-looking panacea in which the evils of modern society and its lack of Catholic morality would be transformed by a system of economically based corporations.[21] Lueger's Catholicism was more pragmatic and was used to unite the previously fragmented Viennese petty bourgeoisie against the anti-clericalism and pro-capitalism of the Liberals. His earliest electoral themes were religious anti-Semitism, a non-plebeian form of populism, and a rabid denunciation of 'corrupt' (i.e. Jewish) capitalism. But the success of Lueger's party lay also in its political *style*, whereby the clubland culture of Viennese politics was replaced with a dynamic, mass-based organization.[22] The movement grew following a series of campaigns aimed at specific groups – teachers, lower government officials and the large and influential block of Viennese landlords – who felt they had a grievance against the city council.[23] Once in office the Christian Socials consolidated their support through a programme of 'communalism' in which the council established its own companies to provide gas, water and electricity and to raise income for the municipal budget. Lueger's corporatist ideas were useful symbols rather than genuine goals; unlike Vogelsang he aimed to reform capitalism, not to replace it. His use of Catholicism was equally pragmatic, since it provided his movement with a 'quasi-religious facade' and an air of moral superiority – as well as votes. Above all, the Christian Social Party displayed a populist and corporatist hue from birth.

[. . .]

The specifically Austrian and Christian Social origins of *the Ständestaat*'s Catholic corporatism were shared by the Heimwehr but were not exclusive to it. Whilst Dollfuss may have said that his state was based on *Quadragesimo Anno*, the latter emphasized the need to eradicate class conflict through 'autonomous' bodies or free associations and said that men should be free to choose the type of government they wanted. This was clearly not the case in the *Ständestaat*. *Quadragesimo Anno* also attacked those employers 'who even abuse religion itself, cloaking their own unjust impositions under its name, that they may protect themselves against the clearly just demands of their employees': a situation which actually developed in the period 1934–8.[24] However, the most telling evidence that the 1934 constitution arose from an anti-democratic tendency in the party which predated the encyclical was the party programme of 1926 which indicated a clear move towards an authoritarian, corporatist and *Stände* policy. When *Quadragesimo Anno* was published in 1931, Christian Social leaders proudly declared that there was no need to alter their 1926 programme since it already conformed to the encyclical's teachings.[25] This was only partially correct: the encyclical had already criticized Italian fascism for misusing the corporate concept for political rather than social purposes, something that was equally true of the Christian Social Party.

As well as corporatism, and indeed running counter to it, the Christian Social Party and its ideology also contained social reformist and federalist strands. During the 1920s, however, the corporatist tendency grew increasingly powerful, thanks partly to the party's structure and partly to the political situation. The structural factor derived from the very nature of the national party, which had been founded in 1907 as an alliance between Lueger's Viennese party and the more conservative Catholic party of the provinces. There were therefore two Catholic movements, the first urban and radical, the second rural and traditional, representing German-speaking, property-owning Catholic farmers, the landed aristocracy and sections of the bourgeoisie.[26]

In the first years of the Republic this division was reflected in the conflict between the monarchist and centralist Viennese wing and the predominantly feder-alist and anti-monarchist provincial factor. With Vienna controlled after 1918 by the Social Democrats, the Christian Social Party's electoral power lay in the provinces. Even so, it was the Viennese wing of Ignaz Seipel which dominated the coalition governments.[27] Conflict between the agrarian federalism of the provinces and the centralism of the party leadership was one feature of Christian Social internal politics in the early 1920s, but differences also surfaced over such crucial issues as *Anschluss* with Germany, relations with the Social Democratic Party, and later those with the Heimwehr. In essence the party functioned as an electoral club of diverse groups which were united in defence of 'Christian values' against the secular Social Democratic Party. Early electoral campaigns were based on this principle – the re-introduction of compulsory religious education in schools, the abolition of Glöckl's education reforms in Vienna, reform of the marriage laws – as well as involving more direct attacks on the fiscal and housing policies of 'Red Vienna' and the Tenants' Protection Act.[28] Slogans were couched in terms of an urban–rural battle between piety and the devil, with Vienna sucking the provinces dry. In the 1927 election campaign political Catholicism was definitely overshadowed by anti-socialism when the party formed an electoral pact with other anti-socialist parties, including the anti-clerical Pan-Germans.[29] Twelve months later, Seipel began his True Democracy campaign, announcing that its main champion was the Heimwehr.[30]

The heterogeneous character of the Christian Social Party, and the shift in polit-ical power from the provinces to the national leadership, help explain its abandonment of democracy in favour of authoritarianism. This is not a complete explanation, however. The notion that Parliament had become a sham also grew after 1927 in the provinces, as the political situation deteriorated rapidly amid increased right-wing fears of a Socialist electoral victory or revolution. Hitherto the Social Democratic Party and the anti-socialists had maintained an uneasy relation-ship in which the former controlled the industrial areas, including Vienna, but remained in opposition in Parliament, while national power was held by a series of coalitions dominated by the Christian Socials in alliance with the Pan-Germans and the Agrarian League. But the size of the Social Democratic Party, its dominance of the capital and its apparent militancy remained constant thorns in the side of the bourgeois parties.[31] One basic problem was economic policy. In 1922 the national government attempted to stop hyper-inflation and stabilize the currency by raising foreign loans and pursuing deflationary policies dictated by the League of Nations. At the same time the Viennese council carried out an experiment in socialist economics based on high taxation and high public sector spending.[32] While the coun-tryside saved, the capital spent.

[. . .]

In relation to this point a number of historians have referred to an *alliance* between the conservatism of the Christian Social Party and the fascism of the Heimwehr. This assumes an independence for the latter which did not exist.[33] The ideological links between the two, already examined, represented only one area of overlap. In political terms their relationship was even closer, for, although regional variations existed within both movements, to all intents and purposes the Heimwehr emerged in the 1920s as the paramilitary wing of the Christian Social Party, sharing rank-and-file members and, in some instances, leaders. In the industrial belt of Upper Styria it also developed a second function as an anti-Socialist trade union force, which brought it the support of sections of Austrian banking and industry.[34] It is in this context that the political influence of the Heimwehr must be seen, for when civil war broke out in February 1934 it was the result of *government* action against the Socialists, in which the Heimwehr acted as an auxiliary force rather than as the main aggressor. Indeed throughout its history the Heimwehr depended upon Christian Social support, particularly the protection of the national government. If a mutual dependence developed after 1927 it was only in part the result of Italian influence, for the Heimwehr provided the manpower to challenge the Social Democratic movement on the streets.[35] This became the main goal of both industry and the Christian Social leadership in the late 1920s and above all after the 1930 election, when it seemed that, despite the depression, the political power of the Socialists could not be defeated within the existing constitution.

[. . .]

The year 1927 marked a watershed in the Republic's history. Prior to the election of that year political tensions had been high, but both sides had restricted their activities to their own areas of support – the Christian Socials and the Pan-Germans were active in the provinces and the Social Democrats in the cities. After 1927 the national government encouraged Heimwehr attempts to challenge the Social Democrats by holding marches and demonstrations in Socialist strongholds in a bid to reclaim the cities or to provoke the Socialists into a violent response which could be forcibly suppressed. The Heimwehr were the obvious choice, for the 1927 general strike had been broken in Styria when Heimwehr units had marched against the strikers and destroyed what the government considered to be a potential revolution. In the autumn of 1927, despite the dubious legality of the Heimwehr's actions and strong rumours that the goal of its Styrian leader, Walter Pfrimer, had been to march on Vienna, Seipel once more arranged meetings with bankers and manufacturers to raise funds for the Heimwehr.[36] At the same time he was striving to increase Christian Social influence within the movement, and beginning to champion it as the protector of 'True Democracy'. He and other members of the government resisted pressure from Britain and France to introduce a general disarmament bill, despite the high number of clashes between the Heimwehr and the Schutzbund [militia established by the Social Democratic Party of Austria] and the threat that, without such a law, foreign loans might not be forthcoming. According to the British ambassador this was because such a bill would have to have covered both movements. Instead raids were carried out by government troops and the Heimwehr on Schutzbund weapon stores; the bulk of what was seized was handed to the Heimwehr.[37]

In this way the Heimwehr came to act as the quasi-legal shock force of the Austrian government. Four months after the movement had publicly rejected 'Western democratic parliamentarism' in favour of a corporate state, the Christian Social chancellor, Vaugoin, invited two of its leaders to join the Cabinet, even though the Heimwehr had, at that time, never stood for election, had no deputies in Parliament and was anti-democratic. Unlike both the Agrarian League and the Pan-German Party, the Christian Social leaders told their members that there was no apparent inconsistency between the Korneuburg Oath and their party's principles.[38] When 14,000 armed Heimwehr men attempted a Putsch in September 1931, the government failed to act until Social Democratic leaders threatened to call out the Schutzbund. Troops took three hours to travel thirty miles from Graz to Bruck an der Mur, enabling the putschists to disperse. The Christian Social governor of Styria dismissed the whole event as 'tipsy twaddle'.[39] Finally in 1932, when the Christian Social/Pan-German coalition collapsed, Dollfuss formed a new government with the support of nine Agrarian League and eight Heimwehr deputies who had been elected in 1930. Fey, a Heimwehr leader, was given the Ministry of Public Security, from which he authorized more raids on the Socialists.[40]

The government's majority of one depended on the Agrarian League and the Heimwehr. According to C. Earl Edmondson, this led to the 'tragedy of Dollfuss's having to allow them (the Heimwehr) to drive a wedge between him and the Socialists, who before Fey's appointment had tacitly tolerated his government'.[41] But Edmondson does not explain why the Heimwehr's influence was so much greater than that of the Agrarian League, which objected to the extent of the fascists' participation; nor does he provide evidence to support his theory that Dollfuss would have preferred a democratic solution to the political dilemma, one which included the Social Democrats. Indeed, Schuschnigg, Dollfuss's successor, wrote that a coalition with the Socialists had been rejected as impractical by the Christian Social leaders since 1931.[42] More telling is Dollfuss's own explanation of his move towards populist authoritarianism: 'Many things will change . . . [We will] do everything step by step to force the Marxists to their knees.'[43] Nor is there evidence in his other speeches and actions to suggest that he was a reluctant ally of the Heimwehr. He was continuing a Christian Social policy of support for the movement. But the Heimwehr remained, as it had always been, the junior partner in the relationship. It was the Christian Social leaders who chose between an alliance with their traditional enemies, the Social Democrats, and so maintaining the parliamentary republic, or jettisoning democracy in favour of fascism. If their predominant fear had been the growth of the National Socialist Party it is difficult to see why they decided to turn first on the one party which might have been able to stem that growth. But fear of socialism was older and much stronger than fear of National Socialism.

[. . .]

The state is said to embody the 'spirit of the people' rather than merely representing a variety of social groups or classes. Underlying this is the belief that there is such a 'spirit of the people' which differentiates one nation from another. In Austria, where concepts of nationality were problematical, this spirit was identified by the Christian Social leadership as German but Catholic, thus separating it from non-Catholic

German nationalism. The explanation was religious but the factors which led to the *Ständestaat* were political and economic and lay in a fear found amongst politicians and businessmen that political power might slip out of the hands of the bourgeois parties. This process began in 1927, intensified in 1930, and was the reason for the increase in support for the Heimwehr from both financiers and the Christian Social leadership. The Heimwehr was not the instigator of policy and its influence appears to have been exaggerated, thus diminishing the role of the Christian Social Party itself in the progression towards fascism. Parliamentary democracy in Austria was destroyed in order to wipe out the Social Democratic movement, not to protect the country against fascism. The result was a form of fascism itself: Austrofascism.

Notes

1   Literally translated: 'State of Estates'.
2   C. A. Gulick, *Austria from Habsburg to Hitler*, Vol. 2 (Berkeley, Calif., 1948), 1443.
3   E. Talos and W. Manoschek, 'Politische Struktur des Austrofaschismus 1934–1938', in E. Talos and W. Neugebauer (eds), *'Austrofaschismus': Beitrage über Politik, Ökonomie und Kultur 1934–1938* (Vienna, 1985), 104.
4   C. Earl Edmondson, *The Heimwehr and Austrian Politics, 1918–1936* (Athens, Ga., 1978), 199; A. Wandruszka, 'Österreichs politische Struktur: Die Christlich-soziale-Konservative Lage', in H. Benedikt (ed.), *Die Geschichte der Republik Öster-reich* (Vienna, 1954), 334–7.
5   R. J. Rath, 'Authoritarian Austria', in P. Sugar (ed.), *Native Fascism in the Successor States 1918–1945* (Santa Barbara, Calif., 1971), 24–43; see also U. Kluge, *Die österreichische Ständestaat 1934–38* (Vienna, 1984) and a review of this work by R. G. Ardelt, *Zeitgeschichte*, vol. 13, no. 3 (December 1985), 109–19.
6   K.-J. Siegfried, *Klerikalfaschismus* (Frankfurt, 1979), 1–7. Similar approaches have been taken by W. Holzer, 'Faschismus in Österreich', *Austriaca* (July 1978), 80 ff. and S. Mattl, 'Die Finanzdiktatur. Wirtschaftspolitik in Österreich 1933–1938', in Talos and Neugebauer (eds), *'Austrofaschismus'*, 133–59.
7   Siegfried, *Klerikalfaschismus*, 23.
8   E. Hanisch, 'Der Politische Katholizismus als ideologischer Träger des "Austro-faschismus"', in Talos and Neugebauer (eds), *'Austrofaschismus'*, 53.
9   Talos and Manoschek, 'Politische Struktur', 97.
10 G. Jagschitz, 'Die österreichische Ständestaat 1934–1938', in E. Weinzierl and K. Skalnik (eds), *Österreich 1918–1938. Geschichte der Ersten Republik*, Vol. I (Vienna, 1985), 501.
11 E. Holtmann, *Zwischen Unterdrückung und Befriedigung* (Vienna, 1978), 15.
12 G. Botz, *Gewalt in der Politik*, 2nd edn. (Vienna, 1978), 237–8.
13 Edmondson, *Heimwehr*, 182.
14 Jagschitz, 'Die österreichische Ständestaat', 498; Martin Kitchen, *The Coming of Austrian Fascism* (London, 1980), 278. On Italy see Adrian Lyttelton, 'Italian fascism', in W. Laqueur (ed.), *Fascism – A Reader's Guide* (London, 1976), 91, 95, 97.
15 Mattl, 'Die Finanzdiktatur', 136–49.
16 Wandruszka, 'Die Christlichsoziale-Konservative Lage', 312–32.
17 John Rath and Carolyn Schum have argued that the Dollfuss-Schuschnigg regime was not fascist because, amongst other things, its attack on civil liberties was less

extreme than those of the Nazi or Italian Fascist states. They comment that although Dollfuss set up a concentration camp in Wöllersdorf in 1933, 'even G. E. R. Gedye, who was anything but a friend of the Dollfuss regime, admits that life was relatively easy (there)'. J. Rath and C. Schum, 'The Dollfuss Regime: fascist or authoritarian?', in S. U. Larsen, B. Hagtvet and J. P. Myklebust (eds), *Who Were the Fascists? Social Roots of European Fascism* (Oslo, Bergen and Tromso, 1980), 252.

18   J. W. Boyer, *Political Radicalism in Late Imperial Vienna* (Chicago and London, 1981), 275. The Viennese franchise was based on a curia system and the right to vote depended on the level of tax paid. In 1885 the lowest threshold was reduced from 10 to 5 gulden, enfranchising lower artisans and shopkeepers.

19   Boyer, *Political Radicalism*, 160–4. Adolf Hitler wrote about Lueger in *Mein Kampf*, comparing his policies and tactics with those of the German nationalist leader Schönerer. In all the important areas in which Schönerer failed, Lueger, he said, succeeded. Adolf Hitler, *Mein Kampf* (Munich, 1939), 105–34.

20   Boyer, *Political Radicalism*, 223–5.

21   ibid., p. 177.

22   Gulick, *Austria from Habsburg to Hitler*, Vol. 1, 26.

23   Boyer, *Political Radicalism*, 419.

24   Gulick, *Austria from Habsburg to Hitler*, Vol. 2, 1425. Gulick also points out that Schuschnigg disowned the association with *Quadragesimo Anno* and that no reference was made to it in the constitution itself.

25   Wandruszka, 'Die Christlichsoziale-Konservative Lage', 336.

26   A. Staudinger, 'Die Christlichsoziale Panel', in Weinzierl and Skalnik, *Österreich 1918–1938*, 250–3. Sections of the Austrian bourgeoisie supported the Pan-German Party, especially in Styria.

27   ibid., 253. The one exception was the 1924 Ramek administration: see Gulick, *Austria from Habsburg to Hitler*, Vol. 1, 701.

28   Staudinger, 'Die Christliche Partei', in Weinzierl and Skalnik, *Österreich 1918–1938*, 250–3; Gulick, *Austria from Habsburg to Hitler*, Vol. 1, 690–3.

29   ibid., p. 711.

30   I. Kerekes, *Abenddämmerung einer Demokratie: Mussolini, Gömbös und die Heimwehr* (Vienna, 1966), 32.

31   One-third of the country's total population of 6 million lived in Vienna. In 1929 national membership of the Social Democratic Party reached a peak of 718,056.

32   J. Lewis, 'Red Vienna socialism in one city, 1918–1927', *European Studies Review*, vol. 13, no. 3 (July 1983), 335–54.

33   See N. Leser, 'Austria between the wars', *Austrian History Year Book*, vol. XVII–XVIII (1981–2), 135.

34   J. Lewis, 'The failure of Styrian labour in the first Austrian Republic', PhD thesis, University of Lancaster, 1984, 207–28.

35   Kerekes, *Abenddämmerung einer Demokratie*, 14. In December 1928 the British ambassador reported a speech by Seipel in Graz in which he said of the Heimwehr 'Its object is to prevent the Social Democrats from having the sole privilege of organising processions and demonstrations in the streets for such a privilege would in the end be misused as a kind of weapon for a terrorist organization', Public Record Office (PRO), Political, Central Austria FO 371 (1928), 12851, C9698, Phipps to Sir Austen Chamberlain, 19.12.1928. This was the same speech in which Seipel produced his 'True-democracy' theory.

36   PRO, FO 371 (1929), 13565 C8732/149/3 Phipps to Henderson, 18.11.1929.

37   ibid. When Seipel resigned as leader of the Christian Social Party in 1930 on grounds of ill health, Schober told the British ambassador that the real cause was his frustration at the dissension within the Heimwehr and the Vatican's veto of his request to become that movement's leader, PRO, FO 317, 14305 (1930), C2968, Phipps to London, 16.4.1930.

38   Gulick, *Austria from Habsburg to Hitler*, Vol. 2, 897. Before the 1930 election the Heimwehr tried to arrange an electoral pact with the NSDAP. When this failed the Vienna and Lower Austria Heimwehr fought a joint campaign in their areas with the Christian Social Party under the label of 'The Christian Social and Heimatwehr Party'. The remaining Heimwehr fought a separate campaign as the Heimatblock. Verwaltungsarchiv, Bundeskanzleramt, Wien Polizeidirektion, Berichte, Karton 15, Pr Zl IV-4602/3/30, 23 Oktober 1930.

39   E. Fischer, *An Opposing Man* (London, 1969), 185.

40   W. Goldinger (ed.), *Protokolle des Klubvorstandes der Christlichsozialen Partei 1932–1934* (Vienna, 1980), 21–4 (sitting of 25 March 1933).

41   Edmondson, *Heimwehr*, 170.

42   K. Schuschnigg, *Im Kampf gegen Hitler* (Vienna, 1969), 132.

43   Goldinger (ed.), *Protokolle*, 212 (sitting of 25 March 1933).

Chapter 20

Sheelagh M. Ellwood

SPAIN: THE 'FALANGE'

■ from **FALANGE ESPAÑOLA, 1933–9: FROM FASCISM TO FRANCOISM**, in M. Blinkhorn (ed.) *Spain in Conflict 1931–1939: Democracy and its Enemies*, London, Beverly Hills and New Delhi, 1986, pp. 206–7, 208, 210–11, 212–14, 215–16, 218, 219, 220–1

The Spanish Falange belongs to that category of 'fascist' movements that strove to publicise their indigenous character and shake off accusations of apeing the two reference fascist movements in Italy and Germany. Sheelagh Ellwood analyses the ideological features of José Antonio Primo de Rivera's (son of the dictator of Spain in the 1920s) movement and its eventual fusion with the traditional Spanish right (both the Carlists and Francoism). Although there were substantial ideological and political differences between Franco and José Antonio, the Falange actively supported the 1936 military uprising and finally became the (only) party of the Francoist regime. It did keep its structure and saw the main tenets of its doctrine embedded in the official ideology of Franco's regime – this was the trade-off for accepting its subjugation to Franco's more authoritarian perception of politics.

O**N 29 OCTOBER 1933** a young Spanish aristocrat, the Marqués de Estella, announced to an expectant audience in one of Madrid's central theatres that democracy was 'the most ruinous system of squandering energy'. 'The liberal State', he continued, had brought economic slavery', whilst socialism meant 'disunity, hatred, separation and forgetfulness of every bond of brotherhood and solidarity between men'. As an alternative to all these evils, he proposed to found a movement which was 'neither rightist nor leftist' and which would redeem Spain from the state of 'moral ruin' into which he considered it to have fallen.[1] The speaker was better known as José Antonio Primo de Rivera, eldest son of the army general who, between 1923 and 1930, had headed a dictatorship which abolished parliamentary democracy while at the same time sustaining the 'liberal' monarchy of Alfonso XIII. By 1933, three years after the exile and death of the dictator and two since the departure of the king, José Antonio Primo de Rivera was well known in Madrid political and professional circles and admired in the upper-class social set he frequented. He was considered a good lawyer, a handsome bachelor and a loyal defender of his father's memory. Indeed, it was the defence of General Primo de Rivera's values and policies which had provided the motive for his son's first experience of organized political activity. In 1930, José Antonio Primo de Rivera was secretary of the Unión Monárquica Nacional, a group which, as its title implies, sought to provide a nationwide channel of solidarity for what was, in fact, a failing monarchy. The UMN saw any alternative to monarchism as being only one step removed from a communist revolution and, by the time the Second Republic was declared on 14 April 1931, the young Primo de Rivera had already made it very clear that his sympathies did not lie with such a regime. The opinions he expressed at a meeting in Bilbao were very explicit on that score:

> There are only two courses open in these transcendental moments: revolution or counter-revolution. Either our traditional order or the triumph of Moscow . . . and Moscow will triumph if the revolution triumphs. It will not be a revolution against the monarchy, but complete subversion of the social order. The conservative republic is only a step (in that direction).[2]

When he announced the creation of his own movement on that October day in 1933, however, he did not propose that it should be either monarchical or *primo-derriverista*. That would have harked back too much to a past which was clearly gone and which no-one had lifted a finger to save. He was proposing something new, something which conceived of Spain as a 'transcendental and indivisible synthesis, with ends of its own to pursue' and which would be the 'efficient and authoritarian instrument at the service of that . . . irrevocable expression of unity which is the Fatherland'.[3] [. . .] When, on 2 November 1933, the new movement was formally given the title of Falange Española (Spanish Phalanx), it was clear that the initials by which it was known – FE – could equally be taken to mean 'fascismo español', 'Spanish fascism'. José Antonio appears to have had no qualms about the possible confusion of the two ideas in the public mind. Ramón Serrano Suñer, José Antonio's close friend, wrote in his memoirs that José Antonio created the Falange 'in response to pressure from those who wished to promote in Spain a copy of the Italian Fascist movement'.[4]

[. . .]

From the outset, the Falange thus had strong right- and left-wing rivals which effectively occupied the political space to which it might otherwise have aspired. The party's propaganda consequently stated repeatedly that it was neither rightist nor leftist. In so doing it fell between two stools, for the social and political context of Spain in the 1930s was one of clearly defined and clearly opposed classes and ideologies which allowed little room for ambiguity. The Falange was too reactionary for the left and too radical for the right; too much like fascism for the working classes, not Catholic enough for the middle classes and too revolutionary for the upper classes. By the end of 1933, its situation was critical. Lack of funds reduced the possibilities of propaganda and recruiting to virtually nothing and made even the maintenance of a place to meet problematical. The Falangist leadership was consequently obliged to look somewhere other than to the parties and sympathizers of the traditional right and left in order to ensure the party's continued material and political existence.

Of the pre-1933 attempts to promote fascism in Spain, only one had survived to the time of the Falange's foundation: the Juntas de Ofensiva Nacional Sindicalista, or JONS, whose leaders were two men of north Castilian origin, Onésimo Redondo and Ramiro Ledesma Ramos. Originally the leaders of two separate groups, they had joined forces in October 1931. The fusion had occurred for much the same pragmatic reasons as that which, in 1933, obliged the Falange to look for allies: lack of both funds and a mass following. The JONS had managed to produce some doctrinal publications in Madrid and the provinces and had established small groups all over the country. In Madrid, the most militant members had been organized into 'assault commandos', for one of the fundamental tenets of the JONS was the legitimacy of the use of violence for the achievement of ideological goals. This, however, had the negative effects of repelling middle-class affiliations and finance and of attracting governmental sanctions, both of which seriously restricted the growth of the JONS. If the JONS had been marginally more successful than the Falange in terms of numbers and presence on a national scale, it was because they were more overtly Catholic in content and less patently upper-class in their discourse and composition. Nevertheless, they had to contend with the same competitors to the right and left and the same unfavourable political climate. Moreover, just as the existence of the JONS limited the Falange's potential for growth, so the foundation of the Falange restricted even further that of the JONS.

Ledesma and José Antonio had talked of joining forces even before the foundation of the Falange, but no agreement had been reached.[5] By the end of 1933, however, recruiting was falling off in the JONS and José Antonio was in danger of becoming a leader without a party. Having reconsidered the advantages to be derived from uniting, the two leaders agreed on the amalgamation of their respective groups on 13 February 1934. The new organization would be called Falange Española de las JONS and would be led by an 'executive committee' composed of Ledesma, José Antonio and the Falangist Ruiz de Aida. In opting for an alliance with the JONS, José Antonio clarified his previously somewhat ambiguous position vis-à-vis fascism, for Ledesma's group had never made any secret of its admiration for Hitler and Mussolini. Three days after the creation of FE de las JONS, José Antonio expressed publicly the view that the new organization could be the vehicle in Spain for the same kind of 'universal attitude of return to one's own self' that fascism represented in Italy.[6]

[. . .]

Ledesma and José Antonio were agreed upon what they saw as the necessity to crush Marxism and upon the inadequacy of the parliamentary system for this purpose, but differed as to what kind of movement they were creating. Whereas Ledesma envisaged a non-Marxist mass movement, capable of channelling the patriotic sentiments of 'people of all classes', José Antonio was intent upon creating an elitist body.

[. . .]

José Antonio was no longer explicit in his monarchism, but he had not severed his relations with his Alfonsine contacts and, in August 1934, he signed a pact with the Renovación Española leader, Antonio Goicoechea. In return for economic assistance, FE de las JONS would stimulate the 'maximum growth of its combative militias' and would in no way obstruct the realization of Renovación Española's programme, including the installation of the monarchy as 'a national and popular regime.'[7] Ledesma's concept of a corporativist state composed of self-governing, classless organizations of 'producers' was incompatible with this notion of a state organized on the monarchical principle.

José Antonio and Ledesma were also in disagreement as to where the party should concentrate its propaganda and recruiting efforts. The former believed that it was in the rural areas, particularly in Castile and Extremadura, that the essence of the 'true' Spain was to be found, whereas Ledesma insisted that the party should, as a 'fascist initiative', prepare to engage battle with the 'subversive organizations' in the capital and the large towns.[8] [. . .]

The rivalry between José Antonio and Ledesma came to a head in January 1935 and was resolved when Ledesma abandoned the party. José Antonio, now in sole and uncontested control, throughout 1935 sought internal and external support for the Falange. The latter was more forthcoming than the former: between June 1935 and June 1936, the party received a substantial monthly subsidy from the Italian Fascist Party.[9] [. . .] The Falange's subsequent call for right-wing unity and the creation of a National Front was ignored by the other rightist parties. Eleventh-hour attempts by José Antonio to reach an agreement with Gil Robles also failed. Consequently, when the Cortes were dissolved in January 1936 and elections called for 16 February, FE de las JONS went to the polls alone. Not one of its candidates was elected.

Paradoxically, the electoral defeat of the Falange and, indeed, of the entire right wing of the political spectrum was precisely the spur that the extreme right needed to legitimate taking the law into its own hands. The right had, in fact polled more votes than in November 1933, but the electoral law favoured coalitions and whereas the right was disunited, the left had formed the alliance known as the Popular Front which was, to all intents and purposes, a re-creation of the 1931 alliance, excluding the Radical Party. The right now began to howl that the victory of the Popular Front was the first step towards the installation of soviet communism in Spain. Since the Falange had been inveighing against Marxism since 1933, the 1936 election result was presented as confirmation that it had been 'right all along'. For the first time in its career, the Falange experienced a noticeable increase in the numbers of its militants as people abandoned the defeated 'moderates' and looked to the extremist postures of José Antonio's party to put up 'energetic' resistance to the Popular Front. From a faltering minority group with some 5000 militants, the Falange became, in less than six months, a party of close to 500,000 members, fired with a desire for revenge.[10] This was the first important stage in a process of quantitative and qualitative change in the Falange. The process was to last until 1939 and leave the party in a position of power which it had proved to be completely incapable of achieving in its first two years of existence.

The Second Spanish Republic was beset from the moment of its declaration in 1931 by conspiracies to overthrow it. One attempt had failed in 1932, and at least one more had been called off at the last moment for lack of support in important sectors of the army. The Falange, too, had proposed a coup d'état in June 1935, for which José Antonio claimed to have the support of an army general; some months earlier, in 1934, he had written two open letters expressing very clearly the view that the army ought to intervene.[11] After the February 1936 elections, the pace of military conspiracy quickened. In an open letter published in May, José Antonio again expressed the willingness of the Falange to participate in a military enterprise the objective of which was the overthrow of the Republic.[12] [. . .] Nevertheless, there was a certain mutual distrust between the military men and the political leaders. Whilst the latter, through multiple secondary channels and contacts, were aware that a *pronunciamiento* was being prepared, they were not included in the conspiracy as the official representatives of civilian support for it. By the same token, the political intriguers were wary as to what kind of regime might come out of a military coup. The instructions from José Antonio circulated to Falange militants in the spring and early summer of 1936 indicate that whilst he favoured the Falange's providing active support for an anti-Republican coup, he was afraid that the party would subsequently be subjugated to the power of the generals, since it was they who possessed the *ultima ratio* of the force of arms.[13]

[. . .]

[Yet] when the rising finally began in Melilla, Spanish Morocco, on 17 July 1936, the Falangists, following a party circular issued in March, presented themselves at the nearest army or Civil Guard barracks to offer 'complete and loyal aid in the tasks assigned by the military leaders for the assistance of the armed forces'.[14]

[. . .]

The immediate military response of the Falange to the rebellion was thus one of well-trained solidarity born partly of necessity and partly of conviction. It was not until the rising turned into war that the full *political* significance of the alliance with the military became apparent. In a war against an external enemy, the legislative and administrative processes of government carry on more or less as normal, albeit on a war footing. In a civil war, however, those processes are seriously disrupted and the structures which exist for their application cease to function or function only partially. Thus, in 1936, the insurgents in Spain simply ceased to consider that 'legality' and 'authority' as defined by the 1931 Constitution were applicable to them. However, since they had failed to take immediately the main power centres of Madrid and Barcelona, they had to improvise the imposition of their own legality in the areas under their control. Initially, this was by sheer force and through the Junta de Defensa (Defence Committee) established in Burgos on 24 July, but the task became more complex as the war advanced and the territory under rebel control expanded.

This situation presented the Falange with the opportunity to assume political leadership in the so-called 'Nationalist' zone. Its only possible rival was the Carlist

Traditionalist Communion over which it now had a considerable numerical advantage.[15] However, the Falange also suffered from a number of important disadvantages. In the first place, the absence of José Antonio was a serious blow to an organization which had cultivated the power of the single, charismatic leader and which had no contingency plan in the event of his disappearance. The subjective and objective gravity of the loss of the central authority was exacerbated when it was known that José Antonio had been executed in Alicante on 20 November 1936. Secondly, whilst the imprisonment, or clandestine location behind the Republican lines, of many provincial and local Falange leaders had had little effect on the military enlistment of party members, it left those who were too young or too old for military service without effective, experienced political leadership. Thirdly, the enormous influx of new militants which occurred after February 1936 continued with the outbreak of the war. By then, the Falangist leaders were more concerned with numerical strength than with ideological conviction and the new militants with their personal safety than with Falangist doctrine. Consequently, far from being the elitist group envisaged by Primo de Rivera, the Falange was turning into a heterogeneous mass led by party cadres who had little time or opportunity for political indoctrination. Fourthly, whereas the leadership of the Traditionalist Communion had clear ideas as to what form their post-war state would take and who would lead it, the Falangists had not. This was the most serious single problem they had to face, for whilst solutions to the others could be improvised for the duration of the war, this one admitted no improvisation and was, moreover, of long-term as well as immediate significance.

[. . .]

Whilst the military aspects of political involvement in the war were uppermost in General Franco's mind, the strictly political aspects concerned his team of collaborators, particularly his brother, Nicolás Franco, who was General Secretary to the Junta Técnica. The existence, alongside the Junta Técnica, of the Falangist Junta de Mando Provisional and the Carlist Junta Nacional de Guerra meant that there were several sources of political power, only one of which was directly responsible to Franco. At the same time, the Junta Técnica was simply an ad hoc solution to an immediate need, lacking both ideology and history. Franco's power was thus based solely on his military prowess and powers of coercion. In the autumn of 1936, Nicolás Franco suggested the creation of a Francoist party, whereby to solve the problem of the plurality of authority and that of the narrowness of Franco's power base. Franco rejected the idea, perhaps afraid that such a party would be too much like Primo de Rivera's unsuccessful Unión Patriótica. Instead, he began to toy with the idea of uniting all the existing parties and assuming the leadership of the resulting 'single party'. At about the same time, General Yagüe mooted the idea of the fusion of Carlists and Falangists, although it is not clear whether he was echoing the *generalissimo*'s sentiments or vice versa. Although available sources give few insights into this, there is reason to believe that there was an important difference between Yagüe's ideas and Franco's. Whereas Franco envisaged himself as head of party, government, armed forces and state in a system to be implemented as a result of winning the war, Yagüe's later political activity suggests that he saw the fusion of the Falange and the Traditionalist Communion as a prior step to negotiating an end to the war and then restoring the monarchy in the person of Alfonso XIII's son, Don Juan de Borbón.[16]

By the beginning of 1937, the idea of uniting the two main political forces in the Nationalist zone was known to Carlists and Falangists and had been discussed openly in the press.[17]

[. . .]

Falangists and Carlists realized that the long-projected amalgamation might take place before the end of the war and attempted to retain the initiative for themselves. [. . .] The provisional head of the Falange, Manuel Hedilla, had known of Franco's intentions since November 1936 and was therefore working towards the creation of a permanent party structure with himself at the head. If the unification of the Falange and the Traditionalist Communion were to take place, the Falange would be in a favourable position to assume the leading roles in the new organization. For, in spite of the war and the prohibition of political activities, the Falange had managed to maintain its pre-war hierarchical structures throughout the country, its press and propaganda apparatus, its social services (run by the women's section) and, of course, its militias. Although the Carlists had also retained some of their pre-war activities, their power was largely limited to the northern provinces and they were now, in any case, numerically inferior to the Falange. If the creation of a single party was designed precisely to absorb and take advantage of existing political forces, it was logical that the Falange's infrastructure should be adopted as that of the new party. This would be interpretable as tantamount to the conquest of the state envisaged by the Falangist doctrine.

Conscious of the importance of such a development, Hedilla called a meeting of the Falange's National Council for 18 and 19 April 1937, in Salamanca, to elect a permanent national chief. In view of the numerous differences and contradictions in the first-hand accounts of the events surrounding the meeting, it cannot be stated with absolute certainty whether Hedilla acted in the knowledge that Franco had decided the date for the unification of all parties, or whether the *generalissimo* took that decision as a result of the clash between different Falangist factions which occurred in Salamanca on the night of 16 April 1937.[18] What is certain is that, on the same day that Manuel Hedilla was elected National Chief of the Falange, he was divested of the post by the public announcement that the Falange and the Traditionalist Communion were to be fused together and that Franco would be the national leader of the new party. All other parties were dissolved and their members automatically incorporated into the new organization. Decree 255, published on 20 April 1937, put the announcement into immediate effect.

[. . .]

The importance of the unification cannot be exaggerated because, in general terms, it laid the *de facto* and *de jure* foundations of a system which, politically, was to remain unaltered until the death of Franco in 1975, and because, for the Falange in particular, it did, indeed, mean the 'conquest of the state', although not in the sense envisaged by Ledesma, José Antonio or Hedilla. It was not that the Falange had taken power, for power still lay in the hands of the armed forces, and ultimately, was Franco's personal prerogative. It had, however, been given access to the status, authority and economic resources it had proved incapable of achieving before July 1936. The war itself had opened the way to the Falange's rise, for a party which both preached and practised a credo of violence was better adapted to a situation of armed conflict than those which functioned within the norms of democratic parliamentarianism. The terms of the Decree of Unification confirmed for the post-war period the priority given to the Falange at the time of the rising.

The two years between the promulgation of Decree 255 and the end of the war in April 1939 saw the consolidation of the Falange's position as *primus inter pares*. The new party adopted the same hierarchical structure as the pre-unification Falange, with a single, charismatic leader – Franco; an executive committee, or Junta Politica; and a consultative body of party delegates – the National Council. The party uniform was the blue Falangist shirt and the Carlist red beret. The party symbol was the Falangist yoke and arrows and the fascist salute of the Falange was adopted as the official salute on 24 April 1937. The party statutes were published on 4 August 1937 and the formation of FET de las JONS was completed with the appointment of Falangist Raimundo Fernández Cuesta as secretary-general on 2 December 1937. When Franco announced his first cabinet, in January 1938, two ministries were occupied by Falange militants: Fernández Cuesta in Agriculture and Pedro González Bueno in Syndical Action and Organization. Whilst this might appear to be very little in a quantitative sense, it was of considerable qualitative significance. In January 1938, Spain was still submerged in a civil war which, to a large extent, had been provoked by the issues of the distribution of land and the power of an organized working class. That Franco should confer on Falange militants the responsibility for these two key areas was far more important than the mere number of ministerial posts they occupied. Under Fernández Cuesta, the ministry of Agriculture reversed the legislation on land reform put into practice by the Republican government in 1936. González Bueno, for his part, initiated the construction of the official, obligatory trade unions which were to replace class-based representation for the next forty years.

By the time the war ended, in April 1939, the Falangist doctrine had been adopted officially as 'the programmatic norm of the new state'.[19] Some of those who had formed the party in 1933 held cabinet posts, whilst others and later militants formed the backbone of the legislative and administrative apparatus of an entire state. Certainly, they had to share power with the representatives of the political currents which had once been their rivals and with the Catholic Church. Certainly, too, their authority was delegated by the supreme power of the *generalissimo*. The Falange did not stand alone, as José Antonio Primo de Rivera had envisaged in 1933, and its place in the post-war spoils system had been achieved, as he had foreseen, in exchange for subjugation to the armed forces. This, however, was the price of survival. When forced to choose between failed fascism or successful Francoism, the Falange had opted without hesitation for the latter.

Notes

1 J. A. Primo de Rivera, 'Discurso de la fundación de Falange Española', in *Obras completes* (Madrid 1945), 17–25.

2 Quoted in A. Gibello, *José Antonio, apuntes para una biografia polémica* (Madrid 1974), 80.

3 Primo de Rivera, op. cit., 22.

4 R. Serrano Suñer, *Memorias* (Barcelona 1977), 473.

5 F. Bravo Martínez, *Historia de la Falange Española de las JONS* (Madrid 1940), 13; R. Ledesma Ramos, *Fascismo en España?* (Barcelona 1968), 123.

6 *Ahora* (Madrid), 16 February 1934.

7 P. Sáinz Rodríguez, *Testimonio y recuerdos* (Barcelona 1978), 375–6; J. M. Gil Robles, *No fue posible la paz* (Barcelona 1968), 442–3.

8 Ledesma Ramos, op. cit., 167.

9 Angel Viñas, 'Berlin: salvad a José Antonio', *Historia 16,* nos. 1 and 2 (May/June 1976); John F. Coverdale, *La Intervención fascista en la guerra civil española* (Madrid 1979), 67, 74; Max Gallo, *Spain under Franco* (London 1973), 48–9.

10 Former Falange secretary, Raimundo Fernández Cuesta, in an interview with the author in Madrid, 15 July 1977. Most of the new recruits came from the Juventud de Acción Popular, although it is not known whether they were instructed or encouraged to join the Falange. See Paul Preston, *The Coming of the Spanish Civil War* (London 1983), 188.

11 On 24 September 1934 José Antonio had written a letter to General Franco and in November of the same year he published a 'Letter to a Spanish soldier'. Both are reproduced in *Obras completas*, 623–6 and 645–53 respectively.

12 'Carta a los militares de España', 4 May 1936, in Primo de Rivera, op. cit., 669–74.

13 Circular 'To all provincial and territorial chiefs', 24 June 1936, in Primo de Rivera, op. cit., 969–72.

14 Quoted in David Jato, *La rebellion de los estudiantes?* (private edn, Madrid 1975), 332–3. This circular does not appear in the *Obras completes* of Primo de Rivera.

15 The Traditionalist Communion was equally convinced that it had a 'natural right' to the political leadership of the Nationalist zone and was not prepared to yield to Falangist aspirations: Martin Blinkhorn, *Carlismo y contrarrevolución en España, 1931–1939* (Barcelona 1979), 367–8.

16 Dionisio Ridruejo, *Casi unas memorias* (Barcelona 1976), 65, refers to Yagüe discussing the idea of unification in the Segovia press in November 1936. Yagüe's subsequent ideas on the role of the party and the possible installation of Don Juan as regent under Falangist tutelage are contained in the personal archive of General Yagüe, which the present writer was able to examine briefly in 1984.

17 For example, in *El Pensamiento Navarro* in December 1936 and in the Falangist *Arriba España* of 6 January 1937.

18 Details of the events in Salamanca between 15 and 20 April 1937 are contained in A. Alcazar de Velasco, *Los siete días de Salamanca* (Madrid 1976), 91–105, 123–282; V. Cadenas Vicent, *Adas del ultimo Consejo Nacional de FE de las JONS (18–19/IV/1937)* (private edn, Madrid 1975), 66–156; M. Hedilla Larrey, *Manuel Hedilla. Testimonio* (Barcelona 1972), 443–94; and S. Dávila, *Jose Antonio, Salamanca y otras cosas* (Madrid 1967), 125–33.

19 Preamble to Decree 255, *Boletín Oficial del Estado*, 20 April 1937.

Chapter 21

Robert Soucy

FRANCE: THE 'SECOND WAVE' OF FASCISM IN THE 1930s

■ from *FRENCH FASCISM: THE SECOND WAVE, 1933–1939*,
New Haven and London, 1995, pp. 26–8, 311, 312–16, 317–20

Robert Soucy has published two major monographs on the rise of French fascism in the interwar period. Although he challenged Zeev Sternhell's contention that fascism was 'neither right nor left', perceiving it as a major reaction to the resurgence of the French left in the 1920s and 1930s, he shared with him the belief that, contrary to the traditional idea of French fascism as an imported phenomenon essentially alien to the intellectual traditions of the country (*thèse immunitaire*), France developed her own unique (autochthonous) brand of fascism in the 1930s. The following excerpt comes from the second monograph, dealing with the 'second wave' of French fascism that emerged in France after the electoral victory of the Popular Front in 1936 (the 'first wave' – the subject of his first book – refers to those fascist movements that emerged after the 1924 victory of the left).

T HE RESURGENCE OF FASCISM IN FRANCE in the early 1930s and its eventual decline in the late 1930s cannot be understood in the absence of some account of the larger historical context in which it operated, particularly the political consequences of the Depression in France. Although France suffered less from the Depression than did Germany, the effects were still grim. As one contemporary later recalled, 'Part-time unemployment prevented the statistics of total unemployment from assuming at once alarming proportions. Widespread anxiety developed slowly; a more and more painful misery settled gradually among the masses. . . . For fear of being thrown into the hell of unemployment, the workers consented almost in silence to incredibly low salaries.'[1] The historian Gordon Wright has noted that the Depression in France developed into the longest and most severe economic crisis France had known for a century and that when the recovery did set in it was slower than in most countries.

Adding to the crisis was the flood of immigrants that began pouring into France in the late thirties, including Jews fleeing from Nazi Germany. As Paula Hyman, David Weinberg, Robert Paxton, and Michael Marrus have shown, anti-immigration feelings were widespread in France in the 1930s, even in some Jewish and liberal circles. Immigration also became a major issue for French fascists, who, while denying that they were racists, protested the arrival of left-wing Jews.[2]

Politically, mass economic hardship led to a resurgence of the left in France, as the extreme left, the Communists, entertained hopes of an impending revolution and the center left, the Socialists and Radical-Socialists, called for more social legislation to alleviate the suffering. The elections of 1932 brought a new Cartel des Gauches (left-center coalition) to power in parliament, and four years later another national election produced an even more left-wing government, the Popular Front, an alliance of Socialists, Communists, and left-wing liberals under the leadership of Léon Blum. The result was that many French conservatives, including many democratic conservatives who called themselves moderates, felt beleaguered.

[. . .]

Since 1875 most French conservatives, supporting the Third Republic rather than an Orleanist or Bonapartist restoration, had relied on political democracy to defend their interests. However, when major threats from the political left and left-center developed in the 1920s and 1930s, some conservatives turned to more authoritarian alternatives. The first wave of organized fascism in France emerged in 1925, following the election of the first Cartel des Gauches in 1924. It receded two years later when a right-center coalition led by Raymond Poincaré stole its thunder by defeating the cartel.[3] With the onset of the Depression in France in 1931 and the election of a new cartel majority in parliament in 1932, a second wave of fascism emerged in France. Not only did the AF and the JP gain new support, but three new fascist movements were launched: the CF (founded earlier but greatly politicized by Colonel de La Rocque after 1931), the SF in 1933, and the Francistes in 1933. In 1936, following the election of the Popular Front, the PPF was also founded.

All of these movements sought to capitalize on public discontent with a parliamentary system that was ineffectual in dealing with the Depression. Between 1932 and 1934, France underwent six successive governments, none able to garner a working parliamentary majority. One cabinet after another was toppled as even Socialists and Radical-Socialists split on whether to raise income taxes and increase government spending, the Socialist solution, or keep taxes low and reduce government spending, the Radical-Socialist solution. One result was a rising public outcry, largely but not solely from the political right, for a revision of the Constitution that would break the stalemate by strengthening the power of the executive and reducing that of the legislature. For conservative revisionists like André Tardieu and François Coty, constitutional revision was meant to favor a conservative executive who would use his additional powers to keep the working classes and their disempowered legislators under control. The positive reaction of the French right-wing press to Hitler's actions against Communist and Socialist organizations in Germany in 1933 was indicative of this spirit.[4]

Some French fascist movements of the period damned parliamentarianism altogether (the royalist AF called the Third Republic the Sow), but most insisted that they were still committed to a republican form of government, albeit to a stronger form of republicanism than that provided by the Third Republic. They advocated constitutional revisions that would not only increase the power of the executive but also create corporatist representative bodies (representing occupational groups rather than regions), which would further reduce the power of the Chamber of Deputies.

[. . .]

In terms of size, the major fascist movements in France between 1924 and 1939 were Charles Maurras's AF, Antoine Rédier's Legion, Georges Valois's Faisceau, Pierre Taittinger's JP, François Coty's SF, Colonel de La Rocque's CF/PSF, and Jacques Doriot's PPF. Henri Dorgères's Greenshirts, although more of a peasant auxiliary to French fascism than a prime mover, was also sizeable. Except for Maurras's AF (whose membership was smaller than that of the others at their peak), all were republican, that is, nonroyalist.

All eight movements criticized Marxism, liberalism, parliamentarianism, internationalism, egalitarianism, feminism, and decadence, and all eight defended socio-economic conservatism, political authoritarianism, paramilitary action, nationalism, hierarchy, paternalism, and the spiritual. All eight were far more nationalist than socialist, advocating a form of class collaboration that would have favored management by replacing the Communist CGT and the Socialist CGTU with corporatist unions, deprived workers of the weapon of the strike, and substituted conservative arbitration (under a right-wing authoritarian state) for collective bargaining.

[. . .]

The leadership of France's major fascist movements, both on the national and local levels, was dominated by individuals from middle-class, aristocratic, and military backgrounds, and the rank and file members were drawn predominantly from petty bourgeois, white-collar, and peasant constituencies. This was true even of the PPF after 1936, a movement whose politburo and central committee, originally packed with ex-Communists, made way for former members of the CF and other extreme rightists and whose original working-class base declined sharply after Doriot shifted to the political right.

France's major fascist movements during the interwar period extolled the petty bourgeois and the peasantry, not the proletariat, as the guardians of French tradition. Despite the big business subsidies that played a major role in funding their activities, they denounced plutocracy and the trusts and promised to protect small businesses from their larger competitors. At the same time, they insisted that capitalism was superior to socialism, praised profit as 'the motor of production,' and denounced bureaucratic interventions into the economy. Castigating the political left for threatening property rights, they called for lower taxes, reduced government spending (true even of the PPF when its program is read carefully), an end to wage hikes, and a revision (upward!) of the forty-hour-week law. The slogan

'Neither right nor left,' which all of these movements employed at one time or another, was fraudulent, typical of the verbal mystifications that French fascists resorted to in their attempts to win over blue-collar workers.

Although anti-Semitism was a major characteristic of German fascism, its role in French fascism was much smaller. As Eugen Weber has noted, there were varieties of fascism in Europe in the 1930s. Some of these varieties were less anti-Semitic than others. To conclude because of the Holocaust that anti-Semitism was the central feature of all fascism during the interwar period not only minimizes the anti-Marxist thrust of Hitler's and Mussolini's policies but also ignores the fact that fascist Italy before 1938 was generally not anti-Semitic and even as late as 1943 it was a haven for Jews escaping Vichy France. If not to be anti-Semitic in the 1920s and early 1930s was not to be fascist, then Mussolini was not a fascist. [. . .]

In France, it was only after the Popular Front came to power in 1936 that La Rocque and Doriot retreated from their earlier opposition to anti-Semitism (although in 1934 La Rocque had been something of a *selective* anti-Semite on the immigration question). There are also important distinctions to be made between religious, cultural, and biological anti-Semitism, however much they reinforced one another in practice. One did not have to believe in biological anti-Semitism in the early 1930s to believe in fascism, as again was demonstrated by Italian fascism. Even the anti-Semitic AF and SF denied that they were racist, insisting that they objected to Jews on cultural and political, not biological, grounds. La Rocque publicly welcomed right-wing Jews into his movement. Not until 1938 did Doriot give the go-ahead to anti-Semites within the PPF to fully indulge their venom, and even then such attacks were largely limited to Algeria. Although after 1936 La Rocque tolerated anti-Semitic articles in some of the PSF's provincial newspapers, especially those published in Algeria and Alsace, it was not until 1938 that he enjoined his followers in Constantine to abstain from all relations with the Jewish community. In 1941 he associated Jews with the de-Christianization of France and with the 'mortal vices' that had led to military defeat in 1940.

Like the first wave of fascism in France, which peaked in 1925, the second wave, which peaked in 1937, was part of a right-wing backlash to an electoral victory of the center-left. Just as Valois and Taittinger founded fascist organizations in 1924 to combat the Cartel des Gauches, La Rocque and Doriot mobilized movements in 1936 to combat the even more leftist Popular Front. In both cases, when the threat from the left was at its greatest, large sums of money flowed into French fascist coffers from business sources, French fascist propaganda and organizational capabilities expanded, and French fascist recruitment drives flourished. When the threat from the left declined, French fascist financial contributions receded, French fascist propaganda and organizational capabilities contracted, and French fascist membership numbers either dropped or – as in the case of the CF/PSF – leveled off.

[. . .]

Changing circumstances made France more permeable to fascism at some times than at others. Some of the same conservatives who supported Poincaré in 1923 supported Valois in 1925 and Poincaré again in 1926. Many so-called moderates abandoned the FR for the CF/PSF after 1936. The once fascist Philippe Barrès

[. . .] joined Charles de Gaulle in London in 1940. The line between democratic and fascist conservatism was crossed in both directions, depending on the situation.

Fascist leaders in France adapted to changing circumstances, just as Hitler did in Germany after 1923, when he chose to abandon paramilitary overthrow for the electoral path to power. As we have seen, to insist that only movements that espouse totalitarianism *before* they come to power be considered fascist would be to deny that both Mussolini's and Hitler's movements were fascist. Moreover, even after these dictators consolidated their power, they were far more totalitarian toward the left than toward the right, making important accommodations with preexisting elites. Colonel de La Rocque was equally opportunistic, as he went from denouncing democracy to professing democracy to denouncing democracy once again.

During the 1930s, La Rocque, Doriot, Renaud, Taittinger, and Bucard all stressed, in spite of their obvious taste for authoritarian solutions, that they were republicans. Fundamentally contemptuous of electoral democracy, political pluralism, and the civil rights of their opponents, they paid lip service to republican institutions and liberties even as they sought to subvert them.

After June 1936, when the paramilitary movements of the extreme right were outlawed, French fascist leaders were careful to temper their public remarks about democracy lest they provoke another ban. At the same time, they made it clear to French conservatives that what they had in store for the political left, should they come to power, was much stronger medicine than that proposed by the democratic right. The PSF promised a more forceful response to the Communist and Socialist threats than did the FR – or than did the FR's major affiliate in Alsace, the Union Populaire Républicaine (UPR). As Sam Goodfellow has pointed out, since the UPR was well organized and had consistently dominated elections in Alsace through 1936, 'there was no need for a new (democratic) conservative party in Alsace, because the UPR already filled that role.' The PSF therefore differentiated itself from the UPR in Alsace with its fascist characteristics.[5] After 1938 especially, that is, after the Popular Front lost its police powers, propagandists for both the PSF and the PPF grew increasingly bold in associating themselves with fascism. This was particularly true of PPF intellectuals like Bertrand de Jouvenel and Pierre Drieu La Rochelle, who openly praised fascist man in Italy and Germany.

But even between 1933 and 1938, contemporaries with any knowledge of fascist ideology no doubt took the disavowals of fascism of the SF, the CF, and the PPF with a large grain of salt. For *members* of these movements to have taken these disavowals at face value would have been especially benighted. When Vinceguide (speaking in 1934 to 450 SF militants dressed in paramilitary uniforms who ended the meeting with the fascist salute) declared, 'We are antifascist,' it is unlikely that the audience took him literally. What Vinceguide, La Rocque, and Doriot insisted upon was the Frenchness of their movements, which led them to reject the label *fascist* lest they be unfairly dismissed as lackeys of France's hereditary enemy across the Rhine. Certainly La Rocque was hardly unique among French fascist leaders in the 1930s in denying any sympathy for Hitlerism, a denial that did not prevent him from praising Mussolini. [. . .]

If in France in the 1930s thousands of French men and women were, in fact, attracted to fascist doctrines, sentiments, and values – as seen especially in the spectacular rise of La Rocque's CF/PSF after 1936 – what then prevented fascism from coming to power in France as it did in Germany? One reason was that the impact of the Depression in France was not as devastating as it was in Germany. Although the economic crisis was severe, many of the unemployed were able to roll with the blow by returning to the farms of relatives. Precisely because the French economy was less industrialized than that of Germany and northern Italy, because its stagnant sector was still heavily spotted with small family farms, it was cushioned against some of the worst effects of the world-wide economic crisis. Had this not been the case, the Popular Front might have attracted even more mass support than it did – which, in turn, would have probably led to an even more intense fascist backlash.

Another reason for fascism's failure to come to power in France in the 1930s was simply the chronology of political events. French fascism's best chance of coming to power was between May 1936 and April 1937, when the Popular Front was most threatening to rightists. By 1936, however, developments in Germany, especially Hitler's Night of the Long Knives of June 1934, had hurt the fascist cause in France. Between 1922 and 1933, fascism abroad, especially in Italy, was regarded benignly by much of the French conservative press. Hitler's repression of the German left soon after he came to power in January 1933 was condoned by many French right-wing newspapers, the same journals that later condoned the violence of the demonstrators during the riots of February 6, 1934, in Paris. However, Hitler's crackdown on dissident German Catholics and conservatives a few months later brought a much more negative response. Nazism in Germany lost its glow for many French conservatives after Hitler ordered the murder of General von Schleicher and his wife and the house arrest of General von Papen in June 1934.

After these events, French fascists were plagued with guilt by association, in spite of their attempts to distance themselves from their political cousins across the Rhine. Hitler became one of French fascism's greatest liabilities, one that was exacerbated by his public tirades against the French. The association of fascism with Hitler, which had been only a minor negative for French fascists before 1933, became a serious handicap afterward.

[. . .]

Why was the CF/PSF particularly, the largest fascist movement in France between 1936 and 1939, unable to topple the Third Republic? There were several reasons besides those already mentioned. One was the existence of the Popular Front, a coalition that had been created precisely for the purpose of preventing a fascist takeover in France. In Italy and Germany, Communists, Socialists, and left-wing liberals had failed to form such a coalition, and fascism had triumphed. French leftists and liberals, benefiting from hindsight, did not make the same mistake. Once in power, the Popular Front banned the paramilitary organizations of the extreme right, handing French fascists a major setback.

Also, on July 12, 1936, a few weeks after the Popular Front came to power in France, civil war broke out in Spain between the Popular Front government in that country and the troops of General Franco. As is clear from even French fascist newspapers of the period, large sections of the French public feared the outbreak of similar violence in France. Had La Rocque launched a paramilitary action at that time, he would have alienated many French conservatives who feared social disorder even more than they feared the Popular Front.

There were other factors as well. Authoritarian conservatives within the French officer corps, even had they contemplated participating in a coup against the Blum government, could not have been certain that the enlisted ranks, being as they were prey to so-called Communist agitators, would not rebel against them. (The Corvignolles, a secret organization within the army, had been formed for the very purpose of counteracting the influence of the 'reds.') In short, the fact that France still had a citizens' army was a partial deterrent to fascism.

Too, in May 1936 a majority of the electorate had just voted for the Popular Front, and any immediate attempt to overthrow this government by force would no doubt have aroused scores of Communists, Socialists, and left-wing liberals to reply with massive force of their own. Leftist militants had physically attacked French fascists throughout the 1930s, disrupting their meetings on a number of occasions, cowing them more often than they were cowed. (Simone de Beauvoir recalled that in 1935 'when militant members of the left and right met in public brawls it was the left that came off best.') The French left knew what had happened across the Rhine when the German left had stood by and done little to stop the Nazis from taking control of the state; it had no intention of doing the same in France. Here again, the timing of events worked against French fascism. Colonel de La Rocque, an experienced military man, wisely backed away from paramilitary action in the summer and fall of 1936, recognizing that such an adventure would have indeed been disastrous for his cause.

Finally, not only most French leftists but also many French centrists and right-ists were hostile toward fascism in 1936. Not all social conservatives shared fascism's taste for military values and its contempt for liberal democracy. Many of these conservatives were confident that the left could be defeated through parliamentary means, as it had been in 1926 and 1934. In 1937, when Doriot called for the forma-tion of a Liberty Front, that is, for democratic and authoritarian conservatives alike to unite against the Popular Front, he was turned down by two of France's leading right-center parties, the Democratic Alliance and the People's Democratic party, both of which were opposed to the polarization of French politics.

[. . .]

The French sociologist Michel Dobry has criticized historians who have argued that France was immune to fascism in the 1930s: *la thèse immunitaire* he calls it. These historians, Dobry writes, not only have displayed a 'surprising amnesia' about the crisis that democratic political culture in France underwent in the 1930s, but also have reacted to the writings of Zeev Sternhell (writings that have challenged *la thèse immunitaire*) in such a way as to 'reveal a passion which . . . appears to be the most certain indication that a sensitive point has been touched on questions that are not exclusively methodological.'[6]

According to Dobry, these historians have created a 'suitably imaginary' model of fascism, one that supports *la thèse immunitaire* by narrowly defining fascism in terms of its results in Italy and Germany, that is, in terms of what it did *after* it came to power in these countries. In doing so, they ignore the many expedient compromises that Italian and German fascists made *before* they came to power, including Mussolini's and Hitler's participation in electoral politics. By applying such an ahistorical model to France, 'they demand of the radical right not only that it define itself with more clarity than original fascism – Italian – but that it undertake everything, immediately and openly.'[7]

Dobry also rejects a classificatory perspective, which views the French extreme right in the 1930s as politically and socially marginal, in favor of a relational perspective, which, by including Colonel de La Rocque and his great mass of followers as an integral and opportunistic part of the extreme right, acknowledges the much larger importance of fascism in France during this period.

This book provides a good deal of evidence in support of Dobry's perspective. Much of the same evidence also bolsters the positions taken by the second school of historians mentioned in the introduction.

After 1936, the meteoric rise of La Rocque's CF/PSF, along with the less successful but well-financed emergence of Doriot's PPF, demonstrated the continuing appeal of the fascist tradition in France, especially when conservatives were confronted with a major threat from the political left.

Not only was France more permeable to fascist ideas in the 1930s than has generally been acknowledged, but French fascism's enormous disgust with decadence, part of a tradition that extends from George Valois's Faisceau in 1925 to Colonel de La Rocque's PSF in 1941, helped paved the way for some of the most repressive and cruel measures of the Vichy regime. When in 1941 La Rocque called for severe punishments for prominent leftists while awaiting the 'integral extirpation of contaminated elements' in French society, he was aiding the realization of what scores of French fascists before him had only preached.[8]

Notes

1   Yves Simon, *The Road to Vichy, 1918–1938* (Lanham: New York and London, 1988), 85–86.

2   Paula Hyman, *Anti-Semitism from Dreyfus to Vichy* (New York: Columbia University Press, 1979); David Weinberg, *Les juifs à Paris de 1933 à 1939* (Paris Calmann-Lévy, 1974); Robert Paxton and Michael Marrus, *Vichy and the Jews* (New York: Basic Books, 1981).

3   Robert Soucy, *French Fascism: The First Wave, 1924–1933* (New Haven: Yale University Press, 1986), 187–90.

4   *Gringoire*, February 10, 1933; *Je suis Partout*, February 4, 1933; *L'Ami du Peuple*, February 7, 9, 1933; *Le Journal*, February 6, 1933; *Le Petit Journal*, February 9, 14, 1933; *L'Echo de Paris*, January 31, 1933; *La Croix*, February 14, 1933; *Le National*, November 18, 1933. These newspapers were critical of Hitler, however, in those areas where they perceived him as threatening German conservatives or French national security.

5   Sam Goodfellow, 'Fascist or Conservative? The Croix de Feu/PSF in Alsace,' Paper presented at the Western Society for French Historical Studies, October 15, 1993.

6   Michel Dobry, 'Février 1934 et la découverte de l'allergie de la société française à la "Revolution fasciste,"' *Revue française de sociologie* 30 (July–December 1989), 511, 512–13.

7   Ibid., 523.

8   Colonel de La Rocque, *Disciplines d'Action* (Clermont-Ferrand: editions du 'Petit Journal,' 1941), 109, 146.

Chapter 22

Richard Thurlow

BRITAIN: THE 'BRITISH UNION OF FASCISTS'

■ from *FASCISM IN BRITAIN: A HISTORY, 1918–1985*, Oxford, 1986, pp. 145–52, 298–300

As in the case of French fascism, fascism in Britain raises a host of complex questions both about the forces that underpinned its emergence and about the reasons for its eventual failure to seize power or exercise significant social and political influence. In the following excerpt Richard Thurlow analyses the ideology of British fascism's most important phenomenon – Oswald Mosley's BUF. Fuelled by the concept of Britain's and Europe's cultural and economic collapse, the BUF aspired to reverse this historical trend by envisioning a radically new political and economic system. The failure of Mosley's efforts to achieve political prominence in 1930s Britain is attributed by the author to a combination of factors, ranging from the personality of the leader himself to the mentality of the British public and the sensible actions of the national government.

T HE BUF WAS ALMOST UNIQUE among fascist movements in that its origin was marked by the publication of a coherent political programme and doctrine, in Oswald Mosley's *The Greater Britain* in October 1932. This outlined the rationale behind Mosley's revolt and the policies needed in his view to reverse Britain's decline. Although ideology came to play a less important role in the movement after 1935, Mosley nevertheless concentrated his energies in this sphere and in communicating his message to the British public, delegating administrative and financial organization to others.

The ideology and the movement

The importance for Mosley of rationally expressing an alternative political strategy to the party system and establishment values has been interpreted by commentators in various ways. Of those who have gone beyond a mere exposition of Mosley's and the BUF's basic ideas, Brewer has concentrated on his conception of crisis and explained it in sociological and psychological terms, rather than in terms of the economic and philosophical ideas from which it was derived.[1] Nugent has argued that a division should be made between the official ideas of the leadership and the less well formulated motivating concepts of the rank and file.[2] Rawnsley, following Billig's distinction between an esoteric and exoteric ideology in the National Front, has suggested that members were recruited through various populist campaigns and then indoctrinated with a secret inner core ideology which emphasized the need for dictatorship, militarism, anti-semitism and the corporate state.[3] Farr has interpreted the emergence of the BUF as a watershed in the history of the British right: the development of a form of fascism with roots deep in a British national tradition which marked an integration of nationalist, socialist, imperialist and racist attitudes and had been formulated in the last stages of the New Party.[4] Skidelsky, in a brilliant and mainly convincing exposition, has analysed the development of Mosley's economic and philosophical ideas in a sympathetic manner, even if he attacked Mosley's establishment opponents in too cavalier a fashion and was not critical enough of his fascist ideas.[5]

All these interpretations have something to commend them, although Brewer's tautologies and arguments are difficult to follow at times, and he has not looked at the most interesting aspects of Mosley's conception of crisis. In this chapter I propose to examine Mosley's fascist ideas in terms of the historical development of his thought and relate this to the fortunes of the movement, and also to assess the practicality of such ideas and the role and function of the ideology to the movement, with some reference to the explanations already outlined.

Several facts need to be firmly emphasized before a detailed analysis of the ideas is undertaken. Firstly, Mosley's conviction that radical alternative economic and political policies were vital to halt what he saw as the inevitable decline and collapse of Britain was a constant and genuine belief which underlies all his actions. Having said that, however, the changing tactical and strategic shifts in policy necessitated by pragmatic political realities possessed one attribute in common. The turn from Conservative to Labour and the flirtations with the Liberals which made him so suspect to the establishment of the 1920s, and his switch to the leadership principle in 1931, all placed Mosley in the centre of events. Britain needed radical new policies which, if they could not be achieved through the democratic process by Mosley and his changing allies, would have to be solved by Mosley the dictator. His iconoclasm and egotism both pointed to Mosley as the big wheel around which all else revolved. In the 1930s he led the fascist revolution of youth against the 'united muttons' of the 'old gangs'.[6] In his old age he argued that there was no substitute for practical experience.[7] His whole political life was dedicated to two propositions: that the British Empire and/or Europe was in danger of collapse without drastic reorganization under firm leadership, and that he alone could provide the heroic flair and drive to restore the power that was being insidiously undermined by external and internal enemies.

Secondly, the distinction between official ideas of the leadership and unofficial fascist ideology of the rank and file was no different from the intellectual coherence of leaders and ideologists in most organizations with the reductionist transmission of such concepts. Fascism was a leadership movement, and although members influenced policy it was Mosley who brought the tablets down from the mountain to the membership. It was not true, for example, that the tactics of political anti-semitism and street violence were accepted by Mosley because of rank and file pressure. Mosley's own concept of personal honour and his rational analysis of the activities of some Jews against the BUF, and their role in British society, convinced him that assaults by enemies on the movement should be resisted by defensive force. Some members left because of the increase in violence and trend towards anti-semitism to which these tactics led; individuals were disciplined and expelled for unprovoked violence, or personally challenging the authority of the leader; but this did not constitute differences between official and unofficial ideology.

Thirdly, the core nature of fascist ideas remained remarkably consistent during the 1930s despite the various campaigns designed to appeal to popular sentiments and prejudices in order to draw people into the movement. Mosley's main statements of his beliefs in *The Greater Britain* (1932, revised 1934), *Fascism – One Hundred Questions Asked and Answered* (1936) and *Tomorrow we Live* (1938), all heavily accentuated the economic critique and political analysis of his alternative vision. Anti-semitism and foreign policy made no appearance in the first work and comprised only four and eight pages respectively out of seventy-two in *Tomorrow we Live*. The marked contrast with the space devoted to these themes in *Action* and *Blackshirt* after 1935, and the virulent political campaigns after 1936, inverted the emphasis between official ideology and populist rhetoric.

With the failure of official BUF ideology to provide a stimulus for recruitment after Rothermere's defection, populist campaigns appealing to local sentiment were the main weapons designed to restore the movement's collapsing fortunes. Racial populism and appeasement were used to recruit followers and those who became committed followers were converted to the basic beliefs of inner fascism. The vast majority of members in the 1930s were never wholehearted supporters of the full ideological package; only a small group of several thousand members were ever that. This gap between the true believers and the single-issue fascists helps to explain the widely differing estimates of numbers made by commentators on the movement in the 1930s.

To argue as Rawnsley does that there were different layers of ideology is correct, but unfortunately he does not take his analysis far enough. Whilst committed fascists believed in leadership, militarism, anti-semitism and corporatism, they did so in an entirely open and non-conspiratorial manner. These beliefs lay just below the surface of fascism and accounted for its notoriety and apparent addiction to physical violence, but the real inner core was something entirely different. This represented the concept of the new fascist man derived from heroic vitalist and creative evolutionist philosophies.[8] Man, through overcoming his own nature, would be able in a disciplined and socially responsible movement to transform himself and his society to create a new stage in the evolutionary development of mankind. This may have been Utopian and the idea only fully rationalized by Mosley after 1945, yet sufficient contemporary evidence exists to suggest that these beliefs were at the root of Mosley's revolt in the 1930s. Both Robert Skidelsky and Nicholas Mosley have examined these ideas, the latter in a critical fashion, and have illuminated the beliefs behind British fascism in the most convincing fashion.[9]

Finally, the nature and content of Mosley's thought deserves special emphasis because its logical structure was far removed from British academic and intellectual traditions. Mosley's powerful mind produced stimulating ideas which were usually expressed in a coherent and rational manner. However, the development of his argument was dependent on continental methods of analysis rather than on British traditions. Although not an original thinker, he was a strong believer in synthesizing ideas, no matter how disparate, to produce new thought at a higher level.[10] While the intellectual justification for this was not developed by Mosley until after 1945, it was characteristic of the way his mind worked in the inter-war period. Thus although British fascism was strongly rooted in relatively weak national traditions, its political expression and intellectual justification were much more strongly influenced by European examples.[11] If Marx's ideas represented a fusion of English economics, French politics and German philosophy, Mosley's system, at a lower level of analysis, represented a fusion of English radical economics, fascist politics and German idealist philosophy. The links were to be in philosophical method, as Mosley's insistence on idealism and psychological roots of behaviour were to contrast with Marx's materialism. For Mosley, Marx's materialism denied man's spiritual and evolutionary potential.

Mosley and other BUF theorists presented their case both in terms of sweeping away the old parliamentary system of government and of the need to replace it with a new fascist conception based on leadership and personal responsibilities. Mosley was perfectly serious when he talked of the need for a revolution.[12] Britain was facing a crisis and was in a steady decline which could only be checked by the forming of an instrument of steel.[13] The immediate problem was to solve growing unemployment, which reached 3,000,000 in the last months of 1932. However, this was only a symptom of the more insidious collapse of British power in the twentieth century which had been accelerated by the First World War. These twin problems demanded radical new economic policies and a new political system of government if Britain were not to decline to the level of Spain.[14] To reverse the situation required a different type of leader and the development of a community imbued with cohesive and coherent national values. Thus for Mosley and the BUF new political, economic and philosophical ideas were necessary to prevent long-term trends turning into terminal decline. The BUF was at base an attempt to defy the trend of history, a 'mutiny against destiny' as James Drennan (W. E. D. Allen) called it.[15] Blackshirts in the Black House in the Rothermere period had an almost chiliastic belief in the BUF attaining power within a few months.

Mosley did not produce a systematic theory of why Britain had declined from her peak as an imperial and industrial power in the eighteenth and nineteenth century until after 1945.[16] He then developed an interesting historical and psychological critique of the British ruling class. In the 1930s the demands of British fascism left him little time for new constructive thought and the intellectual content of his argument against the British ruling class at this time often degenerated to the level of crude propaganda and virulent political abuse. He had lost patience with the British establishment and became totally alienated from the methods of parliamentary government and its apparent inability to solve the fundamental problem of political decline. His failure, outside a small and diminishing coterie of convinced followers, to persuade any political party or government until 1931 to commit themselves to radical policies to fight a war in peacetime against unemployment, convinced him that parliamentary democracy could not solve Britain's fundamental problems. Although some radicals sympathized with this analysis, few of any consequence were prepared to follow Mosley and work outside the system. Mosley therefore concentrated on the economic analysis of the reasons for Britain's decline and the philosophical justification for, and political blueprint of, the proposed fascist Utopia. During the 1930s, apart from some interesting comments on Spengler, Mosley left the historical justification for British fascism to others.

The BUF argued that the principles of British fascism were embedded deep in British history, and that it was the dominant Whig interpretation that had distorted the historical textbooks.[17] Taking their arguments from a recently published modern history of England, they argued that the founding of the history schools at Oxford and Cambridge had been a propaganda stunt to justify the Hanoverian dynasty and were endowed in order to write Whig history.[18] To Bill Allen, for instance, the National government of 1931 was another long Walpolean lassitude, a revived Whigdom. Modern conservatism, despite its turn to Protectionism, had failed to develop national planning to make the policy effective. The BUF by contrast saw itself as a continuation of a tradition which linked feudalism, the guild system, Tudor centralized authority and the spirit behind the achievement of Empire to their own conception of the corporate state.[19]

In particular, it was the vital spirit of endeavour that so characterized the Elizabethan age which the BUF tried to emulate. They believed that the Tudor nation-state concept which had produced the basis of British world supremacy had been undermined during the seventeenth century by the victory of parliament over the centralized authority of monarchy.[20] As a result liberal capitalism and the dominance of powerful vested interests had replaced the needs of the state as the paramount influence on government. As David Baker has shown, other fascists, like A. K. Chesterton, also saw in the Elizabethan age the model for fascist revolt. For Chesterton, it was not the lessons of history but the aesthetic appreciation of the plays of Shakespeare which provided a guide to political action.[21]

This dubious attempt to place the BUF within the mainstream of British history was seen by Mosley as the explanation of why the political establishment had failed to adopt his, or anybody else's, radical policies to solve the immediate problems: the British ruling class had become ossified and was unable to meet the rapidly changing circumstances of the post-war world. His near apocalyptic gloom and doom foreboding was partly based on a rational economic critique, but was also partly a critical reaction to Oswald Spengler's *Decline of the West*. [. . .]

The Sawdust Caesars

Whatever one may think of the highly controversial personality of Sir Oswald Mosley, there is little doubt that his involvement in British fascism proved the last straw for his prospects of a potentially highly successful career within the orbit of high politics. The self-destructive side of his personality, his inability to compromise on issues of policy and principle, his notorious short temper and failure to suffer fools gladly, and his poor judgement of men and events, represented the negative side of a brilliant but erratic man. The establishment rationalized these drawbacks in terms of the narrow Nonconformist puritanical moral ethos into which the great liberal tradition of British politics had sunk by the 1920s. As both Robert Skidelsky and Nicholas Mosley have pointed out, Mosley's revolt went beyond the refusal to play the game of party politics and was justified by him in terms of the need not only for a revolutionary transformation of the political system but in the nature of man himself.

Of course such views were Utopian and unrealistic, given the straitjacket within which the British economy and political system operated within the inter-war period. Mosley's chosen vehicle to spearhead the assault on the establishment, the British Union of Fascists, also failed to live up to such high expectations. It did motivate an interesting collection of talented idealists and political mavericks who were attracted by Mosley's dream in the drab Depression years; it also drew a motley crew of cranks, anti-semites, petty criminals, opportunists, thugs and literal social fascists who recognized an easy ride when they saw it. Mosley's organizational weaknesses, his personal flaws, his counter-productive obsession with secrecy and security-consciousness, and his failure to paper over the developing fissures within the movement after the collapse of membership in 1934, meant that the BUF increasingly attracted at all levels of the movement the deeply alienated or those who had chips on their shoulders. The original revolutionary economic and political programme of *The Greater Britain* increasingly came to play a secondary role to populist campaigns which appealed to local prejudices, of which the whipping up of anti-semitic sentiment in the East End of London was to become the most notorious.

Indeed, although there was a constant ideological core to the BUF in the 1930s, the move from emphasis on a revolutionary economic and political policy to anti-semitism and to preserving the peace of Europe, reflected both the changing sociological base of British fascism and the alteration in political emphasis from a pseudo-left-wing to a radical right organization. The supposed 'third way' in British politics in the 1930s was a shifting alliance of disparate groups and individuals in a movement which appeared to be in constant turmoil and crisis.

Mosley's failure in the 1930s was achieved partly by his own inadequacies, the lack of impact of the BUF, and astute political management by the National government. Mosley was a poor judge of events and had wretched luck in the 1930s. His much-vaunted economic expertise led him to misjudge the nature of the crisis; the mass unemployment of 1929–32 was not the final crisis of capitalism and the economy made a significant recovery in the 1930s. Only in regional blackspots too dependent on staple industries did recovery fail to occur. Even in these areas, apart from the cotton campaign in Lancashire in 1934 the BUF cut little ice. Mosley failed to accept that the British public had deep conservative instincts; that they preferred a slow economic decline to radical reform which would revolutionize the social fabric of the nation.

The Home Office, worried by increased conflict between communists and a rapidly growing fascist movement, began a policy of surveillance of the BUF in 1934. MI5 and Special Branch reported on developments, although their sources of information proved to be not as useful as elsewhere from the fascist political fringe. Mosley's counter-subversion strategy, which compromised the organizational efficiency of the BUF, was specifically designed to minimize damage caused by infiltration by the security service. The available evidence suggests that MI5 had a cosy view of Mosley and his activities in the 1930s; unlike the Communist party the BUF was seen as patriotic and by 1935 they were no longer seen as a threat. Renewed conflict between fascists and communists and Jews in 1936 did lead the government to act to maintain public order and political uniforms were banned. However, only in the special circumstances of spring 1940 did MI5's attitude to Mosley change overnight in the aftermath of the Tyler Kent affair [*Note: Tyler Gatewood Kent worked in the American embassy and stole the top-secret correspondence between President Franklin Delano Roosevelt and Churchill, turning this over to the Nazis at the beginning of the Second World War.*].

The other major aspect of government management of the BUF was the publicity boycott. After the withdrawal of Rothermere's support in 1934 the BUF was given little coverage in the media and that only of a negative kind, associating it with political violence. From then until the publication of his autobiography in 1968, Mosley was kept beyond the pale, a political unperson. He was carefully shunted into a siding of British politics, and the BUF and later political movements associated with him became a dead end. Internment in the war meant that a general attitude of indifference to him was turned into a deep suspicion of his motives and activities; the always hostile view of the political left became an accepted view of society as a whole.

Notes

1   J. Brewer, 'The British Union of Fascists, Sir Oswald Mosley and Birmingham: an analysis of the content and context of an ideology', M.Soc.Sci. thesis, University of Birmingham, 1975, 1–171.

2   N. Nugent, 'The ideas of the British Union of Fascists', in *The British Right*, ed. N. Nugent and R. King (London, 1977), 133–64.

3   S. Rawnsley, 'Fascism and fascists in Britain in the 1930s', PhD thesis, University of Bradford, 1983, 48.

4   B. Farr, 'The development and impact of right wing politics in Great Britain, 1903–32', PhD thesis, University of Illinois, 1976.

5   R. Skidelsky, *Oswald Mosley* (London, 1975).

6   O. Mosley, *The Greater Britain* (London, 1934), 149–51.

7   Idem, *My Life* (London, 1968), 128–36.

8   E. Bentley, *The Cult of the Superman* (Gloucester, Mass., 1944); J. Drennan (W. E. D. Allen), *BUF, Oswald Mosley and British Fascism* (London, 1934), 176–293.

9   Skidelsky, *Oswald Mosley*, 299–316, 465–80; N. Mosley, *Beyond the Pale* (London, 1983), 35–42.

10   O. Mosley, *My Life*, 91.

11   R. Thurlow, 'The Return of Jeremiah', in *British Fascism*, ed. K. Lunn and R. Thurlow (London, 1980), 100–13.

12   *Blackshirt*, Feb. 1933.

13   O. Mosley, *Tomorrow We Live* (London, 1938), 10.

14   *Parliamentary Debates*, vol. 239, 28 May 1930.

15   Drennan, *BUF, Mosley and British Fascism*, 200.

16   O. Mosley, *The Alternative* (London, 1947).

17   A. L. Glasfurd, 'Fascism and the English tradition', *Fascist Quarterly*, 1, 3 (July 1935), 360.

18   G. R. Stirling Taylor, *A Modern History of England 1485–1932* (London, 1932), 28.

19   Drennan, *BUF, Mosley and British Fascism*, 16.

20   Ibid, 30.

21   D. Baker, 'A. K. Chesterton. The making of a British fascist', PhD thesis, University of Sheffield, 1982, 146–217.

PART THREE

The 'regime-model' of fascism

■ Techniques of fascist rule – the exercise of power by the 'regime-model' of fascism

WRITING IN THE 1960S, Ernst Nolte acknowledged the difficulty of deciding on an appropriate, all-embracing definition of fascism by underlining the challenge of distinguishing it from other, more conventional forms of authoritarianism and nationalism (Nolte 1965). If the task of identifying suitable case-studies of fascist *movements* has often confounded comparative research on fascism, producing a short-list of candidates for the *regime* variant has proved an even more unrewarding methodological pursuit. The fundamental problem with the 'fascist regime' lies in the circumstances of its establishment – no such regime was created as a result of majority popular choice or in total opposition to the existing ruling socio-political elites. Even in the cases of Fascist Italy and Nazi Germany, fascist leaderships were admitted to power with the consent of traditional institutions (see Introduction to Section VIII), heading coalition cabinets for an initial period and generally drawing their legitimacy from the support of the political elites, the armed forces and powerful economic interests. Other regimes, such as the dictatorship of José Antonio Primo de Rivera in 1920s Spain, Antonio de Oliveira Salazar's *New State* in Portugal, Ioannis Metaxas' *Fourth of August* regime, Engelbert Dolfuss' *Christian Social State* and Franco's dictatorship – and this is by no means an exhaustive list – could not disguise their more traditionalist authoritarian outlook and structures of support but did display a strong interest in learning from the 'fascist' experience of Italy and Germany (cf. Lipset (8)). Finally, a host of 'puppet' fascist regimes were instituted in many parts of Axis-occupied Europe in the 1940s (Vichy France, Slovakia, France, Greece, Hungary, etc.) as a form of collaborationist self-administration of the territories partaking in the fascist 'new order'.

So, what is a 'fascist regime'? Is it a regime that became the exclusive property of the facist leaderships, through successful consolidation and elimination of initial power-sharing with traditional elites? This definition would restrict the sample to Mussolini's and Hitler's regimes. It might not even be applicable to the reference fascist regime, that of Mussolini, given the latter's co-existence with the monarchy and the Vatican until 1943. Is it a regime with at least one 'fascist' component (movement/party) in its political make-up? Such a broader definition would essentially apply to a number of further cases beyond Italy and Germany: the Dolfuss–Schuschnigg regime with the participation of the *Heimwehr*, General Antonescu's dictatorship with the short-lived co-optation of the fascist Iron Guard, Franco's regime with the participation (albeit dwindling in influence) of the *Falange*, Admiral Horthy's long rule with the co-operation of Gömbös in early 1930s Hungary, and France's Vichy state after the German invasion of 1940. Or, finally, is the 'fascist regime' judged only on the basis of its political features and extent of appropriation of the 'fascist' legacy, as epitomised by Fascist Italy and/or Nazi Germany? In other words, could such a regime constitute an experiment of 'fascism from above', without necessarily resting on a popular movement, new radical leaders and an ideological break with the old, conservative right's more traditional authoritarianism? This definition would be flexible enough to encapsulate the experience of Portugal, Spain under de Rivera, and of most Balkan countries in the 1930s, where figures of the traditional political establishment enjoying the support of the monarchy, the Church and the armed forces seized power and sought societal regeneration through a coupling of authoritarian dictatorship and novel 'fascist' experiments.

The aim of this and of the subsequent three sections on the regime variant of fascism is not to provide equal or extensive coverage for the whole spectrum of 'fascist regimes'. Emphasis on Nazi Germany and Fascist Italy is unavoidable, not only on the basis of the two regimes' high degree of evolution and consolidation but also because of the influence which they exerted on movements and regimes throughout Europe in the interwar period. The selection of excerpts featured in these sections aims to provide a general overview of the administrative peculiarities, political priorities and devices that differentiate the 'fascist regime' from other versions of right-wing authoritarian dictatorship. In particular, emphasis is placed on the way in which certain fascist themes, such as corporatism (see also Eatwell (**4**); O'Sullivan (**13**)), charismatic leadership, racism (Section VI) and social engineering (Section VII) were adapted to the specific circumstances and problems of different countries. This is why the selection includes pieces on Salazar's (Costa Pinto (**27**)) and de Rivera's regimes (Ben-Ami (**47**)), despite the fact that both lacked a popular fascist mass base and manifested a more traditionalist ideological outlook.

The most fundamental problem with the 'fascist regime' is that it lacks an elaborate theory of its own. The theory of *totalitarianism* produced a highly elaborate checklist of attributes (one party, charismatic leader, total control over society, use of terror, etc.) which could be applied primarily to Nazism and Stalinism, with only oblique references to Fascist Italy (Friedrich and Brzezinski (**23**)). No matter how sophisticated the conceptual apparatus of this theory was in describing the techniques of 'totalitarian' rule, its coupling of fascism and communism (two systems not just ideologically opposed but also fundamentally divergent in their worldviews) could not make a serious contribution to an autonomous understanding of the 'fascist regime'. On the other hand, the 'new consensus' approach has been primarily concerned with fascism as an ideological entity and perceives the regime variant as a misleading and unreliable source of information about the true nature of fascist ideology. Essentially, this implies that the experience of fascist rule in the interwar period should not be seen as an accurate paradigm of what generic fascist ideology really stood for (cf. **4**). A criticism of this 'static' view of fascism underpins Robert O. Paxton's 'dynamic' theory of fascism. In contrast to the 'new consensus', Paxton has argued that the experience of fascist rule in interwar Europe is highly relevant to our understanding of fascism's essence, a culmination of its ideological prescriptions, as well as a source of doctrine in itself and evidence of what it aimed to achieve (see **6**).

This debate about the relevance of the regime variant to the overall theory of generic fascism is underpinned by a more fundamental question: the degree of correspondence between *intentions* and *actions* in fascist politics. Even if one accepts the methodological fecundity of studying fascism in time, as both ideological system and political practice, it is by no means clear whether the resultant fascist system of rule reflected the actual intentions of the fascist leaderships and followers or arose out of structural pressures, compromises or political opportunism. The intentionalist–structuralist debate (Introduction, pp. 13–14) has produced a plethora of interpretations on the character of the fascist state and the influences that shaped it. The initial impression that the fascist system was totalitarian, monolithic, successful in exercising extraordinarily high levels of social control and the product of the leader's intentions has been openly challenged by commentators emphasising a series of deficits in the fascist regime's totalitarian pretensions. F. Neumann's groundbreaking account of the Nazi state, published in the midst of the Axis war campaign, underlined its 'statelessness', that is, the absence of a clear and unified structure of administration in the Nazi system (**24**). Robert Koehl (**25**) has taken the argument about the fragmentation and factionalism of Nazi administration further by equating it to a 'feudal' system of rule, whereby loosely demarcated regional and political spheres became the near-exclusive property of individuals loyal to the leadership, without effective powers of central rationalisation and co-ordination. While, however, Koehl perceived this system as the result of a consciously pursued Nazi regression to pre-modern (that is, medieval) modes of exercising power, others have attributed the lack of administrative coherence in the fascist state to structural failures and compromises. D. Thompson (**26**) examines the limitations of the Fascist regime's totalitarian apparatus (for example, the party, the organisation of leisure) and underlines the cracks in the 'consensus' that the system allegedly enjoyed even in its heyday. Similar shortcomings pervaded the organisation of one of the most fundamental devices of fascist totalitarianism – secret police and surveillance. As K.-M. Mallmann and G. Paul contend (**27**), even the Gestapo, the organisation generally viewed as the most fomidable and horrifyingly all-powerful institution of Nazi social coercion, owed most of its reputation to the *impression* that it was 'omniscient, omnipotent, omnipresent' rather than to the actual capacity of the network to supervise the activities of the population – which was far less extensive than previously believed.

In such a system with so many competing factions, overlapping spheres of authority and lack of modern administrative procedures, the significance of charismatic leadership has been extensively documented. In many ways, charisma was the political antidote (or alternative, if one accepts that the fascist state reflected the actual intentions of its elite) to the absence of bureaucratic routine. Ian Kershaw (**28**) illustrates how powerful the carefully choreographed 'cult of the *Führer*' was and how it could compensate for (or actually disguise) the chronic deficiencies of the Nazi state. The importance of the fascist leaderships in Italy and Germany is further demonstrated by their primary role in the shaping of foreign policy – an area that both Mussolini and Hitler prioritised from the early stages of fascist rule. Macgregor Knox (**29**) discusses the dual function of territorial expansion in Fascist Italy and Nazi Germany – as both a reflection of leadership intentions and a powerful political device for expanding domestic control in pursuit of absolute power. Both Knox and Kershaw suggest that the two leaders possessed a distinct ideological vision and successfully controlled the central decision-making mechanisms of their regimes so as to further their cherished goals. Such a view has once again been challenged by structuralist accounts, which tend to emphasise the ability of domestic and international pressures to divert the fascist leaders from their preferred actions (see, for example, Hans Mommsen's (1997) notion of 'cumulative radicalisation', which attributes the growing fanaticism of the regimes to the uncontrollable dynamism of its largely independent and uncoordinated constituent elements, not least the parties and regional leaders). But most structuralists tend to accept the leader's pivotal role in the fascist system, if not as a source of vision for subsequent policy initiatives, at least as the most important arbiter of factional disputes and guarantee of the state's minimum cohesion.

A similar intentionalist–structuralist controversy surrounds the introduction of corporatism in certain 'fascist' regimes. For many experts on fascist ideology corporatism represents one of the most identifiable fascist traits (for example, O'Sullivan (**13**)), associated with the search for a 'third way' beyond liberalism and socialism. In this respect, Salazar's regime in Portugal constitutes an excellent example of how corporatism could be appropriated by a regime with fascist tendencies in order to legitimise the introduction of a new kind of state (the Portuguese *Estado Novo*) and a novel, more organic society. The problem, however, lies in the rationale behind this adoption of corporatism: whether it was motivated by genuine ideological considerations or formed part of an opportunistic strategy of legitimising an otherwise authoritarian dictatorial project. S. Ben Ami (**30**) offers a conceptually sophisticated analysis of Salazar's regime and explores the strengths and limitations of his corporatist experiment in the 1930s.

Chapter 23

Carl J. Friedrich and Zbigniew K. Brzezinski

'TOTALITARIAN DICTATORSHIP' AND FASCISM

■ from *TOTALITARIAN DICTATORSHIP AND AUTOCRACY*,
New York, Washington and London, 1965, pp. 15–16, 17–20, 21–6

C. J. Friedrich and Z. K. Brzezinski have provided one of the most elaborate theoretical expositions of the totalitarian model of analysis. In the following excerpt the
two authors outline the six main features of the 'totalitarian dictatorship', which
they perceive as the 'adaptation of autocracy to twentieth-century industrial society'
– and therefore a novel form of rule. The authors also respond to the criticism
that totalitarianism attempts to compare two diametrically opposed phenomena –
fascism and communism. But equally significant is the final point of this excerpt –
that 'totalitarian dictatorship' should be analysed in close relationship to democracy
(which totalitarian ideology seeks to replace by perverting their programmes).

The general characteristics of totalitarian dictatorship

TOTALITARIAN REGIMES ARE autocracies. When they are said to be
tyrannies, despotisms, or absolutisms, the basic general nature of such regimes
is being denounced, for all these words have a strongly pejorative flavor. When they
call themselves 'democracies,' qualifying it by the adjective 'popular,' they are not
contradicting these indictments, except in trying to suggest that they are good or at
least praiseworthy. An inspection of the meaning the totalitarians attach to the term
'popular democracy' reveals that they mean by it a species of autocracy. The leaders
of the people, identified with the leaders of the ruling party, have the last word.
Once they have decided and been acclaimed by a party gathering, their decision is
final. Whether it be a rule, a judgment, or a measure or any other act of government, they are the *autokrator*, the ruler accountable only to himself. Totalitarian

dictatorship, in a sense, is the adaptation of autocracy to twentieth-century industrial society.[1]

Thus, as far as this characteristic absence of accountability is concerned, totalitarian dictatorship resembles earlier forms of autocracy. But it is our contention that totalitarian dictatorship is historically an innovation[2] and *sui generis*. It is also our conclusion from all the facts available to us that fascist and communist totalitarian dictatorships are basically alike, or at any rate more nearly like each other than like any other system of government, including earlier forms of autocracy. These two theses are closely linked and must be examined together. They are also linked to a third, that totalitarian dictatorship as it actually developed was not intended by those who created it – Mussolini talked of it, though he meant something different – but resulted from the political situations in which the anticonstitutionalist and antidemocratic revolutionary movements and their leaders found themselves. Before we explore these propositions, one very widespread theory of totalitarianism needs consideration.

It is a theory that centers on the regime's efforts to remold and transform the human beings under its control in the image of its ideology. As such, it might be called an ideological or anthropological theory of totalitarianism. The theory holds that the 'essence' of totalitarianism is to be seen in such a regime's total control of the everyday life of its citizens, of its control, more particularly, of their thoughts and attitudes as well as their activities. 'The particular criterion of totalitarian rule is the creeping rape [*sic*] of man by the perversion of his thoughts and his social life,' a leading exponent of this view has written. 'Totalitarian rule,' he added, 'is the claim transformed into political action that the world and social life are changeable without limit.'[3] As compared with this 'essence,' it is asserted that organization and method are criteria of secondary importance. There are a number of serious objections to this theory. The first is purely pragmatic. For while it may be the intent of the totalitarians to achieve total control, it is certainly doomed to disappointment; no such control is actually achieved, even within the ranks of their party membership or cadres, let alone over the population at large. The specific procedures generated by this desire for total control, this 'passion for unanimity' as we call it later in our analysis, are highly significant, have evolved over time, and have varied greatly at different stages.

[. . .]

Totalitarian dictatorship then emerges as a system of rule 'for realizing totalist intentions under modern political and technical conditions, as a novel type of autocracy.'[4] The declared intention of creating a 'new man,' according to numerous reports, has had significant results where the regime has lasted long enough, as in Russia. In the view of one leading authority, 'the most appealing traits of the Russians – their naturalness and candor – have suffered most.' He considers this a 'profound and apparently permanent transformation,' and an 'astonishing' one.[5] In short, the effort at total control, while not achieving such control, has highly significant human effects.

The fascist and communist systems evolved in response to a series of grave crises – they are forms of crisis government. Even so, there is no reason to conclude that the existing totalitarian systems will disappear as a result of internal evolution, though there can be no doubt that they are undergoing continuous changes. The two totalitarian governments that have perished thus far have done so as the result of wars with outside powers, but this does not mean that the Soviet Union, Communist China, or any of the others necessarily will become involved in war. We do not presuppose that totalitarian societies are fixed and static entities but, on the contrary, that they have undergone and continue to undergo a steady evolution, presumably involving both growth and deterioration.[6]

But what about the origins? If it is evident that the regimes came into being because a totalitarian movement achieved dominance over a society and its government, where did the movement come from? The answer to this question remains highly controversial. A great many explanations have been attempted in terms of the various ingredients of these ideologies. Not only Marx and Engels, where the case seems obvious, but Hegel, Luther, and a great many others have come in for their share of blame. Yet none of these thinkers was, of course, a totalitarian at all, and each would have rejected these regimes, if any presumption like that were to be tested in terms of his thought. They were humanists and religious men of intense spirituality of the kind the totalitarians explicitly reject. In short, all such 'explanations,' while interesting in illuminating particular elements of the totalitarian ideologies, are based on serious invalidating distortions of historical facts.[7] If we leave aside such ideological explanations (and they are linked of course to the 'ideological' theory of totalitarian dictatorship as criticized above), we find several other unsatisfactory genetic theories.

The debate about the causes or origins of totalitarianism has run all the way from a primitive bad-man theory[8] to the 'moral crisis of our time' kind of argument. A detailed inspection of the available evidence suggests that virtually every one of the factors which has been offered by itself as an explanation of the origin of totalitarian dictatorship has played its role. For example, in the case of Germany, Hitler's moral and personal defects, weaknesses in the German constitutional tradition, certain traits involved in the German 'national character,' the Versailles Treaty and its aftermath, the economic crisis and the 'contradictions' of an aging capitalism, the 'threat' of communism, the decline of Christianity and of such other spiritual moorings as the belief in the reason and the reasonableness of man – all have played a role in the total configuration of factors contributing to the over-all result. As in the case of other broad developments in history, only a multiple-factor analysis will yield an adequate account. But at the present time, we cannot fully explain the rise of totalitarian dictatorship. All we can do is to explain it partially by identifying some of the antecedent and concomitant conditions. To repeat: totalitarian dictatorship is a new phenomenon; there has never been anything quite like it before.

The discarding of ideological explanations – highly objectionable to all totalitarians, to be sure – opens up an understanding of and insight into the basic similarity of totalitarian regimes, whether communist or fascist. They are, in terms of organization and procedures – that is to say, in terms of structure, institutions, and processes of rule – *basically alike*. What does this mean? In the first place, it means that they are *not wholly alike*. Popular and journalistic interpretation has oscillated between two extremes; some have said that the communist and fascist dictatorships are wholly alike, others that they are not at all alike. The latter view was the prevailing one during the popular-front days in Europe as well as in liberal circles in the United States. It was even more popular during the Second World War, especially among Allied propagandists. Besides, it was and is the official communist and fascist party line. It is only natural that these regimes, conceiving of themselves as bitter enemies, dedicated to the task of liquidating each other, should take the view that they have nothing in common. This has happened before in history. When the Protestants and Catholics were fighting during the religious wars of the sixteenth and seventeenth centuries, they very commonly denied to one another the name of 'Christians,' and each argued about the other that it was not a 'true church.' Actually, and in the perspective of time, both were indeed Christian churches.

The other view, that communist and fascist dictatorships are wholly alike, was during the cold war demonstrably favored in the United States and in Western Europe to an increasing extent. Yet they are demonstrably not wholly alike. For example, they differ in their acknowledged purposes and intentions. Everyone knows that the communists say they seek the world revolution of the proletariat, while the fascists proclaimed their determination to establish the imperial predominance of a particular nation or race, either over the world or over a region. The communist and fascist dictatorships differ also in their historical antecedents: the fascist movements arose in reaction to the communist challenge and offered themselves to a frightened middle class as saviors from the communist danger. The communist movements, on the other hand, presented themselves as the liberators of an oppressed people from an existing autocratic regime, at least in Russia and China. Both claims are not without foundation, and one could perhaps coordinate them by treating the totalitarian movements as consequences of the First World War. 'The rise (of totalitarianism) has occurred in the sequel to the first world war and those catastrophes, political and economic, which accompanied it and the feeling of crisis linked thereto.'[9] As we shall have occasion to show in the chapters to follow, there are many other differences which do not allow us to speak of the communist and fascist totalitarian dictatorships as wholly alike, but which suggest that they are sufficiently alike to class them together and to contrast them not only with constitutional systems, but also with former types of autocracy.

[. . .]

The basic features or traits that we suggest as generally recognized to be common to the totalitarian dictatorships are six in number. The 'syndrome,' or pattern of interrelated traits, of the totalitarian dictatorship consists of an ideology, a single party typically led by one man, a terroristic police, a communications monopoly, a weapons monopoly and a centrally directed economy. Of these, the last two are also found in constitutional systems: Socialist Britain had a centrally directed economy, and all modern states possess a weapons monopoly. Whether these latter suggest a 'trend' toward totalitarianism is a question that will be discussed in our last chapter. These six basic features, which we think constitute the distinctive pattern or model of totalitarian dictatorship, form a cluster of traits, intertwined and mutually supporting each other, as is usual in 'organic' systems. They should therefore not be considered in isolation or be made the focal point of comparisons, such as 'Caesar developed a terroristic secret police, therefore he was the first totalitarian dictator,' or 'the Catholic Church has practiced ideological thought control, therefore . . .' The totalitarian dictatorships all possess the following:

1   An elaborate ideology, consisting of an official body of doctrine covering all vital aspects of man's existence to which everyone living in that society is supposed to adhere, at least passively; this ideology is characteristically focused and projected toward a perfect final state of mankind – that is to say, it contains a chiliastic claim, based upon a radical rejection of the existing society with conquest of the world for the new one.

2   A single mass party typically led by one man, the 'dictator,' and consisting of a relatively small percentage of the total population (up to 10 percent) of men and women, a hard core of them passionately and unquestioningly dedicated to the ideology and prepared to assist in every way in promoting its general acceptance, such a party being hierarchically, oligarchically organized and typi-cally either superior to, or completely intertwined with, the governmental bureaucracy.

3   A system of terror, whether physical or psychic, effected through party and secret-police control, supporting but also supervising the party for its leaders, and characteristically directed not only against demonstrable 'enemies' of the regime, but against more or less arbitrarily selected classes of the population; the terror whether of the secret police or of party-directed social pressure sys-tematically exploits modern science, and more especially scientific psychology.

4   A technologically conditioned, near-complete monopoly of control, in the hands of the party and of the government, of all means of effective mass communication, such as the press, radio, and motion pictures.

5   A similarly technologically conditioned, near-complete monopoly of the effec-tive use of all weapons of armed combat.

6   A central control and direction of the entire economy through the bureaucratic coordination of formerly independent corporate entities, typically including most other associations and group activities.

The enumeration of these six traits or trait clusters is not meant to suggest that there might not be others, now insufficiently recognized. It has more particularly been suggested that the administrative control of justice and the courts is a distinctive trait; but actually the evolution of totalitarianism in recent years suggests that such administrative direction of judicial work may be greatly limited. We shall also discuss the problem of expansionism, which has been urged as a characteristic trait of total-itarianism. The traits here outlined have been generally acknowledged as the features of totalitarian dictatorship, to which the writings of students of the most varied back-grounds, including totalitarian writers, bear witness.

Within this broad pattern of similarities, there are many significant variations to which the analysis of this book will give detailed attention. To offer a few random illustrations: at present the party plays a much greater role in the Soviet Union than it did under Stalin; the ideology of the Soviet Union is more specifically committed to certain assumptions, because of its Marx–Engels bible, than that of

Italian or German fascism, where ideology was formulated by the leader of the party himself; the corporate entities of the fascist economy remained in private hands, as far as property claims are concerned, whereas they become public property in the Soviet Union.

Let us now turn to our first point, namely, that totalitarian regimes are historically novel; that is to say, that no government like totalitarian dictatorship has ever before existed, even though it bears a resemblance to autocracies of the past. It may be interesting to consider briefly some data which show that the six traits we have just identified are to a large extent lacking in historically known autocratic regimes. Neither the oriental despotisms of the more remote past nor the absolute monarchies of modern Europe, neither the tyrannies of the ancient Greek cities nor the Roman empire, neither yet the tyrannies of the city-states of the Italian Renaissance and the Bonapartist military dictatorship nor the other functional dictatorships of this or the last century exhibit this design, this combination of features, though they may possess one or another of its characteristic traits. For example, efforts have often been made to organize some kind of secret police, but they have not even been horse-and-buggy affairs compared with the terror of the Gestapo or the OGPU (afterwards MVD, then KGB). Similarly, though there have been both military and propagandistic concentrations of power and control, the limits of technology have prevented the achievement of effective monopoly. Again, certainly neither the Roman emperor nor the absolute monarch of the eighteenth century sought or needed a party to support him or an ideology in the modern party sense, and the same is true of oriental despots.[10] The tyrants of Greece and Italy may have had a party – that of the Medicis in Florence was called lo stato – but they had no ideology to speak of. And, of course, all of these autocratic regimes were far removed from the distinctive features that are rooted in modern technology.

In much of the foregoing, modern technology is mentioned as a significant condition for the invention of the totalitarian model. This aspect of totalitarianism is particularly striking in the field of weapons and communications, but it is involved also in secret-police terror, depending as it does upon technically advanced possibilities of supervision and control of the movement of persons. In addition, the centrally directed economy presupposes the reporting, cataloging, and calculating devices provided by modern technology. In short, four of the six traits are technologically conditioned. To envisage what this technological advance means in terms of political control, one has only to think of the weapons field. The Constitution of the United States guarantees to every citizen the right to bear arms (fourth amendment). In the days of the Minutemen, this was a very important right, and the freedom of the citizen was indeed symbolized by the gun over the hearth, as it is in Switzerland to this day. But who can 'bear' such arms as a tank, a bomber, or a flamethrower, let alone an atom bomb? The citizen as an individual, and indeed in larger groups, is simply defenseless against the overwhelming technological superiority of those who can centralize in their hands the means with which to wield modern weapons and thereby physically to coerce the mass of the citizenry. Similar observations apply to the telephone and telegraph, the press, radio and television, and so forth. 'Freedom' does not have the same potential it had a hundred and fifty years ago, resting as it then did upon individual effort. With few exceptions, the trend technological advance implies the trend toward greater and greater size of organization. In the perspective of these four traits, therefore, totalitarian societies appear to be merely exaggerations, but nonetheless logical exaggerations, of the technological state of modern society.

Neither ideology nor party has as significant a relation to the state of technology. There is, of course, some connection, since the mass conversion continually attempted by totalitarian propaganda through effective use of the communication monopoly could not be carried through without it. It may here be observed that the Chinese Communists, lacking the means for mass communication, fell back upon the small group effort of word-of-mouth indoctrination, which incidentally offered a chance for substituting such groups for the family and transferring the filial tradition to them.[11] Indeed, this process is seen by them as a key feature of their people's democracy.

Ideology and party are conditioned by modern democracy. Totalitarianism's own leaders see it as democracy's fulfillment, as the true democracy, replacing the plutocratic democracy of the bourgeoisie. From a more detached viewpoint, it appears to be an absolute, and hence autocratic, kind of democracy as contrasted with constitutional democracy.[12] It can therefore grow out of the latter by perverting it.[13] Not only did Hitler, Mussolini, and Lenin build typical parties within a constitutional, if not a democratic, context, but the connection is plain between the stress on ideology and the role that platforms and other types of ideological goal-formation play in democratic parties. To be sure, totalitarian parties developed a pronounced authoritarian pattern while organizing themselves into effective revolutionary instruments of action; but, at the same time, the leaders, beginning with Marx and Engels, saw themselves as constituting the vanguard of the democratic movement of their day, and Stalin always talked of the Soviet totalitarian society as the 'perfect democracy'; Hitler and Mussolini[14] made similar statements. Both the world brotherhood of the proletariat and the folk community were conceived of as supplanting the class divisions of past societies by a complete harmony – the classless society of socialist tradition.

Not only the party but also its ideology harken back to the democratic context within which the totalitarian movements arose. Ideology generally, but more especially totalitarian ideology, involves a high degree of convictional certainty. As has been indicated, totalitarian ideology consists of an official doctrine that radically rejects the existing society in terms of a chiliastic proposal for a new one. It contains strongly Utopian elements, some kind of notion of a paradise on earth. This Utopian and chiliastic outlook of totalitarian ideologies gives them a pseudo-religious quality. In fact, they often elicit in their less critical followers a depth of conviction and a fervor of devotion usually found only among persons inspired by a transcendent faith. Whether these aspects of totalitarian ideologies bear some sort of relationship to the religions that they seek to replace is arguable. Marx denounced religion as the opium of the people. It would seem that this is rather an appropriate way of describing totalitarian ideologies. In place of the more or less sane platforms of regular political parties, critical of the existing state of affairs in a limited way, totalitarian ideologies are perversions of such programs. They substitute faith for reason, magic exhortation for knowledge and criticism. And yet it must be recognized that there are enough of these same elements in the operations of democratic parties to attest to the relation between them and their perverted descendants, the totalitarian movements. That is why these movements must be seen and analyzed in their relationship to the democracy they seek to supplant.

Notes

1   Harold J. Berman, *Justice in the USSR – An Interpretation of the Soviet Law* (Cambridge, 1950; 2nd ed., 1963).

2   George W. F. Hallfarten, *Why Dictators? The Causes and Forms of Tyranical Rule since 600 BC* (New York, 1954); Karl Wittfogel, *Oriental Despotism* (New Haven, 1957), 141ff; C. E. G. Catlin, *Systematic Politics* (Toronto, 1962).

3   H. Buchheim, *Totalitäre Herrschaft – Wesen und Merkmale* (Munich, 1962), 14, 24.

4   W. W. Rostow, *The Stages of Economic Growth: A Non-Communist Manifesto* (Cambridge, 1960).

5   Klaus Mehnert, *Soviet Man in this World* (New York, 1962; German ed., Stuttgart, 1958), 35.

6   Wolfgang Leonhard, *The Kremlin since Stalin* (New York, 1962; Garman ed., 1959), 504ff.

7   Aurd Kolnay, *The War Against the West* (New York, 1938); Friedrich Glum, *Philosophen im Spiegel und Zerspiegel – Deutschlands Weg in den Nationalsozialismus* (Munich, 1954); Neanne Hersch, *Idéologies et réalité* (Paris, 1956); Hellmuth Plessner, *Die Verspätete Nation* (Stuttgart, 1959).

8   Alan Bullock, *Hitler – A Study in Tyranny* (London, 1952), passim.

9   Karl Dietrich Bracher, and Wolfgang Sauer and Gerhard Schulz, *Die Nationalsozialistische Machtergreifung – Studien zur Errichtung des totalitaeren Machtsystems in Deutschland, 1933–34* (Cologne, 1960), 4–5, where Bracher accepts our view. See also comments by Schulz, 371ff.

10 Wittfogel, op. cit., 141 ff.

11 Peter S. H. Tang, *Communist China Today*, vol. 1 (Washington D.C., 1957; 2nd ed. 1961).

12 Ibid.

13 Karl Dietrich Bracher, *Die Auflösung der Weimarer Republik* (Stuttgart, 1955; 2nd ed. 1957).

14 Angelo Tasca, *Nascita e avvento del Fascismo* (Rome, 1950).

Chapter 24

Franz Neumann

'BEHEMOTH': NAZISM AS 'STATELESS' SYSTEM

■ from *BEHEMOTH: THE STRUCTURE AND PRACTICE OF NATIONAL SOCIALISM*, London, 1942, pp. 69–71, 378–80, 381–4

Franz Neumann's study of the National Socialist regime in Germany was published during the Second World War (1942), but it still constitutes a consummate example of structuralist analysis of Nazism. The title of the work (*Behemoth*) is a direct tribute to the Hobbesian analysis of the Long Parliament period in England with the same title. It refers to the absence of unified political power and rational bureaucratic management in the National Socialist state. Neumann stresses that the Nazi regime lacked a clear political theory of its own and cannot qualify as a 'state'. His analysis in the following excerpt highlights the significance of the leadership principle as a mediator between four competing power blocs within the state (military, bureaucracy, industry, party). Neumann also underlines the function of Nazi ideology as a mere exercise in domination and social control, devoid of any programmatic substance.

The rational bureaucracy

THE DOCTRINE OF STATE SUPREMACY had to be abandoned in Germany because the claims of the party conflicted with the claims of the state. Had this situation not existed, nothing could have prevented Hitler from holding to the totalitarian state theory. Today, the doctrines exalting the state, notably Hegelianism, have been thrown overboard.

It may be true, as Hobhouse tried to prove, that Hegel's glorification of the state was the strongest ideological factor responsible for Prussian militarism and the First World War.[1] But Hegel cannot be held responsible for the political theory of National Socialism. A number of Hegelians are still active within the National

Socialist movement; among them some even try to adjust Hegel's theory to the new National Socialist ideology.[2] Their efforts, however are laughable. For no one can doubt that Hegel's idea of the state is basically incompatible with the German racial myth. Hegel asserted the state to be 'the realization of reason', and compared to the theories of Haller and the allegedly liberal doctrines of the *Burschenschaften* (student unions led by the philosopher Fries), his political theory was progressive. Hegel despised them both, for Haller represented a reactionary political move to justify the political power of the most backward strata in society, while the 'liberal' doctrine of the *Burschenschaften* contained the germ of racism, Anti-Semitism, and Teutonic egotism, as even Treitschke could see.[3] Hegel's theory is rational; it stands also for the free individual. His state is predicated upon a bureaucracy that guarantees the freedom of the citizens because it acts on the basis of rational and calculable norms.[4] This emphasis on the rational conduct of the bureaucracy, which is, according to Hegel, a prerequisite of proper government, makes his doctrine unpalatable to National Socialist 'dynamism'.

A few words are required to clarify the notion of 'rational' bureaucracy, as Hegel meant it, and the relation between it and a democratic system. Bureaucratic encroachments are today resented in almost every country as a threat to individual liberty. And if we define democracy solely as an organizational pattern that distributes political power among freely elected representatives, we can readily see that a bureaucracy that is permanent, hierarchically ordered, and subject to arbitrary command must appear as the contradiction of democracy. But democracy is not merely an organizational pattern. It is also a system of values, and the goals it pursues may change. Competitive capitalism aimed exclusively to protect the freedom of society from government interference. In the era of collectivism, which replaced competitive capitalism as a result of profound economic changes, and in which the masses demand recognition of their material status, the system of values represented by liberal democracy proves inadequate. Unemployment insurance, health and disability insurance, housing programmes become necessary and must be accepted as part of the paraphernalia of democracy. In addition, some kind of control over economic activities must be established. Two methods are apparently open for the realization of these new aims. One, a pluralistic solution, involves self-government through private interested parties; the other, a monistic solution, involves bureaucratic regimentation. The choice between the two methods is not easy, all the less so since the ultimate in bureaucratic power is reached only when public and private bureaucracies interpenetrate. Preference for self-government does not necessarily follow from the nature of democracy. It would follow, and indeed it would be the ideal solution, if the private bureaucracies could reach agreement on all major issues without harming the interests of society as a whole. But the expectation is Utopian. Whenever private groups agreed, it was at the expense of society as a whole; the consumer usually suffered, and government interference proved indispensable. Our society is not harmonious, it is antagonistic, and the state will always be the *ultima ratio*. In Germany, as I have tried to show, the pluralist system of private administration sooner or later compelled the government to intervene, and as a result the power of the state bureaucracy increased. Moreover, the parties concerned, such as trade unions, cartels, trade associations, and political groups, tend to become bureaucratic bodies, whose purpose is either to keep their organizations running or to keep themselves on top. Inevitably, the spontaneous desires of the rank and file are sacrificed.

Faced with the choice between two kinds of bureaucracy, the citizenry might prefer the public bureaucracy to the private. For private bureaucracies pursue egoistic group interests, whereas public bureaucracies, even when they are dominated by class interests, tend to serve the general welfare. The reason is that public bureaucracies obey fixed and ascertainable rules, while private bureaucracies follow secret instructions. The public servant is selected by a merit system based on the principle of equal opportunity for each competitor, even though the principle is often perverted in practice. Private bureaucracies co-opt their members and there is no public control of this process.

Max Weber's sociological analysis of bureaucracy, though based on an ideal case, contains a certain amount of truth that applies to any bureaucratic body. Precision, permanency, discipline, reliability, and rationality characterize the bureaucrat who acts 'impersonally', that is, 'sine ira et studio', without hate or passion . . . ; he is motivated by a simple idea of duty, without regard to the person, with formal equality for everyone.[5] It is true that bureaucracy may turn into an anti-democratic force, but whether it does so or not will depend much more on the strength of the democratic forces than on its inner tendencies. Even if it should become reactionary, the bureaucracy will incline towards carrying out its policies legally, in line with the fixed rules according to which it must behave. It will preserve a minimum of liberty and security and thus support the contention that all rational law, regardless of content, has an incontestable protective function.

The rational practices of bureaucracy appear incompatible with National Socialism for the reasons mentioned. The rejection of state supremacy is therefore more than an ideological device intended to conceal the party's betrayal of the army and the civil service; it expresses a real need of the system to do away with the rule of rational law.

We must not be deceived into assuming, however, that centralization of bureaucratic machinery has in any way lessened in Germany, that the party's existence has in any way restricted bureaucratic powers. On the contrary, preparedness and war have noticeably strengthened authoritarian control in the federal, state, and municipal bureaucracies. [. . .]

Has Germany a political theory?

Every political system can be characterized by its political theory, which expresses its structure and aims. But if we were asked to define the political theory of National Socialism, we should be greatly embarrassed. National Socialism is anti-democratic, anti-liberal, and profoundly anti-rational. That is why it cannot utilize any preceding political thought. Not even Hobbes's political theory applies to it. The National Socialist state is no Leviathan. But Hobbes, aside from his *Leviathan* also wrote *Behemoth, or the Long Parliament*, which Ferdinand Toennies edited for the first time from the original manuscript in London in 1889. *Behemoth*, which depicted England during the Long Parliament, was intended as the representation of a non-state, a situation characterized by complete lawlessness. The Leviathan, although it swallows society, does not swallow all of it. Its sovereign power is founded upon the consent of man. Its justification is still rational and, in consequence, incompatible with a political system that completely sacrifices the individual. That was clear to Charles II, who had the *Leviathan* burnt; Clarendon had summed up the book for him in the following words: 'I never read a book which contained so much sedition, treason, and impiety.' That was also clear to Hobbes's contemporaries, especially Johann Friedrich Horn, the German reactionary political theorist, who perceived the revolutionary implications of a political theory that derived sovereign power from the consent of men. Hobbes's *Leviathan* also preserves remnants of the rule of law. The law should be general and should not be retroactive. The whole power of the sovereign is, for Hobbes, merely a part of a bargain in which the sovereign has to fulfil his obligations, that is, preserve order and security so that there may be realized 'the liberty to buy and sell and otherwise contract with one another; to choose their own abode, their own diet, their own trade of life, and institute their children as they themselves think fit'.[6] If the sovereign cannot fulfil his side of the bargain, he forfeits his sovereignty. Such a theory has little in common with National Socialism, absolutistic as it may be.

[. . .]

National Socialism is, we repeat, incompatible with any rational political philosophy, that is, with any doctrine that derives political power from the will or the needs of man. Why that should be so is, I believe, amply proved by the structure of National Socialist society. There exists a fundamental antagonism between the productivity of German industry, its capacity for promoting the welfare of the people and its actual achievements, and this antagonism is steadily deepening. For the past eight years (1933–41) huge industrial machinery in continuous expansion has been set to work exclusively for destruction. The promises given by the regime to the masses are certainly sweet, but many of them have been broken and every essential point of the party programme has been sacrificed. This antagonism must be felt by the masses, which are not simply babes in the woods but have a long tradition behind them, a tradition that imbued them with a critical spirit and made them aware that the primary fact of modern civilization is this very antagonism between an economy that can produce in abundance for welfare but that does so only for destruction.

In such a situation, thought is fatal for the regime – on this point a leading positivist and a leading anti-positivist agree.[7] Thought, if allowed, would turn against oppression and injustice. When John Stuart Mill wrote his essay on Jeremy Bentham, he entitled one of his chapters 'The Danger of Asking the Why'.[8] Bentham's utilitarianism was rejected by a society which felt that critical analysis was dangerous to its existence. In National Socialist Germany thought of any kind, whether positivist or pragmatic, whether idealistic or not, must inevitably have a critical and revolutionary impact.

National Socialism has no rational political theory. But has it an anti-rational one, and is there such a thing as an anti-rational theory? We believe not. There are non-rational religious theories and there is a non-rational magic. But a political theory cannot be non-rational. If it claims to be non-rational, it is a conscious trick. 'And there has arisen . . . blood against formal reason; race against purposeful rationality; honour against profit; unity against individualistic disintegration; martial virtue against bourgeois security; the folk against the individual and the mass.'[9] This description of National Socialist philosophy by one of the leading National Socialist philosophers, Ernst Krieck, now professor at Heidelberg, may be considered authoritative. We have tried to show on many occasions that the so-called non-rational concepts, blood, community, folk, are devices for hiding the real constellation of power and for manipulating the masses. The charisma of the Leader, the superiority of the master race, the struggle of a proletarian race against plutocracies, the protest of the folk against the state are consciously applied stratagems. It may not be exaggerated to say that National Socialism acts according to a most rational plan, that each and every pronouncement by its leader is calculated, and its effect on the masses and the surrounding world is carefully weighed in advance.

From the preceding political systems that lack theoretical justification and that were prevalent in the period of the foundation of the Italian city states and the early seventeenth century, National Socialism is distinguished by its appeal to the people.[10] We have seen that National Socialism has risen to power with the support of the masses. After society has passed the phase of large-scale democracy the appeal to the masses and their support become imperative. No political system can build on nothing or completely erase the past. Every new political system must incorporate certain aspects of the past. National Socialism has transformed institutional democracy of the Weimar Republic into a ceremonial and a magic democracy, a development made necessary by the requirements of totalitarian war, in which the distinctions between civilians and soldiers are annihilated and in which the civilian suffers even more than the soldiers. The socialization of danger,[11] as Harold Lasswell aptly termed this situation, more than ever requires full control over the whole mass of the people and over each aspect of their individual lives. Finally, in order to manipulate the masses, in order to control, atomize, terrorize them, one must capture them ideologically.

[. . .]

These considerations lead us to conclude that National Socialism has no political theory of its own, and that the ideologies it uses or discards are mere *arcana dominationis*, techniques of domination. If that is true, it must, in my opinion, be granted that the German leadership is the only group in present German society that does not take its ideological pronouncements seriously and is well aware of their purely propagandistic nature.

Is Germany a state?

But if National Socialism has no political theory, is its political system a state? If a state is characterized by the rule of law, our answer to this question will be negative, since we deny that law exists in Germany. It may be argued that state and law are not identical, and there can be states without law. States, however, as they have arisen in Italy, are conceived as rationally operating machineries disposing of the monopoly of coercive power. A state is ideologically characterized by the unity of the political power that it wields.

I doubt whether a state even in this restricted sense exists in Germany. It has been maintained that National Socialism is a dual state, that is, in fact, one state within which two systems are operating, one under normative law, the other under individual measures, one rational, the other the realm of prerogative.[12] We do not share this view because we believe that there is no realm of law in Germany, although there are thousands of technical rules that are calculable. We believe that the monopolists in dealing with non-monopolists rely on individual measures, and in their relations with the state and with competitors, on compromises which are determined by expedience and not by law. Moreover, it is doubtful whether National Socialism possesses a unified coercive machinery, unless we accept the leadership theory as a true doctrine. The party is independent of the state in matters pertaining to the police and youth, but everywhere else the state stands above the party (. . .) The army is sovereign in many fields; the bureaucracy is uncontrolled; and industry has managed to conquer many positions. One might say that such antagonisms are as characteristic of democracy as they are of National Socialism. Granting that, there is still one decisive difference. In a democracy and in any other constitutional system, such antagonisms within the ruling groups must be settled in a universally binding manner. The absolutistic king is the real legislator; in his person, legislation, administration, and the judiciary are actually unified. When his absolutistic claim comes into conflict with reality, the state disintegrates, as France before the Revolution of 1789 when the king was absolutistic in name only, while the power was exercised by the bureaucracy, the feudals, the courts, the high bourgeoisie, all of them bitterly fighting each other. In an absolute monarchy, in a constitutional system, and in a democracy, the compromises between various groups claim and have universal validity. It is necessary for the state to coordinate and integrate hundreds and thousands of individual and group conflicts, the process must be accomplished in a universally binding manner, that is, through abstract rational law or at least through a rationally operating bureaucracy. Under National Socialism, however, the whole of the society is organized in four solid, centralized groups [party, army, bureaucracy, industry], each operating under the leadership principle, each with a legislative, administrative, and judicial power of its own. Neither universal law nor a rationally operating bureaucracy is necessary for integration. Compromises among the four authoritarian bodies need not be expressed in a legal document nor must they be institutionalized (like the 'gentlemen's agreements' between monopolistic industries). It is quite sufficient that the leadership of the four wings agree informally on a certain policy. The four totalitarian bodies will then enforce it with the machinery at their disposal. There is no need for a state standing above all groups; the state may even be a hindrance to the compromises and to domination over the ruled classes. The decisions of the Leader are merely the result of the compromises among the four leaderships. The ministerial council for the defence of the realm has no executive apparatus different from that of the four wings of the ruling class.

It is thus impossible to detect in the framework of the National Socialist political system any one organ which monopolizes political power.

The most advanced National Socialist lawyers, Reinhard Höhn[13] and Gottfried Neesse,[14] reject the very concept of the state, and their ideas are widely approved.[15] Both reject the notion of the state's personality as a mere liberal construction, for if the concept of the state is accepted, they argue, those exercising its power are merely its organs. According to them, Germany's political power rests in the Leader, who is not the organ of the state but who *is* the community, not acting as its organ but as its personification. Neesse distinguishes three independent powers of equal rank, the party, the army, and the state (by which he means the bureaucracy); above them is the Leader 'acting not only for the people and in its place but as the people'.[16] He utilizes the party, the army, and the state as his tools only because he cannot do everything personally. We are not concerned with the sophistry of this new theory of transubstantiation implied by the identification of the Leader and the people, but rather with the consequences that derive from such theory. This advanced National Socialist constitutional theory, although attacked even by Carl Schmitt, clearly admits that it is not the state which unifies political power but that there are three (in our view, four) co-existent political powers, the unification of which is not institutionalized but only personalized. It may be readily admitted that in constitutional law, as in any other field, the theories of the people's community and leadership are a mere shield covering the powers of the enormously swollen bureaucratic machines. But at least a grain of truth may be contained in these theories; to wit, that it is difficult to give the name state to four groups entering into a bargain. In fact, except for the charismatic power of the Leader, there is no authority that co-ordinates the four powers, no place where the compromise between them can be put on a universal valid basis.

But if the National Socialist structure is not a state, what is it? I venture to suggest that we are confronted with a form of society in which the ruling groups control the rest of the population directly, without the mediation of that rational though coercive apparatus hitherto known as the state. This new social form is not yet fully realized, but the trend exists which defines the very essence of the regime.

Notes

1   L. T. Hobhouse, *The Metaphysical Theory of the State*, London, 1926.

2   We must make a distinction. There are some who maintain that Hegel is the greatest German political philosopher, but made no attempt to adapt his theory to National Socialism. These merely pay him a compliment and no more: for example, Hans Frank, president of the Academy of German Law, in his 'Die Aufgaben des Rechts', in the *Zeitschrift der Akademie für Deutsches Recht*, 1938, 4. Others attempt to reconstruct Hegel's theory and make it useful to National Socialism, as, for the best example, Karl Larenz, 'Die Bedeutung der völkischen Sitte in Hegels Staatsphilosophie', in the *Zeitschrift für die gesamte Staatswissenschaft*, 1938 (98), 110, where he says, 'It is not the state in the ordinary meaning of the term that was Hegel's most proper and original interest, but the community of life as a whole with a character and a most comprehensive activity of its own'. Hegel would have shuddered at such a definition. Finally, the most influential political theorists reject the Hegelian political philosophy because it glorifies the state. Among these, we can mention Alfred Rosenberg, *Mythos des 20.Jahrhunderts* (1930), 525–7; Otto

Koellreuter, *Volk und Staat in der Weltenschauung der Nationalsozialismus*, Berlin, 1935, 12–15; and above all, Carl Schmitt, *Staat, Bewegung und Volk* (1933), 31–2, in which he says, 'On this thirtieth of January (the day of Hitler's appointment) . . . the Hegelian civil service state of the nineteenth century . . . gave way to another state structure. On this day, one can therefore say, Hegel died.' Then follows the usual compliment to Hegel's greatness.

3   Herbert Marcuse, *Reason and Revolution. Hegel and the Rise of Social Theory*, New York, 1941. I am in complete agreement with Dr. Marcuse's analysis. As for Treitschke's denunciation of the Teutonism of the Burschmschaften, see Heinrich von Treitschke, *Deutsche Geschichte im neunzehnten Jahrhundert*, 3rd ed., 1886, Vol. ii, 383–443.

4   *Philosophy of Right*, trans. by W. Dyde, London, 1896, 289–97.

5   Max Weber, 'Wirtschaft und Gesellschaft', in *Grundriss der Sozialökonomie*, iii, Tübingen, 1922.

6   Thomas Hobbes, *Leviathan*, Molesworth ed., Vol. III, Part II, ch. 21, 199. The following remarks on the political thought of National Socialism are based upon my unpublished manuscript, The Governance of the Rule of Law, written in 1936, available at the University of London, 561.

7   Bertrand Russell, 'The Revolt against Reason', in the *Political Quarterly*, 1935, 5. Max Horkheimer, 'Zum Rationalismusstreit in der gegenwärtigen Philosophie', in *Zeitschrift für Sozialforschung*, 1934 (3), i.

8   *Dissertations and Discussions*, 3rd ed., Vol. i, 332.

9   Ernst Krieck, *Nationalpolitische Erziehung*, 14th ed., Leipzig, 1933, 68.

10 This phenomenon has been observed by Carlton J. H. Hays, 'The Novelty of Totalitarianism in the History of Western Civilization', in *Symposium on the Totalitarian State* (American Philosophical Society), Philadelphia, 1940, 91–103.

11 Harold D. Lasswell, 'The Garrison State', in *The American Journal of Sociology*, 1941 (46), 455–68, esp. p. 462.

12 Ernst Fraenkel, *The Dual State*, New York, 1941.

13 Höhn, *Die Wandlung im staatsrechtlichen Denken*, Hamburg, 1934. 32. Neesse, *Führergewalt*, Tübingen, 1940.

14 Roger Diener, 'Reichsproblem und Hegemonie', in *Deutsches Recht*, 1939, 551–66.

15 Neesse, op. cit. p. 54.

16 'Der Reichsbegriff in Völkerrecht', in *Deutsches Recht*, 1939, 341–4.

Chapter 25

Robert Koehl

NAZI STATE AND NEO-FEUDALISM

■ from **FEUDAL ASPECTS OF NATIONAL SOCIALISM**, *American Political Science Review*, 54 (1960), pp. 152–3, 154–5, 156–8, 161–2, 167, 169–70

Robert Koehl pioneered the analysis of National Socialism as a peculiar regression to feudal relationships. In the following excerpt, he lists a host of 'feudal' features: the ideas of honour (*Ehre*) and loyalty (*Treue*), the imagery of the Teutons, the notion of self-subordination and personal allegiance, the interdependence between leadership and chieftains. For Koehl, such a revival of feudalism in Nazi Germany was a response to the reality of a fragmented society and a means to repair it without directly addressing the causes of its fragmentation.

T HE NOTION THAT 'FEUDALISM' is a 'form of society,' especially a 'stage in development,' can be traced back to Marxist historiography, and from there back to eighteenth century French thinkers. But instead of becoming thoroughly discredited, the notion has recently led to new thinking on the subject which may turn out to be fruitful. In *Feudalism in History*, for example, Rushton Coulborn has combined eight separate papers on feudalism in various parts of the world by different historians, with his own critical and synthetic studies.[1] Though he fails to find even one 'fully developed' feudal society according to his own definition – a not unexpected result – his study contains an amazing amount of suggestive analysis.

His suggestions are particularly valuable in the construction of 'working models' or 'ideal types' as research tools. Even when we remain safely within our own 'fields,' if we are to go beyond highly specialized fact-gathering and at the same time avoid 'presentist subjectivism,' we will need such tools.

Feudalism, above all, is a power-relationship. Its essential ingredients are vassalship and the fief. Vassalship is based on personal dependence and loyalty, while the fief represents a *conditional* proprietary right, often to landed property. The fief is the basis of personal power; it is presumably held subject to limits defined in terms of service to superiors. Feudalism is always marked by 'a dispersal of political authority amongst a hierarchy of persons who exercise in their own interest powers normally attributed to the state, which are often, in fact, derived from its break-up.' Vassals tend to be 'a specialized military class occupying the higher levels in the social scale.' 'The performance of political functions depends on personal agreements between a limited number of individuals. . . . Since political power is personal rather than institutional, there is relatively little separation of functions.'[2]

Coulborn has suggested that feudalism is 'a mode of revival of a society whose polity has gone into extreme disintegration.' 'Political reformers seek to restore the disintegrating state by calling to its aid the personal vassalage relations which have come to permeate its upper ranks.' 'The culture of a jaded civilized society is reinforced in its elemental nucleus, the relationship of man to man, by an ethic drawn from a primitive source.'[3]

It is quite remarkable how much of this applies to the internal politics of National Socialism. Moreover, Nazi thinkers quite consciously tried to model the New Order along feudal lines.

[. . .]

Nazi predilection for Teutonic imagery is well known. There is an essential connection between this love of the archaic and the primitive and Nazi glorification of the medieval Reich-idea. They found in *Gefolgschaft* and *Treue* the basis for a Germanic Reich as opposed to a Roman legalistic structure or a Byzantine theocratic *Machtstaat*. Over-simplifying the scholarly theories of the Germanic origin of feudalism, they asserted that it was the 'sound judgment of the Nordic ethos' which rejected the subjugation of creative talents either to dead laws or to autocratic personal authority. An honorable self-subordination by mutual contract was the genius of the Germanic Reich-idea. Loyalty (*Treue*) and honor (*Ehre*) were made the ultimate values in life for all upholders of the contract, whether lords or vassals.[4]

The *comitatus* (*Gefolgschaft*) for the Nazis was the natural political unit, the model for all political relationships. Indeed, the *Führerprinzip* was a kind of twentieth-century *Gefolgsordnung*. National Socialists denied allegations that the 'leadership principle' was equivalent to unrestrained and arbitrary tyranny on the Byzantine model. The power of a leader was said to be proportional to the confidence and loyalty of his voluntary followers. Far from extolling naked force, the *Führerprinzip* was 'the rediscovery of the basis of political power: loyalty.' And behind that loyalty lay the 'full and honest acceptance of responsibility' by the strong. Thus the National Socialist ideology made much of 'Germanic' feudalism and condemned the modern state both for its autocratic and its bureaucratic elements.[5]

[. . .]

Yet Hitler himself never tired of extolling the 'Reich-idea.' The notion of a German hegemony in central Europe, over Burgundy, Italy, the Low Countries, Denmark and western Slavdom filled him with a sense of grandeur.[6] On the other hand he repudiated Germanization and uniformity for these imperial areas. Indeed, his conception of 'the good old days' included the same ideals which Himmler and

Rosenberg stressed. There had been no bureaucracy. A divisive nationalism had not yet come into being. Central Europe had been sufficiently unified by the respect for Germanic traits and the use of the German tongue so as to permit a large-scale political decentralization by means of viceroys and *Reichsstatthalter*. Everything really important could be dealt with by meetings of leading men and smaller details referred to the local nobility with the security that they would handle matters in the shortest possible order. The great emperors had always retained just enough domains to hold the balance of punitive striking power in the Reich.

The National Socialist doctrines of 'Blood and Soil' are similarly reminiscent of feudal property relationships. R. W. Darré, the Nazi agrarian, called private property rights 'Roman.' The Germanic idea of property, said he, was the right of usufruct and inheritance in return for service rendered to the community. Darré waxed eloquent on the subject of a past and a future 'Germanic aristocracy of the soil.' Without denying the fighting prowess of the medieval German nobility, Darré derived it and aristocratic conceptions of honor and loyalty from its free-peasant foundations rather than the battlefield. The rough honesty and simplicity of the Teutonic spirit were preserved on the land. A 'true communalism' allegedly developed in this class of noble farmers which was based on mutuality; it was purchased neither by the servility of the west-Frankish serf nor the destruction of individuality by the Slavic village community. In fact, 'it was the Germanic genius to combine noble breeding with land-management responsible to the community.' This limited freedom in the use of land was the price paid by the Germans; when modern Germans refused to pay it – because of the 'reforms' of the French Revolution – German property relationships became chaotic, said Darré.[7]

Thus, the first task of National Socialism according to Darré was to free the German peasant from 'the chaos of a market economy.' The famous *Erbhofgesetz* re-created the principle of entail for peasant farms. While it was never possible to apply this law across the board, qualified farmers were 'freed' from indebtedness, past and future, at the same time receiving their 'hereditary estate' as a fief from the Reich. Similarly, just as such farmers became dependent on government loans for farm improvements, so all farmers were required to take part in a cooperative marketing network to 'free them from the chaos of the market.' This *Reichsnährstand* was much more than a compulsory marketing organization, however. As its name implied, it was intended by Darré to be a corporative estate of food producers. Darré meant it to be an autonomous, self-governing unit of a future pluralistic German society. Through its power, vis-à-vis the individual peasant, and vis-à-vis German society, he hoped it would pave the way for a 'New aristocracy of Blood and Soil.'[8]

[. . .]

The last item in our catalogue of Nazi medievalism, while not precisely feudal, is composed of many related elements. National Socialist historians, as well as Rosenberg and Himmler, gave a high place to the Teutonic Order. For them all, the essence of the Order was its elitism. It, too, was an elaboration of the war-band, the self-constituted league of fighting aristocrats. However, only the dedicated were able to sustain the pitiless self-subordination to the higher purposes of the order. It was in the Teutonic Order that the Hegelian synthesis of Germanic pride and

Christian humility was fused to create Prussiandom. The *Ordensritter* was a knight *sans peur et sans reproche*, not for himself, not for Holy Church, but for an Idea. That this Idea was not fully revealed to him, though it had something to do with the future and with Europe as a whole, was an advantage, not a drawback. Quite consciously Rosenberg called upon the NSDAP to make itself the German Order of the twentieth century in the service of the 'unknown god.' Similarly Himmler devised his *Schutzstaffel* or Elite Guard (SS) in the conscious effort to form a new pioneer-nobility for a future German east. He tried to instill in them a natural piety and a worshipful attitude towards the creative forces of nature as a substitute for Holy Church. On their belt buckles he inscribed *Meine Ehre heisst Treue* (My honor is loyalty).[9]

[. . .]

The consequence of these practices for the Nazi empire approximated feudal monarchy. Numerous eyewitnesses have reported that Hitler held his power not as an absolute monarch but through his ability to operate a delicate system of checks and balances.[10] He was a unifying factor for the disparate and competing elements of National Socialism, possessed of a considerable power of his own over the masses and over many leading Nazis which has been termed 'charismatic.' These characteristics are precisely those of the successful feudal monarch like St. Louis. Without precisely encouraging strife among his cohorts, Hitler was capable of remarkable neutrality – an ability to remain above the battle. Thus he could intervene when he had discovered where lay the advantage to his own power and to the Reich as he saw it. He also had the habit of so 'impartially' deciding an issue that aggressor and victim were treated equally, with the result that there was an advantage to activist policy.[11] Since he could not be everywhere, especially in the continuous crisis of wartime, Hitler had to encourage self-reliance and independence, both in his paladins and in the regional chieftains, the *Gauleiter*.

In the last years of the Nazi era there is the most striking evolution along feudal lines. The *Gauleiter* became so fully identified with the interests of their bailiwicks that we find them behaving more like ancient stem dukes in their refusal to recognize the authority of the central government than like *missi dominici*. Hitler had to inveigh against the idea of hereditary Gauleitership, though he did not dare transfer recalcitrant *Gauleiter* where they had personally won the *Gau* for National Socialism.[12] As for the paladins, Göring, Goebbels, Himmler, and the newcomers, Speer and Bormann, had constructed virtually impregnable appanages. The more dependent Hitler became upon their empires for German victory, the more easily they looted the power of rivals like Rosenberg and Ribbentrop, Sauckel and Keitel. They made their systems independent of the central authorities and even of the Führer's support by absorbing some vehicle of power, usually economic, though Goebbels also used the mass media and Himmler the secret police.[13]

[. . .]

In a way then, Nazi 'feudalism' was merely play-acting. Rosenberg acknowledges this in his prison memoirs when he states that the Third Reich was a theatrocracy, a notion he borrows from Jacob Burckhardt.[14] Some Nazis 'lived their parts' better than others. The German middle class, from which the rank and file of supporters came, had turned to a fantasy world and a make-believe language, which they called the 'higher truth' just because they found the level of rationalization in real economic and political life too cruel. 'Cold rationality' and 'the colorless network of self-interest' were the reality, even after an intellectual flight from the scene occurred in the form of National Socialism. Both *petit bourgeois* preoccupation with blood and soil and aristocratic-intellectual preoccupation with 'leadership' disguised the mounting *rational* impersonality of economic forces of which even the cartel chiefs were merely agents.[15]

And yet there was a deeper level of motivation. Unconsciously German industrialists and Nazis alike seemed to be trying to adapt themselves to factors of disintegration within German society.[16] Not merely as a form of protest against the rationalization of the economy and society, nor as a mere flight into fairy-tales, *but as a sincere but primitive effort to hold together a crumbling social order*, Nazi neo-feudalism is worthy of attention.

[. . .]

National Socialism is to be understood, then, as an effort of a disorganized society to repair itself, or rather, as an effort *of certain of its members,* whose own experience and character were the product of the very disorganization they sought to repair. To be sure they conceived of themselves as especially chosen by fate or history for this role; a disintegrating society *does* call forth such types: cutters of Gordian knots, empire-builders, scorners of theory. But only rarely were National Socialists able to escape from their own romanticism and wishful thinking. As a result their constructions were not truly empirical; their *Mythos* was too bound up with their own immediate past. Yet it is sobering to recall that it was only a thorough military defeat by a powerful coalition of three great societies, the United States, the British Commonwealth, and the Soviet Union, that drove these improvisers from the stage. A question universally asked is whether the conditions which made their appearance possible have been radically altered. Much of the current optimism with regard to Germany is based upon explanations of National Socialism which do not stress the neo-feudal or pseudopluralist aspects of Nazism. The optimism is, of course, primarily based on the successes of the German Federal Republic, its economic strength, its relative homogeneity, its political maturity and flexibility. The total collapse of specifically Nazi figures and Nazi legends (i.e., Hitler) is reassuring, but it may indicate the inadequacy of the specific National Socialist response to German social disorganization, rather than a guarantee that another crisis cannot develop in the relationships of the state, the parties, the corporations, and other pressure groups. The German people may well have been inoculated against the superficial aspects of neo-feudalism: medievalism, *Gefolgschaft*, Teutonic Orders, and *Gauleiter*. The question remains whether they have been welded together sufficiently in the fiery furnace of national disaster and in the short period since 1945 to counteract the legacy of their past and the divisive forces of modern industrial society.

Notes

1   Rushton Coulborn, ed., *Feudalism in History* (Princeton, N.J., 1956). See also *From Max Weber, Essays in Sociology*, ed. H. Gerth and C. W. Mills (New York, 1946), 300. Cf. C. Sjoberg, 'Folk and "Feudal" Societies,' *American Journal of Sociology*, LVII (1952), 231–239.

2   F. L. Ganshof, *Feudalism* (London, 1952), xv. Joseph R. Strayer and R. Coulborn, 'The Idea of Feudalism,' in Coulborn, *Feudalism*, 5.

3   Coulborn, *Feudalism*, 364–395, esp. pp. 364, 392.

4   'Der Staat ist nun nicht die Verwirklichung der deutschen Volksordnung schlechthin, sondern er ist aus der Gefolgsordnung heraus gewachsen.' ('The state is not the direct embodiment of the national structure, but rather grew out of the feudal order.') Carl Johanny and Oscar Redelberger, *Rechtspflege und Verwaltung: I. Allgemeiner Teil, Heft 2: Volk. Partei. Reich* (2nd ed., Berlin, 1943), 3–4.

5   Fritz Nova, *The National Socialist Fuehrerprinzip and its Background in German Thought* (Philadelphia, 1943), 1–14, 71–72, 90–94. According to National Socialist critiques of modern western society, a man's chance to act responsibly, indeed a man's *right* to be responsible, had been taken from him in the leveling and anonymous processes of mass democracy. Furthermore, the attempt to create uniform, rationalistic rules of procedure in political affairs had served to conceal the role of decision-making, and thus rendered decision-makers irresponsible.

6   Cf. *Hitler's Secret Conversations 1941–1944* (New York, 1953), 325–329; *Mein Kampf* (New York, 1940), 596–606, 935–943.

7   R. Walther Darré, *Neuadel aus Blut und Boden* (Munich, 1935), 43–47, 62, 67–76.

8   Hermann Reischle and Wilhelm Saure, *Der Reichsnährstand: Aufbau, Aufgaben und Bedeutung* (Berlin, 1934), 15–30, 38–44, 133–152.

9   Karl O. Paetel, 'Die SS, Ein Beitrag zur Soziologie des Nationalsozialismus,' *Vierteljahrshefte für Zeitgeschichte*, II (1954), 1–33; Hans Buchheim, 'Die SS in der Verfassung des Dritten Reiches,' *ibid.*, III (1955), 128–155. Cf. Gerald Reitlinger, *SS: Alibi of a Nation* (London, 1956). In keeping with the development of an elite the Nazis gave up one of the oldest ideals of Prussian education: uniform public education. They tried to substitute for it the special school for the future elite in which not only the aristocratic virtues were encouraged but in which the sense of difference from the *hoi polloi* was reinforced.

10   Hans B. Gisevius, *Bis zum bitteren Ende* (Hamburg, 1947), I, 121–123, 138–139, 155ff. Otto Strasser, *Die deutsche Bartholomäusnacht* (6th ed., Zurich, 1935), 17–33, 47ff., 73–81. Cf. Walter Görlitz and Herbert Quint, *Adolf Hitler* (Stuttgart, 1952), 629–631.

11   *The Memoirs of Alfred Rosenberg*, ed. S. Lang and E. von Schenck (New York, 1949), 231.

12   *Hitlers Tischgespräche* (Bonn, 1951), 250, 252, 254. Cf. Franz Neumann, *Behemoth: The Structure and Practice of National Socialism 1933–1944* (London and New York, 1944), 535; E. Vermeil, 'German Nationalist Ideology in the Nineteenth and Twentieth Centuries,' *The Third Reich* (New York, 1955), 299.

13   A characteristic stage in the development of feudal offices is the assignment of tasks by the leader to table-companions and household employees. Precisely this stage was reached in 1945 Hitler Germany, especially in the Führer-Bunker. Furthermore, whether guilty or innocent, Göring and Himmler were accused in April

1945 by Hitler of that fatal feudal disease: *frondieren*. Each absented himself from the court, in a suspiciously distant corner of the kingdom.

14   Rosenberg, *Memoirs*, 248. Max Weber wrote '. . . when enthusiasm and emotional response are rationally calculated *into* the equation of power, we are not dealing with genuine feudal and/or charismatic power' (from *Max Weber, Essays in Sociology*, 254).

15   Neumann, *Behemoth*, 350–356.

16   Schacht, for example, was an economic rationalist who tried to compromise with chaos; he managed quite successfully from 1933 to 1936. By 1937, however, he and the Nazis disagreed about *the degree* of lawfulness to be preserved (Earl R. Beck, *Verdict on Schacht. A Study in the Problem of Political 'Guilt,'* Florida State University Studies, No. 20 (Tallahassee, 1955), 92).

Chapter 26

Doug Thompson

DEVICES OF THE 'FASCIST CONSENSUS': PARTY AND MASS ORGANISATIONS IN FASCIST ITALY

■ from *STATE CONTROL IN FASCIST ITALY: CULTURE AND CONFORMITY, 1925–43*, Manchester and New York, 1991, pp. 79–84, 87–9, 140–1, 146–51

Doug Thompson's analysis of the way the Italian Fascist regime set up a mechanism for social control and fabrication of 'consensus' underlines the absence of positive, lasting popular identification with the regime, even in cases where evidence of 'momentary appreciation and acceptance' exists. In the following excerpt Thompson discusses the function of two significant institutions (the National Fascist Party and the Dopolavoro – organisation of leisure) in cultivating a culture of conformity and loyalty to Fascism. In both cases, he argues, participation and lack of opposition did not signify 'consensus'. Interestingly, Thompson attributes this failure partly to the fact that large sections of the Italian population had showed little sign of identification with the state and the Italian 'nation' ever since the unification.

The National Fascist Party

THE *PNF* [. . .] GRADUALLY CHANGED its character, and whilst it was still to remain the single most powerful force in the imposition of Fascism as a way of life on the great mass of the Italian people, its hold on real political power declined proportionally to the growing influence of the dictator, Mussolini.[1]

Between 1926 and 1930 membership of the Party remained fairly constant, around the million mark, but towards the end of the decade evidence suggests that it was becoming ever more middle-class in its social composition; indeed, in some of the large cities, including Milan and Rome, working-class membership had dropped to as little as 10 per cent of the whole.[2] In many of the local branches in both smaller towns and countryside the bulk of the members were public employees, and this was noticeably the case in the south.

Though the power of the Party had been on the decline since the time of Farinacci's secretariat in 1925–6, the greatest single blow to its power and its pride came with the general reopening of Party membership in 1932, ostensibly to coincide with the triumph of the *Decennale*. In reality, it happened because in 1932–3 a series of decree laws was passed which demanded Party membership of all those seeking public employment or advancement in public employment and the professions, so that enrolment in the Party became as much a passport to economic security as an indication of Fascist zeal, though for propaganda purposes it was always the latter which was emphasised.[3] As a result of this basic requirement rather than the 'democratisation' of the Party, the membership began to climb rapidly, again most noticeably in the south.[4] It was also the types of employment most affected by these new laws which finally imposed a decisive middle-class, conservative stamp on the Party. From the early 1930s on, personnel from the middle and upper strata of industry, commerce and agriculture, as well as from the lower strata of the urban and rural middle classes, came gradually to dominate the Party and its tutelary organisations in most parts of the country. In effect, this large-scale 'migration' of the old dominant classes under the umbrella of the Fascist State reaffirmed the class nature of Italian society which had been one of its constant features since Unification.

In the mid-to-late 1920s Turati, the Party Secretary, tried to maintain some essential political functions for the Party, though with the main aim of creating a centralised authoritarian State based on mass support. Party organisation improved significantly whilst the role and importance of extremism rapidly diminished. However, the balance between the power of the Party and that of the *Duce* finally tipped in the latter's favour with Turati's departure from office in 1930. Neither Giuriati, his immediate successor, nor the long-serving Starace, was able or indeed willing to resist Mussolini's planned marginalisation of the Party in the political life of the country. Giuriati was responsible for the expulsion of roughly one-fifth of the membership at the time of greatest friction between the State and the Church (late 1930 to mid-1931) in an attempt to purge it of men of dubious loyalty, zeal or style. It was primarily his enthusiasm for this task which cost him his job in December 1931, in the wake of the reaffirmed harmony and cooperation between Pope and *Duce*.

Starace's sweeping reform of the Party's statutes in 1932 (coinciding with the general reopening of Party membership) not only confirmed its slide from power but by incorporating into it many hitherto semi-autonomous groups such as the *GUF* (*Gioventù universitaria fascista* – Organisation of Fascist University Students) and the *FGC* (*Fascisti giovanili di combattimento* – The Fascist Youth for Combat), effectively redefined its role as a bureaucratic machine.[5] In this new guise, Ragionieri argues, it played an essential part in checking social mobility and in establishing consensus around the social and political status quo.[6] The case of women is instructive here for though better organised than ever before in Italian history such organisation confirmed, indeed institutionalised, the traditional, socially and politically inferior role of women in society, though with its attendant flattering propaganda smokescreen.[7] In this new, rapidly emerging role, the Party became a major tertiary sector employer, though advancement from the lower to the middle and upper ranks of the hierarchy was uncommon, vacancies at those levels being filled mainly by rotation and transfers between one region and another.

Under Starace, and particularly after the war in Africa, the Party underwent a steady, irreversible decline in popularity, frequently because it was seen both locally and nationally to be run by people who were intent on feathering their own nests, but also because with its rigid, inflexible approach to social questions in particular it was felt to be something of an anachronism, seeming to be still fighting battles Fascism had already won. Starace, especially, was a target for derision, but he was by no means alone in this, for his secretaryship gave rise to all manner of grotes-queries in which many of the other *gerarchi*, seemingly willingly, became implicated, and these factors too served to increase the growing disaffection with Fascism, among the intelligentsia and the morally more honest sections of society.

Early in 1931, in what proved to be a fundamental shift in policy, Mussolini declared his intention of '*andare verso il popolo*' (going out to the people). This new policy was not overtly political in its means though its intended effects clearly were political, seeking to reach those large sections of society which had steadfastly remained unmoved by the political appeal of Fascism over the preceding decade. Hitherto, the regime had been concerned primarily with the organisation and disci-pline of the masses in the work place, but now it sought to move into the broad areas of leisure and education. So determined and successful was this policy that by the mid-1930s there were many thousands of recreational-educational circles in Italy with several million participants. It was thus that a mass culture came to be forged in Fascist Italy through what was intended to bring about nothing less than the 'taylorization of leisure',[8] in a 'politics of diversion'.[9] However, the petty bour-geoisie, never having previously experienced such organisation, rapidly became the most enthusiastic participants in particularly the *dopolavoro* circles and it was they who came to provide the regime with an acceptable model for that national mass culture which has often (then and since) been disparagingly referred to as the *cultura dopolavoristica* (the 'after work' culture).[10]

In its earlier days the local Party, like the other political parties and *sindacati* prior to their abolition, had acted as a recreation centre for its members, but with the emergence of its new role this function degenerated rapidly in all but a few, mainly remoter areas, and it was in these circumstances that the *dopolavoro* came into its own.

The National Working Men's Clubs' Association

The *Opera nazionale dopolavoro* which in the early and mid-1920s had been confined mainly to the northern cities, became a nationwide Party organisation under Turati.[11] However, it was during the years of the great depression that it really flour-ished, for it assumed the further task of seeking to offset the hardships inflicted on the working classes by unemployment and low wages.[12] Its educational-recreational character remained but financial assistance to members fallen on hard times must be accounted a major factor in its popularity. It gradually extended its range of activi-ties in the 1930s to include popular folklore and festivals,[13] theatre groups, musical groups, group cinema visits and excursions to places of national importance or scenic interest (members received concessionary theatre and cinema tickets as well as reduced train fares) and, of course, sport.[14] It was through these many activities that the regime was able to embrace so many of those belonging to the lower classes, without in any way involving them directly in politics. Through lectures, films, folk-lore, sporting activities and so on, it was able to inculcate a greater sense of patriot-ism, nationalism or 'manly (or womanly) virtues' closely associated through its propaganda with the Fascist ideal. It was indeed as Ragionieri comments:

> The *dopolavoro* was structured in such a way as to overcome the reluctance of the masses to take part in the activities of a Fascist organisation. At the local level, a whole series of groups which had a certain social prestige, such as lawyers and elementary school teachers in particular, were active though often not members of the Party, indeed, even being former mem-bers of the old anti-Fascist parties (ex-Popular Party and Reformist Socialists). In a society which, by this time, was distinguished by the stag-nation of its social relations, the contribution of these groups was becom-ing crucial for gaining acceptance of the social status quo and for presenting it as a natural process of history, redeemed at last by the mod-est conquests which, until a few years before, must have seemed impos-sible, from the 'people's trains' to the summer colonies. In the *dopolavoro*, as indeed in the administration of all large, medium and small Italian groupings, the imperialistic nationalism of Fascism was watered down, but at the same time found a degree of support in an exaggerated local-ism in which a revitalised municipalism of ancient tradition fused with a newer version based on tourist rivalries and sporting competitions.[15]

A fair number of the 'showpiece' *dopolavoro* circles were those managed by large firms such as FIAT, SIP or several of the larger textile companies, where the corpo-rate ideal of Bottai's vision came very much closer to fulfilment than ever it did at the national level. The range of facilities and activities open to employees was in some cases truly impressive and did much to foster the notion of an elite workforce clearly appreciated and cared for by the management. FIAT, in particular, learnt quickly how to swim with the tide, becoming adept at adopting the right posture demanded by the moment. It took a characteristically militaristic view of its role and of its workforce, regarding the latter as front-line troops in the economic war, imposing always a strict discipline on them in the interests of efficient production and social orderliness. SIP (The Hydroelectric Company of Piedmont) was much influenced by American company paternalism in its relations with its workers, making great play of an apparently democratic attitude manifested, typically, in its policy of equal access to the *same dopolavoro* facilities for workers and management. The idea of the firm as an extended family was central to its policy in which loyalty, obedience and dedication were the watchwords.

[. . .]

In the public sector too, railway workers, civil servants and the State bureaucracy were all groups that were well 'looked after' socially and in their leisure time by a government which was anxious to acquire their loyalty and efficiency largely through the inculcation of a sense of gratitude in them.

The channelling of emotions into nationalistic competitiveness associated particularly with football, cycle racing and boxing, probably bound far more individuals to Mussolini and the regime than did any ideology or the overt militarism of so much of Fascist activity.[16] In the 1930s, sport in Italy became big business,[17] and huge public and private funds were invested in facilities, coaching and competitions.[18] Some big firms like FIAT or public service industries such as the national railways organised sports, largely under the tutelage of their own *dopolavoro* circles, to a very high level of professionalism, and became regular recruitment centres for competitors at the national and international levels. Yet the elitism which such lavish spending created also tended to isolate groups of workers from their less fortunate fellows, setting up tensions and rivalries which ensured often that a former local class solidarity was fragmented; a situation which intensified as those who had grown up entirely under Fascism reached adulthood.

On the face of it, Fascist mass culture offered open access to all sections of society, yet on closer inspection the divisions and hierarchies built into the organisation of leisure – class, sex and age – demonstrate that it was far from egalitarian in reality:

> The public of the *dopolavoro* was relegated to the Saturday matinees or special performances, to the upper tiers of the theater, and to the third-class compartments on trains, and the recreational facilities for popular use were often rudimentary. Moreover, the Fascist organisation of leisure introduced a new status differentiation within recreational activities. Distinctions between the amateur and the professional, the dilettante and the expert, were accentuated; the 'high theater' and elite sports were increasingly commercialized and professionalized, whereas the categories of the 'amateur' sportsmen and the dilettante actors of 'passion' not 'ambition' – that is, of those pastimes identified as 'popular' – were formalized. Nor did the OND seek to set up training programs or facilities that would provide access from one realm to another. Finally, low levels of popular consumption remained a barrier to participation and to the extension of facilities that state intervention could only partially overcome.[19] [. . .]

We now come to the question of consensus. De Felice, following the lead of Togliatti, argues that substantially, between 1929 and 1934, wide sections of the lower classes in Italian society gave their support to Mussolini's regime. Their alleged consent was based on the regime's ability to offer them a living wage, a wide-ranging social welfare programme and, through schemes such as land reclamation, the Battle for Wheat and even resettlement elsewhere, to create jobs and some measure of security at a time of world economic recession. Certainly, these must have been positive factors for many in their individual accommodation with the regime. But does acceptance of the benefits purveyed by the regime necessarily add up to approval of it? A whole gamut of responses, ranging from enthusiastic conversion to making the best of a bad job, is clearly possible. Moreover, even within the individual, attitudes are likely to vary from question to question and from moment to moment.

If the regime exploited the great mass of the industrial and rural lower classes – as it surely did – they too, out of necessity, were often only too willing to exploit the regime in whatever ways they could, and did so – as, among others, Revelli, Passerini and Mafai have shown. Bending with the prevailing wind is certainly one way of surviving until it passes. The lack of political opposition, as Passerini argues, should never be confused with consent,[20] especially, one must add, among the great majority for whom political activity was in any case, whatever the circumstances, peripheral to their lives. Under Fascism, as under the preceding cautious democratisation of the Giolittian years or the earlier, more authoritarian forms of Liberalism, the great majority of Italians – the rural peasantry – remained outside politics, entrenched in an age-old culture which centred on work and the business of feeding one's family. Admittedly, Fascism probably intruded more on that way of life than did the previous styles of government, intrusions that were frequently resented but which were not always detrimental to what the peasantry – and perhaps to a lesser extent, the generally more politicised industrial working classes – perceived to be their own best interests.

At this point, a further question arises, namely what degree of consensus was enjoyed by those earlier kinds of government? To which the reply must be almost none. In a sense, the question of consensus – by which we generally mean a more or less continuous sense of harmony between government and governed – is superfluous in a nation which perhaps did not really achieve any true sense of its own identity until some two decades after the Fascist regime had fallen back into history.

The question of consensus, by which term we may be tempted to understand a willing acceptance of the style and purposes of, and an active participation in, the politics of the regime, is then hedged about with a host of provisos. Undoubtedly, at times, particularly in moments of international recognition but equally in moments of national crisis which intensified the economic and social repression of huge sections of society, Mussolini's regime was able to manage information in such a way as to demonstrate the enthusiasm of the masses (e.g. the signing of the Concordat, the conquest of Ethiopia and the rejection of the League of Nations' sanctions) or their tranquil discipline in the interests of the nation (e.g. at the time of the wage reductions following the Wall Street debacle, but even earlier, after 'quota 90'), yet none of this, in the majority of cases, represented anything more than a momentary appreciation or acceptance, as the case may be. On the other hand, in this work of the creation of political myths the regime was actively and enthusiastically supported by the better-off sections of society which were, on the whole, satisfied that their own material interests were being looked after even though through an economic system which was deliberately constructed on the social and cultural poverty of the lower classes. [. . .]

Notes

1   Mussolini himself declared, as late as 10 March 1943, that: 'The Party is the irreplaceable, the necessary link between the State and the people. This is the definition which must be engraved, impressed on our spirits. The Party is the organ which links the State and the people, the linking organ inasmuch as the Party is the State and the people, because if it were otherwise, if it were neither one nor the

other, it could not possibly be the third. These two entities are separate and yet interdependent, having the same essential nature' (*Opera omnia*, XXXI, 166).

2   See E. Ragionieri, *Storia d'Italia,* vol. IV, 3, *Dall'Unità a oggi*, Turin, 1976, 2220–1.

3   As Aquarone demonstrates, Mussolini himself insisted that personnel in ministerial offices should be members of the Party, in a circular to all ministers and undersecretaries, dated 24 March 1932: 'It has come to my notice that in some of the offices of government ministers there are some employees who are not members of the Party . . . I think it necessary that . . . all such personnel be chosen from among members of the Party. Therefore, I should be most grateful if Your Excellencies would arrange for all personnel of whatever grade and in whatever capacity they are employed in ministerial offices to be chosen from amongst employees who, in addition to the requirements of existing orders, are also members of the Party.' *L'organizzazione dello Stato Totalitario*, Turin, 1965, 258, n. 1.

4   Aquarone provides the following statistics for Party membership: October 1932 – 1,007,231; October 1933 – 1,415,407, an increase of just over 40 per cent (ibid., 186).

5   According to Ragionieri *(Dall'Unità a oggi*, 2224 n. 1), other organisations which passed, at the same time, under the tutelage of the Party Secretary, were: *Associazione fascista della scuola (AFS), Associazione del pubblico impiego (AFPI), Associazione dei ferrovieri (AFF), Associazione dei postelegrafonici (AFPT), Associazione degli addetti alle aziende industriali (AFAAI)*. Aquarone *(L'organizzazione*, 264, n. 2) provides a much more extensive list of all those associations which were still being managed by the *PNF* according to the provisions of a later statute, RD, 17 February 1941.

6   E. Ragionieri, *Dall'Unità a oggi*, 2224.

7   G. Biondi and F. Imberciadori report that in 1929 the *Fasci Femminili* were also inaugurated: 'in every locality of the Kingdom and of the colonies, where there is a *Fascio di combattimento,* a *Fascio Femminile* must be set up. To the *Fasci Femminili* are entrusted the tasks of assisting in the carrying out of all relief work organised by the *PNF*, and of spreading the idea of Fascism and of keeping it active in the family circle. All those Italian women who are of irreproachable moral conduct and sure Fascist faith can become members of the Fasci . . .' (cited from G. Rabaglietti, *Le istituzioni del Regime*, Bologna, 1935, 21). See . . . *Voi siete la primavera d'Italia . . . : l'ideologia fascista nel mondo della scuola, 1925–1943*, Turin, 1982, 24, n. 26.

8   V. De Grazia, *The Culture of Consent. Mass Organisation of Leisure in Fascist Italy*, Cambridge, 1981, 44.

9   Ibid., 216, where this phrase is used.

10   De Grazia provides a useful table showing the composition of *OND* membership between 1926 and 1936 in which, up to 1928, salaried workers make up more than 50% of the membership. From 1929 on, however, they are overhauled by manual workers who, from a figure of only 116,000 in 1926, had reached 1,093,000 by 1930, climbing to 1,921,000 by 1936 out of a total membership of 2,755,000. By 1936, something like 20% of the industrial labour force and 7% of the peasantry were enrolled in the organisation. In general, however, it was members of the smaller group who tended to be the office holders and organisers, over and above the 700 or so full-time officials at the national level (see ibid., 55).

11   Ragionieri also provides membership figures for 1939, by which time the organisation could boast 3,831,331 members of whom 1,581,313 worked in industry,

559,048 were in commerce and banking, 879,389 in agriculture, 308,223 transport workers and 503,538 in other sectors, notably State employees. He then quotes E. R. Tannenbaum's cautionary note: 'the figure for industry could be misleading because it included workers in the big firms such as Fiat, Ansaldo and Breda. Among those enrolled from agriculture, two-thirds were farm owners and only one-third were dependent labourers. The probable conclusion is that only a half of the members were workers, while the other half were made up of members of the petty bourgeoisie or at least, who saw themselves as belonging to that social group' (see n. 1, 2227, Dall'Unità a oggi).

12 De Grazia explains that: ' "Reaching out to the people" in practice took two forms: a sizable relief program, provided by public distribution of fuel and bread under the auspices of the party's Ente Opere Assistenziali, or EOA, together with public works projects, which in 1935 had employed about half a million of the several million unemployed; and, second, an intense though increasingly depoliticized activism on the part of the regime's mass organisations. Party headquarters were ordered to remain open day and night, and fascist functionaries, as Mussolini admonished his cohorts through a widely publicized "note" to Parenti, the free-living *federale* of Milan, were to adopt an entirely new populist style – no more nightlife or theatergoing; travel on foot or by motorcycle rather than in chauffeured cars; plain "black shirts of the revolution" at public occasions instead of top hats and fancy dress; a full day at the office listening to "the greatest number of people possible" with "the utmost patience and humanity"; finally, visits to working class neighborhoods on a regular basis to make "physical as well as moral contact" with the working population.' *The Culture of Consent*, 52.

13 De Grazia, ibid., 201–2, argues that 'Clearly rejecting a role in the development of a technological culture, the OND turned its organizational energies and ideological stratagems toward sustaining those very folk traditions that were gradually disappearing with the spread of literacy, urbanization, and improved communications . . . By the early thirties the OND had become the leading celebrant of folk values, virtually ceasing its efforts to engender a more sophisticated identification with the fascist precepts'.

14 See A. Lyttelton, *The Seizure of Power. Fascism in Italy 1919–1929*, London, 1987, 2nd ed., 401–2.

15 E. Ragionieri, *Dall'Unità a oggi*, 2228.

16 A. Aquarone, *L'organizzazione*, 268, reports that: '. . . *Critica fascista* grumbled that in the Fascist youth organisations, with the exception of the *GUF*, "easier access to, and pleasure in, sporting activities have almost entirely and universally precluded every other care and interest which might aim at the inculcation of a culture, however limited, and the arousal of political consciousness, in the mass of their young members; indeed, the *Fascist formation* of these latter . . . has indubitably been found wanting".'

17 V. De Grazia, *The Culture of Consent*, 178.

18 V. De Grazia, ibid., 178, reports that: 'Between 1927 and 1930 more than 1,000 new sports fields were inaugurated; by 1930, the total number of playing fields amounted to 3,289, with marked increases in Piedmont and Lombardy and a not insignificant rise in the more prosperous southern regions, most noticeably Apulia'.

19 Ibid., 186.

20 L. Paserini, *Fascism in Popular Memory*, 65.

Chapter 27

Klaus-Michael Mallmann and Gerhard Paul

COERCION AND TERROR: THE GESTAPO IN THE NAZI SYSTEM

■ from **OMNISCIENT, OMNIPOTENT, OMNIPRESENT? GESTAPO, SOCIETY AND RESISTANCE**, in David Crew (ed.), *Nazism and German Society 1933–45*, London, 1994, pp. 167, 169–70, 172–4, 175–7, 184–5, 187–8, 189

In the following excerpt Mallmann and Paul challenge the traditional representation of the Gestapo (Geheime Staatspolizei) as 'omnipotent, omnipresent, omniscient'. Their extensive research on the organisation and operation of the Nazi secret police encountered a reality of a far-from-all-pervasive mechanism, relying heavily on voluntary denunciations and an inconsistent web of paid or unpaid informers. The two authors' conclusion, that the Nazi regime was incapable of 'comprehensive surveillance or perfect repression', is important in two ways. First, it shows how successful Nazi propaganda was in cultivating the (erroneous) impression that the Gestapo was truly omnipotent, omnipresent and omniscient. Second, it underlines the complicity of many ordinary Germans who – out of fanatical support for, or fear of, the regime – became willing participants in the terror perpetrated by Nazism (cf. Goldhagen (31)).

THE STORY OF THE GESTAPO is not least the story of its perception in the 'distorted mirror' of omnipotence, omniscience and ubiquity. The aura of a perfectly operating secret police was preeminently an image created by means of propaganda, which was meant to intimidate but also to conceal its own structural deficits. Although this picture was in many respects a chimera – as we intend to show – it none the less gave reality its direction, indeed created its own unique reality, thereby furnishing the Gestapo with the aura of the most extreme criminological efficiency, which constituted a not insignificant part of its effectiveness, even though it was fictional. In 1941, at the German Police Convention, (Reinhard) Heydrich praised the fact that 'The secret police, the criminal police and the security forces are shrouded in the whispered secrets of the political crime novel.'[1]

The conceptions of the resistance fighters and of those in exile were also not left untouched by this carefully staged representation of the secret police, tracking down the regime's enemies with instinctual sureness. Right from the beginning this image especially impressed the left because the absence of mass resistance, their own growing social isolation, along with the decimation of their ranks – all this forced them to accept an explanation, which would not shake the basic foundations of their own worldview. The image of the Gestapo fabricated by the regime was just what was needed. The alleged perfection of the secret police's surveillance methods and the supposed efficiency of the Gestapo's omnipotent apparatus offered a 'back door' through which the resistance could escape any confrontation with the reality of the shattered labor movement or the reasons that the possibility of an insurrection were fading. Because their own projections, patterns of interpretation and modes of thinking interfered with their perceptions, distinctly paranoid forms of perception were increasingly produced, which had very little in common with the reality of the state police, which indeed said more about the authors of these reports than about the actual subject being described.

[. . .]

In his 'classical' local study of the Nazi 'seizure of power' in Northeim, William Sheridan Allen concluded that 'The general feeling was that the Gestapo was every-where' even though in this small town in southern Lower Saxony, in addition to the regular police, there had only been one occasional informer for the security police, but not one single permanent Gestapo agent.[2] This model of the SS- or Gestapo-State as an unscrupulous clique dominating the German people, although a historical misrepresentation, provided absolution and so became a founding myth of both German states which managed to establish that Germans had been absolutely over-powered by their 'criminal rulers,' that they had been completely helpless against the 'Nazi Socialist tyranny of violence,' and thus also managed to conjure away the Gestapo and the SS as some kind of social enclave not really part of German society.[3] [. . .]

Especially Jacques Delarue's *History of the Gestapo* – still regarded as a standard work – was taken in by the great claims made by the Nazi police strategists: 'Never before, in no other land and at no other time, had an organisation attained such a comprehensive penetration (of society), possessed such power and, reached such a degree of "completeness" in its ability to arouse terror and horror, as well as in its actual effectiveness.' As the informers of the Gestapo 'spotted or overheard every German's slightest movement,' the omniscience of the Gestapo was for Delarue as unquestionable as its omnipotence, both of which he quite simply derived from the Gestapo's formal functions. According to his circular argumentation at the level of an introductory seminar course: 'in order to carry out its functions, the Gestapo had to be omnipotent.'[4] The tradition of such thrillers extends, unbroken, right into the present. Jochen von Lang's book *Die Gestapo*, which appeared in 1990, conjures up the metaphysical dimensions of this omnipotence as does Adolf Diamant's treatise on the Gestapo offices in Frankfurt and Leipzig.[5] Like their predecessors, both authors mistake intention for reality, confuse the program with the actual practice;

they become completely intoxicated with the monstrosity of the Gestapo, but they do not give a single thought to the investigation of the actual ways in which it worked. Common to all of these studies is the fact that their evaluations are based not upon empirical study but largely upon a system of speculative supposition. The intentions of the Nazi police strategists concerning a comprehensive system of police control over German society has thereby achieved a certain retrospective historiographical reality.

[. . .]

However, some local and regional studies did initiate a new way of looking at the reality of the Gestapo. Whenever the bird's eye view from the Berlin central office was not uncritically reproduced, when attention was focussed upon domination and resistance in an area small enough to be observed in detail, where the local structures of social milieux and the concrete activities of the agencies of persecution became transparent, then the myth of the ubiquitous, efficient Gestapo began to crumble, provided that historians did not try, from the very start, to force the empirical findings into the procrustean bed of the Gestapo's omnipotent significance. Above all, Detlev Peukert's study of the communist resistance in the Rhine and Ruhr areas drew attention to inconsistencies in the historiographic picture of the Gestapo,[6] as did Inge Marssolek and René Ott in their monograph on Bremen.[7] But while these were more or less accidental by-products of local or regional investigations of resistance, which were not based upon a systematic approach to the Gestapo or upon a theoretically informed formulation of the questions, Reinhard Mann's study of Düsseldorf was able, for the first time, to demonstrate statistically the outstanding importance of denunciations within the state police's repertoire of practices.[8] Robert Gellately's work on the Gestapo district office in Würzburg – which appeared in 1990 – reinforced this perspective and, for the first time, brought German society centrally into the analysis of this Nazi institution of domination, although he concentrated his empirical investigation upon the persecution of the Jews and the surveillance of Polish workers.[9] Burkhard Jellonek's Münster dissertation on the repression of homosexuals, which appeared in the same year, limited itself neither to the normative aspect nor to the national level, but rather scrutinized in great detail the local offices in Neustadt, Würzburg and Düsseldorf.[10] Our own study of the district Gestapo office in Saarbrücken, published in 1991, which attempted to reconstruct police methods of proceeding against the various targets of persecution, should also be mentioned.[11] Although these studies certainly by no means redress all the deficits of existing research, they none the less permit – as a kind of interim reappraisal – several observations on the general structure, the methods of functioning and the effectiveness of state police activity at the local level, which cast new light upon the internal mechanisms of the 'Prerogative State' (*Massnahmenstaat*) which, because of their relatively broad empirical basis, can lay some claim to a certain paradigmatic significance. If the Gestapo is not deprecated, as a propagandistically inflated subject, but rather observed in its normality and everyday routine, then it becomes especially clear that its own strength could scarcely have made it capable of playing the role of the ubiquitous 'Big Brother.'

What stands out the most obviously is denunciation, almost overlooked until now, but frightening in its extent; it kept the machinery of terror going, and constituted a centred component of the internal 'constitution' of the Third Reich.

It has become clear in all of these studies that the National Socialist 'Prerogative State' (*Massnahmenstaat*) was certainly no thoroughly rationalized mechanism of repression, in which one gear meshed precisely with the other, keeping the entire population under close surveillance. In quantitative terms alone, the Gestapo at the local level was hardly an imposing detective organization, but much rather an under-staffed, under-bureau-cratized agency, limping along behind the permanent inflation of its tasks and of its own imaginings of the enemy.

[. . .]

In quantitative terms, the Gestapo hardly represented a nursery of National Socialist fanaticism. An analysis of the composition of the personnel of the district offices in Würzburg and Saarbrücken confirms the opinion expressed by Dr Werner Best to the Nuremberg military tribunal that especially the political police was staffed with 'officials of the previous police agencies' and that the proportion of SS 'at first remained very small'.[12] The purging of police ranks was confined to the top level; continuity in personnel remained dominant, as did the secondary virtues of duty and obedience which were deeply engrained in the dependent career civil service.[13] The core of the Gestapo was formed from the Political Department of the Weimar police – operating mostly under the designation IA – that contributed, in particular, its expertise in combating the communists.[14] To increase personnel or to create new district branches – as in Trier or Saarbrücken – the Gestapo turned, above all, to security or criminal police officers, who saw a transfer as an advancement of their careers, which, however, meant that in the field of combatting political opponents, the majority of the officers were self-taught.[15]

Only two of the Gestapo officers in Würzburg, the head of the department and his successor, had joined the Nazi Party before Hitler's accession to power; in 1933, four more followed, the remainder joined only in 1937 and 1939, respectively.[16] So far, at least, as staffing was concerned, the regional office in Saarbrücken was certainly not the domain of the SS or of the party; only about 10 per cent of those employed here belonged to the SS in 1935, while 50 per cent were party members. The number of those who did not belong to any Nazi organization was, at 40 per cent, amazingly high; even the director of Department II – a complete career official – joined the NSDAP only in 1942.[17] This picture of a by no means fanaticized police unit becomes even more heterogeneous when one considers that numerous Gestapo officials in Saarbrücken had been members of republican parties before 1933 and even remained practising Christians.[18] It would be mistaken, in the face of such diversity, to view the Gestapo simply as the agent of Nazi ideology in the years before the war; in 1939, only 3,000 of its roughly 20,000 employees held an SS-rank.[19] More decisive than recruitment from within the Nazi sub-culture were the lines of continuity with the German police upon which the Gestapo could support itself; the fixation upon the authoritarian, nation state, the traditional canon of secondary virtues, the deification of law and order, the mentality of the 'unpolitical' civil servant.[20]

With the war came important qualitative changes in the staff structure of district offices. In Saarbrücken, young criminal police assistants took the places of employees who had been conscripted. A new type of Gestapo official began to rise in the ranks, less technically competent than the criminological experts they replaced, and at the same time far more ideological. Complaints about their insufficient professional training and aptitude remained the order of the day until the end of the war. And the structural changes in qualifications, along with an increasing mobility of staff led to a considerable reduction in the Gestapo's striking power. While the categories of the persecuted steadily expanded (and this increase in the Gestapo's functions had, by itself, greatly overloaded its capabilities), the number of trained criminologists, schooled in interrogation techniques, became an ever smaller minority. This decline in intelligent police practice promoted the replacement of inherited police methods with confessions extorted with the use of force. It was at this point in its history that the reality of the Gestapo began to conform to its popular image as a brutal gang of thugs.[21] [. . .]

[With regard to denunciations] paid informers exposed conspiratorial groups and voluntary denunciations ran dissent to ground. Or in other words, the oppositional impulses and activities of workers were, as a rule, eliminated from within their own ranks; fears of the Gestapo were largely home-made. These plebiscitary strains of terror question the cliché of a society held together by brutal force exercised from above and demonstrate that, as both unpaid denouncers and paid informers, elements of the working class were indispensable wheels in the machinery of persecution who helped in quite concrete ways to shape the *Massnahmenstaat*.

Without the army of voluntary informants from the general population and the state administration, the Gestapo would have been virtually blind. And without the official co-operation of the criminal police, the constabulary and the gendarmes, it would not have been able to carry out the tasks it had been assigned. 'Although there were remarkably few Gestapo people on the ground,' according to Gellately, 'there were many professional and amateur helpers on whom they could rely.'[22] Although the Gestapo was certainly the final authority, in most cases, it was not the driving force. It interrogated, selected, made decisions, deported or delivered cautions; but it was scarcely able to engage in investigations by itself. The widespread collaboration with the regime, the acceptance of terror by society, cancelled this deficit and provided the Gestapo with many ears, in the immediate vicinity of the regime's political opponents. The concept of 'mass crime' therefore has a double meaning; these were crimes that affected masses of Germans, but a large part of the German population also participated in these crimes.

[. . .]

The inadequacies of the Gestapo thus created no real buffer against terror, but rather an opaque, ultimately incalculable domain with no laws, in which, whether or not someone caught up in the machinery of destruction depended, accidentally, upon the person working on the case and his state of mind. It was, therefore, not least the structural weaknesses of this system of terror which contributed to its progressive radicalization. The permanent overloading of this system created fears of threats which found an outlet in preventive measures, thus constructing a vicious circle;

from the concern to eliminate ever new sources of danger there emerged additional tasks, further overloading and a commensurate growth of paranoia.[23] On the other hand, the Gestapo displayed a much lower level of systematic procedure and criminological intelligence than the previous literature suggests and the possibilities for surveillance were by no means so 'totalitarian' that resistance was, from the outset, condemned to catastrophe. The internal fragmentation of the *Massnahmenstaat* and the structural deficiencies of its agencies permitted a variety of free spaces and niches into which people could withdraw. The number of paid informers, the only effective weapon against conspiratorial groups, was limited and could not be increased at will; the Gestapo had no magic wand. The cumulative radicalization with its over-extension of police resources and over-exertion of the Gestapo's own strength even produced the paradox that once the war began, the resistance's chances to be active increased objectively.

Closely inspecting the ways in which the state police approached and disposed of cases and shifted the perspective away from the history of institutions and towards a history of the effects of the *Massnahmenstaat* casts a completely new light upon the possibilities for conspirational resistance, but above all, upon the significance of popular complicity with the regime, upon the popular instrumentalization of terror and upon the disputed issue of whether the 'brown' violence had arisen from within the German population or had simply swept over it. A social history of terror as an integral component of German social history during the Nazi period, that tries to close the gaps between our detailed knowledge of the Gestapo's duties and its real activities and resources, must proceed from the assumption that denunciations were the key link in the interactions between the police and the population, that they were among the most important factors which kept the system of terror going. 'That conclusion,' Robert Gellately quite rightly observes, 'suggests rethinking the notion of the Gestapo as an "instrument of domination"; if it was an instrument it was one which was constructed within German society and whose functioning was structurally dependent on the continuing cooperation of German citizens.'[24] This viewpoint, in turn, in which Germany no longer appears as 'the first occupied territory'[25] and the Gestapo is no longer seen as a foreign institution imposed upon the population, but rather as one rooted in German society, requires a real change in the paradigm which has guided research until recently; instead of the image of a state capable of (almost) perfect surveillance of the whole population we need now to see a society that produced mass denunciations.

[. . .]

[T]he Nazi regime was quite definitely not in the position to engage in comprehensive surveillance or perfect repression. Although the Nazi regime's aspirations were totalitarian, the reality was not. We must therefore agree with Hans Mommsen who concludes that 'The decisive cause of the German catastrophe was not the Nazis' superior manipulative capabilities or their techniques of rule, but rather the lack of resistance in German society to the destruction of politics. The Third Reich can, in this respect, be historicized without thereby questioning the special importance of National Socialism.'[26]

Notes

1   *Völkischer Beobachter*, 17 February 1941.

2   William Sheridan Allen, *The Nazi Seizure of Power. The Experience of a Single German Town, 1930–1935* (Chicago, 1965), 178.

3   See Alf Lüdtke, 'Funktionseliten: Täter, Mit-Täter, Opfer? Zu den Bedingungen des deutschen Faschismus' in Alf Lüdtke (ed.), *Herrschaft als soziale Praxis. Historische und sozialanthropologische Studien* (Göttingen, 1991), 559–90.

4   Jacques Delarue, *Geschichte der Gestapo* (Düsseldorf, 1964), 9, 89, 91.

5   Jochen von Lang, *Die Gestapo. Instrument des Terrors* (Hamburg, 1990); Adolf Diamant, *Gestapo Frankfurt am Main. Zur Geschichte einer verbrecherischen Organisation in den Jahren 1933–1945* (Frankfurt, 1988).

6   Detlev Peukert, *Die KPD im Widerstand. Verfolgung und Untergrundarbeit an Rhein und Ruhr 1933 bis 1945* (Wuppertal, 1980), 116–30, 278–87, 372–81.

7   Inge Marssolek and René Ott, *Bremen im Dritten Reich. Anpassung-Widerstand-Verfolgung* (Bremen, 1986), 176–83.

8   Reinhard Mann, *Protest und Kontrolle im Dritten Reich. Nationalsozialistische Herrschaft im Alltag einer rheinischen Grossstadt* (Frankfurt a.M/New York, 1987), 147–76, 287–305.

9   Robert Gellately, *The Gestapo and German Society. Enforcing Racial Policy, 1933–1945* (Oxford, 1990); see also Gellately, 'The Gestapo and German Society. Political Denunciation in the Gestapo Case Files', *Journal of Modern History*, 6 (1988), 654–94.

10   Burkhard Jellonek, *Homosexuellen im Dritten Reich* (Paderborn, 1990), 176–326.

11   Klaus-Michael Mallmann and Gerhard Paul, *Herrschaft und Alltag. Ein Industrierevier im Dritten Reich* (Bonn, 1991), 175–268, 284–97, 318–26.

12   *Der Prozess gegen die Hauptkriegsverbrecher vor dem Internationalen Militärgerichtshof Nurnberg 14 November 1945–1 Oktober 1946* (= IMG), Vol 20 (Nurnberg, 1948), 142, 160.

13   On the Political Police in Prussia during the Weimar Republic see Christoph Graf, *Politische Polizei zwischen Demokratie und Diktatur. Die Entwicklung der preussischen Politischen Polizei* (Berlin, 1983), 5–107.

14   See Gellately, *The Gestapo and German Society*, 50–7, on the continuity of personnel in Bremen, see Inge Marssolek and René Ott, *Bremen im Dritten Reich*, 176 in Hamburg, see Helmut Fangmann, Udo Reifner, Norbert Steinborn, *'Parteisoldaten' Die Hamburger Polizei im 'Dritten Reich'* (Hamburg, 1987), 51–62, in Munich, see Aronson, *Reinhard Heydrich und die Fruhgeschichte von Gestapo und SD*, 127–76, on the activities of the Political Police see the local examples given by Bernd Klemm (ed), *'Durch polizeiliches Einschreiten wurde dem Unfug am Ende gemacht'. Geheime Berichte der politischen Polizei Hessen über Linke und Rechte in Offenbach 1923–1930* (Frankfurt a M /New York, 1982).

15   On the composition of the personnel in the Ther and Saarbrücken district offices see Mallmann and Paul, *Herrschaft und Alltag*, 181f, 203f.

16   See Gellately, *The Gestapo and German Society*, 58f, 76.

17   Berlin Document Center, NSDAP-Mitgliederkartei, file Eugen Schwitzgebel, Zentrale Stelle der Landesjustizverwaltungen Ludwigsburg, Verschiedenes 10.

18   For more details see Mallmann and Paul, *Herrschaft und Alltag*, 205f, for similar information see also Bernd Hey, 'Zur Geschichte der westfälischen Staats-polizeistellen und der Gestapo,' *Westfälischen Forschungen*, 37, 1987, 67.

19   Robert Lewis Koehl, *The Black Corps: The Structure and Power Struggles of the Nazi SS* (Madison, 1983), 159.

20   On the myth of the Schupo as a republican corps see Peter Lessmann, *Die preussische Schutzpolizei in der Weimarer Republik. Streifendienst und Strassenkampf* (Dusseldorf, 1989), see also Hsi-Huey Liang, *Die Berliner Polizei in der Weimarer Republik* (Berlin/ New York, 1977).

21   See Mallmann and Paul, *Herrschaft und Alltag*, 207f.

22   Gellately, *The Gestapo and German Society*, 72.

23   On the cumulative radicalization, see Mallmann and Paul, *Herrschaft und Alltag*, 264–8.

24   Gellately, *The Gestapo and German Society*, 136.

25   Friedrich Zipfel, 'Gestapo and the SD: A Sociographic Profile of the Organizers of Terror' in Stein U. Larsen, Bernt Hagtvet, Jan P. Myklebust (eds), *Who were the Fascists? Social Roots of European Fascism* (Bergen/Oslo/Tromso, 1980), 263.

26   Hans Mommsen, 'Nationalsozialismus als vorgetauschte Modernisierung' in Walter A. Pehle (ed), *Der historische Ort des Nationalsozialismus. Annäherungen* (Frankfurt a M, 1990), 46.

Chapter 28

Ian Kershaw

CHARISMATIC LEADERSHIP: THE 'CULT' OF HITLER

■ from *THE HITLER-MYTH: IMAGE AND REALITY IN THE THIRD REICH*, Oxford and New York, 1989, pp. 48–9, 50, 52–3, 59–60, 64–6, 67, 70, 77–8, 81–2

One of Ian Kershaw's earlier publications dealt with what he called the 'Hitler-myth', that is, the charismatic basis of the Führer's leadership and the cult which Nazi propaganda erected around it. In the following excerpt Kershaw explains how, in spite of the loss of popularity that plagued the Nazi regime in 1934–6, Hitler himself was largely shielded from popular criticism. As he notes, there was a 'large residual feeling' for the Führer – a result of the carefully choreographed cult of the leader. For Kershaw, the successful remilitarisation of the Rhineland (March 1936) constitutes a turning point in the history of the Nazi regime: from that point onwards Hitler himself fell prey to his own propagandistic image of the infallible leader, chosen by 'Providence'.

THE SEEMINGLY UNENDING torchlight procession, staged by Berlin *Gauleiter* Goebbels, which wound its way past Hitler and Hindenburg as they watched from the balcony of the Reich Chancellery on the evening of 30 January 1933, was meant to signify that Hitler's appointment to the Chancellorship was no normal change of government. The spectacular celebration of Hitler's personal triumph and the 'victory' of his Movement was intended to suggest to the German people that they were witnessing a historic break with the past, the dawn of a new era. And already voices could be heard saying that Hitler would never relinquish the power he had won.

Outside the Nazi Party and its supporters, however, Hitler's elevation to the Chancellorship did nothing overnight to alter existing perceptions. Among those still holding to the Catholic parties, many doubtless shared the sentiments expressed in a leading article on 31 January 1933 in the *Regensburger Anzeiger*, a newspaper aligned to the Bavarian People's Party, that a Hitler Chancellorship marked a 'leap into the dark'. On the Left, especially, the view prevailed that Hitler would be no more than the 'front-man' for a cabinet of reactionaries dominated by Hugenberg, von Papen, and their friends, the direct representatives of Germany's ruling classes. And it was widely presumed that the heterogeneous nature of the catch-all Nazi programme promising all things to all men would quickly result in a far-reaching disillusionment of the NSDAP's mass base and a rapid drop in Hitler's popularity.[1] Away from the clamour of the big city celebrations of the 'seizure of power', Hitler's appointment to the Chancellorship initially did nothing, in those parts of provincial Germany which the Nazis had far from won over by 1933, to break through the wall of profound apathy and scepticism created by the miseries of the Depression and apparently ceaseless and fruitless electioneering and party-political wrangling. Pessimism generally prevailed here: many thought that there was little chance of Hitler bringing about any improvement, some 'that Hitler would not even be as long in office as his predecessor General von Schleicher'.

[. . .]

It was not simply that Hitler now had the prestige of the Chancellorship behind him. Already Nazi propaganda was working to create the impression that Hitler was a new and different kind of Reich Chancellor. And the campaign for the Reichstag election on 5 March provided ample opportunity to bestow fresh attributes on the Chancellor of the 'national uprising', and to emphasize his personal leadership 'genius'. In the 'revised' campaign conditions of early 1933, with the Nazis rampant and their ideological enemies subjected to brutal repression, the 'rally' style of the big city was now extended to the countryside in greater measure than ever before. Hitler's Chancellorship was trumpeted as no mere change of government, but as a 'world-historical event'. Nazi speakers did not tire of portraying Hitler as the last bulwark against the threat of communism, the final hope of peasants and workers, the protector of the Christian religion. Above all, Nazi propaganda appealed to voters to give the new Chancellor a chance: 'Hitler has not betrayed us up to now. We must first give the man time to work.'[2]

[. . .]

[T]he draconian measures adopted by the government – suspension at one fell swoop of the most basic civil rights of the Reich Constitution through the promulgation of an 'Emergency Decree for the Protection of People and State' against 'communist acts of force', and massive police raids rounding up thousands of communists in Prussia in the night of 28 February – encountered little criticism and no small degree of favour among the majority of ordinary, middle-class Germans and among the rural population. The attack on the communists was seen, according to one fairly typical report as 'a long-necessary act of liberation'.[3] The far-reaching significance of the Reichstag Fire 'Emergency Decree' was recognized only by few. Rather, the welcome it received gave Hitler's popularity a new boost on the eve of the election.[4]

Although there were already not a few, even apart from the Left, who were prepared to believe that the Nazis had themselves set fire to the Reichstag, the majority of the population undoubtedly supported the police actions against the

KPD, which now seemed to be tackling 'in the national interest' the problem of the proclaimed 'red danger' at its root.[5] Clearly Hitler stood to gain massively from the degree of anti-communist paranoia which extended way beyond the ranks of the Nazi Movement and, while not created, was doubtless furthered by the openly propagated pro-Moscow stance of the KPD. Hitler had said in opposition that heads would roll in the event of a Nazi take-over of power. Now, in acting with utter ruthlessness, he could be portrayed as the eliminator of a national danger. It was not the last time that brutality and repression in the interests of 'peace and order' would increase Hitler's popularity and function as an important component of the 'Führer myth'.

Nevertheless, in the March election of 1933, held against the back-cloth of the assault on the Left and in the heady atmosphere of what Nazi propaganda styled as the 'national uprising', fewer than half of the voters cast their ballot for the NSDAP. The Nazis had still been unable to make a decisive breakthrough in the electoral blocks of the Left and of political Catholicism. At the same time, however, assisted by a record turn-out, they had garnered a higher proportion of the vote than any other party had ever managed during the Weimar era.

[. . .]

Hitler still had far to go before he won over the majority of those who had not supported him in March 1933. But the birthday celebrations of April 1933 were a step on the way. In the six weeks since the elections, Hitler's image had already been significantly transformed. He was no longer the Party leader opposing the State and polarizing opinion, but rather – according to the now more or less uniform Party propaganda – the symbol of unity of the German people, even for many who continued to see in the NSDAP a Party of particular interests.

During the next few months further important steps were taken in the process of eliminating all possible alternative sources of political allegiance which might counter loyalty to Hitler. The disbanding of the remaining parties removed any lingering possibility of open organizational counter-loyalty. This found its symbolic expression in the extension of the Nazi Party's 'Hitler Greeting' into, increasingly, the standard greeting for all Germans. The simple but constantly employed 'Heil Hitler' became the outward profession of support for the regime – whether given freely, resignedly, or under pressure – while its refusal was a clear sign of political nonconformity. The 'German Greeting', as it was now styled, was both propaganda and coercion: anyone not wishing to be seen as a political outsider, with all the consequences which might follow, was ready to offer at least a half-hearted 'Heil Hitler'; and the sea of outstretched arms at every big rally provided an impressive outward witness to the professed unity of Leader and People.

[. . .]

The eulogy had a hollow ring to it for the many who had yet to see anything of the great benefits of the Third Reich which Nazi propaganda was daily trumpeting. It had become obvious to broad sections of the population during the winter of 1933–4 that the social and economic improvements which had actually taken place scarcely matched the grand claims the Nazis were making. The progress of the Nazi 'economic miracle' was still extremely limited, a fact which was bound up for many with the first disappointments about unfulfilled promises made before the 'seizure of power'. The enthusiasm of summer 1933 about the prospects for the economy had faded. Among the peasantry, sections of the lower middle class, and not least among industrial workers and the millions still unemployed, the feeling grew that the economic reality of the Third Reich bore scant relation to its propaganda.

Reports from all parts of the Reich testify to a significant deterioration in mood – no doubt contributing to the more restrained tone of the celebrations for the Führer's birthday – during the first half of 1934.[6] This was not without effect on attitudes towards Hitler himself. A *Sopade* [Note: the exiled executive of the SPD (German Social Democratic Party) during the Nazi years] report from south-west Germany in late spring 1934 claimed that 'criticism was no longer stopping at Hitler'; one from Saxony declared that the mood was also directed against 'the Führer, the unnatural glorification of whom is declining'; and the Berlin agent concurred that while criticism up to around four weeks earlier had been along the lines that Hitler meant well but had bad counsellors, he was now also coming under attack, and that was the case too in the Labour Service camps and within the SA, where it was gradually being realized 'that Hitler does not want any socialism'.[7] The *Sopade* analysts acknowledged, nevertheless, that their reports did not speak in unison. Other accounts they received still pointed to extraordinary popular adulation of Hitler, extending into the working class.[8] According to a Berlin reporter, Hitler was credited with honest intentions, and it was said he could do nothing for the maladministration of his underlings. This same account accepted that this attitude was only in part a result of the 'systematic Führer propaganda'; it had also to be attributed to the undoubted impact of Hitler's personality on 'ordinary people', 'and Hitler still possesses a great deal of personal trust in particular among the workers'.[9]

As such comments suggest, continuing discontent about social and economic conditions – much of it presumably expressed, not least in the working class, by those who had never wholly been won over to Nazism – was perfectly compatible with recognition of other 'achievements' of the regime, in particular those attributed to Hitler himself. Everyday grievances based on material dissatisfaction, important though they were in forming popular attitudes, by no means necessarily signified total rejection of Nazism or of the Führer, who stood in a sense above and outside the 'system', detached from the 'everyday' sphere of dismal 'normality'.[10] Though by no means unscathed in the light of gathering economic discontent, it seems clear that the 'Hitler myth' could transcend daily material worries and function as a compensatory mechanism. While the euphoria unleashed by a Hitler speech or by a major foreign policy success was of short duration before giving way again to the greyness of everyday life, there was a lasting residual feeling, evidently shared by many, that, whatever the temporary hardships and cares, the Führer was in control and knew the way forward to better times. Unquestionably, therefore, the 'Hitler myth' had a crucial stabilizing and integrating function within the Nazi system in defusing discontent and offering a sphere of 'national' policy and 'national' interest lying outside the normality of 'daily life' which drew even critics of the Regime to support of major aspects of Nazi rule.

[. . .]

Two events in summer 1934 contributed decisively to the further development of the Führer image: the suppression of the so-called 'Röhm Putsch'; and the merging of the offices of Chancellor and Reich President following the death of Hindenburg on 2 August 1934. The remarkable popular reactions to the bloody massacre, ordered by Hitler himself, of the SA leadership on 30 June 1934, [. . .] far from damaging his prestige brought a sharp increase in his popularity [. . .] . The second major impetus to the development of Hitler's image came from Hindenburg's death, which provided the propaganda machine with a further opportunity to exploit the great prestige of the deceased in the interests of the Nazi regime. Press reportage of Hindenburg's death and funeral spoke of him as the 'national myth of the German people', the 'true Ekkehart', the 'monumental memorial from the distant past', whose greatest service had been to pave the way on 30 January 1933 for the 'young National Socialist Movement'.[11]

[. . .]

In 1934–5 the Führer cult also began increasingly to determine the constitutional doctrine of the Third Reich. Leading experts on constitutional law such as Huber, Forsthoff, and Koellreuther now formulated their contrived doctrines of the 'Führer State', legitimizing through mystical notions of the incarnation of the will of the people in the person of Hitler the omnipotence of the Führer and reducing the government to his mere advisory body.[12] As Hans Frank, head of the Nazi Lawyers' Association, put it a few years later: 'Constitutional Law in the Third Reich is the legal formulation of the historic will of the Führer, but the historic will of the Führer is not the fulfilment of legal preconditions for his activity.'[13] The 'Hitler myth', the personality cult surrounding the Führer, had by this time long since caught hold of prominent sections of the bourgeois intelligentsia and social elites, whose contribution to its legitimation – drawing on social standing and supposed intellectual 'gravitas' – was considerable.

The march into the Rhineland on 7 March, despite its risk successfully calling the bluff of the allies, put earlier foreign policy triumphs (e.g. the Saar plebiscite) in the shade. Another piece of 'Versailles', the national trauma, had been removed. Few bothered that it marked the burial of the spirit of collective security which Stresemann had ushered in at Locarno in 1925. The spectacular coup met with almost uniform acclaim and jubilation, and was again advanced – and largely received – as the outstanding achievement of *one* man.

A new wave of elemental adulation of the Führer swept through Germany, stimulated by the surprise dissolution of the Reichstag and the propaganda campaign for the 'election' on 29 March. Though the 'election' was that of a new Reichstag, the entire Party and the propaganda machine directed their fevered campaign at the Führer himself, and at producing a massive new demonstration of loyalty to emphasize the futility of opposition at home and the strength and unity of Germany to the outside world. The long arm of propaganda did not stop at the big city, but extended even into small villages. The alpine villages of Upper Bavaria had huge banners stretching across their streets carrying slogans such as: 'Only one man can pull it off: the Führer! Stay loyal to him!' Houses were decked with garlands of flowers, pictures of Hitler, and other forms of festive decoration. On election day itself, the inhabitants of the villages often marched together, accompanied by brass bands, to the polling station.[14] On 28 and 29 March (1936) the papers carried huge pictures of Hitler and his request for the support of every German in his 'struggle for a true peace.' Quotations from 'words of the Führer' littered the pages. Articles and illustrations let no one forget the Führer's achievement. 'Germany is working again', trumpeted one newspaper as the caption to a full-page illustration of a German worker and below him a motorway stretching into the distance: 'Everywhere hands are active in the common work! One people, one will, one deed! The German people has the Führer to thank for all that!'[15]

[. . .]

What was the effect on the man who was the object of such a daily torrent of adulation? In the 1920s, as we saw, Hitler's self-image was still quite detached from the already present excesses of the Führer cult. Even in the early years of the Third Reich itself, some of this reserve is still just perceptible. Despite the forceful egocentric intolerance towards any form of criticism or opposing opinion, which was a consistent feature of Hitler's character, he appears at least in the first years of power to have retained some distance from the personality cult built up around him. It could be argued that in the years 1933–5, Hitler still saw the cult constructed around his person largely as an essential device for fostering the integration not only of Party members, but of the entire people, and approved of it, while retaining some aloofness from the cult, as a vehicle for the 'stupefication of the masses.'

It is scarcely conceivable, however, that Hitler could have remained impervious to the extraordinary cult which had been created around him, and which was now coming increasingly to envelop him. When did Hitler fall victim himself to the 'Führer myth'? Much points to the heady weeks following the Rhineland triumph as the time when Hitler became a full believer in his own 'myth'. The argument gains support from the recollections of some contemporaries who could observe Hitler from close quarters at this time. Press Chief Otto Dietrich, for example, referred to the years 1935–6 as decisive in Hitler's development, marked by a noticeable change in Hitler's personal conduct, and the memoirs of former Gestapo chief Rudolf Diels point in the same direction.[16] Apart from such testimony, the changing language of his public speeches also suggests the shift in self-perception. Before March 1936 he seldom if ever spoke of himself in the pseudo-mystical, 'messianic', quasi-religious terms which Goebbels and others used. But from the time when, in his speech in Munich on 14 March 1936, he claimed that he walked 'with the certainty of a sleep-walker' along the path which 'Providence' had laid out for him, the mystical relationship between himself and 'Providence' was seldom absent from his major speeches, and the pseudo-religious symbolism and belief in his own infallibility became ingrained in his rhetoric.[17] The style and content of his speeches – the immense claims he now regularly made on himself, and increasingly on the German people – point clearly towards a change in Hitler's self-image. At the Reich Party Rally in 1936 he now spoke himself of a mystical unity between himself and the German people: 'That you have found me . . . among so many millions is the miracle of our time! And that I have found you, that is Germany's fortune!'[18] All the signs are that this was no longer pure rhetoric. Hitler himself was a convert to the 'Führer myth', himself a 'victim' of Nazi propaganda. If one wants to put a date on the conversion, then perhaps 7 March, the date of the successful march into the Rhineland, comes as close as any. What seems certain is that the day on which Hitler started to believe in his own 'myth' marked in a sense the beginning of the end of the Third Reich.[19]

Notes

1　See GStA, MA 106670, RPvOB, 6 Feb. 1933.

2　GStA, MA 106677, RPvOF/MF, 5 Mar. 1933; see also GStA, MA 106682, RPvS, 4 Mar. 1933.

3　See GStA, MA 106672, RPvNB/OP, 5 Mar. 1933, where it was expressly claimed that 'the drastic action against the troublemakers' had satisfied the 'alarmed population' and resulted in a rise in the Nazi vote at the election.

4　For a graphic indication of the fever-pitch anti-communism after the Reichstag Fire, see the editorial of the *Miesbacher Anzeiger* of 2 Mar. 1933, cited in I. Kershaw, *Popular Opinion and Political Dissent in the Third Reich*, Oxford, 1983, 117–18. See also J. Noakes and G. Pridham, eds., *Documents on Nazism*, London, 1974, 174–5.

5　*Völkischer Beobachter*, north German edn, 21 Apr. 1933, and see E. K. Bramsted, *Goebbels and National Socialist Propaganda 1925–1945*, Michigan, 1965, pp 204–6.

6　See the reports, particularly the sections dealing with the economy, for February and April 1934 from Gestapo offices throughout Prussia in ZStA Potsdam, RMdI 25721, 26060. And for Havana, see Kershaw, *Popular Opinion*, pp 46ff, 75ff, 120ff. See also *DBS*, i 9–14, 99–122, reports from 17 May 1934 and 26 June 1934.

7　*DBS*, i 101–2, 26 June 1934.

8　Ibid, i 100–1, 26 June 1934.

9　Ibid, i 10–11, 17 May 1934. See also L. Eiber, *Arbeiter unter der NS-Herrschaft. Textil- und Porzellanarbeiter im nordöstlichen Oberfranken 1933–1939*, Munich, 1979, p 110, and T. W. Mason, *Arbeiterklasse und Volksgemeinschaft*, Opladen, 1975, pp 123, 149 n 233.

10　I have argued this point at greater length in my essay 'Alltägliches und Außeralltägliches: ihre Bedeutung für die Volksmeinung 1933–1939', in D. Peukert and J. Reulecke, eds., *Die Reihen fast geschlossen. Beiträge zur Geschichte des Alltags unterm Nationalsozialismus*, Wuppertal, 1980, 273–92.

11　*Muenchener Neueste Nachrichten,* 3 Aug 1934; J. C. Fest, *Hitler: Eine Biographie*, Ullstein edn., Frankfurt a.M., 1976, 651.

12　See ibid., 146; *Der Nationalsozialismus. Dokumente 1933–1945*, ed. W. Hofer, Frankfurt a.M., 1957, 82–3; *DBS*, v. 525–31.

13　Noakes and Pridham, 254.

14　*Münchner Neueste Nachrichten*, 29 Mar. 1936.

15　Ibid., 28 Mar. 1936.

16　O. Dietrich, *Zwölf Jahre mit Hitler*, Cologne/Munich, n.d. (1955), 44–5; R. Diels, *Lucifer ante Portas. Zwischen Severing und Heydrich*, Zurich, n.d. (1949), 48–50, 58–9, 61–2.

17　M. Domarus, ed., *Hitler. Reden und Proklamationen 1932–1945*, Wiesbaden, 1973, 606, and see also pp 16–19.

18　*Der Parteitag der Ehre vom 8. bis 14. September 1936*, Munich, 1936, 246–7.

19　See Fest, 713–14; A. Bullock, *Hitler. A Study in Tyranny*, Pelican edn., Harmondsworth, 1962, 375.

Chapter 29

Macgregor Knox

FASCIST REGIME AND TERRITORIAL EXPANSION: ITALY AND GERMANY

■ from **CONQUEST, DOMESTIC AND FOREIGN, IN FASCIST ITALY AND NAZI GERMANY**, *Journal of Modern History*, 56 (1984), pp. 43–5, 46–57

Territorial expansion constituted a fundamental similarity between the Nazi and the Italian fascist regimes. Knox has pinpointed the origins of this common propensity in comparable ideological traditions of indigenous nationalism (myth of the nation, glorification of national history, cult of violence and war, etc.) and in the personal visions of the two leaders, as well as in the idiosyncratic circumstances of the interwar period in the two countries. In his view, the two regimes' emphasis on territorial expansion combined a similar ideological propensity with the desire for 'conquering' (i.e. transforming in a radical direction) the domestic system. In this sense, expansion served the need to speed up the process of domestic consolidation and to free the two leaders from the last remaining vestiges of the old order.

MUSSOLINI'S TRANSITION TO ACTIVE expansionism aroused less resistance than Hitler's; the Duce's chosen victims seemed less capable of defending themselves. Nevertheless, the decision to attack Ethiopia has found a variety of interpretations. Determinists have argued that the Depression and consequent need to reflate the economy prompted expansion. Another popular claim is that Mussolini sought to 'relaunch' a flagging regime and cement the loyalty of the younger generation by foreign adventure.[1] Renzo De Felice, while rejecting the economic argument and demonstrating convincingly that the regime was at the height of its popularity, has suggested that failure in transforming society at home impelled Mussolini into previously unsought imperial adventure. The decision for war, in all these views, was a choice for second best, and Ethiopia no more than a target of opportunity that German revival impelled the frightened French to offer Mussolini. Finally, Jens Petersen has argued that what happened between 1932 and 1935 was that international alignments at last permitted Mussolini to implement a long-held expansionist program. German rearmament and French fear (to which one must add the Depression's severing of financial dependence on Washington) at last gave Mussolini his chance.[2]

Mussolini's repeated, almost monotonous references to the goal of empire from 1918 on support the last interpretation. But it was more than a foreign policy program that moved him to action. War, Mussolini insisted both as Socialist and as Fascist, was linked to revolution. Only war, whose uncivilizing effects he well remembered, could help break the old society's resistance to the new paganism, make Italy the 'militarist' nation he demanded,[3] and further undermine monarchy and Church. Foreign adventure was also internal forward policy, not the mere 'social-imperialist' defense of order at home characteristic of more staid authoritarian regimes.

The choice of Ethiopia was long overdetermined. Fascism, as part of its historic mission, had to avenge Adua, the humiliating defeat of its great precursor Crispi. Mussolini's interest in 'profiting from an eventual dissolution of the Ethiopian empire' dated from at least 1925, and concrete planning began in November 1932.[4] Once it had conquered East Africa, the 'prisoner of the Mediterranean' might hope to lever the British out of the Sudan and Egypt.[5] Finally and most importantly, Ethiopia was the one enemy Mussolini's flankers and the European powers would reluctantly permit him to conquer. The flankers also felt the shame of Adua, and assumed that the Italy that had stood up to Austria-Hungary could defeat a land-locked, half-tribal, half-feudal kingdom with perhaps a quarter of Italy's population. And the other powers were ultimately disposed to tolerate an Italian aggression outside Europe that did not directly touch their own possessions.

Mussolini nevertheless faced and overcame major obstacles in launching his Fascist imperial war. Internally, he had to sap the tenacious resistance of the army. That hierarchy remained wedded to its Alpine priorities and dubious of the advantages of empire; the Austrian crisis of July 1934 emphasized the need to keep Italy's guard up in Europe. Both Marshal Pietro Badoglio, the chief of the vestigial interservice general staff, and General Federico Baistrocchi, the dynamic army chief of staff and undersecretary for war, were initially hostile to the project, which originated in the colonial ministry under Mussolini's aegis.[6] Once he had converted Baistrocchi and partially neutralized Badoglio by mobilizing navy and air force support, Mussolini still faced the king and a conservative Establishment that abhorred risk. The Duce complained in 1936 that the monarch bore no responsibility for victory: '*He* didn't want to go – I had to force him.' First-hand evidence of the king's attitude is lacking, but Mussolini's June 1935 complaint to his field commander in East Africa about 'grumblers and defeatists – more on high than below' suggests that king and Establishment were indeed recalcitrant.[7] Even Fascists wavered. The ex-secretary of the Party, Giovanni Giuriati, allegedly told the king that Mussolini's policy would lead to 'national disaster.' And Britain's apparent intention of fighting Mussolini in the Mediterranean if he went ahead produced warnings from Badoglio and the military of 'a disaster that would reduce us to a Balkan level.'[8] Even the Duce's son-in-law and future foreign minister, Galeazzo Ciano, temporarily gave way to despair after the League imposed sanctions.[9] Only the Church, which looked forward to civilizing the heretical Copts, and much of the public, which believed the regime's tales of Ethiopian and British provocations, and of an East African el

Dorado, remained stalwart for aggression. Much later, Mussolini complained that many, many important people came to him and said, 'You have already done great things. Now [you should] pull in your oars.'[10]

[. . .]

Victory indeed had consequences. Mussolini, as 'founder of the empire,' could now impose on his subordinates, without being laughed at, the reverence he aspired to. His subsequent policy – Spanish intervention, the racial laws, the campaign against the bourgeoisie, the annexation of Albania, and the plunge into war in 1940 – was only possible thanks to domestic reinforcement through African victory, and the license for aggression which increasing German preponderance brought. Far from representing a falling off from the famous 'realism' that his propagandists and some historians have ascribed to him, Mussolini's later policies were simply ever more risky attempts to implement his program within his own lifetime. It was his mission to remake 'the character of the Italians through combat.' Revelation of a long-held vision, not the 'involution' of personality and will that some scholars have discerned, presided over Italy's road to the Second World War.[11]

African victory naturally did not remove all obstacles. Mussolini put the League of Nations's sanctions to good use in convincing the great economic interests that autarky – the breaking of Italy's remaining ties to the world market – was the only feasible course. And although autarky proved 'too tight a shirt' for the export industries, the increasing stream of armaments contracts helped ease the pain. Italy's massive dependence on imported energy and strategic raw materials made genuine autarky impractical, but furnished yet another argument for expansion. In both domestic and foreign policy, Mussolini moved with increasing self-confidence. He plunged into Spain apparently without consulting the king; when Baistrocchi objected and Badoglio grumbled, he sacked one and ordered the other to show public approval. Spain, however, provided anything but the expected easy victories, and the disaster at Guadalajara in March 1937 allowed the king to level veiled reproaches at Mussolini.[12] But the humiliation passed with the summer 1937 victories in the Basque country. By early 1938, the German example – Hitler made himself commander-in-chief of the armed forces on February 4 – prompted emulation. The Party, presumably on Mussolini's secret instructions, pushed through Chamber and Senate a bill creating both Duce and king 'First Marshals of the Empire.' This demotion of the monarch to Mussolini's level produced wrath at the Quirinal.[13] Mussolini also promulgated in 1937–38 laws that formally wrote the Party into the constitution, and in January 1939 the Chamber of Deputies became the Chamber of Fasci and Corporations. Only the Senate remained as a relic of the liberal-monarchical past, and it owed its considerable staying power to its life tenure and royal appointment.

Mussolini and his entourage began looking forward with increasing anticipation to the removal of the king, perhaps even as early as the end of the Spanish war. It was only right, the Duce commented cynically in 1936 when exempting the king's foreign assets from the nationalization that League sanctions made necessary, to leave him 'a well-protected nest-egg.' The fate of monarchies was frequently an uncertain one.[14] The Duce's private remarks suggest an ever-growing resolve to smash the internal and foreign-policy restraints the monarchy still imposed.[15]

The military, like the monarchy, also failed to show the necessary enthusiasm for Mussolini's increasing risk-taking. Although he had achieved de facto direction of the armed forces during the Ethiopian war, Mussolini remained a prisoner of their institutional structures. Major surgery, such as the 1933 and 1936–37 plans for a tri-service defense ministry that would restrict the services' autonomy, was impossible without disturbing the interservice balance and tampering with the monarchy's prerogatives.[16] Both the rigidity of service promotion procedures and the caste resistance of the senior generals inhibited the injection of fresh and necessarily Fascist blood into the higher reaches of the military. In strategic planning, Mussolini had his way for a while. In 1937 and 1938 the army, under Baistrocchi's successor Pariani, made grandiose plans, with navy cooperation, for an assault on Egypt from Cyrenaica. But after the shock of Munich Badoglio reasserted his prerogatives, and killed the plan. If France were also hostile, Italy was too weak to seize Suez. Badoglio's refusal to permit planning 'that d(id) not correspond to the situation' meant that when the situation changed, Italy had no plans. In the event, Mussolini had to trick his generals and admirals into war in 1940 with the assurance that they need not fight.[17]

Less dangerous for Mussolini than the recalcitrance of monarchy and military, but still inconvenient, was the Church. The Vatican, despite its compromise with Mussolini, made difficulties about what Pius XI denounced as 'pagan state idolatry.' Naturally, the Church overwhelmingly supported the Ethiopian campaign and Mussolini's allegedly anti-Bolshevist intervention in Spain. It evinced qualified approval even of the annexation of Albania.[18] But when Mussolini's concern with the 'purity of the race' came home from the colonies, and in deference to the Germans attacked Jews as well as blacks, the Vatican became uneasy. The Church was not averse to religious discrimination, and avant-garde Jesuits urged segregation of the Jews, but the pseudo-biological provisions of the 1938 racial laws included Catholic converts.[19] At the same time, the German alliance and the increasing risk of general war added to the Church's reservations about the regime. War – apart from the predictable loss of life and destruction – would either result in Axis defeat, endangering Italy and the Lateran pacts, or a victory that would bring pagan racist revolution in earnest. Hence the papal protests and peace messages against which Mussolini increasingly railed between 1938 and 1940.

The upper middle classes, too, began to distance themselves subtly from Mussolini as he moved to implement his vision. It required the shock of defeat to consummate the divorce Italian-style between the regime and what Mussolini described as a bourgeoisie riddled with 'cowardice, laziness, [and] love of the quiet life.' But the origins of that divorce lay in Mussolini's post-Ethiopian activism both at home and abroad. Italy's forced 'non-belligerence' in September 1939 was thus not an example of Mussolini's purported realism, but rather the Establishment's last victory over the regime's expansionism. The pope and Badoglio, Ciano and the diplomats, industrialists and king, all coalesced to hold back Mussolini and the Party enthusiasts. But the victory was a Pyrrhic one. Mussolini remained in control of the machinery of government. Only a coup, which the king briefly contemplated in March 1940, could remove him. When the king failed to move, the members of the quasi-coalition of 'moderates' remained prisoners of their separate bargains with the Duce, and of their own cautiously expansionist appetites.

The great German victories in the West in May 1940 enabled Mussolini to activate that expansionism with the promise that Italy need not fight. He himself sought instead a swift but decisive conflict that would free Italy from its Mediterranean imprisonment and give him the prestige to crush his flankers. That was why the regime insisted – contrary to common sense, which dictated the mobilization of all strands of Italian nationalism – that this war was '*la guerra fascista*.' It was a war of internal as well as foreign conquest. And when Italy's independent war ended in the winter of 1940–41 in disaster at Taranto, in the Albanian mountains, and in the sands of Beda Fomm, Mussolini's revolutionary project died with it.[20] The regime survived until the 'moderate' Fascists revolted against Mussolini and the king and generals overthrew him in July 1943. But the crushing defeats of 1940 and Italy's humiliating new status as first satellite of the Reich had broken the prestige Mussolini needed for internal transformation. In the end, the flankers, emboldened in defeat, repudiated the regime in the name of the same Italian nationalism, and interests, that had once led them to support it.

Hitler fortunately also failed, but his failure was less humiliating and infinitely bloodier than Mussolini's. Hitler had written in *Mein Kampf* that Germany would 'either be a world power, or cease to be.' He almost achieved the first, and barely failed at the second. His starting point in blending revolution and territorial expansion was his discovery in November 1937 that Germany's growing if foreseeably temporary preponderance in armaments had not convinced Blomberg, Fritsch, and Neurath that Germany could, should, and must fight. Their lamentable lack of faith emerged from the alarmed protestations at the November 5, 1937 Reich Chancellory conference at which Hitler revealed for the first time that he intended to seize Austria and smash Czechoslovakia, situation permitting, as early as 1938. Fritsch and his subordinate Beck did not merely object to the risks involved, but above all to Hitler's implicit claim to be Germany's sole font of strategic leadership. Regrettably, the first civilian since Bismarck to impose on the army both civilian control, and Clausewitz's heretical notion that war was a tool of politics, turned out to be Hitler.

The dictator confirmed his November 5 prediction of war two weeks later in a speech to Party officials: new tasks awaited Germany, 'for the living space of our Volk is too narrow.' And he again stressed the identity of foreign and domestic policy. Just as the National Socialists had 'led the nation upwards' internally, so they would achieve for Germany abroad 'the same rights to existence as other nations.'[21] Two months later, he dismissed both Blomberg and Fritsch, and for good measure, Neurath and the ambassador to Italy, Hassell. Blomberg's mesalliance with an ex-prostitute, and damaging though bogus SS charges of homosexuality against Fritsch allowed Hitler to dispense with both, and take over Blomberg's position in person. He had breached the Establishment's last citadel, strategy and foreign policy.

In the aftermath of the February 4 coup, many high officers seethed with indignation at the preposterous accusations against Fritsch, but foreign policy came to Hitler's aid. Political developments in Austria allowed him to distract the army with a job to do: the Anschluss. The resulting personal triumph allowed him to brush off Army pressure for Fritsch's reinstatement, while the public, consulted in the first plebiscite since the Rhineland coup, returned an overwhelming vote of confidence. Foreign policy had first demanded domestic upheaval, then blessed it with success.

But obstacles remained. The credulous acceptance of the Führer's mission and quasi-supernatural gifts by Keitel and Jodl was not yet general in the officer corps. Throughout the summer, as preparations to attack Germany's next victim, Czechoslovakia, went forward, Hitler gave vent to a stream of complaints against the generals. Most of them 'had rejected (his leadership), and continued to reject it.' They 'as yet did not understand the meaning of the new age,' and were far inferior in élan to his trusty Gauleiters. Delays in the army-supervised construction of the *Westwall* fortifications led him to threaten to turn the job over to Martin Bormann, 'whom he could at least rely on.'[22] Fritz Todt, another Party luminary, actually got the job. And several months later, Hitler apparently intimidated a reluctant Admiral Raeder with the not entirely incredible threat that if further delays slowed the gargantuan naval program, he would turn procurement over to Todt.[23]

The real issue of the summer, however, was what Hitler characterized as '*Angst* and cowardice in the army': the refusal of Beck and the hesitation of other senior officers to accept his strategic leadership and the risks the Czech enterprise would involve. Fortunately for Hitler, Beck was relatively isolated both in his high assessment of the risk of general war and his dogged insistence on the coresponsibility of the army chief of staff for strategic decisions. Nevertheless, Hitler felt obliged to harangue his top commanders twice in mid-August to counteract Beck's influence and steel their nerves for the coming struggle. Conveniently for Hitler, Beck cracked under the strain of isolation and resigned. His successor Halder plotted in secret, but made no attempt at open contradiction.[24] Even more fortunately for Hitler, the West surrendered Czechoslovakia without fighting. Bloodless triumph cut the ground from under doubters and plotters. Munich also raised Hitler higher in the public esteem than ever before – the German people had nationalist triumph without war.[25]

The crisis had other effects besides strengthening Hitler internally. He had passionately sought war against the Czechs, both to steel the young, and to test the newly minted Wehrmacht. Only at the last moment had he accepted a negotiated surrender of the Sudetenland. On the evening of September 27, Hitler had watched motorized units on their way to the border roll through central Berlin, as he had ordered. The public stood, silent and sullen; no cheers or 'German greetings' honored the Führer's appearance at the Reich Chancellery balcony.[26] The delirious scenes of August 1914 did not repeat themselves. After the euphoria of the Anschluss, this may have come as a shock. The unfeigned enthusiasm of German crowds for Chamberlain added insult to injury.[27] Hence Hitler's post-Munich rage at the British ('we will no longer tolerate the supervision of governesses') and his diatribe to German press representatives on November 10 demanding indoctrination that would 'free the Volk of doubts that make it unhappy' and inculcate '*fanatical* belief' in final victory. The nation must stand like 'formed-up troops' behind his decisions. The 'intellectual strata' – by which he meant those educated Germans, including officers, who still refused to accept him on faith – were unfortunately still necessary: 'otherwise one could exterminate them, or whatever.'[28]

Hitler could have been under no illusion that propaganda alone would consolidate internal unity behind him. As he harangued the press, the SS and police were supervising the cleanup of the debris from synagogues and Jewish shops burned out in the *Kristallnacht* pogrom. Hitler had inspired that action as a hint of things to come and as a salutary release for Party radicalism, but he was too shrewd a judge of public and elite opinion to associate with it openly. Generals were still heard to mutter about hanging 'this swine, Goebbels,' who was ostensibly responsible.[29] The time of the Jews was nevertheless coming, Hitler hinted in his January 30, 1939 Reichstag speech. That of the churches, he had said privately the previous August, had not yet come; he still had 'too many other problems.'[30]

Yet as his insistence on his cyclopean building program and his acceleration of the already breakneck pace of naval construction suggest, Hitler had already left the confines of the interwar German state far behind (symptomatically, Germany proper now became the '*Altreich*'). The immense Nazi eagle with a globe in its claws that Hitler ordered to crown his gigantic Berlin great hall was no mere ideological metaphor. Germany, he told a group of senior officers in early February 1939, was bound for world mastery; the triumphs of 1938 were not the end of the road but the beginning. Germany could best preserve the reputation and prestige acquired since 1933 by 'without letup exploiting every opportunity, however small, to move immediately towards a new success.'[31] He would tolerate no more 'warning memoranda' – an apparent reference to Beck's attempts to thwart him the previous summer. The alleged 'hothouse intellectualism' of the general staff since Schlieffen's day was outdated; he demanded 'believing officers' with 'trust and blind confidence.'[32]

The next major success, Hitler decided shortly after his bloodless absorption of rump Czechoslovakia in mid-March, must come in war against Poland. The origins of that war, which contrary to Hitler's intentions eventually became a world war, have inevitably provoked vast controversy. But until Tim Mason's work on the regime's relationship with the industrial workers, few scholars have had much to say about the internal ramifications of Hitler's decision. Mason has opened the question up by suggesting that Hitler took the plunge largely to escape the economic and political crisis rearmament had created. Conquest was 'an end in itself,' an improvised defensive 'flight forward' to escape intolerable domestic problems. The argument is not overly convincing.[33] Hitler had passionately wanted to fight in 1938, before the crisis reached full intensity. Politically, the regime was hardly on its last legs, either in the public or in the official mind. Mason's arguments for social and political crisis echo with the liturgy of the class struggle, but fail to address at least some of the evidence. The Ruhr miners, on whose efforts all of German industry relied, had a lower absentee rate in 1938 than in 1929, and later showed remarkable aptitude for supervising slave labor.[34]

As for the economic crisis, the evidence does not suggest that anyone except a narrow circle recognized it as such. Hitler merely argued, in prodding his generals toward war, that Germany could hold out only 'for a few more years.'[35] This was less a prediction of imminent catastrophe than a ploy to egg the reluctant onward by reminding them of difficulties that they had helped him create. Mason has also claimed in support of his thesis Hitler's remarks in both 1937 and 1939 that Germany faced a choice between expansion and degeneration. But those remarks were Hitler's standard justification, fixed since 1921–22, of the need for *Lebensraum*.[36] The economic strains of 1938–39 were for him no more than confirmation of that insight.

But the foremost difficulty with Mason's theory is that it isolates the events of 1938–39 from those preceding, and thus interprets as cause a phenomenon that is first of all effect. As Jost Dülffer has pointed out, the internal crisis was a consequence of Hitler's ever-increasing demands on the economy for armaments and for the immense building program.[37] Those demands led directly to war, with no need for an intervening deus ex machina in the form of internal crisis. Only war could transmute armaments into *Lebensraum* and world mastery. Only war, along with the new Reich's cyclopean monuments and incessant propaganda, could fully nationalize the masses. The 1938–39 crisis was above all a symptom of Hitler's offensive forward thrust towards war and revolution, rather than a driving force behind it.

As for the timing of the attack on Poland, three considerations were decisive. First and least important was the pact with Stalin, which secured Germany's rear and checkmated the remaining doubters among the generals. Second came a broader consideration, which Hitler repeatedly emphasized in his 1939 harangues to his military leaders. Rearmament had created a brief window of opportunity for Germany; after 1941–42 that window would close as the other powers caught up. Finally, of course, came Hitler's ever-growing obsession with the short time left to him personally; as he told his generals 'in all modesty' in November 1939, he alone possessed the nerve (*Entschlusskraft*) to fulfill Germany's mission.[38]

He lost no time putting war to use. Within the Reich, he secretly ordered the killing of the congenitally ill and insane in state institutions. Poland offered an even greater opportunity to implement his internal programs for Germany – using Poles as 'laboratory rabbits.' As Heydrich crudely explained to the army, 'we want to spare the little people, but nobility, clergy, and Jews must be killed.'[39] The generals recoiled in pious horror, then sheepishly yielded responsibility for the occupied territories.

The generals did make a brief stand on the sole issue they could not evade: Hitler's demand, made immediately after Poland's collapse, for an immediate offensive to smash the French and British. The military's resistance, which included yet another hesitant Putsch conspiracy in which Halder again took fleeting interest, was the last twitch of the organized German Establishment. It was short-lived. This time, no one dared openly question Hitler's strategic judgment as Beck had done; instead, the generals took refuge in technical arguments that inevitably lost force as army readiness improved and French ineptitude and de-moralization became apparent. Hitler's tirades terrorized Brauchitsch and Halder, and the repeated weather postponements of the attack allowed the generals to prepare it with even more of the thoroughness that was their trademark. The pathetic April 1940 showing of the British and French in Norway did the rest. When army and Luftwaffe crossed the western borders on May 10, the doubters had long fallen silent or joined the ranks of the converted.

In mid-January, even before the Wehrmacht rolled, Hitler had made clear to some of his associates the internal consequences of victory: 'The war is in this respect, as in many other matters, a favorable opportunity to dispose of it (the church question) root and branch.' In the ancient world entire peoples had been liquidated, and the Soviet Union was setting the example in the present. But the old German 'proclivity for mysticism' still thwarted him:

> If he did nothing now against the rebellious parsons, then it was not least
> out of concern for the Wehrmacht. There they ran to the field chaplains,

and a trooper who was brave with the good Lord was always more useful to him than one who was cowardly without Him. But here the indoctrination of the SS, which was now proving in war that ideologically schooled troops could be brave even without the Lord, would outline the necessary development.[40]

In conversation with Rosenberg, his religion expert, Hitler foresaw the possibility of smashing the churches by force ('ein harter machtpolitischer Eingriff') – but this could only take place when Germany was 'fully independent internationally'; 'otherwise the resulting blaze of internal political controversy could cost us our existence.'[41]

The Wehrmacht's crushing victory over France in May–June 1940 did not secure the full measure of freedom Hitler sought, but he now commanded the confidence of the military elite as never before or after. Symptomatic of that confidence was the pleasurable anticipation with which many senior generals prepared to tackle the next intriguing military problem Hitler set them: the destruction of the Soviet Union and the physical elimination of its 'Jewish-Bolshevik intelligentsia.' A few had doubts, but now took refuge not in plotting but in irony. Fedor von Bock, who had wanted to hang Goebbels in 1938, saw off a fellow army group commander with a cryptic 'Well, see you in Siberia.'[42] The public, sullen during the phony war, suddenly went 'berserk with success'; in the words of one jaundiced eyewitness, after the French collapse Germany's cafes were full of 'beer-soaked old pinochle players dividing up continents over their steins.'[43]

Nevertheless, Hitler still lacked the prestige to impose his vision in its entirety inside Germany. The attack on the Soviet Union was thus more than merely a response to Churchill's incomprehensible obduracy and to United States support for Britain, or another momentous step in Hitler's foreign policy *Stufenplan*. It was also a further mighty thrust towards the internal barbarization of Germany itself. *Lebensraum* and foreign policy 'freedom' would enable him at last to crush that 'reptile,' the churches.[44] The war of racial annihilation in the East would harden German youth to destroy the old society at home, while the lavish rewards of victory would still whatever unquiet consciences remained.

But even while the Wehrmacht struck deep into Russia, the Bishop of Münster, Count Galen, raised his voice publicly against the euthanasia program, and the regime had to suspend it. Hitler raged in private. This, too, would appear on the churches' final bill. He had, he noted privately in October 1941, also had to put up with the Jews for a long time; now, though he left it unsaid, extermination had begun.[45]

That last foundation of his program was indeed all that remained once the Wehrmacht failed to take Moscow in November–December 1941. In Jodl's words, 'long before anyone else in the world, Hitler suspected or knew that the war was lost,' and that suspicion drove him to give the Final Solution an ever higher priority, a priority that soon eclipsed the fighting of the war itself.[46] Internally, SS and Party vied in radicalism, while furtive half-knowledge of Germany's Eastern crimes and of coming retribution bound the public to the regime to the end. What remained of the Establishment had lost in 1938–40 all capacity to put the brakes on Hitler. The final despairing gesture of some of its members, the botched bomb plot of July 20,

1944, if anything strengthened the regime. Barbarous revenge ended the history of Prussia, while miraculous survival fleetingly refurbished Hitler's defeat-tarnished charisma.[47] Hitler's revolution, unlike that of Mussolini, had at least made itself irreversible from within. And the temporary allies who met across the rubble of Greater Germany could not restore Bismarck's Reich, even had they wished it.

Notes

1   Franco Catalano, *L'economia italiana di guerra* (Milan, 1969), 7; Giorgio Rochat, *Militari e politici nella preparazione della campagna d'Etiopia* (Milan, 1971), 105–7.

2   R. De Felice, *Mussolini il fascista*, (Milan, 1966), 359; *Mussolini il duce*, 1 (Milan 1974): 179, 466–7; Petersen, 'Die Aussenpolitik des faschistischen Italien als historiographisches Problem,' *Vierteljahrshefte für Zeitgeschichte* (VfZG), 22 (1974): 417–57.

3   *Opera Omnia di Benito Mussolini*, ed. by E. and D. Susmel (Florence, 1951–62 – henceforward *OO*), 26: 308 (August 24, 1934) (the 'discorso del carro armato').

4   See Rochat, *Militari e politici*, 26–33.

5   Pompeo Aloisi, *Journal (25 juillet 1932–14 juin 1936)* (Paris, 1957), 382 (May 8, 1936).

6   For details, Rochat, *Militari e politici*, Chaps. 1, 2.

7   Luigi Federzoni, *L'Italia di ieri per la storia di domani* (Milan, 1967), 233 (also Attilio Tamaro, *Venti anni di storia* (Rome, 1953–54), 3: 217, note 98a); *OO*, 42: 107 (June 26, 1935).

8   Badoglio to Mussolini, September 1935, in Rochat, *Militari e politici*, 229.

9   Alessandro Lessona, *Memorie* (Florence, 1958), 239–40.

10 *OO*, 44: 325 (April 17, 1943).

11 Mussolini's words: Galeazzo Ciano, *Diario 1937–1943* (Milan, 1980), November 13, 1937. For the involution thesis, which resembles the folk wisdom of the day ('. . . se dopo l'Etiopia, si fosse fermato. . . .'), De Felice, *Mussolini il duce*, 2, Chap. 3.

12 M. Knox, *Mussolini Unleashed* (Cambridge, 1982), 30.

13 De Felice, 'Mussolini e Vittorio Emanuele III Primi Marescialli dell'Impero,' in University degli Studi di Messina, *Scritti in onore di Vittorio De Caprariis* (Rome, n.d.), 347–68.

14 De Felice, *Mussolini il duce*, 2 (Milan 1981): 16 (in general, 14–21).

15 See particularly ibid., 40, and Giuseppe Bottai, *Diario 1935–1944*, ed. Giordano Bruno Guerri (Milan, 1982), entries for June 23, July 12, and June 13, 1938.

16 Knox, *Mussolini Unleashed*, 17–18.

17 Ibid., 18–19, 58, 119–23.

18 Ibid., 11.

19 See De Felice, *Storia degli ebrei italiani sotto il fascismo* (Turin, rev. ed. 972), 204–5, 286–87.

20 Knox, *Mussolini Unleashed*, Chaps. 3 and 6, and Conclusion.

21 M. Domarus, *Hitler: Reden und Proclamationen*, 2 vols (Wiesbaden 1973), 760 (November 21, 1937).

22 G. Engel, *Heeresadjutant bei Hitler* (Stuttgart, 1974), 20, 26, 32 (April 20, June 25, April 18, 1938).

23 J. Dülffer, *Weimar, Hitler und die Marine. Reichspolitik und Flottenbau 1920–1939* (Düsseldorf, 1973), 500–1, 512, 541.

24   K.-J. Müller, *Das Heer und Hitler Armee und nationalsozialistisches Regime 1933–1940* (Stuttgart, 1988), Chaps. 7, 8; Williamson Murray, *The Change in the European Balance of Power, 1938–39* (Princeton University Press, forthcoming), Chaps. 5–7.

25   Ian Kershaw, *Der Hitler-Mythos* (Stuttgart, 1980), 123.

26   See Telford Taylor, *Munich* (New York, 1979), 877.

27   See the editors' remarks in '*Es spricht der Führer*,' pp. 230–31.

28   'Governesses': speech at Saarbrücken, October 9, 1938, Domarus, *Hitler*, 956: the rest from H. von Kotze, H. Krausnick, eds., '*Es spricht der Führer*' (Gütersloh, 1966), 283, 281–2.

29   Fedor von Bock, quoted in Müller, *Heer*, 385.

30   Domarus, *Hitler*, 1058; Engel, *Heeresadjutant*, 30 (August 6, 1938).

31   All from J. Thies, *Architekt der Weltherrschaft. Die "Endziele" Hitlers*, (Düsseldorf, Droste, 1976), 116.

32   Quoted in Müller, *Heer*, p. 383.

33   See Mason, 'Innere Krise und Angriffskrieg 1938/1939,' pp. 158–88 in *Wirtschaft und Rüstung am Vorabend des Zweiten Weltkrieges*, ed. F. Forstmaier and H. E. Volkmann (Düsseldorf, 1975); also his *Arbeiterklasse und Volksgemeinschaft*, 119ff. For the criticisms, Jost Dülffer, 'Der Beginn des Krieges 1939: Hitler, die innere Krise, und das Machtsystem,' *Geschichte und Gesellschaft*, 2 (1976): 443–70, and Ludolf Herbst, 'Die Krise des nationalsozialistischen Regimes am Vorabend des Zweiten Weltkrieges und die forcierte Aufrüstung,' VfZG, 26 (1978): 347–92 (see particularly pp. 376–82). For public opinion, see Kershaw, *Mythos*, 123–5, which suggests that only fear of war marred the popularity Hitler had achieved through foreign success in 1938–39.

34   John Gillingham, 'Ruhr Coal Miners and Hitler's War,' *Journal of Social History*, Summer 1982, 637–53.

35   Hitler speech summary, August 22, 1939 (probably from stenographic notes by Canaris), *Akten zur deutschen auswärtigen Politik*, Serie D (Baden-Baden, Frankfurt, 1950–) (henceforth ADAP, D) 7: 168. A second version, written that evening by Admiral Boehm, suggests even less urgency: 'perhaps 10–15 years.' Mason prefers the Lochner document (ADAP, D, 7: 171–2 note), which ascribes to Hitler a lament that 'the Four Year Plan (has) failed and we are finished, without victory in the coming war.' But the Lochner version will not bear much weight; its provenance, its divergences from all other accounts, and its piquant fabricated details (a Goring war-dance on the conference table) mark it as an Abwehr/resistance concoction for Western consumption. (On the sources, see Winfried Baumgart, 'Zur Ansprache Hitlers vor den Führern der Wehrmacht am 22. August 1939,' VfZG 16 (1968): 120–49.)

36   Mason, 'Innere Krise,' pp. 182–4.

37   Dülffer, 'Beginn des Krieges,' p. 464.

38   ADAP, D, 7: 168 (August 22, 1939) and 8: 348 (November 23, 1939).

39   Müller, *Heer*, 427.

40   All from Engel, *Heeresadjutant*, 71–2 (January 20, 1940); see also p. 52 (July 8, 1939).

41   Rosenberg, *Tagebuch*, 98 (January 19, 1940).

42   See Helmut Krausnick, 'Kommissarbefehl und "Gerichtsbarkeitserlass Barbarossa" in neuer Sicht,' VfZG 25 (1977): 685, 718–20, 757, and Andreas Hillgruber, 'Das Russland-Bild der fuhrenden deutschen Militärs vor Beginn des Angriffs auf die Sowjetunion,' pp. 296–310 in *Russland – Deutschland – Amerika*, ed. Alexander

Fischer et al. (Wiesbaden, 1978) (Bock quotation: p. 306).

43   Friedrich Percyval Reck-Malleczewen, *Diary of a Man in Despair* (New York, 1970), 109, 103.

44   'Reptile': *Monologe*, 337 (August 11, 1942).

45   Ibid., 108 (October 25, 1941). Hitler frequently remarked that the ideal solution would be to let the churches die out naturally (ibid., 40–1, 67, 82–5), but he clearly intended to help them along (see especially ibid., 272).

46   Jodl memorandum, October, 1946, in Percy Ernst Schramm, *Hitler: The Man and Military Leader* (Chicago, 1971), 204; Hillgruber, *Hitlers Strategie. Politik und Kriegsführung 1940–41* (Frankfurt am Main, 1965), 551–4 and note 84; Hildebrand, 'Weltmacht oder Niedergang: Hitlers Deutschland 1941–1945,' in *Weltpolitik II 1939–1945*, ed. Oswald Hauser (Göttingen, 1975), 308–13.

47   Kershaw, *Mythos*, 186–91.

Chapter 30

Antonio Costa Pinto

SALAZAR'S *ESTADO NOVO*: THE NATURE OF A 'PARA-FASCIST' REGIME

■ from *SALAZAR'S DICTATORSHIP AND EUROPEAN FASCISM: PROBLEMS OF INTERPRETATION*, Boulder, 1995, pp. 147–9, 165–70

Antonio Costa Pinto's account of salazarismo and his *Estado Novo* (New State) in Portugal is one of the most conceptually sophisticated works on (para)fascism, analysing a regime that presents a series of taxonomical problems for any model of generic fascism. The author describes it as a 'constitutionalised dictatorship', a 'civilian police dictatorship', while he depicts Salazar himself as an ultra-conservative integralist believer in social Catholicism. Although the following excerpt deals exclusively with Portugal as a case of 'fascism from above' (no party, no charismatic leader), its conclusions are also relevant to the study of other para-fascist dictatorships of the interwar period (for example, Greece).

Fascism and Salazarism – problems of interpretation

A **S SOON AS THE REPUBLICAN** regime was overthrown [*Note: on 25 May 1926 by a military junta, headed by General Oscar Carmona, who became President of Portugal in 1928*], the Military Dictatorship immediately found negative solutions for some of the problems most worrisome for the conservative bloc. The Democratic Party was ousted from power and its leaders exiled, the working class lost its right to strike and the unions' room for legal maneuvering was considerably restricted. Revolutionary action against the dictatorship was carried out almost exclusively by the republicans, with the exception of a failed general strike in 1934, when Salazar established the corporatist system. The Catholic Church blessed the 1926 coup and immediately offered up its secular members for possible ministerial positions, albeit cautiously in view of the presence of many republican officers and civilians.

Salazarism grew out of the Military Dictatorship established in 1926. The Dictatorship imposed by the military was permeated by a succession of conspiracies, palace coups and even revolutionary attempts, which clearly expressed the fight for leadership within the vast conservative coalition on which it was based. The difficulties in consolidating an authoritarian regime came one after the other, given the political diversity of the conservative bloc and its ability to penetrate the armed forces. Curiously, it was under the Military Dictatorship that the Fascists enjoyed some influence; given their presence in the young officer class, they attempted to create some autonomous organizations and played a role in driving out the republican military component. It was this 'limited and self-devouring pluralism', mediated by the military, that Salazar gradually came to dominate.

The National Union (UN) was legally established in 1930. It was an 'anti-party' which aggregated the civilian forces that supported the new regime. In 1933 a new Constitution declared Portugal a 'Unitarian and Corporatist Republic', creating a compromise between liberal and corporatist principles of representation. The former were eliminated through subsequent legislation and the latter limited and relegated to the background. The result was a Dictatorship of the Prime Minister and a National Assembly dominated by the UN through non-competitive elections. To avoid any loss of power, even to a House dominated exclusively by the government party, the executive was made almost completely autonomous. General Carmona remained as President to guarantee military interests. The censorship services eliminated any suggestion of political conflict and devoted their attention both to the opposition and, initially also, to the Fascist minority of Rolão Preto that insisted on challenging the new regime. The political police were reorganized and used with remarkable rationality. All this was done 'from above' without any particular Fascist demagogy and the process depended more on Generals and Colonels than on Lieutenants, and more on the Ministry of the Interior than on 'the mob'. By 1934, after a few hitches, liberalism had been eliminated and the old republican institutions replaced.

The more rebellious fascist leaders were exiled but most of them 'got jobs' in minor positions, especially with the onset of the Spanish Civil War, which frightened the regime. The great republican figures were forgotten in exile after the brief optimism caused by the Spanish popular front. One by one the anarcho-syndicalist leaders went to prison or died in Spain leaving the leadership of the clandestine opposition to the small and young communist party.

The regime institutionalized by Salazar was admired by many on the fringes of the European radical right, above all by those of Maurrazian and traditional Catholic origins, given the very similar cultural origin of the 'New State'. This identity transcended a mere 'order' program but did not include the 'totalitarian', 'pagan' aspects that were bringing Nazi Germany and Fascist Italy closer and closer. *It is within the ideological spectrum of the radical right as well as in anti-liberal social Catholicism that the cultural and political origins of Salazar's regime are to be found.* [. . .]

The political system of Salazarism

In 1935, a delegate of the CAUR (*Comitato d'Azione per l'Universalità di Roma*), Baldi-Papini, visited Portugal and sent a long report back to Rome expressing his views on Salazar's regime and quoting from conversations with Portuguese political leaders.[1] Placing the process of the overthrow of the liberal order and Salazar's rise to power in a historical context, Papini stressed the differences with Italian fascism. In Portugal, 'a policing operation by the Army was enough, while in Italy there was a civil revolution with all its bloodshed, its March and its collective spirit of regeneration. Thus, no Duce, no elite, no doctrine, no revolutionary faith born and cemented in the battlefield had filled the soul of the people from the very start'.[2]

Referring to Salazar, he emphasized that 'the leader and founder of the "New State" took no part in the movement and eventually created a "personal regime without a personality"'. After analyzing its institutions and recognizing the mark and inspiration of Fascism here and there, he concluded: 'in short, while Fascism is a system of thought rather than a system of government, the "New State" is merely a system of government to which an idealized content is imparted'.[3]

A 'constitutionalized dictatorship'

The institutions of the *Estado Novo*'s political system were essentially defined by the 1933 constitution. It was a constitution that represented an early compromise with conservative republicans and was thus weak in its liberal principles and strong in its corporatist and authoritarian dimension. Rights and liberties were formally maintained, but were actually eliminated by government regulations. Freedom of association was maintained, but parties effectively eliminated through regulation. The UN never had formal status as a single party, although from 1934 on it was one.

The UN president would be Salazar, who would nominate the National Union deputies to parliament. The constitution maintained the classic separation of powers, and gave relatively few powers to the chamber of deputies and none to the corporatist chamber, making the government autonomous from any control. Theoretically the members of the corporatist chamber ought to have been designated by the corporations, but in reality Salazar would nominate most of them. The constitution maintained a president of the Republic elected by direct suffrage and a president of the council of ministers, and Salazar was only answerable to the first. During the early years this would be the only constitutional threat to Salazar. The president of the Republic was always a general, a legacy of the Military Dictatorship that would eventually cause some problems to the dictator, especially after 1945. In sum, the definition of a 'constitutionalized dictatorship', to use a phrase of the time, reflected the real nature of the regime.

Reduced to mere 'advisory councils', both the Chamber of Deputies and the Corporatist Chamber represented, as did the single party, the regime's 'limited pluralism'. The contradictions between those favoring a restoration of the monarchy and republicans, between integral and moderate corporatists, cut across the chambers. In the 1950s different lobbies arose among defenders of agricultural and industrial interests.

The *Estado Novo* inherited the repressive apparatus set up by the Military Dictatorship and strengthened it. Censorship, established in 1926, was reorganized and later controlled by the propaganda services. The same occurred with the political police, which was transformed into the true backbone of the system. The growing autonomy of the political police was progressively decreed until it ended up answerable only to Prime Minister Salazar. Aside from repressing the clandestine opposition, controlling access to public administration was of central importance. Mechanisms to control judiciary power were increased. Political crimes, for example, were placed under the jurisdiction of special military courts, and special judges were nominated. Furthermore, the political police were given ample powers to determine prison sentences.

In 1936, with the basic outlines of the legal system consolidated, Salazar authorized the founding of a militia, the Portuguese Legion, and also set up youth and women's organizations dependent on the ministry of education. A fascistic choreography thus emerged more clearly.

One important problem remained, namely, relations with the military. Throughout the regime's long life this was the institution that Salazar was most sensitive about and the one he most feared. Nonetheless it is clear that the subordination of the military hierarchy to the regime was a fact on the eve of the Second World War. The process was slow, and numerous tensions arose, but the movement to co-opt and control the military elite was the central element in the consolidation of Salazarism.

Salazar's 1938 speech at an officers' demonstration symbolically marked the victory of 'a civilian police dictatorship' over the old Military Dictatorship implanted in 1926.[4] In political-administrative terms, the two most important steps of this control process went from the arrival of Salazar in the War Ministry in mid-1936, after several previous attempts disallowed by Carmona, to the reform of the Armed Forces in 1937.

After taking charge of the War portfolio in 1936, Salazar had a final, albeit tentative word on all high-level promotions and transfers. In spite of the 'temporary' nature of his position, Salazar was Minister of War until the end of the Second World War. It was as Minister of War that he presented his reform bill for the Armed Forces in 1937. It constituted the most significant piece of legislation for ensuring government control over the Armed Forces. This reform provoked the most important quantitative and qualitative reduction in the Armed Forces to occur since the First World War. In the years that followed the officers corps would decline by 30%. Already significantly affected by resignations and transfers into the reserves of those implicated in the dozens of attempted coups and revolutions after 1926, it reached 'the lowest levels registered since 1905'.[5] Apart from this control 'from above', a number of legislative measures strengthened ideological and police control over the Armed Forces. These measures heralded the political hegemony of the Dictator's aide for the Armed Forces, Captain Santos Costa. He was promoted Sub-secretary of State and his domain went unchallenged until the late 1950s.

Salazarism was no affront to international order. Its nationalism was based on the legacy of the past and on its colonial patrimony. Its system of alliances was based on the Anglo-Portuguese Alliance which was never questioned and which ensured the English government's discrete support of the dictatorship. The geography and progress of the Second World War determined Portugal's noninvolvement. Salazarism focused on maintaining neutrality and continuing the old system of alliances.

As far as the political system is concerned, little or nothing changed with the profound alteration of the international order after 1945. The only concession was the opening for the emergence of a legal opposition a month at a time every four years for which no constitutional reform was necessary. In 1958, following the 'scare' provoked by the presidential candidacy of a dissident general, Humberto Delgado, the President was indirectly and 'organically' elected by the National Assembly and the representatives of the Municipal Chambers.

Salazar: a 'strong' dictator

Many studies of modern dictatorships ignore the leader. In the case of the 'New State' it would be a mistake to do so. Salazar had a world view and ran the whole institutional design of the regime. Once he became the unchallenged leader little legislation, be it the most important or the most trivial, was passed without his approval.[6]

Salazar played no part in the 1926 coup d'etat. Nor was he listed as a candidate for dictator during the last years of the parliamentary regime. He was born to a poor rural family in a village in central Portugal, in Vimieiro near Santa Comba Dão. Oliveira Salazar received a traditional Catholic education and completed most of his intellectual and political education before the 1st World War. He attended a seminary but abandoned the ecclesiastical path on the eve of the fall of the Monarchy in order to study law at the University of Coimbra. A reserved and brilliant student, he led the best known Catholic student organization at Coimbra, the CADC. His friendship with the future cardinal patriarch, Cerejeira, dates from this time. He pursued a university career as a professor of economic law and his only political activity under the liberal Republic occurred within the strict limits of the social Catholic movement. He was one of the leaders, but not the only one, of the Catholic Center and was elected deputy by the party in the early 1920s.

It was because of his expertise in finance and his membership in the Catholic Center that his name was suggested a number of times for Finance Minister immediately after the 1926 coup. As it was of course in that capacity that he joined the Military Dictatorship in 1928. His rise within the government was initially due to the ample powers he negotiated on his arrival at the finance ministry. Only later did he turn his attention to the political institutions.

The image that Salazar cultivated was that of a reserved puritanical and provincial Dictator, an image which held sway until his death and one which he never attempted to change. As a young Catholic militant he left Portugal only once to take part in a Catholic congress in Belgium. After taking power, he made a single trip to Spain to meet with Franco. He ruled over a 'colonial empire' but never visited a single colony during the 36 years of his consulship. He never went to Brazil, the 'brother country', either. He flew once and didn't like it. Yet it would be a mistake to assume that his provincialism implies a lack of political culture. Salazar was an 'academic' dictator who closely followed international politics and the ideas of the times.

Salazar always evinced some ideological traits connected with his cultural background: he was a traditional anti-liberal Catholic integralist in a context of secularization and accelerated modernization. For him the latter were symbolic of the First Republic. He was ultra-conservative in the most literal sense of the term.

He steadfastly defended his rejection of democracy and its ideological heritage, favoring an 'organicist' vision of society based on traditional and Catholic foundations. As national leader he was aware of the inevitability of modernization but was always acutely aware of the threat it represented.

In their systematic and cartesian simplicity, his speeches provide a good indication of his political thought.[7] He always spoke to the elite. When the District Governors mobilized the peasants, Salazar maintained, come hell or high water, his principles. Everything else derived from or was added to this. He was a professor of finance and had clear ideas about the management of a State's balance sheet. Portugal's dictator rejected the Fascist model of charismatic leadership both out of ideological training and political choice; not for pragmatic reasons and even less out of suitability to any characteristic nature of Portuguese society, the social structure of which was not unlike many of those which underwent a populism closer to Fascism. As a 'strong' dictator he rarely decentralized decisions and relied above all upon a docile administration.

Notes

1   CAUR, *Relazione sulla Missione Compinta dall' Aw. U. Baldi Papini in Portogallo*, Agosto 1935, Miniculpop, Busta 404, ACS, Roma. On this organization of Italian fascism see M. A. Ledeen, *Universal Fascism* (New York 1972).

2   Idem.

3   Idem.

4   See Maria Carrilho, *Forças Armadas es Mudança Política em Portugal no Séc. XX* (Lisbon 1985), 423, and Jose Medeiros Ferreira, *O comportamento Político dos Militars. Forças Armadas e Regimes Políticos em Portugal no Séc. XX* (Lisbon 1992), 175–202.

5   Idem, 422.

6   We are still waiting for a good biography of Salazar, meanwhile see the one written by one of his Ministers, Franco Nogueira, *Salazar*, 6 vols. (Coimbra 1977–85).

7   For the 1930s, see Oliveira Salazar, *Discursos*, Vol. I (Lisbon 1935).

SECTION VI

■ Fascism and anti-Semitism

NAVOIDABLY, THE EXPERIENCE of the two reference fascist regimes – Italian Fascism and Nazism – has dominated the process of theorising about fascism. If, as some commentators seem to suggest (e.g. 6, 10), the Italian and German variants are the two most extreme and developed cases of fascism, then they should be more suitable for educing general criteria as to what constitutes the fascist experience. The problem, however, lies in distinguishing those attributes that were derived from fascist intentions from those elements already inherent in the cognitive model of German or Italian nationalism. To take one conspicuous example, Nazism was impregnated by an eliminationist form of racial anti-Semitism – which Nazi policy-making pursued with horrific diligence and unprecedented brutality – while Italian Fascism endorsed this ideological trait belatedly and far less wholeheartedly. Similar distinctions apply to the ideological discourse of the other fascist movements and regimes. The Romanian Iron Guard espoused a virulent anti-Semitic discourse, while the leadership of the Hungarian Arrow Cross proclaimed themselves 'a-Semitic', promoting the vision of a Jew-free Hungary but stopping short of emulating the aggressive eliminationist discourse of Nazism. Should we then infer from this confused landscape that active anti-Semitism was a defining attribute of generic fascism? In his 'discursive theory' of fascism Griffin has argued that while generic fascism is intrinsically racialist, it is not *necessarily* anti-Semitic, at least not in the Nazi fanatic sense of the word (Griffin 1993b: 48–9). This explanation excludes anti-Semitism from the nucleus of the 'fascist minimum' but raises a host of issues about the production of extreme anti-Semitic tendencies in *certain* fascist cases. If anti-Semitism was not a de facto fundamental element of the fascist experience, it is not self-evident whether its zealous sponsoring by Nazism and a host of other fascist and collaborationist movements/regimes emanated from specific generic *fascist* values or from particular long-term traits of national traditions and contexts.

It is important at this point to remember that anti-Semitic prejudices, of either mild or extreme character, have inhered in the model of Christian European culture for many centuries, starting off in the form of religious intolerance but gradually developing a social and a political slant. D. Goldhagen's controversial but hugely popular account of Nazi anti-Semitism records the way that conventional bigotry against the Jews reigned supreme in German society (sometimes, as he argued, even employing direct references to the desirability of a *Judenfrei*, Jew-free, Germany) for a significantly long time prior to the emergence of the Nazi movement (**31**). Similar clichéd anti-Semitic prejudices were evident in most European societies in the nineteenth and early twentieth century, especially amongst conservative and nationalist circles. What, however, provided a calamitous pertinence to this sort of discourse in the interwar period was the psychological association forged between European Jewry and two cataclysmic events: the triumph of Bolshevism in Russia and the world economic crisis of 1929. Jews were now reviled for their alleged collusion with international communism in a world-wide conspiracy to bring down the capitalist system and thus facilitate the spread of Bolshevism throughout Europe and the whole world. The publication of the fabricated *Protocols of the Elders of Zion* in the early 1920s acted as a confirmation of the suspicions about Jewish intentions which were rife in sections of European society. The Abel interviews of more than five hundred early Nazis highlights that strong anti-Semitic beliefs were reflected in the discourse of half the respondents as the main reason for joining the NSDAP. However, a significant number declared that they came to an endorsement of anti-Semitism through resentment at defeat in the First World War, the 1918 revolution and the Weimar Republic, which they were ready to accept as indications of an international Bolshevik-Jewish conspiracy (Merkl 1975).

Be that as it may, an influential part of the historiography of fascism has put forward the view that the centrality of eliminationist anti-Semitism in Nazi Germany (both in ideological and decision-making terms) is a sufficient reason for extricating Hitler's movements and regime from any generic discussion of fascism. The seminal work of M. Burleigh and W. Wippermann on Nazi anti-Semitism (**32**) has provided an elaborate justification of this methodological distinction, echoing Gilbert Allardyce's earlier critique of treating Nazism, Italian Fascism and a host of other movements/regimes as offspring of the same phenomenon of 'fascism' (**1**). A similar exclusion of Nazism from the discussion of generic fascism was even encouraged by a prominent member of the school of the 'new consensus', albeit originating from a different methodological consideration. Sternhell's model (see **14**) emphasised the dissident Marxist themes in fascist ideology that could not accommodate Nazism's primary emphasis on racial-biological anti-Semitism. This line of interpretation provided an acceptable and plausible framework for conceptualising other fascist movements and regimes – including Italian Fascism – as either more benign or essentially dissimilar to the Nazi case. A group of Italian historians, with Renzo De Felice and A. James Gregor (1979a, 1979b) as their most prominent spokespeople, identified the potential benefits of such an analysis of Nazism in presenting Mussolini's movement as more forward-looking, modernising and humane. As J. Steinberg shows (33), the limitations of Fascist anti-Semitic (the 'race' legislation of 1938) and overall racialist policies (for example, the apartheid regime instituted in Ethiopia after 1936) contrasted quite sharply with the demonic systematisation and horrifying efficiency of similar policies pursued by Hitler's regime.

The importance of this debate is not simply confined to the historical understanding of anti-Semitism itself, either within indigenous societies or in the ideological discourse of individual fascist movements and regimes. If the Nazi obsessive fascination with biological racialist themes is to be taken as the defining characteristic of the National Socialist worldview, then any attempt to devise a generic definition of fascism should de facto exclude Nazism from its scope. Such an approach is, as mentioned earlier, in line with Sternhell's theory of fascist ideology as a synthesis of dissident Marxist and radical right-wing themes to which Hitler's movement does not really conform. Yet, Sternhell's model is rather unusual in the historiography of generic fascism; most other disciples have instead endeavoured to produce an ideological minimum of fascist ideology that is capable of reconciling other common fascist themes with Nazi lethal anti-Semitism. An interesting attempt in this direction is offered by the recent study of fascism by M. Neocleous (34). Squaring the methodological vicious circle of the alleged uniqueness of Nazi *Vernichtung* (eliminationist) policy, Neocleous argues that this constituted a unique and extreme articulation of a fundamental shared fascist commitment to nationalism in its most organic and exclusive sense. The benefits of such an approach lie in the conjunction of a generic understanding of fascism with the specificity of national intellectual traditions and beliefs. In this sense, the burden of accounting for the deviation of the Nazi case-study is shifted from the generic theory of fascism to a careful analysis of indigenous values in the longer term and how they were promulgated by the fascist discourses.

In the end, even the most tenacious national 'myths' cannot evade the invigorating challenge of critical reassessment. The gradual questioning of conventional views about the attitudes of the Italian Fascist and French Vichy regimes towards indigenous Jewish populations has already been discussed in the Introduction (pp. 14–16, 22–6, 35–9). A sample of these findings is represented in this section with two excerpts, one for each respective country. E. M. Robertson records the increasing importance of racialism in Mussolini's foreign policy, discussing its role in both the colonial pursuits of the regime in Libya (1928–32) and Ethiopia (1936 onwards), and in Europe through the introduction and implementation of the racial legislation after 1938 (35). Eventually, race did matter for Italian Fascism, if in a less sinister way than for Nazism. A similar reappraisal of the indigenous roots of anti-Semitism in France has led to a growing questioning of another myth – that of an overwhelming French resistance to the sort of persecution that the Nazi occupiers and their domestic collaborators inflicted upon the French Jewish community. In this respect, Susan Zuccotti's work (36) is representative of the latest stages of a major revision of modern French history – a revision which made its appearance in the early 1970s with Robert O. Paxton's account of Vichy France (**41**), but has come of age in the last two decades, and especially after the so-called 'Sternhell controversy' (Introduction, pp. 22–4).

Chapter 31

Daniel Jonah Goldhagen

GERMAN ANTI-SEMITIC TRADITION, NATIONAL SOCIALIST REGIME AND 'ORDINARY GERMANS'

■ from *HITLER'S WILLING EXECUTIONERS: ORDINARY GERMANS AND THE HOLOCAUST*, London, 1997, pp. 77–82, 87–90, 127–8

So much has already been said about Daniel Goldhagen's international best-seller *Hitler's Willing Executioners* that any preface would sound superfluous (see Introduction pp. 39–41). His view that 'eliminationist anti-Semitism' was so deeply ingrained in German collective consciousness even before the rise of the Nazis – and had made massive inroads into all sections of German society – has given rise to a series of acrimonious debates ever since the book first appeared in 1996. For Goldhagen, the 'leap to genocide' of the 1930s and 1940s did not mark a qualitative departure, in the sense that the Nazis simply manipulated the eliminationist mentality of the overwhelming majority of Germans towards 'the Jews'. In this sense, they were 'active participants', willing executioners of a project whose ideological presuppositions they had culturally endorsed since the nineteenth century. Interestingly, Goldhagen shifts the burden of evidence to those who might want to prove that the Germans did not share this eliminationist mentality; the absence of any clear indication of active mass opposition to the regime's genocidal policies is regarded by the author as a direct endorsement of his own controversial thesis.

T HIS BOOK'S APPROACH yields a new understanding of antisemitism that holds it to have had greater continuity and to have been more ubiquitous in German society during the modern period than others have maintained.

[. . .] The purpose of the discussion has been to establish and focus on the *central features* of antisemitism in nineteenth-century Germany (and not on the exceptional divergences from the norm), because the central features were the ones that would shape the history of twentieth-century Germany:

1   From the beginning of the nineteenth century, antisemitism was ubiquitous in Germany. It was its 'common sense.'

2   The preoccupation with Jews had an obsessive quality.

3   Jews came to be identified with and symbolic of anything and everything which was deemed awry in German society.

4   The central image of the Jews held them to be malevolent, powerful, a principal, if not the principal, source of the ills that beset Germany, and therefore dangerous to the welfare of Germans. This was different from the medieval Christian view, which deemed the Jews to be evil and the source of great harm, but in which the Jews always remained somewhat peripheral. Modern German antisemites, unlike their medieval forebears, could say that there would be no peace on earth until the Jews were destroyed.

5   This cultural model in the second half of the nineteenth century coalesced around the concept of 'race.'

6   This brand of antisemitism was unusually violent in its imagery, and it tended towards violence.

7   Its logic was to promote the 'elimination' of Jews by whatever means necessary and possible, given the prevailing ethical constraints.

The purpose of this account more generally is to demonstrate two points: that the cognitive model of Nazi antisemitism had taken shape well before the Nazis came to power, and that this model, throughout the nineteenth and early twentieth centuries, was also extremely widespread in all social classes and sectors of German society, for it was deeply embedded in German cultural and political life and conversation, as well as integrated into the moral structure of society.[1] The foundational concept for German popular political thought, the *Volk*, was conceptually linked to, and partly dependent upon, a definition of Jews as the *Volk*'s antithesis. Built into the concept of *Volk* was a deprecation of Jews, who embodied all the negative qualities and ideals which were absent from the *Volk*, including moral ones. Thus, the conceptual and moral foundation of German political existence incorporated the perniciousness of the Jews, which guaranteed still greater staying power and political potency to the antisemitic cultural cognitive model.

The discussion here further illustrates the argument put forward in the previous chapter that antisemitism, while undergoing important changes in its character during the nineteenth century and while always having been widely present in German society, became more or less *manifest*, in response to varying developments in German society, especially to the fortunes of the economy.[2] In light of this history – which, despite cycles of great antisemitic agitation, quiescence, and then renewed agitation, was characterized by a continuity of cognitions and accusations about Jews – it would be false to believe that the changes in the degree of German antisemitic expression indicate that Germans became antisemites, then rejected antisemitism, only to adopt its precepts whole again, etc. The evidence, moreover, of a public discussion which was overwhelmingly antisemitic, presenting for the German people's consideration virtually only negative images of Jews, and negative images that portrayed the Jews as poisonous, evil, eternally strange, as subversive infiltrators, destroyers, and demon-like in their aims and powers – a discussion in which the German people were *active participants* – can leave little doubt that the cognitions and emotions about Jews dominant in society were given no reason during the course of the nineteenth century to evaporate. Since the vast majority of Germans had little or no contact with Jews, and certainly did not know Jews well, the only Jews whom they actually met and came to know were the ones represented in the antisemitic speeches, writings, caricatures, and discussions on which they were nurtured. Folktales, literature, the popular press, and political pamphlets and cartoons, the bearers of potent antisemitic images, provided the poisonous *Bildung* about Jews that was at the core of German culture.[3]

In the nineteenth century, those who agitated for the emancipation of the Jews hardly spoke for the majority of Germans; they won their battle but barely.[4] Built into emancipation itself – an emancipation that proceeded upon a cultural model of Jews derived from hostile Christianity – was the belief that Jews would disappear; since Jews refused to do so, the false promises of emancipation created all but a structural guarantee that antisemitism would develop new virulence (as Jews, to use the idiom of the day, invaded the Germans' home and became the objects of great envy because of their meteoric rise from pariah status), would metamorphose itself cognitively to account for the changing conditions of German society and the position of Jews within it, and, since economic troubles and social dislocations were bound to occur, would intensify and become activated politically. This was the nineteenth-century antisemitic legacy that was to inform twentieth-century German society and politics.

It is no wonder that in light of this evidence, no one has yet been able to *demonstrate* that the vast majority of Germans, or even significant minorities (save for small elite groups), had at any time renounced their cultural heritage of an anti-Jewish animus, had freed themselves of the cognitive model of Jews that governed Germany. It is not enough to assume and assert it, or to trace the writings of a few liberal intellectuals, as other interpreters of German antisemitism have done. As I have argued, demonstrating this – namely providing *evidence* that the scope and intensity of antisemitism had atrophied – should be the analytical burden when discussing the degree to which Germans were antisemitic. It remains unmet. The fact was that as the 1920s and then the Nazi takeover approached, the German people were more dangerously oriented towards Jews than they had been during any other time since the dawn of modernity.

By the eve of the First World War, a discourse – namely a discussion structured by a stable framework with widely accepted reference points, images, and explicit elaborations – had for over thirty years been in place with regard to the Jews. The consolidation of this discourse, the forging of a common set of assumptions and beliefs about Jews, the solidifying of the Jews as a cultural and political symbol, one of decomposition, malignancy, and willful evil, meant that it was well-nigh impossible to discuss Jews except in its frame of reference. In the antisemitic publications of the late nineteenth century, when some new accusation against, or argument about, the Jews would appear, the construction would then be incorporated into subsequent editions of other antisemites' works that had initially been published prior to the novel contribution to the corpus of anti-Jewish thought.[5] The German discourse in some sense had as its foundation the extremely widespread, virtually axiomatic notion that a '*Judenfrage*,' a 'Jewish Problem,' existed.[6] The term '*Judenfrage*' presupposed and inhered within it a set of interrelated notions. Jewish

Germans were essentially different from non-Jewish Germans. Because of the Jews' presence, a serious problem existed in Germany. Responsibility for the problem lay with the Jews, not the Germans. As a consequence of these 'facts,' some fundamental change in the nature of Jews or in their position in Germany was necessary and urgent. Everyone who accepted the existence of a 'Jewish Problem' – even those who were not passionately hostile to the Jews – subscribed to these notions, for they were constitutive of the concept's cognitive model. Every time the word '*Judenfrage*' (or any word or phrase associated with it) was uttered, heard, or read, those partaking in the conversation activated the cognitive model necessary to understand it.[7]

Change of some sort was seen as necessary, yet the Jews' nature, because of their 'race,' was understood by Germans to be unchangeable, since the prevailing German conception of the Jews posited them to be a race inexorably alien to the Germanic race. Also, the 'evidence' of their senses told Germans that the majority of Jews had already assimilated, in the sense of having taken on the manners, dress, and idiom of modern Germany, and so the Jews had already been given every possible chance to become good Germans – and failed.[8] This axiomatic belief in the existence of the 'Jewish Problem,' more or less promised an axiomatic belief in the need to 'eliminate' Jewishness from Germany as the 'problem's' only 'solution.'

The toll of these decades of verbal, literary, institutionally organized, and political antisemitism was wearing down even those who, true to Enlightenment principles, had resisted the demonization of the Jews. The eliminationist mind-set was so prevalent that the inveterate antisemite and founder of the Pan-German League, Friedrich Lange, could with verity declaim the universal belief in the 'Jewish Problem,' rightly pointing out that the means to the 'solution,' and not the existence of the 'problem' itself, was the only remaining subject of doubt and disagreement: 'I assert that the attitude of the educated Germans towards Judaism has become totally different from what it was only a few years ago . . . The Jewish Problem is today no longer a question of "whether?" but only one of "how?"'[9] The axiom that Jews were harmful and that they must be eliminated from Germany found renewed, intense expression in an unexpected context, during a time when national solidarity is typically forged and hardened, and social conflicts are dampened and deferred – namely the national emergency of full-scale war.

During World War I, Germans accused the Jews of not serving in the military, of not defending the Fatherland. Instead, Jews were alleged to have been staying safe at home and using the wartime conditions to exploit and immiserate the Germans for their own profit on the black market. The upsurge against the Jews was so extreme that in 1916 the Prussian authorities conducted a census of Jews in the armed forces in order to assess the Jews' martial contribution – a humiliating measure providing stunning testament to the Jews' precarious social position and to the ongoing belief in the centrality of the 'Jewish Problem.'[10] It is precisely because Jews had long been considered dangerous aliens that the closing of Germans' ranks in social solidarity produced not a diminution of social animosity towards the Jews, but an upsurge in antisemitic expression and attacks. The more perilous the times, so drove the anti-Semitic logic, the more dangerous and injurious the Jews must be. Franz Oppenheimer summarized the attitudes of Germans towards Jews, attitudes that Jews could not favorably alter no matter how fervently they might dedicate themselves to the German cause: 'Don't fool yourselves, you are and will remain Germany's pariahs.'[11] German antisemites had always been somewhat autistic in their conception of Jews. The autism was to grow worse.

[. . .]

When the fateful days of Hitler's assumption of the office of German Chancellor came on January 30, 1933, the Nazis found that they did not have to remake Germans at least on one central issue – arguably the most important one from their point of view – the nature of Jewry. Whatever else Germans thought about Hitler and the Nazi movement, however much they might have detested aspects of Nazism, the vast majority of them subscribed to the underlying Nazi model of Jews and in this sense (as the Nazis themselves understood) were 'Nazified' in their views of Jews. It is, to risk understatement, no surprise that under the Nazi dispensation the vast majority of Germans continued to remain antisemitic, that their antisemitism continued to be virulent and racially grounded, and that their socially shared 'solution' to the 'Jewish Problem' continued to be eliminationist. *Nothing* occurred in Nazi Germany to undermine or erode the cultural cognitive model of Jews that had for decades underlain German attitudes and emotions towards the despised minority among them. Everything publicly said or done worked to reinforce the model.[12]

In Germany during the Nazi period, putative Jewish evil permeated the air. It was discussed incessantly. It was said to be the source of every ill that had befallen Germany and of every continuing threat. The Jew, *der Jude*, was both a metaphysical and an existential threat, as real to Germans as that of a powerful enemy army poised on Germany's borders for the attack. The character, ubiquity, and logic of action of German antisemitism during the Nazi period is captured brilliantly by Melita Maschmann in a confessional memoir written to her lost, former childhood Jewish friend. A devoted member of the girls' division of the Hitler youth, Maschmann was not the progeny of country bumpkins, being the daughter of a university-educated man and a woman who had grown up in a prosperous business family. She begins telling of her youthful understanding of Jews by observing that the regnant conception of 'the Jews' had no empirical basis.

> *Those* Jews were and remained something mysteriously menacing and anonymous. They were not the sum of all Jewish individuals. . . . They were an evil power, something with the attributes of a spook. One could not see it, but it was there, an active force for evil.
>
> As children we had been told fairy stories which sought to make us believe in witches and wizards. Now we were too grown up to take this witchcraft seriously, but we still went on believing in the 'wicked Jews.' They had never appeared to us in bodily form, but it was our daily experience that adults believed in them. After all, we could not check to see if the earth was round rather than flat – or, to be more precise, it was not a proposition we thought it necessary to check. The grownups 'knew' it and one took over this knowledge without mistrust. They also 'knew' that the Jews were wicked. The wickedness was directed against the prosperity, unity and prestige of the German nation, which we had

learned to love from an early age. The anti-semitism of my parents was
a part of their outlook which was taken for granted. . . .

For as long as we could remember, the adults had lived in this
contradictory way with complete unconcern. One was friendly with
individual Jews whom one liked, just as one was friendly as a Protestant
with individual Catholics. But while it occurred to nobody to be ideologically hostile to *the* Catholics, one was, utterly, to *the* Jews. In all this
no one seemed to worry about the fact that they had no clear idea of who
'*the* Jews' were. They included the baptized and the orthodox, yiddish
[*sic*] speaking second hand dealers and professors of German literature,
Communist agents and First World War officers decorated with high
orders, enthusiasts for Zionism and chauvinistic German nationalists.
. . . I had learned from my parents' example that one could have anti-
semitic opinions without this interfering in one's personal relations with
individual Jews. There may appear to be a vestige of tolerance in this
attitude, but it is really just this confusion which I blame for the fact that
I later contrived to dedicate body and soul to an inhuman political
system, without this giving me doubts about my own individual decency.
In preaching that all the misery of the nations was due to the Jews or that
the Jewish spirit was seditious and Jewish blood was corrupting, I was
not compelled to think of you or old Herr Lewy or Rosel Cohen: I
thought only of the bogeyman, '*the* Jew.' And when I heard that the Jews
were being driven from their professions and homes and imprisoned in
ghettos, the points switched automatically in my mind to steer me round
the thought that such a fate could also overtake you or old Lewy. It was
only *the* Jew who was being persecuted and 'made harmless.'[13]

Maschmann's account conveys, better than any scholarly analysis of which I
know, the central qualities of German antisemitism: its hallucinatory image of the
Jews; the specter of evil that they appeared to Germans to be casting over Germany;
Germans' virulent hatred of them; the 'abstract' character of the beliefs that
informed the treatment which its bearers accorded *real* Jews; the unquestioned
nature of these beliefs; and the eliminationist logic that led Germans to approve of
the persecution, ghettoization, and extermination of Jews (the evident meaning of
the euphemism 'made harmless'). Maschmann leaves no doubt that antisemitism in
Germany was, for many, like mother's milk, part of the Durkheimian collective
consciousness; it was, in this woman's astute account, 'a part of their outlook which
was taken for granted.' The consequences of these views, of this ideological map,
can be seen in the wild success of the unfolding eliminationist antisemitic persecution that began with the Nazis' assumption of power.

[. . .]

The eliminationist ideology, derived from the German cultural cognitive model of
Jews, was at the root of the policies of the 1930s which the German people
supported. The genocidal program of the war was grounded in the same ideology
and set of cognitions. It was a more extreme 'solution' to a problem, the diagnosis

of which had long been agreed upon in Germany. Seen in this light, the leap from supporting the eliminationist policies of the 1930s to supporting a genocidal 'solution' is not as great as it has been almost universally supposed to have been.[14] Overcoming the ethical inhibitions to wholesale slaughter of this kind was for some a substantial task. Yet the motivational foundation for such a radical 'solution' had long been in place, requiring Germans to have the courage of their convictions and to place their trust in Hitler, their *Führer*, that he indeed would solve the 'problem' while ensuring Germany's long-term welfare. It is thus no surprise that as knowledge of mass and systematic killings of Jews spread widely throughout Germany, Germans expressed little more than unease – born of the residual fear that such a frightening measure would be bound to provoke in a people brought up on the commandment 'Thou shall not kill,' and of dread at the thought of what those putatively powerful beings, the Jews, would do to them should the Germans fail.[15] The alternative to victory on the battlefield, according to the hallucinatory understanding of the world that the former Hitler Youth, Heck, shared with his countrymen, was 'the endless night of Bolshevik-Jewish slavery, [which] was too horrible to contemplate.'[16] Equally fearful for Germans to contemplate were the consequences should their nation fail in its program to exterminate the Jews.

These unsurprising yet comparatively slight misgivings aside, ordinary Germans were poised in 1939 to have their racial antisemitism channeled in a genocidal direction and *activated* for a genocidal enterprise. Did their antisemitism and eliminationist ideology prepare them to take their convictions to their logical, most radical extreme? Would they, when finally confronted with the 'evil' that most of them had known only from afar, be willing to expurgate it in the only manner that would be 'final'? The theoretical framework elucidated here for understanding antisemitism suggests that they would have, because such a 'solution' had as its ideational foundation the same demonized view of the Jews that underlay the various highly popular measures of the 1930s which the regime and ordinary Germans in all walks of life had already taken in order to degrade and immiserate Jews and to exclude them from German society.

Notes

1   Rainer Erb and Werner Bergmann, *Die Nachtseite Der Judenemanzipation: Der Wiserstand gegen die Integration der Juden in Deutschland, 1780–1860* (Berlin: Metropol, 1989), agree that almost all Germans during the period of their study (1780–1860) to a greater or lesser degree held the 'shared conviction in the perniciousness of the Jews' and that the exterminatory calls grew out of this common cultural model (p. 196).

2   Rosenberg, 'Anti-Semitism and the "Great Depression", 1873–1896', in Herbert A. Strauss, ed., *Hostages of Modernization: Studies on Modern Antisemitism, 1870–1933/39* (Berlin: Walter de Gruyter, 1993), 19–20.

3   See Alfred D. Low, *Jews in the Eyes of the Germans: From the Enlightenment to Imperial Germany* (Philadelphia: Institute for the Study of Human Issues, 1979), for rich material from written expressions of antisemitism; for pictorial depictions of Jews, see Eduard Fuchs, *Die Juden in der Karikatur* (Munich: Albert Langen, 1921).

4   Werner E. Mosse, 'From "Schutzjuden" to "Deutsche Staatsbürger Jüdischen Glaubens": The Long and Bumpy Road to Jewish Emancipation in Germany', in Pierre Birnhaum and Ira Katznelson, eds., *Paths to Emancipation: Jews, States and Citizenship* (Princeton: PUP, 1995), writes: 'In fact, during the decades that followed (emancipation) it became axiomatic – and not without justification – that the bulk of the population, particularly in rural areas where most Jews resided, disliked them and was hostile to their further emancipation' (p. 72).

5   Klemens Felden, 'Die Uebernahme des antisemitischen Stereotyps als soziale Norm durch die bürgerliche Gesellschaft Deutschlands (1875–1900)' (Ph.D. diss., Ruprecht-Karl-Universität, Heidelberg, 1963), 47.

6   See Werner Jochmann, 'Die Ausbreitung des Antisemitismus in Deutschland, 1914–1923,' in *Gesellschaftskrise und Judenfeindschaft in Deutschland, 1870–45* (Hamburg: Hans Christians Verlag, 1988), 99. Alex Bein, *The Jewish Question: Biography of a World Problem* (New York: Herzl Press, 1990), dates the upsurge in the use of the concept 'Jewish Problem' to around 1880: 'In the large number of writings that appeared at that time, the concept "Jewish Question" was again primarily used by foes of the Jews, to whom the existence of the Jews and their conduct appeared at least problematic and perhaps even dangerous' (p. 20).

7   Jews' linguistic usage was also constrained by the cognitive and linguistic models of the day, so they too were compelled to include '*Judenfrage*' in their social lexicon as well as their printed one. 'The Jewish Lexicon' of 1929 defined '*Judenfrage*' as 'the totality of the problems arising out of the coexistence of the Jews with other peoples.' This idiosyncratic, neutral definition denies the Jews' responsibility for the 'problems' that the term's cognitive model ascribed to them. Even if the editors of this lexicon would not acknowledge and codify the true meaning of the term, when Jews heard or read the term, they, as members of this society, undoubtedly understood its full implication. See Leonore Siegele-Wenschkewitz, 'Aus ein ander setzungen mit einem Stereotyp: Die Judenfrage im Leben Martin Niemöllers,' in Ursula Büttner, ed., *Die Deutschen und die Judenverfolgung im Dritten Reich* (Hamburg: Hans Christians Verlag, 1992), 293. On the use of the term 'Jewish Problem' by Germans and Jews, see Bein, *The Jewish Question*, 18–21.

8   Beginning in the late nineteenth century, Germans began to focus on the eastern European Jews who were living in Germany as revealing the essence of Jewishness. Steven Aschheim writes in *Brothers and Strangers: The East European Jew in Germany and German Jewish Consciousness, 1800–1923* (Madison: University of Wisconsin Press, 1982): 'While the caftan Jew embodied a mysterious past, the cravat Jew symbolized a frightening present' (p. 76). 'Race,' in their minds, linked the eastern Jews to the German Jews. Thus, the eastern Jews 'served as a constant reminder of the mysterious and brooding ghetto presence' and were seen by the antisemites as the 'living embodiment of a fundamentally alien, even hostile, culture' (pp. 58–59), reinforcing the Germans' cultural cognitive model about Jews.

9   Peter G. J. Pulzer, *The Rise of Political Anti-Semitism in Germany and Austria* (New York: John Wiley & Sons, 1964), 288. In keeping with the usage here, 'Jewish Problem' has been substituted for 'Jewish Question,' which appears in the translation quoted.

10   See Jochmann's treatment of Germans' attacks on German Jews during the war in 'Die Ausbreitung des Antisemitismus in Deutschland, 1914–1923,' pp. 101–117; and Saul Friedländer, 'Political Transformations During the War and

their Effect on the Jewish Question,' in Herbert A. Strauss, ed., *Hostages of Modernization: Studies on Modern Antisemitism 1870–1933/39* (Berlin/New York: Walter de Gruyter, 1993), 150–164. The attacks were so vicious, their themes becoming cultural truisms during Weimar, that the Jewish community believed itself compelled to respond with statistical proof that belied the antisemitic charges. See Jacob Segall, *Die deutschen Juden als Soldaten im Kriege, 1914–1918: Eine statistische Studie* (Berlin: Philo-Verlag, 1921).

11   Quoted in Jochmann, 'Die Ausbreitung des Antisemitismus in Deutschland, 1914–1923,' p. 101.

12   A number of general analyses of German antisemitism and attitudes towards the persecution of the Jews exist. Naturally, they do not all agree with one another or with the conclusions presented here. The most important secondary analysis is David Bankier, *The Germans and the Final Solution: Public Opinion under Nazism* (Oxford: Blackwell, 1992). It contains far greater empirical support for my positions than space permits me to offer here, and indeed puts forward aspects of the argument that I am making here, though significant differences remain between Bankier's understanding and mine. The absence from the book, for example, of a theoretical or analytical account of antisemitism or a more general discussion of the nature of cognition, beliefs, and ideologies and their relation to action leads Bankier to interpret the evidence in ways that can be contested. For a sample of the existing literature, see the many publications of Ian Kershaw, including 'Antisemitismus und Volksmeinung: Reaktionen auf die Judenverfolgung,' in Martin Broszat and Elke Fröhlich, eds., *Bayern in der NS-Zeit* (Munich: R. Oldenbourg Verlag, 1989), vol. 2, 281–348; *Popular Opinion and Political Dissent in the Third Reich: Bavaria, 1933–1945* (Oxford: Oxford University Press, 1983), chaps. 6, 9; 'German popular opinion and the "Jewish Question," 1939–1943: Some Further Reflections,' in Arnold Paucker, ed., *Die Juden im nationalsozialistischen Deutschland: The Jews in Nazi Germany, 1933–1943* (New York: Leo Baeck Institute, 1986), 365–386; see also Otto Dov Kulka and Aron Rodrigue, 'The German Population and the Jews in the Third Reich: Recent Publications and Trends in Research on German Society and the "Jewish Question,"' *Yad Vashem Studies* 16 (1984), pp. 421–435; Kater, 'Everyday Anti-Semitism in Prewar Nazi Germany'; and Robert Gellately, *The Gestapo and German Society: Enforcing Racial Policy, 1933–1945* (Oxford: Clarendon Press, 1990). Two published documentary sources which are repeatedly used in many of these studies are *Deutschland-Berichte der Sozialdemokratischen Partei Deutschlands (Sopade), 1934–1940*, vols. 1–7 (Salzhausen: Verlag Petra Nettelbeck and Frankfurt/M: Zweitausendeins, 1980); and *Meldungen aus dem Reich, 1938–1945: Die geheimen Lageberichte des Sicherheitsdienstes der SS*, ed. Heinz Boberach, vols. 1–17 (Herrsching: Pawlak Verlag, 1984).

13   Melita Maschmann, *Account Rendered: A Dossier of My Former Self* (London: Abelard-Schuman, 1964), 40–41.

14   Even Bankier, *The Germans and the Final Solution* (. . .)

15   See Kershaw, *Popular Opinion and Political Dissent in the Third Reich*, 370.

16   Alfons Heck, *The Burden of Hitler's Legacy* (Frederick, Colo.: Renaissance House, 1989), 87.

Chapter 32

Michael Burleigh and Wolfgang Wippermann

THE 'UNIQUENESS' OF NAZI RACIALISM

■ from *THE RACIAL STATE: GERMANY 1933–1945*, Cambridge, 1991, pp. 44–51, 305–7

Although Michael Burleigh's and Wolfgang Wippermann's authoritative monograph concerns Nazi racial policy, it also contains one of the strongest statements in favour of Nazism's 'uniqueness' and against the soundness of generic theories of fascism. The featured excerpt highlights the 'specific' character of Nazism as an ideology-driven quest for the 'creation of a hierarchical racial new order'. In pursuing this sui generis utopia, the regime combined racial legislation against 'alien' groups (Jews, Sinti and Roma, Slavs) with racial-hygienic measures (targetting the mentally ill, the disabled, 'asocials', etc.).

Racial legislation

'ABOVE ALL, I CHARGE the leadership of the nation, as well as its followers, to a rigorous adherence to our racial laws and to a merciless resistance against the poisoner of all peoples – international Jewry.'[1] This was one of the last sentences Hitler committed to paper. It is from his 'Political Testament', dictated in a bunker beneath the ashes and collapsing masonry of Berlin. Which racial laws did he have in mind, shortly before the end? Certainly, those which were directed against the Jews, described here as 'the poisoner of all peoples'.[2] The first anti-Jewish laws were promulgated in April 1933, in the wake of the unsuccessful boycott action earlier that month. Legislation was designed to fulfil the twofold objective of assuaging rabid grassroots Party activists, while not alienating either Hindenburg, or the Nazis' conservative coalition partners, by appearing to license disorder. Legislation commenced with the Law for the Restoration of the Professional Civil Service of 7 April 1933, followed by measures against Jewish physicians, teachers, and students, on the 22nd and 25th of the same month.[3] The former sanctioned the dismissal of both the politically undesirable and 'non-Aryans' from the public service; the latter attempted either to remove Jews from, or to restrict their access too, the professions, while encouraging 'Aryans' to dispense with the services of Jews. All of these measures were hastily cobbled together, with a number of concessions to Hindenburg regarding categories of exemption, notably war veterans. The Nazis seem to have been taken by surprise by the number of Jews who could claim exemption on these grounds. Between 1933 and 1939 these measures were then extended to cover the 'dejewification' of other occupational groups, a process which will be described in detail in the chapter on the persecution of the Jews below.

The next wave of anti-Semitic legislation, in 1935, was designed to achieve legal discrimination, segregation, and precision in the question of who was a Jew. Discrimination began with the Military Service Law of May 1935 which made 'Aryan' ancestry mandatory for service in the armed forces.[4] The Nuremberg Laws, promulgated after hasty consultations during the Party Rally that September, were the product of several circumstances:[5] firstly, Hitler's desire to announce something more substantial to the Party faithful than a law forbidding Jews to hoist the national flag; secondly, the desire of the legal profession and registry officials for greater clarity concerning how to define a Jew. As a commentator in the journal of the League of German Jurists crisply observed:

> While logic and consistency have traditionally been a special province of jurists and lawyers, it appears that since the seizure of power these faculties have eluded them. In looking through our racial laws it becomes apparent that we are lacking a certain conceptual clarity in using such terms as 'race', 'racial hygiene', 'eugenics', and others which fall into the same category. They are frequently used with different and contradictory meanings.[6]

Finally, the Party leadership was under pressure from both grass-roots activists and committed anti-Semites like Streicher, or the Reich Physicians Leader, Gerhard Wagner, to regulate marital and sexual relations between 'Aryans' and Jews. Under the ensuing Law for the Protection of German Blood and Honour, Jews were forbidden to marry or have extra-marital sexual relations with 'Aryan' partners. Under the Reich Citizenship Law, Jews were redefined as 'subjects', while 'political rights', which by this time were notional, were restricted to 'citizens of the Reich'. Although the official spokesmen of German Jewry were relieved that years of insecurity and uncertainty were apparently over, the Nuremberg Laws had officially rendered the Jews second-class citizens. These laws were accompanied by intensive discussions upon who was to be considered a Jew. The result was the First Supplementary Decree of the Reich Citizenship Law of 14 November 1935, which specified the criteria for determining who was a full or part Jew.[7] Ironically enough, these criteria were based upon a religious, rather than a scientific, definition of race.

These anti-Semitic laws, and the subsequent decrees on their implementation, continue to preoccupy historians. This interest is warranted, for in addition to shedding light on the *ad hoc* way in which the regime legislated, these measures ultimately created a pseudo-legal basis for later policies, including mass murder. However, while Hitler may have regarded these laws as being the most significant creation of his regime, they were not unique. Anti-Semitic legislation was accompanied by other laws and decrees, whose object was the 'racial hygienic improvement' of the 'body of the German nation'.[8] Both 'alien' races and 'racially less valuable' members of the German population were excluded from their positive provisions. 'Elements' of 'lesser racial value' in the German population were subject to a series of 'negative' measures, ranging from compulsory abortion, castration, and sterilisation, via commitment to asylums, and on to murder. These racial hygienic laws and measures were part of a continuum ranging from the progressively more covert measures taken against the Jews to initiatives in social policy and welfare which the regime publicised at every opportunity. The connections were both immanent, and central to the thinking of the politicians and experts in racial hygiene who were responsible for these measures. Consequently, it is impossible to study either anti-Semitic or racial hygienic measures in isolation, the two were indivisible parts of the whole. Hence the following account of initiatives in 'social policy' is designed to bring out the underlying racial objectives.

One of the earliest, and most popular, initiatives in this field was the Law for the Reduction of Unemployment of 1 June 1933.[9] This introduced marriage loans which couples could then pay off by having children. However, the loans were conditional upon the woman giving up paid employment. This had been the goal of a campaign against so-called 'double earners' waged by both the Nazis and the Catholic Centre Party during the Weimar Republic. However, the desire to disburden the labour market of married women workers, in the interests of reducing the number of unemployed men, was no longer the primary object of policy-makers. The Law was also designed to force women back into their 'original' role as wives and mothers, in line with Nazi and conservative thinking about the 'natural' role of women. However, the Law also had a racial objective. According to the first decree on its implementation of 20 June 1933, loans could be refused 'if one of the prospective marriage partners is suffering from a hereditary or mental or physical illness which renders their marriage undesirable to the whole national community'.[10] A second supplementary decree, issued a month later, stipulated that all applicants for a marriage loan would have to undergo medical examination.[11] This opened a way for the racial registering of the population. Further philogenerative welfare measures, such as travel concessions and tax benefits for large families introduced in October 1934 and September 1935, were explicitly denied to persons deemed to be of 'lesser racial value'.[12] A general decree dated 26 September 1935 stipulated that only 'citizens of the Reich according to the Reich Citizenship Law of 15 September 1935 and their children, in so far as they are free from hereditary mental or physical illnesses' should be allowed to take advantage of these welfare measures.[13] From this time onwards, social policy was indivisible from the 'selection' of 'alien' races and those of 'lesser racial value'.

Initially, members of 'alien' races were 'only' subject to discrimination, loss of civic rights, and progressive economic ruination. By contrast, those sick and socially disadvantaged persons who were classified as being of 'lesser racial value' immediately suffered physical and psychological terror. The legal basis for this was supplied by the Law for the Prevention of Hereditarily Diseased Progeny of 14 July 1933,

which came into force on 1 January 1934.[14] This permitted the compulsory sterilisation of persons suffering from a series of allegedly hereditary illnesses as well as
chronic alcoholics. Applications for sterilisation could be made by the persons themselves, but also by their legal guardians, physicians, and asylum or public health
authorities. The decision to sterilise a person was taken by the newly-established
Hereditary Health Courts, whose verdicts could only be challenged in a Higher
Hereditary Health Court. If the appeal failed, then the sterilisation operation was
carried out, regardless of the wishes of the person concerned or of those who raised
objections on their behalf. In reality, persons were sterilised who were neither ill
nor 'hereditarily ill', in the senses specified by the law. Their 'illness' consisted in
being classified as 'asocial' or 'community aliens'. The law contained no provision
for this last practice. Plans to include the 'asocial' within its provisions had been
explicitly shelved, because of the imminence of separate legislation concerning these
categories of person. The drafting of a law on the 'asocial' was under way when the
law on compulsory sterilisation was promulgated.[15]

The Law against Dangerous Habitual Criminals, which was promulgated on 24
November 1933, was a first step in this direction. This permitted the detention and
compulsory castration of certain types of criminal as defined by 'racial-biological'
investigation. Similar measures were then incorporated into the Law on the Punishment of Juvenile Offenders of 22 January 1937. A 'racial-biological' examination
determined the duration and conditions of the sentence, a practice which was then
applied to adult offenders too. To this end, a number of 'criminal-biological research
centres' were established in various cities. Along with the illegal misapplication
of compulsory sterilisation, measures like these were to be incorporated into the
projected law on the 'asocial'. However, like its analogue – a law on 'Gypsies' – no
comprehensive law on the 'asocial' was ever promulgated. This was due not to the
collapse of the Third Reich, but rather, as was the case with the Jews, to the fact
that the regime preferred to solve the 'question' without resorting to formal
legislation or decrees.

The transition from the pseudo-legal to the totally illegal persecution of both
'alien' races and those of 'lesser racial value' occurred from approximately 1935
onwards. In that year the regime introduced two important racial-hygienic laws. The
Law for the Alteration of the Law for the Prevention of Hereditarily Diseased
Progeny of 26 June 1935 sanctioned compulsory abortion, up to and including
the sixth month of pregnancy, for women who had been categorised as 'hereditarily
ill' by the health courts.[16] This law represented a qualitative radicalisation of existing
racial-hygienic measures. The Law for the Protection of the Hereditary Health of
the German People, issued on 18 October 1935, was designed to register, and hence
more effectively exclude, 'alien' races and the 'racially less valuable' from the
'national community'.[17] The law made possession of a 'certificate of fitness to marry'
mandatory for all prospective marriage partners. The certificate was issued by public
health authorities. They could refuse a certificate to those who were allegedly
suffering from either 'hereditary illness' or contagious diseases, notably those which
were sexually transmitted. This practice gradually made it possible to register and
hence 'select' the whole German population. It also enabled health and registry
offices to encompass statistically members of 'alien' races not covered by the
Nuremberg Laws. Therefore this so-called Marriage Health Law represented an

important link between the racial-anthropological and racial-hygienic measures of the regime. This connection requires some elaboration.

The first supplementary decree on the Law for the Protection of German Blood and Honour of 14 November 1935 stipulated that not only Jews were forbidden to marry or have sexual relations with 'persons of German blood'.[18] More generally, marriages could not be contracted if 'offspring likely to be prejudicial to the purity of German blood' were anticipated. A circular issued by the Reich and Prussian Minister of the Interior on 26 November 1935 on the implementation of the law specified which marriages the regime had in mind, namely those between persons of German or related blood, and 'Gypsies, negroes or their bastards'.[19] This point was taken up by Stuckart and Globke in their official commentary on the Nuremberg Laws.[20] According to them, 'in Europe', 'Gypsies, negroes, or their bastards' were normally counted alongside Jews as 'earners of non German or related blood'.

In the following period, further social legislation was promulgated, all of which contained racial anthropological and racial hygienic provisions, i.e. the exclusion of both 'alien' races and those of 'lesser racial value' in the German population. These measures included decrees on child benefits, the Income Tax Law of 27 February 1939,[21] and the decrees 'for the protection of marriage, the family, and mother-hood' issued in 1942 and 1943 which increased maternity benefits.[22] By contrast, no further racial legislation was promulgated. There were various reasons for this. Firstly, existing decrees and legislation were formulated so elastically that they could simply be applied to further groups of people without having to introduce new laws. Secondly, the Nazis did not regard it as either necessary or opportune to advertise their persecution of 'alien' races or the 'racially less valuable' through formal legislation. Finally, to legislate would have involved introducing order into the struggle over competences taking place between the rival agencies involved in racial policy, an issue which will occupy us below.

[. . .]

The essential elements of the resulting barbaric Utopia had been considered long before Hitler achieved political power. Racial ideologies were not solely concerned with a return to some imagined past social order. They also reflected the desire to create a future society based upon the alleged verities of race. Hitler took over existing ideas and converted them into a comprehensive programme for a racial new order. Without doubt, racial anti-Semitism was the key element in a pro-gramme designed to achieve the 'recovery' of the 'Aryan Germanic race'. Various racial-hygienic measures were designed to achieve this goal. These ranged from compulsory sterilisation to murdering the sick, the 'asocial', and those designated as being of 'alien race'. The extermination of the Jews was crucial to these policies. In Hitler's mind they were not only 'racial aliens', but also a threat to his plans for the 'racial recovery' of the German people. They were both a 'lesser race' and one bent upon destroying the 'racial properties' of Hitler's 'Aryans'.

Under the Third Reich, this racial-ideological programme became the official dogma and policy of the State. Racism replaced the Weimar Republic's imperfect experiment in political pluralism. Along with the political parties and trade unions, the Nazis also endeavoured to destroy the existing social structure. Although there were undoubtedly social classes in Nazi Germany, it was a society organised increasingly upon racial rather than class lines. The regime's racial policies struck at people whether they were rich or poor, bourgeois, peasants, or workers.

As we have seen, this racial new order was based upon the 'purification of the body of the nation' of all those categorised as being 'alien', 'hereditarily ill', or 'asocial'. That meant Jews, Sinti and Roma, the mentally and physically handicapped, 'community aliens', and homosexuals. Obviously there were major quantitative and qualitative differences in the degree of persecution to which these groups were subjected. Jews, as the racial group whom the Nazis regarded as the greatest threat, undoubtedly constituted the largest single group of victims and were persecuted in the most intensive and brutal manner. Persecution undoubtedly had different specificities. This should not result in attempts either to relativise or to overlook the sufferings of others, let alone a ghoulish and profoundly inhuman competition to claim the right to having been most persecuted. All of these people were persecuted for the same reasons, although the degree of persecution was bound up with how threatening the regime perceived them to be.

The regime's 'national community' was based upon the exclusion and extermination of all those deemed to be 'alien', 'hereditarily ill', or 'asocial'. These 'elements' were subject to constant and escalating forms of selection. The 'national community' itself was categorised in accordance with racial criteria. The criteria included not merely 'racial purity' but also biological health and socio-economic performance. Members of the 'national community' were also compelled to reproduce through a series of measures ranging from financial inducements to criminal sanctions. The inducements contained in the regime's social legislation were also conditional upon an individual's racial 'value', health, and performance.

For biological reasons, women were particularly affected by the regime's attempts at racial selective breeding. Women's worth was assessed in terms of their ability to produce as many Aryan, healthy, and capable children as possible. Women were therefore reduced to the status of mere 'reproductive machines'. Racially motivated anti-feminism represented a significant departure from traditional Christian-Conservative anti-feminism. The Nazis' hierarchically organised, racist society, with healthy, 'Aryan' German man at the apex, began to rival the existing social order. However, it failed to supersede it for a variety of reasons. The first is that changes on this scale required longer than twelve years to be realised, a fact which makes any generalisations concerning the impact of the regime on German society difficult. Secondly, there were disagreements within the ruling cartel about the forms, radicalism, and tempo with which a consensually approved racial programme should be implemented. Finally, political and military considerations forced the regime to establish priorities and to postpone some of its plans until the post-war period. In other words, social policy was heavily influenced by military, economic, and domestic-political considerations, not least by the desire to integrate and pacify the population in a wartime crisis.

The main object of social policy remained the creation of a hierarchical racial new order. Everything else was subordinate to this goal, including the regime's conduct of foreign affairs and the war. In the eyes of the regime's racial politicians, the Second World War was above all a racial war, to be pursued with immense brutality until the end, that is until the concentration camps were liberated by invading Allied armies. All of these points draw attention to the specific and singular character of the Third Reich. It was not a form of regression to past times, although the regime frequently instrumentalised various ahistorical myths to convey the idea of historical normalcy. Its objects were novel and *sui generis:* to realise an ideal future world, without 'lesser races', without the sick, and without those who they decreed had no place in the 'national community'. The Third Reich was intended to be a racial rather than a class society. This fact in itself makes existing theories, whether based upon modernisation, totalitarianism, or global theories of Fascism, poor heuristic devices for a greater understanding of what was a singular regime without precedent or parallel.

Notes

1   'Hitlers Testament', *Der Prozess gegen die Hauptkriegsverbrecher vor dem Internationalen Militärgerichtshof*, Nuremberg, 14 November 1945–1 October 1946 (Nuremberg, 1947–9), Vol. 41, 552.

2   For a collection of anti-Semitic laws and decrees see Joseph Walk, *Das Sonderrecht für die Juden im NS-Staat. Eine Sammlung der gesetzlichen Massnahmen und Richtlinien* (Karlsruhe, 1981). There are also editions of the major laws and decrees by Helmut Eschwege, *Kennzeichen 'J'. Bilder, Dokumente, Berichte zur Geschichte der Verbrechen des Hitlerfaschismus an den deutschen Juden 1933–1945* (Frankfurt am Main, 1979); Kurt Patzold (ed.), *Verfolgung, Vertreibung, Vernichtung. Dokumente des faschistischen Anti-semitismus 1933–1942* (Leipzig, 1983); Hans-Dieter Schmid *et al.*, *Juden unterm Hakenkreuz. Dokumente und Berichte zur Verfolgung und Vernichtung der Juden durch die Nationalsozialisten 1933–1945* (Düsseldorf, 1983), Vols. 1 and 2.

3   'Gesetz zur Wiederherstellung des Berufsbeamtentums vom 7. April 1933', *Reichsgesetzblatt 1933*, Part 1, 175, reprinted in Schmid *et al.*, *Juden unterm Haken-kreuz*, Vol. 1, 78f. For a detailed discussion of this law see Uwe Dietrich Adam, *Judenpolitik im Dritten Reich* (Düsseldorf, 1979), 46ff.

4   'Wehrgesetz vom 21. Mai 1935', *Reichsgesetzblatt 1935*, Part 1, 611; reprinted in Schmid *et al.*, *Juden unterm Hakenkreuz*, Vol. 1, 86.

5   'Reichsbürgergesetz' and 'Gesetz zum Schutz des deutschen Blutes und der deutschen Ehre vom 15. September 1935', *Reichsgesetzblatt 1935*, Part 1, 146f.; reprinted in Schmid *et al.*, *Juden unterm Hakenkreuz*, Vol. 1, 97f.

6   Falk Ruttke, 'Erb- und Rassenpflege in Gesetzgebung und Rechtssprechung des Dritten Reiches', in *Deutsches Recht*, 25 January 1933, 25–7, cited by Karl A. Schleunes, *The Twisted Road to Auschwitz: Nazi Policy toward German Jews 1933–1939* (London, 1970), 120.

7   'I. Verordnung zum Reichsbürgergesetz vom 14. November 1935', *Reichs-geset-zblatt 1935*, Part 1, 1333f.; reprinted in Schmid *et al.*, *Juden unterm Hakenkreuz*, Vol. l, 102.

8   As yet there has been no comprehensive study of Nazi racism. In recent years there has been considerable interest in racial hygiene and health policy under the Nazi regime. On this see Kurt Nowak, *Euthanasie und Sterilisation im Dritten Reich. Die Konfrontation der evangelischen und katholischen Kirche mit dem 'Gesetz zur Verhütung erbkranken Nachwuchses' und der 'Euthanasie'-Aktion* (Göttingen, 1978); Gerhard Baader, Ulrich Schultz (eds.), *Medizin und Nationalsozialismus* (Berlin,

1980); Walter Wuttke-Groneberg, *Medizin im Nationalsozialismus. Ein Arbeitsbuch* (Tubingen, 1980); Ernst Klee, *'Euthanasie' im NS-Staat. Die 'Vernichtung lebensunwerten Lebens'* (Frankfurt am Main, 1983), *Dokumente zur 'Euthanasie'* (Frankfurt am Main, 1985), *Was sie taten — was sie wurden. Artze, Juristen und andere Beteiligte am Kranken- oder Judenmord* (Frankfurt am Main, 1986); Benno Müller-Hill, *Murderous Science: Elimination by Scientific Selection of Jews, Gypsies, and Others, Germany 1933–1945* (Oxford, 1988); Peter Weingan, 'Eugenik, eine angewandte Wissenschaft im Dritten Reich', Peter Lundgreen (ed.), *Wissenschaft im Dritten Reich* (Frankfurt am Main, 1985), 314–49; Gisela Bock, *Zwangssterilisation im Nationalsozialismus* (Opladen, 1986); Alfons Labisch, Florian Tennstedt, *Der Weg zum Gesetz über die Vereinheitlichung des Gesundheitswesens* (Düsseldorf, 1986); Heidrun Kaupen-Haas (ed.), *Der Griff nach der Bevölkerung. Aktualität und Kontinuität nazistischer Bevölkerungspolitik. Schriften der Hamburger Stiftung für Sozialgeschichte des 20. Jahrhunderts*, 1 (Nordlingen, 1986); Christian Ganssmüller, *Die Erbgesundheitspolitik des Dritten Reiches* (Cologne, 1987); Hans Walter Schmuhl, *Rassenhygiene, Nationalsozialismus, Euthanasie* (Göttingen, 1987); Peter Weingart, Jürgen Kroll, Kurt Bayertz, *Rasse, Blut und Gene. Geschichte der Eugenik und Rassenhygiene in Deutschland* (Frankfurt am Main, 1988); Peter Emil Becker, *Zur Geschichte der Rassenhygiene. Wege ins Dritte Reich* (Stuttgart, 1988); Robert N. Proctor, *Racial Hygiene: Medicine under the Nazis* (London, 1988); Paul J. Weindling, *Health, Race and German Politics* (Cambridge, Cambridge University Press, 1989).

9   'Gesetz zur Verminderung der Arbeitslosigkeit vom 1. Juni 1933', *Reichsgesetzblatt 1933*, Part 1, 323ff.

10   'Erste Durchführungsverordnung über die Gewährung von Ehestandsdarlehen vom 20. Juni 1933', *Reichsgesetzblatt 1933*, Part 1, 377–88.

11   'Zweite Durchführungsverordnung über die Gewährung von Ehestandsdarlehen vom 26. Juli 1933', *Reichsgesetzblatt 1933*, Part 1, 515.

12   'Runderlass des Preussischen Ministers des Innern vom 4. Mai 1934 über Fahrpreisermässigungen für kinderreiche Familien', *Zentralblatt für Jugendrecht und Jugendwohlfahrt. Organ des deutschen Instituts for Vormundschaftswesen*, 26 (1934), 55f.; 'Einkommenssteuergesetz vom 16. Oktober 1934', *Reichsgesetzblatt 1934*, Part 1, 1005–31; 'Verordnung über die Gewährung von Kinderbeihilfen an kinderreiche Familien vom 15. September 1935', *Reichsgesetzblatt 1935*, Part 1–, 1160.

13   'Durchführungsbestimmungen zur Verordnung über die Gewährung von Kinderbeihilfen an kinderreiche Familien vom 26. September 1935', *Reichsgesetzblatt 1935*, Part 1, 1206ff.

14   'Gesetz zur Verhütung erbkranken Nachwuchses vom 14. Juli 1933', *Reichsgesetzblatt 1933*, Part 1, 529ff. Arthur Gütt, Ernst Rüdin, Falk Ruttke, 'Gesetz zur Verhütung erbkranken Nachwuchses vom 14. Juli 1933' (Berlin, 1934).

15   For the following see Patrick Wagner, 'Das Gesetz über die Behandlung Gemeinschaftsfremder', *Feinderklärung und Prävention. Kriminalbiologie, Zigeunerforschung und Asozialenpolitik. Beiträge zur nationalsozialistischen Gesundheits- und Sozialpolitik*, 6 (Berlin, 1988), 75–100; Ernst Klee, *'Euthanasie' im NS-Staat*, 38ff.; Detlev Peukert, 'Arbeitslager und Jugend-KZ. Die "Behandlung Gemeinschaftsfremder" im Dritten Reich', in Detlev Peukert, Jürgen Reulecke (eds.), *Die Reihen fast-geschlossen. Beiträge zur Geschichte des Alltags unterm Nationalsozialismus* (Wuppertal, 1981), 413–34; J. Hellmer, *Der Gewohnheitsverbrecher und die Sicherheitsverwahrung 1934–1945* (Berlin, 1961); Karl-Leo Terhorst, *Polizeiliche plan-massige Überwachung und polizeiliche Vorbeugungshaft im Dritten Reich* (Heidelberg, 1983).

16 'Gesetz zur Änderung des Gesetzes zur Verhütung erbkranken Nachwuchses vom 26. Juni 1935', *Reichsgesetzblatt 1935*, Part 1, 1035ff.

17 'Gesetz zum Schutze der Erbgesundheit des deutschen Volkes vom 18. Oktober 1935', *Reichsgesetzblatt 1935*, Part 1, 1246ff.

18 '1. Durchführungsverordnung zum Gesetz zum Schutz des deutschen Blutes und der deutschen Ehre vom 14. November 1935', *Reichsgesetzblatt 1935*, Part 1, 1334ff.

19 'Runderlass des Reichs- und Preussischen Ministers des Innern vom 26. November 1935', *Ministerialblatt für Preussische innere Verwaltung*, 1935, 1429–34. Compare also 'Runderlass der Reichsministers des Innern vom 3. Januar 1936', in Pätzold (ed.), *Verfolgung, Vertreibung, Vernichtung*, 121f.

20 Wilhelm Stuckart, Hans Globke, *Kommentar zur deutschen Rassengesetzgebung* (Munich, 1936), Vol. 1, 55.

21 'Einkommenssteuergesetz vom 27. Februar 1939', *Reichsgesetzblatt 1939*, Part 1, 297–320.

22 'Ausführungsverordnung zum Gesetz der erwerbstätigen Mutter vom 17. Mai 1942', *Reichsgesetzblatt 1942*, Part 1, 324ff.; 'Verordnung zum Schutz von Ehe, Familie und Mutterschaft vom 9. Marz 1943', *Reichsgesetzblatt 1943*, Part 1, 140f.

Chapter 33

Jonathan Steinberg

PARTNERS IN GENOCIDE?
ANTI-SEMITISM AND THE
AXIS ALLIANCE

■ from *ALL OR NOTHING: THE AXIS AND THE HOLOCAUST 1941–1943*, London and New York, pp. 220, 222–3, 224–5, 226–7, 228, 229, 240–1, 242, 243

In the concluding paragraph of his monograph *All or Nothing* Jonathan Steinberg affirms that Fascist Italy and Nazi Germany 'differed less in structure than in thoroughness and purpose'. His comparative analysis of anti-Semitic policies in the two Axis countries encountered significant differences: the Nazi regime was more consistent, uniform and intolerant of 'flexible' policy and had to deal with a more prominent and sizeable Jewish community within its jurisdiction; by contrast Mussolini wavered, lacked the brutal determination of Hitler, failed to impose a culture of loyalty and eventually targeted a smaller, but more integrated Jewish population. Steinberg does admit that 'something went horribly wrong in Italy' (the rise of Fascism) – much earlier than in Germany. However, he also notes that the social and political conditions in Nazi Germany were far more conducive to the horrors of the Final Solution than in Italy.

D OES IT FOLLOW, THEREFORE, that Germans hated Jews and Italians did not? There does seem to have been remarkably little Italian anti-semitism. Jewish communities on Italian soil had, of course, an ancient lineage. The Roman Jewish community can trace its continuous existence with some certainty to the days of the Roman Republic when Jews were called 'liberti', the 'freed', because they were so difficult to enslave.[1] In the ensuing 1,800 years they had suffered all the persecutions, forced conversions, exclusions and deprivations which are common to Jewish history everywhere. What made Italian Jews different from co-religionists elsewhere was not the Jews but the environment in which they lived.

[. . .]

Jews became patriotic Italians and took part in the wars of national liberation. The architect of unification, Count Cavour, employed the Jew Isaaco Artom as his private secretary and Jews fought on the barricades and in the services. Jews became propagandists for the new Italy. German-speaking Jews who were Austrian subjects in cities like Trieste turned themselves into Italian-speaking patriots. One of them, Hector Schmitz, became one of Italy's greatest novelists under the name Italo Svevo. Felice Venezian founded the Dante Alighieri Society, the Italian equivalent of the British Council or US Information Service. Jews identified strongly with the Italian monarchy. As the great historian Arnaldo Momigliano noted in a lecture at Brandeis, in 1984, 'It explains why my grandmother used to cry every time she listened to the *"Marcia Reale"* – the Royal Hymn of the Italian Monarchy – and if you can cry at such atrocious music, you can cry at anything.'[2]

[. . .]

They [Italian Jews] made up less than 1 per cent of the Italian population and blended easily into the surrounding Italian environment. In Rome the Jews of the ghetto and Trastevere spoke the *Ramanesco* of other slum dwellers mixed with the occasional Hebrew phrase and had their distinctive cuisine and habits. Elsewhere, as in Ferrara and cities further north, Jews divided into three distinctive groups, symbolized by the three different synagogues: *la scola tedesca* (ashkenazic), *la scola spagnola* (sephardic) and *la scola italiana* (Italian) but, as any reader of Giorgio Bassani's wonderful *The Garden of the Finzi-Contini* will recall, ashkenazic Jews in Ferrara had become by the 1930s no less Italian than their sephardic or Judaeo-Italian co-religionists.[3]

To Jews from northern Europe, then and now, Italian Jews, like the countless jokes about Jews in China and Japan, 'did not look Jewish'. As Primo Levi remarked in his last book, this fact cost many of them their lives in the Nazi death camps. They could not communicate; they spoke no Yiddish: 'The Polish, Russian, Hungarian Jews were stupefied that we Italians did not speak it; we were suspect Jews, not to be trusted . . . it was not comfortable to be an Italian Jew.'[4]

Jewish identity had become attenuated by the twentieth century. Dan Vittorio Segre recalls that knowledge of Hebrew, the rituals and practices of Judaism had become little more than symbolic acts of identity in his well-to-do north Italian family.[5] Nello Rosselli, one of the founders of the anti-fascist movement *Giustizia e Libertà*, summed up the situation of many Italian Jews in a speech of 1924: 'I am a Jew who doesn't go to temple on the sabbath, who doesn't know Hebrew, and who doesn't observe any part of the religion. . . . I am not a Zionist and am not, therefore, an integral Jew.'[6]

Jewishness for well-educated Italian Jews had become the smile of the Cheshire Cat, just visible as it disappeared. Mixed marriages between Jews and non-Jews had become extremely common. In practice, according to the census of 1938, 43.7 per cent of marriages involving Jews were marriages in which one partner was not Jewish. Even the office for Demography and Race was struck by the figure and commented: 'The percentage of Jews of both sexes who marry persons of other races and religions in Italy is markedly higher than in other countries of Europe.'[7]

Jews spread out into various professions and activities but nowhere achieved that prominence in, say, banking or the professions, as in Hungary, the type of prominence which provoked anti-semitic comment or defensive measures. Certainly, as H. Stuart Hughes notes in his *Prisoners of Hope. The Silver Age of the Italian Jews*,[8] there were many important writers who were Jews, but nothing in Alberto Moravia's work or Carlo Levi's is specifically 'Jewish'. Even Primo Levi, who has become for our generation the very symbol of Jewish survival in the holocaust, saves his soul in Auschwitz not by Torah but by Dante. *If This Be a Man* explores the dilemma of Italian Jewry. A man with the most Jewish of names, 'Levi', finds himself in a Nazi concentration camp for no other reason than his Jewishness, but his Jewish identity has become so tenuous that he turns to the supreme Christian poetic work for solace at his moment of need. Italian Jews, in truth, 'did not look Jewish'.

[. . .]

When Italy joined Nazi Germany in the Anti-Comintern Pact of 6 November 1937 Jews began to get nervous. A month after the treaty was signed, Ciano wrote in his diary: 'The Jews are flooding me with insulting anonymous letters, accusing me of having promised to persecute them. It's not true. The Germans have never mentioned this subject to us.'[9] The rumours reached such a level that the Italian Foreign Ministry issued an official denial on 14 February 1938:

> the recent polemics in the press have been such as to arouse the impression in certain foreign circles that the Fascist government is on the point of initiating an anti-semitic policy. Responsible circles in Rome are in a position to affirm that such impressions are completely erroneous.[10]

That was simply false and many people knew it. At precisely the same time the Ministry of War had begun to make lists of Jews in the officer corps. Some time in 1937–38 Mussolini changed his attitude to the Jews. People at the time, and some scholars after the event, assumed that the introduction of anti-semitic legislation had been a condition of the establishment of the Axis. Meir Michaelis, whose *Mussolini and the Jews* investigates this question, states categorically that 'the entire ample documentation in this field, in fact, contains not the least hint of German interference in Italy's domestic Jewish question during the period under review (that is, 1936–38)'.[11]

Mussolini hated the impression that he, the master in such matters, had become Hitler's pupil, and by August the fascist press, as Bottai noted in his diary on 10 August 1938

> were engaged in a journalistic attempt to show a continuity in the racist thinking of the Duce. But people remember the pages of his conversation with Ludwig. They remember that the writer, chosen to receive historic confidences, is a Jew, that the first biographer of Mussolini was a Jewess and that he has nominated many Jewish senators.[12] [. . .]

If the Germans cannot be directly blamed for Mussolini's sudden conversion to the Nuremberg Laws, they and the atmosphere they created in Europe certainly played a part. In May 1938 the Hungarian regime of Prime Minister Bela Imredy passed the first of several discriminatory laws which step by step first segregated the rich, powerful and fiercely loyal Magyar Jewish community and ultimately destroyed it.[13] Early in 1939 Hungary, too, signed the Anti-Comintern Pact. Meir Michaelis may be right that no proof exists that the Germans intervened to force Mussolini to promote anti-Jewish legislation, but they had no need to intervene. Everybody in Europe knew what Nazism meant for the Jews. To ally with that state was at the very least to condone racial persecution. Respectability in the Anti-Comintern club required commitment and the Horthy regime in Hungary, the Antonescu regime in Rumania and the Duce's regime in Italy met that requirement. The Jews paid the dues for the regime's new association.

On 6 October 1938 the Fascist Grand Council approved the text of the racial laws which as Royal Decree Number 1728 became law on 17 November. Jews suddenly turned into second-class citizens, forbidden to serve in the armed forces or the state bureaucracy, to teach in state schools and universities, to own or manage companies engaged in military production or employing more than a certain number of employees, to have 'aryan' domestic servants and so on.[14] These were Nuremberg Laws but Italian-style, that is, shot through with inconsistencies and riddled with exemptions for this or that category of persons 'who deserved well of the state', such as the families of those killed in battle, holders of high decorations for valour and the like. A committee of the Department of Demography and Race in the Ministry of the Interior met to consider the thousands of applications for 'discrimination', the term for honorary exemption from the burden of Jewishness.

The files of 'Demorazza', as the department was called, make depressing reading. Jewish generals, admirals, distinguished lawyers and bankers, war widows, semi-literate tradespeople, all wrote begging petitions on the special *carta bollata* (officially stamped paper), which the citizen has to use to approach the Italian state. The anonymous letter, a peculiar vice of Italian public life, added to the misery of the Jews by raising all sorts of unsubstantiated charges. Files filled up with letters of support or opposition. But the main impression was of a pervasive moral degradation. A full admiral, whose family fought for Italy in 1848, and who was a former inspector general of naval armaments, submitted a humble petition begging for the restoration of his Italian citizenship because as an engineer officer in the First World War he had not received the 'War Cross', a medal which conferred automatic exemption under the law of 17 November 1938. He adds that his wife and children are Catholic but he is of *la religione ebraica*.[15] I only found one example of backbone. A young air force lieutenant resigned his commission and returned his decorations.[16] The rest outdid themselves in servility and professions of loyalty to a regime which had betrayed and humiliated them.

The Jewish fascists were doubly desperate, deprived at a stroke of the King's pen of their party and their state. Susan Zuccotti gives the number of Jewish members of the fascist party at nearly 5,000, which would amount to 10 per cent of the Jewish population.[17] Just as not all Jews were equally Jewish, so there were fascists and fascists. By 1938, as Camillo Boitani explained to me, a party membership had become a document like a birth certificate, a piece of evidence one needed to be admitted to competitions for state employment or for certain careers in the armed services. Nobody checked if dues were paid or if membership had been renewed.[18] It had come to be known as the *tessera del pane*, the bread ticket. Certainly one did not have to join, but many did. It made life more convenient and involved no great sacrifice of principle for most people. After all, had not 'He' (i.e. Mussolini) saved Italy from bolshevism?

[. . .]

The 'Laws' ruined lives and brought misery to thousands of patriotic Italian Jews, but often, as Evi Eller told me, the behaviour of the local population 'mitigated' the force of the 'Laws'. The Ellers had migrated from Hungary in 1925 and settled at Orano near Fiume, a region that today belongs to Yugoslavia. Her father, who ran a small garage, became an Italian citizen in 1937. The following year the 'Laws' deprived him of his citizenship and forced Evi, then 20, to give up her university course in classics and Italian at Padua. Mr Eller was forced to sell his business and Evi, as a Jew, was immediately dismissed from her job as supply teacher at the *liceo* in near-by Abbazia. The local people helped them in whatever way they could. Tradesmen somehow never got round to sending the Ellers a bill. The grocer gave them free vegetables. When Evi began to offer private coaching for school exams, her first pupil was the nephew of the captain of the fascist militia: 'When the others saw that, they too found the courage to send their children to me for lessons.'[19]

Thousands of Jews, Italian and foreign, tell similar stories: acts of kindness here, moments of courage there, gratuitous assistance from total strangers somewhere else. Without that remarkable practical compassion many more Jews would have perished when the holocaust hit Italy than actually did. [. . .]

The officials who controlled the Jewish concentration camp at Ferramonti in Calabria turned it into the largest kibbutz on the European continent. Barracks were divided into kosher and non-kosher and the *maresciallo* of the carabinieri even learned some Yiddish to communicate with the prisoners. Prisoners were addressed as *signore* and the Jewish doctors provided clinics for the surrounding peasant villages. The commandant risked his life in 1943 to get permission to allow his prisoners to go free before the German troops retreating from Sicily fell upon the Jews and destroyed them.[20]

[. . .]

Not all Italians behaved this way and there are stories of betrayal, denunciation and treachery. Italian humanity was selective. Jews were often extremely badly treated by the regime. Mussolini encouraged the spread of anti-semitic propaganda and made fanatics like Telesio Interlandi, editor of a paper called *La Difesa della Razza* (the Defence of the Race) into respected figures. Institutes published racist studies and professors who should have known better gave lectures. Italy was not free of anti-semitism, either clerical or racial, but somehow it never seized the imagination of the Italian people.

No explanation of the Italian attitude to the Jews from 1938 to 1945 can ever be satisfactory. Most end by citing aspects of what we loosely call national character. National character certainly exists. The rich compound of language, habits, tradition, architecture, social structure, laws, history, climate and geography that give a place its specificity is undeniably 'out there' in reality. Every traveller senses such differences expressed in the details of daily life – from the size of the tablespoons to the sounds of the streets.

[. . .]

Jews in Germany were certainly vulnerable in a way that Jews in Italy were not. They were prominent, numerous, identifiable, and concentrated. Italian Jews were almost literally the opposite. Germans had a set of attitudes and values which heightened imagined distinctions between Gentile and Jew; Italian values minimized them. Germans despised trade and commerce and political fixing as *Kuhhandel* (horse-trading), activities at which Italians excelled. Germany had a very brief experience of constitutional democracy; Italy had a rooted, liberal tradition, however corrupt and deformed. The German aristocracies had social and economic power, especially embodied in the Junker class and the great East Elbian estates. After all, one of them, Paul Ludwig Hans Anton von Beneckendorff und von Hindenburg, was the President of the German Republic who named Adolf Hitler – the 'Bohemian Corporal', as he contemptuously called him – Chancellor of the Reich in 1933. The Italian aristocracy broke into local groupings lacking homogeneity and divided by the struggle between church and state. The upper German social strata excluded Jews; the Italian did not. Finally, the single most characteristic institution in the history of Prussia-Germany had been the army. As Georg Heinrich von Behrenhorst had put it in the eighteenth century, 'The Prussian monarchy is not a country which has an army, but an army which has a country, in which – as it were – it is just stationed.'[21] The single most characteristic institution in Italy was the church.

The smaller question – why did Italian officers and diplomats refuse to co-operate in the holocaust while their German opposite numbers did? – can, I hope, now be answered. The two strands of the argument, the 'events' as they unfolded and the 'explanations' which have compared structures, behaviours and beliefs, converge at this point. Italian officers behaved as they did because they served in a traditional, monarchist, liberal, gentlemanly, masonic, philo-semitic and anti-fascist service. The professional diplomats, even those who had come from the fascist movement, shared those values, and, then, there was always in the background the church. The worse the war went the more they asserted those values of *civiltà italiana* against the monstrous demands of their Axis partner. German officers acted as they did because traditions of obedience and rigidities of thought made any other action unthinkable, because by 1941–42 Hitler's ideology had fused with their own prejudices and assumptions, because their culture had an almost Manichaean dualism which excluded Jews and other *Untermenschen* from the human race, because the Nazi regime had a dark apparatus of repression and terror from which nobody, not even a four-star general, could feel exempt. Ambassador Guelfo Zamboni told me that in Salonica even *Generaloberst* Löhr, Supreme Commander South East, trembled when the SS came.[22] Italian officers and diplomats could conspire because the risks were less. Nobody obeyed in Italy anyway; because Mussolini could, even at the end, still hear a human voice and react, because they knew that their conspiracy made sense nationally.

[. . .]

Hitler inflicted more misery on his fellow human beings than anybody in the history of the human race. He may not have been more vicious than some great evil-doers in the past but he had more terrible means at his disposal. Yet, as I have tried to show, it is more than naive, it is dangerous to see Hitler as uniquely guilty. While he was undoubtedly mad, his madness came in forms which seemed attractive and right to millions of his fellow countrymen. His resentments were theirs; his prejudices and preferences like their own. He used the engines of a modern state to murder and enslave millions, but that engine functioned smoothly to the end. In the SS files, I found pay-slips complete with the correct deductions and provision for pensions dated 30 April 1945. The Nazi state ticked over until there were no typewriters to pound or gas to put in gas chambers.

[. . .]

Something went terribly wrong in Italy too and the rise of fascism was really 'prior' to the emergence of Nazism. Hitler always acknowledged his debt to Mussolini and rightly. Mussolini invented the modern mass movement of the right. He learned his techniques from Lenin and drew his ideology from the accumulating detritus of irrationalism, voluntarism, futurism and anti-modernism in all its poisonous variants. The fascist regime had secured its power, jailed its enemies and begun to build its great Roman monuments while Hitler's party lurked in the shadows of the Weimar Republic, not able to collect 3 per cent of the votes.

The two regimes had much in common. The Axis was less 'unnatural' than many Italians wished to believe. They differed less in structure than in thoroughness and purpose. Hitler never wavered in his determination to destroy Jewry. Mussolini never fixed his attention on anything for very long. Hitler's views on politics remained constant from 1920 to the last days in the bunker; Mussolini changed his direction with each passing wind. For Mussolini power itself seemed to be the end; for Hitler it was but a means.

Notes

1 Milano, Attilio, *Storia degli ebrei in Italia* (Turin, 1963) p. 9.
2 Momigliano, Armando Dante, 'The Many Worlds of Vito Volterra', lecture delivered Brandeis University, 30 April 1984, 8 (typescript copy given to me by the author).
3 Momigliano, A. D., 'The Many Worlds', 3.
4 Levi, Primo, *I sommersi e i salvati* (Turin, 1986) p. 78.
5 Segre, Dan Vittorio, *The Memoirs*, 27–29.
6 Cited in Renzo De Felice, *Storia degli ebrei sotto il fascismo* (Turin, 1972). 89.
7 ibid., 17.
8 Hughes, H. Stuart, *Prisoners of Hope. The Silver Age of the Italian Jews 1924–1974* (Cambridge, Mass., 1983) especially 9 ff. where Hughes very sensitively poses the question 'what is left of identity when language and religion are gone?'.
9 Michaelis, Meir, *Mussolini and the Jews. German-Italian Relations and the Jewish Question in Italy, 1922–1945* (Oxford, 1978).
10 'Informazione Diplomatica', no. 14, 14 February 1938, in Meir Michaelis, *Mussolini*, 141.

11   ibid., 158.

12   G. Bottai, *Diario, 1935–1944*, ed. by Giordano Bruno Guerri (Milano, 1982), 10 August 1938.

13   Katzburg, Nathaniel, *Hungary and the Jews 1920–1943* (Ramat-Gan, 1981), 101–04 and Randolph L. Braham, *The Politics of Genocide. The Holocaust in Hungary*, 2 vols (New York, 1981) vol. 1, 122–27.

14   The most complete account of the racial laws of 1938 is to be found in Renzo De Felice's *Storia degli ebrei sotto il fascismo* (Turin, 1972) in which all the most important documents are published in an appendix. Susan Zuccotti in *The Italians and the Holocaust* offers an excellent and readable account in English of the laws and their application in chapter 3, 28–51.

15   Guido, Segre, ammiraglio di squadra, 2 November 1938, ACS SPD CR 1922–45 480R B. 144, f. 315.

16   Valfredo, Segre, to S. E. Valle, 5 September 1938 with Mussolini's marginalia, ibid.

17   Zuccotti, Susan, *The Italians*, 27.

18   Boitani, Camillo, interview, Rome, 2 April 1988. See also Paolo Monelli, *Roma 1943* (Rome, 1946), 23 ff. for an entertaining account of the fraudulence of party membership.

19   Eller, Evi, interview, Rome, 4 April 1988.

20   Bandler, Paul, interview, Rome, 28 March 1988; see also the fascinating account of the concentration camp in Calabria by Carlo Spartaco Capogreco, *Ferramonti. La vita e gli uomini del piu grande campo d'internamento fascista (1940–1945)* (Florence, 1987). Dr Capogreco, who is Calabrian, not Jewish, was intrigued by the ruins of the camp and decided to reconstruct this forgotten chapter of the history of Calabria. It is a fine, humane and moving work.

21   Cited in Christian Graf von Krockow, *Warnung vor Preussen* (Berlin, 1981), p. 213, n. 5; C. B. A. Behrens, *Society, Government and the Enlightenment. The Experiences of Eighteenth-century France and Prussia* (London, 1985), 182–83.

22   Interview with Ambassador Guelfo Zamboni, Lido dei Pini, 9 April 1988.

Chapter 34

Mark Neocleous

RACISM, FASCISM AND NATIONALISM

■ from *FASCISM*, Milton Keynes, 1997, pp. 27–30, 31–7

Mark Neocleous puts forward a highly convincing counter-argument to the views of Burleigh and Wippermann (**32**) about the significance of anti-Semitism in fascist ideology. While for the latter Nazi virulent racialism constituted the defining element of Hitler's *Weltanschauung* and thus undermines the validity of generic fascism, Neocleous suggests that the outwardly different policies of the regimes in Germany and Italy towards race were in fact 'different ideological mechanisms for substantiating (similar) nationalist claims'. For him racism and anti-Semitism – far from being an essentially 'German peculiarity' – emanate from the same 'xenophobic core of nationalism'. Therefore, Hitler's fanatical pursuit of anti-Semitism derived from a general concern for the 'racial foundations of the nation', while Mussolini's seemingly bewildering conversion to anti-Semitism in the late 1930s related to similar concerns about the future of the Italian nation in an expanding colonial empire.

HERE WE NEED TO ADDRESS the question of race. Extending a point made by Peter Gay, we can say that race was everywhere by the end of the nineteenth century, saturating social, political and scientific thought. Yet however much those who spoke of race thought (and still think) they were engaged in a purely scientific activity, even 'the most neutral use of the word "race" could not conceal the invidious element lurking in the background', namely, their contribution to the cultivation of hatred.[1] For the purpose of differentiating between races is never simply to show that races exist, that is, that there are human groups whose members possess common physical characteristics. Nor is it to show that there is a continuity between physical type and character and that individual behaviour depends on the racial group to which the individual belongs. It is in fact to politicize the pseudo-scientific activity by ranking the races hierarchically and reworking political structures such that institutions and processes which depend on and support racial differences are maintained and strengthened. With this last point racial theory joins racist practice.[2] However much the argument turned on the scientific measurement of skulls and other physical characteristics, all commentators agreed that what was carried in the blood was a set of characteristics and capacities linking individuals in some indefinable way, some mystical fashion, to other members of their race. What racism produces – *völkisch* or otherwise – is, in essence, a *biological mysticism*.

The Nazis took these ideas and gave them a political charge that they otherwise lacked, in two ways. First, the Nazis sought to go beyond *völkisch* groups by grounding the racism of their ideas in a strong conception of movement and party. The reason for grounding the movement in a National Socialist German Workers' Party (NSDAP) was that the party form would also serve to frighten the 'folkish sleepwalkers' away. Left on their own, the Nazis believed, *völkisch* ideas are like religious conceptions of the world: spiritually powerful but politically nebulous and without any organizational means for realizing their force. For Hitler, the concept *völkisch* was 'uncleanly defined': 'in view of its conceptual boundlessness the ideal is no possible basis for a movement'. What was needed was an instrument which would enable the *völkisch* world-view to fight, a militant organization willing to mobilize the masses and produce the necessary leadership. Second, the struggle between races was seen as a struggle of the eternal will for superiority, serving the aristo-cratic principle of nature. The state would be the means to the preservation of this inequality and the racial foundation of society.[3]

Now, there are several issues at stake here. First, there is the claim that Nazi biological racism and anti-Semitism reflects a substantial difference between German and non-German thought and culture. The problem with such a claim is that it rests on a simplistic distinction between styles of *national* thought. Clearly *völkisch* thought had a resonance in Germany that it failed to achieve elsewhere, but there are dangers in reducing it to something *peculiarly* German. As Geoff Eley points out, until 1914 the term *Volk* had the same double connotations of 'national' and 'popular' found in other countries as well,[4] and a large number of the contributors who assisted in turning *völkisch* thought into virulent racism were non-German. Admittedly Arthur de Gobineau, who made racial doctrine popular with his *Essay on the Inequality of the Human Races* (1853–5), was more widely read in Germany than in his native France (hence the creation of the Gobineau Society in Germany), and Houston Stuart Chamberlain, whose *Foundations of the Nineteenth Century* (1898–1900) combined racial science with a mysticism and a political programme, was of English origin but identified with the Germans and was taken up by them in return.[5] But this hardly justifies the claim that there is something specific in *German* thought and culture which enables us to explain the role of racism and anti-Semitism in fascism.[6]

The approach to Nazism which tries to explain it with reference to 'German thought', 'German culture', 'German militarism', 'German authoritarianism', 'the German cultural cognitive model of society', or, for that matter, anything else deemed the essence of 'the German character', runs the risk of perpetuating the myth of German peculiarity, the idea that Nazism was the outcome of a German deviation from an otherwise 'normal' type of European development.[7] Such an approach not only fails to grasp the essential relation between Nazism and other forms of fascism, but also obliterates the important exchange of ideas that occurred across Europe and contributed to the success of fascism. Moreover, such arguments concede to fascism its own central claim: that nations are natural phenomena which shape our character and which thus determine our place in history. Rejecting the claim that Nazism can be understood through German peculiarity does not mean that one makes no reference to historical specificity; it *does*, however, mean that our major conceptual tool for the understanding of fascism is not reduced to national 'peculiarities'.

The question, then, is how to incorporate the phenomenon of Nazism and its biological racism and anti-Semitism into the account of fascism being developed here. One way is through the idea of the nation and the virulent nationalism found in fascist thought. In Hitler's *Mein Kampf* there is a continual oscillation between race and nation, as though distinguishing between them makes no difference. In the Chapter on 'Nation and Race' he distinguishes between 'culture-bearing' and 'culture-creating' *races*, only to refer to them later as culture-bearing and culture-creating nations, a transition made via the concept of a 'people'. Sometimes his oscillation between the two results in both being reduced to the blood. Indeed, Clause 4 of the Programme of the German Workers' Party as it was transformed into the NSDAP in February 1920 states that 'Only members of the nation may be citizens of the State. Only those of German blood, whatever their creed, may be members of the nation'.[8] And early Nazi ideologues such as Walther Darré wrote that 'the choice is now between nationalism and inter-nationalism; that is, between anti-semitism and pro-semitism'.[9]

Hitler's oscillation between race and nation is not surprising given his prime propaganda technique of reducing everything to one simple proposition, but there is more than propaganda at stake here. *Volk* is a notoriously slippery concept, shifting as it does between 'people', 'nation' and a 'natural' racial community of blood and soil (which are, in turn, all equally slippery). The oscillation masks the fact that *nationalism* is the real driving force behind Nazism, as it is with fascism in general. The precondition of the existence of a higher racial humanity is not the state but the nation; thus the importance of the state lies in the relative utility it possesses for the nation.[10] Moreover, when Hitler talks about the nation, he frequently does so in language that would not be out of place in Mussolini and Gentile's account of the state: 'the underlying idea is to do away with egoism and to lead people into the sacred collective egoism which is the nation'.[11] As a political programme Nazism set itself against the Weimar Republic, the Marxist and social democratic left, unemployment and economic collapse, and the Versailles Treaty. In this it shared the ideological ground with the range of conservative, reactionary and counter-revolutionary forces on the political right generally. In Weimar Germany these forces often took the form of *völkisch* organizations or parties. As a political force Nazism had to appeal to these groups as well as rally the masses. To do this it frequently invoked nationalism rather than racism for, despite their *völkisch* character and the 'nebulous abstraction' (as Griffin calls it), of a rejuvenated *Volk* at the centre of their thought, the central thread connecting all the groups on the political right in Weimar Germany was *nationalism*. In Arthur Moeller van den Bruck's *The Third Reich*, for example, it is German nationalism that is the means of expressing

German universalism, for it will enable the Third Reich to be a genuine 'third way' between capitalism and socialism. This third way will be achieved by incorporating the proletariat through a return to the values of the *Volk*, to be established by making the proletariat part of the nation. This approach is representative of the range of conservative revolutionaries who played a crucial role in undermining Weimar democracy. Likewise, the programme of the DNVP was committed to national rebirth in which racial origins were to be protected 'for the sake of national unity'. Its reference to 'spiritual unity' is a reference to the unity of the nation. Just as this nationalism was to be the protection against Bolshevism, the solution to the crisis of Weimar democracy and thus the saviour of Germany, so it was with nationalism rather than racism that the Nazis sought to win the support of both other forces and the German people.[12]

[. . .]

In one sense, then, the central issue behind racial discourse is the threat to the nation. In the case of Nazism, as the fear for the nation was transformed from *völkisch* anxiety to political programme the issue concerned not so much the question of racial inter-mingling as the threat posed to the nation and national unity by such intermingling. Hitler's concerns over race are in fact concerns over the racial foundations of the nation.[13] His biologism applies to the nation as to the race: it is the nation that is variously described as containing 'symptoms of disease', 'poisoning', 'creeping sick-ness', 'toxins', 'plague', 'parasites' and an 'alien virus'.[14] Nazism thus consolidates the centrality of nationalism to fascism by rationalizing the territoriality of some species on the natural basis of the nation-state. In Nazism the nation becomes a unit filled with blood.[15]

   Thinking of nationalism's relationship to fascism in this way also partly explains the place of the Jew in Nazism. In *Mein Kampf* Hitler attacks the Jews for a variety of reasons — their conspiratorial nature, their participation in Bolshevik power and centrality to Marxism, their control of finance and capital — but the crux of his attack, and the basis of his fear, is that 'the Jew is a parasite in the body of other peoples'. This account of the Jew is founded on the fact that Jews have no home of their own, that is, the Jew is 'a parasite in the body of other nations and states'. As Hannah Arendt argues, one of the means by which the Jews are understood by Nazism, and one of the reasons why the Jews are regarded as a threat, is that the Jews are a nation-less people, a non-national element in a world of nations. In other words, the Jew has no nation. The Jew is a foreigner like no other foreigner, for not only is the Jew not at home in Germany, but the Jew is not at home anywhere. Being a foreigner is the *essence* of the Jew rather than a transitory state. As such, the Jew poses a double threat. On the one hand, the Jew stubbornly refuses to adopt the mode of being, to adhere to the political form through which rootedness should be expressed. Instead the Jews insist on being a 'community' within other nations. On the other hand, being a non-national nation means that the Jews are equally an inter-national nation, in that their nationless state allows them to drift across the borders of other, real, nations. Since the nation is to be the basis of salvation, the medium through which rejuvenation and revitalization could occur, the Jews' nationless status threatens this salvation from within, so to speak.[16] Moreover, the Jew's preaching of universal human values also undermines the nation, for the Jew appears intellectually committed to a universalism which pits free will and the idea of choice – through a commitment to either universal liberal values of Enlightenment reason or Marxist internationalism – against the mythic status of national boundaries. Both physically and intellectually, the Jew defies the truth on which all nations rest their claims: the naturally ascribed character of nationhood and the naturalness of national entities.[17]

Now, I am not seeking to elide the differences between nationalism and racism; nor do I wish to reduce the latter to the former. Equally I am not arguing that racism is of no significance to our understanding of fascism. I am arguing that claims which point to the biological racism and anti-Semitism of the Nazis as the ground of a fundamental difference between Italian fascism (as 'fascism proper') and Nazism fail to register the fact that the biological racism and anti-Semitism of Nazism emerges from the xenophobic nature of nationalism. However one characterizes the distinctive feature of the kind of nationalism found in fascism – 'integral' nationalism, 'radical' nationalism and 'ultra' nationalism are all fairly common – it is the logic of nationalism and the logic of racism which share fundamental features; nationalism is *necessarily xenophobic* – that is, xenophobia is part of the logic of nationalism – and thus always remains an invitation to anti-Semitism and racism. As Peter Pulzer shows in his work on the rise of political anti-Semitism, anti-Semitism was historically a by-product of nationalism: 'nationalism had, by the beginning of the nineteenth century, become the main driving force behind anti-Semitism'.[18] In effect, the theoretical and historical roots of racism and anti-Semitism lie in nationalism.

Thinking of Nazism in this way assists in interpreting the Nazi regime itself. There has been a tendency to attribute the 'success' of Nazism to its anti-Semitism: put simply, by focusing on the Jews in particular the Nazis are said to have tapped into some kind of popular vein of resentment and encouraged the 'scapegoating' of the Jews for the ills suffered by Germans. Such an interpretation has become widespread in academic writings on Nazism and has a certain common-sense appeal. But the scapegoat thesis in fact fails to explain anything. This fact is succinctly expressed by a post-WWI joke reported by Arendt: 'An anti-semite claimed that the Jews had caused the war; the reply was: Yes, and the bicyclists. Why the bicyclists? asks the one. Why the Jews? asks the other'.[19] The scapegoat thesis has the appearance of an explanation, but in fact leaves the question begging. Historical research partially bears this out. In their campaigning and propaganda the Nazis often played down their anti-Semitism, favouring instead a focus on the importance of national revival – the party manifesto of 1930 insists that the party will 'allow a nation once more to rise up' and will train the nation to have an 'iron determination' so that 'in future the importance of our nation . . . corresponds to its natural worth'.[20] An analysis of the ideology of rank-and-file Nazis revealed that while those joining the party showed clear prejudices, anti-Semitism figured as the *major* prejudice in only a minority. Some 60% of activists barely mentioned anti-Semitism at all, with some even dissociating themselves from the party's anti-Semitism. This research reveals the inadequacy of explaining anti-Semitism with the scapegoat thesis. If the thesis does not apply to those inside the party, it is not likely to apply to those outside. Likewise, if the thesis has any explanatory power it must lie in being able to explain the anti-Semitism of those entering the party after 1929 in the midst of the economic crisis, when the search for a scapegoat would be at its peak. Yet it would appear that those joining the party in this period were the least anti-Semitic.[21] What appealed to those who supported the Nazis was its ultranationalism combined with one or more of a range of other issues: anti-communism, the repeal of war reparations, the revoking of the Versailles Treaty, the curb on excessive profiteering by industry, a strong leadership to bring an end to the struggles and crises of the Weimar period and, undoubtedly for some, anti-Semitism. Arno Mayer may not be far off the mark in claiming that 'anti-Semitism did not play a decisive or even significant role in the growth of the Nazi movement and electorate'.[22]

Placing the nation and nationalism at the heart of our understanding of Nazi ideology is not meant to ignore the issue of race and anti-Semitism, but to give it a new theoretical direction. This would enable a rethinking of the shift to racism and anti-Semitism made by the fascist regime in Italy. It is now commonplace to claim that for the most part race was not an issue in fascism in Italy, a claim which is especially appealing to those who continue to try and separate Nazism from fascism as a means of making fascism respectable and thus, logically, acceptable once more.[23] This rests on the general assumption that Mussolini's 'conversion' to racism and anti-Semitism in the late 1930s came about under pressure from the Nazis and was never convincing, even to most fascists, and that until the late 1930s Mussolini appeared to criticize the Nazis for their racism, arguing that fascism and national pride have no need of the 'delirium' of race.[24] The claim generally made is that racism and anti-Semitism were never done very well by the Italian fascists, supposedly because they never really believed in them. Thus even when the Italian fascist state introduced racial laws in 1938 forbidding mixed marriages and excluding Jews from military service and large landholdings, Jewish war veterans and those who had participated in the fascist movement were exempt. And Jews who could show Italian nationality were protected by Italian embassies in Nazi-occupied Europe.[25] These details are meant to show that fascist racism and anti-Semitism are some kind of aberration, due to the negative influence of the Nazis and thus nothing really to do with fascism. Thinking of anti-Semitism and racism as a by-product of nationalism, however, raises questions about such claims.

First, fascist racism and anti-Semitism in Italy were as much an outcome of a concern over the best method for policing the colonies and the necessity for justifying the domination of the colonies as they were the result of pressure from the Nazis. But the worry over the colonies was, in effect, a worry that the nation was being undermined. When in November 1938 the publication *Partito e Impero* raised questions about the role of the party given the expanded nature of the Empire following the conquest of Ethiopia, the answer it gave rested on the mobilization of the people: the function of the party is

> never to allow the Italian people to rest, to urge them on, to foster among them the urge to expand indefinitely in order to survive, to instill in them a sense of superiority of our race over the blacks . . . In short, we must try to give the Italian people an imperialist and racist mentality.

For Mussolini the necessity of stressing the domination of the Italians over the Africans was the catalyst for the development of a formal doctrine of racial superiority. Likewise, the intention behind the outlawing of conjugal relations between Italians and colonial subjects or foreigners with cultural and legal customs similar to those of the colonial subjects (April 1937), and marriages between Italian citizens of Aryan stock and members of a different race (November 1938), was to prevent the birth of racially mixed children who might pollute the Italian nation.[26] Similarly, anti-Semitism became a key issue because Mussolini identified Jewish aggression, power and corruption at the heart of the nation as a genuine concern for fascism. There followed a whole range of books debating the nature of fascist anti-Semitism and racism. But whatever differences there were between the authors of these books, they all thought of the Jewish problem in terms of the threat to the nation. *Il Popolo d'Italia*, reviewing a book by Paolo Orano in May 1937, insisted that the Jews had to decide whether they were merely guests in Italy or Italians of Jewish religion. And one solution to the Jewish problem – of being a non-national nation – presented in a government document of February 1938 and thought to have been written by Mussolini, was to create a Jewish state in some part of the world. The solution to a people existing as a state within the state was to create for them a state of their own. In other words, a racist mentality developed from the continued expansion of the nation; as with its Nazi counterpart, Italian fascist racism and anti-Semitism were the by-product of nationalism.

Second, far from becoming a pseudo-racist and anti-Semite in the late 1930s under the influence of the Nazis, Mussolini was increasingly using the language of race from 1918. As racism became more a policy of the Italian state in the late 1930s, Mussolini and other fascists justified it by claiming – correctly – that they had *always* talked of race. In April 1921, in a speech in Bologna, Mussolini claimed that 'Fascism was born . . . out of a profound, perennial need of this our Aryan and Mediterranean race' and went on to suggest that fascism sought to impart to Italians a sense of 'racial solidarity' in order to turn all Italians into 'one single pride of race'. From this point on the term 'race' appeared regularly in his writings and speeches, and the term was used widely in the writings of other Italian fascists in this period.[27] The specific use of the concept is revealing, however. For 'race' and 'racial pride' here mean very little other than 'nation' and 'national consciousness'. Hence Mussolini's claim that 'before I love the French, the English, the Hottentots, I love Italians. That is to say I love those of my own race, those that speak my language, that share my customs, that share with me the same history'. As Gregor notes, the racism manifested by Mussolini in fascism's formative years was little more than a euphoric nationalism.[28] This is equally true of his anti-Semitism. His anti-Semitic remarks – such as his claim in 1919 that the Jewish bankers of London and New York were bound by the chains of race to Moscow and that 80 per cent of the leaders of the Soviets were Jews – were commonplace in nationalist circles at the time.[29] In other words, Mussolini became a racist and anti-Semite as he became a nationalist and fascist. Admittedly, Mussolini's racism and anti-Semitism appear to lack the biologism found in Nazism, focusing instead on race formation as a political and cultural process. But this does not mean that there are categorical differences between Nazism and fascism. Nazi race doctrine was in many ways remarkably unoriginal, rooted in doctrines common in the nineteenth century. Like all doctrines, racism has its own nuances and varieties, but to separate out 'biological' racism into a world of its own is dangerous: it encourages the belief that some forms of racism are somehow better or more respectable for having nothing to do with biology, disguising the fact that all forms of racism rest on an obscure and superficial biological reductionism in the first place.[30]

If this is the case, then what explains the place of the state and race in Italian fascism and German Nazism is not the dominant cultural and intellectual trajectories and milieux that existed in those countries. Far from being the product of national peculiarity, the concepts of state and race are different ideological mechanisms for substantiating nationalist claims. Much of the recent and convincing work on nationalism has pointed to the synthetic nature of nations, to their status as imagined communities – imagined as both inherently limited and sovereign. This has the virtue of drawing our attention to the fact that nations are necessarily cultural artefacts; they are imagined because members of even the smallest nation will never know or meet their fellow members. For nationalists this need not matter because what links us as nationals is not our meeting or knowing but our participation in some kind of 'national spirit'. The nation supposedly links us as individuals to a universal and collective force, of world-historical importance. As such 'nationalism thinks in terms of historical destinies'. On this reading, the nation has little to do with borders, forms of government or nationality as such, but is in fact a form of community based on sentiment, emotion and instinct.[31]

For fascism the concepts of race and the universal state perform the same function. That is, the state and race in fascism work alongside the idea of the nation, combining with the nation to link the individual to a higher, spiritual and universal force. Like the nation, the race and state are imagined ethical communities in fascist thought, growing from the nation, sustaining national power against its enemies and contributing to the ideology of state power by disguising that power as a manifestation of both our 'natural' collective identity and our unity with a 'spiritual' force. To Nairn's point noted above – that, seen in sufficient *historical* depth, fascism tells us more about nationalism than any other episode – we can thus add the following: seen in sufficient *theoretical* depth, nationalism tells us a great deal about fascism.

Notes

1   Peter Gay, *The Cultivation of Hatred: The Bourgeois Experience, Victoria to Freud*, Vol. III (London: HarperCollins, 1994), 73–5, 82–3.

2   Tzvetan Todorov, *On Human Diversity: Nationalism, Racism, and Exoticism in French Thought*, trans. Catherine Porter (Cambridge, MA: Harvard University Press, 1993), 90.

3   Adolf Hitler, *Mein Kampf* (1925, transl. Ralph Mannheim – Boston: Houghton Mifflin Co., 1943), 362–3, 378–85, 460–1.

4   Geoff Eley, *Reshaping the German Right: Radical Nationalism and Political Change after Bismarck* (Ann Arbor: University of Michigan Press, 1991), 185–6.

5   On Gobineau, see Michael D. Biddiss (ed.) *Gobineau: Selected Writings* (London: Jonathan Cape, 1970); and Biddiss, *Father of Racist Ideology: The Social and Political Thought of Count Gobineau* (London: Weidenfeld & Nicolson, 1970). For Chamberlain, see Roderick Stackelberg, *Idealism Debased: From Völkisch Ideology to National Socialism* (Kent, OH: Kent State University Press, 1981), Part Three.

6   Moreover, in his attempt to present European racism as leading to the final solu-
     tion, Mosse obliterates the national context in which writers such as Benedict
     Morel in France and Cesar Lombroso in Italy worked. And in his concern to point
     out the continued dangers of such thinking, Mosse himself moves from the German
     context and points to the way in which American groups who 'want to segregate
     Negro from white . . . embrace the volkish ideology' without justifying this leap
     or sensing any difficulties in doing so. See George Mosse, *Toward the Final Solution:
     A History of European Racism* (London: Dent & Sons, 1978), 82–3; Mosse, *The Crisis
     of German Ideology: Intellectual Origins of the Third Reich* (New York, 1964), 10.
7   For a general account of the problems of focusing on 'German peculiarity' see
     David Blackbourn and Geoff Eley, *The Peculiarities of German History: Bourgeois
     Society and Politics in Nineteenth-Century Germany* (Oxford: Oxford University Press,
     1984). For a wider discussion in the context of state and class in Britain, see Mark
     Neocleous, *Administering Civil Society: Towards a Theory of State Power* (London:
     Macmillan, 1996), ch. 4.
8   The Programme is reprinted in J. Noakes and G. Pridham (eds), *Nazism
     1919–1945, Vol. 1: The Rise to Power 1919–1934* (Exeter: University of Exeter,
     1983), 14–16.
9   In 1923; cited in Anna Bramwell, *Blood and Soil: Walther Darré and Hitler's 'Green
     Party'* (Bourne End: Kensal Press, 1985), 36.
10   Hitler, *Mein Kampf*, 290–3, 389, 392, 395, 403–7, 442.
11   Hitler, interview with the *New York Times*, 10 July 1933, cited in Alan Bullock,
     'The Political Ideas of Adolf Hitler', in International Council for Philosophy and
     Humanistic Studies, *The Third Reich* (London: Weidenfeld & Nicolson, 1955), 362.
12   See the 'Program' of the DNVP from 1931 reprinted in Kaes *et al.*, *Weimar Republic
     Sourcebook*, 348–52. For Moeller van den Bruck, see Kaes *et al.*, *Weimar Republic
     Sourcebook*, 332–4, and Fritz Stern, *The Politics of Cultural Despair: A Study in the Rise
     of the Germanic Ideology* (New York: Doubleday & Co., 1965), Part III.
13   Hitler, *Mein Kampf*, 327, 339, 393.
14   Ibid., 231–3, 243, 304, 337. See also Chapter 5 of [Neocleous'] book.
15   Ernst Bloch, *Heritage of Our Times*, trans. Neville and Stephen Plaice (Cambridge:
     Polity, 1991), 91–2.
16   Hitler, *Mein Kampf*, 150, 303–5, 623. Hitler was still thinking of the Jews in this
     way in 1945. See François Genoud (ed.), *The Testament of Adolf Hitler: The Hitler–
     Bormann Documents, February–April 1945*, trans. Colonel R. Stevens (London: Icon
     Books, 1962), 60. Hannah Arendt, *The Origins of Totalitarianism* (San Diego, CA:
     Harcourt Brace and Co. 1973), chs 2 and 3; see also the appropriation and
     reworking of her account by Zygmunt Bauman, *Modernity and the Holocaust*
     (Cambridge: Polity Press, 1989).
17   Bauman, *Modernity and the Holocaust*, 55.
18   Peter Pulzer, *The Rise of Political Anti-Semitism in Germany and Austria* (London:
     Peter Halban, 1988), 221. My intention here is thus diametrically opposed to that
     of those who seek to separate nationalism from fascism – see, for example,
     Anthony D. Smith, *Theories of Nationalism*, 2nd edn (London: Duckworth, 1983),
     Appendix B – and those who seek to salvage some kind of civic nationalism from
     the wreckage brought about by the history of nationalism in the twentieth century
     – see, for example, Michael Ignatieff, *Blood and Belonging: Journeys into the New
     Nationalism* (London: Vintage, 1994).
19   Arendt, *Origins of Totalitarianism*, 5.

20   'Manifesto of the NSDAP, 1930', in Noakes and Pridham (eds), *Nazism 1919–1945*, Vol. 1, 72.

21   See Theodore Abel, *Why Hitler Came to Power* (Cambridge, MA: Harvard University Press, 1986), first published in 1938; Peter H. Merkl, *Political Violence Under the Swastika: 581 Early Nazis* (Princeton, NJ: Princeton University Press, 1975), 453, 498–507; John Hiden and John Farquharson, *Explaining Hitler's Germany: Historians and the Third Reich* (London: Batsford, 1983), 41–4.

22   Arno J. Mayer, *Why Did the Heavens Not Darken?: The 'Final Solution' in History* (London: Verso, 1990), 108. Henry Ashby Turner points out that Hitler 'soft-pedaled or left altogether unmentioned his anti-Semitism when speaking to men of big business, having recognized its unpopularity in those circles' – *German Big Business and the Rise of Hitler* (Oxford: Oxford University Press, 1985), 343 and 348.

23   See the Conclusions of [Neocleous'] book.

24   Cited by Emil Ludwig, *Talks with Mussolini*, transl. Eden and Cedar Paul (Boston: Little, Brown and Co., 1933), 69–70.

25   Mosse, *Toward the Final Solution*, 200, 230.

26   Luigi Preti, 'Fascist Imperialism and Racism', in Roland Sarti (ed.), *The Ax Within: Italian Fascism in Action* (New York: New Viewpoints, 1974). The account of Mussolini's racism and anti-Semitism has been adopted from Preti's article and Denis Mack Smith, *Mussolini* (St Albans: Granada, 1983), 256–8.

27   A. James Gregor, *The Ideology of Fascism: The Rationale of Totalitarianism* (New York: Free Press, 1969), 246–7, from where the citations from Mussolini's speech are taken.

28   Ibid., 248, 256.

29   Mussolini, June 1919, cited in Gregor, *Ideology of Fascism*, 250.

30   The 1938 *Manifesto of Fascist Racism* is indicative of the ambiguities concerning 'race' and the pretence that it can be non-biological. The document concedes that 'the concept of race is a concept essentially biological', but also denies that fascist racism is the same as 'German' racism. A *purely* biological concept of race would mean undermining the concept of the nation – for races would then be conceived of like classes in Marxism, as transcending and thus threatening national boundaries. But when the *Manifesto* tries to rework the biology of race through the idea of population and history it is still reduced to talking about the pure 'Italian race' rooted in the blood of Italian families. The Manifesto is reproduced as 'Appendix A' of Gregor, *Ideology of Fascism*. In that book (pp. 265–82) Gregor gives a good account of the Manifesto's complexities, including Mussolini's description of the *Manifesto* as a German text translated into bad Italian (p. 277).

31   Benedict Anderson, *Imagined Communities: Reflections on the Origin and Spread of Nationalism*, revised edn (London: Verso, 1991), 149.

Chapter 35

E. M. Robertson

ITALIAN FASCISM AND RACISM

■ from **RACE AS A FACTOR IN MUSSOLINI'S POLICY IN AFRICA AND EUROPE**, *Journal of Contemporary History*, 23 (1988), pp. 38–44, 46, 51, 53–4

Like Burleigh and Wippermann (**32**), E. M. Robertson considers race as a fundamental difference between Nazism and Italian Fascism. But, he continues, Mussolini's regime did in fact possess a certain 'racist' core, evident in its colonial policy in Libya, Somalia and (after 1935) Ethiopia. What still remains puzzling is Mussolini's attitude towards the Jews – its shift from seeming acceptance to discrimination and persecution from 1937–8 onwards. In Robertson's view the key to understanding this change lies in the role of Austria for the relations between Fascist Italy and Nazi Germany in the 1930s. As long as the two regimes were antagonistic and suspicious of each other's foreign-policy intentions, Mussolini regarded Austria (with its relatively large Jewish population) as a bulwark against Nazism (both German and Austrian) and was therefore intent on upholding the country's independence from Germany. With the gradual rapprochement, however, between the two fascist leaders after 1936, Austria's independence lost its political significance for Mussolini. By the time of the Anschluss the scene had been already set for the extension of the Fascist regime's earlier racist policy to the Jews.

U NTIL RECENTLY, MOST ITALIAN and non-Italian authorities on Mussolini's Italy have claimed that a sense of racial superiority in a biological sense is alien to Italians and that it found little or no expression in Italian policy either before or after Mussolini came to power. We are told that it was only in 1938, some two years after the community of fate between Italy and Germany had been sealed, that Mussolini, aping his brother dictator Adolf Hitler, introduced anti-semitic legislation. One of the striking differences between nazi Germany and fascist Italy is, according to established opinion, the question of race.[1] Mussolini certainly believed in the superiority of Latin culture over Teutonic barbarity, and in an effusion made against nazi Germany, probably after the murder of Dollfuss on 25 July 1934, he is reported to have said that Hitler's racial theories were so absurd that, if carried to their logical conclusion, the Laplanders could claim to be the 'bearers of the highest culture'.[2] Whereas nazi ideologues held that Germans were the master race by virtue of unique genetic characteristics, most fascist theorists held that the martial qualities of virulence, vitality and violence could be inculcated into their own people through discipline and training. A country in order to remain healthy, so Mussolini boasted early in 1935, needed a war every twenty-five years.[3] Mussolini, however, did not hold that breeding and sexual habits were of no account in determining a nation's (or an individual's) moral fibre and will to fight. Just before the outbreak of the Ethiopian war, he ordered an inquiry into the population structure in Britain. We learn from two sources, Aloisi's and Ciano's diaries, that he laid great stress on the results of this inquiry. In England, there was a surplus of women over men, of the aged over young, because of sexual inhibitions; hence the nation was morally decadent and incapable of fighting.[4] The Americans were also, according to Mussolini, hopeless as soldiers because of the high proportion of Jews and blacks.[5] After the Ethiopian war, sexual habits and 'racial hygiene' were, as will be seen, to be controlled, at least in theory, by the state in Italy.

[. . .]

According to fascist principles, Croats, Slovenes, Germans, Jews and even Arabs and Ethiopians could all be assimilated into Italian culture, in which moral consciousness based on a common historical identity, not on purity of blood, was accepted as the criterion for establishing the legitimacy of the regime. Opposition to Hitler's racial ideas on the part of Italian fascists found its most vehement expression in a propaganda organization, known as 'the Society for the Universality of Rome', which was founded in the summer of 1933. In opposing the nazi creed, the Italian authorities used this society to spread their culture to non-Italians, especially within the Mediterranean world.[6] It can be claimed, however, that Mussolini, far from being encouraged to espouse racial doctrines, was prevented from so doing mainly because of his quarrel with nazi Germany.

There can be no gainsaying that those historians who lay stress on the incompatibility of fascism and racism can make a plausible case from the available evidence when the argument is applied to Europe. Two scholars, G. Bernardini and Meir Michaelis, are, however, at one in rejecting the view that Mussolini was just aping Hitler and currying German favour when, in the summer of 1938, he decided to extend racial discrimination from Africa to Italy. Bernardini maintains that Judeophobia, which is something different from, but can degenerate into, biological anti-semitism, was implicit, not only in fascist political philosophy but also in the teachings of the Post-Tridentine church. In fact, on 11 February 1932, Pope Pius XI drew Mussolini's attention to the underlying Christian aversion inherent in Judaism which found its most militant expression in bolshevism. The Pope did, however, pay homage to Jews living inside Italy, especially certain rabbis.[7] While Bernardini stresses the ideological and indigenous element in Italian racism, Michaelis also argues that Mussolini was not copying Hitler and that Hitler never even tried to inveigle Mussolini into accepting racial theories. Michaelis does, however, claim that there was an integral relationship between Mussolini's racial policy in Europe and Ethiopia, and he is correct in so doing.[8] But Michaelis did not make fullest use of some excellent studies on Mussolini's colonial policy in East Africa, Libya and the Middle East as a whole. This is understandable, for he was writing primarily about Europe.[9]

Mussolini's racial attitude overseas only became practical politics in the period after the subjugation of Northern Somalia in 1928 and the conquest of Cyrenaica in 1932. He could now turn to extending Italy's frontiers both in Europe and Africa and consolidating Italian rule.[10] On 3 January 1933, the day on which he sanctioned a plan for an eventual invasion of Ethiopia, he made a highly significant remark to one of his leading diplomats, Baron Pompei Aloisi. The French, he said, had committed an appalling blunder in Tunisia by permitting sexual relations between the natives and Europeans. The result was bound to be a nation of half-castes. Hence, he ordered General Emilo De Bono, his Colonial Minister, to take a much tougher line than that adopted by the French and also by Marshal Badoglio, at that time Governor-General of Tripolitania and regarded by Mussolini as being too soft on racial matters. Later Mussolini banned a novel depicting a love affair between an Italian girl and an African. But Mussolini was not only concerned with miscegenation. He told Aloisi that the spectacle of an Italian taxi-driver taking a tip from an Arab, or of a Sicilian boy polishing the shoes of a wealthy native, was an abomination.[11] The stage was set for the introduction of the first laws of July 1933 discriminating against blacks, which will be considered presently. The question must first be asked whether racial discrimination in the Italian empire ran parallel to similar development laws in Africa and anti-Jewish and later anti-semitic policies in Europe.

The Jews in Italy were a small minority, numbering approximately 40,000–50,000. Except in Trieste, they belonged to what is called the Sephardic family of Jews, and they spoke a Romance language among themselves known as Ladino. They are not to be confused either with the Ashkenazi Jews of Northern Europe who spoke Judeo-German (or Yiddish) or with those Jews who spoke various Arabic dialects among themselves and who lived mainly in Muslim areas of North Africa and the Middle East. Michaelis is right in contending that the Jews in Italy drew their inspiration from Garibaldi and the Risorgimento, a movement which went hand in hand with emancipation. Some of them, such as the Luzzatti family, were Hebrew scholars of great eminence who were proud to regard Italy as their home. Many Jews had also served, or were still serving, with distinction in the Italian armed forces.[12] Hence Mussolini himself drew a distinction between two groups of Jews: 'Italian Jews', whose primary loyalty lay with their co-religionists in other parts of the world, especially Palestine, and 'Jewish Italians', who put Italy first. While Mussolini's preference lay with Jewish Italians, he did not reject Zionists, provided that they lived outside Italy. Zionism was a useful political weapon which he could use against the British in Palestine, against the Germans in Austria and, if necessary, against the Pope.[13]

[. . .]

It is hardly a coincidence that the first official attack on the Jews in Italy was launched in the *Popolo d'Italia* late in March 1934.[14] This took place soon after Mussolini's famous speech of 18 March in which he declared that Italy was about to embark on a policy of cultural and economic expansion in Asia and Africa. In Europe there was nothing to do. This caused alarm in Turkey, which had recently joined the League. He also left his listeners in no doubt that, if the disarmament negotiations broke down, Italy might have no recourse other than to withdraw from the League of Nations which, from the Italian point of view, was badly in need of reform. Mussolini's speech did in fact lead to a change in policy. Convinced that Italy must act before she got left behind in an all-out arms race, the first concrete measures for transforming Eritrea into a base for war against Ethiopia were undertaken in April 1934.[15] But in 1934 Mussolini did not drive home his attacks on the Jews. In this connection, one of Michaelis's theses concerning Germany is open to criticism. Michaelis rightly contends that Mussolini's aim was to reconcile Hitler and the Jews. To do this he had first to persuade Hitler to abandon his crude anti-clerical and anti-semitic policy and, second, to launch a minor attack on the Jews, whom in 1933–4 he still regarded as the more powerful of two antagonists locked in needless conflict.[16]

Austria, and not Hitler's general policy of anti-semitism, is more likely to be the key to Mussolini's policy towards the Jews in Europe. The 200,000 Austrian Jews constituted the one and most reliable political group which would at all times and in every circumstance resist an *Anschluss* (union) with nazi Germany, which Mussolini sought either to prevent or at least to delay.[17] But the Austrian Jews stood mainly on the left of the political spectrum, where they were supported by the Czechs for whom Mussolini had nothing but contempt. This might explain why Mussolini requested Dollfuss, the Austrian Chancellor, to add a 'dash' of anti-semi-tism to his policy – a course which would render it less easy for Dollfuss to link up with the Social Democrats, who were crushed in February 1934. Later that year, the Austrian nazis, and not the Social Democrats, constituted the main threat to Italian interests.[18] Hence, from the spring of 1934 until 1938, Mussolini had nothing to gain from attacks on the Jews in Europe. It was only after the *Anschluss* of March 1938, when there were no longer any Austrian Jews to protect, that Mussolini was in a position to go over to a fully fledged policy of anti-semitism.

[. . .]

The Jews were not the only Semites against whom Mussolini had to contend. Late in 1931, troops under Graziani, including Eritrean Christians, massacred the Senussi, a strict Muslim brotherhood in Cyrenaica, where it is estimated that one third of the population was killed. The Italians had made themselves so unpopular that at a world Islam congress held in December 1931 in Jerusalem fascist Italy was vehemently condemned. Also, Senussi refugees were active in disseminating anti-Italian propa-ganda from Egypt. Since Jewish immigration into Palestine was also condemned at this congress, circumstances favoured co-operation between Mussolini and the Zionists.[19] For a time Mussolini did, in fact, toy with the idea of obtaining an Italian mandate over Palestine, where perhaps a small Arab and Jewish state could be estab-lished. In the summer of 1935, he proposed support for the Zionists in Palestine in return for Zionist aid for the transfer of either Iraq or Syria as a mandate to Italy.[20] But Mussolini realized that the task of building up a new Roman Empire would prove impossible if the Arabs, who were beginning to organize themselves on an international level, were solidly against him. In order to give Italy a better image, a meeting of students from all over the Middle East was held in Rome in December 1933. The Propaganda Fide of the Roman Catholic Church gave this congress its blessing.[21]

[. . .]

After the capture of Addis Ababa on 5 May 1936, the Italians ignored a German request for economic concessions in Ethiopia.[22] Italy alone was to exploit to the full the resources of that country. But because of the ferocity of armed resistance, even in the neighbourhood of Addis Ababa, the Italians were not able to enjoy the fruits of their conquest. In these circumstances, far tougher laws were introduced against miscegenation. In June 1936, citizenship was denied to mulattoes of unknown parentage, regardless of whether or not they were 'worthy' of it. In April 1937, in the wake of a reign of terror under Graziani, all conjugal relations were forbidden between Italians and natives, except prostitutes. Laws were also passed for the segregation of living quarters and transport. It was above all enacted that Italians should not be seen by the natives performing menial tasks. Those who did so were described as 'moral half-castes'. The colour bar also applied to Indian, but not Japanese, traders in Ethiopia.[23]

[. . .]

At first, racial issues gave rise to serious quarrels within the Italian government. The colonial ministry enlisted Arab-speaking Italians from Egypt as officials in Italian East Africa. This made it easier for the Italian authorities to encourage the building of mosques and to recruit Ethiopian Muslims, who spoke Arabic as a second language, into the armed forces. The favours shown to the Muslims, according to Trimingham, enhanced their sense of dignity. It also occasioned a quarrel with the Vatican, which saw in Islam the major obstacle to missionary endeavour. The quarrel with the Church was to be intensified after the introduction of racist legislation into Italy in the summer of 1938.[24] There was also a serious human problem. Because of the rebellious conditions in the Empire, well over 250,000 Italian soldiers and workers were needed. In order to provide Italian men with family life and creature comforts, a campaign was launched in the home country to attract Italian women to join the colony. Before their arrival in Ethiopia, they had to be schooled in the arcane arts of racial hygiene. Racial hygiene meant there must be no sexual relations with non-ethnic Italians within the peninsula, and the only group which could conceivably be described as ethnically alien – apart from the gypsies – was the Jews. Italian women were required to set their men a good example in having no sexual relations with Africans. But an appeal had to be made to all Italians, not just the women. Hence, early in August 1938, a journal was established in Rome called *La Difesa della Razza*. Its editor was a notorious leader of the anti-semitic faction within the Fascist Party, Telesi Interlandi. In this journal, a black Ethiopian woman was depicted side by side with a Jewish male. Both were caricatures of humanity. Next to them, and separated by a sword, was the bust of an Aryan male, representing the ideal Italian. In the autumn of 1938, legislation was finally introduced against all Semites and Hamites both in Italy and in her colonies.[25]

Admittedly, the reason given for introducing the racial laws was the need to 'uphold imperial prestige'. But does this mean that Mussolini was not influenced by nazi racial ideas? According to Ulrich von Hassel, the German ambassador to Rome, Mussolini was so impressed by the strength of nazi Germany after his visit to that country in September 1937 that he realized that nothing could be gained for Italy by an alignment with Britain and France. The only alternative was to toe the nazi party line completely and fatalistically.[26] The laws took effect at the time of the pogrom in Germany of 9 and 10 November. Henceforward, both Hitler and Himmler officers regarded fascist Italy not only as Germany's ally, but as her partner in the 1940s fate and glory. No such honourable role was, needless to say, accorded to the Japanese. But the nazi leaders misunderstood ordinary Italians, many of whom, of every political allegiance, displayed the most remarkable moral courage in sheltering Jews from the holocaust.[27]

One question remains. Could Mussolini discriminate against all Semites, including Arabs, and also promote pan-Arab and pan-Islamic movements? Italo Balbo, Italian Governor of Libya, was opposed to Mussolini's anti-semitic laws and favoured conferring full Italian citizenship on the Arabs. Under his rule, this colony was incomparably better governed than was Ethiopia. But, in a theatrical manner, 20,000 Italian settlers sailed for the colony in October 1938. By 1940, the Italian colony numbered over 100,000, compared with only 3000 Italian colonists in Ethiopia. Violent protests against the seizure of Arab land could be heard in countries as far away as Iraq.[28] The annexation on 7 April 1939 of another predominantly Muslim country, Albania, also caused disquiet in North Africa and the Middle East. The Libyan Jews, after the landing of German troops in February 1941, were savagely persecuted. It can be claimed that as a result of first Italian and later German propaganda, the Arabs themselves fell victims to some of the worst features of European Judeo-phobia and that in response many Zionists became militantly intolerant towards the Arabs. At all events, the Jews in Libya were subjected to a violent pogrom in 1945, as a result of which the survivors left for Palestine. A similar fate awaited those Jews who remained in the Yemen.[29]

Finally, what conclusions can be drawn from this brief survey? First, as a result of the Italian occupation and defeat in Ethiopia in 1941, racial and cultural resentment spread more rapidly from North Africa and the Middle East to tropical Africa than it might otherwise have done. Second, the British and French, in order to defend their imperial interests against Italy, started to recruit Africans into their armies. During the campaign for the liberation of Ethiopia in 1941, African troops proved that they were capable of defeating whites on equal terms. This must have caused dismay among the whites of Kenya and Southern Africa. If Mussolini's conquest did not mark the beginning of decolonization, a term which does not lend itself to a clear definition, it certainly gave it an added stimulus. It may even have determined the form it would take. Army officers, rather than intellectuals, spearheaded revolutions in Africa.

Notes

1   L. Villari, in *Italian Foreign Policy under Mussolini* (New York 1956), is partly responsible for giving credence to this view. It is not upheld by Renzo De Felice in his *Storia degli ebrei Italiani sotto il Fascismo* (Turin 1972), 242–7. For a full account, see Meir Michaelis, *Mussolini and the Jews: German–Italian Relations and the Jewish Question 1922–1945* (Oxford 1978), especially 120–8.

2   Ulrich von Hassell, *Vom anderen Deutschland aus den nachgelassenen Tagebüchern 1938–1944* (Zurich 1946), 28 November 1938, 28.

3   Baron P. Aloisi, *Journal (25 juillet 1932–14 juin 1936)*, introduction and notes by Mario Toscano (Paris 1957), 6 February 1935, 255.

4   Galeazzo Ciano, *1937–1938 Diario* (Rocca S. Casciano – 8–1948) entries for 3 and 6 September 1937, 12–13, and Aloisi, op. cit., 23 May 1936, 386. See also M. Knox, 'Fascist Italy Assesses its Enemies', in E. R. May (ed.), *Intelligence Assessment between the Two World Wars* (Princeton 1984), 363–5.

5   M. Knox, 'Conquest Foreign and Domestic in Fascist Italy and Nazi Germany', *Journal of Modern History*, 56 (1984), 26, discusses Mussolini's sense of inferiority.

6   P. V. Cannistraro and D. Wymot, Jr, 'On the Dynamics of Anti-Communism as a Function of Fascist Foreign Policy 1933–1943', *Il Politico: rivista di scienze politiche*, XXXVIII (1973), 652–3.

7   G. Bernardini, 'The Origins and Development of Racial Anti-Semitism in Fascist Italy', *Journal of Modern History*, 49, 3 (September 1977). An English translation of the text of Mussolini's account of his interview with the Pope on 11 February 1932 can be found in P. C. Kent, *The Pope and the Duce* (London 1981), 192–5.

8   Michaelis, op. cit., 125–6.

9   R. Pankhurst, 'Fascist Racial Policies in Ethiopia: 1922–1941', *Ethiopian Observer*, XII, 4 (1969); 'The Secret History of the Italian Fascist Occupation of Ethiopia 1935–1941', *African Quarterly*, XVI, IV (April 1977); 'Economic Verdict on the Italian Occupation of Ethiopia 1936–1941', *Ethiopian Observer*, XIV, 1 (1971); also 'A chapter in Ethiopia's Commercial History during the Fascist Occupation 1936–1941', ibid. D. Mack Smith, *Mussolini's Roman Empire* (London 1976) discusses Italian apartheid, 122–3.

10 See Giorgio Rochat, *Militare e politiche nella preparazione della Campagna d'Etiopia: studio e documenti 1932–1936* (Milan 1971), 30 ff.

11 Aloisi, op. cit., 3 January 1933, 46, and 2 April 1934, 185.

12 Michaelis, op. cit., 5 ff. Also *Encyclopaedia Judaica* (*EJ*) under 'Italy'.

13 P. C. Kent, op. cit., 39–40, and G. Carocci, *La Politica estera dell'Italia fascista* (Bari 1969), chap. XIX.

14 Michaelis, op. cit., 59–62.

15 Aloisi, op. cit., 18 March 1934, 184. For reform of League, ibid., 169. For military decisions taken in April 1934, see G. Rochat, op. cit., 40, 68–9.

16 Michaelis, op. cit., 59–61, 64–6.

17 *EJ* under 'Austria', and E. M. Robertson, *Mussolini fondatore dell'Impero* (Bari 1979), chap. 3.

18 E. M. Robertson, ibid., 238–9, and Michaelis, op. cit., 90–2.

19 Royal Institute of International Affairs (RIIA), 'Survey 1934', 105, note 1.

20 Michaelis, op. cit., 88.

21 Aloisi, op. cit., 17 and 22 December 1933, 168, 169.

22 K. Hildebrand, *Vom Reich zum Weltreich: Hitler, NSDAP und koloniale Frage 1919–1945* (Munich 1969), 892–3.

23 Pankhurst, 'Fascist Racial Policies', op. cit., 274–6, and 'Economic Verdict', op. cit., 55–6.

24 P. C. Kent, 'The Catholic Church in the Italian Empire, 1936–38', in *Historical Papers Communications Historiques* (1984). J. Spencer Trimingham, *Islam in Ethiopia* (London 1965), claims that the Italian occupation gave the Muslims of Ethiopia dignity, independence and tranquillity, 275–76.

25 Pankhurst, 'The Secret History of the Italian Occupation', op. cit., describes the armed opposition against Italian rule. Japanese traders, see his 'Economic Verdict', op. cit., 55–6, and his 'Fascist Policies', op. cit.

26 Hassell, op. cit., 28 November 1938, 28.

27 E. M. Robertson, 'German Military Planning and the Response of the Powers, 1938–early 1939', in H. W. Koch (ed.), *Aspects of the Third Reich* (London, 1985), 214–15. For the moral courage of Italians, see H. S. Hughes, *Prisoners of Hope: The Silver Age of Italian Jews 1924–1974* (Boston, MA 1983), 63.

28 C. G. Segré, 'Italo Balbo and the Colonialization of Libya', *Journal of Contemporary History*, 1, 3–4 (July–October 1972), 3–4, G. Wright, The Ordeal of Total War, 1939–1945 (Toronto: Harper Collins, 1968), chap. 15.

29 H. E. Golberg, 'The Libyan Pogrom 1945', *Plural Societies*, 8, 1; also *EJ* under 'Libya', and R. Gavin, *Aden under British Rule 1839–1967* (London 1975), 232.

Chapter 36

Susan Zuccotti

ANTI-SEMITISM IN VICHY FRANCE

■ from *THE HOLOCAUST, THE FRENCH AND THE JEWS*,
London, 1993, pp. 80–3, 85–9

Susan Zuccotti's analysis of the fate of France's Jewish population under the Vichy regime asks two equally interesting questions: why as many as 24 per cent of the Jews perished and why a significant 76 per cent survived. Her research encountered a culture of complicity of Vichy officials to the Nazi eliminationist designs, often precipitating and facilitating Nazi claims in that direction – a point that was emphatically put forward by Robert O. Paxton in the early 1970s (41). As for the attitudes of the French public, Zuccotti came upon a mixed picture: while many French joined collaborationist organisations (for example, the Milice) and fanatically targeted members of the Resistance and the Jewish community, many more either shielded Jews actively or helped them indirectly through what Stanley Hoffmann called 'informal assistance' or through closing their eyes and failing to fulfil their duty as potential informers of the Vichy authorities.

MORE THAN 24 PERCENT of the approximately 330,000 Jews in France at the end of 1940 were deported or died within the country during the Holocaust. They totaled nearly 80,000 men, women, and children. More than 77,000 of them were murdered in deportation, executed in French prisons, or killed from starvation, exhaustion, and disease in French internment camps. The reasons for their deaths have been discussed. Certainly the German occupiers of France bear the primary responsibility. Following the general policy initiated by Adolf Hitler and defined by Heinrich Himmler, Reinhard Heydrich, Adolf Eichmann, and others, German anti-Jewish agents in France rounded up Jews or, much more frequently, demanded that French police perform the dirty work. Nazis then organized the deportations and murdered Jews when they arrived in the east.

The French government at Vichy, however, and many French civilians share the burden of guilt. Vichy politicians began preparing racial laws before any had been decreed by the German occupiers of the northern zone, and quite apart from any German demands. Vichy bureaucrats decreed and performed detailed censuses of Jews in France, and later made the data available to those who would arrest and deport them. Vichy police rounded up and interned foreign Jews in the southern zone at a time when their counterparts in the German-occupied north remained quite free. At first Jews were seized because they were enemy nationals, but long after the armistice they were still being held, often in life-threatening conditions, *explicitly* because they were Jews.

French offenses did not end with racial laws and internment. Vichy officials at the highest levels ordered French police to round up mostly foreign Jewish men in Paris in 1941 and made no protest when they and many French Jewish men were deported in March 1942. In July 1942, those same French authorities ordered the arrests in Paris of more foreign Jews, this time including women and their often French-born children. French police duly complied by seizing 12,884 people. Officials then demonstrated appalling contempt for human life by depositing more than 8,000 prisoners in the Vélodrome d'Hiver, with little preparation for their maintenance. Prior to the arrests, Pierre Laval, the head of government, had urged the Nazis to deport the children, before the Germans had decided what to do with them. They were deported.

Also in July, Vichy authorities agreed to supply the Nazis in the north with foreign Jews from the south, from the so-called free zone where the Germans had as yet no jurisdiction. These Jews too were deported. First to be delivered were recent Jewish immigrants already in Vichy internment camps. Most were refugees from the Third Reich or from German-occupied countries in the east; they included the German Jews expelled from their homes in October 1940 and dumped by the Nazis in France. They were followed by other immigrants especially arrested throughout the unoccupied zone for that purpose. More than 11,000 people were sent north to Drancy before the Germans occupied the southern zone in November. The expulsions occurred in conditions that replicated exactly those of the Nazi deportation trains. French police locked men, women, and children into cattle cars, with little food or water, soiled straw on the floor, and a bucket for their bodily functions. As in the Third Reich, social workers and other civilians of goodwill were not permitted to alleviate their suffering.

Under more or less severe German pressure, Vichy officials then proceeded to order French police to make more and more roundups. Jews from Poland, the Greater Reich, and the Soviet Union were joined by Jews from Romania, Bulgaria, Belgium, the Netherlands, Greece, and, ever more frequently in 1944, French Jews as well. This gradual escalation had a devastating effect, for Jews who perceived that they did not fit into a category eligible for arrest often neglected to hide and were caught when the rules changed. In addition, news of a roundup in one city, if it was known at all, was often perceived as a local aberration rather than a warning. Meanwhile, Vichy officials ordered gendarmes to guard Drancy and other places where Jews were confined and to accompany deportation trains to the French–German frontier. The manpower supplied made arrests and deportations possible. As seen in Nice in September 1943, understaffed Nazis functioned poorly without help.

And French civilians? Journalists fed the vast anti-Semitic propaganda machine, convincing citizens that Jews were their enemy and the cause of all their troubles. Tens of thousands of collaborators joined Fascist leagues or the Milice, in whose ranks they hunted for Resistants, escaped Allied prisoners of war, draft evaders, and Jews.[1] Informers flourished, persuaded that betrayal was their patriotic duty. Gendarmes and municipal police obeyed orders, warning a few friends, perhaps, of a pending arrest, or turning their backs while a few charming little children and their mothers escaped, but knocking down other doors, searching apartments, interrogating neighbors, and catching their prey. And many average citizens, if they did not actually condone what they saw, simply closed their eyes to it, grateful, perhaps, that they could believe themselves morally uninvolved.

The converse of the terrible death rate is the fact that 76 percent of the Jews in France, or some 250,000 people, survived. How did that happen?

Some of the explanation lies with the physical characteristics of the country and in the complex chronology of the persecution itself. Unlike Belgium and the Netherlands, where overall Jewish deportation and death rates were much higher, France is a large country with extensive tracts of remote, often mountainous terrain favorable to hiding.[2] France also borders two countries that were neutral during the Second World War and were able, if not always willing, to receive fugitives. Also in comparison to Belgium and the Netherlands, far fewer German personnel were allocated to France after the armistice in relation to the size and population of the country. Those devoted to hunting Jews were not numerically adequate to perform the task.[3] They could not hope to comb the country thoroughly without French cooperation.

For the leaders of Nazi anti-Jewish units, securing that cooperation became a constant problem, requiring patience, tact, cajoling, prodding, threats, and compromise. Most of all, it required time – valuable time, especially in 1943, that Heinz Röthke and Alois Brunner could have used to plan their own anti-Jewish raids. For with regard to the Jews, Laval had his own agenda: that French Jewish adults and their children should not be arrested and deported, and that French police should not be used in major roundups unless they were so ordered by their own superiors, for clearly defined actions.

Laval frequently compromised on these principles. He allowed French police to arrest *individual* Jews, including citizens, for specific or alleged violations, and he tolerated limited daily arrests of Jews without charges by special anti-Jewish units like the Permilleux service in Paris or the Milice elsewhere. Vichy officials protested only slightly when their wishes were ignored, and French gendarmes continued to guard trains that they knew were carrying French Jews. In 1944, Laval even permitted French police to participate in roundups of native Jews on specific lists. But until then, French Jews, with the tragic exception of the children of immigrants, clearly benefited from a limited protection. Without it, more would have been arrested and the overall Jewish death rate would have been higher.

The existence of an Italian occupation zone in southeastern France between November 1942 and September 1943 also affected survival rates by buying time for the Jews. Some 50,000 people lived free from danger there for many months. The menace of deportation returned when the Italians withdrew, and many were caught unprepared, but each day that had passed without arrests meant fewer arrests overall.

The passing of time had other consequences. Jews and non-Jews alike had time to learn about the deportation of women, children, and old people incapable of labor and to ponder its meaning. Jews were able to make plans and secure false papers. Non-Jews could reflect and ask themselves whether the official anti-Semitic and anti-foreign rhetoric that they perhaps applauded in the abstract justified the dreadful suffering of human beings that they heard about and sometimes even observed personally. Churchmen of goodwill had time to exercise a moral leadership, speaking out against deportations and encouraging alternative attitudes and behavior. And perhaps most important of all, the Allies had time to win victories and convince the French that the Germans were not invincible, the Vichy regime might not last forever, and collaboration might not be the most opportune route to follow. Laval himself seems not to have heeded the warning. In early 1944, when he surely knew that Auschwitz meant certain death for most and that the Germans would lose the war, he actually intensified rather than diminished French police pressure on native Jews. Members of the Milice and other fanatic collaborators were delighted. But many municipal police and gendarmes, along with prefects, mayors, and other local Vichyite bureaucrats, certainly read the handwriting on the wall and made some adjustments.

[. . .]

Finally, Jewish survival in France depended upon attitudes within the non-Jewish community. Whether hidden by rescue organizations or making their own arrangements for family members, many Jews had to find willing hosts. Many more who simply moved independently to a new address needed help with documents plus some assurance that they would not be reported as 'newcomers.' Dependence upon at least a mild tolerance was total. Survival rates in France suggest that large numbers of Jews received it.

In 1977, the researcher and historian Lucien Steinberg came to a similar conclusion:

> I would like to emphasize that the majority of the Jews saved in France do not owe their rescue to Jewish organizations. The various Jewish bodies which worked with such great dedication managed to save only a few tens of thousands, while the others were saved mostly thanks to the assistance of the French population. In many cases, groups of Jews lived in small villages. Every one of the Jews was convinced that no one in that area knew their true identity; after the war it turned out that everyone knew that they were Jews.[4]

The young Stanley Hoffmann encountered similar informal assistance during the war and judged it to be representative. Years later, he wrote:

> In my memory, the schoolteacher – now seventy-five, and still vibrant – who taught me French history, gave me hope in the worst days, dried my tears when my best friend was deported along with his mother, and gave false papers to my mother and me so that we could flee a Gestapo-

infested city in which the complicity of friends and neighbors was no longer a guarantee of safety – this man wipes out all the bad moments, and the humiliations, and the terrors. He and his gentle wife were not Resistance heroes, but if there is an average Frenchman, it was this man who was representative of his nation.[5]

The historian and former Jewish Resistant Léon Poliakov agreed, writing in 1949 of 'the good sense . . . the profound humanity of the immense majority of the French people.'[6]

In 1940, such attitudes might not have been predictable. The resentment of Jews and foreigners that had permeated the general population throughout the depression years of the 1930s had been exacerbated by the military defeat and by the Vichy regime. Few French men and women protested when foreign Jews, along with many other refugees and immigrants, were interned in the south. Few knew, or cared to know, when they starved or froze to death in French camps, well out of public view. Few protested the racial laws or worried about economic and psychological suffering that they rarely witnessed. Not many were concerned about the arrests in Paris in 1941 of mostly foreign Jewish young men. Nor did they worry when those same usually young men were deported between March and July 1942, allegedly for labor. After all, more than a million and a half young French prisoners of war were already in German prison camps. Why, the argument ran, should the French worry about immigrants, many of them without papers, when they had all they could do taking care of themselves?

Attitudes changed when suffering became unavoidably visible. They changed also when the victims were no longer strong young men, but *families*. When women, children, and old people were packed into sealed freight cars and delivered to the Nazis, many French men and women experienced a sense of shame. That shame was deepened by the public protests of churchmen who finally broke the silence and reminded the French to think for themselves. And so the climate of sullen resentment shifted into one of benign neglect, vague goodwill, and, occasionally, active support.

EIF child rescuers Shatta and Bouli Simon well understood that non-Jewish attitudes changed when persecution acquired a visible and personal dimension. Shatta Simon recalled after the war:

> The Germans [after they occupied the southern zone] must have noticed that very often their arrest plans were thwarted because the French living among Jews whom they knew could hardly keep from warning them of great danger; thus they [the Germans] operated with [French] people brought to town from elsewhere, who had to deal with people whom they did not know and to whom they were indifferent.

Toward the end of 1943, the Simons went to the local prefect, whom they called a Pétainist, and asked quite openly for 150 ration cards for Jewish children hiding in Christian institutions. They explain, 'We had the experience that in that region we could talk clearly to the French, even the collaborators, when it was a question of children: they always agreed that they should be saved.'[7] The prefect not only agreed to supply the cards regularly but arranged that the Simons should not have to carry them through the streets. He asked the mayor of Moissae to deliver them!

That prefect was replaced in 1944 by one known to be much more fanatically fascist. Several German divisions were stationed in the area, and two Resistants had just been hung. Shatta Simon went to the new prefect and asked him to continue what his predecessor had done for Jewish children. She relates, 'He closed all the windows, and then said to me in a whisper, "O.K., but don't tell anyone that I have been nice to you."'[8] The response seems very human, very normal. It is in many ways easier to understand than a refusal.

Those willing to help had an ability to perceive the human dimension that lay beyond the bureaucratic jargon. They were skeptical of political rhetoric and propaganda and able to think independently. They demonstrated, in the last analysis, a respect for human life, a tolerance of diversity, and a willingness to ignore regulations that threatened the survival of others. Some broke important rules, guiding illegal fugitives across frontiers or taking others into their homes or schools and keeping them alive. They were immensely courageous. They were also not numerous. More people acted in less dramatic but equally crucial ways. Police did not try too hard to find individuals on their lists. Others leaked information about pending arrests. Petty bureaucrats overlooked suspicious documents, issued new ones with few questions, or investigated newcomers in their area only superficially.

And then there were those who helped by simply doing nothing. Shopkeepers, teachers, priests and pastors, mailmen, bus drivers, municipal employees – hundreds of thousands of French men and women, scattered throughout the country, could not help but notice that there was a new face in town. They helped by asking no questions, by minding their own business. They created an environment conducive, with a strong dose of good luck, to survival.

Perhaps no case of survival cited in this book is more typical than that of Mr. and Mrs. Caraco, middle-class French Jews of modest means who were able to live independently without organized assistance. Despite warnings from their daughter in the Jewish rescue service, they were slow to perceive their danger. They left Marseille after the indiscriminate roundups there in January 1943, but they insisted on registering as Jews in their new village. For a time, they benefitted from their citizenship and from the few anti-Jewish forces in rural areas. Later they benefitted from luck – when the Nazis came for them, they were out. And finally, they benefitted from a benevolent environment. Their neighbors told the Germans that they had moved away, and then told the Caracos of the visit. There was no outstanding act of courage, no spectacular rescue, but the Caracos did not need that. Children needed that, as did the elderly, the handicapped, the foreign and totally different. In addition to good luck, the Caracos needed only a vague goodwill – a lack of overt hostility – but that was indispensable. And that they found [Note: this story is told in Chapter 9 of Zuccotti's book].

It is useful to recall that both Jews and non-Jews who decided to be helpful in France rarely understood that they were directly saving lives. Rumors of gas chambers and deliberate extermination were vague and inconsistent, dismissed as enemy propaganda or as simply unbelievable. Instead, rescuers and more casual helpers often risked their lives to spare Jews the sufferings of deportation to camps known to be harsh and cruel, where families would be dispersed and where children and the elderly, at least, might die. Because of that generosity, tolerance, and fundamental humanity, 250,000 people were able to survive.

Notes

1 Henry Rousso, *La Collaboration: Les noms, les themes, les lieux* (Paris: M.A. editions, 1987), 131, 138–39, and 156, estimates that of the three major leagues during the war, the *Parti populaire français* had some 20,000 to 30,000 adherents; the *Rassemblement national populaire*, 20,000; and the *Mouvement social révolutionnaire*, 15,000. As seen in chap. 2, the Milice had some 29,000 adherents in the autumn of 1943. Some of these came from the leagues.

2 In the Netherlands, about 105,000 Jews died, or 75 percent of a community of about 140,000. In Belgium, approximately 24,000 Jews died, or nearly 42 percent of a community in October 1940 of some 57,000. (The prewar Jewish population of Belgium had been about 90,000, but nearly half of these fled into France when the Germans invaded.) These statistics are from Michael R. Marrus and Robert O. Paxton, 'The Nazis and the Jews in Occupied Western Europe,' in *Unanswered Questions: Nazi Germany and the Genocide of the Jews*, François Furet, ed. (New York: Schocken, 1989), 172–98, 190, 195.

3 There were fewer than 3,000 German civilians at work in occupied France in August 1941, compared with just over 3,000 in the Netherlands (ibid., 175). The figures are cited from a contemporary study prepared by Werner Best, then head of the military administration civil staff in France. By mid-1942, according to the same authors, there were just three battalions of German police in France, or 2,500 to 3,000 men. That statistic is from Michael R. Marrus and Robert O. Paxton, *Vichy France and the Jews* (New York: Basic Books), 241.

4 Lucien Steinberg, 'Jewish Rescue Activities in Belgium and France,' *Rescue Attempts during the Holocaust: Proceedings of the Second Yad Vashem International Historical Conference*, Jerusalem: April 8–11, 1974 (Jerusalem: Yad Vashem, 1977), 603–14, 614.

5 Stanley Hoffmann, 'In the Looking Glass: Sorrow and Pity?' in *Decline or Renewal: France since the 1930s* (New York: Viking, 1974), 60.

6 Léon Poliakov, *L'étoile jaune* (Paris: Editions du Centre, 1949), 93.

7 Shatta and Bouli Simon testimony [n.d.], CDJC, DLXXII–46 (16 pp.).

8 Ibid.

PART FOUR

Societal attitudes to fascism

Support, conformity, opposition and resistance

SECTION VII

■ Society and attitudes to fascism – support, conformity and resistance

THE FASCIST PROJECT was an extraordinary exercise in all-pervasive social engineering. Through its transformation from movement to regime fascism sought the loyalty not only of its supporters but of the totality of the national population. In promoting an ultra-nationalist utopia, fascism aspired to embody and promote the 'national interest' in a holistic, uncompromised manner unmatched by any previous social or political force in national history. Finally, in its fundamental opposition to communism, fascism also aspired to transcend its national limits and command loyalty on an international scale as a counterbalance to Bolshevik internationalism. Through the multiple process of accumulating and overwriting traditional allegiances, it aspired to become much more than a simple ideological and political alternative alongside other oppositional forces; it aimed to reconfigure existing loyalties in a new model, a new 'conception of life' (Mussolini 1932), which gravitated towards fascism, its historic leader and its ideology. The regime variant of fascism aspired to offer much more than simply a transient strategy of political management. Rather, it claimed to offer a morally superior point of reference for the whole nation, embracing all levels and expressions of its life as a historic, socio-economic, political and cultural entity.

In Section V we underlined the significance of using institutionalised coercion, terror and sophisticated methods of surveillance for ensuring the political durability of the fascist regime (see Mallmann and Paul (**27**)). Such a predominantly coercive function, however successfully administered, served as the basis for a postwar questioning of the legitimacy of the fascist claim that its power also rested on popular consent. Postwar anti-fascist historiography thrived on an analytical model which divided the population into two uneven groups: the resisters (majority) and the collaborators (minority). In Italy, the myth of the *Resistenza* facilitated the act of salvaging a sense of national pride from the loathsome period of Fascist rule and thus ensured a smooth political transition to a post-fascist, liberal and democratic era. For France, the powerful imagery of anti-Nazi struggle promoted the de-legitimisation of the Vichy regime as a political edifice established through external compulsion, contradicting the wishes of the majority of the population and failing to generate popular consensus with regard to its goals and practices. This historical interpretation, based on a morally conspicuous Manichean choice between the 'evil' of fascism and the 'good' of the country, served Marxist and liberal historiography equally. For the left, the idea that the resistance was effectively organised, systematised and carried out through surviving communist and socialist networks helped enforce the representation of the working class en bloc as ideologically and actively opposed to the fascist totalitarian project. As Giuliano Procacci (a prominent communist politician and historian of the *Resistenza*) wrote, the left was best suited to assume leadership of anti-fascist resistance as it possessed an elaborate organisational structure, experience of mass mobilisation and an ideologically cogent discourse of opposition to the Fascist regime (Procacci 1970). At the same time, the dominant liberal interpretation of fascism as essentially the offspring of the petty bourgeoisie's support for order, security and strong leadership left the anti-fascist prestige of the urban and rural working class largely unscathed. Even in Germany, where – in contrast to Italy and France – evidence of popular and systematic resistance activity against Nazism is scant, historians such as Martin Broszat (1981) emphasised a plethora of non-conformist dispositions to the regime, primarily in the form of verbal criticism, but also in terms of active disobedience and non-participation in Nazi-inspired projects such as leisure and youth clubs, anti-Semitism, etc.

Nevertheless, from the 1960s onwards the crude distinction between resistance and collaboration or consensus was challenged from a host of novel historiographical viewpoints. First, the pursuit of new methodological avenues in analysing societal attitudes to fascism produced a growing interest in a 'history from below'. Popular attitudes, oral history and emphasis on the everyday life of individuals and groups under fascism suggested a more nuanced reality of public perspectives on fascism, where the model of 'resistance-versus-collaboration' represented two opposites but failed to account for the attitudes of the majority. It was gradually becoming apparent that apathy, ideological confusion, and rejection of moral choices were far more common amongst the populations than outright support for either side. The pioneering work of Luisa Passerini on oral history revealed a high degree of passive consensus amongst large sectors of the Italian working class towards the Fascist regime. Passerini noted that it was heuristically problematic to generalise about the working class as a whole: there were significant geographic, economic and generational cleavages amongst its members which facilitated different responses to Fascism, from active participation in the *Resistenza* to a-political indifference and (opportunistic or fanatical, incidental or consistent) collaboration (Passerini 1979, 1987). Even if this did not amount to positive ideological support for the regime, it did nevertheless reflect the absence of a clear class-consciousness (which would have rendered anti-fascism an automatic response to the establishment of Mussolini's regime) and a relative vulnerability of the working class to conformist attitudes in return for material and other concessions. In this light, the claim of Renzo De Felice that the Fascist regime enjoyed a long period of 'consensus' in the 1920s and 1930s, peaking during the Ethiopian campaign of 1935–6, epitomised the historiographical need to reassess the nature of the 'resistance' narratives. Although De Felice's motives behind his conscious revision of the 'myth of the resistance' were politically questionable, they exposed the inadequacies of a view of the *Resistenza* as an 'uninterrupted core of anti-fascism' enjoying the near-universal support of the working class (Passerini 1979: 87ff.). Without an awareness of the inroads made by the Fascist regime – through either coercion or manipulation or simply as a result of living in a routine – the 'consensus' generated during the Ethiopian war is reduced to an incomprehensible lapse of consciousness, which certainly does not do justice to the far deeper social attitudes that fostered its temporary strength. B. Wanrooij (37) shows in particular how the appeal of Fascism to specific sections of the population can be understood as a 'generational' phenomenon. This said, as T. Abse (38) points out, the majority of Italian workers did not display a positive or enduring allegiance to Fascism, remaining either indifferent and passive or hostile to the regime's efforts to 'go to the people' and purchase their loyalties (cf. 26).

The historiographical landscape is equally interesting with regard to Germany. The absence of a popular resistance movement during the Nazi period is instructive in two ways. First, it illustrates the success of the Nazi suppression and disruption of the (highly elaborate prior to 1933) socialist and communist networks of mass activity. Second, it attests to the existence of a wide-ranging template of popular and elite consensus for the regime which overshadowed sporadic and uncoordinated acts of non-conformity and active insubordination. While the elite consensus (see Section VIII) had already started to crumble by 1936–7, inducing isolated acts of resistance (such as the efforts of certain military and diplomatic groups to oppose Hitler's plans to invade Czechoslovakia in the summer of 1938 or attack Poland in 1939 – see 43), popular support or passive endorsement continued well into the war, only to be severely undermined by the bare necessities of defeat in the war and the agonising collapse of the regime in 1943–5. D. Goldhagen's work on 'Hitler's willing executioners' (31) constitutes a statement, however exaggerated and flawed, about the high degree of the German public's support for the Nazi projects. Popular 'consensus' for the Nazi regime was not simply the negative product of institutionalised coercion and terror; it rested on a mixture of fear of the alternatives to Nazism and an instinctive sense of allegiance to the leadership. As D. Peukert (39) illustrates, the Nazi movement recruited supporters and members from all social classes (including the working class), in spite of the numerically superior representation of the middle class and of the 'losers' of the Depression amongst its ranks. Conformity or apathy, however, should not be confused with active support. The initial postwar view of the Nazi regime as monolithic and all-pervasive has been widely challenged, revealing areas which Nazism failed to penetrate. J. Stephenson's work on the attitudes of women under Nazi rule (40) came across a far-from-uniform response to the efforts of the movement/regime to organise women, with apathy and lack of involvement reigning supreme.

Finally, this section features two more excerpts that shed light on social attitudes to fascism in France and Spain. Robert O. Paxton's piece (**41**) exposes the
limited character and recruitment of the French resistance movement amidst a
general social milieu of apathy, *attentisme* and occasional collaboration. In the
second excerpt, on Spain, R. Carr (**42**) analyses the complex motives that fuelled
the desire of individuals and groups in the Spanish population in the 1930s to fight
on either side of the bloody civil war.

Chapter 37

Bruno Wanrooij

ITALIAN FASCISM AS A 'GENERATIONAL' PHENOMENON

■ from **THE RISE AND FALL OF ITALIAN FASCISM AS A GENERATIONAL REVOLT**, *Journal of Contemporary History*, 22 (1987), pp. 401, 402–4, 405–9, 410, 411, 413–14

Bruno Wanrooij's analysis of Italian Fascism as a 'generational revolt' (a term first used by J. J. Linz) actually refers to two generational conflicts – one (earlier) within Italian society and one (later) within the Fascist movement itself. On the one hand, the revolt of the *novecento* generation against socialism and liberalism (in particular, its detestation for the patriarch of Italian liberalism, Giovanni Giolitti) prefigured the rise of Fascism as a 'young' force in Italian politics from 1919 onwards. On the other hand, the emergence of a new wave of young Fascists in the 1930s caused a generational friction within Fascism itself, this time between the old elite around Mussolini and the younger disciples. As the gap between the two groups widened after 1935, Fascism itself entered a period of crisis that pushed large sections of the younger generation to the path of disaffection with the regime.

MANY OBSERVERS HAVE NOTICED the great interest with which, during the 1930s, the leaders of the Soviet Union, nazi Germany and fascist Italy followed the political development of young people. Youth had made a major contribution to the rise to power of new regimes in these countries, and the preservation of the preferential relationship between youth and the political leadership was considered essential to the success of the revolutions that had taken place. In Italy this relationship was invested with particular importance; whereas the concept of class had been at the centre of the ideological framework of the October Revolution, and race was the key element in nazi ideology, the fascists had come to power 'raising the banner of youth'.[1]

[. . .]

The social conditions underlying the generation conflict were experienced first by the middle classes in Italy. The extension of time spent in education created a contrast between the financial and social dependence of young people and their biological and psychological independence. For this reason, the aspirations of the younger generation in the first part of this century were in reality those of middle-class youth. Only later did these conditions extend to other classes.

Some of the reasons why fascism was identified with the aspirations of youth in the post-war period can be traced back to earlier developments. For a number of reasons, young intellectuals during the first decade of the twentieth century began to turn away from socialism, to the ideals of which many of them had adhered in the 1890s.[2] Culturally, the rise of an idealist philosophy made socialism look anti-quated, because it was associated with positivism. The reformist strategy that had been adopted at the Rome party congress in 1900 seemed too cautious to young people, many of whom were strongly influenced by the model of heroic, individu-alistic action as portrayed in the novels of Gabriele D'Annunzio.[3] At least as important for the political development of young intellectuals was the fact that the success of the socialist movement began to endanger their privileged position which depended upon their traditional role, of intermediaries between the ruling groups and the working class.

Although intellectuals during this period were no longer drawn to socialism, they were not attracted by the ruling class either, which was accused of not defending its interests with sufficient vigour. The parliamentary system was criticized as a source of corruption and of mean-spirited compromises. Fierce attacks were directed against the policy of Prime Minister Giovanni Giolitti, who wanted to main-tain state neutrality in labour conflicts in the hope of thereby overcoming the traditional gap between the working class and the Italian state. The criticism of socialist reformism on the one hand, and of the political system on the other, was voiced in *Il Regno* and *La Voce*, small intellectual periodicals published in Florence by Giuseppe Prezzolini and his friends.

Conscious of the weaknesses of the existing ruling class, and eager to contribute to the formation of a new elite, Prezzolini found allies in the emerging new class of the industrial bourgeoisie, which condemned attempts to find a compromise between the interests of capital and labour, and proposed the replacement of the political class, then still composed of members of the liberal professions, with a parliamentary coalition of industrialists.

The ideas on the formation of a new elite were based largely on theories which had been elaborated by such eminent scholars as Vilfredo Pareto and Gaetano Mosca. The lack of any serious proposal to promote social mobility indicates, however, that we are dealing with an attempt to speed up circulation within the existing ruling class. In this context, the political struggle necessarily took the form of a struggle between generations.[4]

A similar development took place in the socialist party, where young maximal-ists opposed the leadership of the older reformists. At the congress of Reggio Emilia of 1912, the young revolutionary socialists, led by Benito Mussolini, emerged victo-rious. The new party line which they imposed was strongly influenced by the ideas of Georges Sorel; it emphasized the role of an active minority, but disregarded the necessity for serious mass organization.

As is well known, the differences within the opposed camps resulted in an explosion over the issue of Italy's participation in the war. Mussolini was expelled from the socialist party because of his propaganda in favour of intervention and his insistence on the revolutionary character of war. What is significant, from our point of view, is that, after his expulsion, Mussolini made an appeal to youth, urging them to decide on a new course in history.[5] The young intellectuals who had gathered around *La Voce* and had long been critical of the government's lack of energy, now began to see Mussolini as a possible ally. Giovanni Papini, who had been a close collaborator of Prezzolini, expressed the hope that the war would create the conditions for a radical change in the ruling class.[6] University students played a major role in the violent demonstrations in favour of intervention, directing their attacks explicitly against the older generation. One of them, Paolo Marconi, wrote in his diary:

> Between parents and sons a frightful struggle is going on. We are descended from a generation of bastards that neither made Italy nor created the Italians. Down with old age! Today a young man can only be a revolutionary. He who is not a revolutionary is not young.[7] [. . .]

For them, the experience of war became a basis for the interpretation of all subsequent events.[8] Of course, this experience did not necessarily lead to an identity of ideas, but it did create a common ground for the divergent interpretations of reality expressed by all those who shared it. In this sense, Marc Bloch has defined a generation as a *communauté d'empreinte*.[9]

Giuseppe Bottai, an important leader of the fascist party, was well aware of the impact the war had had on his personal and political formation, when he wrote in 1935:

> For us, to make war and to become men was the same thing. War and youth exploded simultaneously. We did not need any will-power, no solemn decision, no exception to normality in order to make war. One cannot avoid puberty. War has been our puberty.[10]

Bottai identified himself with the values and symbols of this war that had become *his* war.

[. . .]

Mussolini was well aware of the potential political force of the youth movement and paid great attention to its demands and complaints. His efforts were not without success. Less than three months after the creation of the fascist movement, he was able to write that many young people had joined it, attracted by its dynamism, its open-mindedness, and its struggle for a radical change in society.[11] The active role in the fascist movement played by futurists and members of the assault troops' organizations reinforced Mussolini's attempts to make fascism the expression of the war generation. Moreover, the violent style of fascist political action offered those young people who, for reasons of age, had not participated in the war, the opportunity to show their courage.[12] The enthusiasm of students for fascism was so great that in November 1921 they accounted for 13.1 per cent of the movement's total membership.[13]

On the basis of these figures, Juan Linz has defined fascism as a 'generational revolt'.[14] Fascism, a late-comer on the political scene, could gain a mass base only by directing its appeal to a younger generation which had not yet been attracted by the existing parties. In order to avoid the risk of isolation, the fascist leaders were compelled to identify with the aspirations of the 'new romantics' who, after the war, were waiting for a second 'age of heroes'.[15] Although fascism certainly did not express the feelings of all young people, and other parties, like the newly-founded communist party, gained a certain popularity among youth,[16] the concept of fascism as a paradigmatic expression of the political ideas of the younger generation was accepted even by its opponents. According to Alberto Cappa, fascism represented the violent reaction of the younger generation against the conservatism of their fathers.[17]

Aiming at a redistribution of political power along generational lines, Mussolini sought to undermine the cohesion of the existing social groups and classes. The contrast between the 'revolutionary' programme of the fascist movement of 1919 and the violent attacks against all revolutionary movements can be explained as an attempt to weaken the links between the working class and the organizations. The generational revolt created the pre-conditions for rapid change within the ruling class, but left the social equilibrium essentially unaltered. The continuous appeal to the values of the war served as a justification of the attempt to restore the authority of the 'heroic petty bourgeois lieutenants'.[18]

The seizure of power by the fascist party in October 1922 resulted in a considerable rejuvenation of the political class. In the parliamentary elections of 1924, 82.3 per cent of the fascist candidates had no parliamentary experience; 35.9 per cent were less than thirty years old.[19] Fascists could therefore claim that they had brought youth to power. At the same time, however, the seizure of power revealed a potential conflict between the necessity to restore order and the spontaneity of the youth revolt. The conservative allies of fascism emphasized the need to slow down the revolutionary process.[20] The fascists refused to abandon their preferential relationship with youth, but gradually suppressed the remaining autonomy of the youth movement. The fascist student organizations were reorganized and subjected to the authority of the party secretary. In 1923, fascist students were practically forced to give up their protest against the university reforms which abolished the privileges of the war veterans.[21]

Under these circumstances, the more radical fascists such as Roberto Farinacci were able to gain the support of a considerable number of young people. Their proposals regarding a radical change of the political class and a purge in the state administration attracted all those who wanted to make money out of their early membership of the fascist movement. As the so-called *intransigenti* based their plans for the future of fascist society on the hierarchy that had been established during the revolutionary period, they were unable to convince the young fascists who had not participated in this action. This is why, in the long run, the reformist fascists who gathered around Giuseppe Bottai and his periodical *Critica fascista* proved more successful.

The *revisionisti* recognized the limits of the existing fascist elite and therefore accepted temporary collaboration with the political personnel linked with the pre-fascist governments. They were to be allowed to continue to do their work on condition they formally accepted the principles of fascist policy. In future, however, these persons were to be replaced by a new elite, consisting of young fascists who would combine an unswerving loyalty to the fascist cause with a thorough knowledge of state administration. The creation of a new elite thus became the main theme in the writings of reformist fascists. The prospect of becoming part of this new fascist ruling class was at the base of the support offered by young intellectuals to the fascist regime.[22]

Through the myth of youth, which continued to be at the centre of fascist ideology, the regime tried to separate young workers from the older members of the working class. While some political leaders and many of the trade-union leaders recognized that it would be extremely difficult to gain the support of the working class as a whole, they hoped that at least among its young members, who had no memory of the violent repression of the working-class movement, it would be possible to create some form of consensus. The concept of youth, in fact, was supposed to unite young people belonging to the elite and young members of the working class under the sun of an imaginary 'springtime of beauty'.[23] The dreary social and economic conditions of the working class, however, were in sharp contrast with this image. Moreover, young workers who entered the production process at an early age fairly soon acquired a sense of class consciousness. Although the importance of new forms of organization of leisure can hardly be underestimated, the main purpose of the mass organization of working-class youth remained the creation of a new, disciplined type of worker.[24]

The distinction between different age groups was of greater importance in the upper classes, where university students in particular were reminded time and again of their responsibilities as the future ruling class. In the second half of the 1920s, it became more difficult for young people to identify with the fascist leaders with whom they no longer shared the experiences of war and revolution. In consequence, their demands to be admitted to the leadership became more pressing. Though some of the fascist leaders recognized the need to preserve the original character of fascism and proposed to make way for new young leaders, the realization of their plans proved extremely difficult. They were opposed by those in power, who refused to recognize that they were now regarded as old.[25] Another problem was the lack of any institutionalized mechanism for the renewal of the party cadres. The myth of youth thus became a threat to the established order.

The leaders in power reacted to this threat by pointing out that the concept of youth could not be restricted to a certain age group, but applied to all those possessing a number of spiritual qualities, such as enthusiasm, optimism and faith. The right of young people to demand special privileges based on their age alone was rejected by the fascist ideologist Camillo Pellizzi on the grounds that, unlike the war generation, they had not earned them.[26] Many of the early fascists agreed that the 'absolute apriorism' in favour of youth should be abolished,[27] and maintained that the eventual renewal of the ruling class should take place on the principle of 'Power to the Elders'.[28] The press attacked youth with such fierceness that on a number of occasions the party secretary felt the need to intervene and prescribe more moderate language.[29]

[. . .]

Mussolini [. . .] denied the existence of a generation struggle in fascist society and underlined the continuity between the war generation and the young people who had grown up under fascism. His views were summarized in the 'Firm Points about Youth', published by the fascist party in 1930. In this document, he declared that the fascist regime should remain one of youth and that, therefore, all other things being equal, it should prefer the nomination of a thirty-year-old to that of someone older. The creation of the new elite should be the result of continuous selection among members of the youth organizations. In the meantime, the political, social and cultural organizations of fascism should offer youth the possibility of apprenticeship.[30] The press predictably reacted very positively to the 'Firm Points about Youth' and underlined Mussolini's aspiration to continue the revolutionary course of fascism. In reality, however, the totalitarian control over youth was reinforced, whereas the advantages of the new system applied to only a small minority.

Despite the introduction of the propaganda slogan 'Make Way for Youth', the problem of the renewal of the ruling class remained substantially unsolved. Eighty of the 145 new deputies appointed in 1934 had entered the fascist party before 1922; twenty-seven had joined that year, and only thirty-eight had become members at a later stage.[31] Even among the leaders of the fascist student groups in 1931, 57.3 per cent had entered the party before 1923 whereas only 13 per cent had come from the fascist youth organizations.[32]

The failure of the new policy and the existence of a considerable number of unemployed intellectuals persuaded the regime to open up new possibilities for discussion. The elaboration of its ideology served the need to distinguish fascist Italy from the capitalist countries in crisis, and, at the same time, made it possible to reaffirm the special relationship between fascism and youth. The contribution of the students to the ideological debate was useful preparation for their future role as a ruling class and fulfilled a long-felt need:

> We should give youth a myth because youth needs to have a blind faith in something and wants to be at the centre of events. At present intellectual youth – as such – feels spiritually uncertain because it is confronted with two great events, war and revolution, in which it did not take part and to which it made no contribution. Youth is searching for something it feels instinctively, but is not yet able to define.[33]
> [. . .]

The well-known Italian historian Renzo De Felice has described the years 1936–40 as a period of psychological detachment which need not necessarily have led to the crisis of 1943.[34] However, as the fascist regime had been unable to improve the condition of the majority of the population and had granted privileges to only a small coterie, these psychological aspects acquired a particular meaning. This is even more true for intellectual youth, which had based its support for fascism on an uneasy equilibrium between revolt and conformity, in which the idea of belonging to an elite was the decisive element. The gradual elimination of all possibilities for discussion, which followed the rapprochement with nazi Germany, deprived students of their main instrument for participation in the development of fascist society. Disagreement with more or less important aspects of political and social life could thus be transformed into active anti-fascism. The war against Ethiopia was at the start of this process.

Young intellectuals, even those who criticized other aspects of the regime, like the young people who gathered around Ruggero Zangrandi, had been among the most enthusiastic supporters of the invasion of Ethiopia. They hoped that the war would again set in motion the revolutionary process. War had the added advantage of giving them a chance to win approval for courage shown on the battlefield. Thus, they could finally overcome their sense of inferiority and prove themselves the equals of the older generation which had risked its life for the country and the fascist cause.

[. . .]

The political options of 1938, the intervention in the Spanish Civil War, the alliance with nazi Germany and the subsequent introduction of anti-semitic laws, were rejected by a growing minority of the younger generation, which deplored the decreasing chances of promoting an autonomous interpretation of fascist ideology. For some years, the myth of youth was absent from fascist propaganda. It was only during the second world war, when military defeats had annihilated the prestige of the regime, and when contact with harsh reality had persuaded many young people to abandon the illusion of an improved fascism, that Mussolini tried to breathe new life into fascism and explain that only the younger generation would be able to bring about a radical renewal of the system.[35] The temptations of irrationality and a desperate sense of moral coherence persuaded a number of young people to follow Mussolini into the cruel adventure of the Republic of Salò. In general terms, however, by 1942 the fascist generations had come to an end, as was clearly stated by the communist leader Palmiro Togliatti:

> The majority of the fascist leaders was young during the other war. This generation was confronted in the after-war period with a great economic, political and moral confusion. A part of it followed fascism, expecting a social revolution and a renewal of the nation's life. The best fascists of this generation, in one way or another, have disappeared. The others have become bourgeois, rich, bureaucrats. Once more we have arrived at one of these points which historians call a turn of generations.[36]

An indication of this change can be found in the words of a young anti-fascist, Ernesto Treccani: 'I became an anti-fascist because I was young.'[37]

Among the characteristics of the 'classical' fascist dictatorships, Mihaly Vajda has drawn attention to the substitution of the representatives of the ruling class in the political elite by members of a new fascist elite.[38] For a number of reasons, this substitution was never completed in Italy. The preferential relationship with youth which the fascist leaders tried to preserve indicates, nevertheless, the nature of the fascists' plans for the future, and created a link between the *Realpolitik* of the fascist regime and the totalitarian aspirations of the fascist movement which found a common goal in the creation of a 'new man'.

At the same time, the fascist interpretation of the concept of generation, according to which the members of a social and cultural elite represented a whole generation, indicates the limits of the fascist revolution and its elite character. The imaginary unification of the younger generation against the 'old' social and political order constituted an argument against the theory of class struggle.[39]

The political formation of young people under fascism was strongly influenced by the model of the generation struggle. Hence, for a long time they were unable to see that their criticism was in reality directed against the ruling class and not against the older generation in general. Nevertheless, the growing importance of the generation struggle during the 1930s can be considered as an indication of the crisis of the fascist ruling class.[40]

Notes

1   Benito Mussolini, 'Discorso agli arditi di Trieste' (1918), *Opera omnia* (Florence 1951–1963), X, 140–42.

2   Vilfredo Pareto, at that moment still a supporter of an alliance between liberalism and socialism, wrote in 1897 that almost all intelligent young people in Italy and France grew up as socialists: Vilfredo Pareto, 'Cronaca', *Ecrits politiques*, II, *Reazione Libertà Fascismo 1896–1923* (Geneva 1974), 193–7. The 'idealism' of students has been noted in a more recent period by Frank Parkin, 'Adolescent Status and Student Politics', *Journal of Contemporary History*, 5, 1 (January 1970), 150–3. The activities of large groups of young intellectuals of bourgeois origin in the socialist movement have been interpreted by Antonio Gramsci as an 'unconscious' attempt to restore the hegemony of their class: Antonio Gramsci, *Quaderni del carcere* (Turin 1975), 396–7. The political development of French youth in the first decade of this century has been studied by Philippe Beneton, 'La génération de 1912–1914. Image, mythe et réalité', *Revue française de science politique*, 21, 5 (1971), 981–1009.

3   Cf. G. A. Borgese, *Gabriele D'Annunzio* (Naples 1909), Carlo Sahnan, *Miti e coscienza del decadentismo italiano* (Milan 1980), 29–105, and George L. Mosse 'The Poet and the Exercise of Political Power', *Yearbook of Comparative and General Literature*, 22 (1973), 32–41. A personal recollection of this period can be found in Carlo Rossetti, 'Filippo Turati e il socialismo italiano', *Quaderni di Giustizia e Libertà*, 3 (1932), 1–41. According to H. Stuart Hughes, who proposes the year 1905 as a watershed in intellectual history, the estrangement between intellectuals of different ages was a general phenomenon in Europe: H. Stuart Hughes, *Consciousness and Society: The Reorientation of European Social Thought 1890–1930* (rev ed, New York 1977), 337–44.

4   Cf. on the elite theories and their application in Italy Eugenio Ripepe, *Gli elitisti italiani* (Pisa 1974), Ettore A. Albertoni, *Gaetano Mosca. Storia di una dottrina politico. Formazione e interpretazione* (Milan 1978), and Francis Vecchini, *La pensée politique de Gaetano Mosca et ses différentes adaptions au cours du XXème siècle en Italie* (Paris 1968). Cf. on Pareto Giovanni Busino, *Gli studi sul Vilfredo Pareto oggi. Dall'agiografia alla critica (1923–1973)* (Rome 1974).

5   Benito Mussolini, 'Audacia', *Il Popolo d'Italia*, 1, 1 (1915) and *Opera omnia*, op cit, VII, 5–7.

6   Giovanni Papini, quoted in Eugenio Gann, *Cronache di filosofla italiana 1900–1943* (Rome–Bari 1975), 313.

7   Paolo Marconi, 'Io udii il comandamento', *Dal diario e dalle lettere di un eroe ventenne* (Rome 1919), 65–6, 2 March 1915.

8   According to Lambert, who bases his ideas on empirical research done by Piaget, the critical age for the formation of a political consciousness is between eighteen and twenty-six years. Historical events of particular importance can create a gap between those who have experienced them during this critical period and others. T. Allen Lambert, 'Generations and Change Towards a Theory of Generation as a Force in Historical Process', *Youth and Society*, (1972), 21–45.

9   Marc Bloch, *Apologie pour l'histoire ou métier d'historien* (Paris 1974), 150–1.

10   Giuseppe Bottai, *Diario* (Milan 1982), 216–17.

11   Benito Mussolini, 'Il "fascismo"', *Popolo d'Italia*, 6, 180 (1919) and *Opera omnia*, op cit, XIII, 218–20.

12   The availability of young people between fifteen and twenty years old for violent action has been noted by Ferruccio Vecchi, *Arditismo civile* (Milan 1920), 77–84.

13   *Il Popolo d'Italia*, 8 November 1921.

14   Juan B. Linz, 'Some Notes Toward a Comparative Study of Fascism in Sociological Historical Perspective', in Walter Laqueur (ed), *Fascism: A Reader's Guide* (Harmondsworth 1979), 52–4.

15   Dino Grandi, 'I nuovi romantici', *La libertà economica*, 20 October 1919 and *Giovani* (Bologna 1941), 91–3.

16   Paolo Spriano has underlined the enthusiasm of young people for communism, which had gained great prestige as a result of the October Revolution: Paolo Spriano, *Storia del partito comunista italiano* (Turin 1976), I, 43–5.

17   Grildrig (pseud Alberto Cappa), *Le generazioni nel fascismo* (Turin 1924), 4–9. The young political thinker and editor Piero Gobetti emphasized in a review the existence of groups of young intellectuals who abhorred the style and the contents of fascist politics: Piero Gobetti, 'La lotta delle generazioni', *La rivoluzione liberate*, 25 September 1923 and *Scritti politici* (Turin 1960), 522–3.

18   F. T. Mannetti, 'Al di là del comunismo' (1920), *Teoria e invenzione futurista* (Verona 1968), 415–16.

19   Jens Petersen, 'Elettorato e base sociale del fascismo italiano negli anni venti', *Studi storici*, 16, 3 (1975), 650.

20   Cf. Ettore Ciccotti, 'Tempo secondo', *Giornale d'Italia*, 16 January 1923 and *Il fascismo e le sue fasi, Anarchia – Dittatura – Deviazioni* (Milan 1925), 268–73.

21   Cf. Archivio Centrale dello Stato (ACS), *Mostra della Rivoluzione fascista*, b. 16. The relationship between fascism and youth in the period before the seizure of power has been studied, among others, by Maria Cristina Giuntella, 'I Gruppi universitari fascisti nel primo decennio del regime', *Il movimento di liberazione in Italia*, 107 (1972), 12–13. The best study on fascist education is Michel Ostenc, *L'éducation en Italie pendant le fascisme* (Paris 1980).

22   Cf. Roberto Cantalupo, *La classe dirigente* (Milan 1926), 81.

23   The first lines of the fascist anthem are 'Youth, youth! Springtime of beauty'.

24   Cf. Pietro Caporelli, *Il fascismo e i giovani* (Rome 1932), 68–9. Cf., on the organization of leisure, Victoria de Grazia, *The Culture of Consent. Mass Organization of Leisure in Fascist Italy* (Cambridge 1981).

25   Cf. Giuseppe Bottai, 'Corradini e il dramma delle generazioni' (1927), *Incontri* (Milan 1943), 297.

26   Camillo Pellizzi, 'Elogia della gavetta', *Il Resto del Carlino*, 44, 301 (1928), 2.

27   Germano Segreti, 'I giovani', *Critica fascista*, 3 (1929), 48–9.

28   Luigi Passerini, 'Preoccupazioni e ansie dei giovani. Discussioni utili', *Corriere emiliano*, 175, 186 (1930).

29   Cf. Philip V. Cannistraro, *La fabbrica del consenso. Fascismo e mass media* (Rome–Bari 1975), 443–5.

30   Partito nazionale fascista, *Foglio d'ordini*, 64 (20 January 1930). The continuity of generations under fascism was exemplified in the ceremony of the *leva fascista*.

31   Renzo De Felice, *Mussolini il duce*, vol I, *Gli anni del consenso 1929–1936* (Turin 1974), 312 footnote.

32   ACS, Gruppi umversitari fascisti, b 6.

33   Carlo Scorza, 'Relazione sui FGC, sui GUF, sulla Milizia universitaria' (11 July 1931). Quoted in Alberto Aquarone, *L'organizzazione dello stato totalitario* (Turin 1965), 513.

34   Renzo De Felice, *Mussolini il duce*, II, *Lo Stato totalitario 1936–1940* (Turin 1981), 3–4, 218.

35   Benito Mussolini, 'Al direttorio nazionale del PNF' (1942), *Opera omnia*, op cit, XXXI, 71–6.

36   Palmiro Togliatti, 'Generazioni vecchie e giovani nel partito fascista' (1942), *Opere*, IV, 2 (Rome 1979), 242–4.

37   Ernesto Treccani, quoted in Ettore A. Albertoni et al (eds), *La generazione degli anni difficili* (Bari 1962), 273.

38   Mihaly Vajda, *Fascism as a Mass Movement* (London 1976), 15.

39   Herbert Moller, 'Youth as a Force in the Modern World', *Comparative Studies in Society and History*, 10, 3 (1968), 254–6.

40   Cf. Antonio Gramsci, *Quaderni del carcere*, op cit, 115.

Chapter 38

Tobias Abse

FASCISM AND WORKING CLASS: WORKERS UNDER ITALIAN FASCISM

■ from **ITALIAN WORKERS AND ITALIAN FASCISM**, in Richard Bessel (ed.) *Fascist Italy and Nazi Germany: Comparisons and Contrasts*, Cambridge, 1996, pp. 40, 42–3, 48–51, 56–7, 57–60

Tobias Abse's work on the attitudes of the Italian working class to Fascism has exposed a series of significant limitations to the regime's claim that it enjoyed the support ('consensus', to use Renzo De Felice's much-debated term) of the majority of the Italian population. Abse maintains that the Italian working class remained 'stubbornly recalcitrant' throughout the life span of Mussolini's rule, displaying no sign of lasting loyalty to the regime. In spite of Fascism's efforts to purchase the allegiance of the proletariat (including the opening up of the PNF's membership and the establishment of Fascist trade unions and of the Dopolavoro), working-class participation in the regime's social sphere remained limited and far from enthusiastic. This pattern, Abse stresses, was accentuated during the war as a result of food shortages and the damage caused by the Allied bombardments, generating great anger at the regime and acts of outright dissent (for example, the strikes of 1943).

T HE ITALIAN WORKING CLASS'S experience of fascism was very different from the German working class's experience of Nazism. The sort of questions that Tim Mason asked himself in the Epilogue to the English edition of *Social Policy in the Third Reich*, the questions that led him to doubt the value of his earlier analyses centred on class relations, do not need to be asked in the Italian instance. This was a working class which broke with the regime, not one that followed – or appeared to follow – the dictator to the bitter end. If the behaviour of the German population, civilian and military, from early 1943 to May 1945 might be described as 'incomprehensible',[1] the same cannot be said of their Italian counterparts. This difference in behaviour between the two working classes might be attributed in part to the differing levels of efficiency reached by the two dictatorships – Mussolini's Italian Fascism was an authoritarian regime which made a large number of compromises with the existing political and economic elites, compromises which went far beyond any the Nazis made, and it had no real equivalent to the Gestapo or the SS, for the OVRA was little more than a slightly better organised version of the political section that had always existed within the traditional police. Therefore repression did not reach German levels: if political murders of anti-Fascists occurred in 1920–5 and again in 1943–5, for the bulk of the regime's existence *squadrismo* gave way to very traditional police methods; imprisonment and internal exile, not death, were the standard penalties for political dissidence. Therefore, there is a certain plausibility in Mason's argument that 'the crucial difference lay in the capillary character and the greater executive power of the various German administrative machines'.[2]

[. . .]

In this context it is hardly surprising that Italian Fascism never really gained any widespread consensus or support amongst the industrial working class of northern and central Italy, with the sole, if extremely interesting, exception of Trieste (where the Fascists rallied a large section of the ethnically Italian workers alongside the Italian petty bourgeoisie in an alliance against the Slav workers who were more inclined to the political Left). The exception reinforces the general argument. Trieste, it must be remembered, was not only ethnically divided, it had also been under Habsburg, not Italian, rule before 1918 and its political culture owed more to the rival nationalisms of Austria-Hungary than to the anti-statist, anti-militarist traditions of the Italian workers' movement. The industrial cities were the strongholds of anti-Fascist resistance in the undeclared civil war of 1921–2, when the *Arditi del Popolo* of Livorno, Piombino and La Spezia fought back against the Fascist squads with far more organisation and determination than the leaderless and largely unarmed *braccianti* (landless labourers) of Ferrara and Reggio Emilia. Many historians have been too ready to assume that the behaviour of the rank and file can be deduced from the proclamations of party leaderships – that the rank and file in the militant cities of northern and central Italy followed to the letter the absurd pacifism of the Milanese middle-class intellectual Filippo Turati, who from the safety of a parliamentary forum solemnly instructed Socialists to turn the other cheek to the tide of Fascist barbarism, or the equally absurd sectarian bombast of the Neapolitan engineer Amadeo Bordiga that Communists should form no alliances in the fight against Fascism. It did not. Even if the only national dynamic behind an armed united front against the Fascists came from the Anarchists, whose leader Errico Malatesta argued for it throughout 1921–2, at the local level *sovversivi* [Note: literally *subversives*] of every stripe – Socialists, Communists, Anarchists, Syndicalists, Republicans – rallied to the defence of their neighbourhoods and fought the Fascists square by square, street by street, turning whole districts of cities like Livorno into 'no go' areas for the Fascists and their allies in the security forces.

[. . .]

[A]ny discussion of the relationship between the working class and the regime, any further exploration of this theme that seeks to ascertain the extent to which the *tradizione sovversiva* survived between 1922 and 1943 has to address a number of more general issues: the extent to which the mass organisations of the Fascist regime, such as the Fascist trade unions, the Fascist youth organisation and the Fascist leisure organisation, changed workers' attitudes; the effects of Taylorism and rationalisation (so important in the German case), insofar as they affected Italian industry, on the working class; and the extent to which Fascism was able to create a new working class from peasants or women without prior political traditions.

The Fascist mass organisations were designed to facilitate the integration of the lower classes – the industrial workers and peasants – into the nation-state, the project in which the Liberals had shown themselves such failures before 1922. Of all the Fascist mass organisations, the Fascist trade unions were the most obvious means through which the industrial proletariat might have been won over to the new regime. The Pact of Palazzo Vidoni between the employers and the regime, together with the anti-strike legislation of 1926, had left the Fascist trade unions as the only legal representatives of the Italian working class. However, the Fascist trade unions did not profit from this legal monopoly to any great extent. It is true that they tried to assert their autonomy between 1926 and 1928, often denouncing the employers and occasionally calling strikes to demonstrate their potential power, but the employers were able to ignore their empty threats and appeal directly to Mussolini, who was not prepared to risk his alliance with the industrialists for the sake of the pride of Fascist trade-union bureaucrats. Once the unified corporative organisation was divided into seven separate bodies in 1928, the Fascist unions were left virtually impotent, whatever vestigial beliefs in workers' participation may have lingered on in the minds of former Syndicalists within the bureaucracy. The drastic wages cuts in 1927 had weakened the Fascist unions early in their existence, and the decrees which sanctioned additional pay cuts in 1930 and 1934 further undermined their credibility in the eyes of their potential constituency on the factory floor. The massive growth in unemployment in the industrial centres during the 1930s was another indication of the unions' powerlessness; Corner argues that unemployment remained around 50 per cent for years in some provinces,[3] and unions that can neither defend wages nor defend jobs have no possible source of legitimacy. While the trade-union bureaucrats would have liked to have posed as the workers' champions, if only to increase their own prestige in relation to the leaders of other Fascist organisations, the regime gave them little opportunity to do so and frequently did deals with major employers over their heads – as was the case in Turin, where Agnelli preferred to deal with the Fascist party rather than with the Fascist unions. Whilst desperate workers may have turned to the Fascist unions as well as to other Fascist organisations in search of financial assistance in the early 1930s, this is not a reflection of any genuine consensus around bodies which had signally failed to defend either their wages or their jobs.

While the Fascist trade unions were the mass organisation which targeted the workers as workers, the Fascist youth organisations – the ONB (Opera Nazionale Balilla) until 1937, the GIL (Gioventù Italiana del Littorio) after 1937 – were likely to have had by far the greatest impact on working-class children brought up under Fascism. Whilst the population of certain agricultural provinces of southern Italy had a minimal contact with Fascist youth organisations, the same cannot be said of the industrial north. By June 1939 70 per cent of six- to twenty-one-year-olds in Turin were members of Fascist youth organisations.[4] Amongst the ninety-four Italian provinces Turin had the tenth place, Genoa the eleventh and Milan the fourteenth in terms of the percentage of the relevant age group joining the GIL in May 1939.[5] However, it would be wrong to assume that, because a large percentage of working-class youth had been through the Fascist youth organisations at some stage in their lives, they had been turned into devoted Fascists. Two reports on youth organisations in the province of Turin drawn up by the provincial party secretary in the 1930s make interesting reading in this connection. In November 1931 it was reported to Starace that 'unfortunately instead of diminishing, the detachment between Fascism and the youth sector seems to be growing . . . [There] is an aversion to what Fascism represents and a repulsion for the idea of coming closer and understanding what Fascism really means.' In 1937 the provincial secretary sounded equally depressed: 'The young Fascists are deserting the meetings . . . Only the books are full of members, but the truth is that the young no longer go to the groups.' Nor was Turin atypical – the situation was the same elsewhere in the industrial north, as this 1936 report from the Ligurian province of Savona, commenting on recent ceremonies involving the youth groups, makes abundantly clear: 'The Fasci Giovani were a joke from all points of view . . . Discipline did not exist and I was forced to resort to severe punishment to get them to show up at meetings.'[6] Tannenbaum has emphasised that in the larger towns working-class youths belonged to different branches of the Fascist youth organisation from their middle-class contemporaries because of the geographical divisions between the classes. Tannenbaum also emphasises that even in the late phase, after 1939 when GIL membership was mandatory regardless of parents' wishes, this was only so for those still at school.[7] (Previously, working-class parents with leftist sympathies, less concerned about their children's career prospects than middle-class professionals, had been amongst the most obstructive.) This meant that vast numbers of working-class teenage boys, who left school before their middle-class counterparts, escaped its influence.

The third of the Fascist mass organisations that might have had a major effect on the working class and its attitude to the regime was the Fascist leisure organisation, the Opera Nazionale Dopolavoro (OND). The OND had the largest membership of any of the mass organisations, representing a very important part of the attempt to create a consensus for the regime, especially in the 1930s.[8] Under the inspiration of Mario Giani, a former director of Italian Westinghouse who claimed to have been influenced by American examples, the Fascist trade unions had originally seen the provision of workers' leisure facilities as a means of competing with the Socialists, who had built up an extensive network of cultural and educational organisations. The competition was in no sense a fair one; when in the early 1920s Fascist violence forced the closure of many of the Socialist clubs and societies, those buildings and facilities that had not been physically destroyed by the squads were often re-opened as part of this new Fascist Dopolavoro. In April 1925 Mussolini agreed to the Fascist unions' demands to set up a national Dopolavoro organisation, the OND, with Mario Giani at its head, but took its effective control away from the Fascist trade unions lest what he regarded as an unruly element, with a dangerous ex-Syndicalist component, use it to threaten his power base. The new organisation initially had a productivist and largely apolitical image, which gained it the support of employers, at least in principle, although few rushed to set up Dopolavoro sections in their own plants. In April 1927 Augusto Turati, the Fascist party Secretary, became OND leader, sacked Giani and turned the OND into a fully fledged auxiliary of the Fascist party. However, its image remained a rather austerely productivist rather than actively political one during the late 1920s and it was only in the 1930s under Achille Starace's direction that it became primarily recreational, concentrating on sports rather than technical instruction, and gained a genuine mass membership as a consequence. It ought to be stressed that its greatest success was amongst the salaried petty bourgeoisie rather than the working class, but nearly 40 per cent of the industrial work force, a minority but a very significant minority, had been recruited into the Dopolavoro by 1939. Despite its rhetoric about breaking down class divisions, it is worth noting that a number of its activities, including the more expensive sports such as skiing and motorcycling, were only really open to its non-working-class members. Nonetheless, the outings and sports activities organised by the Dopolavoro proved genuinely popular with large numbers of workers, who enjoyed the chance to visit other parts of Italy or to play football, a game whose popularity rose under Fascism, aided by the two Italian world cup victories of the 1930s.

However, these activities did not turn workers into ideologically convinced supporters of the Fascist regime. Corner puts this argument very forcefully, observing that 'Fascism had nothing to offer beyond the odd film or theatre production, generally of very low quality which the workers dismissed immediately as *roba dei fascisti* (more or less "Fascist rubbish"). This dismissal was based often less on ideological grounds than on the fact that the rhetorical material of Fascism was, in most cases, boring and laughable. Where it was not, it was not explicitly Fascist and therefore did nothing to reinforce the image of Fascism.'[9]

[. . .]

The Second World War affected Italian workers in a multiplicity of ways. Of these, the expansion of the war industries is perhaps the most obvious. However, it should be emphasised that the switch from peacetime to war-time production in Italy had to a large extent started in 1936, not 1940, with the invasion of Abyssinia, not the fall of France.[10] In the years 1935–9 11.8 per cent of Italy's national income had been spent on war preparations, compared with 12.9 per cent in Nazi Germany, and the mere 6.9 per cent in France and 5.5 per cent in Britain. Admittedly Italy pushed this up to 18.4 per cent of national income in 1939–40, but such a level of mobilisation was not really sustainable. The agreement between Agnelli and Mussolini to plan the development of war production reached on 24 October 1940 only achieved its targets in 1942. Italy's war economy proved less successful in the Second World War than in the First. If the 1938 figure for industrial production is represented as 100, 1940 saw Italy achieve 110, before falling back disastrously to 89 in 1942 and 70 in 1943.[11] [. . .]

Food, or rather the lack of it, was a crucial aspect of the Italian working-class experience of the Second World War. The appearance of rationing, which started in May 1939 with restrictions on the serving of coffee in bars, was a sign of the imminence of war. Pasta rationing came in the autumn of 1940 and as the war went on the situation deteriorated with further restrictions in 1941. In the autumn of 1941 bread was rationed – 200 grams per head per day. This gave rise to much discontent and the regime reacted in November by increasing the bread ration for various categories it considered to be more deserving (or perhaps to possess greater potential for rebelliousness): for instance, the ration for miners and dockers was raised to 500 grams. The dire economic situation made such politically expedient decisions difficult to sustain for any length of time and in March 1942 the standard bread ration was reduced to 150 grams a head. War increased the gap between rich and poor and between town and country. In the countryside food consumption remained at more or less the prewar levels. For those deprived by poverty or geography of ready access to the black market, particularly for the poorer sections of the urban working class, life became harder and harder. By January 1943 the ration card of a worker in the Biella wool industry could enable him only to obtain food whose calorific value was an inadequate 1,000 calories a day.

Important as food shortages were in their effect on working-class morale, what really brought the war home to Italian workers in the most deadly way possible was the bombing. The impact of the bombing on the Italians cannot be measured in purely numerical terms, that is in terms of the casualties it caused. In the entire course of the Second World War 64,000 Italians were killed in bombing raids – only very slightly more than the 60,000 killed by bombs in Britain and far fewer than the number of German civilians killed in Allied bombing raids, which totalled somewhere between 600,000 and 700,000. Furthermore, of those killed in the Allied raids, only 21,000 had been killed by 8 September 1943, about half of the British total of such fatalities by that date. The crucial point is that the reaction of the Italian population to the bombing raids was very different from that of the German population to the Allied bombs, or indeed of the British population to the German bombs. In Italy bombing raids did not have the effect of unifying the population behind their own government and increasing their hostility towards the enemy, which was the majority reaction in Germany. In Italy the bulk of the anger aroused by the bombing was not directed, as the Fascist authorities had hoped, against the British and the Americans, who after all were genuinely responsible for the casualties in the most immediate, direct and physical sense; instead it was aimed against the Fascist regime and its alliance with Nazi Germany, a phenomenon that is virtually incomprehensible unless we assume the persistence of the *tradizione sovversiva* amongst significant groups within the working class. Given the extent to which the population, especially the lower classes, identified the Fascist regime with Mussolini, the remarks made about his speeches during these years give a good indication of popular morale. As early as June 1941 police informants reported Mussolini being described as 'a man in decline', by February 1942 they were saying 'he's old' and by August 1942 'he's finished'.[12] The reaction to Mussolini's broadcast of 2 December 1942, which caused panic by urging the rapid evacuation of bombed cities, was even more interesting. Police informants reported that it was widely believed that 'the voice heard on the radio is not the *Duce's* voice'.[13] In short the myth of the *Duce* himself as all-powerful leader, a myth that permeated large sections of the working class in the course of the *ventennio* (the twenty years of Fascist dictatorship), had started to crumble, giving new heart to those workers who had never wavered in their opposition.

These subterranean currents of discontent that had expressed themselves in grumbling on the trams or slogans written on walls late at night in 1941 and 1942 rose to the surface in the spring of 1943. The outbreak of mass strikes in Turin and Milan in March and April 1943 was one of the most remarkable episodes in Italy's wartime experience, more remarkable in comparative perspective than the Resistance itself, since these strikes were directed at a native Fascist regime, not a foreign occupier. These strikes preceded the king's dismissal of Mussolini on 25 July by some months and cannot be linked in time with the disaffection of the traditional elites to which the king's action gave concrete expression. The working class acted alone, to some extent under the leadership of the clandestine Communist party, but without any support from the other social groups. The workers' action may be seen as prompting the subsequent action of the elites, who began to feel that if they did not act to remove Mussolini by conspiracy the workers would remove him by mass strikes and demonstrations, and that such events would lead not just to political change but to dramatic social upheaval, sweeping aside capitalism along with Fascism. It should also be emphasised that the strikes broke out before the Allied landings in Sicily and not as a result of them – no Italian territory had been invaded in March. It is arguable that the strikes' organisers were influenced more by the course of the war in the East – by the Soviet triumph over the Nazis at Stalingrad – than by that of the war in the West – by Italy's defeats in North Africa. While by 1943 the regime was identified in the popular imagination with the increasingly hated Germans, the strikes of 1943, unlike the mass strikes of 1944, were directed against the native Fascist regime, not against German occupation.

Food shortages, bombing and the military defeats in North Africa do not provide a sufficient explanation for the re-emergence of working-class militancy on this scale. The causes lay not just in the material conditions of 1943 but in the failure of Italian Fascism over two decades to win the lasting allegiance of a stubbornly recalcitrant working class, despite deploying a combination of repression, propaganda and mass organisations of a type that no previous Italian regime had had at its disposal. The strikes demonstrated the very fragile basis of Mussolini's conversion of the Italians to nationalism at the time of the victory over Abyssinia in 1936 – a conversion which some, but not MacGregor Knox, see as already reversed by June 1940.[14] And they demonstrated the enormous strength of the old subversive traditions which had outlasted twenty years of Fascist dictatorship and which now identified themselves with the Soviet Union.[15]

Notes

1   Tim Mason, *Social Policy in the Third Reich. The Working Class and the 'National Community'* (Providence and Oxford, 1993), 276.

2   Mason, *Social Policy*, 277.

3   Paul Corner, 'Italy', in Stephen Salter and John Stevenson (eds.), *The Working Class and Politics in Europe and America 1929–1945* (London and New York, 1990), 160.

4   Edward R. Tannenbaum, *Fascism in Italy. Society and Culture 1922–1945* (London, 1973), 139.

5   T. H. Koon, *Believe, Obey, Fight. Political Socialization of Youth in Fascist Italy, 1922–1943* (Chapel Hill and London, 1985), 183.

6   All quotations taken from Koon, *Believe, Obey, Fight*, 114.

7   Tannenbaum, *Fascism in Italy*, 160.

8   The membership figures were 280,000 in 1926, 2,780,000 in 1936 and 5 million in 1940: Renzo De Felice, *Mussolini il duce*, vol. 1, *Gli anni del consenso, 1929–1936* (Turin, 1974), 198.

9   Corner, 'Italy', 164.

10   The remainder of this essay draws heavily on my chapter on 'Italy' in Jeremy Noakes (ed.), *The Civilian in War: The Home Front in Europe, Japan and the USA in World War II* (Exeter, 1992), which develops many of these ideas at greater length and with more illustrative detail.

11   Valerio Castronovo, 'L'industria di guerra 1940–1943', in Francesca Ferratini Tosi, Gaetano Grassi and Massimo Legnani (eds.), *L'Italia nella seconda guerra mondiale e nella resistenza* (Milan, 1988), 237–56.

12   Nicola Gallerano, 'Gli Italiani in guerra 1940–1943: Appunti per una ricerca', in Tosi, Grassi and Legnani (eds.), *L'Italia nella seconda guerra mondiale*, 320.

13   Ibid.

14   MacGregor Knox, *Mussolini Unleashed, 1939–1941. Politics and Strategy in Fascist Italy's Last War* (Cambridge, 1982), 108–12.

15   While it may seem very strange that a left-wing tradition which owed so much to Anarchism identified so heavily with Stalin and the Soviet Union, the reality of popular Stalinism has to be faced. 'Baffone viene' – 'the man with the big moustache (i.e. Stalin) – is coming' was a popular Resistance wall slogan. Enrico Mannari, 'Tradizione sovversiva e comunismo durante il regime fascista 1926–1943: Il caso di Livorno', in *La classe operaia durante il fascismo* (Milan, 1981), 868–9, cites wall slogans in praise of Stalin in Livornese factories in December 1941, September 1942, November 1942 and April 1943. As Paul Ginsborg has argued recently: 'Russia's charisma in this period can not be overstressed. Tens of thousands of Italian workers looked to Russia for their model and to the Red Army for the decisive contribution to the creation of Communism in their own country. Stalin was a working-class hero, Togliatti his trusted emissary in Italy': *A History of Contemporary Italy. Society and Politics 1943–1988* (Harmondsworth, 1990), 54.

Chapter 39

Detlev J. K. Peukert

FASCISM AND THE CRISIS OF MODERNITY: NSDAP MEMBERS AND SUPPORTERS

■ from *INSIDE NAZI GERMANY: CONFORMITY, OPPOSITION AND RACISM IN EVERYDAY LIFE*, London, 1989, pp. 27, 32–4, 35–6, 37–9, 40–1, 42

Detlev Peukert's work on interwar German society is underpinned by the belief that the rise of the NSDAP was both a symptom of a crisis (caused by rapid modernisation) and a perceived solution to it that – unlike socialist revolution – 'did not tamper with the structures of society'. Peukert deals with the social base of the Nazi movement and the reasons behind its mass following after 1928. The conclusion he reaches is that the NSDAP had a predominantly inter-class character, with an over-represented middle class, but also a significant number of working-class followers, young ex-soldiers, unemployed and other 'losers' of the Depression.

THE NAZI MOVEMENT [. . .] succeeded in assuming power even though it likewise never obtained a majority in free elections and in no sense offered a seriously worked-out political programme. Hitler, however, was able in 1933 to convert these very weaknesses into strengths. The fact that the National Socialist movement had got bogged down at about 40 per cent of the vote, after making sensational advances between 1930 and the spring of 1932 – and indeed lost votes heavily in the Reichstag elections of November 1932 – ultimately made it seem a respectable alliance partner for the old power elites in business, public administration and the military, which until then had been sceptical about their ability to control the Nazi mass movement.[1]

The fact that the NSDAP had no firm, consistent political programme enabled it all the more easily to entice a wide range of groups in the population with a variety of promises, so long as it could conjure up the prospect that, once armed with the dignity of power and the instruments of propaganda, it would effect a fundamental break with the old Weimar 'system' and a general national 'awakening'.

[. . .]

[I]f our aim is to explain the everyday experience and behaviour of Germans in the thirties, then we cannot be satisfied merely with snatching a right-wing glimpse into the antechambers of the aged President of the Reich or a left-wing glimpse into the counting-houses of the industrialists of the Ruhr: we must take account of the crisis of the Weimar Republic in all its complexity. At the beginning of the thirties the German political system collapsed for the second time in a dozen years. We may therefore speak with good reason of a deep-seated crisis in the political system which went far beyond elections and parties and which was in many ways a crisis of German industrial class society as a whole.

Whereas the political system under the imperial monarchy relied on giving the middle class preferential treatment, and making the workers' ghettoised existence at best bearable by means of gradual economic improvements, to the rigorous exclusion of all political influence, the Weimar Republic was originally based on the positive inclusion of those sections of the working class represented by Social Democracy and the trade unions. It was the middle classes' loss of their privileged role, but more especially the economic humiliations of the years of inflation, that first impelled them to make moves to detach themselves from the political system. Though the bourgeois bloc governments of the stabilisation period (1924–28) again swung back more strongly towards the socio-political pattern of the monarchy, upgrading the role of the middle classes and reinforcing their anti-working-class prejudices, nevertheless they too were forced to preserve a state of equilibrium vis-à-vis the workers and their Social Democrat representatives. In addition, the deep structural crisis in German agriculture radicalised the traditionally right-wing conservative agrarian leaders and led to a mass recruitment of farmers into the Nazi Party.

With the end of the economic boom, the twin pillars of the political system, the middle classes and the social settlement with labour, began to totter. To the alarm of business, the system of social-welfare concessions to labour, which had been viewed as a temporary and tactical measure, was beginning to be taken as a fixture. (Thus leaders of heavy industry were furious when almost all of the Reichstag parties came out in favour of relief for the metal workers locked out during the Ruhr iron dispute of 1928; fears of a so-called trade-union state were reawakened.)[2] However ready the SPD and ADGB (Allgemeine Deutsche Gewerkschaftsbund) might be to make compromises at their supporters' expense, their mere existence remained a potential obstacle to social-welfare retrenchment during the crisis. The KPD, despite gaining electoral votes, had isolated itself to such an extent through its 'Revolutionary Trade Union Opposition' (RGO) and 'social fascism' tactics that the great menace it seemed to pose was rated as very minor by sober, realistic entrepreneurs. But its potential, too, seemed dangerous enough to many.

The dismantling of the welfare state was being demanded, especially by representatives of heavy industry in the Rhineland and Westphalia, even before the onset of the world economic crisis. After 1929 it became the standard feature of all capitalist strategies for dealing with the crisis. Workers' parties and trade unions would have, at the very least, to be kept in check. Such aims, however, did not necessarily mean that the ultimate goal was terrorist dictatorship on the National Socialist pattern (though even those in big business who had not voted for the NSDAP before 1933 were pleased to note the outlawing and persecution of the KPD, SPD and trade unions). Almost throughout the period of crisis the political options favoured by industrialists oscillated among authoritarian, corporatist solutions, restoration of the monarchy, presidential dictatorship and the like; only a minority backed the NSDAP.[3] By the summer of 1932 the worst point of the crisis had been passed. Welfare retrenchment and the lowering of living standards went ahead within the framework of the Republic up till the end of 1932. After 1933 the National Socialists, though they wiped out the labour movement and certainly sought to preserve the low levels in living standards caused by the crisis, did not carry out the general assault on wages that had been forecast by the left. The Papen government had already met the wishes of business in full.

Panic of the middle strata: the dynamics of the movement

A factor that was more significant in the rise of fascism than the industrialists' strategy of solving the economic crisis on the backs of the workers was the set of processes within the middle and lower-middle social strata which caused broad sections of white-collar employees, public officials, tradesmen and small businessmen and peasant farmers to become detached from their traditional political allegiances and to join the National Socialist movement.[4] They were accompanied by sections of the younger, socially disorientated 'war generation', ex-soldiers who had failed to reintegrate themselves into society, people whose careers had foundered and long-term unemployed who had no links with the labour movement. The ranks of the Nazi movement were also swollen by a large number of groups and individuals 'between the classes', whose lives had been shattered by the social and economic dislocations of the Depression. An advance hint of these processes of radicalisation was given by rumblings within the bourgeois party system even before the onset of the world economic crisis.[5] Millions of people who had previously not voted, or who had supported the bourgeois parties, declined the blandishments of these parties in the Reichstag elections of 1930 and became radicalised into the ranks of the NSDAP. This mass movement occurred before big business came out in favour of the NSDAP on any large scale. If we wish to explain Nazism, then, we must start by explaining the causes of these mass shifts of alignment.[6]

[. . .]

Who actually were the active Nazis? The Party's statistical data for 1935, on which most historical investigations are based, are fairly general. They indicate that the lower-middle classes were over-represented and workers under-represented, though the latter still constituted between one-fifth and one-quarter of the total membership. But whether or not some social groups were over- or under-represented in Nazi ranks, we must appreciate that significant proportions of all social groups were involved. Although numerically dominated by the middle strata, the movement in fact had an inter-class character. In any case, the life-stories, experiences and attitudes that lie concealed behind these abstract social categories can be reconstructed only from autobiographical documents. Despite all provisos as to the extent to which information obtained from individuals can be generalised to cover a movement of millions, such reports give a pretty clear idea of the range and nature of the experience of the 'old guard'. Many of them were people whose lives and careers were unstable or indeed shattered. These early NSDAP members had often abandoned their businesses for economic reasons, or had failed to settle back into civilian life after the lost world war, or had undergone frequent changes of job or profession, or had experienced frequent or long-term unemployment. What made the situation more acute was the fact that the majority of them were members of a 'shattered intermediate generation' (K. D. Bracher's term) whose whole sense of purpose in life had been overshadowed by the uncertainties of post-war crisis and world recession. Not all National Socialists had first-hand experience of this insecurity and loss of status. But some had, and the others saw it as a constant potential threat – a sign that 'order' had begun to waver and that there could be no prospect of a return to normality unless there was a radical break with the past. For the unemployed worker, the failed small businessman, the young man who saw no hope of better training or social advancement – and, at the same time, for those members of the upper-middle class who saw their life-style and social values threatened – the loss of perspective and meaning in everyday life caused by the crisis could not, objectively speaking, be abolished by active participation in the National Socialist movement; but it could be made easier to bear.

[. . .]

What was important was the fact that Nazi Party supporters had a pressing need to experience a sense of 'heightened' significance, which stood 'in contrast to the *Lebenswelt* [life-world] of a generation bereft of an outlook and opportunities',[7] and that they met this need in the hectic campaigns of the Nazi movement and in the Party ceremonies with their quasi-religious ritual.

In addition, in the street battles before 1933 NSDAP supporters could give aggressive vent to the inner injuries and frustrations they had sustained in their lives. The very style of the subsequent descriptions of these battles with the Communist *Rotfront* clearly shows the mechanism of projection, channelling and discharge of aggression: it is always the others who are the first to use violence; it is therefore 'just' – i.e. legitimised by this violence – to fight back even more brutally.[8]

Admittedly, only the relatively small group of 'old guard' Nazis was fired by such experiences and clusters of motives in concentrated form. But similar situations and frameworks of expectation can also be found among the wider membership of the NSDAP, those who voted for the Party and those non-Nazi Germans who, after Hitler was appointed Chancellor of the Reich, were carried away by the stage-managed excitements of the national 'awakening'.[9]

To the middle class and to a growing number of people between the social classes, bourgeois society in the Weimar Republic offered no outlook or prospects. Traditional loyalties broke down under the pressure of anxieties about loss of status. But the radicalising of the middle classes did not lead towards forms of interest-group trade unionism (though after the November revolution there had been first moves in this direction among white-collar employees), nor towards a strengthening of the democratic left on the lines of Roosevelt's New Deal in America.[10] It led to a mass movement, highly modern in its structures, which had borrowed its ideological precepts from the chauvinistic, anti-modern, anti-Marxist, anti-Semitic and antidemocratic pseudo-theories of the closing years of the nineteenth century. Its hatred was directed against 'modernity' itself, the Weimar 'system' *tout court*; and against its two representatives, capital as well as the proletariat. Yet it would be incorrect to write off fascism as simply an ideological regression into medieval darkness. Its sources were very contemporary ones; although it sometimes employed empty, outdated rhetoric and ritual, its dynamics sprang from the contradictions of the inter-war years.

The fascist ideological mix[11]

Older interpretations of the 'panic of the middle classes' concentrated on the problems of the old middle-class social strata, peasant farmers, tradespeople and craftsmen. Since these categories of employment were becoming increasingly fossilised in industrial society, and since the share in the labour market they represented was declining, a link with the fossilised anti-modern ideology of fascism readily suggested itself. But such a line of argument scarcely works for the modern middle class: the expanding groups, growing in long-term importance, which consisted of white-collar employees in commerce, social and public service and technological jobs. Not only did these groups, like the old middle classes, have privileges to defend against the remorseless march of socio-economic change; they might also, counting on change, either demand a betterment in their position or view a temporary lowering in their status, given the particular weakness of Weimar society with its burdens of reparations and the Versailles sanctions, as a highly outrageous and 'unjust' result of the 'system'. In other words, the social basis of National Socialism also encompasses the new, rising middle class, bewildered at living through exceptional times.

But why, in that case, a backward-looking ideology? On the one hand, it offered the prospect of uniting the old and new middle classes, which had been held together under the monarchy on the basis of nationalistic and authoritarian formulae. On the other hand, though, we must not underestimate the 'modern' elements in National Socialist ideology either: its choreographing of the masses, its glorification of technology, its defence of the 'dignity of labour'. With these, after 1933, went the razzmatazz about the Autobahn and the Volkswagen, architectural gigantism in factories and public buildings, public-relations boasts about achievements in technological and military hardware, and rationalisation in industrial relations and new regulations affecting work and training.

[. . .]

The triad of factors cited as giving rise to National Socialism — hostility to progressive politics, the glorification of pseudo-medieval ideology, and a social basis in a moribund middle class — makes it easy to lose sight of the fact that the Nazis' perverted vision of modern society not only displayed features of fossilisation but also had roots in wholly modern social groups and their associated ideologies. This mixed social basis, consisting of the old and the modern middle class, young people without a clear outlook or prospects in life,[12] long-term unemployed and *déclassés*, must be borne in mind if we are to explain the strange combination of archaic and brand-new elements within Nazi politics and ideology.

These groups, with goals in life that were uncertain or quite vague, experienced particularly acutely the upheavals caused by the modernisation process of the 1920s – which the whole society went through – while remaining particularly in the dark about their causes. Here we can give only an incomplete list of these upheavals: the rationalisation of production, with the growth of assembly-line work and the introduction of ingeniously segmented work processes; associated job insecurity, even during periods of boom,[13] along with changes in job descriptions and alterations in gender-specific divisions of labour;[14] seismic upheavals in traditional social stratification, particularly in status hierarchies, which meant a relative decline by the old middle-class groups and a rise in status (albeit viewed as the opposite) by the new middle-class groups; the introduction of a new model in social policy, combining state intervention and corporatism (viz. large unions and big business), which was still going through its birth traumas when it was first hit by crisis and breakdown and had no protective backing of economic prosperity;[15] longer-term changes in processes of socialisation and in relationships between generations, expressed particularly in the upsurge of youth movements and in the general youth cult of the twenties;[16] changes in cultural life, shown in the highly visible breakthrough of modernism in art, architecture and design and in formal and political experimentation in literature, theatre and film;[17] changes, too, in socio-cultural styles, encapsulated in the term 'the Roaring Twenties', with new forms of sexual self-expression, new dances, new fashions, 'sinful' big-city life (much deplored by conservative cultural critics; eyed from the provinces with both mistrust and fascination), a new consumer culture (offering thrills for those with money and disappointments for those with none), and the 'loss of values' that was widely bemoaned at the time;[18] and, last but not least, changes in the system of authority and in political culture, which even the Republic's half-hearted attempts at democratisation had helped bring about.

[. . .]

The labour movement was a helpless bystander at these developments; the crisis in the political system could not be exploited to help form an alternative bloc on the left. When the National Socialist movement took shape out of the radicalised middle classes, the prospect of an escape from the crisis was offered which did not tamper with the structures of society. The NSDAP was at once a symptom, and a solution, of the crisis.

Notes

1   Bracher, Sauer and Schulz, *Die nationalsozialistische Machtergreifung* (3 vols.), 2nd edn., Frankfurt/Berlin/Vienna, 1971; Erich Matthias and Rudolf Morsey (eds.), *Das Ende der Parteien 1933*, 2nd edn., Königstein, 1979; Wolfgang Luthardt (ed.),

Sozialdemokratische Arbeiterbewegung und Weimarer Republik. Materialien zur gesell-schaftlichen Entwicklung 1927–1933 (2 vols.); Wolfgang Schieder (ed.), *Faschismus als soziale Bewegung*, Hamburg, 1976; Gerhard Schulz, *Aufstieg des National-sozialismus. Krise und Revolution in Deutschland*, Frankfurt, 1975.

2   Michael Schneider, *Unternehmer und Demokratie*, Bonn-Bad Godesberg, 1975; Bernd Weisbrod, *Schwerindustrie in der Weimarer Republik*, Wuppertal, 1978.

3   Dirk Stegmann, 'Kapitalismus und Faschismus in Deutschland 1929–1934', *Gesellschaft*, no. 6, Frankfurt, 1976, 19–91; Henry A. Turner, *German Big Business and the Rise of Hitler*, New York, 1985.

4   Heinrich August Winkler, *Mittelstand, Demokratie und Nationalsozialismus 1918–1933*, Cologne, 1972; Jürgen Kocka, *Angestellte zwischen Demokratie und Faschismus*, Göttingen, 1977.

5   Cf. the role of the Wirtschaftspartei (Economic Party) or the remoulding of the Deutsche Demokratische Partei (DDP, German Democratic Party) into the Deutsche Staatspartei (German State Party). Larry E. Jones, 'The Dissolution of the Bourgeois Party System in the Weimar Republic', in Richard Bessel and E. J. Feuchtwanger (eds.), *Social Change and Political Development in Weimar Germany*, London, 1981, 268–88.

6   Winkler, op. cit.; Kocka, *Angestellte*, op. cit. [. . .]

7   Christoph Schmidt, 'Zu den Motiven "alter Kämpfer" in der NSDAP', in D. Peukert and J. Reulecke (eds), Die Reihen fast geschlossen (Woppertal, 1981) 37. On the Führer cult, see also: Wolfgang Horn, *Der Marsch zur Machtergreifung. Die NSDAP bis 1933*, 2nd edn., Düsseldorf, 1980. For many sophisticated detailed insights into the National Socialist movement, now see also the work by the GDR historians Kurt Pätzoldt and Manfred Weissbecker, *Geschichte der NSDAP 1920–1945*, Cologne, 1981. Graphic source material is in: Ernst Deuerlein (ed.), *Der Aufstieg der NSDAP in Augenzeugenberichten*, Munich, 1974; Conan Fisher, *Stormtroopers: A Social, Economic and Ideological Analysis 1929–1935*, London, 1983.

8   Cf. Klaus Theweleit, *Mannerphantasien* (2 vols.), Frankfurt, 1977; Peter Merkl, *Political Violence under the Swastika: 581 Early Nazis*, Princeton, 1975; Mathilde Jamin, *Zwischen den Klassen*, Wuppertal, 1984; Richard Bessel, 'The Role of Political Terror in the Nazi Seizure of Power', *Acta Universitatis Wratislaviensis*, no. 484, Wroclaw, 1980, 199–216; Eve Rosenhaft, *Beating the Fascists? The German Communists and Political Violence 1929–1933*, Cambridge, 1983.

9   George L. Mosse, *The Nationalisation of the Masses*, New York, 1975; id., *Ein Volk, ein Reich, ein Führer. Die völkischen Ursprünge des Nationalsozialismus*, Königstein, 1979; Rainer Lepsius, *Extremer Nationalismus. Strukturbedingungen vor der national-sozialistischen Machtergreifung*, Stuttgart, 1966; Kurt Sontheimer, *Antidemokratisches Denken in der Weimarer Republik*, Munich, 1962.

10   Kocka, *Angestellte*; id., *Die Angestellten in der deutschen Geschichte 1850–1980*, Göttingen, 1981; Winkler, op. cit.

11   The standard works on fascist ideology are still: Ernst Nolte, *Three Faces of Fascism*, New York, 1966; Eberhard Jäckel, *Hitlers Weltanschauung*, new edn., Stuttgart, 1981. See also: Mosse, *Volk*, op. cit. My discussion does not seek to provide an outline of Nazi ideology, but only to trace certain connections between Party ideology and everyday anxieties, experiences and projections on the part of the National Socialist masses.

12   An up-to-date survey is: Hermann Giesecke, *Vom Wandervogel bis zur Hitlerjugend. Jugendarbeit zwischen Politik und Pädagogik*, Munich, 1981. Cf. also the report by

Klaus Schönekäs, *Jugend auf dem Weg ins Dritte Reich*, working paper no. 9 of the Institut für historisch-sozialwissenschaftliche Analysen, Frankfurt, 1980.

13   Charles S. Maier, 'Between Taylorism and Technology: European Ideologies and the Vision of Industrial Productivity in the 1920s', in *Journal of Contemporary History*, vol. V, 1970, 27–61; Peter Hinrichs, *Um die Seele des Arbeiters. Arbeitspsychologie, Industrie- und Betriebssoziologie in Deutschland 1871–1945*, Cologne, 1981; cf. also Wilhlem Treue (ed.), *Deutschland in der Weltwirtschaftskrise in Augenzeugenberichten*, 2nd edn., Munich, 1976.

14   Tim Mason, 'Women in Germany, 1925–1940: Family, Welfare and Work', in *History Workshop Journal*, nos. 1 and 2, 1976; Annemarie Troger, 'Die Frauen im wesensgemässen Einsatz', in Frauengruppe Faschismusforschung (ed.), *Mutterkreuz und Arbeitsbuch. Zur Geschichte der Frauen in der Weimarer Republik und im Nationalsozialismus*, Frankfurt, 1981, 246–72.

15   Ludwig Preller, *Sozialpolitik in der Weimarer Republik*, 2nd edn., Düsseldorf, 1978.

16   Giesecke, op. cit.; John R. Gillis, *Youth and History: Tradition and Change in European Age Relations, 1770–Present*, London, 1981; Walter Laqueur, *Young Germany: A History of the Youth Movement*, New York, 1975.

17   Walter Laqueur, *Weimar. A Cultural History*, New York, 1975; Peter Gay, *Weimar Culture: The Outsider as Insider*, New York, 1968.

18   On the 'out of phase' relations between social-structural change, value systems and forms of socialisation, see: Talcott Parsons, 'Demokratie und Sozialstruktur in Deutschland vor der Zeit des Nationalsozialismus', in id., *Beiträge zur soziologischen Theorie*, 2nd edn., Neuwied, 1968, 256–81.

Chapter 40

Jill Stephenson

FASCISM AND GENDER: WOMEN UNDER NATIONAL SOCIALISM

■ from *THE NAZI ORGANISATION OF WOMEN*, London, 1981, pp. 11–16, 17–20

Jill Stephenson's work on women in Nazi Germany has revealed a picture that contradicts the traditional perception of a monolithic, unified system of social control exercised by Hitler's regime on German society. In spite of the existence of a peculiar Nazi organisation of women (NS-Frauenschaft) and the persistent efforts of the regime's officials to win over the female population, Stephenson asserts that 'women . . . were peculiarly resistant to National Socialism'. Surviving allegiance to family and Church, coupled with a general dislike for organised activities, made German women far less accessible and vulnerable to Nazi propaganda or compulsion.

THE PARADOXICAL CHARACTER of the NSDAP, as a revolutionary force pledged to restore Germany to a mythical past from which it could develop towards an ideal present and future, attracted to it from 1919 those who wanted to return to the point where, they felt, Germany had taken a wrong turning. Unification in 1871 had been part of the 'correct' development, as far as it had gone, but the ensuing rapid industrialisation had brought urbanisation and the politicisation of the working class by Marxist Social Democrats. It had also, by its insatiable demand for cheap and docile labour, brought large numbers of women into exhausting, dirty and even dangerous work which threatened the healthy development of the 'race' by damaging and debilitating Germany's mothers. The massive increase in women's employment outside the home in the thirty or so years before the First World War[1] had also, by this analysis, threatened family life in other ways, by diverting housewives and mothers from their essential duties in the home for much of their life. Women were too busy or too tired to learn how to run a home in an orderly way, to protect their own health as childbearers, and to care adequately for their children. Improved methods of birth control from the later nineteenth century had led women to try to mitigate their problems by restricting the size of their family[2] – yet again, in the Nazi view, endangering the future of the 'race'. The quality of German life, too, was under threat, with women, 'the guardians of German culture', distracted by work, political agitation and the growth of a consumer society from their alleged age-old function of cherishing the nation's distinctive songs, dances, costumes and crafts.

The Nazi revolution would restore women to the idyllic destiny from which they had been diverted before the First World War and which was, said the Nazis, deliberately derided by the Marxists, internationalists, liberals and feminists who seemed, in the post-war period, to have emerged as the victors from Germany's pre-war political and social conflicts. And if women had been deflected from their destiny – which was only the fulfilment of the instinctive aspirations of the female nature, it was said – even before the war, the experience of the war and the trauma of the revolutionary upheavals in a number of Germany's cities in 1918–19 convinced increasing numbers of men and women that the circumstances of post-war Germany would only intensify the distortion. The kind of changes that could be achieved to counteract modern evils through the new parliamentary system would do no more than tinker with the symptoms, for example, the 'filth' that was given free rein in literature and drama by the lifting of censorship.[3] Nothing less radical than a revolution – *a national* revolution, not a Marxist one – could bring Germany back to the path of 'correct' development. This was what the Nazi Party was fighting for in *Kampfzeit* (time of struggle, up to 1933). Axiomatically, women could not participate actively in the struggle, since allowing them to do so would be simply to follow the false example set by the Nazis' adversaries. One of the spectres that remained with Nazi activists for years was the horror of women's participation in the attempted revolution of 1918–19, and Rosa Luxemburg – although she was a victim rather than a perpetrator of violence – became a symbol of the evils threatening German society. Years later, she and others were remembered with fear and loathing as an example of what National Socialism was pledged to prevent.[4]

These sentiments contributed to the development of what may cautiously be called the Nazi view of women's role in the nation and in the party. As Hans Frank was to say, there were as many 'National Socialisms' as there were leaders[5] and the variations on the theme of women's place were legion. But it is generally safe to say that in the Nazi view women were to be 'wives, mothers and homemakers', they were to play no part in public life, in the legislature, the executive, the judiciary or the armed forces. Hitler himself frequently expressed opposition to women's participation in politics, claiming that it sullied and demeaned the female nature, as he saw it.[6] It was partly Hitler's personal attachment to the image of women as mothers of the nation which delayed and then vitiated the introduction of labour conscription for women during the Second World War, although in his *Götterdämmerung* mentality early in 1945 he was prepared to see women enlisted as soldiers and sent to the front. While Nazi leaders differed about the extent to which women should be employed outside the home and to which they could usefully contribute to the Party's campaigns, they generally accepted that from earliest childhood girls should be brought up to accept motherhood as their 'natural calling', and that all other roles they might assume or functions they might exercise should be consistent with childbearing and child-rearing. Again, this preoccupation derived largely from increasing anxiety in Nazi and non-Nazi circles alike in the 1920s about Germany's falling birth-rate.[7]

While growing numbers of men were drawn to National Socialism in the 1920s because of these ideas among others, there were women, too, who found the Nazis' traditionalist approach to women's role attractive. For them, it was enough to sympathise with and support the Party's 'fighting menfolk', and although small numbers of women joined the new local branches of the NSDAP which sprang up all over the country from the mid-1920s, most pro-Nazi women regarded it as inconsistent with their own and the Party's view of women's role to join a political party. But there were, almost paradoxically, a number of women with distinctly feminist views who gravitated to National Socialism because of its anti-Marxism, its ultra-nationalist and racist aspect, or for local or family reasons. It is clear that they either ignored the Party's pronouncements about women's role or else refused to take them seriously. In the critical years between 1930 and 1933 the Party gave them plenty of encouragement in their self-delusion at a time when its leadership was hoping to make a favourable impact on the female voter in its bid for power the legal way. Gregor Strasser, the Party's organisational chief at this time until his unexpected resignation in December 1932, particularly seemed to welcome and encourage women's participation in election campaigns. And so women supporters of National Socialism in the 1920s, up to 1933, might or might not wholeheartedly support the Party's general view of women's place in society, and might or might not be members of the NSDAP.

Women's group activity developed something of a split personality because it embraced these different kinds of women. It also started and grew spontaneously and in a variety of forms because the inherent male chauvinism of the movement led to exclusive concentration on the men's struggle against the Weimar 'system'. Often enough, a woman whose husband or brother was a Party member would join in giving *ad hoc* support to the men in the area, providing food, making and mending uniforms, or, as in Hanover in 1922, for example, making a flag bearing the Party's symbol.[8] These activities set the tone for what would throughout the rest of the Nazi era be known as 'womanly work', the kind of mundane, practical assistance which women, as homemakers, could readily provide, and which men really could not be asked to contemplate. This division of labour reflected the Party's general view of women's functions and underlined its insistence on the segregation of the sexes at work and at play. Women's talents and capacities were different from men's, and, like men's, they should be utilised to the full and not squandered in vain attempts by women to take over men's work or emulate men's achievements. Because of initial neglect of women's contribution to the Party's work, which led to its growth independently of male control, this segregationist policy led perhaps not to 'secondary racism',[9] but certainly to organisational apartheid. The male chauvinist mentality of the NSDAP's men ensured that women who were attracted to the Party were condemned to 'separate development', which allowed them to work out their role in the Party's service to a great degree as they chose.

The evolution of Nazi women's groups of different kinds caused problems for the Party once it belatedly acknowledged their existence and assistance, in the later 1920s. To solve these, Gregor Strasser ordered the dissolution of all existing women's groups in 1931 and created, in their stead, the *NS-Frauenschaft* (*NSF* – Nazi Women's Group), the first official Nazi women's organisation under central Party control. Strasser's role here and in the subsequent development of the NSF casts interesting light on his character and methods. Unlike many leading Nazis he clearly felt that the women's organisation could contribute usefully to the Party's work; this was no doubt why he was at pains to create a uniform, harmonious organisation out of the diverse warring factions which had evolved in the 1920s. Others, too, valued the 'women's work'. The SA depended on women's soup kitchens to feed its members when they were on duty, especially if they were unemployed, and for a time the SA welcomed the rudimentary first-aid service provided by Nazi women for 'heroes' hurt in brawls.[10] As the Depression hit Germany's larger towns particularly hard from 1930 onwards, welfare work by women who collected money, cast-off clothing and household utensils, who gave material and moral support to the families of political detainees, and who provided food and warm clothing for destitute Germans, whether they were Party supporters or not, was regarded as vital in both practical and propaganda terms.[11]

As the Party's apparatus and ambitions grew, so it came to create new, permanent institutions to replace the voluntary, *ad hoc* work done by women enthusiasts. The SA in Berlin, for example, developed its own specialist medical corps and increasingly – and ungratefully – rejected the assistance which women's groups continued to provide. The founding of the Nazi welfare organisation (*NS-Volkswohlfahrt* – NSY) in Berlin in winter 1931–2 similarly led to a downgrading of the spontaneous assistance for long provided by women's groups. And in July 1932 the order that the Hitler Youth should have a monopoly of organising Nazi girls threatened to deprive the NSF of its traditional function of bringing the young into the movement, under the guidance of their elders. After tooth-and-nail resistance from the women, this order was enforced in 1933, but only by replacing the existing leadership in the NSF in the first of a series of changes which culminated in the appointment of Gertrud Scholtz-Klink as NSF leader in February 1934. By the time she took office, the women's organisation had been shorn of most of the functions it had exercised in the *Kampfzeit*, and in spite of official propaganda to boost its image it never recovered from these losses. The demarcation disputes in which the NSF became involved, with the NSV and the Hitler Youth especially, during the 1930s and into the war, were a reflection of the extent to which NSF leaders refused to be reconciled to these losses, and to which they recognised the damage they had inflicted on the NSF's authority and prestige. For the rest of the Third Reich, the NSF was to concentrate on winning over the uncommitted 'valuable' female population to National Socialism, in Germany itself and in the new possessions Germany acquired in the later 1930s and early 1940s. Here, it suffered not only as a result of the restricted role which the Party Leadership now allowed it, but also from the strange limbo in which the NSDAP, of which it was a part, found itself from 1933. The substantial support which the Party had won in elections in 1932–3, was still the support of a minority of the electorate, and many of these voters, influenced by the catastrophic economic circumstances prevailing in Germany in the early 1930s, could hardly properly be classed as 'Nazis'. For many, the NSDAP was the party of last resort in desperate times. Failure to recognise this was one factor which seduced the NSDAP into a grandiose but doomed attempt to win the co-operation and approval of the mass of 'Aryan' Germans for every measure of Hitler's Government in peace and war, by persuasion and with a minimum of coercion. There was also the optical illusion created by the rush of opportunists to join the Party and its affiliated organisations, including the NSF, after Hitler's appointment as Chancellor on 30 January 1933. But most of all, the Party found itself confirmed to this utopian purpose by Hitler's betrayal of it. By taking over the machinery of the State intact, Hitler and a few chosen henchmen were able to govern through traditional German institutions.

[. . .]

The NSDAP had always drawn the bulk of its support from the various elements in the middle class. Even in the Depression the organised working class 'remained unimpressed by Nazi slogans', although some proletarian women became Nazi supporters.[12] With the destruction of communist and socialist organisations as the first priority of *Gleichschaltung*, working-class women, like the men, lost their main focus of group activity. Some working-class women, like women of other classes, belonged to Church groups, and most did not belong to organisations of any kind; this applied especially to women in rural areas. The NSF would find the dead weight of apathy on the part of the traditionally unorganised virtually impossible to mobilise, and continuing influence of the Churches extremely hard to undermine. And it immediately forfeited the interest of working-class women who had engaged in some kind of group activity by the way in which it constructed the DFW (Deutsche Frauenwerk) exclusively on the remains of middle-class women's groups which would quickly become expendable but which provided a ready-made basis – with members, funds, premises, magazines – for a new all-embracing combine. From the start, the middle-class character of the DFW, in terms of its immediate membership, inherited from the old groups, in terms of its leadership, attitudes and activities, denied it the support of more than a handful of working-class women, and contradicted its stated aim of bringing all German women under its aegis. The limited appeal of the DFW ensured that its ambition to become the mass organisation of German women would never be realised.

But if the Party and its women's groups were middle-class in orientation and appeal, this did not mean that all, or even most, middle-class women were attracted to them. There were enthusiasts, and there were also women who joined because they regarded membership as a useful insurance policy, particularly if they had a professional career to conserve. Often enough they merely paid their subscription and were classed, on investigation, as 'inactive' members; it was a continuing source of frustration to NSF and Party officials that women from the 'educated classes' generally held aloof from the women's organisation. And middle-class women were certainly not in the forefront of those responding to Party and NSF appeals for volunteers to help the German war-effort from 1939. Only a minority of women – in contrast with men – tends to favour single-sex activity, and a single-sex monopoly organisation with a heavy emphasis on propaganda and indoctrination at once made itself unattractive to large numbers of women, whatever their class. Some women joined no doubt because they wanted to be members of a music group or sports club or sewing circle, and had to choose between the Nazi-sponsored one, under DFW control, or nothing. But, even so, German women were, contrary to popular view,[13] peculiarly resistant to National Socialism, and probably, because of their relative inaccessibility, much more resistant than men. And there was another reason: German women, like women elsewhere, remained more attached than men to religion. The spiritual authority of the Churches, particularly the Catholic Church in rural areas, retained the allegiance of large numbers of women in the face of competition from the NSF. It was hardly a contest: the Nazis could not hope to win against one of the traditional forces in society which many had believed they were coming to power to safeguard against atheistic Marxism.[14] Unable to use coercion to win recruits to the DFW, the NSF found, uncomfortably, that it was largely preaching to a converted minority, still cut off from the antagonistic or, more likely, uninterested 90 per cent and more of the female population of Germany. [. . .]

It was perhaps fitting that the women's organisation should revert, towards its end, to something akin to what its predecessors had been in the 1920s, small local groups working in difficult circumstances to mitigate distress, this time among fellow citizens who were victims of air-raids or the more or less willing subjects of evacuation policies. With shortages and the rupture of the communications network towards the end of the war, the NSF's activities must have borne an uncanny resemblance to those of the Kampfzeit, with little or no central control of individual local policies. And it was clearly in emergency circumstances, in small groups of dedicated activists, that the Nazi women's work flourished. The extent of central authority effectively wielded by Gertrud Scholtz-Klink from her office in Berlin had always depended on the degree to which a Gauleiter had or had not intervened, but the chains of command in the women's organisation had been established at an early stage and had at least nominally held until well into the war. Their purpose had been to try to ensure that the work of the women's organisation throughout the country was conducted in a uniform way, to serve at the local level the demands of the regime as enunciated by the NSDAP and detailed by the staff of bureaucrats gathered in Gertrud Scholtz-Klink's central office. This contrasted sharply with Strasser's creation of the NSF in 1931 as essentially the women's branch of the Party, serving its needs at the local level. Strasser had himself set in motion the centripetal forces, which would ultimately and stultifyingly culminate in a top-heavy administrative centre whose edicts were intended to determine the nature of local women's group activity everywhere. But this conclusion was the logical one only to men, like his successors, with minds less flexible than his own. Unimaginative men with totalitarian aspirations produced a bureaucratic jungle in the women's organisation, as elsewhere; but here they were helped by their choice, as women's leader, of an unimaginative woman. No doubt the obsession with order and uniformity – which competing jurisdictions and a barrage of paperwork successfully vitiated – was yet another deterrent to potential recruits to the women's organisation at the local level. Those who joined up and stayed the course had as their reward a brief taste of initiative and freedom from the centrally-imposed straitjacket in the last months of the war, before the total eclipse.

Notes

1   *Statistisches Jahrbuch für das Deutsche Reich*, 1927, 25.

2   D. V. Glass, 'Family Planning Programmes in Western Europe', *Population Studies*, 1966, 225; J. Peel, 'The Manufacturing and Retailing of Contraceptives in England', *Population Studies*, 1963–4, 117, 122.

3   Jill Stephenson, *Women in Nazi Society*, London, 1975, 10.

4   *NSDAP Hauptarchiv* (hereafter HA), reel 13, fol. 254, Gau History Halle-Merseburg, 1; Berlin Document Center, *Akten des Obersten Parteigerichts*, 2684/34, letter from Walter Buch to Dr Krummacher, 20 September 1933.

5   Quoted in Joachim C. Fest, *The Face of the Third Reich*, London, 1970, 164; Dorte Winkler, *Frauenarbeit im 'Dritten Reich'*, Hamburg, 1977, 28, also makes this point.

6   Stephenson, 12 n23.

7   Stephenson, 38–40; F. Grosse, review of Ernst Kahn, *Der Internationale Geburtenstreik*, Frankfurt, 1930, in *Die Arbeit*, 1931, 308.

8   Institut für Zeitgeschichte Archive, MA 736, Bruno Wenzel, *Zur Frühgeschichte der NSDAP in Niedersachsen*, n.d.

9   David Schoenbaum, *Hitler's Social Revolution*, London, 1967, 187.

10   Conan Fischer, Heriot-Watt University, has been kind enough to give me information about this.

11   Mrs Cecilia Smith, Edinburgh University, is writing a thesis on the Nazi welfare organisation, the NSV. She was kind enough to give me information about this.

12   H. A. Winkler, 'German Society, Hitler and the Illusion of Restoration 1930–33', *Journal of Contemporary History* (October 1976), 2.

13   Joachim C. Fest, *Hitler*, London, 1977, 369, writes of 'growing hordes of sharply politicized women' supporting the NSDAP in 1928. David Pryce-Jones, 'Mothers for the Reich', *Times Literary Supplement*, 2 July 1976, propagates several of the myths.

14   See Winkler, op. cit., for a discussion of the support the NSDAP won from those who wanted a return to the pre-1914 system.

Chapter 41

Robert O. Paxton

VICHY FRANCE: RESISTANCE AND COLLABORATION IN THE NAZI NEW ORDER

■ from *VICHY FRANCE: OLD GUARD AND NEW ORDER 1940–1944*, New York, 1972, pp. 291–3, 294–5, 357–9, 364–8, 370–2

Although published in the early 1970s, Robert Paxton's *Vichy France* is still regarded as the work that challenged successfully two major themes in postwar French historiography on fascism: the notion of overwhelming resistance to the fascist new order and the idea that Vichy France spared France the Nazi wrath that befell other occupied countries (such as Poland). Paxton underlines that the majority of the French population remained demoralised and passive during occupation. As for the 'shield theory', Paxton eloquently highlights that the Vichy regime did nothing to mitigate or reverse Nazi demands for French labour or to shelter the French Jews from persecution. That eventually France and her Jewish community suffered relatively less than Poland and eastern European Jews can be attributed to factors for which, as Paxton stresses, the Vichy regime 'can claim no credit'.

Threats to the social order – resistance

THE VICHY REGIME came into existence mastering a movement of resistance to the armistice in the colonies. Its very credibility as a legitimate regime depended on its continuing ability to neutralize anti-German activists. From the moment it persuaded Generals Noguès and Mittelhauser in North Africa and the Middle East to accept the armistice on 25 June 1940 up through its first year of existence, Marshal Pétain's regime had been quite successful. Although the internal Resistance had begun to trouble public order after the summer of 1941, the Gaullist movement was probably weaker in France after the loss of Syria to Britain in July 1941 than before.

Active opposition to an authoritarian and widely supported regime is a minority business at best. Resistance requires a clear target, and in the unoccupied part of France it was not altogether clear to a lot of anti-German Frenchmen whether Vichy was an enemy too. Resistance also requires some hope, and until late in the war, throwing the Germans back across the Rhine seemed beyond mortal strength. Resistance, finally, means accepting lawlessness on behalf of a higher good and the replacement of routine by a life of relentless improvisation. Only the young and the already outcast can adapt easily to a life of extended rebellion, and that is why the Resistance in France contained a disproportionate share of the young, Communists, and old street-fighters from the prewar protofascist leagues. The active resistance's outlaw status, in turn, magnified the fears it aroused in solid citizens.

It was with an act of assassination that active resistance first thrust itself upon French public consciousness. The shooting of the naval cadet Alfons Moser on the subway platform of Barbès-Rochechouart in Paris on 21 August 1941 [was significant, as was] the sickening toll of hostages whom the Germans shot following the subsequent assassinations of that autumn. The point is that active resistance to the German occupation stepped upon the stage firmly linked to the Bolshevik menace. Marshal Pétain's speech of August 11, 1941, and the extensive security legislation of that week cemented that identification, as did the German propaganda label of 'Communist' attached to the hostages they shot. Pétain, Darlan, and Goebbels tacitly agreed to link all active resistance to bolshevism.

While direct action by the Resistance subsided after the fall of 1941 — 1942 was the time at which the Gaullists and the internal Resistance began to coordinate their organizations — resistance took on a more militant and alarming cast again after November 1942. It was Hitler who did most to mobilize young people for the Resistance by trying to mobilize them for work in German factories. Laval's efforts to placate Gauleiter Sauckel with volunteers having failed, the Service du Travail Obligatoire began summoning whole age classes of young Frenchmen in draft contingents to go to work in German factories in February 1943. Young men faced the choice of taking the train to Germany or the path to the mountains. Thousands who could get to remote areas chose the mountains, and encampments of young men, the *maquis*, sprang up in the Alps, the Massif central, and the Pyrenees. The camps had, of course, to eat and to defend themselves. They supported themselves at least in part by raids on sources of money and supplies. They raided offices of the STO [*Service du Travail Obligatoire*, Compulsory Labour Service] and burned draft files. It is not inconceivable that a few more sinister renegades joined them. The *guerrilla*, which Pétain and others had feared in 1940 would destroy France, had begun.

The issue of premature violence divided even the active Resistance. General de Gaulle publicly deplored the assassinations of 1941 for their waste of life for the sake of no immediate gain. The Resistance was always torn between those preparing for action on some still-distant D-day and those taking action at once. Deeper there lay the division between those who wanted only to chase the Germans out and those who wanted also to change French society root and branch. There was a muted civil war within the armed Resistance in 1943 and 1944 between those Resistance groups solidly staffed by army officers and the *francstireurs* partisans.

[. . .]

The prospect of liberation by the sword, under the auspices of 'brigands,' was anything but alluring to many Frenchmen. Some 45,000 volunteered for the infamous Milice [*Note: police force operating under the Vichy regime*] in 1944, partly, perhaps, to escape from labor service, partly for fanaticism, but at least in part to help defend 'law and order.' Counting police and military guard units as well, it is likely that as many Frenchmen participated in 1943–44 in putting down 'disorder' as participated in active Resistance. Almost every Frenchman wanted to be out from under Germany, but not at the price of revolution.

Under these conditions, the number of active Résistants was never very great, even at the climactic moment of the Liberation. After the war, some 300,000 Frenchmen received official veterans' status for active Resistance service: 130,000 as deportees and another 170,000 as 'Resistance volunteers.' Another 100,000 had lost their lives in Resistance activity. This brings the total of active Resistance participation at its peak, at least as officially recognized after the war, to about 2 percent of the adult French population.[1] There were no doubt wider complicities. But even if one adds those willing to read underground newspapers, some two million persons, or around ten percent of the adult population, seem to have been willing to take even that lesser risk. Let nothing said here detract from the moral significance of those who knew what they had to do. But the overwhelming majority of Frenchmen, however they longed to lift the German yoke, did not want to lift it by fire and sword. [. . .]

Was Vichy a lesser evil?

In the end, one must make some overall judgment of the immediate results of collaboration for Frenchmen. With all its one-sided social favors and with all its complicity in the brutal last stages of nazism's paroxysm, did it not save many Frenchmen from still worse direct German administration? Was it not better to have Frenchmen administering Frenchmen than the tender ministrations of a gauleiter? Did not the Vichy regime save France from 'Polandization'? Did it not 'éviter le pire'?

Marshal Pétain elected to base his defense in 1945 on pragmatic material grounds, and most of the Vichy ministers followed his example. This defensive terrain was marked out for Pétain by Henri Massis, the old Action Française pamphleteer, in the declaration drafted for Pétain when the retreating German armies carried him off to Germany in August 1944:

> For more than four years, resolved to remain in your midst, I tried every day to serve the permanent interests of France. Loyally, but without compromise, I had only one goal: to protect you from the worst. . . . If I could not be your sword, I tried to be your shield.
>
> Sometimes my words or acts must have surprised you. Know that they hurt me more than you yourselves realized. But . . . I held off from you some certain dangers; there were others, alas, which I could not spare you.[2]

In his one statement before the High Court of Justice, Marshal Pétain developed the shield theory further:

> I used my power as a shield to protect the French people. . . . Every day, a dagger at my throat, I struggled against the enemy's demands. History will tell all that I spared you, though my adversaries think only of reproaching me for the inevitable. . . . While General de Gaulle carried on the struggle outside our frontiers, I prepared the way for Liberation by preserving France, suffering but alive.[3]

Pierre Laval, in his turn before the High Court, claimed that his government had managed to 'éviter le pire,' to act as a 'screen' between the conqueror and the French population. The refrain was taken up by succeeding defendants before the High Court and by a stream of self-exculpating memoirs.[4]

Despite these partisan origins, the material advantage theory has been quite widely accepted. Robert Aron, trying to strike a reasonable balance on the basis of the trial records, the only sources available in 1954, argued that life was easier statistically speaking, for Frenchmen than for others in occupied Europe. The reproaches against Vichy, he said, are moral rather than material.[5]

In its most widespread form, the material advantage thesis argues that Vichy kept France from 'Polandization,' and everyone knows that the Poles suffered more in World War II than the French. Nazi contempt for Slavic Untermenschen makes Poland an invalid comparison with France, however. Nazi purists might well cast aspersions upon French 'mongrelization' and lack of racial self-consciousness, but they did not contemplate French extinction. The shield theory must be understood in terms of actual German demands, rather than in terms of vaguely infinite possibilities of evil. It can be validly tested only in comparison with fully occupied Western countries like Belgium, Holland, or Denmark, or other collaborating regimes like Quisling's Norway. If incomplete occupation or the existence of a quasi-autonomous indigenous administration spared France any of the rigors of direct German rule, those favors should show up in comparison with fully occupied Western countries without an indigenous collaborationist regime.

One can suppose two ways in which Vichy France could have suffered less than France under a gauleiter. The German occupation authorities might have asked for less in order to reward and solidify a useful collaborationist regime. Or if the German occupation authorities asked no less of France than of fully occupied Western nations, the Vichy regime might have been better able or more willing to refuse excessive demands than would a gauleiter. A hard comparative look at the material conditions of life in Western occupied countries fails to show any important advantage for France, either granted by or extorted from Berlin.

[. . .]

Vichy's effectiveness as a 'shield' has been most persistently claimed in the areas of forced labor for German factories and the Jewish Final Solution. Laval claimed after the war that while the Germans took 80 percent of Belgian workers to Germany, they took only 16 percent of French workers.[6] As for Jews, Xavier Vallat, who had been Commissaire aux Questions Juives in the Vichy government from 29 March 1941 to 6 May 1942, claimed in his trial that Jews were better off under Vichy than under a gauleiter.

> So, the basic question is this: was it better that the French government concern itself with the Jewish problem or leave the entire material and moral responsibility for it to the occupation authorities?
>
> As for me, I think it was better that the French Government got into it. . . .
>
> At a time when out of 4,343,000 native Jews who lived in Austria, Belgium, Czechoslovakia, Germany, Greece, Holland, Luxemburg, in Poland, and in Yugoslavia only 337,500 survived – that is to say that 0,2% of the Jews disappeared, the figures given for France [by the Anglo-American Commission of Enquiry on the Palestine Question, 1946] . . . prove that if, alas, most of the foreign Jews died in deportation, 95% of the Jews of French nationality are fortunately still living. That is my answer.[7]

Unfortunately the shield was less successful in either case than the Vichy defense claimed.

If few French workers went to Germany in the earlier stages of the war, it was because Polish and then Russian prisoners of war and women were the mainstay of German forced labor. Only when those sources were exhausted by the very brutality of their treatment was volunteer labor replaced by forced labor in the Western occupied countries. In April 1942, Hitler appointed Fritz Sauckel, former gauleiter of Thuringia, to the office of plenipotentiary for foreign labor and authorized him to impose conscription of labor on occupied Belgium, Holland, and France.

It would be a striking justification for the Vichy shield theory if at this point the Germans had asked less of collaborationist France or if Laval had proven able to win concessions for his new ministry. The Germans asked no less of the Occupied Zone of collaborationist France than of totally occupied Belgium and Holland, and much more of France than of collaborationist Norway and Denmark (who contributed little to foreign labor working in the Reich).[8] Only the Paris embassy, among German agencies, seems to have been worried about the political cost to Vichy of forced labor in 1942. Rudolf Schleier, Abetz' second-in-command at the Paris embassy [Note: Otto Abetz was the German ambassador in Vichy France], warned Laval on 24 April 1942, through Consul-General Krug von Nidda, of what was coming and urged Vichy to counter the blow by making the volunteer system much more effective. At first Laval took this advice, permitting the establishment on May 1, 1942, of permanent German recruitment offices in Lyon, Marseilles, and Toulouse, enjoying the full support of French labor offices.[9] These efforts to increase French volunteer labor for Germany did not prevent the eventual introduction of forced labor in France, however. In fact, France became the largest single supplier to Germany of foreign male labor in all occupied Europe in 1943, east or west. Sauckel's Anordnung Nr. 4 of 7 May 1942, instituting forced labor in the west, makes no distinction between the French Occupied Zone and other occupied areas. And after November 1942, all of France was occupied. By November 1943,

1,344,000 French males were working in German factories, slightly ahead of the Russian and Polish male contingents. French women workers, at 44,000, came in third place, well behind the Russian and Polish women. Moreover, on January 5, 1944, Sauckel said he planned to draft an additional million Frenchmen to work in Germany. The German government spared Frenchmen none of the agonies of forced labor.[10] There remains the possibility that Pierre Laval, working within the quasi-autonomy of Vichy, delayed or mitigated the application of forced labor to the unoccupied zone. His old associate Pierre Cathala tried to prove after the war that Laval had managed to 'éviter le pire' with his famous Auvergnat peasant horse-trading: 'Sauckel wants men, I will give him legal texts,' Laval is supposed to have said.[11]

Cathala's claims don't stand. Sauckel got legal texts and men too.

Never a man to leave the initiative to others, Laval was ready with a counter-proposal when Sauckel came to Paris in mid-June 1942 to apply the new German labor policy to France. France enjoyed a unique tactical position in occupied Europe with respect to manpower. Two million able-bodied young Frenchmen were already in Germany as prisoners of war, and Laval now threw them into the bargaining scales with the notorious relève schemes, the release of one prisoner of war for every three French workers who volunteered to work in Germany. Hitler accepted this plan after a telephone conference with Sauckel on 15 June, and Laval worked out the details with Sauckel on the spot.

Laval clearly thought he had gained something, as the volume of French propaganda shows. The return of war prisoners, however few, touched the deepest emotions of both the French public and Pétain himself. Laval marked the political importance of the relève by going in person to greet the first trainload of returning prisoners at Compiègne on August 11, with maximum publicity. The other thing Laval thought he had gained was French sovereign control over one more area of threatened German direct administration.

And so the French government worked frantically to meet the quota of French volunteer workers. It supplied the names and addresses of specialists, arranged the closing of inefficient shops, and extended the work week, all measures designed to release a skilled labor pool for the relève. More strikingly, Laval asked German authorities secretly for a letter threatening direct German forced labor if the relève did not work. He and Pétain thought this would help convince the reluctant.[12] Although the relève got off to a slow start, with only 19,000 skilled workers signed up by 7 October, Vichy's strenuous efforts had recruited 181,000 workers by 21 November, of whom 90,000 were specialists.[13]

Even if Laval had managed to stave off direct forced labor until 1944 by means of the relève, it would have been a questionable bargain. In concrete terms, it was not really the three-for-one exchange which propaganda claimed. Laval and Sauckel agreed on 15 June that France would supply 400,000 workers, including 150,000 with special skills. The relève applied only to skilled workers; i.e., a maximum of 50,000 prisoners would be freed in return for eight times that many volunteer workers. Moreover, the exchange returned mostly farm boys to France at the expense of men with such vital industrial skills as lathe-turning, a short-term gain perhaps for French food production but a bad bet for the French future in Europe. The Germans, in turn, merely lowered the expense of keeping French war prisoners. The net result was that Vichy wound up doing Sauckel's job about as well as Sauckel could have done it himself. Most damning of all, the *relève* didn't buy any French exemption from forced labor in the long run anyway.

[. . .]

Two forces finally did save a number of Frenchmen from the STO. In fact, of the million men Sauckel asked for in January 1944, only 38,000 French workers actually went to Germany in the remaining months before the Liberation. Vichy can take credit for neither of these effective barriers. One was Albert Speer, who struggled for influence against Sauckel in 1943–44. Speer, whose approach was technocratic rather than punitive, believed that it was more effective for workers to produce for Germany in their own countries than to be brought to Germany where they had to be fed, supplied and protected from Allied bombardment. [. . .] The other real barrier to the STO was the *maquis*. It became very difficult to compel young French skilled workers to go to Germany after the beginning of 1944 and virtually impossible after the Allied invasion of Normandy in June 1944. Vichy can take no credit for either of these shields, of course. They would have developed and worked as well, all other things being equal, under a gauleiter.

[. . .]

There remains the somber business of the Jewish Final Solution. [. . .]

It is true that the unoccupied zone of France provided a refuge of sorts for tens of thousands of Jewish refugees from Germany and Eastern Europe for the first two years. Republican France having taken over from England the role of Europe's refuge haven in the late nineteenth century, German Jews and then, after September 1939, Polish Jews, followed a well-worn path to the west. The fact that the armistice and the division of France into two zones kept many of these refugees one jump ahead of the German armies was not the result of any Vichy sentimentality about the refugees. In fact, Vichy objected vigorously when the Germans delivered more expatriate Jews into the unoccupied zone in the fall of 1940. After protest, Vichy acquiesced in Article 19 of the armistice, which empowered Germany to demand the extradition of German citizens who had sought refuge in France. Under this provision, such prominent figures as Herschel Grynspan (who had assassinated a German diplomat in Paris in 1938) and the socialist economist and Weimar minister Rudolf Hilferding were delivered back into German hands – an ominous first warning about the precariousness of asylum in Vichy France. Moreover, Vichy did everything possible to encourage the further emigration of Jewish refugees. At a time when French Jews were being uprooted from the economy, there was no possibility of foreigners settling. Vichy also revoked some recent citizenships, enlarging the number of Jews in France without the protection of citizenship. Finally, Vichy gathered destitute Jewish refugees into work camps. Although Pétain spared them the yellow star, thousands were waiting behind barbed wire when the Germans came into the unoccupied zone in November 1942. Only those with money had managed to use southern France as a springboard for safer havens. For the rest, the French tradition of refuge made the unoccupied zone a trap.

The possibilities of sheltering Jews in southern France were far greater, say, than in the ghetto of Amsterdam. Furthermore, by the time the Germans actually arrived in southern France, in November 1942, there had been ample time for emergency arrangements. The final irony is that Italian-occupied Alpine France provided the cover in 1943 that Vichy refused. Many French citizens did the same, but the Vichy authorities deserve none of their credit. Vichy bears the guilt for not having used its opportunity for the kind of escape operation that the totally occupied Danes managed to carry out by moving almost the entire Jewish population by small boat to Sweden in September 1943. [. . .]

Notes

1   Gordon Wright, 'Reflections on the French Resistance,' *Political Science Quarterly* LXXVII: 3 (September 1962), 336–49, summarizes this information usefully in English. Other estimates put the total active Resistance at 45,000.

2   Georges Blond, *Pétain* (Paris, 1966), 468–69, attributes this text to Henri Massis.

3   République française. Haute Cour de Justice. *Procès du Maréchal Pétain* (Paris, 1945), 9.

4   *Le Procès Laval*; Guy Raïssac, *Combat sans merci* (Paris, 1966), 403. Among memoirs, see, e.g., Yves Bouthillier, *Le Drame de Vichy* (Paris, 1950), I, 138, on 'la politique du bouclier,' and II, 280; Pierre Pucheu, *Ma Vie* (Paris, 1948), 287; Pierre Cathala, *Face aux réalités* (Paris, 1948), 102–5; Raïssac, *Combat*, 370.

5   Robert Aron, *Histoire de Vichy* (Paris, 1954), 736. See also Guy Raïssac, *Combat*, 23, 348, on Vichy leaders' 'louable desseins de tempérer les épreuves.'

6   Laval testimony in *Procès Pétain*, 206. Less absurd but erroneous figures were published later in Pierre Laval, *Laval parle*. Notes et mémoires rédigés par Pierre Laval dans sa cellule (Paris: Les editions du cheval ailé, 1948) 130, and Pierre Cathala, *Face aux réalités* (Paris, 1948), 102, where it is claimed that while 50 to 80 per 1,000 of the total population of Belgium, Holland, and Poland were sent to work in German factories, only 13 per 1,000 of the French population were forced to work in Germany. Cathala, 105, then repeats Laval's claim to have 'saved 4/5 of the French.'

7   *Le Procès de Xavier Vallat présenté par ses amis* (Paris, 1948), 117–18.

8   Edward L. Homze, *Foreign Labor in Nazi Germany* (Princeton, N.J., 1966), 148, 200.

9   Schleier (Paris) 449 to Krug von Nidda (Vichy), 24 April 1942; Schleier (Paris) 526 to Krug von Nidda (Vichy), 5 May 1942. Centre de Documentation Juive Contemporaine, Paris, document nos. CLXXXIV–23, 24.

10   Homze, 195. Sauckel's Anordung Nr. 4 is found in T–120/5636/E407359–68.

11   Pierre Cathala, *Face aux réalités* (Paris, 1948), 97 ff.

12   Schleier (Vichy) 1842 to Paris, 6 October 1942 (T-120/5367/ E407490–91). Schleier talked to Pétain too.

13   The whole labor question is best followed in the files of the German embassy in Paris: Deutscher Botschaft, Paris – T–120/5635H, 5636H, 5637H, and in Edward L. Homze, *Foreign Labor in Nazi Germany* (Princeton, 1966), chap. 9. Homze's data, drawn mostly from Berlin materials, needs to be supplemented with the local perspective of the Paris embassy.

Chapter 42

Raymond Carr

SPAIN IN THE 1930S: A DIVIDED SOCIETY AND THE COMING OF THE CIVIL WAR

■ from *THE SPANISH TRAGEDY: THE CIVIL WAR IN PERSPECTIVE*, London, 1993, pp. 64–87

Raymond Carr's *The Spanish Tragedy* is a passionately drafted account of Spain's turbulent path to the civil war and to Francoism in the 1930s. The author focuses on how historical forces and developments affected society, trying to understand the motivations of individuals and social groups who fought passionately on either side of the left–right divide. Here Carr reviews the political trajectory of four individuals from different social backgrounds and regions of Spain. His conclusion is that reactions to the civil war cannot be adequately explained on the basis of class, geography or age groups – loyalties were selective, inconsistent, sometimes even confused, and fraught with contradictions, even inside rigid groups such as the Church and the armed forces.

A FTER TWO CONFUSED WEEKS the generals' rising divided Spain into two zones: 'red' and 'white'. Spaniards only gradually realized that they were cut off from each other as telephones, railway trains, letters and road traffic stopped at the frontiers of the zones. The failure of the rising in Barcelona, Valencia, Alicante and Malaga secured Catalonia and the Levante for the government; the centre stood with Madrid while Old Castile fell to the rebels. The northern coastal provinces, the Basque Provinces and Asturias, remained with the government; Galicia, which was left politically, fell to the insurgents in a matter of days. Santander and its province presented an opposite case. It had voted for the right throughout the Republic; both the monarchists and the Falangists were strong locally. But Mola's preparations had gone awry. The garrison was apathetic and a major loyal to the government saved the day.

The two zones did not correspond neatly either with previous political loyalty or with social class, and without the concept of 'geographical loyalty' the Civil War is incomprehensible. Those caught in either zone had to conform, escape, or risk imprisonment or shooting. Thus the bullfighters' union in Madrid supported the government; but in Vitoria the bulls were killed in honour of General Franco's wife. While the two greatest Spanish actresses took opposite sides, those theatre companies caught on tour in the rebel zone had no alternative but to earn a living by performing propagandist plays and classical drama in Nationalist cities.

Although class division was thus cut across by the accidents of war and conquest, nevertheless a division emerged, where free choice was possible. In spite of Falangist propaganda for a national, classless revolution, the unionized workers supported the Popular Front; the rich, the aristocrats and *upper*-middle classes of the old pre-1931 political and economic establishment sought protection with the Nationalists. Thus many senior civil servants and almost all diplomats defected from the legal government; the directors of the Bank of Spain who represented private shareholders vanished from Madrid.

It was the allegiance of the middle class proper – amorphous and ill-defined, including the 'traditional' middle class that fed the professions, the civil service and the army – that was in doubt. It was partly for this reason that the Communists were to expend such effort in reassuring them that the Popular Front was a respectable, moderate, democratic concern, determined to protect the property of the 'little' man. If the Communist assertion that the Republic represented *merely* a bourgeois revolution against feudalism had been true, then bourgeois loyalty would have been secured for the Popular Front. But the Republican experience in the spring and summer of 1936, in words if not in deeds, went beyond this. The allegiance of the middle classes was therefore selective. The Spanish middle class as a whole had not suffered, as had the German bourgeoisie after 1919, a dramatic deterioration in their living standards and a blow to their national pride that turned them towards Nazism. Yet the milder depression and the increasing threat of 'proletarianization' was not without its effects. Many small-time traders and professionals, historically a bulwark of Republican radicalism, saw in the strong government promised by the Nationalists a security against descent in the social scale. The 'sufferings of the middle class' had long been a standard theme. These sufferings were now seen not, as in the past, as inflicted on the modest man by his indifferent superiors, but as a price paid for working-class advances. Gerald Brenan noted 'the look of triumph on the faces of the workmen' in the streets of Malaga; this was a painful affront to traditional middle-class values, as was the cheaply produced pornography which seemed in some way to be connected with the advance of democracy.

In general, older middle-class professionals and intellectuals often sympathized with the Nationalists, driven by distaste for the proletarian style of the Popular Front: the vogue for Soviet films and literature was uncomfortably un-Spanish. The younger intellectuals, in so far as they had not been influenced by Falangism, sided with the Republic with enthusiasm – for instance, the poets Alberti and Hernández. The more prominent, older established writers had lost faith in the Republic by 1936. Others, like Antonio Machado, a schoolmaster in a poor province and the purest poetic talent in Spain, stayed with the Republic till he crossed the border in 1939 to die, broken, in France.

But the tepid and doubtful sympathy of the older generation did little to diminish the hostility of the Nationalists to intellectuals as such: they were abused in

Nationalist propaganda as a 'dissolvent' element, as representatives of 'anti-Spain' influenced by the pernicious currents of a Europe in democratic decline.

The Nationalists were indeed correct in emphasizing the European inspiration of the younger generation of intellectuals, a generation which had made intellectuals a force in Spanish life as never before or since. In Ortega's words, they had restored Spanish culture to 'the place in Europe it had lost for centuries' and there is a sense in which, for a short time, intellectuals replaced the old political elite which had vanished in the twenties. Azaña was deeply influenced by French radical thought. Negrin, later Prime Minister of the Republic, is a typical representative of the middle generation of Spanish intellectuals loyal to the Republic. He had studied physiology in Germany and was a representative 'of the first European generation' in Spain; he became a Socialist because he considered the party the most 'European' party.

If the middle classes were divided, neither did the mass of the peasantry act as a bloc, driven by economic hardship to support the declared enemies of the 'powerful ones'. The small farmers of Valencia and Alicante, relatively prosperous, were to show little enthusiasm for the social experiments of the Popular Front government in whose territory they remained till the end. The peasants of the Castilian heartland joined the Nationalists and provided, with Navarre and Galicia, the bulk of its army. This peasant basis of the Nationalist army was to be of great significance. To a certain extent it made the war a war of the countryside against the great cities, of the rural, conservative heartland against the 'progressive' periphery (except for the greatest Castilian city, Madrid). It was the Nationalists who spoke of the Castilian and Navarrese peasant as the 'moral reserve' of the nation.

As in the case of the middle classes in general, the allegiance of the peasantry was selective. In the civil wars of Mexico, Russia, China and Vietnam the allegiance of the peasantry was clear; but, as Professor Malefakis points out, this was not the case in Spain. 'In Spain . . . the Civil War was also to a very significant degree a fratricidal conflict of peasant against peasant'. The sons of the Catalan *rabassaire* fought against the families of the Castilian small farmer. As for the day labourers of the south-west, their allegiance was not in doubt. They murdered (or witnessed the murder by FAI militants of) their landlords; but they quickly fell under the military dominance of the Nationalists and their revolutionary potential was therefore neutralized.

While no one can deny the class nature of the Civil War, all attempts to break down allegiances *solely* in terms of class, professional interest, status or age neglect the fact that men act by temperament as well as by interest; that in the same social situation different men perceive their interests differently; that class interests may be overlaid by religious affinities or regional interest. Where the mass of the middle class supported the Popular Front as it did in Catalonia, that allegiance was given as much out of nationalist enthusiasm as in support of a bourgeois revolution: the Popular Front would support the hard-won Catalan autonomy now effective in the Generalidad, an autonomy which the Nationalists would destroy. Only the businessmen of the *Lliga* put their class interest above the defence of Catalonia. In contrast, conservative, pious Basque peasants fought for the Republic because it was the guarantor of Basque autonomy.

The assertion that all *Africanista* officers were enthusiastic rebels, not least because their promotion was blocked by Azaña's legislation, is an oversimplification.[1]

Africanistas were among the most enthusiastic and dedicated conspirators; yet many, like General Riquelme and Colonel Jurado, fought for the Republic; so did Lieutenant-Colonel Romero Bassart – his African services for which he was promoted did not prevent him becoming the political ally of the CNT in Malaga. Moscardo, the hero of the Alcazar, had seen his promotion blocked by Azaña's legislation; but so had Major Perez Farras who went with the first CNT columns to the Aragon front. Colonels Aranda and Asensio had seen men promoted above their heads: Aranda saved Oviedo for the Nationalists, Asensio became Largo Caballero's military *éminence grise*.

The ultimate tragedy of a civil war is that it is often a war of brother against brother. The Perez Salas family had five brothers in the army. Four served the Republic in important commands; the fifth joined the rising and became a lieutenant-general in Franco's army. As it turned out, he made a wise choice: his brother Joaquin was shot by the victors in 1939 and another went into permanent exile.

One simple fact must be stated over and over again; if *all* officers had joined the rising it might well have been successful in a matter of days. As we have seen, in Madrid the officer corps was deeply divided and its divisions doomed the conspiracy of the younger activists to failure.

Though it would be fashionable exaggeration to speak of a generational conflict, on *both* sides the tensions of the summer of 1936 revealed the pull of youth movements on older statesmen. The Revolution of October 1934 had been, according to the Socialist intellectual Araquistain, 'the work of younger proletarians'; it was the Socialist Youth (amalgamated with the Communist Youth) that encouraged Largo Caballero's move to the left, and which after July 1936 became a dominant force in the loyal towns. It was the younger generation of CNT leaders who organized the great Madrid building strike of June 1936.

The generation gap was apparent on the other side of the barricades. Young Falangists hid their pistols from their parents in hollowed-out books; Gil Robles was under constant pressure from his own youth movement, attracted by the wilder spirits of the Falange to which it ultimately deserted. Among the Carlists the abrasive leader of the Carlist Youth, Fal Conde, outdistanced in his harsh militancy the older, more accommodating Conde de Rodezno. It was the younger officers who were the most militant conspirators; in Pamplona it was Captain Barrera who organized the garrison conspiracy, later to be taken over by General Mola. In the key rising in Morocco the older, senior officers were loyal to the government; it was an affair of majors and captains organized by a colonel. 'In the military sphere, as in the civil,' wrote Jose Maria Fontana, a Catalan Falangist, 'the bulk of the [Nationalist] movement was *cosa de gente joven* – a young people's affair.' If these young enthusiasts imagined they were making a world safe for the under-forties, they were sadly mistaken.

II

I have chosen four biographies to illustrate how the acceleration of political change after 1931 and the process of mass politicization changed men's lives and determined their choices in July 1936. Manuel Cortes was born in 1905 (the rainless year that reduced the poor to starvation) in the Andalusian hill *pueblo* of Mijas. In this remote area – the road was frightful and there was no telephone – its two thousand inhabitants made a living out of the esparto grass of the surrounding hills, the produce of vineyards, and from smuggling tobacco. There were smallholders, tenant farmers, sharecroppers and eight hundred day labourers working on the surrounding estates. Since childhood Cortes saw little but poverty, backbreaking work and the oppression of the local cacique and his cronies. Before 1923 elections were 'a form of terror' and under the dictatorship of Primo even mild political satire was stamped on and the village ruled by an irascible retired major.

Thus up to 1930 the *pueblo* had no real experience of politics. Suddenly, with the fall of Primo de Rivera, politics burst in. Cortes set about organizing a branch of the Landworkers' Federation (FTT) affiliated to the UGT. It grew rapidly. The landless labourers joined *en masse*; the tenant farmers, sharecroppers and smallholders needed some persuasion to see that their interests were not in conflict with the hopes of the landless. The enemies of both were the 'powerful ones' of the village *camarilla* who had monopolized both political power and land. Suddenly, in April 1931 with the declaration of the Republic, the powerful ones were stripped of their political power. Cortes, the self-educated, socialist village barber, became first town councillor and then mayor of Mijas.

Economic power remained unaltered; it was still in the hands of the powerful. 'A lot was done about education and very little about the land.' The unions doubled the wages of the day labourers but agrarian reform stayed in the government offices at Malaga; smallholders were often too frightened to join the union or form a cooperative to challenge the landowners. In the 'Two Black Years' the landowners had it their own way. After the Popular Front victory they fought a bitter rearguard action; they simply refused to employ labour even if it meant tearing up their own vines. 'Let the Republic find you work, let the Republic feed you.' 'The landlords are attempting to stage a boycott in order to crush the labourers. . . . That's the way the bourgeoisie is here, intransigent. For them a Socialist is the very devil himself. They could never understand that they were driving the masses towards violent solutions far more extreme than any the Socialist party, for my part, would have advocated. But that's how they are, reactionary, traditionalist, frightened of any change – and with a terrible fear of the proletariat.' But now the proletariat was losing its fear of them. On May Day 1936 the local rich escaped lynching only through Cortes' influence and astuteness as mayor.

Manuel Cortes hated violence and despised the gun-toters of the CNT. But he equally believed that the Republic had been weak. 'The Republicans were always thinking about legality. Look at the business of claims I've described. That sort of legality and paperwork existed in everything.' To Cortes, even after the Popular Front victory in February 1936, the revolution remained in the hands of a new brand of Republican bureaucrats without the strength to make a clean sweep of 'everything that was old'. 1931–6 was a disillusioning experience for an overworked mayor, without funds to pay unemployment benefits and in constant battle with recalcitrant employers on the one side and extremists who lacked 'seriousness' on the other. But even if the Republic had been a disappointment there could be no doubt where his loyalties lay in July 1936. He had seen oppression all his life. He now fought for the Republic against the 'powerful ones'.

Manuel Hedilla was born three years before Manuel Cortes in a village of the northern province of Santander; his father was a civil servant whose death left his mother a hard-up widow working to keep her family 'respectable'. Educated in Catholic schools in Bilbao, he was apprenticed in the shipyards. Uninterested in politics, his whole effort was concentrated on earning enough money to support his mother. As a ship's engineer he could do this but the post-war shipping slump left him unemployed. He was saved by the ambitious public works programme of Primo de Rivera, becoming a transport contractor on the new tourist road in Cuenca. Primo de Rivera's fall put him out of a job once more and he came to Madrid to set himself up as a garage and lorry proprietor; once more he failed, a victim of the depression. All his early life, therefore, had been one long and lonely struggle to gain a decent, middle-class competence. The highest wage he earned before 1936 was six hundred pesetas a month, on which he supported a wife and two sons.

From Madrid Hedilla came back to his native province to become an engineer in a Catholic dairy farmers' cooperative and under the influence of a Capuchin monk he joined the Traditionalists. He soon joined the Falange and set about organizing a National syndicalist union. It was an uphill task. The Falange had no funds and was fighting the powerful UGT (Unión General de Trabajadores) unions and their closed shop policy: recruitment in taverns brought in only marginal workers. Hedilla changed his job once more (he considered his employers 'red' because they were only feeble supporters of his struggle with the UGT) and became a supervisor in a glass factory. By the spring of 1936 his small band of enthusiasts was persecuted, its meetings broken up by the unions or prohibited by the civil governor. Jose Antonio had warned in November 1935 that the coming struggle might be 'more dramatic' than a mere electoral contest. The Santander Falange managed to get fifty rifles from a sympathetic officer.

Hedilla was a walking contradiction. His whole ambition had been to become an independent entrepreneur; his failure to do so, combined with an intense sympathy for the working class and a hatred of the UGT for 'politicizing' the struggle for better conditions, turned him into a radical Falangist. This was the only position that combined an attack on liberal capitalism with a rejection of the Marxism which his Catholic background made unacceptable. Hedilla fought the attempt of conservative Falangist sympathizers to set up an employers' union; he was a strong supporter of Jose Antonio's radical line. 'The Falange wants to dismantle the capitalist system so that its benefits may go to the producers.' As a National Councillor he helped draw up a report on unemployment. 'The principal cause of unemployment is the principle of liberal individualism that informs the present economic system . . . the profit motive.' Banks, usury, absentee landlords, multiple stores must vanish once the economy had been reorganized 'organically'. In the end, as we shall see, Hedilla failed to impose his populist radicalism on the Nationalist state; his conservative enemies won out in April 1937.

The two Manuels, Cortes and Hedilla, could not have been more of a contrast: one a self-educated free thinker, the other a Catholic schoolboy; one with a passionate belief in education, the other believing that higher education had already gone too far and that the liberal professions should be 'dignified' by restricting university entrance. One was a Marxist who had no time for the CNT and its contempt for 'serious' politics, the other had a sneaking sympathy with anarchist direct action. Yet they shared characteristics common to the best spirits on each side. They were austere men. Hedilla neither smoked nor drank, and possessed only one suit. They both believed they should serve their cause for no reward. They were both patient organizers and persistent propagandists by example and persuasion: Cortes in his barber's shop trying to persuade smallholders to combine with land-less workers; Hedilla in taverns struggling to convert socialists to the true unionism.

Hedilla and Cortes came from modest backgrounds. Juan Ansaldo was an aristo-cratic air force officer, a friend of Primo de Rivera's family, at home on golf courses, bathing beaches and at 'La Pena', the White's of Madrid. He was a passionate monar-chist, a pious Catholic and a brave and determined conspirator whose aeroplane was constantly used to carry messages and persons in repeated plots. From the day the Republic came into being he was convinced that it must be overthrown by force. And for Ansaldo there was only one force that could accomplish this: the army.

He was an active supporter of Sanjurjo's abortive coup in August 1932 and on its failure immediately set about with his monarchist friends 'to put in train a new national rising'. Again it must be a military rising ordered 'from above' by generals who could immediately take over the administration by declaring a state of war. Civilians could only be 'auxiliary elements capable only of secondary missions'. He was an active member of Renovación Española, to him a mere 'camouflage for the preparation of a military plot'. He was 'maddened' by generals like Franco who hid their intentions and would not act; he despised Gil Robles and the 'legal' right as 'monarchists of weddings and baptisms' unwilling, as they were, to risk life and fortune for the cause.

For a time he joined the Falange, because it appeared the only instrument of the violence he sought; he insisted on reprisals in the gang warfare of the militia. The 'intellectuals' of the movement could tolerate neither his monarchism nor his violence; he could not bear Jose Antonio's distaste for political murder and his leader's 'court of *littérateurs* and poets'. He was expelled from a movement which he had come to consider weak in numbers and purpose.

He found in Calvo Sotelo's National Bloc a more congenial home: it was, to him, a 'cover-up for and stimulus to the military coup'. He organized its militia, took a sporting pleasure in eluding the police and sending up balloons with monar-chist slogans. He soon found himself at odds with most of the Bloc's leaders who could not 'abandon their political mentality', i.e. put their trust in Ansaldo's guer-rillas. No one lived up to his expectations: above all Franco, whom he came to hate with his refrain 'the time has not yet come'. When the time came Ansaldo botched it. He was sent to Portugal to fly out General Sanjurjo to become the Head of State of Nationalist Spain, the Monck who would restore the monarchy. On a poor airfield he crashed and Sanjurjo was killed. The 'Franquito' he despised, and the Falangists whom he had come to see as 'foreign' fascists, triumphed.

It is impossible to understand the history of the Republic without remembering that throughout its life men like Ansaldo and his rich monarchist friends, meeting in smart restaurants and drinking 'select wines', had no other aim but to destroy it. After every failure they began again, collecting funds, approaching officers, talking in the bars of Biarritz and St Jean de Luz of the 'day'. Ansaldo, it is true, was extreme in his persistent plotting. Other rightists at times believed they might defeat the revolution by legal means: Gil Robles or even Lerroux might save Spain. But, like

Ansaldo, they never abandoned 'the way of force', if legalism – as it did with Gil Robles' failure to win a crushing victory in February 1936 – yielded no dividends. The activists were let down time and time again. But even failure had its uses. To defend itself the Republic closed down newspapers, arrested politicians and prohibited meetings. 'All this accentuated the discrepancy between its [the Republican government's] theoretical democratic base and its authoritarian actions.' The attempt to repress the activist right and the revolutionary left discredited the Republic as a democratic regime; but repression failed to stamp out conspiracy and the persistence of violence discredited the Republic and 'proved' that it could not maintain 'order'.

Cortes, Hedilla and Ansaldo were conscious and committed militants. Pepe S.[2] was a militant *malgré lui*. 'The revolution is like a hurricane,' wrote the Mexican novelist Azuela, 'if you're in it you're not a man . . . you're a leaf, a dead leaf, blown by the wind.' So it was with Pepe S.

The father of Pepe S. was a retired provincial doctor, a Catalan by origin, who was an enthusiastic follower of Lerroux. In the last years of the dictatorship the son came to Madrid University to study law and found himself 'shouting slogans' in the streets with his fellow students. 'I was not politically minded but, like most students of my generation, I looked on Primo de Rivera as a shameful ruler. He was bankrupting the country and throwing our best intellectuals, like Unamuno, out of their jobs. Though my father had always opposed Catalan nationalism – he thought Macià[3] a lunatic and we never spoke Catalan at home – my cousins were in the *Esquerra* and hated Primo. So I was glad to see the back of Primo and King Alfonso. A Republic must be better than they had been.'

In 1932 Pepe S.'s father was hit by the depression because most of his income in retirement came from a small farm let out to an insolvent tenant. The son was forced to work in a bookshop at the 'humiliating' job of delivering books to customers. He could not earn enough money, by changing jobs, to marry his sweetheart whom he had been courting for three years. He could not bring himself to join any party. He was 'muddled'; he was 'frightened'. His father, by this time, had moved with his leader to the right.

In June 1936, depressed and out of a job, he went to stay with his sweetheart's family in Saragossa. There the rising of 18 July caught him. After a month's hesitation whether he should try to get back to his own home near Barcelona or stay in Nationalist Spain, he volunteered for the Nationalist army and served throughout the war without distinction in an office job. Yet by family tradition – his father and grandfather were Republicans – economic status and nationality he should have fought on the other side.

He failed to get a commission; 'perhaps because I was not enthusiastic enough or perhaps because all my own family were for the Popular Front.' (Even so, his cousin was imprisoned in Lerida by the Popular Front.) In 1950 he was an embittered minor civil servant, the fate of many a 'geographical loyalist'.

Notes

1   *Africanistas* were officers who had served in the Moroccan campaigns; they were the army's most professional and war-hardened officers and formed a group

interest against 'sedentary' officers who were regarded by the *Africanistas* as little better than civil servants. Nevertheless the division can be exaggerated.

2 A pseudonym: the person concerned was interviewed in 1950 and may still be alive.

3 Macià was the founder of Estat Catalá which in the twenties proposed self-determination for a Catalan state in an Iberian Federation. He later became the first President of the Generalidad.

■ Fascism and social elites – complicity and antagonism

ELITE SUPPORT FOR THE FASCIST leaderships was significantly more than a weighty vote of confidence in fascism in what amounted to a passport out of political wilderness; it was the vehicle for the transformation of fascism from a non-mainstream movement of political 'outsiders' into a trustworthy formula for the reorganisation of the existing regime. For, it has to be emphasised again, fascism never acquired power autonomously, as a result of either majority popular will or the individual actions of its leadership. Even in Germany, where the fascist component (NSDAP) enjoyed wide electoral support under the Weimar system, it did not attain parliamentary majority in the two 1932 elections – and it even failed to come near to a majority in the elections conducted under its aegis in early 1933. The same applies to the second and third most popular (in terms of voting preference) fascist movements in interwar Europe, the Arrow Cross in Hungary and the Iron Guard in Romania, which reached an impressive 25 per cent and 15 per cent of the vote in the late 1930s respectively. Even in the case of Italian Fascism, the PNF achieved a small but politically significant parliamentary repesentation in 1921 by participating in Giolitti's liberal *listone*, having been co-opted by significant sectors of the mainstream Italian political establishment. In the rest of the countries, fascist parties commanded the voting allegiance of very small minorities of the electorate and did not constitute a direct challenge to the stability of the parliamentary system or to the status of the elite groups.

Such an overall failure of the fascist movements to achieve overwhelming levels of electoral support (with only a few notable exceptions, still falling short of majority) is hardly surprising; what is indeed bewildering is that, on the eve of the outbreak of the Second World War, so many European states, from the Iberian peninsula to Romania and Greece, were governed by regimes that were fascist, included a strong fascist component, or openly imitated the 'fascist' style of politics epitomised by Fascist Italy and Nazi Germany (see Payne (5)). This overwhelming endorsement of fascist or quasi-fascist politics obviously had little to do with popular support and parliamentary arithmetic – after all, in many countries liberalism amounted to a flawed parliamentary system, largely divorced from real executive power that depended on the support of powerful extra-parliamentary elite sectors, political and military. In this context, the assumption of (or inclusion in) power by the fascist leaderships was far from inevitable. Fascist parties continued to appear extreme in their ideological goals, and the subversive activities of their more militant members (for example, the SA in Germany, the *squadri* in Italy and the *Legionari* in Romania) were just a slightly more useful threat to the stability of the system – useful only in the sense that they targeted the socialist/communist organisations, whose political agenda was anathema to conservative elite groups. As for the 'fascist' activist style of politics, the populism of their discourse and the largely 'plebeian' lineage of its leaders, traditional elite sectors remained in most cases largely unimpressed, clearly falling short of any enthusiastic endorsement of their political functionality in the longer term.

How, then, did a meagre statistical possibility become an acceptable solution in interwar Europe? Early Marxist historiography had from the very beginning argued in favour of understanding fascism as a puppet regime, propelled to power through the wishes of industrial elites and their political partners to operate in a less accountable and restrictive framework and thus promote their monopolistic interests under the guise of a populist regime. An elaboration of this argument was provided by the theory of *caesarism*: a political arrangement in which the autonomy of the traditional groups would be enhanced and legitimised by the charisma and popular appeal of the fascist leaders personally without alteration of the existing real configuration of power behind the scenes. For liberal historiography, however, such a blanket dismissal of the fascist regime as a tool of monopoly capitalism was problematic. Instead, emphasis was placed on exploring the degree to which the fascist seizure and exercise of power constituted a break with the previous bourgeois regimes. In the 1960s Hans Mommsen (1966, 1977) referred to the 'complicity' of the elite sectors of German society in transforming Hitler from a radical, unacceptable 'bohemian lance-corporal' (as President Hindenburg used to refer to him) into an attractive solution to the Weimar Republic's parliamentary and constitutional deadlock. Evidence of such complicity abounds elsewhere – from the political and military establishment in Italy to the intrigues of the monarchs in the Balkan states and the positive attitude of the Church leaders in Spain, Portugal and Austria. This evidence helps us to reconceptualise the fascist take-over, not as a real *seizure* of power (as perhaps Mussolini would have wanted through his March on Rome), but rather as a *capitulation* of the bourgeois system to the short-term appeal and/or functionality of the fascist leaders. Given that, at least initially, the appointed fascist leaderships operated within coalition cabinets alongside powerful traditional figures of the bourgeois establishment, there was at least some continuity in the transition to fascist rule.

The excerpts in this section shed light on the origins and eventual limitations of this continuity. M. Blinkhorn (43) explores the nature of the relationship between conservative right and fascism. K.-J. Müller's essay on the conservative opposition to the Nazi regime (44) illustrates why the initial identity of goals between Hitler and conservative elites was eroded by 1936–7 but failed to produce an effective 'resistance' force against Hitler. H. A. Turner (45) explores the role of German big-industry bosses in bringing Hitler to power and consolidating his authority. A. Lyttelton (46) documents the complex developments that led King Victor Emmanuel III to the decision to appoint Mussolini in October 1922. Finally, S. Ben-Ami (47) focuses on the complicity of the royal and military elites in Spain in the establishment of Primo de Rivera's dictatorship – a regime that, in his opinion, created a political mould for 'fascism from above' that inspired similar experiments in other 'peripheral' European states experiencing a 'crisis of modernisation' (for example, in the Balkans) throughout the 1930s.

Chapter 43

Martin Blinkhorn

FASCISTS AND CONSERVATIVES: BETWEEN ALLIANCE AND RIVALRY

■ from **ALLIES, RIVALS, OR ANTAGONISTS? FASCISTS AND CONSERVATIVES IN MODERN EUROPE**, in Blinkhorn (ed.) *Fascists and Conservatives*, London, 1990, pp. 2–3, 4, 5–6, 7, 8–9, 13

With this essay Martin Blinkhorn introduces a collection of essays on the relationship between conservative right and fascism in interwar Europe. After indicating the inconsistent use of the term 'fascism' in the literature, Blinkhorn discusses how the emergence of fascism owed a lot to previous authoritarian ideas, but also differed from conventional authoritarianism in being generally more extreme. He concludes by noting that the (accurate) distinction between fascism and conservatism became gradually more problematic, given the adoption of 'fascist' symbols, policies and discourses by authoritarian regimes throughout Europe in the 1920s and 1930s.

L ET US TAKE FASCISM FIRST,[1] and begin with what is (almost) incontrovertible: namely, that Italian fascism provides us with models of both a fascist movement and a fascist regime. More or less simultaneously with the emergence of fascism in Italy, there also emerged in other European countries, especially those, like Italy, affected by war, demobilization and revolution or left-wing militancy – Germany, Austria, Finland, parts of the Balkans – significant popular movements with sufficient in common with Italian fascism quickly to be bracketed with it. Then, as time passed and as fascism in Italy ceased to be a mere movement and became a securely established regime, the term 'fascism', and the values, goals etc. associated with it, began to be *deliberately* adopted by new, imitative movements, from London to Athens and from Lisbon to Helsinki.

So far, so good. The picture soon becomes blurred, however, by a number of additional and related factors. It is necessary to recognize, first, that on the interwar European right there existed a plethora of organizations with authoritarian goals, some actually founded before 1914, others newly emerging, some working through parliamentary machinery, others extra-parliamentary and paramilitary in character; and that within the political world of the right, the increasingly modish labels 'fascism' and 'fascist' were employed with little consistency. Secondly, during the course of the interwar period the whole of central, southern and eastern Europe succumbed to rightist, authoritarian regimes of one sort or another, of which few actually called themselves 'fascist' or 'national socialist' but most praised aspects of Italian fascism and Nazism and borrowed selectively from the examples they provided. Third, liberals and leftists, fearful of a general authoritarian trend of which Italian fascism was reckoned to be the standard-bearer, themselves began to apply the term 'fascism' loosely (but understandably) to a variety of right-wing movements, parties and regimes, by no means all of which saw *themselves* as 'fascist'.

To produce a rigorous and consistent definition of 'fascism' against such a background is difficult, perhaps impossible – if only because no single definition will satisfactorily embrace both movements and regimes. Since no definition of 'fascism' can ever be universally accepted or objectively 'correct', what is needed is rather a valid and useful *working approach* which will assist our understanding of the right in general, and of the complex relationships within it. For our purpose it would probably be wisest to suggest (1) that movements and (much more rarely) regimes adopting the labels 'fascist', 'national socialist' and 'national syndicalist', or associating themselves with these causes, present no taxonomic problem; (2) that other movements of the authoritarian right – those, for example, with Catholic origins which claimed not to be 'fascist' – must be considered empirically, in terms of both their subjective and their objective relationship to the radical right; and (3) that ostensibly 'non-fascist' regimes of the right present the most difficulty, since many rightist regimes, not excepting those of Mussolini and Hitler, represented a compromise between self-confessed fascism/national socialism and other forces.

[. . .]

To state what is admittedly obvious, the early twentieth century was an unprecedentedly volatile and turbulent period in the history of Europe. Between the later nineteenth century and the Second World War, although the details and the pace of process differed considerably from country to country, the dominant classes throughout much of the continent – and those who represented them politically – found themselves facing the arrival of mass politics, political democracy, popular pressure for social reform, and the possibility, at the very least, of left-wing revolution. Two major historical events, the First World War and the Russian Revolution, massively influenced both the sociopolitical realities of Europe and the individual and collective political consciousness of its inhabitants. In the response of Europe's established elites to these and related challenges, fascism – that is, fascist movements and fascist ideas – sometimes played an important and complex role. Complex, since fascism, where it appeared, was at one and the same time a symptom and a product of contemporary change; a possible weapon whereby conservatives might deal with some of the other, unappealing aspects of change, notably the challenge of the left; and a possible threat in itself.

Already before 1914, the confident control of Europe's incumbent elites, variously aristocratic and *haut bourgeois*, 'conservative' and 'liberal', was wavering.

Industrialization and urbanization, the capitalist transformation of agriculture, population migration, cultural modernization and secularization: these and related
contemporary phenomena were breaking down existing forms of hierarchical and
clientelist politics, confronting the politically dominant with the uncertainties of
popular politics, the often unwelcome prospect of more genuine democracy, and
the fast-advancing threat of socialism. Under these pressures, confidence in existing,
mainly liberal-parliamentary, principles and practices was liable to falter.

Throughout much of Europe, 'constitutional' conservatism was already, before
fascism became a reality, subject to varying degrees of subversion by ideas and organizations of an authoritarian or corporatist character. [. . .] [F]or example, how in
the decade before the birth of fascism much of the German right was ideologically
Pan-Germanized; how strong was the influence of the Italian Nationalist Association,
elitist social theory and the 'Return to the Statute' school in Italy; how Maurassian
ideas extended beyond France – where indeed their practical importance may if
anything have been overstated by historians – to influence conservatives in, for
example, Greece and more particularly Portugal. In Austria, the conservative
Christian Socials took with them into the 1920s a populist corporatist, chauvinist
tradition, effectively mobilized by Karl Lueger, whilst in Spain the 'alternative
conservatism' of Catholic traditionalism continuously beckoned any conservatives
whose loyalty to the liberal system was at all shaky.

[. . .]

In much of postwar Europe, conservatives found themselves operating within a
suddenly altered political world in which the control of established elites was overturned or at least seriously threatened. The advent of the Weimar Republic may not
have brought down Germany's social and institutional elites, but it deprived them
of political dominance and seemed thereby to threaten their total destruction.
Austrian conservatives found themselves left with a rump state of questionable
national identity, in which socialism was ominously powerful. In Italy, the advent of
virtually universal male suffrage and proportional representation thrust the country's
'liberal' and Catholic elites into a mass-political arena for which they were ill-
prepared. Greece and Romania [. . .] found their polities transformed, the former
by the arrival of several hundred thousand refugees from Asia Minor, the latter
through the country's doubling in size and population, and its loss of ethnic homogeneity. In both Romania and the newly independent state of Finland conservative
anti-socialism was rendered all the more intense by the proximity of the Soviet
Union. In situations such as these, in which liberal parliamentarism no longer offered
a guarantee of lasting social hegemony, established elites and elements within conservative and sometimes even 'liberal' political parties were liable to find their devotion
to parliamentarism wavering.

[. . .]

The appearance, out of the same postwar crisis – of which they were indeed the
creatures – of fascism, Nazism and kindred radical-rightist movements complicated
this situation immeasurably. It would be absurd to suggest that Italian fascism, the

National Socialist German Workers' Party (*Nationalsozialistische Deutsche Arbeiter-partei*: NSDAP), the Austrian Heimwehr, the Romanian student nationalists and other 'new' movements of the 1920s owed *nothing* to previous right-wing authoritarian ideas and organizations; on the contrary, in almost every instance a common ideological base is visible. Nevertheless in important respects – both ideological and social – they were *different*. For one thing, they were, in Geoff Eley's words, 'more extreme in every way': shriller in their nationalism, more plebeian in composition and style, less respectful of tradition and of established hierarchies, more violent in their behaviour and, specifically and crucially, their anti-leftism. In some, though admittedly not all, cases, they possessed something of a leftist ancestry themselves, and employed as one weapon in their mixed armoury a quasi- or pseudo-leftist rhetoric. This was certainly true of the two movements which must inevitably shape our perceptions of 'fascism', namely, Italian fascism and the NSDAP. At the very least what we may now classify as 'fascist' movements tended to differentiate themselves from what Mosley, in the next decade, was to label the 'old gang' of conservative and liberal politicians and notables. Whatever may have happened later, these were genuine differences, both subjectively and objectively speaking.

The more or less spontaneous emergence of radical-rightist movements in the 1920s – spontaneous in the sense of being autochthonous and non-imitative – was later, mainly after the onset of economic depression in 1929, followed by the much more deliberate, even calculated, foundation of fascist, national socialist, or clearly *fascisant* movements inspired by the example and supposed success, first of Italian fascism and later of Nazism. The British Union of Fascists, the Juntas de Ofensiva Nacional Sindicalista (JONS) and Falange Española in Spain, Norway's Nasjonal Samling, Portuguese National Syndicalism, the Parti Populaire Français: these are just a few examples of the imitative fascism of the 1930s. It is important to stress the obvious, but all too often ignored, distinction between organizations such as these, and their predecessors which grew, so to speak, organically out of the postwar environment.

[. . .]

The fact remains that in many [countries] [. . .] conservative parties and the interests they represented shifted perceptibly rightwards after 1919. [. . .] The relationship of this process to fascism is far from straightforward. Fascism's achievement of power in Italy probably could not have occurred without the complaisance of a variety of elite groups, conservative-liberal politicians, etc. While regarding Mussolini's movement with considerable suspicion, these elements were nevertheless impressed by its patriotism, youthful energy, mass base and strike-breaking capacity, and convinced that, even if given a taste of power, it could be manipulated in the establishment's interests.

[. . .]

It is not, however, simply a matter of what attitude conservative parties, their supporters and the interests they represented took towards autonomous fascist parties. The installation of the Fascist regime in Italy, especially after the erection of a dictatorship in January 1925, created a model which served not merely for would-be imitators such as Mosley or Quisling but also, albeit usually in a more selective way, for elements within the conservative right itself. This operated in a variety of contexts, affecting conservative parties within parliamentary systems as well as authoritarian regimes with non-fascist, essentially conservative, origins. [It is interesting to see] the extent to which fascism and national socialism ate into Nordic conservatism, inspiring a rash of *fascisant* splinter-groups and interest associations, and in particular infecting conservative youth movements. [Note], however, that constitutional conservatives successfully beat off the radical-rightist challenge. In Spain, the Confederación Española de Derechas Autonomas (CEDA), on behalf of policies which its leaders insisted were not fascist, employed a 'style' which certainly was; here too the party's youth movement, the Juventud de Acción Popular (JAP), suffered at the very least what Stanley Payne has called 'the vertigo of fascism' – and arguably more. Explicitly authoritarian movements of the conservative right were naturally even more prey to fascist influence, in terms of both style and acceptance of extreme solutions; just as Italian Nationalism and conservative Catholicism quickly found a home in the Fascist regime, so in Spain the monarchist right under the Second Republic developed its own brand of 'monarcho-fascism' and leaders such as Calvo Sotelo happily donned the 'fascist' label. The Austrian Heimwehr, while implicitly fascist in style and operation throughout its existence, adopted an explicitly fascist programme in 1930.

[. . .]

Such developments created, during the course of the 1920s and 1930s, a situation at once simple and confused. For many on the left it was simple: since the 'objective' role of interwar right-wing authoritarianism was the defence of capitalism through the violent destruction of the left, all its manifestations could be regarded as 'fascist' whether they accepted the label or not; to put it another way, 'fascism' referred to the role of certain kinds of regime rather than to a particular kind of political movement or set of ideas, and 'fascists' were all those who, by whatever route and with whatever ideological inspiration, sought to create or perpetuate such regimes. Given the fate suffered by leftists at the hands of various kinds of rightist regime, not all of which devotees of analytical rigour would regard as fascist, such an attitude is at least understandable. For those seeking a more rigorous understanding of 'fascism', confusion reigned, since the differences among a whole host of rightist movements and parties, and an increasing number of rightist regimes, tended to be subtly nuanced and constantly shifting.

On the basis of what has been examined so far, it is clearly reasonable to confirm the existence of a distinction, at the level of ideas and movements, between the radical or 'fascist' right and the conservative right, even when the latter gave birth to authoritarian movements of its own. However, for the reasons just discussed, not merely was a boundary between fascists and authoritarian conservatives never drawn with total clarity, but it became more blurred with every year that passed. Matters become more difficult still, however, when we come to examine the fascist-conservative relationship in the context of those regimes to which fascist or national socialist movements made a major contribution or, indeed, which they actually created.

[. . .]

It cannot seriously be denied that as movements, parties and political ideologies, conservatism and fascism occupied very different positions within the early and mid-twentieth century European right, converging at some points and conflicting at others.[2] In certain circumstances, especially characteristic of the 1919–45 period, convergence outweighed conflict, and the uneasy coupling of fascism and conservatism spawned a new kind of political regime. With fascists often showing a tendency to succumb to a cosy conservatism, and conservatives sometimes embracing the rhetoric (or more) of fascism, such regimes exhibited a kaleidoscopic variety of tendencies of which the rarest was what might be termed 'pure' fascism. In many cases, genuine – that is to say self-consciously radical – fascists were a negligible force and any 'fascist' element at most merely cosmetic. Elsewhere, notably in Spain, assorted conservatives proved capable of displacing radical fascism. In Fascist Italy, surely the paradigmatic fascist regime, conservatives co-existed with fascists, survived largely unscathed, and when given the opportunity overthrew the Fascist regime. Only in Germany did the conservative right come close to being devoured by the tiger it had chosen to ride.

Notes

1   The general bibliography on fascism is now vast. The following is intended merely as a selective guide: F. L. Carsten, *The Rise of Fascism* (London, 1967), S. G. Payne, *Fascism: Comparison and Definition* (Madison, Wis, 1980), N. O'Sullivan, *Fascism* (London and Melbourne, 1983), M. Kitchen, *Fascism* (London, 1976), J. Weiss, *The Fascist Tradition. Radical Right-Wing Extremism in Modern Europe* (New York, 1967), E. Weber, *Varieties of Fascism* (Princeton, NJ, 1964), S. J. Woolf (ed), *Fascism in Europe* (London, 1981) [an earlier edition appeared in 1968 as *European Fascism*], S. J. Woolf (ed), *The Nature of Fascism* (London, 1968), A. J. Gregor, *Interpretations of Fascism* (Berkeley, Calif, 1974), W. Laqueur (ed), *Fascism: A Reader's Guide. Analyses, Interpretations, Bibliography* (London, 1976), H. R. Kedward, *Fascism in Western Europe 1900–45* (New York, 1971), N. Poulantzas, *Fascism and Dictatorship* (London, 1979), M. Vajda, *Fascism as a Mass Movement* (London, 1976).
     On the fascist-conservative relationship, see H. Rogger and E. Weber (eds), *The European Right. A Historical Profile* (London, 1965), E. Nolte, *Three Faces of Fascism* (London, 1963), Barrington Moore Jr, *Social Origins of Dictatorship and Democracy. Lord and Peasant in the Making of the Modern World* (London, 1967).
     Two recent volumes examine in detail the social base of fascism: S. U. Larsen, B. Hagtvet and J. Myklebust (eds), *Who Were the Fascists? Social Roots of European Fascism* (Bergen, Oslo and Tromso, 1980) and D. Muhlberger (ed), *The Social Basis of European Fascist Movements* (London, New York and Sydney, 1987).

2   On conservatism see H. Rogger and E. Weber (eds) *The European Right. A Historical Profile*, N. O'Sullivan, *Conservatism* (London, 1976), J. Weiss, *Conservatism in Europe, 1770–1945* (London, 1977), R. Kirk, *The Conservative Mind* (London, 1954), S. P. Huntington, 'Conservatism as an ideology', *American Political Science Review*, vol. LI (1957), pp. 454–73, C. Rossiter, 'Conservatism', in D. L. Sills

(ed), *International Encyclopedia of the Social Sciences* (New York, 1968), Vol III, pp. 290–4, P. Viereck, *Conservatism Revisited* (New York, 1965). See also two issues of the *Journal of Contemporary History* devoted to 'A century of conservatism', vol 13, no 4 (October 1978) and vol 14, no 4 (October 1979).

Chapter 44

Klaus-Jürgen Müller

CONSERVATIVE ELITES AND HITLER: FROM SUPPORT TO OPPOSITION

■ from **THE STRUCTURE AND NATURE OF THE NATIONAL CONSERVATIVE OPPOSITION IN GERMANY UP TO 1940**, in H. W. Koch (ed.) *Aspects of the Third Reich*, Houndmills and London, 1985, pp. 135–6, 142–7, 151–2, 153–4, 156–7, 166–7, 175–7

Klaus-Jürgen Müller's discussion of the 'national conservative opposition' to Hitler focuses on the causes of the conservative elite's gradual estrangement from the regime and the limitations of its oppositional project. For Müller, even at the zenith of disillusionment with Nazism (the Blomberg–Fritsch affair, the Czech crisis of 1938 and the Polish crisis of 1939), the conspirators failed to formulate a coherent alternative policy and did not seriously contemplate the overthrow of the regime – with which they shared a series of objectives from the beginning. Thus, Müller argues, the 'anti-war party' had the trappings of a 'built-in opposition' to the system – not of a resistance opposed to the Nazi regime and its goals.

WHAT IS KNOWN AS 'national conservative resistance' is fundamentally an independent phenomenon in so far as it represents a specific manifestation of the attitude of traditional elites towards National Socialism and the Nazi regime. In this respect a further examination is introduced of the wider framework of the attitudes of traditional power elites in a political and social environment which is experiencing profound secular change. From such a proposition the conservative opposition is conceived as being a specific symptom of politico-social change. It is therefore a question of the activity and attitudes of opposition groups from the areas of the traditional, national conservative ruling elites, mainly those of the military, diplomatic and upper administrative groups from within and (with few exceptions) also outside the apparatus of state.

[. . .] [T]here must also be an attempt to define this national conservative resistance in exact conceptual terms. In the case of the traditional ruling elites, the commonplace term 'opposition' already presents a few difficulties. What does 'opposition' mean in these contexts? What does 'resistance' mean? What is the fundamental difference between 'opposition' and 'resistance'?

Is every contradiction of any high-ranking state functionary on any important political question immediately to be termed 'opposition' within the NS *Führer* state, especially when fundamental aspects of the ruling system, as invested in the functionary concerned, have been accepted and the conventional procedures (lectures, memoranda) adhered to? Is it 'opposition' when actual or implicit agreement on aims exists, although divergences of method are both apparent and expressed? Does the concept of 'opposition' presuppose not only contradiction and dissent, but also a certain basic consent, whereas 'resistance' is distinguished from 'opposition' precisely by the lack of basic consent?

[. . .]

Hitler's government was formed at that time on the basis of an 'entente' between substantial organisations of the traditional power elites and the leaders of the National Socialist mass movement. All of the groups which formed this 'entente' saw in it particular advantages for themselves. The old elites no longer felt capable of maintaining their traditional positions by themselves, or of realising their political objectives either inwardly or outwardly. They lacked, in addition, any basis within society. Hitler, however – or so it seemed to the defenders of the idea of an 'entente' with the NS movement – was able to give them the necessary basis with the masses and thereby solve for them the problem of integration. Hitler, for his part, had to accept that he was unable to get to power on the strength of his own organisation. The events of 9 November 1923 had shown the impossibility of any *coup d'état*: the November elections of 1932 had shown the hopelessness of obtaining power through a parliamentary majority. The mass movement had brought Hitler to the threshold of power, but only the old power elites, who still held the decisive posts within the state apparatus, could help him across it. They alone could procure for him any share of power.

For the military elite, who were not in a position during this phase of rapid politico-social change to achieve any substantial basis of legitimation and action on their own, conditions from now on seemed to be assured for the realisation of most of their fundamental objectives: in home politics there was the recreation and securing of that traditional division of power within both state and society which had been considered since 1918 to be particularly threatened; in foreign politics there was the regaining of the 'great power status' of the Reich, defined as military power politics; and finally, in military politics, there was the permanent and total mobilisation of society, called by the euphemistic name 'defense capacity of the nation', which was considered to be the incontrovertible prerequisite of any status as a great power, given the conditions of an industrial-technological era.

There were also advantages, *mutatis mutandis*, for the non-military elites, who saw their basis in society rapidly dwindling as parliamentary and social change increased and as the power structures, monopolised by the conservative bourgeoisie, were eroded. In this entente the army were allotted, according to their own self-appraisal, a privileged status; Hitler paraphrased this with the formula of the 'two pillars' on which the regime rested – army and party – thereby, through clever tactics, cunningly limiting the expectations of the military.[1] But in foreign ministry circles also, despite the indolence of the Reich foreign secretary von Neurath, 'who considered it more important merely to be in attendance rather than to put through any sensible foreign policy',[2] a tradition of joint responsibility and sharing of power endured. This was embodied by Ernst von Weizsäcker who, on his appointment as secretary of state (February 1938) described this concept with the metaphor that it was a matter of 're-engaging the neutral gear of the Foreign Office to the state engine so that it would help to pull'.[3]

For the representatives of the traditional power elites, this entente promised to create those prerequisites which seemed necessary for the successful attainment of their main objectives. Because of the nature of the entente with the National Socialists in the coalition, the twofold objective described above, with its foreign and home policy components, took on a decisive function in the relationship between the traditional ruling groups and the National Socialist regime. The future development of this relationship was thenceforward fundamentally governed by the degree of fulfilment, or as the case may be, disappointment, of those expectations which had united the elites within the collaboration implicit in the 1933 entente. In concrete terms this meant that this relationship developed, in domestic policy, according to the measure of attainment (or failure) of any joint decision-making power within the state, which assumed a greater importance for the military than for the upper ranks of diplomats; in foreign policy, according to the guarantee (or endangering) of success in the aspiration to be a great power.

A suitable interpretative framework has thus been constructed which enables a sufficiently precise historical definition of the phenomenon 'national conservative opposition' to be made. What is formulated in Hüttenberger's conceptual system as 'resistance' by integral units of a ruling body against other more represented in the historic fact of the national conservative opposition as a definite complementary feature of the entente of the traditional elites with Hitler and his movement. National conservative opposition was thus a specific phenomenon of conflict within the framework of this entente. At the same time, differentiation between national conservative 'opposition' and the resistance of 'a prioristic opponents' becomes possible. Those opposition groups' very being (like that of the National Socialists themselves) in principle allowed them no choice between opposition, neutrality or coalition (or perhaps collaboration) with the National Socialists: groups like the Jews, to whom the NS racist ideology allowed of no possible option; or groups for whom there was no option on philosophical or religious grounds, such as, for instance, Christian fundamentalists. This applies also to supporters of political movements who, like Communists or anarchists, were fighting in principle against the existing[4] social order; irrespective of whether it was a National Socialist or a middle-class parliamentarian order. Therefore the whole spectrum of this particular phenomenon of conflict, which was a complementary feature of the entente of the traditional ruling classes with NS leaders, needs to be fully described because of its varying stances, ranging from those inherent in to those opposed to the system. Also the form, as well as the degree of intensity, of different reactions by individual representatives of those traditional elites to the various demands made by the regime must be fully evaluated. In this respect the following additional analytical categories must be introduced. First, the phenomenon of conflict is to be analysed from the point of view of which of the two essential objectives appeared to be most endangered in the eyes of a cross-section of representatives of the elites; the 'entente' character of the system or the great-power conception in world politics, or both? Given that this consideration of objectives was of all-consuming fundamental importance, it can, for example, be shown as quite plausible that while certain immoral practices and features of the regime in the first years of the Third Reich certainly caused disquiet and criticism in military and diplomatic circles and in the ranks of the upper civil service (as, for example, the suppression of political and ideological opponents, and various anti-semitic and anti-religious measures which directly violated all ideas of tolerance and human rights), it was not until the *va banque* game of 1938 or the intrigue against Fritsch, and immediately prior to the ambitions of the *SA* Chief of Staff Röhm in national defense policies, that any politically significant moves were made by the opposition.

Second, the question has to be asked, by whom and in what way was this endangering of objectives behind the backs of the traditional elite effected? In other words, opponents and dangers must be assessed. With this answered, the possibility then exists of describing and explaining with more precision the breadth of the respective reactions in cases of conflict, and therefore the gradual development from, for instance, defensive assurance of an individual position to offensive stabilisation of the position (such as 'the purging of "radical" elements from the regime' or their elimination from the decision-making process in foreign policy) and thence to plans and attempts to destabilise and overthrow the system. In this respect it was of considerable significance whether certain threats to the essential objectives, as envisaged by representatives of the elites, emanated from individuals and certain groups within the NS movement or from Hitler himself. The quality of their reaction was significantly governed by this: the following three examples show variant combinations.

1   The Röhm affair[5] of June 1934: why did the murder of some conservative adherents in the course of the elimination of the *SA* leadership not produce any significant political reaction on the part of the elected representatives of the officer corps? The answer is clear when the interpretive framework is referred to: Röhm's policy was, for the *Reichswehr* leadership, the first threatening attack on the inner-political position of the army both in its capacity as the monopolist of national strength and as one of the two constituent 'pillars' of the regime. Röhm and his *SA*, with their internal and military political aspirations, were endangering the 'arrangement' of 1933. Hitler, on the other hand, had by his action shown himself to be a loyal partner to the alliance who was merely stabilising the system of the 'two pillars'. Seen in this light, the passivity over the murders, the decision to accept Hitler as Hindenburg's successor and the oath to Hitler are all quite logical.[6] [The decision to fuse the offices of Chancellor and President was made by unanimous cabinet decision on 1 August 1934 and sanctioned by a plebiscite. The result of the latter caused some disquiet in the NS leadership because the votes in favour of it were 3 million down compared with the plebiscite of November 1933 which endorsed Germany's withdrawal from the League of Nations. *Ed.*]

2   In certain phases of the German–Polish crisis, which in turn led to the outbreak of the Second World War, the conduct of the secretary of state, von

Weizsäcker, was influenced for quite a long time by the conviction that the Reich foreign minister, von Ribbentrop, was the only warmonger, while Hitler had merely fallen prey to an erroneous, if fatal, assessment of the international situation; it was just a matter of correcting this by means of informative manipulation. The secretary of state therefore did all he could to gain influence over Hitler's decisions, to the exclusion of the foreign minister. One thing he tried was to persuade the British to issue a warning to Hitler, so that he would have no illusions at all about the reaction of the British government to any German aggression against Poland. This warning was, on the one hand, to be discreet, that is, it should not be made public in order to save the *Führer*'s prestige (every kind of destabilisation of the system was to be avoided) and, on the other hand, it was to be effected, if possible, without the involvement of the foreign minister. Weizsäcker even went so far as to suggest to the British ambassador that he should discredit Ribbentrop.[7] It was a classic case of contra-diplomacy within the framework of a system-adherent power struggle for influence with Hitler.

3   Another example is the Blomberg–Fritsch crisis (winter 1938).[8] If, in the opinion of some national conservative representatives during the Röhm affair and in certain phases of the Polish crisis, it seemed that Hitler could either be relied upon to defend the entente character of the regime or could not himself be numbered among the radical warmongers, he nevertheless played a less distinct role in the Blomberg–Fritsch crisis, at least in the eyes of many of the military. It was mainly the Gestapo and *SS/SD* who had perpetrated a treacherous coup against the army in the intrigue against Fritsch. Hitler's conduct, however, was now at best unfathomable; the solutions, in staff and organisation, which he eventually imposed no longer enabled him to appear to be an arbiter favourable to the army. The Fritsch crisis was therefore a decisive turning point for certain key figures in the later resistance, as is shown in the cases of Admiral Canaris and General Oster.[9] [However, the suggestion that Hitler should assume direct supreme command came from none other than the retiring Field Marshal von Blomberg. *Ed.*]

[. . .]

Before the Blomberg–Fritsch crisis, certain activities took place on two levels which were frequently claimed by writings exclusively aligned to aspects of the resistance to be evidence of determined resistance, but which a closer perusal shows were anything but that. First there were the activities of the internal political information and news service, built up by the then Lt. Colonel Oster under the auspices of the *Abwehr* and accepted and supported by Canaris, which mainly focused its attention on those party organisations (particularly the *SS* and *SD)* which were opposed to the army, and on their criminal machinations.[10] Oster had extended the information facilities which were at his disposal in his official *Abwehr* post by building up a loosely connected network of information sources. He kept in touch with countless individuals who were fundamentally critical of the party or of the regime, and who were mainly from the rightist conservative circles, such as Gisevius, Schlabrendorff,

Halem, Kleist-Schmenzin and Beppo Römer, who were known to him from time spent together in the *Freikorps* or because of social or in-service contacts. (Römer in fact was to end up as a Communist. *Ed.*] They were relevant to his purpose and possessed countless interesting and valuable contacts. But this was by no means that 'significant inter-cooperative and vast organisation of a conspiracy begun in the second half of the thirties'.[11] There can be no question of this being a 'conspiracy', in the sense of a conspiratorial organisation pledged to overthrow the status quo or determined upon a *coup d'état*. On the contrary, the truly discerning eye can see a sort of very loose 'old boy network', made up of former *Freikorps* members and right-wing conservatives, extended by accidental or socially established contact with critically aligned individuals, which together formed the basis of Oster's internal political system of information and contact. But it was nothing more than that.

[. . .]

The Blomberg–Fritsch crisis[12] in more ways than one forms a decisive landmark in the history leading up to the later military opposition. In the first place, for many national conservatives, already critical of isolated events as well as of certain tendencies developing in the regime, it was a turning point and the beginning of an increasing disillusionment with the nature of the regime itself. At this point some decisive moves were made in the direction of later resistance activities. In the second place, the crisis also had the effect of a catalyst: many different individuals who had previously only been in loose contact with one another now, for the first time, united in closer and more direct association. A more exact analysis shows that it was still in no way a case of the formation of a kind of unified, coherent opposition grouping, but a move towards activities and cooperation on very different levels, with extremely diverse motives, objectives and methods, carried on by a whole variety of persons and groups.[13]

[. . .]

Thus the Fritsch crisis mainly brought about a climax in the internal political struggle for power which was inherent in the system, but was in no way a conspiracy aimed at the overthrow of the system, even in its initial stages.

It was not until the Sudeten crisis,[14] between April and September 1938, that further crucial moves were made. In this international crisis there arose for the first time a few loosely-knit organisational groups which could be termed an 'anti-war party'. They lent a new dynamism both to the trends of evolutionary regime reform and to those of violent regime purging. These three components – anti-war party, evolutionary regime reform groups and violent regime purge groups – provided the phenomenon which was often called (in much too unspecific and abbreviated a way) 'the German opposition' or 'the German resistance'. It was a very complex structure which was prohibitive of any all-inclusive label giving the idea of a united movement.[15] Concepts such as 'plot', 'conspiracy' or 'anti-Hitler fringe' can be considered as only very indistinct approximations; they fall well short of the truth and do not possess the analytical strength and selectivity required in this matter.

The outstanding representatives of this 'anti-war party' in the international crisis of 1938 were, on the military side, the chief of the general staff, Beck,[16] then his successor General Halder[17] and the *Abwehr* chief Admiral Canaris;[18] on the German diplomatic side it was secretary of state von Weizsäcker.[19] The partial and short-term combination of efforts towards the prevention of war, together with indications of the internal political power struggle (in its evolutionary-reformative form), and above all the political motive structure of the 'anti-war party', and the consequent effects of these three components, were all crucial factors in determining the nature of the activities and the limits of capacity for action of these elements.

For all four representatives of the 'anti-war party' the central issue of their external political objectives was the idea of a German great power status in central and eastern Europe. This objective was self-evident and beyond question. It went beyond any mere revision of the Treaty of Versailles. What was intended was a fundamental reshaping of the central European scene envisaging German hegemony. As far as the methods with which such a concept was to be carried out were concerned, there was also agreement in principle between these individuals. None of them denied the possibility of the involvement of military power or even of war. Moreover, military power and its possible deployment was an integral part of their calculations, even if in varying degrees of importance. Again, they were in agreement over the stipulation that such a policy should never lead to an all-out European war. Limited and politically controlled martial conflicts were not excluded from this concept, even if they were not a foregone conclusion in any plans. A combination of diplomacy (assurance through alliances and agreements between the great powers) with military deployment was the basis of the concept on which these men, with all their individual differences, were agreed.

[. . .]

The nature of the anti-war party and its opportunities can be further clarified by an analysis of its structure. Its actual nucleus – and this word is not used in the sense of its organisation but as an identification of the principal representatives of that central and all-exclusive objective, prevention of war – consisted of the high-ranking officers already mentioned and, in the diplomatic field, Weizsäcker. From him emanated activities which ran parallel to those of Canaris and Beck, and which – so it seems – took place partly and temporarily in coordination with them. Beneath this small central group there was the circle around Oster and Gisevius. For them, in contrast to the Beck–Canaris–Weizsäcker group, the efforts to prevent a war rapidly became a vehicle for considering a *coup d'état*. For them the overthrow of the regime was the prime objective, in the face of which the prevention of war took on a secondary and instrumental function. In their oppositional aspirations they were more radical, but in their means and possibilities, because of their subsidiary posts within the apparatus of power, they lacked any significant opportunities for influence. For this reason they were constantly on the lookout for a general who would be prepared to support their subversive manifesto, and to cooperate with Beck and Canaris. They were also concerned with broadening the basis of their campaign, if possible by the involvement of more high-powered statesmen. With this in mind they made contact with Schacht, put out feelers to Brauchitsch and made overtures to some younger members of the foreign office who were critical of the regime.[20]

On a third level there was a string of individuals who were activated by both these groupings in complete independence of each other. They took over (as previously mentioned) various supportive functions for the anti-war party, either as emissaries on secret diplomatic missions or for the purpose of exercising influence internally on various high-ranking officials. They were made up both of individuals from the critical and dissatisfied national conservative milieu who found themselves outside the apparatus of state, such as Kleist-Schmenzin, and of men who fulfilled functions at a wide range of levels within the state service, such as Count Schwerin. the brothers Kordt or, on a higher political plain, Schacht. These were people with a wide variety of oppositional attitudes. Many had their own, highly individual, political ideas which (as Kleist-Schmenzin did, for example) they expounded on their own account to their foreign counterparts in completely independent extensions of their allotted foreign missions. This contributed in no small way to the fact that the view of the German opposition was made no clearer, and even became more distorted.[21] Within the framework of our enquiry, they nevertheless play a subsidiary but instrumental role as 'auxiliary organs' with the anti-war party or the subversion groups. They did not, however, possess any oppositional importance in their own right.

[. . .]

These sort of activities (especially in view of the conditions prevalent in a totalitarian regime) should rather be considered as built-in opposition, as opposition in traditional political parlance, namely as attempts to introduce and carry out an alternative policy. That is not to say that the ethically significant intention of preserving peace for Europe and the Reich should be considered any less important; it is merely that, for these activities, the term 'opposition' is simply not appropriate in the sense of a resistance opposed to the system; it was rather opposition as an attempt to put through an alternative policy within the system. This in turn clarifies the nature of the activities of the anti-war party in this phase. These consisted of bringing influence to bear on the process of decision-making both by means of normal procedures along official channels with peripheral measures based on the usual diplomatic political tactics, and also of activities which would be considered as a kind of counter-diplomacy: an interplay with allies and representatives of states with which the Reich leadership was in controversy at the time but which were likewise interested in the prevention of war. Whatever form the attempts at gaining effective influence on the central foreign policy decision-making process may have taken – information, counter-information, occasional false information, back-room talks and talks to gain opposite effect – it nevertheless all remained the type of opposition inherent in the system.[22] In this phase of development before the outbreak of war there was no earnest consideration or even preparation for war prevention using measures likely to destabilise the system. In May 1939, when Goerdeler reported to his British counterparts that the German army was still prepared for the overthrow of the regime but that it was a question of choosing the right time, that although he himself was ready for action, 'the leaders of the whole movement . . .

still considered it too early', then this was either an assessment of the situation stemming from his own pipe-dreams or a conscious delivery of false information [such
as a completely falsified version of Hitler's speech to his generals of 22 August 1939
designed to harden British attitudes against any compromise solution. *Ed.*] by which
he intended to make the British take some action.[23] Gisevius states here, quite rele-
vantly, with bitter self-criticism: 'In these dramatic days before the outbreak of war
there is absolutely nothing heroic to be reported about the attitude of the German
opposition . . . we must be content with the simple fact that nothing notable has
been done.'[24] This was the situation as expressed by that small group of radicals
opposed to the system, but it was equally, if not more, relevant to the antiwar party
which wished to retain the system. Their efforts had been in vain on at least three
accounts. First because of the lack of coordination in their activities, they provided
their foreign counterparts across a broad front with a confused and even contradictory view of things.[25] Second, many of their interventions and much of their advice
were contradictory and even countermanding.[26] Third, the greatest reason for the
failure of their efforts lay in the fact that they failed to recognise Hitler's absolute
war intentions. Weizsäcker still believed for a long time in summer 1939 in a 'huge
bluff on Hitler's part with the intention in the end still of giving in',[27] and that their
Prusso-German revisionist and 'great power' views coincided almost completely, in
the case of Poland, with Hitler's immediate objectives as he continued his course of
confrontation with the Reich's eastern neighbour. Canaris furthered the anti-Polish
nationality and Ukrainian policy while Weizsäcker, at the end of 1938, tried to
distract Ribbentrop and Hitler from the Czechoslovak problem and on to the question of Poland (Danzig and the Corridor) and some time later he advised 'being
clearer to the Russians in Moscow on the question of the division of Poland'.[28] There
can be no question but that all this contributed not only to the fatal momentum of
the developing crisis between Munich and the outbreak of war, but also to the final
futility of all efforts of the anti-war party.

Notes

1   See M. Messerschmidt, *Die Wehrmacht im NS-Staat. Zeit der Indoktrination* (Hamburg, 1969), passim.

2   Quoted from R. A. Blasius, *Für Grossdeutschland – gegen den grossen Krieg. Ernst v.
Weizsäcker in den Krisen über die Tschechoslowakei und Polen* (Cologne/Vienna, 1981),
24 (also the relevant literature cited there on E. v. Weizsäcker).

3   Ernst v. Weizsäcker, *Die Weizsäcker-Papiere*, ed. by L. E. Hill (Berlin, 1974).

4   Huttenberger, 'Voruberlegungen zum "Widerstandsbegriff"', 133.

5   On the Röhm affair see K.-J. Muller, *Das Heer und Hitler. Armee und nationalsozialistisches Regime 1933–1940* (Stuttgart, 1969), Chapter III, as well as his
'Reichswehr und "Röhm-Affäre"', in *Militärgeschichtliche Mitteilungen* 3 (1968),
107–44 and Ch. Bloch, *Die SA und die Krise des NS-Regimes 1934* (Frankfurt, 1970).

6   On this point see Blasius, *Für Grossdeutschland*, *passim* and the literature mentioned
there.

7   Ibid., 120, 121, 125. See special emissary Henderson's letter to Lord Halifax of
21 August 1939, about Weizsäcker's suggestion that General Ironside should send
a warning letter from the British prime minister to Hitler: 'His visit might at least

help to discredit Ribbentrop', *Documents on British Foreign Policy 1919–1939*, ed. by E. L. Woodward and R. Butler (London, 1946) (in future abbreviated to *DBFP*), 3rd series, vol. vii, no. 117, 109.

8   See K.-J. Müller, *Das Heer und Hitler* (Stuttgart, 1969), Chapter iv, 'Blomberg-Skandal und Fritsch-Krise', as well as H. C. Deutsch, *Das Komplott oder die Entmachtung der Generale. Blomberg- und Fritsch-Krise. Hitlers Weg zum Krieg* (Zurich, 1974).

9   B. Scheurig, *Henning von Tresckow. Eine Biographie* (Hamburg, 1973, 1980). H. Graml, 'Der Fall Oster', in *Vierteljahrshefte für Zeitgeschichte* (Munich, 1966), 26–39. General Beck noted at the time his impression that the Fritsch case 'had opened a chasm between Hitler and the officer corps, especially in respect of mutual trust, which could never again be bridged', *Bundesarchiv-Militärarchiv* no. 28/3, sheet 43–5, note of 29 July 1938; cf. H. Höhne, *Canaris, Patriot im Zwielicht* (Munich, 1976).

10   On this, see especially Hohne, *Canaris*, Chapter 8, along with the most recent literature.

11   With reference to the inter-connections of personnel, especially informative is: Hoffmann, *Widerstand*, Chapter ii; the quotation is from there.

12   See on this and on the following, Deutsch, *Das Komplott*, as well as the relevant chapters in Hoffmann, *Widerstand* (Chapter vi) and Müller, *Heer und Hitler* (Chapter vi). For Canaris see Höhne, *Canaris*, 244ff.

13   The background to which these developments took place was the increasingly critical attitude which prevailed in sections of the national-conservative milieu, who were disappointed with the development of the regime. The rapidly spreading dissatisfaction in these circles, which had helped in 1933 to carry the 'national rebirth' as far as possible, is however, in no way to be labelled 'opposition'. At best it was the root-base for a possible formation of such opposition, but nothing more, even if many of these disappointed national-conservatives were inclined to profess themselves to be an 'opposition', especially when describing to counter-parts abroad the whole mood of their circles, even though completely misunderstanding the true nature of the existing power relationships (see, as example, the comments of Koerber to Mason MacFarlane, *DBFP*, 3rd series, vol. ii, no. 595, 65). Beck, Canaris and Hossbach, on the other hand, were completely free of such illusions at this time.

14   On this and on the following see H. K. G. Roennefarth, *Die Sudetenkrise in der international Politik. Entstehung, Verlauf, Auswirkung*, vol. 2 (Wiesbaden, 1961); as well as K.-J. Müller, *Ludwig Beck*. Studieu und Dokumente zur politisch-utilitärischen Vorstellungswelt des Generalstabschefs des deutschen iteeres, 1933–1938 (Boppard, 1980), Chapter v and vi, and R. A. Blasius, *Grossdeutschland*, passim (along with the most recent literature). Also K. G. Robbins, *Munich* (London, 1978) and E. H. Carr, *The Twenty Years' Crisis* (London, 1939), first edition only.

15   This suggests mainly the work by Hoffmann, *Widerstand*.

16   For this and for the following, in detail, see Müller, *Ludwig Beck*; a synopsis of the findings in this book in K.-J. Müller, *Armee, Politik und Gesellschaft* in Deutschland, 1933–1945 (3rd edn, Padeborn, 1981), the paragraph headed 'Generaloberst Ludwig Beck. Generalstabchef des deutschen Heeres 1933–1938. Einige Reflektionen und neuere Forschungsergebnisse', 51–100.

17   See G. R. Ueberschär, 'Generaloberst Halder im militärischen Widerstand', 1938–1940', in *Wehrforschung*, I (1973), H. I, 20–31.

18   See, in addition, Höhne, *Canaris*, passim.

19   See Blasius, *Grossdeutschland*.

20   On the role of the brothers Theo and Erich Kordt in the foreign office, about the circle around these two and their contacts with other oppositionists see Blasius, *Grossdeutschland*, 55f., 141ff. (with corresponding sources and literature).

21   On this point, see S. Aster, *Second World War, 1939* (London, 1973), as well as B.-J. Wendt, *München 1938. England zwischen Hitler und Preussen* (Frankfurt, 1965).

22   See the résumé of the analysis by Blasius, *Grossdeutschland*, 162: Weizsäcker, 'it is true, despised the Nazi regime, but, because of his attitude during the crises concerning Czechoslovakia and Poland is not to be considered as a "man of resistance" against Hitler. Weizsäcker was counting on the common sense of the *Führer*, and, in order to influence the *Führer*'s decisions, he thought it necessary to wrestle with the "war-monger" Ribbentrop.'

23   Quotation from Aster, *Second World War*, 230f.

24   Hans B. Gisevius, *Bis zum bitteren Ende* (Hamburg, 1947), 403f.

25   This is shown most impressively by the findings evaluated in Aster, *Second World War*. In addition, the British also had dealings to attend to with Hitler's official emissaries, who came to London outside the normal diplomatic channels, such as Wiedemann, Reichenau, etc.

26   For example, Schwerin suggested to the British that they should send a part of the fleet into the Baltic as a demonstration, while, at the same time, Weizsäcker was busy persuading Hitler, by reason of detente, not to send a German fleet to Danzig. (On the Schwerin mission: Aster, *Second World War*, 235, 237f.)

27   *Weizsäcker-Papiere*, 163 (31 August 1939).

28   On Canaris see Höhne, *Canaris*, 302f., 320ff., as well as Groscurth, *Tagebucher*, 171, 173 ('The great Reichstag speech of the Führer now sets in motion our work ag016.nst Poland. That is good and is about time, too') and pp. 178ff.; on Weizsäcker see *Weizsäcker-Papiere*, 150ff., 175f. (quotation p. 157, entry of 30 July 1939); on Halder: see in Müller, *Heer und Hitler*, 545f., 567 the supporting proof of Halder's innate anglophobia and his essential agreement on the need for a settlement of the question of the eastern borders; on 15 October 1965 Halder wrote to the author: 'That England was, in fact, the key protagonist in the struggle between the western powers and Germany, I have never doubted.'

Chapter 45

Henry A. Turner Jr

INDUSTRIAL ELITES AND THE RISE OF NATIONAL SOCIALISM

■ from **BIG BUSINESS AND THE RISE OF HITLER**, *America Historical Review*, 75 (1969), pp. 56, 58, 59–70

One of the most persisting 'legends', in Henry A. Turner Jr's words, about the rise of Nazism in Germany is the alleged financial and political backing of Hitler by the leadership of German industry. In the following excerpt Turner challenges this conventional assumption by stressing the limited (in material terms), inconsistent and half-hearted support that the Nazis received from industrialists prior to Hitler's appointment in January 1933. That eventually many big-industry bosses turned to Hitler, as late as December 1932, is attributed by Turner to their frustration with Chancellor Kurt von Schleicher and their impression that, by helping Hitler, they effectively heralded the return of their favourite, Franz von Papen, to power (Papen became Vice-Chancellor in Hitler's cabinet). For Turner, the support of the industrialists for Hitler became a significant factor after the latter's appointment, helping him to retain – but not to acquire – power.

DID GERMAN BIG BUSINESS SUPPORT Adolf Hitler's climb to power? A quarter of a century after the demise of the Third Reich, this remains one of the major unresolved questions about its inception. [. . .] None of the new evidence contradicts the widespread impression that German big businessmen were unenthusiastic about the Weimar Republic. Most were not, as is often assumed, unreconstructed monarchists; they displayed, on the whole, a surprising indifference to governmental forms. What offended them about the new state was its adoption of costly welfare measures, its introduction of compulsory arbitration in disputes between labor and management, and, most particularly, the influence it accorded to the prolabor Social Democratic party, which was most pronounced in the

government of the largest federal state, Prussia. Despite abundant objective evidence
that the republic, at least during its years of prosperity, provided generally favorable conditions for business enterprise, Germany's business leaders continued to eye
it with misgiving. Their attitude had much in common with that of the army: they,
too, refused to commit themselves to the new state, regarding it as a potentially
transitory phenomenon, while viewing themselves as the guardians of something of
more permanent value to the nation – in their case, *die Wirtschaft*, the industrial
sector of the economy.[1]

In spite of its reserved attitude toward the new German state, big business was
nevertheless politicized by the changes resulting from the Revolution of 1918.
Whereas in the Empire its leaders had been able to influence governmental policy
without wholesale commitment to partisan politics, in the republic they found it
necessary to assume a more active political role.[2] In far greater numbers than in the
Empire, they joined the ranks of the *bürgerlich*, or nonsocialist, parties and sought
places in the Parliaments for themselves or their spokesmen.[3] For most big businessmen, politics was more a matter of interests than of ideology.[4] When they took
the trouble to describe their political outlook, the words that reoccurred with
greatest frequency were 'national' and 'liberal.' The term 'liberal' has always been
problematical in German usage, but in business circles of this period it was more so
than usual, as was revealed by one businessman who, writing to an acquaintance,
explained: 'As you well know, I have always been liberal, in the sense of Kant and
Frederick the Great.'[5]

[. . .]

A number of legends about industrial support for the Nazis have been perpetuated
by previous literature and, largely by virtue of repetition, have come to be accepted
as fact. According to one of these legends, large sums of money flowed to the Nazis
through the hands of Alfred Hugenberg, the reactionary press lord who became head
of the Right-wing German National People's party in 1928.[6] This allegation probably derives from Hugenberg's role in the campaign against the Young plan in 1929.
As one of the organizations supporting that campaign, the Nazi party did receive a
share of the funds that Hugenberg helped to raise at the time.[7] There is not a trace
of documentary evidence, however, that any of Hugenberg's resources were thereafter diverted to the Nazis.[8] Indeed, this seems highly unlikely: as the leader of a
party that was itself beset by financial problems, Hugenberg had little motive to share
any funds he received from big business, least of all with a party that was taking votes
away from his own.[9] The amount of big business money at Hugenberg's disposal
has, in any event, been grossly exaggerated. Contrary to the widespread belief that
he was one of the foremost spokesmen of big business throughout the republican
period, most of the industrial backers of his party had opposed his election as its
chairman in 1928, rejecting him as too inflexible, too provocative, and too high-
handed for their tastes.[10] In the summer of 1930 a large segment of his party's
industrial wing took issue with his opposition to Heinrich Brüning's cabinet and
seceded to join the new Conservative People's party.[11] Even among those who did
not take that step, there was a strong movement to replace Hugenberg with a more

moderate man. As a result, Hugenberg, who had enjoyed wide support from big business during the first decade of the republic, was forced, during its last years, to rely increasingly upon the backing of agricultural interests.[12]

Another persistent legend concerns Emil Kirdorf, long universally regarded as a kind of industrial *alter Kämpfer*.[13] Kirdorf, an octogenarian survivor of the beginning phase of German heavy industry in the 1870's, was the first really noteworthy business figure to join the Nazi party, entering in 1927. But despite the tributes lavished upon him by Hitler and the party press during the Third Reich, he was far from a loyal Nazi. In 1928, only a little over a year after joining the party, Kirdorf resigned in anger, a fact that the Nazis long succeeded in concealing from historians.[14] Eventually, it is true, he rejoined the party, but only in 1934, when on personal orders from Hitler Kirdorf's records were rewritten to make his membership seem uninterrupted. But during the crucial years 1929–1933 Kirdorf was a supporter of the German National People's party, not the Nazi party. Nor is there any evidence that Kirdorf contributed appreciable sums to the Nazis during the struggle for power. Since he had retired from all active business posts even before joining the party for the first time in 1927, he had no access to corporate or associational funds.[15] Anything he gave had to come from his own pocket, and he was not known as a man who spent his money either gladly or lavishly. Kirdorf's reputation as a patron of National Socialism rests not on documented facts but on a myth created in large measure by the Nazis themselves following his reentry into the party, when they appropriated the aged industrialist as a symbol of respectability.

The reason for Kirdorf's resignation from the party is indicative of the attitude of most big businessmen toward National Socialism in the years before Hitler achieved power. Kirdorf did not withdraw because the Nazis were antidemocratic, aggressively chauvinistic, or anti-Semitic (even though he, like most business leaders, was himself not an anti-Semite). What drove him out of the party was the social and economic radicalism of the Left-wing Nazis. Like millions of other Germans of middle-class background, including big businessmen, Kirdorf was attracted to Nazism by its assertive nationalism and its implacable hostility toward Marxism, but, like most big businessmen, he was at the same time repelled by the fear that the National Socialists might eventually live up to their name by turning out to be socialists of some kind. Hitler, who began earnestly to court the business community in 1926, went to great pains to allay this fear. In 1927, at the request of Kirdorf, he wrote a pamphlet that was secretly printed and then distributed in business circles by the old industrialist.[16] In the pamphlet, as in his speech before the Düsseldorf *Industrie-Klub* in January 1932, Hitler sought to indicate that there was no need to fear socialism from his party. It is safe to assume that he said much the same thing in his numerous other meetings with representatives of big business.[17] His efforts, however, were repeatedly compromised, as in the case of Kirdorf, by the radical noises emanating from the Left Wing of the Nazi party.[18]

As a consequence, most of the political money of big business went, throughout the last years of the republic, to the conservative opponents, of the Nazis.[19] In the presidential campaign of 1932 most of the business community backed Paul von Hindenburg against Hitler, despite the Nazi leader's blatant appeal for support in his *Industrie-Klub* speech.[20] In the two Reichstag elections of 1932, big business was overwhelmingly behind the bloc of parties that supported the cabinet of Franz von Papen, the first government since the Revolution of 1918 to arouse enthusiasm in business circles.[21] If money could have purchased political power, the republic would have been succeeded by Papen's *Neuer Staat*, not by Hitler's *Drittes Reich*. But the effort to transform marks into votes proved a crushing failure.

There were, to be sure, exceptions to this pattern. Certain big businessmen did give money to the Nazis, particularly after the 1930 Reichstag election showed them to be a major political factor. Some of these contributions can best be described, however, as political insurance premiums. This was clearly the case, for example, with Friedrich Flick, a parvenu intruder into the ranks of the Ruhr industrialists, who by the early 1930s had managed to secure a dominant position in the country's largest steel-producing firm, the United Steel Works (*Vereinigte Stahlwerke*). Flick's speculative transactions and his questionable dealings with the Brüning cabinet left him vulnerable to attacks from the press and apprehensive about the attitude of future cabinets toward his enterprises.[22] His solution was to spread his political money across the political spectrum, from the liberal and Catholic parties to the Nazi party. Flick may be a deplorable example of the politically amoral capitalist, but he was by no means an enthusiastic supporter of National Socialism prior to 1933. Nor is there any indication that he was especially generous toward the Nazis. According to the records he produced at his war crimes trial in Nuremberg, the Nazis received little more than token contributions in comparison to the sums that went to their opponents.[23]

The political activities of the I. G. Farben chemical trust were characterized by much the same pattern as those of Flick. From its formation in 1925, the company maintained contact with all the nonsocialist parties and made financial contributions to them. According to the postwar accounts of one official of the trust, the Nazis were added to the list in 1932. That same official estimated the total contributions for one of the Reichstag election campaigns of 1932 (it is not clear whether he was referring to the July or November elections) at approximately 200,000 to 300,000 marks. Of this, he reported, no more than 10 to 15 percent had gone to the Nazis.[24] I. G. Farben, like Flick, had special reason to be concerned about maintaining the good will of the political parties. In its case, this concern arose from heavy investments in elaborate processes designed to yield high-grade synthetic gasoline. Since the costs of production were initially high, the company could hope to break into the domestic market only if a protective tariff were imposed on oil imports. Such a tariff had been put into effect by the Brüning cabinet and maintained by the Papen regime, but in view of Germany's obviously chronic political instability, the tariff question remained a source of considerable anxiety to the leadership of the firm. When attacks on Farben appeared in the Nazi press in 1932, concern developed about the attitude of what was by then the country's strongest political party. Two minor officials were, accordingly, sent to Munich in the autumn of 1932 to sound out Hitler on the project.[25] Much has been made of this episode by some writers, who have inferred that it produced a deal that brought Farben behind the National Socialist movement at a crucial time.[26] From all available evidence, however, the firm's representatives came away with only vague assurances from Hitler that he would halt the attacks in the party press.[27] The Nazis apparently received at most the small share of the relatively modest political funds described above, although even this may, in view of the ambiguity of the evidence, have been granted earlier, at the time of the summer election campaign, and thus quite independently of the Munich meeting with Hitler. There is, in any case, no evidence that the chemical combine wanted a Nazi triumph or threw its financial support decisively to National Socialism. All indications are, in fact, that the leaders of Farben, acutely aware of their firm's dependence on exports, were apprehensive at the prospect of a take-over of the government by a party that preached economic autarky.[28]

As in the cases of Flick and I. G. Farben, most of the big business money that found its way to the Nazis was not given simply, or even primarily, with the aim of bringing them to power. Whereas Flick and Farben were seeking to buy political insurance against the eventuality of a Nazi capture of the government, others were attempting to alter the nature of the Nazi movement. This they hoped to accomplish by giving money to 'sensible' or 'moderate' Nazis, thereby strengthening that ele-ment and weakening the economically and socially radical tendencies that had always been the chief obstacles to cooperation between big business and National Socialism. There was, however, no agreement as to who the 'sensible' Nazis were. Thyssen, one of the few who really wanted a Nazi triumph, was nevertheless concerned about radicalism in the party. He sought to counteract it by subsidizing the man he regarded as the bulwark of moderation, Hermann Goring, who used at least a considerable portion of Thyssen's money to indulge his taste for lavish living.[29] Hermann Bücher, head of the large electrical equipment concern, *Allgemeine Elektrizitats-Gesellschaft*, tried to combat Nazi radicalism by giving financial aid to Joseph Goebbels's rival in Berlin, storm troop leader Walter Stennes, in his short-lived revolt.[30] Surprisingly, the directors of the principal organization of the coal industry, the *Bergbau-Verein*, saw their 'moderate' Nazi in Gregor Strasser — usually classified as a leader of the Left Wing — and for a time channeled funds to him.[31] Still others gave money to Walther Funk, the former editor of a conservative financial newspaper, who bore at least the title of economic adviser to Hitler and who was regarded in some business quarters as a 'liberal' Nazi and a potential moderating influence.[32]

Not all attempts to alter the Nazis' economic and social attitudes involved finan-cial contributions. Kirdorf, for example, maintained cordial personal relations with Hitler even after resigning from the party in 1928, and sought to exert influence on the Führer by making clear his objections to the Left-wing Nazis and to the radical planks in the party program.[33] Much the same attempt was made by the *Keppler-Kreis*, the group of businessmen assembled in the spring of 1932 at Hitler's request by one of his advisers, Wilhelm Keppler. Later, during the Third Reich, after this group was appropriated by Heinrich Himmler and transformed into his *Freundeskreis*, it became a source of enormous contributions for the SS.[34] But prior to the acqui-sition of power by the Nazis, it was merely an advisory body, seeking, without success, to bring about a commitment of the party to conservative economic policies; it did not serve as a channel for business contributions.[35]

The question of whether the Nazis were aided appreciably by the big business money that did reach them from those who were seeking either to buy protection or to alter the nature of the party cannot at present be definitively answered: igno-rance about Nazi finances is a major handicap that deserves far more attention than it has received. But it is known, from Goebbels's diary and other sources, that the Nazis were plagued by acute money problems until the very moment of Hitler's appointment as Chancellor.[36] It thus seems clear that the sums received were not sufficient to solve the party's financial problems. The significant point, in any case, is that the funds reaching the Nazis from big business were but a small fraction of those that went to their opponents and rivals. On balance, big business money went overwhelmingly against the Nazis.

In spite of all this, it is nevertheless true that most business leaders were favorably inclined toward the new cabinet installed on January 30, 1933, with Hitler as Chancellor. It has been alleged that this was only the expression of attitudes already discernible at least as early as November, when, following the poor showing of the Papen bloc at the polls, some businessmen had, at the instigation of the *Keppler-Kreis*, petitioned Hindenburg to appoint Hitler Chancellor. But the attitude of those who signed the petition was not typical of the outlook of big business in November 1932; nor did the list of signatories include any major business figures, aside from Thyssen, who had for some time made no secret of his support for the Nazis. Another signatory, Hjalmar Schacht, is often assigned to the ranks of big business, but as of 1932 he is more properly classified as a political adventurer.[37]

The change of outlook occurred for most businessmen in December 1932; its primary cause was Kurt von Schleicher. It is difficult to exaggerate their distrust and fear of the man who became Chancellor on December 3. They were hostile to him in part for his role in bringing down Papen, the one Chancellor they had admired and trusted. But even more important was Schleicher's apparent indifference to orthodox economic principles and traditional class alignments. Shortly after becoming Chancellor he caused the gravest apprehension in business circles by announcing that he was neither a capitalist nor a socialist. He also flirted openly with the trade unions, raising the specter of an alliance of the military and the working class against the propertied elements of society. As a result, Germany's big businessmen feared that Schleicher might turn out to be a socialist in military garb.[38] It was more from a desire to be rid of him than from enthusiasm for what was to replace him that they applauded the events of January 1933.

Contrary to what has often been asserted, big business played no part in the intrigues of that month. Much has been made of the role of Baron Kurt von Schroeder, the banker at whose home in Cologne Hitler and Papen met on January 4 to conspire against Schleicher. Schroeder was, however, not acting as an agent of big business. His importance lay in the fortuitous fact that he was acquainted with both Papen and Keppler, Hitler's adviser, and could thus serve as a convenient intermediary between two sides anxious to join forces.[39] Nor is there any evidence that the meeting at his house began a flow of business money to the Nazis, as has repeatedly been alleged.[40] Money was, in any event, not what mattered in January 1933. What counted was influence with Hindenburg, and big business had little or none of that. From the President's *Junker* standpoint, even the most powerful bankers and industrialists were little better than shopkeepers.

Most of the leaders of big business were, to the very end, under a basic misapprehension about the nature of the new cabinet taking shape in January 1933. Their information came mainly from Papen and his circle, and they were led to believe that what was coming was a revival of the Papen cabinet, with its base widened through the inclusion of the Nazis. Even when it was learned that Papen would be Vice-Chancellor under Hitler, big business continued to assume that he would be the real leader of the new government.[41] In the eyes of the business community, January 30, 1933, seemed at first to mark the fall of the hated Schleicher and the return of the trusted Papen, not the advent of a Nazi dictatorship.

By the time the leaders of big business were disabused of this illusion, they were ready to make their peace with Hitler. One factor in this turn of events was the ability of the new Chancellor, as the legally installed head of government, to appeal to their respect for constituted authority. But even more important, once he was in office Hitler demonstrated that he was, as he had always reassured them, not a socialist. He therefore had no difficulty in extracting large sums from big business, starting with the campaign for the Reichstag election of March 1933. These contributions unquestionably aided Hitler significantly. But they aided him in the consolidation of his power, not in its acquisition. He had achieved that without the support of most of big business, indeed in spite of its massive assistance to his opponents and rivals.

These observations are in no sense intended as an exoneration of German big business. Its political record in the period that ended with the establishment of the Third Reich is hardly praiseworthy. In numerous ways its leaders contributed indirectly to the rise of Nazism: through their failure to support the democratic republic; through their blind hostility to the Social Democrats and the labor unions; through their aid to reactionary forces, most conspicuously the Papen regime; and through the respectability they bestowed upon Hitler by receiving him into their midst on a number of occasions. Some contributed more directly, by giving money to the Nazi party, or at least to certain Nazis. None of this, however, should be allowed to obscure the central fact that the great majority of Germany's big businessmen had neither wanted a Nazi triumph nor contributed materially to it.

The last statement, it should be emphasized, does not necessarily apply to the German business community as a whole. There are, in fact, indications that Hitler received considerable support from small- and middle-sized business.[42] This is not surprising, for it was there that the real and potential entrepreneurial victims of the Great Depression were to be found. The giant businesses of the country knew from past experience that their importance to the national economy was so great that no government could afford to let them go bankrupt; in fact, the cabinets of the republic repeatedly came to the aid of ailing big business concerns rather than face the sharp increase in unemployment that their collapse would entail.[43] Smaller, less visible firms could expect no such protection from the abrasive mechanisms of cyclical contraction; for their owners and managers, economic extinction was a real possibility, with the consequence that they were often genuinely desperate men. But the fact nevertheless remains that these small- and middle-sized businessmen can by no stretch of the imagination be included in the ranks of German big business, or, to use Marxist terminology, 'the monopoly capitalists.' Therefore, unless one is willing to accept the simplistic *cui bono* approach, according to which the eventual economic beneficiaries of Hitler's acquisition of power must necessarily have supported him beforehand, or the sophistic distinction between subjective and objective roles in history that is so popular in Marxist circles, it must be concluded that during its rise to power National Socialism was, in socioeconomic terms, primarily a movement not of winners in the capitalist struggle for survival but of losers and those who feared becoming losers. [. . .]

Notes

1   This theme runs through the speeches of big businessmen during the entire republican period. Many of these can be found in the *Veröffentlichungen* of the national association of industry, the *Reichsverband der Deutschen Industrie* (Berlin, 1919– 1932).

2   Two recent studies of the political role of big business in the Empire are Lamar Cecil, *Albert Ballin: Business and Politics in Imperial Germany, 1888–1918* (Princeton, N.J., 1967); and Hans Jaeger, *Unternehmer in der deutschen Politik (1890–1918)* (Bonn, 1967).

3   See Ingolf Liesebach, 'Der Wandel der politischen Führungsschicht der deutschen Industrie von 1918 bis 1945' (diss., University of Basel, 1957).

4   On February 18, 1919, Albert Vögler, a prominent figure in the steel industry who had been elected to the National Assembly as a delegate of the German People's party, caused considerable consternation among his fellow deputies by announcing in his maiden speech to the chamber: 'I speak here as the representative of an industry . . .' (*Verhandlungen der verfassunggebenden deutschen Nationalversammlung*, CCCXXVI, 137). Thereafter, the parliamentary spokesmen of big business tended to be more discreet in their public statements.

5   Karl Zell, member of the *Vorstand* of *Kronprinz A.G. für Metallindustrie*, to Witkugel, April 27, 1933, Papers of the German People's party (*Deutsche Volkspartei*), No. 151, *Deutsches Zentralarchiv*, Potsdam.

6   This view was first widely circulated by the journalist Konrad Heiden in *Adolf Hitler: Das Zeitalter der Verantwortungslosigkeit* (2 vols., Zurich, 1936–1937), I, 268–272. Since then it has been repeated in many other studies of Hitler's rise, including the most recent book by Karl Dietrich Bracher, *Die deutsche Diktatur: Entstehung, Struktur, Folgen des Nationalsozialismus* (Cologne, 1969), 176.

7   There is documentation on the finances of the plebiscite against the Young plan in two collections in the *Deutsches Zentralarchiv*, Potsdam: *Alldeutscher Verband*, No. 501; *Stahlhelm*, No. 25.

8   The only evidence ever cited to support the allegations about Hugenberg's aid to Hitler is a passage in Thyssen, *I Paid Hitler*, 102–103. But as Bullock has observed (*Hitler: A Study in Tyranny* (London, 1952), 157), that passage is unclear as to when the alleged financing of Hitler took place. Since the passage was not written by Thyssen or even seen by him prior to publication, there are, moreover, grounds for doubting its authenticity.

9   See the papers of the German National People's party, *Deutsches Zentralarchiv*, Potsdam; see also Reusch Papers; Klein Papers.

10 There is evidence of this opposition in the papers of Hugenberg's predecessor as party chairman, Count Kuno von Westarp, now in the possession of his family in Gartringen, West Germany; in the Reusch Papers; and in the files of the *Verein Deutscher Eisen- und Stahlindustrieller*, R 13 1/1064, 1065, *Bundesarchiv*, Koblenz; see also Manfred Dorr, 'Die Deutschnationale Volkspartei 1925 bis 1928' (diss., University of Marburg, 1964), 448, n. 131.

11 On the revolt against Hugenberg in 1930, see [. . .] Emil Kirdorf, *Erinnerungen, 1847–1930*, copy in the Emil Kirdorf Papers, now at the *Gelsenkirchener BergwerksA.G.*, Essen, 226–233.

12 By the time Hugenberg was appointed a minister by Hitler in 1933, with responsibility for both agricultural and economic affairs, he clearly functioned as a

spokesman of the agricultural interests and thus as an opponent of industry, espe-
cially on the question of tariff policy which sharply divided the two at that time
(Dieter Petzina, 'Hauptprobleme der deutschen Wirtschaftspolitik 1932/33,'
Vierteljahrshefte für Zeitgeschichte, xv (1967), 45–55).

13   See K. D. Bracher, *Die Auflösung der Neimarer Republik* (Villingen, 1960), 292, 334;
     Bullock, *Hitler*, 133; Eberhard Czichon, *Wer verhalf Hitler zur Macht? Zum Anteil der
     deutschen Industrie an der Zerstdrung der Weimarer Republik* (Cologne, 1967), passim;
     Konrad Heiden, *Der Fuehrer* (Boston, 1944), 340–342, 356; G. W. F. Hallgarten,
     Hitler, Reichswehr und Industrie (Frankfurt, 1954), passim; Louis P. Lochner, *Tycoons
     and Tyrant: German Industry from Hitler to Adenauer* (Chicago, 1954), 97–98; Franz
     Neumann, *Behemoth: The Structure and Practice of National Socialism* (New York and
     London, 1942), 360; Gerhard Schulz, in K. D. Bracher et al., *Die nationalsozial-
     istische Machtergreifung* (Cologne, 1960), 394.

14   I have dealt in greater detail with this and other aspects of the case of Kirdorf in
     'Emil Kirdorf and the Nazi Party,' *Central European History*, I (1968), 324–344.

15   According to one legend still very much an article of faith in East German histor-
     ical circles, Kirdorf in 1931 prevailed upon the bituminous coal cartel (*Rheinisch-
     Westfälisches Kohlensyndikat*) to impose a levy of five (in some versions fifty) pfen-
     nigs on each ton of coal sold, the proceeds to go to the Nazis (see Czichon, *Wer
     verhalf Hitler*, 19). No documentary evidence has ever been introduced to support
     this allegation. It was challenged from a number of quarters when it first appeared
     in the postwar German press in 1947. (A collection of this material is located in
     the papers of the de-Nazification trial of Fritz Thyssen, *Hauptakte*, 283–286,
     Hessisches Hauptstaatsarchiv, Wiesbaden.) Overlooked by all who have repeated the
     allegation is the fact that Kirdorf's active role in the coal cartel had come to an
     end in April 1925 (Walter Bacmeister, *Emil Kirdorf. Der Mann. Sein Werk* (2d ed.,
     Essen (1936)), 100).

16   See Henry Ashby Turner, Jr., 'Hitler's Secret Pamphlet for Industrialists, 1927,'
     Journal of Modern History, xL (1968), 348–374.

17   Similar statements by Hitler appear in the recently discovered stenographic record
     of two conversations he had in the spring of 1931 with a business-oriented news-
     paper editor (Edouard Calic, *Ohne Maske: Hitler-Breiting Geheimgespräche 1931*
     (Frankfurt a.M., 1968), 35–36).

18   Instances of this are too numerous to recount in full, but two more examples can
     be cited. In February 1926 Hitler delivered a lengthy speech before the Hamburg
     Nationalklub von 1919 (see Werner Jochmann, *Im Kampf um die Macht: Hitlers Rede
     vor dem Hamburger Nationalklub von 1919* (Frankfurt a.M., 1960)). Three years later
     a Nazi spokesman in Hamburg reported that the speech was still remembered
     favorably in business circles but that there was general alienation from the Nazi
     party as a consequence of the radical stance of the local leadership and the party's
     Revolverpresse (Friedrich Bucher to Hitler, July 20, 1929, *Reichsleitung, Personalakte
     Hüttmann*, Berlin Document Center). During the early part of 1932, Hitler sought
     to cultivate allies in big business circles, addressing industrial groups and insti-
     gating, through his adviser Wilhelm Keppler, the formation of an advisory group
     of businessmen, the later *Freundeskreis*. The effects of these efforts were largely
     undone, however, by a campaign pamphlet for the summer Reichstag election,
     Wirtschaftliches Sofortprogramm der N.S.D.A.P. (Munich, 1932), which alarmed busi-
     nessmen, by virtue of its anticapitalist slogans and its call for deficit spending and
     governmental controls aimed at ending unemployment. In September Hitler

informed leading business circles through Schacht that distribution of the pamphlet had been stopped and that the remaining copies had been destroyed, but much damage had already been done by that time (Schacht to Reusch, September 12, 1932, No. 400101290/33, Reusch Papers).

19   In his conversation with the journalist Richard Breiting in May 1931, Hitler boasted that the Nazi party already enjoyed the financial backing of 'Krupp, Schröder, and others from big industry' (Calic, *Ohne Maske*, 27). Only a few pages later, however, he told of his plans to win over big business, revealing that he regarded this as a task yet to be accomplished (*ibid.*, 28–29, 35, 37–38). Further doubt is cast on the accuracy of Hitler's claim by the well-known coolness of Gustav Krupp von Bohlen und Halbach toward National Socialism prior to Hitler's appointment as Chancellor, an attitude recognized by authors of the most varied persuasions and confirmed by Krupp's private correspondence in the Krupp Papers (see Czichon, *Wer verhalf Hitler*, 53; Hallgarten, *Hitler, Reichswehr und Industrie*, 117; Lochner, *Tycoons and Tyrant*, 139) [. . .].

20   This is conceded even by Hallgarten (*Hitler, Reichswehr und Industrie*, 106). There is documentation on the fundraising campaign in the papers of the industrialist who headed it, Carl Duisberg, cofounder of I. G. Farben and chairman of its board of overseers and its administrative council (*Autographen-Sammlung von Dr. Carl Duisberg, Werksarchiv, Parbenfabrik Bayer*, Leverkusen).

21   There is abundant documentation to this effect in the Klein Papers, Krupp Papers, and Reusch Papers, as well as in the informative diary of Hans Schaffer, State Secretary in the Ministry of Finance, now located in the archive of the *Institut für Zeitgeschichte*, Munich. See also Hans Radandt, '"Freie Wahlen" und Monopol-kapital,' *Zeitschrift für Geschichtswissenschaft*, IX, No. 6 (1961), 1321–22 [. . .].

22   This emerged clearly from the testimony and documentary evidence in the Flick trial at Nuremberg in 1947. (See the published excerpts in Nuremberg Military Tribunals, *Trials of War Criminals before the Nuremberg Military Tribunals under Control Council Law No. 10* (15 vols., Washington, D.C., 1949–1953), VI, *passim.*) [. . .]

23   For a summary, see *Trials of War Criminals*, VI, 382–383. The full documentation can be found in Record Group 238 (World War II War Crimes Records), Case 5, Dokumentenbuch Flick I, National Archives (hereafter cited as NA).

24   See the affidavits of Max Ilgner, Microcopy T-301 (Records of the Office of the U.S. Chief Counsel for War Crimes, Nuremberg, Military Tribunals, Relating to Nazi Industrialists), roll 13/NI-1293, *ibid.*; T-301/55/NI-7082, *ibid.*

25   See *Trials of War Criminals*, VII, 536–554 [. . .].

26   Czichon, *Wer verhalf Hitler*, 50; Albert Norden, *Die Nation und wir: Ausgewählte Aufsätze und Reden 1933–1964* (2 vols., East Berlin, 1965), I, 322; Arthur Schweitzer, *Big Business in the Third Reich* (Bloomington, Ind., 1964), 102.

27   See *Trials of War Criminals*, VII, 536–554; see also the full testimony in Record Group 238, Case 6 (German transcript), XXIV, XXV, XXXIV, NA; interroga-tion of Butefisch, 1947, T-301/71/NI-8637, *ibid.* [. . .].

28   At a meeting of Farben's 'Working Committee' (*Arbeitsausschuss*) on April 15, 1932, the relationship between the firm's plans for agreements with foreign companies and the autarkist slogan, 'Protection of the German Market' (*Schutz des deutschen Marktes*), was discussed. Director August von Knieriem emphasized that it was the company's policy to oppose both autarky and state controls of any kind, pointing out that Carl Bosch, one of the founders of the combine, had recently made a similar statement to the press (Nachtrag I zu den Dokumentenbüchern

Gattineau (excerpt from the stenographic record of the meeting), Record Group 238, Case 6, NA).

29   Thyssen, *I Paid Hitler*, 100. This statement in the book is confirmed by the stenographic record of the interviews with Thyssen on which the book was based.

30   This is revealed by Bucher's correspondence with Reusch in No. 400101290/5, Reusch Papers.

31   See the book written by the intermediary between Strasser and the *Bergbau-Verein* (properly *Verein für die bergbaulichen Interessen*), Heinrichsbauer, *Schwerindustrie und Politik* (Essen: West Verlag, 1948), 39–52. Czichon (*Wer verhalf Hitler*, 54) cites the as yet unpublished memoirs of Günther Gereke to the effect that the industrialist Otto Wolff also subsidized Strasser in 1932 at the request of Wolff's friend, General Kurt von Schleicher, who hoped thereby to make Strasser more independent of Hitler.

32   At Nuremberg in 1948 Flick described Funk as a 'liberal thinking man' and a 'man of liberal outlook' (see Record Group 238, Case 10 (German transcript), XV, 5584, NA). According to testimony of his former assistant, Otto Steinbrinck, Flick was among those who aided Funk (Case 5 (German transcript), XV, 4981, *ibid.*). Funk also received small subsidies from two young public relations agents of I. G. Farben, who acted independently of each other in providing funds for the maintenance of his Berlin office in 1932 (see affidavit of Ilgner, May 1, 1947, T-301/55/NI-7082, *ibid.*). Ilgner stated that he ceased payments when he discovered that Funk was also receiving money from Gattineau for the same purpose. According to Heinrichsbauer (*Schwerindustrie und Politik*, 42, 44), the *Bergbau-Verein* also subsidized Funk.

33   Turner, 'Kirdorf and the Nazi Party,' pp. 335–336.

34   Klaus Drobisch, 'Der Freundeskreis Himmler,' *Zeitschrift für Geschichtswissenschaft*, VIII (1960), 304–328.

35   [. . .] See the documentation on the beginnings of the *Keppler-Kreis* in the privately printed memoirs of Emil Helfferich, one of the founding members, *Bin Leben* (4 vols., Hamburg and Jever, 1948–1964), IV, 9–26.

36   Some writers have contended that Goebbels's diary, *Vom Kaiserhof zur Reichskanzlei: Eine historische Darstellung in Tagebuchblättern* (Munich, 1934), shows the finances of the Nazis to have improved markedly in January 1933, following the meeting of Hitler with Papen at the house of the banker Schroeder. Shirer, William Lawrence, *The Rise and Fall of the Third Reich: A History of Nazi Germany* (New York: Simon and Schuster, Inc., 1959), 179, for example, citing Goebbels's entry of January 16, writes: 'he reported that the financial position of the party had "fundamentally improved overnight." There is, however, no mention of finances in that entry; the overnight change in the Nazis' fortunes referred to by Goebbels was clearly the result of the party's successes the day before in the state elections of Lippe, not of capitalists' contributions. The same erroneous interpretation has been given to this diary entry by Bracher (*Auflösung*, 694, n. 33). Bracher cites as well a second entry, that of January 5, in which Goebbels remarked that the financial situation of the Berlin *Gau* had somewhat improved (*Vom Kaiserhof*, 235). It is hardly likely, however, that the Hitler–Papen meeting of January 4 could have, as Bracher infers, had such an immediate material effect on the treasury of the local Berlin organization only one day later. In any event, by January 6 Goebbels was again bemoaning the 'bad financial situation of the organization' (*ibid.*, 236).

37 [. . .] Albert Schreiner, 'Die Eingabe deutscher Finanzmagnaten, Monopolisten und Junker an Hindenburg für die Berufung Hitlers zum Reichskanzler (November, 1932),' *Zeitschrift für Geschichtswissenschaft*, IV, No. 2 (1956), 366–369; also, Czichon, *Wer verhalf Hitler*, 41–42. A comparison of the list of those who signed the petition with the list of those considered as potential signers by the organizers of the project reveals, however, that the great majority apparently refused to sign (see Record Group 238, PS-3901, NA; excerpt in International Military Tribunal, *Trial of the Major War Criminals before the International Military Tribunal, Nuremberg, 14 November 1945–1 October 1946* (42 vols., Nuremberg, 1947–1949), xxxiii, 531–533) [. . .] .

38 There is ample evidence of this in a wide variety of sources. For examples, see the letter of the manager of the *Deutscher Industrie- und Handelstag*, Eduard Hamm, to Otto Most, December 10, 1932, in which Hamm wrote of rumors to the effect that the cabinet would be revamped on a parliamentary basis in a 'certain soldier-worker direction,' R ll/10, *Bundesarchiv*, Koblenz; speech of Krupp to the *Hauptausschuss* of the *Reichsverband der Deutschen Industrie*, December 14, 1932, reported in a communication of the *Reichsverband* of December 15, No. 400101220/13, Reusch Papers; excerpts from the speech of the manager of the *Reichsverband*, Jakob Herle, January 2, 1933, Herle to Reusch, January 4, No. 400101220/14, *ibid*.; Reusch's letters to Hamm, December 22, 31, 1932, No. 40010123/25, *ibid*.; Duisberg to Herle, January 9, 1933, *Reichsverband der Deutschen Industrie, Allgemeiner Schriftwechsel mit der Geschaftsführung, Werksarchiv, Farbenfabrik Bayer*, Leverkusen; Hugo Stinnes to Klein, January 18, 1933, Klein Papers. Some of the leading Ruhr industrialists had an additional reason for hostility toward Schleicher, for they suspected he had used to buy himself a newspaper (*Tägliche Rundschau,* Berlin) some of the money they had given him during the July election campaign in support of the parties backing Papen (see Kurt von Schleicher Papers, HO8–42/22, *Bundesarchiv*, Koblenz; Reusch to Fritz Springorum, October 12, 1932, No. 400101290/36, Reusch Papers).

39 The nature of Schroeder's role emerges clearly from the correspondence preceding the meeting (T–301/3/NI–200–16, NA). Schroeder's lack of standing in big business circles prior to 1933 is attested to by the almost complete absence of his name from the correspondence of major industrial figures cited elsewhere in this article. As is shown by a series of postwar interrogations, his industrial role began only during the Third Reich, largely as a result of his Nazi contacts (NI-226–49, *ibid*.).

40 Hallgarten (*Hitler, Reichswehr und Industrie*, 116) has alleged that immediately after the meeting a consortium of industrialists gave a million marks to the SS and paid the most pressing election debts of the Nazi party. As evidence, he cites an undocumented assertion by the journalist Konrad Heiden, plus a postwar affidavit by Schroeder. In the affidavit Schroeder mentioned payment of a million marks a year to the SS by the *Freundeskreis*, but stated that this began only in 1935 or 1936, specifying that no such payments to the Nazis were made prior to then by that group (this document, which Hallgarten cites by its exhibit number in the Flick trial, is better known as PS-3337). Two further supporting references offered by Hallgarten lead to an English translation of an excerpt from the same affidavit by Schroeder and pages '1353 ff.' of a volume containing only 1099 pages. Bracher has accepted Hallgarten's interpretation and offered as additional evidence a quotation from Thyssen, *I Paid Hitler*, which refers not, as Bracher indicates, to

the effects of the Cologne meeting, but to the aftermath of Hitler's speech before the *Industrie-Klub* almost a year earlier (Bracher, *Auflösung*, 694, n. 33). If the Cologne meeting had opened the coffers of big business to the Nazis, there would hardly have been need for Hitler's appeal for funds to the leaders of industry on February 20, 1933 (see *Trials of War Criminals*, VII, 555–568).

41   [. . .] As late as March, Reusch described the new government as 'Herr von Papen's work of political unification' and promised further support of Papen (Reusch to Kurt von Lersner, March 4, 1933, No. 400101293/12, Reusch Papers). The expectation of a new Papen cabinet was widespread in late January (see Ewald von Kleist-Schmenzin, 'Die letzte Möglichkeit: Zur Ernennung Hitlers zum Reichskanzler am 30. Januar 1933,' *Politische Studien*, X (1959), 91).

42   Two recent studies show this to have been the case during the Nazi party's early years: Georg Franz-Willing, *Die Hitlerbewegung: Der Ursprung 1919–1922* (Hamburg, 1962), 177–198; Werner Maser, *Die Frühgeschichte der NSDAP: Hitlers Weg bis 1924* (Frankfurt a.M., 1965), 396–412. A study written at the time and based on the business press concluded that the same pattern had characterized the last years before 1933: Ernst Lange, 'Die politische Ideologie der deutschen industriellen Unternehmerschaft' (diss., University of Greifswald, 1933), 36, 80. This was also the view of Theodor Heuss, *Hitlers Weg: Eine historisch-politische Studie über den Nationalsozialismus* (Stuttgart, 1932), 122.

43   There is much documentation on this in the papers of the *Reichswirtschaftsministerium*, now located in the *Deutsches Zentralarchiv*, Potsdam.

Chapter 46

Adrian Lyttelton

THE 'MARCH ON ROME': FASCIST TRIUMPH OR CAPITULATION OF THE LIBERAL SYSTEM?

■ from *THE SEIZURE OF POWER: FASCISM IN ITALY 1919–1929*, London, 1973, pp. 85–93

Adrian Lyttelton's masterly study of the Fascist 'seizure of power' in Italy is highly revealing about the confused political and psychological atmosphere in which the actions of the main protagonists in the dramatic events of October 1922 took place. Lyttelton underlines the technical and strategic inadequacies of the 'ill-conceived' March on Rome; but he also acknowledges its significance as a sort of 'psychological warfare' against the state. More important, however, were the attitudes and actions of the political and military establishment. Lyttelton shows that prominent 'Liberal' politicians had been reconciled to the idea of bringing Fascism into the government; that the military was torn between loyalty to the state and Fascist sympathies (see the case of Marshal Diaz); that the local authorities, especially in the provinces, failed to act promptly; and that the King, long impatient with the parliamentary deadlock, shifted his attitude from opposition, to containment of Fascism.

T HE PLAN FOR THE MARCH ON ROME had been drawn up in a secret meeting on 24 October in a Naples hotel. The plan called for the occupation of public buildings throughout north and central Italy as the first stage in the seizure of power; in the second stage three columns would concentrate on the roads leading into Rome, at S. Marinella, Monterotondo and Tivoli, and converge on the capital. If the Government resisted, the Ministries were to be occupied by force.[1] In reality, the March on Rome, in the strict sense, was a colossal bluff. The city was defended by 12,000 men of the regular army, under the loyal General Pugliese, who would have been able to disperse the Fascist bands without difficulty. Many of the Fascists failed to arrive at their points of concentration; they were travelling by train and were stopped by the simple expedient of taking up a few yards of track. Those who did arrive were poorly armed and they were short of food. They could do nothing except hang around miserably in the torrential autumn rain. The grandiose 'pincer movement' on Rome could never have been carried out with any chance of success.[2]

Anti-Fascist historians have quite rightly devoted much attention to puncturing the myth of the March on Rome, as part of a general depreciation of the 'revolutionary' claims of Fascism. However it should be remembered that the seizure of power by 'force' in a modern State is never possible, except when the army or police carries out the *coup*, unless the will to resist of the Government forces has been undermined. Even the Bolshevik Revolution could only succeed because the soldiers of the regular army would not fight for the established government. This does not mean to say, however, that power would simply have fallen into the hands of the Bolsheviks without the determined action of the small groups of Red Guards. The problem can be clarified better by reference to the famous book by Curzio Malaparte, *Technique of the coup d'état*. The exaggerations and inaccuracies of this work have often been pointed out; the notorious thesis of Malaparte that 'what governments have to fear are the tactics of Trotsky, not the strategy of Lenin' was angrily rejected by Trotsky himself as superficial, and the description of the tactics owes much to fantasy. Although Malaparte sensed well enough the importance of disorder, or the existence of what can only be termed rather vaguely a revolutionary atmosphere, he did not unfortunately allow this perception to modify his thesis.[3]

Nevertheless if one refuses to accept Malaparte's view of coup technique as a kind of magic, effective in all historical circumstances, his book can be read with profit. There *is* a 'technical' element in the seizure of power, and it is likely to be more important in the case of a movement like Italian Fascism, whose motive force was weak, both ideologically and socially, when compared with that behind the major revolutions. Malaparte was right to call attention to technique, even though he overrated its importance. The March on Rome can best be viewed neither as a 'revolution', nor as a simple piece of mass choreography, but as psychological warfare. Within the complex of the Fascist operations of the twenty-seventh and twenty-eighth, it is helpful to distinguish the March on Rome proper, which was not, and could not have been, carried out until all possibility of resistance had vanished from the 'first act' of the plan, which consisted in the seizure or isolation of prefectures and police headquarters, railway stations, post and telegraph offices, anti-fascist newspapers and circles and Camere del Lavoro. This programme corresponds more or less to Malaparte's description of the objectives of the new style of *coup*, except, of course, that it was only carried out in provincial centres and not in the capital itself. Neither Balbo, with his romantic temperament, nor Mussolini, who remained all his life surprisingly ignorant of military affairs and logistics, were likely to be altogether hard-headed in their plans; yet there are indications that the seizure of power in the provinces was, realistically, viewed by some Fascists at least as the vital stage in the insurrection. The Prefect of Naples reported to the Government on 26 October that:

From a trustworthy agent comes the following report on the Fascist action; there exist 4 different plans, to be put into effect subsequent to general mobilization: first, a converging March on Rome, the occupation of public offices, buildings, etc.; 2nd, simultaneous occupation of offices and public services of principal cities which would be held as hostages; 3rd, a feint converging manoeuvre on Rome to compel the concentration of larger contingents with object of carrying out instead the 2nd plan; 4th, mobilization ordered only with purpose of impressing public opinion and putting pressure on members of government and thus reaching objectives without striking a blow. He added, however, that he had some reason to believe that now it was a matter of plan no. 3.

According to the record kept by Balbo of the meeting at the Hotel Vesuvius on the twenty-fourth, officially, the first of these alternatives was adopted.[4] However the third alternative, which the Prefect's informant believed to have been adopted, was so much more realistic that it does seem probable that, in the minds of some Fascist leaders, the first phase was really the most important in the operation. Was Mussolini himself of this opinion? He had certainly only committed himself to the operation in the belief that the Government and the Army would not put up an effective resistance. One cannot, therefore, take his military proposals too literally. It is probable that, while leaving the detailed execution to his subordinates, he regarded the occupation of the provincial cities as an important security and bargaining point, in case his assessment should prove wrong. What needs emphasis is that the March on Rome was almost inconceivably ill-planned if the intention really had been to seize the central State machine by force – when the only way would have lain in a rapid *coup de main*, not in a ponderous concentration. But politically it was essential to avoid surprise. The Government and the King could not be threatened too directly; they must instead be put in a position where they would have to take a positive initiative to restore order.

Where Malaparte's interpretation is best founded is in his criticism of the Government's counter measures. These, thanks to the competence of the War Minister Soleri and General Pugliese, were, as we have seen, adequate for the protection of Rome. But in the provinces it was a different matter. General Pugliese himself, anxious to avoid bloodshed, had pointed out that to prevent the concentration of large masses of Fascists, it would be necessary to co-ordinate his dispositions for the defence of Rome with a general plan for the whole of Italy. Such a plan was never drawn up. The Government's instructions to the Prefects were that they should hand over their powers to the local army command in case of grave disorders.

The defects of this system were that it left the initiative in the hands of the Fascists, and that the assignment of responsibility for preventing the take-over of public buildings and other strategic points was likely at the critical moment to be uncertain. Unless the Prefect was unusually astute and handed over power to the Army before the Fascists went into action, both he and the local military commander would find themselves in a difficult position. The Prefect might well feel reluctant to order the police to open fire or to take other decisive action, when he knew that his instructions allowed him to evade the responsibility for repression; on the other hand, the military commander would take over without full knowledge of the political situation or the forces at his disposal, and would be forced to expel the Fascists from strategic points they had already occupied, rather than merely defending them.[5]

The importance of the 'technical' defects of the Government's measures is shown by at least two contemporary documents. The first is the letter in which Camillo Corradini informed Giolitti of the start of Fascist mobilization on 27 October. Corradini, as a former Under Secretary of the Interior who before that had been a permanent official of the same ministry, had an unrivalled knowledge of the workings of the Government machinery in the provinces. His comments are therefore especially worthy of note:

> The uncertainty is greatest among the police and prefectoral authorities. The Government has prescribed resistance including in case of necessity the use of arms. In other words the Government does not see the insurrectionary character of this whole movement, since in such a case it cannot be a question of a mere matter for the police, but of a real movement which should be treated as such, and therefore arrest of the leaders, military government, etc. If this doesn't occur there will be minor disasters, victims without any result, and with the certainty that sporadic acts here and there will not prevent the favourable results of the insurrection and will only embitter and increase the movement. That is my impression. At Rome they don't understand a thing, and what is worse they give uncertain and contradictory information. At Milan, for example, they are in doubt even as to whether the telegraph and telephone offices should be guarded and they telephone from Rome that protection should be confined to the offices dependent on the Ministry of the Interior, as if these offices, cut off from their communications could represent anything, and as if this powerful centre of life could do anything without its own means of communication.

The failure to provide for the defence of the communications system is here singled out by Corradini in terms which suggest the partial validity of Malaparte's analysis, which in this particular was based on his own direct experience of the Fascist occupation of Florence.[6] The second document is the record kept by General Pugliese of his meeting with Facta, the Minister of the Interior, Taddei, the War Minister, and Soleri on the night of the March (27–8 October). Facta and Taddei, faced with the reports from Perugia and Florence of the occupation of the prefectures, telephones and post offices, 'expressed their pained surprise that the armed forces should not have been able to prevent this'. 'The commander of the division replied firmly that this could happen only on account of the lack of precise orders on the attitude to be taken when faced with Fascist violence.' Pugliese pointed out that his suggestions for liaison between the military and political authorities had not been taken up, except for Rome, and that 'therefore the arbitrary Fascist occupations at Perugia and Florence regretted by the ministers Facta and Taddei were the responsibility of the political authority, which, having retained the powers for the protection of public order and absolute control over all the local armed forces, during the whole day of 27 October had been unable to prevent them or to react, and had allowed trains loaded with militia to leave undisturbed for Rome.'[7]

From a strict military or strategic point of view all this was no doubt irrelevant; not only in Rome, but in the great northern cities, Milan, Genoa, Turin, and even in the Fascist stronghold, Bologna, the authorities, alerted in time, were able to maintain control of the situation without much difficulty. However the Fascist action was successful in creating an atmosphere of confusion and an impression of the widespread collapse of State power which during the critical night of 27–8 October could not fail to have a grave psychological effect. For this we have the testimony of Facta's *chef de cabinet*, Efrem Ferraris:

> at the Viminale, the telephones which linked the prefectures to the Ministry gave no respite and after midnight the news became alarming. In the night I witnessed, in the silence of the great rooms of the Viminale, the disintegration of the authority and power of the State. On the large sheets of paper which I kept in front of me, there grew ever thicker the names of the occupied prefectures that I was noting down, the indications of invaded telegraph offices, of military garrisons who had fraternized with the Fascists, providing them with arms, of trains requisitioned by the militia which were directed, loaded with armed men, towards the capital.[8]

Thus at Perugia the Prefect surrendered to the Fascists; at Florence the prefecture was not occupied, but it was cut off and unable to communicate since the Fascists had occupied the railway station and the telegraph office.[9] At Pisa the occupation of the prefecture was prevented, but a large number of Fascists were able to leave undisturbed for the point of concentration; elsewhere in Tuscany this was the general pattern, and the Tuscan Fascists were also able to acquire a notable quantity of arms, including machine-guns.[10] In the Po Valley, except at Bologna, the situation was not much better. At Cremona, Farinacci was anxious to prove himself second to none in decision and toughness. His squads were the first, with those of Pisa, to attack. They began by cutting off the electric light, and in the subsequent darkness and confusion they surprised the police station and the prefecture and occupied all the other key points. Later on, the prefecture was retaken by the Army and it was here that the Fascists suffered their heaviest casualties, eight dead and thirteen wounded. But reinforcements arrived from the province and the situation remained confused, without the military being able or willing to re-establish complete control.[11] At Mantua, the Prefect claimed that after a brief skirmish between the *Guardia Regia* and the Fascists, he was compelled to give way by 'the preponderance of the Fascist forces', several thousand strong and armed with machine-guns.[12] In Alessandria the Fascists broke into the barracks, capturing rifles and machine-guns, and seized the public buildings, holding the Prefect prisoner.[13] In Bergamo, in Venice and almost all the provincial capitals of the Veneto, and in Trieste, the Fascists seized the post and telegraph offices, and often the prefectures as well.[14] The South on the whole stayed quiescent until victory was certain, but the *ras* Caradonna occupied Foggia, disarming the local garrison and seizing large quantities of arms.[15]

It is true that from an orthodox strategic point of view all these local and unconnected successes were irrelevant: but to conclude that 'the seditious movement not only had not been victorious, but must be considered a complete failure on the military plane'[16] is surely to miss the point. The military and political planes of action were not separate but complementary and the partial successes of the military move-ment had their importance.

We must now return to Rome, the central government and the King. All that has been said does not, of course, alter the fact that this was the point of decision. At 8 pm on 27 December, when the King arrived in Rome from his country resi-dence of S. Rossore, he told Facta that the Crown must be able to decide in full liberty, and not under the pressure of Fascist rifles. His determination to resist seemed evident. It was not out of character; Victor Emmanuel had behaved as a correct constitutional monarch, and in 1919 he had courageously resisted Nationalist and anti-parliamentary pressures. To more than one visitor, he had then repeated that he was ready to take a rifle and go down into the piazza in order to defend parliament against a hypothetical military coup.[17] But by October 1922 everything looked very different. The long and painful parliamentary crises had had their effect; in the last stages of the parliamentary crisis of July the King had scarcely concealed his impatience at the protracted failure to find any effective government. In the month before the March, the insouciance of Facta had also deeply perturbed him; on 14 October he had urged Facta to summon Parliament immediately[18] and, reading between the lines, it is easy to see that he was irritated by the Prime Minister's persistent neglect to consult him or keep him fully informed. Twice, on 24 and 25 October, Facta assured him that the project of a March on Rome had been aban-doned; this was not calculated to give the King much confidence in the Government's preparations or power of decision. He was bound, in addition, to be preoccupied with avoiding a violent conflict, especially when all the leading Liberal politicians had shown themselves persuaded of the necessity of giving the Fascists a share in government.[19]

Nevertheless, on the evening of the twenty-seventh, he still saw his duty, in plain terms, as resistance. Why did he change his mind? To this central question, whose importance vividly illustrates the role of the individual in historical crisis the answer cannot be certain. The King was an extremely taciturn man, not given to indiscretions, and the reasons for his volte-face remain a mystery: one can only guess at them.

The explanations which Victor Emmanuel gave of his refusal to sign the emer-gency decree in 1945 are vitiated by their purpose as Royalist propaganda: and all his retrospective statements, indeed, are marked by a desire to put his decision in the best light possible, according to the different dates when they were offered. The excuse that he quite literally ceded to *force majeure*, convinced that the garrison of Rome was too small and too unreliable to resist the Fascist attack, will not hold. However some part of these several statements may be helpful in understanding the King's state of mind: 'At difficult moments everyone is capable of indecision . . . few or none are those who can take clear decisions and assume grave responsibili-ties. In 1922 I had to call "these people" to the Government because all the others in one way or another, had abandoned me'; on other occasions the King spoke of his desire to 'avoid bloodshed given the news from the provinces which were already in the hands of the Fascists', and said that if he had acted otherwise, 'it would have been civil war'.[20] Both these elements in his apologies do seem to correspond to what we know of his feelings and of the actual situation in 1922; in a telegram of 26 October to Facta he had spoken of his desire 'to avoid shocks' by 'associating

Fascism with the Government in a legal form' and we have seen that he had some reason for believing that Facta had deliberately left the unwelcome burden of decision to him.[21] On the night of the twenty-eighth itself, Facta's conduct was extraordinary. First he offered the resignation of the Cabinet to the King, a gesture which goes some way further towards excusing the latter's hyperbolic assertion that he had been 'abandoned': then, with rather excessive sang-froid, Facta retired to bed.[22]

It seems plain that the King's decision must have looked greater and more serious at the end of the night than at the beginning. If the Government counter-measures had been immediately effective, if the occupations had been prevented or the leaders of the movement arrested, the proclamation of martial law might have resolved the situation without a general conflict: by the morning this had become much more doubtful.

By themselves, these considerations might not, however, have been enough to make the King give way. Probably if he had been sure of the loyalty of the Army, he would have given orders for the troops to re-establish order.

With the failure of the civil power to act in time, the Army also found itself, like the King, in a position of unwanted responsibility. Certainly some generals did their duty, even in spite of their personal sympathy with Fascism; this was true, for example, of General Sani, commander of the Bologna Army Corps. But the Army commanders were bound to be influenced by the strong Fascist sympathies of a great part of the officer corps, and the presence in the Militia of a good number of retired and half-pay generals. Finally, there is good reason to believe that Marshal Diaz himself, the president of the Army Council and virtually Commander-in-Chief, was more closely involved with Fascism. He was in Florence on the afternoon of 27 October, when the Fascist mobilization started; there does not seem to have been any pre-arranged agreement between him and the leaders of the movement, as Balbo had to intervene hastily on his arrival to prevent the local squads from assaulting the prefecture, where Diaz was the Prefect's guest. 'Instead I told them to organize a great demonstration for the Duke of Victory in the streets of Florence where he would pass. I ordered them to make contact with the Fascist railwaymen in the station . . . to prepare at all costs a train to take Diaz to Rome at any moment he might desire.'[23] It is very interesting to note Balbo's concern that Diaz should be in Rome. Diaz left Florence finally, by train, on the afternoon of the twenty-eighth: but, aside from the fact that, as De Felice points out, the King could have consulted Diaz indirectly, it seems likely that the Marshal may in fact already have made a secret journey to Rome on the evening of the twenty-seventh. Salvemini noted in his diary that 'Diaz was at Florence on the afternoon of 27 October; he had received favourably a demonstration of enthusiasm by the Fascists, and had conceded an interview to the Florentine newspaper *La Nazione* in which he had expressed his full faith in the Fascist movement, and had rushed *by car* to Rome to inform the King that the Army would not fight against the Fascists.'[24] This version receives confirmation in the *Giornale di Roma* of 29 October: this also reports that Diaz came to Rome on the twenty-seventh by car. The newspaper adds the circumstantial detail that the owner of the car was the Liberal deputy Dino Philipson, who was prominent among the financial backers of Fascism. Whether they actually saw the King remains uncertain: but if one accepts that he came to Rome, and more or less secretly, it could hardly have been for any purpose other than influencing the outcome of the crisis. The story of General Pecori Giraldi, told two years later, becomes more credible:

> 'The Marshal replied that in that night His Majesty had questioned numerous personalities. Among these was the Marshal of Italy, Diaz, and also himself. The Sovereign was gravely preoccupied about the attitude that the Army would take. To Marshal Diaz he addressed the precise question: "What will the Army do?" "Majesty", replied Marshal Diaz, "the army will do its duty, however it would be well not to put it to the test". I – added General Pecori Giraldi – made almost the same reply'.[25]

The King was bound to be doubly anxious about the attitude of the Army in view of his fears that his cousin the Duke of Aosta, who had turned up in Umbria, suspiciously near the scene of operations, might have designs on the throne.

But when all objective elements, the indecisiveness of the government, the partial success of Fascist tactics, the open collusion of some generals, the advice of Diaz, the fear of the Duke of Aosta, have been added up, there remains a margin of doubt which must be ascribed to the character of Victor Emmanuel. By temperament he was a pessimist, and he had little confidence in either his advisers or his subjects. He was keenly conscious that, more intelligent than the general run of monarchs, he did not have the presence or the warmth to inspire personal devotion. Finally his sceptical nature doubted, not altogether wrongly, the solidity of the Kingdom of Italy; the old lands of the Crown of Savoy were one thing, but not all Italians were Piedmontese or Sardinian.[26] All authority depends on confidence; and the King, rational to a fault and with a low opinion of man in general, had none. He gave way, one can suggest, because to him the evidence of his solitude had become overwhelming: the only man who could do anything was convinced of his impotence.

Notes

1 L. Repaci, *La marcia su Roma. Mito e realtà* (Rome, 1963), i, 445–8.

2 Ibid., 465–72, 481–7.

3 C. Malaparte, *Technique du coup d'état* (Paris, 1948).

4 ACS, Uff. cifra tel. in arrivo (26 October), n. 28224; Italo Balbo, Diario (Milan: Mondadori, 1932), 195–8. Balbo, it must be remembered, had every motive to emphasize the heroic aspect of the March on Rome.

5 Repaci, *Marcia*, 2, 282–3.

6 Valeri, *Da Giolitti a Mussolini* (Milan: Mondadori, 1967), 172–3.

7 Repaci, *Marcia*, i, 506–7.

8 E. Ferraris, *La Marcia su Roma veduta dal Viminale* (Rome, 1946), 95.

9 Repaci, *Marcia*, i, 497; 2, 429, 500–1.

10 ACS, Uff. cifra tel. in arrivo (28 October) 1 am n. 28224, Prefect of Siena.

11 Repaci, *Marcia*, i, 498–9, 539; ACS, ibid. (27 October) 11.45 pm n. 28217, Prefect of Cremona.

12 ACS, ibid., n. 28252 11.10 am (28 October).

13 ACS, ibid., n. 28268 10 am (28 October); ibid. n. 28282, 28320.

14   ACS, ibid., n. 28428 (29 October), Prefect of Bergamo; Repaci, op. cit., i, pp. 537–9.
15   ACS, ibid., n. 28374 (29 October).
16   Repaci, *Marcia*, i, 503–4.
17   R. Vivarelli, *Il dopoguerra in Italia e l'avvento del fascismo* (Naples, 1968), 461n.
18   Repaci, *Marcia*, 2, 51.
19   Ibid., 66–8.
20   P. Puntoni, *Parla Vittorio Emanuele III* (Milan, 1958), 40, 288.
21   Repaci, *Marcia*, ii, 69.
22   Ibid., i, 504–5.
23   Ibid., i, 501.
24   Salvemini, *Scritti sul fascismo*, edited by N. Valeri–A. Merola (Milan: Feltrinelli, 1966), ii, 60. N.B. also Salandra's evidence (*Diario* (Milan: Pan, 1969), 271) [. . .]
25   Repaci, *Marcia*, ii, 386.
26   Ibid., 392 (F. Cocco Ortu).

Chapter 47

Shlomo Ben-Ami

MONARCHY AND THE MILITARY IN SEARCH OF DICTATOR: PRIMO DE RIVERA'S DICTATORSHIP

■ from *FASCISM FROM ABOVE: THE DICTATORSHIP OF PRIMO DE RIVERA IN SPAIN, 1923–1930*, Oxford, 1983, pp. 65–7, 68–73, 74–5

In his study of Primo de Rivera's dictatorship Shlomo Ben-Ami is particularly concerned with the causes of the rebellion (which he associates with a general social crisis, caused by rapid modernisation) and the techniques of coup d'état (master-minded by the military and the monarchy). In this respect, Ben-Ami argues, Primo's dictatorship was the precursor of 'proto-fascist' regimes established in the Balkans a few years later. Note that the author sees *Primoderriverismo* as a 'failed revolu-tion', inspiring the opponents of the Second Spanish Republic (including Franco) in the 1930s.

PRIMO DE RIVERA belonged to the 1898 military generation whose major, and deeply frustrating experience, was the loss, to the overwhelming supremacy of the United States, of the remnants of Spain's empire. This was a generation permeated with a profound sense of humiliation and defeat as well as with a feeling of alienation towards civilian society, a society either unwilling or unable to comprehend, or to identify with, the military set of values (loyalty, disci-pline, devotion, patriotism, sacrifice, order, unity, etc.). Primo de Rivera's rebellion was anchored in this typically Spanish sort of militarism determined by inward-chan-nelled nationalism rather than by unrealistic expansionist dreams; it therefore set about fighting the enemy from within – syndicalism, socialism, communism, sepa-ratism, politics, etc. – rather than a non-existent foreign foe.[1] It was to the Nation, not to any given 'temporary' government that the military came to feel they owed allegiance.[2]

Yet, if the mechanism of the pronunciamiento and the inbred praetorian philos-ophy to which it responded were not new, the public atmosphere that surrounded it, its incisive identification with a terrified bourgeoisie in the socially turbulent

Catalonia, its leader's awareness of, and affinity with, European anti-parliamentarian trends, and the presence of the 'communist' fear in conservative minds[3] were indicative that perhaps something new and probably more up to date with European post-War anti-democratic tendencies was being born. In other words, was Primo de Rivera only a successor of generations of 'Spanish' pronunciamientos or was his take-over also indicative of his country's incorporation into horizontal European socio-political processes such as the so-called 'crisis of democracy'? A panegyrist of the Dictator had a positive answer to advance: 'The coup d'état and the Dictatorship are not the consequence of a caprice of General Primo de Rivera, but a response – in addition to the factors that are specific to Spain – to the general current being now manifested throughout the world against parliamentary democracy and for a strong, durable and independent executive power.'[4]

The concept that a rebellion against a 'dissolving' constitutional legality is a patriotic move rather than a punishable rebellion was basically inherited from the traditional *golpista* philosophy. It now acquired, however, an up-to-date sophistication. For the 'catastrophist' right of the Second Republic, Primo de Rivera, rather than the nineteenth century's pronunciamientos, would be the example to imitate and improve upon. The Dictatorship would be remembered by *Acción Española* as a *révolution manquée.*[5] But the view would be rejected that it was 'the consequence of the myth of Don Juan'. Rather, it would be claimed, it was 'a mysterious nationalist reaction, an avant-garde of that which is now looming, with greater violence in the Spanish horizon'.[6] Primo de Rivera was 'the real herald and imitator of the movement of patriotic exaltation now redeeming us. He was the propagator of the anti-democratic practices, now so fashionable.'[7] Mussolini had set the pattern. Primo's was 'the second attempt made in Europe to advance the primacy of moral, social and economic problems, and put aside merely political issues'.[8]

That a general takes over violently the reins of power should not *per se* be indicative of the nature and historic significance of his act. The technique of the *coup d'état* might not have changed, but the social cleavages, and the bitterness of the political contest to which his rebellion was a response, developed in such a way that they helped mould a novel type of military rule. [. . .] [T]he rather traditional mechanisms of seizure of power resorted to by some royal dictatorships in the inter-war period should not exclude them automatically from being considered as potential founders of 'modern' dictatorships, that is dictatorships that respond to crises inherent in modernizing pressures, and that rather than a system of *pouvoir à l'état pur* set up a regime based on practices of mobilization and controlled national consensus.[9] One might say that, like the regimes of Metaxas in Greece, King Alexander's dictatorship, and Stojadinović's proto-fascist essay in Yugoslavia, and similar attempts in inter-war Romania under the auspices of King Carol, *Primoderriverismo* started as an attempt to uphold by means of violence and through non-democratic methods, gradually assuming fascistic traits, the interests of the propertied classes, the unity and the 'dignity' of the fatherland. And, like the Greek, Romanian, and Yugoslav dictatorships, Primo de Rivera's initial success rested upon active royal support, indeed upon a violation of the constitution by a monarch fearful and scornful of democratic procedures.[10]

Dictatorships such as these came to power during, and indeed were the product of, the transition of their countries from tradition to modernity. Rapid structural changes – enhanced by western investments, and reflected in industrialization, rail-road building, the emergence of a market economy and of urban middle and working classes – were taking place in Balkan societies during the first quarter of the twentieth century.[11] The old socio-political order was being undermined by indus-trialization and its concomitant social changes, but the new one had not yet been established. It was the dangerous questioning of the legitimacy of the old order that brought these regimes to power. Under the impact of demographic changes, social pressures, and the emergence of new political forces resting on mobilized, rather than on manipulated, opinion, it became evident in countries such as Spain, Greece, Yugoslavia, and Romania – to mention only select examples of countries where dictatorships were produced by a threatened establishment in order to stave off or control change[12] – that politics could no more be exclusively resolved in terms of personalities and electoral rigging. Parliament was palatable to conservative minds in these countries so long as it did not try to play British or French kinds of politics. Sections of the ruling establishments, by over-exaggerating the puissance of the social menace, felt they would be unable to cope with it if they restricted themselves to parliamentary politics. The dictatorships they produced were the last gasp of a conservatism fearful of the social and political strains that accompanied industrial-ization.[13] To put it in the words of a contemporary enemy of the Spanish dictator: 'The military rebellion of Primo de Rivera was not just one of those many devices adopted by the old regime in order to preserve its authoritarian pre-eminence; it also responded to the transformation of Spain. It was the last-ditch defence of a retro-gressive social state.'[14]

Which is why *Primoderriverismo*, like the Balkanic 'establishment fascist' regimes,[15] at least in their initial stages, rested on the conservative establishments, whom they pretended to guard against the threats of change. Whereas fully-fledged fascism emerged as a revolution from below, the recruiting ground of which was among alienated, revolutionary elements, these regimes did not come to power through mass mobilization, but rather by means of traditional devices such as *coups d'état* or palace manoeuvres. They started, as did indeed also Francoism,[16] as a counter-revolutionary, defensive reaction, which would finally bet on a revolution from above to neutralize that of below.

Such leaders as Metaxas, Stojadinović, Călinescu, and Primo de Rivera looked to Mussolini for inspiration probably also with a spirit of mimicry. 'Please convey to His Majesty the king of Italy, to Mussolini, and to the Italian navy', asked Primo de Rivera, on the day of his *coup d'état*, from Alberto Pizzo, 'my sympathy for the example they have set to all the peoples who know how to save and redeem them-selves.'[17] He owed much to Mussolini's influence, he declared on another occasion. Actually, he said, it was 'Mussolini's seizure of power' that showed him what he 'ought to do' in order 'to save' his own country.[18] King Alfonso complemented the analogy by comparing his role in Primo's *coup d'état* to that of Vittorio Emmanuele in Mussolini's seizure of power. He accepted the Dictatorship, he said – 'just as Italy took refuge in Fascism from the communist threat' – in order 'to curb anarchy' and 'the licentiousness of parliament'.[19]

The nakedly military character of Primo's take-over, to use the words of a contemporary British observer,[20] has been overemphasized as a point of difference from Mussolini's civilian revolution. Yet, without under-estimating the powerful civilian momentum of Italian Fascism, was it not the sympathy Mussolini enjoyed in military circles and in the royal court which paved the way for the Fascist take-over, the March on Rome being no more than a fiasco? It is often forgotten that Mussolini's seizure of power had all the aspects of a *coup d'état*; the military Quadrumvirate that supported it in Rome, the army's decision not to oppose actively the *coup*, Mussolini's ability to pose as a loyal monarchist – these were no less important to its success than the famous Fascist 'élan'. The same British observer argued surprisingly that 'had there been a parallel movement in Spain, its centre of gravity would have been in the industrial region of Catalonia and its headquarters in Barcelona, as Signor Mussolini's are in Milan' [*sic*]. In fact, precisely this is a strong point of analogy between Primo's 'revolution' and that of Mussolini.[21] A panegyrist of the Spanish Dictatorship was later to equate the role of Barcelona in Primo's seizure of power with that of Covadonga in the Reconquest. It was from the Catalan capital that 'the *reconquista* against the invasion of liberal doctrinarism' had started.[22] In less figurative terms, to curb or liquidate proletarian militancy, an ideal for which Spain's business community had made plainly clear it was ready to engender a dictatorship, was a major *raison d'être* – just as it was in the case of Mussolini – for Primo's take-over.[23] Nor did Catalan industry, scattered as it was in undercapitalized, small family firms, differ from that class of small and medium-sized industrialists who, finding themselves in acute economic difficulties, provided Mussolini with a power base in northern Italy. It was, moreover, the breakdown of Giolittian democracy in Italy and the shaking of the mythical omnipotence of a parliamentary system based on 'oligarchy and *caciquismo*' in Spain, as well as the transition, admittedly more discernible in Italy than in Spain, of both regimes from exclusively manipulatory tactics to mobilizing practices, that created the pre-conditions for a Dictatorial take-over in both countries.[24]

It should be stressed, however, that Primo de Rivera was to be the founder of a syncretic dictatorship. His historical mentors were also various. He combined his military tradition, the regenerationist myth of Costa's 'iron surgeon', Maura's 'revolution from above', and the 'urgent' need to 'disarm anarchist syndicalism that was just about to take possession of our homes',[25] in order to produce a 'revolution' that amalgamated archaic with up-to-date models.

Primo was presented as the legitimate executor of the regenerationist myth: 'He who comes to cure the sick has started already to operate; politicians and political parties are being uprooted from power and the enterprise of recuperation has started.'[26] Like Pavía's *coup* against the politics of the 'anarchic' Republic and Sidonio Paes's rebellion against the Byzantine politics of the Portuguese Republic, and, indeed, like Franco's drive 'to Solder the nation' that had been 'divided by the political parties', Primo de Rivera's pronunciamiento was imbued with an overwhelming passion against 'polities' and 'políticos'.[27]

He ruled out immediately upon his arrival in Madrid the possibility of setting up a government of 'political men', not just because this would have been inconsistent with his attempt to mount a campaign of diverted mobilization, the scapegoats of which were the políticos; but also because this would have entailed a non-radical solution in the eyes of the people, eager to see a 'revolution from above'. 'Revolution from above', Primo observed, was 'a phrase that reflected the ideas that Antonio Maura had inculcated in the popular conscience.'[28] So far, such a revolution had been thwarted by parliamentary liberalism; Primo would give it a renewed chance to succeed. He did not fail to seize upon the legacy of Maura – who the Traditionalist Vázquez de Mella had hoped vainly would become 'a Mussolini before Mussolini' – in order to present his rule as the culmination of a respectable movement of opinion committed to the restructuring of the Spanish state on healthy foundations of citizenship, controlled mobilization, a local government law based on a corporative franchise that might 'solve' the Catalan problem, and a campaign against the vices of petty politics. Significantly, Maura's 'revolution from above' was also a source of inspiration to the future leader of Spain's brand of 'dynamic fascism', José Antonio Primo de Rivera.[29]

[. . .]

Ortega y Gasset, an outstanding protagonist of the revolution from above, saw the reason for Spain's tragic 'invertebration' in the lack of directing elites. A disenchanted liberal, Ortega was also popularized by the Dictator for his own needs. The military were long convinced of the futility of 'polities'. The instability of the parliamentary system as reflected in the 'endless' series of 'crises' was there to prove their point.[30] Ortega, of course, was no supporter of a *cuartelazo* (*coup d'état*) as the adequate response to the 'crisis of parliamentarism'. Yet, in February 1920, he expressed his view that 'a government of the military would have the advantage of putting an end to this parliamentary farce that so disgusts us'. 'It is up to the military', he continued, 'to impose silence and order upon this political gibberish, smiting the ministerial counsels, and taking hold of power if the crown is reluctant to grant it to them in goodwill.'[31] In his vigorous demand for a regime based on 'unity, agility, competence and personal responsibility' – 'virtues that are alien to the parliamentary organism' – Ortega enabled the military to claim intellectual legitimacy for their anti-parliamentarianism. Parliaments, Ortega would argue, had been invaded by 'la populacheria', 'turbulence', and by a 'plebeian taste for scenes of cheap dramatics'. This was the reason why the high and small bourgeoisie, he wrote, wanted nothing 'but to see the boat sailing', and they would rather have at the helm a 'strong hand'.[32]

   Would the Dictatorship create the elite pleaded for by Ortega to replace sterile parliamentarism? On the morning of 14 September, when an ecstatic crowd accompanied the would-be Dictator to the train which was to take him from his Barcelona military and civilian power-base to assume power, under the king's invitation, in Madrid, everything seemed possible. But, the task of making 'the boat sail with a strong hand at the helm' could, and would, be immediately put into practice.

Notes

1   Bragulat Julio Busquets, *Pronunciamientos y golpes de Estado en España* (II) (Barcelona, 1982), 137–9.

2   Cf. the case of the Prussian army in J. W. Wheeler-Bennett, *The Nemesis of Power: The German Army in Politics 1918–1945* (New York, 1964), 5, 200 [. . .].

3   Araquistan Luis de, *El ocaso de un régimen* (Madrid, 1930), 224–5.

4   Martín Revesz, *Frente al Dictador* (Madrid, nd), 60. *The Economist*, 22 Sept. 1923 was aware of the overall implications of Primo's *coup*; it was 'a further blow to the stability of Europe, because it will lower by several points more the prestige of parliamentary systems of government'. Cf. Menéndez Pidal, *Los Españoles ante la historia* (Madrid, 1971), 225: he saw the trend towards dictatorship in Spain in the 1920s as an assertion of Spanish traditional exclusivism, that was further enhanced by the inspiration received from European models.

5   Raul Morodó, 'Una revisión de la Dictadura: Acción Española' in *Cuadernos Económicos de I. C. E.*, no. 10 (1979), 91–108.

6   *Acción Española*, 1 Feb. 1932, 429. See also ibid., 16 Mar. 1933, pp. 99–106.

7   F. Bonmati, *El principe Don Juan de España*, quoted in Bernardo Díaz Nosty, *La irresistible ascención de Juan March* (Madrid, 1977) p. 113.

8   Aurelio Joaniquet, Calvo Sotelo, *Una vida fecunda, un ideario político, una doctrina económica* (Santander, 1939), 56 [. . .].

9   Franz Neumann wrote about the 'simple dictatorship' that exercises power through absolute control of the traditional means of coercion (the army, the police, the bureaucracy). This limitation is due less to self-imposed restraints than to the absence of any need for more sophisticated and extensive controls, to which dictatorships that emerge out of a crisis of democracy would have to resort. See his 'Notes on the Theory of Dictatorship', in *The Democratic and the Authoritarian State: Essays in Political and Legal Theory* (London 1964), 235–6.

10   [. . .] For the origins of the Romanian royal dictatorships see Henry L. Roberts, *Rumania. Political Problems of an Agrarian State* (Archon Books, 1969), 170–260; Robert Lee Wolff, *The Balkans in our Time* (Harvard University Press, 1967), 101–18, 126–32; Eugene Weber, 'Romania' in Hans Rogger and Eugene Weber, *The European Right. A Historical Profile* (University of California Press, 1966), 550–2. For the Yugoslavian case, see J. B. Hoptner, *Yugoslavia in Crisis 1924–1931* (New York, 1962), 32–4; Vladimir Dedijer *et al*, *History of Yugoslavia* (McGraw-Hill Book Company 1974), 513–46. For the origins of Metaxas's seizure of power, see the excellent study of Harry C. Cliadakis, 'Greece 1935–1941: The Metaxas Regime and the Diplomatic Background to World War II' (Ph.D. dissertation, University of New York, 1970), 47–74.

11   For the structural changes, see L. S. Stavrianos, 'The influence of the West on the Balkans', and Trian Stoianovich, 'The Social Foundations of Balkan Politics 1750–1941', in Charles and Barbara Jelavich (eds.), *The Balkans in Transition. Essays on the Development of Balkan Life and Politics since the Eighteenth Century* (University of California Press, 1963), 184–226.

12   For a short discussion of the problem of 'transitional dictatorships', see Howard J. Wiarda, *Dictatorship and Development. The Methods of Control in Trujillo's Dominican Republic* (University of Florida Press, Gainesville, 1970), 188–9 [. . .].

13   This 'model', sometimes applied to the origins of Mussolini's rise to power, seems to me more emphatically relevant to the cases mentioned in this paragraph. Cf. Barrington Moore, *Social Origins of Dictatorship and Democracy* (Boston, 1967), 445; John Kautsky, *The Political Consequences of Modernization* (New York, 1972), 210; Alan Cassels, 'Janus: The Two Faces of Fascism' in Henry Turner (ed.), *Reappraisals of Fascism* (New York, 1975), 69–92. A. F. K. Organski, *The Stages of Political Development* (New York, 1965), makes the useful distinction between the syncretic fascism that emerged in newly industrialized nations and the totalitarian National Socialism.

14   Rodrigo Soriano, *A los hombres con verguenza*, in Romanones Archive, Leg. 54, no. 20.

15   The term is used by Professor Pribicevič to define the inter-war dictatorships in the Balkans, see Centre for Mediterranean Studies, American Universities Field Staff, *The Identification of Pre-Fascist Elements in Certain Modern Societies. Summary of Seminar Proceedings* (Rome, 1971), 62–5.

16   Cf. C. Viver Pi Sunyer, *El personal político de Franco (1936–1945)* (Barcelona, 1978), 55–6.

17   Martinez de la Riva, *Las jornadas*, 58.

18   *L'Etoile belge*, 9 June 1926.

19   Quoted in J. Cortés-Cavanillas, *Alfonso XIII. Vida, Confesiones y Muerte* (Barcelona, 1982), 290 [. . .].

20   *The Economist*, 22 Sept. 1923.

21   *The Economist*, 22 Sept. 1923 [. . .].

22   W. G. Oliveiros, 'La nueva Cataluña en la nueva España', *La Nación*, 1 June 1927.

23   See Sergio Vilar, *Fascismo y militarismo* (Barcelona, 1978), 152–8 [. . .].

24   For the breakdown of Giolittian parliamentarism, see Christopher Seton-Watson, *Italy from Liberalism to Fascism 1870–1925* (London, 1967), 596–312; A. Lyttelton, *The Seizure of Power. Fascism in Italy 1919–1929* (London: Weidenfeld & Nicolson, 1973), 15–41.

25   Bueno, Manuel, *España y la monarquía*, Estudio político (New York, 1925) 121–2, 142; Gandarías, Manuel, *Perfiles síquicos del Dictador Primo de Rivera y bosquejo razonado de suobra* (Cadiz, 1929) 27.

26   Ejército y Armada, 14 Sept. 1923.

27   For the origins of Sidonio Paes's seizure of power, see Jesus Pabón, *La revolución portuguesa, de don Carlos a Sidonio Paes* (Madrid, 1941). For Pavía, see Stanley G. Payne, *Politics and the Military in Modern Spain* (Stanford, Calif., 1967), 36–7.

28   Primo's article in *The Times*, 20 Mar. 1930.

29   Juan Beneyto Pérez and José Maria Costa Serrano, *El Partido* (Zaragoza, 1939), 77.

30   Fifteen different cabinets served in the years 1917–23. Especially politically unstable were the months that preceded the *coup d'état*. The result of the switching of chairs was that when Primo de Rivera put the lid on the parliamentary system only three of the ministers had been in office from the beginning of October 1922. See G. Maura Y Gamazo, *Bosquejo histórico de la Dictadura* (Madrid, 1936), pp. 18–19 [. . .].

31   *El Sol*, 13 Feb. 1920.

32   Ortega y Gasset, *Invertebrate Spain* (London, 1937); 'Vieja y nueva política. Conferencia en el teatro de la Comedia, en Madrid, el 23 de marzo do 1914' in José Ortega y Gasset, *Discursos políticos* (Madrid, 1974), 63–102 [. . .].

References

The following titles have been used in the Introduction to the volume, as well as in the smaller introductory pieces to each section.

Adamson, W. L. (1993) *Avant-Garde Florence: From Modernism to Fascism* (Cambridge, MA: Harvard University Press)

Alatri, P. (1963) *Le origini del fascismo* (Rome: Editori Reuniti)

Allardyce, G. (1979) 'What Fascism is Not: Thoughts on the Deflation of a Concept', *American Historical Review*, 84, 367–88

Aquarone, A. (1965) *L'organizzazione dello Stato Totalitario* (Turin: Einaudi)

Aquarone, A. (1981) 'The Totalitarian State and Personal Dictatorship' in E. A. Menze (ed.) *Totalitarianism Reconsidered* (Port Washington: Kennikat Press), 84–103

Arendt, H. (1958) *The Origins of Totalitarianism* (New York: Meridian Books)

Aron, R. (1954) *Histoire de Vichy* (Paris: Fayard)

Azzi, S. C. (1991) 'The Historiography of Fascist Foreign Policy', *The Historical Journal*, 1, 187–203

Bartov, O. (1987) 'Historians on the Eastern Front: Andreas Hillgruber and Germany's Tragedy', *Tel Aviver Jahrbuch für deutsche Geschichte*, 16, 327–43

Bartov, O. (1991) 'Soldiers, Nazis and War in the Third Reich', *Journal of Modern History*, 63, 44–60

Bartov, O. (1996) 'Savage War', in M. Burleigh (ed.) *Confronting the Nazi Past: New Debates on Modern German History* (London: Collins & Brown), 125–39

Battaglia, R. (1953) *Storia della Resistenza italiana (8 settembre 1943–25 aprile 1945)* (Turin: Einaudi)

Beetham, D. (1983) *Marxists in Face of Fascism* (Manchester: Manchester University Press)

Ben-Ami, S. (1979) 'The Forerunners of Spanish Fascism: Union Patriotica and Union Monarquica', *European Studies Review*, 9, 49–80

Ben-Ami, S. (1983) *Fascism from Above: The Dictatorship of Primo de Rivera in Spain, 1923–1930* (Oxford: Oxford University Press)

Berger, S. (1995) 'Historian and Nation-Building in Germany after Reunification', *Past and Present*, 148, 187–222

Berger, S. (1999) 'Historians and the Search of National Identity in the Reunified Germany' in S. Berger, M. Donovan and K. Passmore (eds) *Writing National Histories: Western Europe since 1800* (London: Routledge), 252–64

Bertram, G. (1980) *Collaborationism in France during the Second World War* (Ithaca: Cornell University Press)

Bessel, R. (1996) (ed.) *Fascist Italy and Nazi Germany: Comparisons and Contrasts* (Cambridge: Cambridge University Press)

Blackbourn, D. (1991) 'The German Bourgeoisie', in D. Blackbourn and R. J. Evans (eds) *The German Bourgeoisie: Essays on the Social History of the German Middle Class from the Late Eighteenth to the Early Twentieth Century* (London: Routledge – 2nd edn, 1993), 1–46

Blackbourn, D. and Eley, G. (1984) (eds) *The Peculiarities of German History* (Oxford: Oxford University Press)

Blackbourn, D. and Evans, R. J. (1991) (eds) *The German Bourgeoisie: Essays on the Social History of the German Middle Class from the Late Eighteenth to the Early Twentieth Century* (London: Routledge – 2nd edn, 1993)

Blinkhorn, M. (ed.) (1990) *Fascists and Conservatives: The Radical Right and the Establishment in the Twentieth Century Europe* (London: Unwin Hyman), 71–97

Boca, A. Del (1969) *Ethiopian War, 1935–41* (Chicago: University of Chicago Press)

Boca, A. Del (1976) *Gli italiani in Africa orientale* (Rome and Bari: Laterza)

Bosworth, R. J. B. (1979) in R. J. B. Bosworth and G. Cresciani (eds) *Altro Polo: A Volume of Italian Studies* (Sydney: Frederick May Foundation for Italian Studies, University of Sydney)

Bosworth, R. J. B. (1983) 'Italian Foreign Policy and its Historiography' in R. J. B. Bosworth and G. Rizzo (eds) *Altro Polo: Intellectuals and Their Ideas in Contemporary Italy* (Sydney: Frederick May Foundation for Italian Studies, University of Sydney), 52–96

Bosworth, R. J. B. (1998) *The Italian Dictatorship: Problems and Perspectives in the Interpretation of Mussolini and Fascism* (London and New York: Arnold)

Bracher, K. D. (1956) 'Stufen totalitärer Machtergreifung', *Vierteljahrshefte für Zeitgeschichte*, 4, 30–42

Bracher, K. D. (1960) *Die nationalsozialistische Machtergreifung. Studien zur Errichtung des totalitären Herrschaftssystems in Deutschland 1933/34* (Cologne: Westdeutscher Verlag)

Bracher, K. D. (1971) *The German Dictatorship* (London: Weidenfeld & Nicolson)

Bracher, K. D. (1976) *Zeitgeschichtliche Kontroversen um Faschismus, Totalitarianismus und Demokratie* (Munich: Piper)

Bracher, K. D. (1980) *Totalitarianismus und Faschismus. Eine wissenschaftliche und politische Begriffskontroverse* (Munich and Vienna: C. Hanser)

Broszat, M. (1970) 'Soziale Motivation und Führer-Bindung der Nationalsozialismus', *Vierteljahrshefte für Zeitgeschichte*, 18, 392–400

Broszat, M. (1981) *The Hitler State: The Foundation and Development of the Internal Structure of the Third Reich* (London and New York: Longman)

Burleigh, M. and Wippermann, W. (1991) *The Racial State: Germany 1933–1945* (Cambridge: Cambridge University Press)

Burrin, P. (1993) *La France á l'Heure Allemande: 1940–1944* (Paris: Seuil)

Caplan, J. (1977) 'Theories of Fascism: Nicos Poulantzas as Historian', *History Workshop Journal*, 3, 83–100

Carr, E. H. (1987) *What is History?* (London: Penguin, 2nd edn)

Carsten, F. L. (1964) *The Rise of Fascism* (London: Batsford)

Cassels, A. (1969) *Fascist Italy* (London: Routledge and Kegan Paul)

Cassels, A. (1975) *Fascism* (New York: Crowell)

Chabod, F. (1963a) *History of Italian Fascism* (London: Weidenfeld & Nicolson)

Chabod, F. (1963b) *Storia della politica estera italiana dal 1870 al 1896. Le premesse* (Bari: Laterza)

Charini, R. (1991) 'The "Movimento Soziale Italiano": A Historical Profile' in L. Cheles, R. Ferguson and M. Vaughan (eds) *Neo-fascism in Europe* (London and New York: Longman), 43–65

Childers, T. (1983) *The Nazi Voter: The Social Foundations of Fascism in Germany, 1919–1939* (Chapel Hill: University of North Carolina Press)

Clark, M. (1977) *Antonio Gramsci and the Revolution that Failed* (New Haven: Yale University Press)

Clark, M. (1999) 'Gioacchino Volpe and Fascist Historiography in Italy' in S. Berger, M. Donovan and K. Passmore (eds) *Writing National Histories: Western Europe since 1800* (London: Routledge) 189–201

Conan, E. and Rousso, H. (1994) *Vichy, un passé qui ne passe pas* (Paris: Fayard)

Corner, P. (1975) *Fascism in Ferrara 1915–1925* (London: Oxford University Press)

Costa Pinto, A. (1986) 'Fascist Ideology Revisited: Zeev Sternhell and his Critics', *European History Quarterly*, 16, 465–83

Croce, B. (1941) *History as the Story of Liberty* (London: Allen and Unwin)

Croce, B. (1944) *Per la nuova vita dell'Italia. Scritti e discorsi 1943–44* (Naples: Reuniti)

Czichon, E. (1972) *Wer verhalf Hitler zur Macht?* (Cologne, 3rd edn)

Dahrendorf, R. (1967) *Society and Democracy in Germany* (Garden City: Anchor Books)

De Felice, R. (1965–97) *Mussolini* (Turin: Einaudi)

—— (1965) *Mussolini il rivoluzionario*

—— (1966) *Mussolini il fascista*, 1: *La conquista del potere, 1921–1925*

—— (1968) *Mussolini il fascista*, 2: *L'organizzazione dello Stato Fascista, 1925–1929*

—— (1974) *Mussolini il duce*, 1: *Gli anni del consenso 1929–1936*

—— (1981) *Mussolini il duce*, 2: *Lo Stato Totalitario, 1936–1940*

—— (1990) *Mussolini l'alleato*, 1: *L'Italia in guerra, 1940–1943* (2 vols)

—— (1997) *Mussolini l'alleato*, 2: *La guerra civile 1943–1945*

De Felice, R. (1970) (ed.) *Il fascismo. Le interpretazioni dei contemporanei e degli storici* (Bari: Laterza)

De Felice, R. (1975) *Intrervista sul fascismo*, ed. by M. Ledeen (Bari: Laterza)

De Felice, R. (1977) *Interpretations of Fascism* (Cambridge, MA and London: Harvard University Press)

De Felice, R. (1979) 'Italian Historiography since the Second World War', in R. J. B. Bosworth and G. Cresciani (eds) *Altro Polo: A Volume of Italian Studies* (Sydney: F. May Foundation)

De Felice, R. (1988) *Storia degli ebrei sotto il fascismo* (Turin: Einaudi, 4th edn)

De Felice, R. (1995) *Rosso e nero* (Milan: Baldini & Castaldi)

De Grand, A. J. (1995) *Fascist Italy and Nazi Germany: The 'Fascist' Style of Rule* (London and New York: Routledge)

Degras, J. (1965) (ed.) *The Communist International 1919–1943* (Oxford: Oxford University Press)

Die Zeit, Zeit-dokument 'Die Goldhagen-Kontroverse', January 1996

Dinitroff, G. (1982) *Gegen Faschismus und Krieg. Ausgewählte Reden und Schriften* (Leipzig: Reclam)

Dorpalen, A. (1985) *German History in Marxist Perspective. The East German Approach* (London: Tauris)

Eatwell, R. (1992) 'Towards a New Model of Generic Fascism', *Journal of Theoretical Politics*, 4, 161–94

Eatwell, R. (1993) 'Fascism', in R. Eatwell and A. Wright (eds) *Contemporary Political Ideologies* (London: Pinter), 169–91

Eatwell, R. (1995) 'The Holocaust Denial: Study in Propaganda Technique' in L. Cheles, R. Ferguson and M. Vaughan (eds) *The Far Right in Western and Eastern Europe* (London and New York: Longman), 120–46

Eatwell, R. (1996a) 'On Defining the "Fascist Minimum": The Centrality of Ideology', *Journal of Political Ideologies*, 1, 303–19

Eatwell, R. (1996b) *Fascism: A History* (London: Vintage)

Eichholtz, D. (1971–96) *Geschichte der deutschen Kriegswirtschaft, 1939–1945*, 3 vols (East Berlin: Akademie-Verlag)

Eichholtz, D. and Gossweiler, K. (eds) (1980) *Faschismus-Forschung: Positionen, Probleme, Polemik* (Berlin: Akademie-Verlag)

Eley, G. (1983) 'What Produces Fascism: Pre-industrial Traditions or the Crisis of the Capitalist State', *Politics and Society*, 12, 76–82

Evans, R. J. (1989) *In Hitler's Shadow: West German Historians and the Attempt to Escape from the Nazi Past* (London: Tauris)

Fargon, L. P. (1991) *Il libro della memoria. Gli ebrei deportati dall'Italia 1943–1945* (Milan: Mursia)

Fischer, F. (1967) *Germany's Aims in the First World War* (New York: Chatto & Windus)

Fischer, F. (1974) *World Power or Decline: The Controversy over Germany's Aims in the First World War* (New York: Norton)

Fischer, F. (1975) *War of Illusions: German Policies from 1911 to 1914* (New York: Norton)

Fischer, F. (1986) *From Kaiserreich to Third Reich: Elements of Continuity in German History, 1871–1945* (London and Boston: Allen & Unwin)

Frey, H. (1999) 'Rebuilding France: Gaullist Historiography, the Rise–Fall Myth and French Identity (1945–58)' in S. Berger, M. Donovan and K. Passmore (eds) *Writing National Histories: Western Europe since 1800* (London: Routledge), 205–16

Friedländer, S. (1987a) 'Some Reflections on the Historication of National Socialism', *Tel Aviver Jahrbuch für deutsche Geschichte*, 16, 310–24

Friedländer, S. (1987b) 'West Germany and the Burden of the Past: The Ongoing Debate', *Jerusalem Quarterly*, 42, 3–18

Friedrich, C. J. (1954) 'The Unique Character of Totalitarian Society', in C. J. Friedrich (ed.) *Totalitarianism* (New York: Grosset & Dunlap), 47–60

Friedrich, C. J. and Brzezinski, Z. K. (1956) *Totalitarian Dictatorship and Autocracy* (Cambridge, MA: Harvard University Press)

Fulbrook, M. (1999a) 'Dividing the Past, Defining the Present: Historians and National Identity in the Two Germanies' in S. Berger, M. Donovan and K. Passmore (eds) *Writing National Histories: Western Europe since 1800* (London: Routledge), 217–29

Fulbrook, M. (1999b) *German National Identity after the Holocaust* (London: Polity Press)

Galli della Loggia, E. (1996) *La morte della patria. La crisis dell'idea della nazione tra Resistenza, antifascismo e Repubblica* (Rome and Bari: Laterza)

Gaulle, C. de (1954–9) *Memoires de guerre*, 3 vols (Paris: Plon)

Gentile, E. (1975) *Le origini dell'ideologia fascista, 1918–1925* (Rome and Bari: Laterza)

Gentile, E. (1986) 'Fascism in Italian Historiography: In Search of an Individual Historical Identity', *Journal of Contemporary History*, 19, 251–74

Gentile, E. (1994) 'La nazione del fascismo. Alle origini del declino dello stato nazionale' in G. Spadolini (ed) *Nazione e nazionalità in Italia. Dall'alba del secolo ai nostri giorni* (Rome and Bari: Laterza), 65–124

Gentile, E. (1995) *La via italiana al totalitarismo. Il partito e lo stato nel regime fascista* (Rome: La Nuova Italia Scientifica)

Gentile, E. (1997) 'Renzo De Felice: A Tribute', *Journal of Contemporary History*, 32, 139–51

Gentile, G. (1928a) 'The Philosophical Basis of Fascism', *Foreign Affairs*, 6, 290–304

Gentile, G. (1928b) *Fascismo e cultura* (Milan: Fratelli Treves)

Germino, D. L. (1959) *The Italian Fascist Party in Power: A Study in Totalitarian Rule* (Minneapolis: University of Minnesota Press)

Goglia, L. (1988) 'Note sul razzismo coloniale fascista', *Storia Contemporanea*, 19, 1223–66

Goldhagen, D. (1996) *Hitler's Willing Executioners: Ordinary Germans and the Holocaust* (London: Little, Brown & Co.)

Gordon, B. (1980) *Collaborationism in France during the Second World War* (Ithaca: Cornell University Press)

Gramsci, A. (1966) *Socialismo e fascismo. L'Ordine Nuovo 1921–1922* (Turin: Einaudi)

Gramsci, A. (1971) *Selections from Prison* (London: Weidenfeld & Nicolson)

Grazia, V. De (1981) *The Culture of Consent: Mass Organisation of Leisure in Fascist Italy* (Cambridge: Cambridge University Press)

Grazia, V. De (1991) *How Fascism Ruled Women: Italy 1922–1945* (Berkeley: University of California Press)

Gregor, A. J. (1974a) *Interpretations of Fascism* (Morristown, NJ: General Learning Press)

Gregor, A. J. (1974b) *The Fascist 'Persuasion' in Radical Politics* (Princeton: Princeton University Press)

Gregor, A. J. (1976) *The Ideology of Fascism: The Rationale of Totalitarianism* (New York: Free Press)

Gregor, A. J. (1979a) *Italian Fascism and Developmental Dictatorship* (Princeton, NJ: Princeton University Press)

Gregor, A. J. (1979b) *Young Mussolini and the Intellectual Origins of Fascism* (Berkeley: University of California Press)

Griffin, R. (1993a) 'Fascism' in W. Outhwaite and T. Bottomore (eds) *The Blackwell Dictionary of Social Thought* (Oxford: Basil Blackwell), 223–4

Griffin, R. (1993b) *The Nature of Fascism* (London: Routledge)

Griffin, R. (1995) (ed) *Fascism* (Oxford and New York: Oxford University Press)

Griffin, R. (1998) *International Fascism: Theories, Causes and the New Consensus* (London: Arnold)

Hagtvet, B. and Kühnl, R. (1980) 'Contemporary Approaches to Fascism: A Survey of Paradigms' in S. U. Larsen, B. Hagtvet and J. P. Myklebust (eds) *Who Were the Fascists? Social Roots of European Fascism* (Bergen, Oslo, Tromso: Universitetsforlaget), 26–51

Hallie, P. (1979) *Lest Innocent Blood Be Shed: The Story of the Village of Le Chambon and How Goodness Happened There* (New York: Harper & Row)

Hamilton, A. (1971) *The Appeal of Fascism: A Study of Intellectuals and Fascism 1919–1945* (London: Blond)

Hayes, P. M. (1973) *Fascism* (London: Allen & Unwin)

Hayes, P. M. (1992) 'The Triumph of Caesarism: Fascism and Nazism' in Hayes (ed.) *Themes in Modern European History, 1890–1945* (London and New York: Routledge), 174–204

Hennessy, A. (1979) 'Fascism and Populism in Latin America' in W. Laqueur (ed.) *Fascism: A Reader's Guide* (Harmondsworth: Penguin)

Herf, J. (1984) *Reactionary Modernism: Technology, Culture and Politics in Weimar and the Third Reich* (Cambridge: Cambridge University Press)

Hildebrand, K. (1973) 'Hitlers Ort in der Geschichte der preussisch-deutschen Nationalstaates', *Historische Zeitschrift*, 217, 584–632

Hildebrand, K. (1976) 'Geschichte oder "Gesellschaftsgeschichte"? Die Notwendigkeiten einer politischer Geschichtschreibung von den internationalen Beziehungen', *Historische Zeitschrift*, 223, 328–57

Hildebrand, K. (1979) 'Hitlers "Programm" und seine Realisierung' in M. Funke (ed.) *Hitler, Deutschland, und die Mächte. Materialien zur Aussenpolitik des Dritten Reiches* (Düsseldorf: Droste), 63–93

Hillgruber, A. (1973) 'Politische Geschichte in moderner Sicht', *Historische Zeitschrift*, 216, 529–52

Hillgruber, A. (1986) 'Der Zusammenbruch im Osten 1944–5 als Problem der deutschen Nationalgeschichte und der europäischen Geschichte', in Hillgruber, *Zweierlei Untergang: Die Zerschlagung des Deutschen Reiches und das Ende des europäischen Judentums* (Berlin: Propyläen)

Hillgruber, A. (1988a) 'Das Russlandbild der führenden deutschen Militärs vor Beginn des Angriffs auf die Sowjetunion' in A. Hillgruber (ed.) *Die Zerstörung Europas. Beiträge zur Weltkriegsepoche, 1914 bis 1945* (Berlin: Propyläen), 256–72

Hoffmann, P. (1996) *The History of the German Resistance, 1933–1945* (Montreal: McGill-Queen's University Press, 3rd edn)

Hoffmann, S. (1974) *Decline or Renewal? France since the 1930s* (New York: Viking Press)

Horkheimer, M. (1997) *Dialectic of Enlightenment* (London: Verso)

Iggers, G. (ed.) (1991) *Marxist Historiography in Transformation* (Oxford: Berg)

Ipsen, C. (1996) *Dictating Demography: The Problem of Population in Fascist Italy* (Cambridge: Cambridge University Press)

Jäckel, E. (1972) *Hitler's Weltanschauung: A Blueprint for Power* (Middletown, CT)

Jackson, J. (1999) 'Historian and the Nation in Contemporary France' in S. Berger, M. Donovan & K. Passmore (eds) *Writing National Histories: Western Europe since 1800* (London: Routledge), 239–51

Jarausch, K. H. (1979) ' "From Second to Third Reich": The Problem of Continuity in German Foreign Policy', *Central European History*, 12, 68–82

Juenger, E. (1922) *Der Kampf als inneres Erlebnis* (Berlin: ES Mittler & Sohn)

Jung, E. J. (1927) *Die Herrschaft der Minderwertigen. Ihr Zerfall und ihre Ablösung durch ein neues Reich* (Berlin: Deutsche Rundschau)

Kershaw, I. (1995) *The Nazi Dictatorship: Problems and Perspectives of Interpretation* (London: Edward Arnold, 4th edn)

Kershaw, I. and Lewin, M. (1997) (eds) *Stalinism and Nazism: Dictatorships in Comparison* (Cambridge: Cambridge University Press)

Knowlton, J. and Cates, T. (1993) (eds) *Forever in the Shadow of Hitler? Original Documents of the Historikerstreit, the Controversy concerning the Singularity of the Holocaust* (Atlantic Highlands, NJ: Humanities Press)

Knox, M. (1984) 'Conquest, Domestic and Foreign, in Fascist Italy and Nazi Germany', *Journal of Modern History*, 56, 1–57

Knox, M. (1995) 'The Fascist Regime, its Foreign Policy and its Wars: An Anti-anti-Fascist Orthodoxy?', *Contemporary European History*, 4, 13–31

Knox, M. (1996) 'Expansionist Zeal, Fighting Power, and Staying Power in the Italian and German Dictatorships' in R. Bessel (ed.), *Fascist Italy and Nazi Germany: Comparisons and Contrasts* (Cambridge: Cambridge University Press), 115–33

Knox, M. (2000) *Common Destiny: Dictatorship, Foreign Policy, and War in Fascist Italy and Nazi Germany* (Cambridge: Cambridge University Press)

Koch, H. W. (1972) (ed.) *The Origins of the First World War* (London: Macmillan)

Koch, H. W. (1985) 'Hitler's Programme and the Genesis of Operation "Barbarossa"', in Koch (ed.) *Aspects of the Third Reich* (Houndmills and London: Macmillan), 285–322

Kocka, J. (1988) 'German History Before Hitler: The Debate about the German Sonderweg', *Journal of Contemporary History*, 23, 3–16

Kocka, J. (1990) 'Nur keinen neuen Sonderweg', *Die Zeit*, 19 October 1990

Kuczynski, J. (1972) *Klassen und Klassenkämpfe im imperialistischen Deutschland und in der BRD* (Frankfurt: Verlag Marxistische Blätter)

Kühnl, R. (1980) 'Contemporary Approaches to Fascism: A Survey of Paradigms', in S. U. Larsen, B. Hagtvet and J. P. Myklebust (eds) *Who Were the Fascists? Social Roots of European Fascism* (Bergen, Oslo, Tromso: Universitetsforlaget), 26–51

Kühnl, R. (1987) (ed.) *Vergangenheit, die nicht vergeht* (Cologne: Pahl-Rugenstein)

Landy, M. (1986) *Fascism in Film: The Italian Commercial Cinema, 1931–1943* (Princeton: Princeton University Press)

Laquer, W. (1976) (ed.) *Fascism: A Reader's Guide* (1st ed.; 2nd ed. 1979 by Penguin: Harmondsworth)

Laqueur, W. (1996) *Fascism: Past, Present and Future* (Oxford: Oxford University Press)

Larsen, S. U., Hagtvet, B. and Myklebust, J. P. (1980) (eds) *Who Were the Fascists? Social Roots of European Fascism* (Bergen, Oslo, Tromso: Universitetsforlaget)

Latour, A. (1981) *The Jewish Resistance in France* (New York: Holocaust Library)

Lazare, L. (1996) *How Jewish Organizations Fought the Holocaust in France* (New York: Columbia University Press)

Levy, C. (1999) 'Historians and the "First Republic"' in S. Berger, M. Donovan and K. Passmore (eds) *Writing National Histories: Western Europe since 1800* (London: Routledge), 265–78

Linz, J. J. (1979) 'Some Notes towards a Comparative Study of Fascism in Sociological Historical Perspective' in W. Laqueur (ed.) *Fascism: A Reader's Guide. Analyses, Interpretations, Bibliography* (Harmondsworth: Penguin), 29–39

Linz, J. J. (1980) 'Political Space and Fascism as Late-Comer', in S. U. Larsen, B. Hagtvet and J. P. Myklebust (eds) *Who Were the Fascists? Social Roots of European Fascism* (Bergen, Oslo, Tromso: Universitetsforlaget), 153–89

Lipset, S. (1963) *Political Man: The Social Bases of Politics* (London: Mercury Books)

Lottman, H. (1986) *The Purge: The Purification of French Collaborators after World War II* (New York: William Morrow)

Lozek, G. and Richter, R. (1980) 'Zur Auseinandersetzung mit vorherrschenden bürgerlichen Faschismustheorien' in D. Eichholtz and K. Gossweiler (eds) *Faschismusforschung. Positionen, Probleme, Polemik* (Cologne: Pahl-Rugenstein), 417–51

Ludwig, E. (1982) *Talks with Mussolini* (New York: AMS Press)

Lyttelton, A. (1979) *The Seizure of Power: Fascism in Italy 1919–1929* (London: Weidenfeld & Nicolson, 2nd edn)

Lyttelton, A. (1996) 'The "Crisis of Bourgeois Society" and the Origins of Fascism' in R. Bessel (ed.) *Fascist Italy and Nazi Germany: Comparisons and Contrasts* (Cambridge: Cambridge University Press), 12–22

Macartney, M. H. H. (1944) *One Man Alone: The History of Mussolini and the Axis* (London: Chatto & Windus)

Mack Smith, D. (1969) *Italy: A Modern History* (Ann Arbor: University of Michigan Press)

Mack Smith, D. (1981) *Mussolini* (London: Weidenfeld & Nicolson)

Maier, C. (1988) *The Unmasterable Past: History, Holocaust, and German National Identity* (Cambridge, MA: Harvard University Press)

Maiocchi, R. (1999) *Scienza italiana e razzismo fascista* (Firenze: La Nuova Italia)

Marrus, M. R. and Paxton, R. O. (1981) *Vichy France and the Jews* (Stanford: Stanford University Press)

Martel, G. (1999) 'The Revisionist as Moralist – A. J. P. Taylor and the Lessons of European History' in G. Martel (ed.) *The Origins of the Second World War Reconsidered: A. J. P. Taylor and the Historians* (London: Routledge), 1–12

Marwick, A. (1970) *Nature of History* (London: Macmillan)

Mason, T. (1968) 'The Primacy of Politics – Politics and Economics in National Socialist Germany' in S. J. Woolf (ed.) *The Nature of Fascism* (London: Weidenfeld & Nicolson), 165–95

Mason, T. (1975) *Arbeiterklasse und Volksgemeinschaft. Dokumente und Materialen zur deutschen Arbeiterpolitik, 1936–1939* (Opladen: Westdeutscher Verlag)

Mason, T. (1981) 'Intention and Explanation: A Current Controversy about the Interpretation of National Socialism' in G. Hirschfeld and L. Kettenacker (eds) *Der 'Führerstaat'. Mythos und Realität. Studien zur Struktur und Politik des Dritten Reiches* (Stuttgart: Klett-Cotta), 23–42

Mason, T. (1993a) 'Whatever Happened to "Fascism"?', in T. Childers and J. Caplan (eds) *Reevaluating the Third Reich* (New York and London: Holmes & Meier), 253–62

Mason, T. (1993b) *Social Policy in the Third Reich: The Working Class and the National Community* (Providence, RI and Oxford: Berg)

Mayda, G. (1978) *Ebrei sotto Salò. La persecuzione antisemita 1943–1945* (Milan: Feltrinelli)

Meinecke, F. (1950) *German Catastrophe: Reflections and Recollections* (Cambridge, MA: Harvard University Press)

Merkl, P. H. (1975) *Political Violence Under the Swastika: 581 Early Nazis* (New Jersey: Princeton University Press)

Merkl, P. H. (1980) 'Comparing Fascist Movements' in S. U. Larsen, B. Hagtvet and J. P. Myklebust (eds) *Who Were the Fascists? Social Roots of European Fascism* (Bergen, Oslo, Tromso: Universitetsforlaget), 752–83

Michaelis, M. (1978) *Mussolini and the Jews: German–Italian Relations and the Jewish Question in Italy 1922–1945* (Oxford: Oxford University Press for the Institute of Jewish Affairs)

Michaelis, M. (1989) 'Fascism, Totalitarianism and the Holocaust: Reflections on Current Interpretations of National Socialist Anti-Semitism', *European History Quarterly*, 19: 85–103

Milward (1979) *War, Economy and Society* (Berkeley: University of California Press)

Milza, P. (1987) *Fascisme français, passé et présent* (Paris: Flammarion)

Mommsen, H. (1966) *Beamtentum im Dritten Reich. Mit ausgewählten Quellen zur national-sozialistischen Beamtenpolitik* (Stuttgart: Deutsche Verlagsanstalt)

Mommsen, H. (1977) 'Ausnahmezustand als Herrschaftstechnik des Nationalsozialist-ischen-Regimes' in M. Funke (ed.) *Hitler, Deutschland und die Mächte. Materialien zur Aussenpolitik des Dritten Reiches* (Düsseldorf: Droste), 30–45

Mommsen, H. (1979) 'National Socialism: Continuity and Change' in W. Laqueur (ed.) *Fascism: A Reader's Guide. Analyses, Interpretations, Bibliography* (Harmondsworth: Penguin), 151–92

Mommsen, H. (1995) 'Noch einmal: Nationalsozialismus und Modernisierung', *Geschichte und Gesellschaft*, 21, 391–402

Mommsen, H. (1997) 'Cumulative Radicalisation and Progressive Self-Destruction as Structural Determinants of the Nazi Dictatorship' in I. Kershaw and M. Lewin (eds) *Stalinism and Nazism: Dictatorships in Comparison* (Cambridge and New York: Cambridge University Press), 75–87

Moore, B. (1966) *The Social Origins of Dictatorship and Democracy* (Boston, MA: Beacon Press)

Moore, B. (1978) *Injustice: The Social Bases of Obedience and Revolt* (London: Macmillan)

Mosse, G. L. (1964) *The Crisis of German Ideology* (New York: Grosset & Dunlap)

Mosse, G. L. (1979) 'Towards a General Theory of Fascism' in Mosse (ed.) *International Fascism: New Thoughts and New Approaches* (London and Beverly Hills: Sage Publications), 1–41

Mühlberger, D. (1980) 'The Sociology of the NSDAP: The Quest of Working-Class Membership', *Journal of Contemporary History*, 15, 493–512

Mühlberger, D. (1991) *Hitler's Followers: Studies in the Sociology of the Nazi Movement* (London: Routledge)

Munslow, A. (1997) 'E. H. Carr (1892–1982) *What is History?*', *History Reviews*, November 1997

Mussolini, B. (1932) 'Political and Social Doctrine of Fascism', translated in M. Oakeshott (1949) (ed.) *The Social and Political Doctrines of Contemporary Europe* (New York: Praeger), 164–79

Neumann, F. (1967) *Behemoth: The Structure and Practice of National Socialism* (London: Frank Cass, 2nd edn)

Neocleous, M. (1997) *Fascism* (London: Open University Press)

Nipperdey, T. (1985) '1933 and Continuity of German History', in H. W. Koch (ed.) *Aspects of the Third Reich* (Houndmills and London: Macmillan), 489–508

Nolte, E. (1965) *Three Faces of Fascism: Action Française, Italian Fascism, National Socialism* (London: Weidenfeld & Nicolson)

Nolte, E. (1985) 'Between Myth and Revisionism? The Third Reich in the Perspective of the 1980s' in H. W. Koch (ed.) *Aspects of the Third Reich* (Houndmills and London 1985: Macmillan)

Nolte, E. (1987) *Das Europäische Bürgerkrieg, 1917–1945. Nationalsozialismus und Bolschevismus* (Berlin: Propyläen)

Nora, P. (ed.) (1984–92) *Les lieux de mémoire* (Paris: Editions Gallimard, 7 vols); trans-lated as Nora (1996–8) *Realms of Memory: The Construction of the French Past* (New York: Columbia University Press, 3 vols)

Organski, A. F. K. (1965) *The Forms of Political Development* (New York)

Organski, A. F. K. (1968) 'Fascism and Modernization', in S. J. Woolf (ed.) *The Nature of Fascism* (London: Weidenfeld & Nicolson), 19–41

O'Sullivan, N. (1983) *Fascism* (London and Melbourne: Dent)

Painter, B. W. (1990) 'Renzo De Felice and the Historiography of Italian Fascism', *American Historical Review*, 95, 113–35

Passerini, L. (1979) 'Work Ideology and Consensus under Italian Fascism', *History Workshop*, 8, 84–92

Passerini, L. (1987) *Fascism in Popular Memory: The Cultural Experience of the Turin Working Class* (Cambridge: Cambridge University Press)

Passmore, K. (1997) *From Liberalism to Fascism: The Right in a French Province, 1928–1939* (Cambridge: Cambridge University Press)

Pavone, C. (1991) *La guerra civile. Saggio storico sulla moralità nella Resistanza* (Turin: Bollati, Boringheri)

Paxton, R. (1997) *French Peasant Fascism: Henry Dorgères's Greenshirts and the Crises of French Agriculture, 1929–1939* (Oxford: Oxford University Press)

Paxton, R. O. (1972) *Vichy France: Old Guard & New Order, 1940–1944* (New York: Columbia University Press)

Paxton, R. O. (1998) 'The Five Stages of Fascism', *Journal of Modern History*, 70, 1–23

Payne, S. G. (1961) *Falange* (Stanford: Stanford University Press)

Payne, S. G. (1980a) *Fascism: Comparison and Definition* (Madison: University of Wisconsin Press)

Payne, S. G. (1980b) 'Social Composition and Regional Strength of the Spanish Falange' in S. U. Larsen, B. Hagtvet and J. P. Myklebust (eds) *Who Were the Fascists? Social Roots of European Fascism* (Bergen, Oslo, Tromso: Universitetsforlaget), 423–34

Payne, S. G. (1986) 'Fascism and Right Authoritarianism in the Iberian World: The Last Twenty Years', *Journal of Contemporary History*, 21, 163–78

Payne, S. G. (1997) *A History of Fascism, 1914–45* (London: UCL Press)

Perfetti, F. (1984) *Il dibattito sul fascismo* (Rome: Bonacci)

Peukert, D. J. K. (1989) *Inside Nazi Germany: Conformity, Opposition and Racism in Everyday Life* (Harmondsworth: Penguin)

Poulantzas, N. (1974) *Fascism and Dictatorship: The Third International and the Problem of Fascism* (London: Secker & Warburg)

Procacci, G. (1965) 'Crisi dello stato liberale e origini del fascismo', *Studi Storici*, 6, 221–37

Procacci, G. (1970) *History of the Italian People* (London: Weidenfeld and Nicolson)

Puhle, H.-J. (1981) 'Deutscher Sonderweg. Kontroverse um eine vermeintliche Legende', *Journal für Geschichte*, 4, 44–70

Quartararo, R. (1980) *Roma tra Londra e Berlino. La politica estera fascista dal 1930 al 1940* (Rome: Bonacci)

Quazza, G. (1976) *Resistenza e storia in Italia: problemi e ipotesi diri cerca* (Milan: Il Mulino)

Radel, J.-L. (1975) *Roots of Totalitarianism: The Ideological Sources of Fascism, National Socialism and Communism* (New York: Crane, Russak & Co.)

Rauschning, H. (1939) *The Revolution of Nihilism* (London: Heinemann)

Rauschning, H. (1940) *Voice of Destruction* (New York: Putnam)

Reich, W. (1946) *The Mass Psychology of Fascism* (London: Souvenir)

Rémond, R. (1982) *Les Droites en France. De la première Restoration à la Ve République* (Paris: Aubier)

Riall, L. (1994) *The Italian Risorgimento: State, Society, and National Unification* (London: Routledge)

Ritter, G. (1969–73) *The Sword and the Scepter: The Problem of Militarism in Germany* (Coral Gables, Florida: University of Miami Press)

Robinson, R. A. H. (1981) *Fascism in Europe, 1919–1945* (London: Historical Association)

Robinson, R. A. H. (1995) *Fascism: The International Phenomenon* (London: Historical Association)

Rochat, G. (1973) *Il colonialismo italiano* (Turin: Loescher)

Rogger, H. and Weber, E. (1965) (eds) *The European Right: A Historical Profile* (London: Weidenfeld & Nicolson)

Romeo, R. (1950) *Il Risorgimento in Sicilia* (Bari: Laterza)

Romeo, R. (1963) *Dal Piemonte sabaudo all'Italia liberale* (Turin: Einaudi)

Romeo, R. (1978) *L'Italia unita e la prima guerra mondiale* (Rome and Bari: Laterza)

Rousso, H. (1991) *The Vichy Syndrome: History and Memory in France since 1944* (Cambridge, MA: Harvard University Press)

Rumi, G. (1974) ' "Revisionismo" fascista ed espansione coloniale (1925–1935)' in A. Aquarone and M. Vernassa (eds) *Il regime fascista* (Bologna: Il Mulino), 435–64

Rusconi, G. E. (1993) *Se cesiamo di essere una nazione. Tra ethnodemocrazie regionali e cittadinanza europea* (Bologna: Mulino)

Salomone, A. W. (1964) 'The Risorgimento and the Political Myth of the "Revolution that Failed"', *American Historical Review*, 68, 38–53

Salvatorelli, L. (1923) *Nazionalfascismo* (Turin: Gobetti)

Salvemini, G. (1925) *Dal Patto di Londra alla Pace di Roma* (Turin: Einaudi)

Salvemini, G. (1952) *Mussolini Diplomatico* (Bari: Laterza)

Salvemini, G. (1953) *Prelude to the Second World War* (London: Gollancz)

Sarfatti, M. (1994) *Mussolini contro gli ebrei* (Turin: Zamorani)

Sarfatti, M. (1999) *Gli ebrei nell'Italia fascista* (Turin: Einaudi)

Sarti, R. (1970) 'Fascist Modernisation in Italy: Traditional or Revolutionary?', *American Historical Review*, 75, 1029–45

Schapiro, L. (1972) *Totalitarianism* (New York: Praeger)

Schieder, W. and Dipper, C. (1976) (eds) *Das spanische Bürgerkrieg in der internationalen Politik* (Munich: Droste)

Schoenbaum, D. (1966) *Hitler's Social Revolution: Class and Status in Nazi Germany, 1933–1939* (London: Weidenfeld & Nicolson) – new edn (1997) (London: Norton)

Schöllgen, G. (1991) *A Conservative against Hitler: Ulrich von Hassell, Diplomat in Imperial Germany, the Weimar Republic and the Third Reich, 1881–1944* (Basingstoke and London: Macmillan)

Sheehan, J. J. (1981) 'What is German History? Reflections on the Role of the Nation in German History and Historiography', *Journal of Modern History*, 53, 1–23

Smith, W. D. (1986) *The Ideological Origins of Nazi Imperialism* (Oxford: University Press)

Sontheimer, K. (1968) *Antidemokratisches Denken in der Weimarer Republic* (Munich: Nymphenburger Verlagshandlung)

Soucy, R. (1986) *French Fascism: The First Wave, 1924–1933* (New Haven: Yale University Press)

Soucy, R. (1995) *French Fascism: The Second Wave, 1933–1939* (New Haven: Yale University Press)

Spengler, O. (1934) *The Hour of Decision, Part One: Germany and World-historical Evolution* (New York: A. A. Knopf)

Steinberg, J. (1990) *All or Nothing: The Axis and the Holocaust, 1941–42* (London: Routledge)

Steinmetz, G. (1999) 'German Exceptionalism and the Origins of Nazism: The Career of a Concept' in I. Kershaw and M. Lewin (eds) *Stalinism and Nazism: Dictatorships in Comparison* (Cambridge: Cambridge University Press), 251–84

Stern, F. (1961) *The Politics of Cultural Despair* (Berkeley: University of California Press)

Sternhell, Z. (1979) 'Fascist Ideology' in W. Laqueur (ed.) *Fascism: A Reader's Guide. Analyses, Interpretations, Bibliography* (Harmondsworth: Penguin), 325–406

Sternhell, Z. (1980) 'Strands of French Fascism' in S. U. Larsen, B. Hagtvet and J. P. Myklebust (eds) *Who Were the Fascists? Social Roots of European Fascism* (Bergen, Oslo, Tromso: Universitetsforlaget), 479–500

Sternhell, Z. (1983) *Ni Droit Ni Gauche: L'Idéologie Fasciste en France* (Paris: Editions du Seuil)

Sternhell, Z. (1986) *Neither Right nor Left: Fascist Ideology in France* (Berkeley and Los Angeles: University of California Press)

Sternhell, Z. (1987) 'Fascism' in D. Miller (ed.) *The Blackwell Encyclopedia of Political Thought* (Oxford: Basil Blackwell)

Sternhell, Z. (1994) *The Birth of Fascist Ideology: From Cultural Rebellion to Political Religion* (Princeton: Princeton University Press)

Struve, W. (1973) *Elites against Democracy: Leadership Ideals in Bourgeois Political Thought in Germany, 1890–1933* (Princeton, NJ, Princeton University Press)

Stürmer, M. (1983) 'Kein Eigentum der Deutschen: die deutsche Frage' in W. Weidenfeld (ed.) *Die Identität der Deutschen* (Munich and Vienna: C. Hanser), 83–101

Stürmer, M. (1990) *Die Grenzen der Macht. Begegnung der Deutschen mit der Geschichte* (Berlin: Siedler)

Sugar, P. F. (1971) (ed.) *Native Fascism in the Successor States, 1918–1945* (Santa Barbara, CA: ABC-Clio)

Sweets, J. F. (1986) *Choices in Vichy France: The French Under Nazi Occupation* (New York: Oxford University Press)

Tasca, A. (1950) *Nascita e avvento del fascismo* (Florence: La Nuova Italia)

Taylor, A. J. P. (1961) *The Origins of the Second World War* (London: Hamilton)

Taylor, A. J. P. (1971) 'War Origins Again', in E. M. Robertson (ed.) *The Origins of the Second World War: Historical Interpretations* (London and Basingstoke: Macmillan), 136–41

Tranfaglia, N. (1973) *Dallo stato liberale al regime fascista* (Milan: Feltrinelli)

Tranfaglia, N. (1984) *Labirinto italiano: radici storiche e nuove contraddizioni* (Turin: Celid)

Tranfaglia, N. (1996) *Un passato scomodo: fascismo e postfascismo* (Bari: Laterza)

Trevelyan, G. M. (1923) *The Historical Causes of the Present State of Affairs in Italy* (Oxford: Oxford University Press)

Turner, H. A., Jr (1975) 'Fascism and Modernisation' in H. A. Turner (ed.) (1975) *Reappraisals of Fascism* (New York: New Viewpoints) 117–39

Unger, A. L. (1972) *The Totalitarian Party: Party and People in Nazi Germany and Soviet Russia* (London and New York: University of Cambridge Press)

Vajda, M. (1976) *Fascism as a Mass Movement* (London: Allison & Busby)

Villari, L. (1959) *The Liberation of Italy, 1943–1947* (Appleton, WI: C. C. Nelson Publ. Co.)

Vincent, A. (1992) *Modern Political Ideologies* (Oxford: Blackwell)

Viroli, M. (1995) *For Love of Country: An Essay on Patriotism and Nationalism* (Oxford: Clarendon Press)

Vivarelli, R. (1967) *Il dopoguerra in Italia e l'avvento del fascismo (1918–1922)*, 2 vols (Naples: Istituto italiano per gli studi storici)

Vivarelli, R. (1981) *Il fallimento del liberalismo. Studi sulle origini del fascismo* (Bologna: Il Mulino)

Vivarelli, R. (1991) *Storia delle origini del fascismo: l'Italia dalla grande guerra alla marcia su Roma* (Bologna: Mulino)

Vivarelli, R. (1999) 'A Neglected Question: Historians and the Italian National State (1945–95)' in S. Berger, N. Donovan and K. Passmore (eds) *Writing National Histories: Western Europe since 1800* (London: Routledge), 230–5

Volpe, G. (1931) *L'Italia in cammino. L'ultimo cinquantennio* (Milan: Fratelli Treves, 3rd edn)

Ward, D. (1999) 'From Croce to Vico: Carlo Levi's *L'orologio* and Italian Anti-Fascism' in R. J. B. Bosworth and P. Dogliani (eds) *Italian Fascism: History, Memory and Representation* (Houndmills and London 1999), 64–82

Weber, E. (1964) *Varieties of Fascism* (Princeton, NJ: Van Nostrand)

Weber, E. (1979) 'Revolution? Counter-Revolution? What Revolution?' in W. Laqueur (ed.) *Fascism: A Reader's Guide. Analyses, Interpretations, Bibliography* (Harmondsworth: Penguin), 488–531

Wehler, H.-U. (1975) *Modernisierungstheorie und Geschichte* (Göttingen: Vandenhoeck und Ruprecht)

Wehler, H.-U. (1985) *The German Empire 1871–1918* (Leamington Spa: Berg)

Wehler, H.-U. (1995) *Angst vor der Macht? Die Machtlust der neuen Recht* (Bonn: Friedrich-Ebert-Stiftung)

Wehler, H.-U. (1997) 'The Goldhagen Controversy: Agonising Problems, Scholarly Failure and the Political Dimension', *German History*, 15, 80–91

Weißmann, K. (1993) *Rückruf in die Geschichte. Die deutsche Herausforderung. Alte Gefahren – Neue Chancen* (Frankfurt am Main: Ullstein)

Weißmann, K. (1995) *Der Weg in den Abgrund. Deutschland unter Hitler 1933–45* (Berlin: Propyläen)

Weindling, P. (1996) 'Understanding Nazi Racism: Precursors and Perpetrators' in M. Burleigh (1996) (ed.) *Confronting the Nazi Past: New Debates on Modern German History* (London: Routledge), 66–83

Weisberg, R. H. (1996) *Vichy Law and the Holocaust in France* (New York: University Press)

Wells, H. G. (1933) *The Shape of Things to Come* (London: Hutchinson)

Willson, P. (1993) *The Clockwork Factory: Women and Work in Fascist Italy* (Oxford: Oxford University Press)

Wippermann, W. (1976) *Faschismustheorien: zum Stand der gegenwärtigen Diskussion* (Darmstadt: Wissenschaftliche Buchgesellschaft)

Wippermann, W. (1983) *Europäischer Faschismus im Vergleich, 1922–1982* (Frankfurt am Main: Suhrkampf)

Wippermann, W. (1997) *Wessen Schuld? Vom Historikerstreit zur Goldhagen-Kontroverse* (Berlin: Elefanten Press)

Wiskemann, E. (1966) *The Rome–Berlin Axis* (London: Collins, 2nd edn)

Wiskemann, E. (1970) *Fascism in Italy* (London and Basingstoke: Penguin, 2nd edn)

Wistrich, R. S. (1976) 'Leon Trotsky's Theory of Fascism', *Journal of Contemporary History*, 11, 157–84

Wohl, R. (1991) 'French Fascism, Both Right and Left: Reflections on the Sternhell Controversy', *Journal of Modern History*, 63, 91–8

Woolf, S. J. (1968) (ed.) *The Nature of Fascism* (London: Weidenfeld & Nicolson)

Woolf, S. J. (1981) (ed.) *Fascism in Europe* (London: Methuen)

Zapponi, N. (1994) 'Fascism in Italian Historiography, 1986–93: A Fading National Identity', *Journal of Contemporary History*, 29, 547–68

Zittelmann, R. (1991) *Hitler: Selbstverständnis eines Revolutionärs* (Hamburg and New York: Berg)

Zittelmann, R. (1995) *Wohin treibt unsere Republik* (Berlin: Propyläen)

Zuccotti, S. (1987) *The Italians and the Holocaust: Persecution, Rescue, Survival* (London: Halban)

Zuccotti, S. (1993) *The Holocaust, the French and the Jews* (New York: Basic Books)

Further reading

The following titles listed here complement the works featured in the Reader – and do not include text reproduced in this reader. Further bibliographical references can be found in the Introduction to this volume (and the section titled *References*).

General

General works on the nature of fascism

Gregor, A. J. (1974) *Interpretations of Fascism* (Morristown, NJ: General Learning Press)

Gregor, A. J. (1976) *The Ideology of Fascism: The Rationale of Totalitarianism* (New York: Free Press)

Griffin, R. (1998) *International Fascism: Theories, Causes and the New Consensus* (London: Arnold)

Linz, J. J. (1979) 'Some Notes Towards a Comparative Study of Fascism in Sociological Historical Perspective' in W. Laqueur (ed.) *Fascism: A Reader's Guide. Analyses, Interpretations, Bibliography* (Harmondsworth: Penguin) 29–39

Linz, J. J. (1980) 'Political Space and Fascism as Late-Comer', in S. U. Larsen, B. Hagtvet and J. P. Myklebust (eds) *Who Were the Fascists? Social Roots of European Fascism* (Bergen, Oslo, Tromso: Universitetsforlaget), 153–89

Comparative works on fascist movements/regimes

Bessel, R. (ed.) *Fascist Italy and Nazi Germany: Comparisons and Contrasts* (Cambridge: Cambridge University Press)

Brooker, P. (1991) *The Faces of Fraternalism: Nazi Germany, Fascist Italy and Imperial Japan* (Oxford: Clarendon Press)

Hayes, P. M. (1973) *Fascism* (New York: Free Press)

Kedward, H. R. (1971) *Fascism in Western Europe, 1900–45* (New York: New York University Press)

Laqueur, W. (1979) *Fascism: A Reader's Guide. Analyses, Interpretations, Bibliography* (Harmondsworth: Penguin)

Laqueur, W. (1996) *Fascism: Past, Present, Future* (New York: Oxford University Press)

Merkl, P. H. (1980) 'Comparing Fascist Movements' in S. U. Larsen, B. Hagtvet and J. P. Myklebust (eds) *Who Were the Fascists? Social Roots of European Fascism* (Bergen, Oslo, Tromso: Universitetsforlaget), 752–83

Mosse, G. L. (1979) (ed.) *International Fascism: New Thoughts and New Approaches* (London and Beverly Hills: Sage Publications)

Robinson, R. A. H. (1981) *Fascism in Europe, 1919–1945* (London: Historical Association)

Weber, E. (1964) *Varieties of Fascism* (Princeton, NJ: Van Nostrand)

Woolf, S. J. (1968) (ed.) *The Nature of Fascism* (London: Weidenfeld & Nicolson)

Interpretations of fascism

Arendt, H. (1958) *The Origins of Totalitarianism* (New York: Meridian Books)

Caplan, J. (1977) 'Theories of Fascism: Nicos Poulantzas as Historian', *History Workshop Journal*, 3, 83–100

Carsten, F. L. (1979) 'Interpretations of Fascism', in W. Laqueur (ed.) *Fascism: A Reader's Guide. Analyses, Interpretations, Bibliography* (Harmondsworth: Penguin)

Felice, R. De (1977) *Interpretations of Fascism* (Cambridge, MA and London: Harvard University Press)

Gentile, E. (1990) 'Fascism as Political Religion', *Journal of Contemporary History*, 25, 229–51

Poulantzas, N. (1974) *Fascism and Dictatorship: The Third International and the Problem of Fascism* (London: Secker & Warburg)

Radel, J.-L. (1975) *Roots of Totalitarianism: The Ideological Sources of Fascism, National Socialism and Communism* (New York: Crane, Russak & Co.)

Ideology

General

Mosse, G. L. (1979) 'Towards a General Theory of Fascism', in Mosse (ed.) *International Fascism: New Thoughts and New Approaches* (London and Beverly Hills: Sage Publications), 1–41

Sternhell, Z. (1979) 'Fascist Ideology', in W. Laqueur (ed.) *Fascism: A Reader's Guide. Analyses, Interpretations, Bibliography* (Harmondsworth: Penguin), 325–406

Weber, E. (1979) 'Revolution? Counter-Revolution? What Revolution?' in W. Laqueur (ed.) *Fascism: A Reader's Guide. Analyses, Interpretations, Bibliography* (Harmondsworth: Penguin), 488–531

Italy

Gentile, E. (1975) *Le origini dell'ideologia fascista, 1918–1925* (Rome and Bari: Laterza)

Gentile, E. (1996) *The Sacralization of Politics in Fascist Italy* (Cambridge, MA: Harvard University Press)

Lyttelton, A. (1973) (ed.) *Italian Fascisms from Pareto to Gentile* (London: Cape)

Roberts, D. D. (1979) *The Syndicalist Tradition in Italian Fascism* (Manchester: Manchester University Press)

Sternhell, Z. (1994) *The Birth of Fascist Ideology: From Cultural Rebellion to Political Revolution* (Princeton: Princeton University Press)

Germany

Birken, L. (1995) *Hitler as Philosophe: Remnants of the Enlightenment in National Socialism* (Westport, CT and London: Praeger Publishers)

Hamilton, A. (1971) *The Appeal of Fascism: A Study of Intellectuals and Fascism 1919–1945* (London: Blond)

Kershaw, I. (1991) *Hitler* (London and New York: Longman)

Kershaw, I. (1998) *Hitler, 1889–1936: Hubris* (London: Allen Lane)

Kershaw, I. (2000) *Hitler, 1936–45: Nemesis* (London: Allen Lane)

Smith, W. D. (1986) *The Ideological Origins of Nazi Imperialism* (Oxford: Oxford University Press)

Struve, W. (1973) *Elites against Democracy: Leadership Ideals in Bourgeois Political Thought in Germany, 1890–1933* (Princeton, NJ, Princeton University Press)

France

Sternhell, Z. (1980) 'Strands of French Fascism' in S. U. Larsen, B. Hagtvet and J. P. Myklebust (eds) *Who Were the Fascists? Social Roots of European Fascism* (Bergen, Oslo, Tromso: Universitetsforlaget), 479–500

Spain

Preston, P. (1999) 'The Absent Hero: José Antonio Prima De Rivera' in Paul Preston (ed.) *Comrades! Portraits from the Spanish Civil War* (London: HarperCollins), 73–108

Thomas, H. (1966) 'The Hero in the Empty Room: José Antonio and Spanish Fascism', *Journal of Contemporary History*, 1, 174–82.

Britain

Baker, D. (1996) *Ideology of Obsession: A. K. Chesterton and British Fascism* (London: Tauris Academic Studies)

Skidelsky, R. (1975) *Oswald Mosley* (London: Macmillan)

Thorpe, A. (1989) (ed.) *The Failure of Political Extremism in Inter-War Britain* (Exeter: University of Exeter Press)

Varieties

Spain

Blinkhorn, M. (1975) *Carlism and Crisis in Spain, 1931–1939* (Cambridge: Cambridge University Press)

Ellwood, S. M. (1990) 'Falange Española and the Creation of the Francoist "New State"', *European History Quarterly*, 20, 209–25.

Payne, S. G. (1961) *Falange* (Stanford: Stanford University Press)

Payne, S. G. (1990) 'Political Violence During the Spanish Second Republic', *Journal of Contemporary History*, 25, 269–88

Preston, P. (1990) *The Politics of Revenge: Fascism and the Military in Twentieth-Century Spain* (London: Routledge)

France

Irvine, W. D. (1991) 'Fascism in France and the Strange Case of the Croix De Feu', *Journal of Modern History*, 63, 271–95

Milza, P. (1987) *Fascisme français, passé et présent* (Paris: Flammarion)

Mosse, G. L. (1972) 'The French Right and the Working Classes: Les Jaunes', *Journal of Contemporary History*, 7, 185–208.

Paxton, R. O. (1997) *Peasant Fascism. Henry Dorgères's Greenshirts and the Crises of French Agriculture, 1929–1939* (Oxford: Oxford University Press)

Rémond, R. (1982) *Les Droites en France. De la première Restoration à la Ve République* (Paris: Aubier)

Soucy, R. (1986) *French Fascism: The First Wave, 1924–1933* (New Haven: Yale University Press)

Britain

Lewis, D. S. (1987) *Illusions of Grandeur: Mosley, Fascism and British Society, 1931–81* (Manchester: Manchester University Press)

Lunn, K. and Thurlow, R. C. (1980) (eds) *British Fascism: Essays on the Radical Right in Inter-War Britain* (New York: St Martin's Press)

Austria

Carsten, F. L. (1977) *Fascist Movements in Austria from Schönerer to Hitler* (London: Sage)

Kitchen, M. (1980) *The Coming of Austrian Fascism* (London: Croom Helm; Montreal: McGill-Queen's University Press)

Pauley, B. F. (1981) *Hitler and the Forgotten Nazis* (Chapel Hill: University of North Carolina Press)

Hungary and the Balkans

Higham, R. and Veremis, Th. (1993) (eds) *The Metaxas Dictatorship: Aspects of Greece 1936–40* (Athens: The Hellenic Foundation for Defense and Foreign Affairs)

Ioanid, R. (1990) *The Sword of the Archangel: Fascist Ideology in Romania* (Boulder and New York: East European Monographs)

Sakmyster, T. L. (1994) *Hungary's Admiral on Horseback: Miklós Horthy, 1918–1944* (Boulder and New York: East European Monographs)

Sugar, P. F. (1971) (ed). *Native Fascism in the Successor States, 1918–1945* (Santa Barbara, CA: ABC-Clio)

Vatikiotis, P. J. (1998) *Popular Autocracy in Greece, 1936–41: A Political Biography of General Metaxas* (London: Frank Cass)

Regime

Germany

Bracher, K. D. (1979) 'The Role of Hitler: Perspectives of Interpretation', in W. Laqueur (ed.) *Fascism: A Reader's Guide. Analyses, Interpretations, Bibliography* (Harmondsworth: Penguin), 193–212

Broszat, M. (1981) *The Hitler State: The Foundation and Development of the Internal Structure of the Third Reich* (London and New York: Longman)

Frei, N. (1993) *National Socialism Rule in Germany: The Führer-State 1933–1945* (Oxford and Cambridge, MA: Blackwell)

Hayes, P. (1992) 'The Triumph of Caesarism: Fascism and Nazism', in Hayes (ed.) *Themes in Modern European History, 1890–1945* (London and New York: Routledge), 174–204

Hildebrand, K. (1984) *The Third Reich* (London: Routledge)

Kershaw, I. (2000) *The Nazi Dictatorship: Problems and Perspectives of Interpretation* (London: Arnold, 4th edn)

Kershaw, I. and Lewin, M. (1997) (eds) *Stalinism and Nazism: Dictatorships in Comparison* (Cambridge: Cambridge University Press)

Kitchen, M. (1995) *Nazi Germany at War* (London and New York: Longman)

Mason, T. (1968) 'The Primacy of Politics – Politics and Economics in National Socialist Germany' in S. J. Woolf (ed.) *The Nature of Fascism* (London: Weidenfeld & Nicolson), 165–95

Michalka, W. (1983) 'Conflicts within the German Leadership on the Objectives and Tactics of German Foreign Policy, 1933–1939', in W. J. Mommsen and Kettenacker (eds.) *The Fascist Challenge and the Policy of Appeasement* (London: Allen & Unwin), 48–60

Weinberg, G. L. (1970) *The Foreign Policy of Hitler's Germany: Diplomatic Revolution in Europe, 1933–1936* (Chicago: Chicago University Press)

Weinberg, G. L. (1980) *The Foreign Policy of Hitler's Germany: Starting World War II, 1937–1939* (Chicago: Chicago University Press)

Williamson, D. G. (1995) *The Third Reich* (Harlow: Longman)

Italy

Cassels, A. (1969) *Fascist Italy* (London: Routledge & Kegan Paul)

Cassels, A. (1970) *Mussolini's Early Diplomacy* (Princeton: Princeton University Press)

Gentile, E. (1984) 'The Problem of the Party in Italian Fascism', *Journal of Contemporary History*, 19, 51–74

Germino, D. L. (1959) *The Italian Fascist Party in Power: A Study in Totalitarian Rule* (Minneapolis: University of Minnesota Press)

Grand, A. J. De (1996) *Fascist Italy and Nazi Germany: The 'Fascist' Style of Rule* (New York: Routledge)

Mack Smith, D. (1982) *Mussolini's Roman Empire* (London and New York: Longman)

Morgan, P. (1995) *Italian Fascism, 1919–1945* (Basingstoke: Macmillan)

Whittam, J. (1995) *Fascist Italy* (Manchester: Manchester University Press)

Wiskemann, E. (1966) *The Rome–Berlin Axis* (London: Collins, 2nd edn)

Wiskemann, E. (1970) *Fascism in Italy* (London and Basingstoke: Penguin, 2nd edn)

Spain and Portugal

Ellwood, S. M. (1987) *Spanish Fascism in the Franco Era: Falange Espanola de las Jons, 1936–76* (New York: St Martin's Press)

Gallagher, T. (1979) 'Controlled Repression in Salazar's Portugal', *Journal of Contemporary History*, 14, 385–402

Graham, H. (1989) 'The Franco Regime', *The Historical Journal*, 32, 757–61

Graham, L. (1975) *Portugal: Decline of an Authoritarian Order* (London and Beverly Hills: Sage)

Linz, J. J. (1976) 'An Authoritarian Regime: Spain' in S. G. Payne (ed.) *Politics and Society in Twentieth Century Spain* (New York: New Viewpoints), 160–207

Payne, S. G. (1987) *The Franco Regime, 1936–1975* (Madison: University of Wisconsin Press)

France

Aron, R. (1954) *Histoire de Vichy* (Paris: Fayard)

Race

Bernardini, G. (1977) 'The Origins and Development of Racial Anti-Semitism in Fascist Italy', *Journal of Modern History*, 49, 431–53

Friedländer, S. (1997) *Nazi Germany and the Jews* (New York: HarperCollins)

Graml, H. (1992) *Antisemitism in the Third Reich* (Oxford and Cambridge, MA: Blackwell)

Michaelis, M. (1978) *Mussolini and the Jews: German–Italian Relations and the Jewish Question in Italy 1922–1945* (Oxford: Oxford University Press for the Institute of Jewish Affairs)

Michaelis, M. (1989) 'Fascism, Totalitarianism and the Holocaust: Reflections on Current Interpretations of National Socialist Anti-Semitism', *European History Quarterly* 19, 85–103

Pulzer, P. (1988) *The Rise of Political Anti-Semitism in Germany and Austria* (London: Halban)

Weindling, P. (1996) 'Understanding Nazi Racism: Precursors and Perpetrators' in M. Burleigh (1996) (ed.) *Confronting the Nazi Past: New Debates on Modern German History* (London: Routledge), 66–83

Winock, M. (1998) *Nationalism, Anti-Semitism and Fascism in France* (Stanford: Stanford University Press)

Zuccotti, S. (1987) *The Italians and the Holocaust: Persecution, Rescue, Survival* (London: Halban)

Zuccotti, S. (1997) 'The Italian Race Laws, 1938–1943: A Reevaluation' in J. Frankel (ed.) *Studies in Contemporary Jewry: An Annual* (Oxford: Oxford University Press), 133–52

Society

The social base of fascism

Abse, T. (1986) 'The Rise of Fascism in an Industrial City: The Case of Livorno 1918–1922' in D. Forgacs (ed.) *Rethinking Italian Fascism: Capitalism, Populism and Culture* (London: Lawrence and Wishart), 52–82

Andreski, S. (1980) 'Fascists as Moderates' in S. U. Larsen, B. Hagtvet and J. P. Myklebust (eds) *Who Were the Fascists? Social Roots of European Fascism* (Bergen, Oslo, Tromso: Universitetsforlaget), 52–5

Childers, T. (1983) *The Nazi Voter: The Social Foundations of Fascism in Germany, 1919–1939* (Chapel Hill: University of North Carolina Press)

Corner, P. (1975) *Fascism in Ferrara 1915–1925* (London: Oxford University Press)

Lackó, M. (1980) 'The Social Roots of Hungarian Fascism: The Arrow Cross' in S. U. Larsen, B. Hagtvet and J. P. Myklebust (eds) *Who Were the Fascists? Social Roots of European Fascism* (Bergen, Oslo, Tromso: Universitetsforlaget), 395–400

Lyttelton, A. (1996) 'The "Crisis of Bourgeois Society" and the Origins of Fascism' in R. Bessel (ed.) *Fascist Italy and Nazi Germany: Comparisons and Contrasts* (Cambridge: Cambridge University Press), 12–22

Mühlberger, D. (1987) (ed.) *The Social Basis of European Fascist Movements* (London: Croom Helm)

Mühlberger, D. (1991) *Hitler's Followers: Studies in the Sociology of the Nazi Movement* (London and New York: Routledge)

Noakes, J. (1971) *The Nazi Party in Lower Saxony, 1921–1933* (London: Oxford University Press)

Passmore, K. (1998) *From Liberalism to Fascism: The Right in a French Province, 1928–1939* (Cambridge: Cambridge University Press)

Payne, S. G. (1980b) 'Social Composition and Regional Strength of the Spanish Falange' in S. U. Larsen, B. Hagtvet and J. P. Myklebust (eds) *Who Were the Fascists? Social Roots of European Fascism* (Bergen, Oslo, Tromso: Universitetsforlaget), 423–34

Webber, G. C. (1984) 'Patterns of Membership and Support for the British Union of Fascists', *Journal of Contemporary History*, 19, 575–606

Gender

Bock, G. (1998) 'Ordinary Women in Nazi Germany: Perpetrators, Victims, Followers, and Bystanders' in D. Ofer and L. J. Weitzman (eds) *Women in the Holocaust* (New Haven, CT: Yale University Press), 85–100

Caldwell, L. (1986) 'Reproducers of the Nation: Women and the Family in Fascist Policy' in D. Forgacs (ed.) *Rethinking Italian Fascism: Capitalism, Populism and Culture* (London: Lawrence and Wishart), 110–41

Corner, P. (1993) 'Women in Fascist Italy: Changing Family Roles in the Transition from an Agricultural to an Industrial Society', *European History Quarterly*, 23, 51–68

Nash, M. (1995) *Defying Male Civilization: Women in the Spanish Civil War* (Denver: Arden Press)

Stephenson, J. (1996) 'Women, Motherhood and the Family in the Third Reich' in M. Burleigh (ed.) *Confronting the Nazi Past: New Debates on Modern German History* (London: Collins & Brown), 167–83

Stephenson, J. (2001) *Women in Nazi Germany* (Harlow and New York: Longman)

Population politics

Ipsen, M. (1996) *Dictating Demography: The Problem of Population in Fascist Italy* (Cambridge: Cambridge University Press)

Quine, M. S. (1996) *Population Politics in Twentieth Century Europe: Fascist Dictatorships and Liberal Democracies* (London and New York: Routledge)

The role of the elites

Abraham, D. (1986) *The Collapse of the Weimar Republic: Political Economy and Crisis* (New York: Holmes and Meier, 2nd edn)

Broszat, M. (1987) *Hitler and the Collapse of Weimar Germany* (Leamington Spa: Berg)

Irvine, W. (1974) 'French Conservatives and the "New Right" during the 1930s', *French Historical Studies*, 4, 534–60

Müller, K.-J. (1987) *The Army, Politics and Society in Germany, 1933–45: Studies in the Army's Relation to Nazism* (Manchester: Manchester University Press)

Turner, H. A., Jr (1985) *German Big Business and the Rise of Hitler* (New York: Oxford University Press)

Conformity, resistance and collaboration

Bertram, G. (1980) *Collaborationism in France during the Second World War* (Ithaca: Cornell University Press)

Conan, E. and Rousso, H. (1994) *Vichy, un passé qui ne passe pas* (Paris: Fayard)

Dahrendorf, R. (1967) *Society and Democracy in Germany* (Garden City: Anchor Books)

Gordon, B. (1980) *Collaborationism in France during the Second World War* (Ithaca: Cornell University Press)

Grazia, V. De (1981) *The Culture of Consent: Mass Organisation of Leisure in Fascist Italy* (Cambridge: Cambridge University Press)

Grazia, V, De (1991) *How Fascism Ruled Women: Italy 1922–1945* (Berkeley: University of California Press)

Griffiths, R. (1980) *Fellow Travellers of the Right: British Enthusiasts for Nazi Germany: 1933–39* (London: Constable)

Hoffmann, P. (1996) *The History of the German Resistance, 1933–1945* (Montreal: McGill-Queen's University Press, 3rd edn)

Latour, A. (1981) *The Jewish Resistance in France* (New York: Holocaust Library)

Mason, T. (1993b) *Social Policy in the Third Reich: The Working Class and the National Community* (Providence, RI and Oxford: Berg)

Passerini, L. (1979) 'Work Ideology and Consensus under Italian Fascism', *History Workshop*, 8, 84–92

Passerini, L. (1987) *Fascism in Popular Memory: The Cultural Experience of the Turin Working Class* (Cambridge: Cambridge University Press)

Schoenbaum, D. (1967) *Hitler's Social Revolution: Class and Status in Nazi Germany, 1933–1939* (London: Weidenfeld & Nicolson) – new edn (1997) (London: Norton)

Sweets, J. F. (1986) *Choices in Vichy France: The French Under Nazi Occupation* (New York: Oxford University Press)

Index

Numbers in bold correspond to chapters authored by the indexed scholars.